425

TEACHING IN

SECONDARY SCHOOLS

THIRD EDITION

BY *Nelson L. Bossing*

PROFESSOR OF EDUCATION, UNIVERSITY OF
MINNESOTA · FORMERLY PROFESSOR OF
EDUCATION AND DIRECTOR UNIVERSITY
HIGH SCHOOL, UNIVERSITY OF OREGON

HOUGHTON MIFFLIN COMPANY Boston · New York · Chicago
Dallas · Atlanta · San Francisco **The Riverside Press Cambridge**

The Riverside Press

CAMBRIDGE MASSACHUSETTS
PRINTED IN THE U.S.A.

To My

Father and Mother

PREFACE TO THIRD EDITION

EDUCATION as a science is young; as a profession it is just beginning to find itself: consequently, the theory and practice of education has not crystallized. In education, as in similar fields of applied knowledge, we must be unusually sensitive to the many changes which are taking place in our knowledge and in our social philosophy. Much of our educational practice is experimental and exploratory, and with the accretion of experience, is subject to re-evaluation and re-interpretation.

Textbooks in education written to guide the young neophyte into a clear understanding of the principles and practices of teaching, or to provide inservice stimulation for the teacher at work, must reflect the many changes which result from tested experience and thought as these affect educational theory and practice. Few books in this area can escape the occasional need of some revision to bring them into harmony with current developments. The author claims no exception for *Teaching in Secondary Schools*. There were some aspects of instruction just emerging at the time this book was written which now have become much more clearly defined. The author does admit a feeling of satisfaction that he had anticipated many of these developments.

In this edition the text has undergone major changes to insure that it is abreast of the latest facts bearing upon every phase of methodology. For example, the interrelations of teaching method and the curriculum have made advisable two new chapters in that area. The section on Problems of Method has undergone radical change to conform to recent trends and developments. It has seemed desirable to introduce an extended chapter discussion on Practices and Reviews. The emergence of television as an important adjunct of our culture, with many educational possibilities, has required its consideration in the chapter with its near relative the radio. The unique place of the teacher in modern education has suggested a more extended consideration of the teacher in a textbook devoted to the teaching art.

No chapter has remained unchanged. The bibliographical

material at the end of each chapter has been completely revised. Section headings have been cast in question form to conform to better pedagogical practice.

If the long popularity enjoyed by this book is enhanced by this revision, much credit will be due the many users of this text, students, experienced teachers and instructors, who have contributed their suggestions for its improvement. To all these the author is greatly indebted.

This edition is made available to the members of the teaching profession, both actual and prospective, with the earnest hope that it will be found as helpful as the enthusiastic reception accorded the earlier editions would indicate has been true of it.

Minneapolis, Minnesota   NELSON L. BOSSING

CONTENTS

Part I

BASIC CONSIDERATIONS FOR SECONDARY EDUCATION

Part II

ORGANIZATION OF CURRICULUM MATERIALS FOR INSTRUCTION

vii

Part III

THE PROBLEM OF METHOD

Part IV

TEACHING TECHNIQUES OF THE CLASS PERIOD

Part V

MANAGEMENT TECHNIQUES IN TEACHING

Part VI

THE TEACHER IN EDUCATION

LIST OF TABLES

Part

I

BASIC CONSIDERATIONS

FOR SECONDARY SCHOOL EDUCATION

1

What is the Function of the Secondary School in a Democracy?

1. How Has the Secondary School Evolved?

Past and present interrelated

The high school teacher who aspires to be successful will do well to understand the modern secondary school in its historical perspective. Like many other social institutions, the present-day secondary school represents an evolutionary development. It is a product of many forces that have played upon it, molded its form, and determined its essential characteristics; and, like most institutions of society at the threshold of a new transition period, it has not divested itself completely of the outworn trappings of its past. As a result, many hangovers in the way of organizational form, curriculum, and concept of function — often meaningless and sometimes definitely contradictory — are found to exist side by side in schools in neighboring communities and even within the same school unit.

Nor should we necessarily expect to find a new institution completely divorced from historical origins. Newness per se does not have inherent within itself the essence of value. Intelligent social evolution requires the survival of those institutional values that have proved their worth in racial or social experience. The primary question must be their timeliness, their adaptability for the present.

Unless the teacher has a sympathetic understanding of this evi-

3

dent confusion and its causes, and can thereby keep a sense of perspective in the midst of it all, and select for development those elements in the situation which have value and practicability in the present, inefficiency and dissatisfaction with the profession of teaching must inevitably result.

Stages in secondary school development

At least three secondary institutions have formed a line of succession in the evolution of the American high school. The first of these, the Latin-Grammar school, was brought to America by our first colonists. It represents a direct transplantation from Europe. It embodied the social, political, and educational outlook of its native soil. The secondary schools of Europe were then, and to a great extent still are, the restricted schools of the classes. Only the well-to-do could or did send their children to the Latin-Grammar school. This school was distinctly a college-preparatory institution in Europe, and that remained its rather exclusive mission in early colonial history. As the name clearly implies, the Latin-Grammar school was heavily freighted with the ancient Latin classics and formal rhetoric. Very early in their life in the New World, many of the colonists sensed the inappropriateness of the Latin-Grammar school for the exigencies of pioneer life. Relatively few were able to afford a college education. Even fewer found it possible to follow a life of leisure and cultural interest as did the upper classes in the homeland. A natural demand arose, therefore, for a type of education on the level of the Latin-Grammar school that would contribute more practical worth to the life of these early colonial pioneers.

The dissatisfaction found definite expression in the advocacy by Benjamin Franklin, in 1743, of a secondary school known as the Academy. Franklin was anxious to establish a school that would emphasize a general type of training for those not able to continue their education through the college. The curriculum would focus attention upon such subjects as English, mathematics, morality, geography, and history — the last to include commercial history and natural history. The curriculum suggested by Franklin was a radical innovation. Unfortunately, when finally Franklin's Academy was organized in 1751, the curriculum represented something of a compromise with Franklin's friends, who could not conceive of a secondary school without the time-honored ancient languages. Languages, therefore, were included for those who wished to study them. In fact, Franklin's Academy opened for instruction with three departments — the Latin school, the English school, and the Mathematical school. From this time forward the Academy developed rapidly, ushered in a wide range of subject matter in the curriculum, and soon surpassed the rapidly waning Latin-Grammar school.

At least two major influences brought about the downfall of the Academy. First, with the decline of the Latin-Grammar school, the colleges began to cast about for a suitable preparatory training-medium for their students. The Academy proved to be the logical agency. It gradually lost its original character and became in essence a substitute for the Latin-Grammar school as the agency for preparation of college entrants. Its curriculum became narrow and predominantly classical in content. The second major factor in the eclipse of the Academy was the cumulative public insistence upon free public education at the secondary level. The Academy was from the first traditionally a private tuition school. The first school created in response to these demands was organized at Boston in 1821, as the Boston English Classical School. The school was free and was available for those who did not plan to go to the Latin school; i.e., for those who did not contemplate college attendance. Its curriculum was similar to that of Franklin's Academy except for the complete absence of foreign languages. The development of the high school, however, was slow. The next thirty years saw fewer than forty free public high schools established, while the Academy reached its peak of development about 1850 with over six thousand units.[1] After 1875 the Academy declined rapidly and the free public high schools came into the ascendancy.

Unfortunately, the usurpation of the place of first importance by the high school made it the object of concern by those interested in the adequate preparation of entrants to college. As a consequence the high school, at the beginning of the twentieth century, had degenerated into a preparatory school for the colleges and remained dominantly that prior to World War I. The impetus given by

---

[1] For a more detailed consideration of the Academy, see Mulhern, James, *A History of Education,* pp. 475–478. New York: The Ronald Press Company, 1946. Also Monroe, Paul, *Founding of the American Public School System,* pp. 390–410. New York: The Macmillan Company, 1940.

World War I and its intensification by World War II, to a rethinking of the meaning of our democracy and a program of education adequate to its needs, has projected America into an effort to reshape the program of secondary education to meet the demands of a democratic society.

Growth and development

The growth of the public high school has been phenomenal. The 1947–48 enrollment of the public high school given by the Office of Education in its 1950 report,[2] listed 25,484 public high schools with an enrollment of 5,653,305 pupils. This is approximately one million less pupils enrolled than in 1939–40. The Report estimates, however, that by 1965 there will be upwards of 11,000,000 pupils in the high school grades, 9–12. To get a true picture of the size of the total public secondary school enrollment for 1947–48 it is necessary to include the 3,551,126 enrolled in grades 7–8, now generally considered a part of the secondary school. That would bring the 1947–48 enrollment for grades 7–12 to 9,204,431 pupils.

This rapid development, however, has not taken place without its accumulation of problems. As previously indicated, prior to World War I the secondary school was essentially college preparatory in its emphasis. A study completed in 1921 by Counts,[3] revealed the serious consequences for a democratic conception of education of college-entrance domination of the high school curriculum. Counts found that the character of the high school population startlingly reflected the narrow purpose of the school curriculum. For the most part only those pupils attended whose parents were able to contemplate the possibilities of a college education for their children. The recent and broader emphasis given the curriculum of the secondary school has had a considerable part in the phenomenal growth in high school attendance since 1920, and particularly within the past ten years.

[2] *Biennial Survey of Education in the United States, 1946–48*, chapter I. *Statistical Summary of Education, 1947–48*, pp. 22, 24. Washington: Office of Education, 1950.

[3] Counts, G. S. *The Selective Character of American Secondary Education.* Supplementary Educational Monographs, No. 19. University of Chicago, 1922.

2. What Is the Place of the Secondary School in Modern Educational Organization?

Educational organization evolving

The summary picture thus far presented of the fortunes of the secondary school cannot but suggest the lack of stability within the form of educational organization. While the secondary school through the Latin-Grammar, Academy, and high school has carried with it by implication a lower form of educational organization, as well as a higher (college) form, the outlines of these have not been sharply defined. Rapidly these organizational outlines are being brought into clear perspective. The more clearly defined these lines of cleavage are and the more extensive the units involved, the greater the need on the part of the teacher for a thorough appreciation of the place and nature of the task of the modern high school in a democratic society.

Much like Topsy, our educational system has just grown. Considerable confusion still exists both as to the organizational form and the significance of the parts. The fact that no country in the world previously has undertaken to educate its citizenry on the broad scale attempted in America, or to make that education at all levels potentially possible for the remotest individual, has led to much of our difficulty, inasmuch as we have had no landmarks to guide us. Even worse, the tendency to forget the uniqueness of our educational experiment has led to confusion on the part of many who see a well-defined and coordinated secondary school curriculum in vogue in Europe, but have not paused to inquire into the function of the secondary school in continental education.

Present organization and tendencies

The educational ladder consists of three principal divisions, somewhat clearly defined in major outlines: they are the elementary, secondary, and higher educational levels. The lines of demarcation between these divisions are not so sharply determined. Graphically the divisions may be set down roughly as most commonly recognized by educational leaders.

Elementary $\left\{ \begin{array}{l} \text{Kindergarten — Age } 5 \text{ — Grades sub.} \\ \text{Primary — Ages } 6\text{–}8 \text{ — Grades } 1\text{–}3 \\ \text{Intermediate — Ages } 9\text{–}11 \text{ — Grades } 4\text{–}6 \end{array} \right.$

Secondary
{ Junior High School — Ages 12–14 — Grades 7–9
  Senior High School — Ages 15–17 — Grades 10–12
  Junior College — Ages 18–19 — Grades 13–14

Higher — Professional and Technical Training — Ages 20+ — Grades 15+

While these divisions are the ones commonly accepted in educational theory they do not represent the accepted mode of practice, inasmuch as the eight-year elementary school still predominates and the Junior College is yet in its infancy. Besides, a further development gaining headway at the present would extend education two years below the kindergarten, recognized as the preschool period, change the secondary divisions into the high school, grades 7–10, and the community college, grades 11–14, and at the other extreme would provide a flexible system of adult education not contemplated in the third major division or higher education. These divisions do, however, aid the high school teacher to localize his problem.

3. What Is the Task of Education in a Democracy?

Had our forefathers possessed a well-defined conception of democracy and the peculiar functions of the school within a democratic society, much of the struggle in secondary education recorded in the previous pages would have been avoided. The vicissitudes of the American secondary school reflects the persistent efforts of an awakening democratic spirit to free itself from inherited educational ideas suited to an older authoritarian European society but incompatible with the educational needs of a democratic people.

Meaning of education

Such evidence of confusion as to the purpose of secondary education, revealed throughout the history of the secondary school in America and further indicated in the unsettled scope of its organization, naturally forces the teacher to question the true function of education at this level. Indeed, a prior question would appear to demand an answer; namely, "What is the meaning of education?" No teacher can hope to succeed until he understands the meaning of the whole as well as the relationship of its parts. In other words, he must comprehend clearly the general purpose and function of education. He must see, too, the purpose of each major division as it relates to the larger outreaches of education. The writer has no further objective in this chapter than to suggest for purposes of recall important data that need to be considered, and to insure a common understanding upon which to base a methodology of teaching at the secondary level. The imperative need on the part of the teacher of a well-defined conception of education is accepted as fundamental.[4]

Education may be thought of as having two important and complementary facets: the one is concerned with education as a process of growth or development, and the other is concerned with education as in relation to purposes and goals. The teacher must always think of education as a process. He must constantly keep before him such questions as: "How do boys and girls grow or develop from what they are to something else?" "How do these changes take place?" "What can I do about it?" It is important for the teacher to keep in mind that education is a process by which the learner, often stumblingly, and sometimes with painful slowness, acquires different competencies. Further, it should be recognized that whatever is sought through education must be attained by a growth process. It is the function of the teacher to carefully and patiently guide the learning processes so that desirable changes in the behavior patterns of youth take place.

It is not enough for the teacher to be fully aware that education is a process by which growth and development are attained. It is equally important that the teacher should have definitely in mind the direction which this growth should take. Change does not occur except in some direction. Education must be concerned with the direction in which this change takes place in order to insure that all behavioral changes may represent the acquisition of personal and socially desirable behavior competencies.

The dual nature of education, now fully accepted, is recognized in the statement of the purpose of education in a democratic society given in the now famous *Report of the Commission for the Reorganization of the Secondary School.*[5] Here the over-all purpose of education was stated to be:

[4] The author discusses the meaning of education for a democratic society in much more detail in *Principles of Secondary Education,* chapters X and XI. New York: Prentice-Hall, Inc., 1949.

[5] *Cardinal Principles of Secondary Education,* p. 9. U.S. Bureau of Education, Bulletin 35, 1918.

To develop in each individual the knowledge, interests, ideals, habits and powers whereby he will find his place and use that place to shape both himself and society toward ever nobler ends.

A more comprehensive statement from a contemporary writer agrees in general, but serves to amplify the point of view just quoted. Counts says: [6]

The end of education is to be found in neither the one period nor the other (child or adult), but rather in the growth of the power of the learner to cope with this environment — a growth which is nurtured through a direct participation in the life of the group and through a vicarious participation in the racial experience. . . . The child should be equipped to perform many of the activities adults perform, but often on a more generous scale and according to an improved pattern. Even so, the aim is not to prepare him for adult life, but to give him mastery over his world and to make him a guardian of the spiritual possessions of the group.

A definition of education

The discussion thus far has implied education as the agency by which the individual is molded into a socially efficient member of a democratic society. No doubt that point of view must remain central. However, sociality alone does not make up the complete picture of one's life. An adequate definition should comprehend other things besides, though the final appraisal of education must be made in terms of its significant contribution to social values. For the purpose of pointing a conception that may be basic and dynamic in this book, *the function of education is conceived to be the adjustment of man to his environment, which contemplates man's adaptation to and the reconstruction of his environment to the end that the most enduring satisfactions may accrue to the individual and to society.* It can scarcely be gainsaid that the problem of adjustment to the physical, social, and spiritual forces of our environment is basic in its very nature and cosmic in its outreach. Adaptation is imperative for the individual who would survive. Since man has steadily succeeded, with increasing momentum, in the creation for himself of the highly artificial environment that he

[6] Counts, G. S. "Some Notes on the Foundations of Curriculum Making" in the *Twenty-Sixth Yearbook* of the National Society for the Study of Education, Part II, *Foundations of Curriculum-Making*, pp. 74–75. Bloomington, Ill.: Public School Publishing Company, 1926. Quoted by permission of the Society.

has been pleased to call civilization, the problem of adaptation has assumed a place of primary importance. When man lived in more primitive states, the social adaptations required of him were few and elemental. Likewise the adaptations to his physical world were not numerous or difficult. Simple shelter sufficed. Food was for the most part easily available. The warmer the climate, the less vigorous were the adaptive demands upon him. By the same token, the more complex the environmental situation imposed upon man by his artificial wants and created values becomes, the more imperative and far-reaching becomes the demand for a reconstruction of his environment so that the new wants thus stimulated may be satisfied. Primitive man found the chase supplied his wants for food, clothing, and, in no small part, his shelter. As his wants grew more numerous, it became necessary to reconstruct his environment by cultivation of the soil, manufacture, and the transformation of his physical world to provide more commodious and comfortable shelter. This change affected his social environment. Free nomadic life is incompatible with cultivated crops and imposing non-movable properties. New adaptations to new social environments, and the creation of new modes of social thought and behavior, are rendered necessary as compensations for new values accepted and new satisfactions to be attained.

Unfortunately, we have thought of the adjustment function too literally in terms of social reactions alone. Even at that we have thought of these social adjustments on far too restricted a plane. We have acted as though the greatest satisfactions of life could be attained in the realm of the material. More and more, thoughtful leaders in education raise warning voices against this serious limitation upon our prevailing educational outlook. To one of the world's greatest teachers and thinkers are attributed the words: "Man shall not live by bread alone." A cursory study of the history of the thought-life of the race will reveal how extensively man has given thought to the nature of the cosmos and his relationship to it. One cannot escape, furthermore, the realization of the profound effect that man's view of the universe and his acceptance of his relationship to it have had upon social thought and behavior. Yet, almost by common consent, this vital aspect of man's complete adjustment to his environment has been neglected by the school.

All too often the individual as he reaches maturity has not been able to recognize any great ongoing spiritual forces in the universe, much less to identify himself with them. He does not feel the urge of a great spiritual dynamic, nor is he able to link himself with any cosmic forces that give purposiveness, vital meaning, and a timeless quality to life. As a result he has found his adjustment inadequate and his integration with his world incomplete.

The school must recognize the seriousness of this mission in its educational outlook. The program of the school must make possible the integration of the personality around some great cosmic principle that elevates man to a destiny far beyond that of sensuous satisfactions alone.

Threefold function of the school

Education, implied in such a definition, means a threefold function of the school.

First, the school must become the directive agency by which the child is enabled to adapt himself efficiently to the environment into which he has been born. The writer recalls quite vividly a classroom discussion on the place of motivation in the educational process. The professor in charge of the class, a nationally known educator, after dwelling upon the importance of motivation in efficient learning, mentioned many of the abuses that had developed where teachers, more enthusiastic than wise, had carried to extremes this valuable educational principle. He then summarized the discussion with this trenchant statement:

> Remember that the doctrine of interest is important for learning and should be utilized wherever possible. It is even more important to remember that the child has been born into an artificial structure of civilization. The child is not by nature interested at this tender age in complete adjustment to this highly artificial social institution. But whether he can be motivated by natural interests or not, he must be taught conformity to the demands of this artificial civilization or society will brand him a misfit and ruthlessly cast him aside.

The school must acquaint the youthful citizen with the nature of this institution of which he is and will be with the coming years much more a part. It must provide him with the requisite knowledge and skills for successful adaptation to the patterns of living required in a democratic society. Every major social camp has set up certain guides or regulations (rules of the road), conformity to which it is believed will enable its members to live more efficiently and happily together. These regulations are expressed both in written laws and unwritten conventions and customs which youth should understand.

Second, the school must assume responsibility for the development within the individual of new interests, aspirations, and the power to sense new values, both individual and social, the attainment of which must inevitably bring new permanent satisfactions and cause society to reach even higher levels of living than now enjoyed. It is here that the "reconstruction" principle finds much confusion of thought among some educators, as well as with the laity. There are those who maintain, not without cogent reasoning, that the school is the agent of society solely for the perpetuation of itself. It receives its support and right to exist from this selfsame society, and this is frequently interpreted to mean the perpetuation of the institutional *mores* of a political group or the social conventions, customs, and modes of social thought of a given community. We, therefore, find frequent expression of this conception of the function of the school in American life.

This confusion arises in part from a failure to distinguish sharply between the functions of the school as the educational agency of an authoritarian versus a democratic society. In older European autocratic countries the ideal was to perpetuate from generation to generation, with as little change as possible, the pattern of life set by authoritarian governments. In a democracy, on the other hand, the rules by which people live are determined by the direction and the consent of all its members. The genius of a democracy is its constant alertness to ways in which the patterns of living may be changed to continually improve and enrich the life of all. Another grave source of difficulty is the failure of many to recognize that in a world of increasing tempo of change, a democracy must depend upon the school to so educate the oncoming generations of its youth that they will be aware of the significance of the changes taking place in our culture, and will acquire the essential competencies to change, reconstruct, where needed, the patterns of life for the common good. It is because we have not seen clearly the uniqueness of the reconstruction principle of education in a democracy that we suffer such unnecessary disparity between our "cultural lag" and those highly desirable modifications of our modes of living which democracy in theory should enable its members to attain.

That much freedom and liberality in the interpretation and application of the "reconstruction" principle "to the end that the most enduring satisfactions may accrue to the individual and society" is essential to the welfare of society would seem to need no argument. It is only by the development of an appreciative but critical attitude toward present modes of thought and behavior that new ideas are possible and improved ways of doing things are made available. The school cannot fulfill its true function if it is not free to evaluate every phase of human knowledge, point out weaknesses and fallacies even in our most cherished modes of thought and behavior, and either offer suggestions for improvements or, better still, see that the ongoing generation has the equipment necessary to effect desirable changes. The readiness to reconstruct environment in the direction of desired ends, even the wholesome spirit of adventure, should characterize the school's approach to its educational responsibilities.

Third, an important function of the school is concerned with the development of the affective nature of man. This responsibility of the school has been sadly neglected. Indeed, even now the few voices raised in behalf of this educational need are like voices crying in the wilderness. We have been prone to assume our educational obligations discharged when an intellectual awareness concerning the problems of adjustment has been established, and the techniques by which their solution could be achieved were properly inculcated in the learner. Educational leaders have been greatly disturbed to find these cherished assumptions incorrect in experience. Knowledge of correct forms of social behavior has not, per se, insured the exercise of these desirable behavior patterns; in fact, plenty of evidence is available to show the direct contrary. The debilitating effect of high-heeled shoes upon the health of women has long been accepted and taught in school hygiene, but why do those with this knowledge still persist in the injurious practice? With our school physiologies devoting, on the average, a chapter to the harmful effects of narcotics, with particular reference to tobacco, why is it that most adolescent boys, to say nothing of the girls, will undergo considerable physical discomfort to acquire the ability to smoke cigarettes with a nonchalance that would do credit to a veteran? Our schools have persistently taught the duties of citizenship. It would be difficult to maintain that our adult citizens do not understand the technique of voting, nor that they do not have full knowledge of the significance of the ballot as the bulwark of a democratic society, yet it is a disturbing fact that seldom do as many as fifty per cent of the eligible voters exercise their franchise even in national elections. In off presidential years it is not uncommon to find that as few as thirty per cent of the eligible voters register their convictions at the polls.

While a resident in Chicago, as a graduate student, the writer often frequented a famous club, a semi-underworld organization, where gathered some of the most colorful characters of Chicago's underworld to participate in forum discussions of political and social problems of the moment. In no unselected group anywhere would one be likely to find as high a percentage of college trained men and women. The writer has seldom heard from any platform as chaste English or as fluent oratory as graced these forum discussions, yet by our accepted standards these people had not squared their behavior with the conduct patterns taught them in the schools. Obviously more important controls operated in their lives than the knowledge and skills taught them.

To the late psychologist, G. Stanley Hall, is attributed the words: "Our intellect is a mere speck afloat on a sea of feeling." Apropos of this quotation Briggs further comments: [7]

There is no depreciation of it, not the slightest, in a recognition of the incontrovertible fact that, along with the speck of intellect, often dissolving or profoundly modifying it, is an ocean of feeling. This must be a concern, too, of any comprehensive curriculum. We feel more, both qualitatively and quantitatively, than we think. "One emotion will cover a multitude of ideas." . . . But reaction, intellectual or physical, is seldom determined directly by thinking or action that is original. As a result of inheritance and experience, sometimes singly but usually multiple, every one develops a large number of more or less generalized attitudes, which condition and, to a large extent, determine all future responses. . . . Having been made ill by oysters, one tends to acquire toward oysters, Scotch Highlanders, or steel-link puzzles, attitudes that will persist until modified by rationalization or, what is more likely, by another actual experience with different results.

Briggs has put his finger upon a tender spot in our educational thought and progress. We have failed to take into account in any adequate way the training of man's affective life. It is not enough to insure correct knowledge. That knowledge must have a definite

[7] Briggs, Thomas H. *Curriculum Problems*, pp. 51–54. New York: The Macmillan Company, 1926.

feeling-set. Positive and full-charged attitudes must accompany intellectual awareness if education is to be effective. It may be that in certain situations education should become primarily concerned with the affective state. At least the school will recognize the proper development of the affective life as a natural part of the total education of the learner.

Objectives of education in a democracy

At this point we are prepared to consider briefly the question, "What are the objectives of education for a democracy?" The attempt to formulate a statement of objectives for the American public schools has received much attention, particularly during the past three-quarters of a century. Educators are becoming increasingly aware that only as the unique purposes of goals of education for a democracy are clearly perceived by all engaged in education, can boys and girls be insured those competencies necessary for their effective participation in a democratic society. Possibly the best statement of objectives of education formulated by a representative and highly influential body of educators is that prepared by the Educational Policies Commission of the National Education Association. It is widely used, and will probably continue for a long time to influence the direction of educational thinking. The objectives are given below: [8]

The Objectives of Self-Realization

The Inquiring Mind. The educated person has an appetite for learning.
Speech. The educated person can speak the mother tongue clearly.
Reading. The educated person reads the mother tongue efficiently.
Writing. The educated person writes the mother tongue effectively.
Number. The educated person solves problems of counting and calculating.
Sight and Hearing. The educated person is skilled in listening and observing.
Health and Knowledge. The educated person understands the basic facts concerning health and disease.
Health Habits. The educated person protects his own health and that of his dependents.

[8] Educational Policies Commission, *The Purposes of Education In American Democracy*, pp. 50, 72, 90, 108. Washington: National Education Association, 1938. For a more complete discussion of objectives see Bossing, Nelson L.,

Public Health. The educated person works to improve the health of the community.

Recreation. The educated person is participant and spectator in many sports and other pastimes.

Intellectual Interests. The educated person has mental resources for the use of leisure.

Esthetic Interests. The educated person appreciates beauty.

Character. The educated person gives responsible direction to his own life.

The Objectives of Human Relationships

Respect for Humanity. The educated person puts human relationships first.

Friendships. The educated person enjoys the rich, sincere, and varied social life.

Cooperation. The educated person can work and play with others.

Courtesy. The educated person observes the amenities of social behavior.

Appreciation of the Home. The educated person appreciates the family as a social institution.

Conservation of the Home. The educated person conserves family ideals.

Homemaking. The educated person is skilled in homemaking.

Democracy in the Home. The educated person maintains democratic family relations.

The Objectives of Economic Efficiency

Work. The educated producer knows the satisfaction of good workmanship.

Occupational Information. The educated producer understands the requirement and opportunities for various jobs.

Occupational Choice. The educated person has selected his occupation.

Occupational Efficiency. The educated producer succeeds in his chosen vocation.

Occupational Adjustment. The educated producer maintains and improves his own efficiency.

Occupational Appreciation. The educated producer appreciates the social value of his work.

Personal Economics. The educated consumer plans the economics of his own life.

Consumer Judgment. The educated consumer develops standards for guiding his expenditures.

Principles of Secondary Education, pp. 289–299, 308–325. New York: Prentice-Hall, Inc., 1949.

Efficiency in Buying. The educated consumer is an informed and skillful buyer.

Consumer Protection. The educated consumer takes appropriate measures to safeguard his interests.

The Objectives of Civic Responsibility

Social Justice. The educated citizen is sensitive to the disparities of human circumstance.

Social Activity. The educated citizen acts to correct unsatisfactory conditions.

Social Understanding. The educated citizen seeks to understand social structures and social processes.

Critical Judgment. The educated citizen has defenses against propaganda.

Tolerance. The educated citizen respects honest differences of opinion.

Conservation. The educated citizen has a regard for the nation's resources.

Social Application of Science. The educated citizen measures scientific advance by its contribution to the general welfare.

World Citizenship. The educated citizen is a cooperating member of the world community.

Law Observance. The educated citizen respects the law.

Economic Literacy. The educated citizen is economically literate.

Political Citizenship. The educated citizen acts upon an unswerving loyalty to democratic ideals.

4. What Is the Task of Secondary Education in a Democracy?

Relation of elementary to secondary school

To gain a satisfactory picture of the function of the secondary school, it is necessary to see in perspective the main outlines of the elementary school.

The elementary school child comes to this stage of his educational career direct from the home. He enters the portals of the school with but one important acquired tool with which to begin his educational career. Every normal child from an American home brings with him a working knowledge of the spoken language used as a medium of exchange of ideas within the school. The degree of proficiency with which the child uses the language is dependent upon the quality of speech habits of the home. The acquisition of other forms of language expression, as well as the perfection of the one he uses, is one of his immediate tasks. A second characteristic of the newly entered child is his lack of social adjustment. He comes to the school frequently with nonsocial or unsocial attributes. If he is an only child, the probabilities are that he has not been exposed thoroughly to the socializing influences of childhood companions. If, in addition, he is unfortunate enough to have over-indulgent parents, his social experience will have developed in him pronounced unsocial behavior-patterns, as well as undesirable attitudes. In any event the social experience of the elementary school child is very limited. Again the child in all probability has never been regimented seriously. His indulged individualism brings to the school an undisciplined will and a consequent lack of purposeful coordination.

Tasks of the elementary school

The school, therefore, has four main tasks during this elementary period. *First,* the child must become moderately proficient in the use of language tools. In addition to the development and refinement of the spoken language he is made acquainted with at least four additional language facilities; namely, reading, writing, listening, and the language of number symbols. These will occupy much of the curricular activities of the first six years of the school experience of the child.

The *second* main task of the elementary school is that of socialization at the rudimentary levels. The integrating function of the elementary school centers about the fusing of dissimilar elements into a common unity. By the time the child is ready to leave the elementary school he should have learned how to live cooperatively with others, to show a reasonably intelligent respect for the rights of others, and to exhibit in his general behavior the elementary qualities of a responsible citizen of his group.

The *third* task of the school is to insure that the child has come to understand something of the larger world about him. The child of our contemporary society cannot be oblivious to his outside world. The radio and television, to say nothing of the movie and the newspaper, bring him into contact with many different aspects of his culture, some strange and contradictory to the approved pattern of life to which he is accustomed. As this is written the radio, television and newspapers are featuring the testimony of hoodlums and gangsters as a Senate Investigating Committee uncovers the seamy side of a segment of American life.

The *fourth* task of the elementary school is to help the child as he nears the end of this period of education to become oriented toward the next major division of the school system, the school of adolescence. The maturing child should now begin to discover his emerging interests and attitudes, and see the secondary school as a larger opportunity for his exploration and expression.

The secondary school pupil

With the completion of the elementary school the child has achieved a certain degree of integration with the group. He identifies himself with the group, has taken on some of the general characteristics of his playmates, and, on the main issues of life that confront children of this age, assumes a similar point of view and now possesses a certain amount of common knowledge with those of this age-level. The worst of his rugged individualism and unsocial or anti-social behavior has been worn down so that, within latitude, he is now a rudimentary social being after the accepted pattern of his elders.

Again, he has acquired a basic knowledge of the tool subjects: his mother tongue — speaking, writing, reading, listening and the language of numbers. These important acquisitions transplant the individual into a vastly enlarged world. Now there are in his keeping the keys that unlock the secret recesses of human thought without respect to time, place, or the quality of the ideas revealed.

The tabloid newspapers, magazines ranging from the intellectually stimulating to those that are mere drivel and worse; books that present a world panorama of different peoples, of contemporary and ancient times, their culture and customs, as well as those books that warp personality and foul the wellsprings of human thought at its sources — all these are at once both the priceless and the hazardous possession of the boy or girl who has successfully completed the work of the elementary grades and now stands at the threshold of the secondary school.

More than that, the advent of youth to the secondary school means exposure to an enlarged social horizon, intimate contacts at times with groups that differ sharply in the standards of personal conduct and modes of social thought accepted. In spite of the tendency of our modern economic and industrial life to destroy community consciousness and break down unity within social groups, a large degree of homogeneity still persists within communal districts. Within any urban center may be found rather well-defined strata of social life. The wealthy proprietary group segregates itself in one part of the residential district, the professional and clerical folk find common ground in another, and the industrial workers and laborers form a community with lines of social cleavage more sharply defined than in the two groups previously mentioned. Racial groups show even more definite tendencies in this direction when they exist in considerable numbers in a given community. The elementary school usually serves one of these groups predominantly or almost exclusively; so definitely are these segregations evident at times that unfortunately they are reflected in the type of school facilities provided. Rarely does the secondary school follow such narrow divisional lines. Larger in unit of student population cared for, the high school cuts across artificial barriers and brings these groups of divergent social standards and outlook together. So widely do these groups differ in social point of view at times that a major problem in thought adjustment is faced by those thus sharply made aware of the differences that exist in standards of thought and conduct among the representatives of these various groups.

Last but not least among the forces which converge upon the pupil at this stage is that most profound of all — the physiological change that comes with adolescence. Adolescence has been defined as "that period in the life of the boy or girl which extends from the beginning of puberty through the maturation of the reproductive function." This definition calls attention to but one phase of the adolescent period, albeit the most fundamental one.

As a supplement to the definition given above is the statement of a recent writer: [9] "Adolescence or youth . . . extends from puberty to the attainment of full height and weight and the cessation of growth. It is the period in which the person moves out from the home circle, and becomes physically and mentally independent." This definition assumes that during adolescence, physiological and mental development, in addition to the growth of the sex function, reach approximate maturity. Physiological and mental growth do not necessarily exactly parallel pubertal growth. Indeed, in most cases maturation extends into post-pubertal years so that adolescence encompasses the period from the beginning of puberty

[9] Anderson, John E. *The Psychology of Development and Personal Adjustment*, p. 64. New York: Henry Holt and Company, Inc., 1949.

to the emergence of the individual into the possession of the mature physical, mental and social powers that stamp him an adult.

It is usually assumed that this period extends approximately from ages twelve to twenty. For practical purposes of obtaining a picture of the general nature of the adolescent period these age limits may be accepted, though in some instances full adolescent development may not be reached before twenty-five. It is well for the high school teacher to be aware, however, when confronted with specific school situations, that these years are approximations only, and that while they enable him to draw useful deductions for teaching purposes, the variations in the time of the beginning and maturation of the reproductive function and in the time of general growth make the application of teaching principles at this period extremely difficult. If in a class of juniors in the senior high school there are boys and girls who entered the pubertal stage of adolescence at the age of twelve, and if there are others in the same group who, at the age of sixteen, have just arrived at the pubertal stage, the problems of the teacher are greatly intensified. A vast gulf separates the educational needs of these extreme groups.

Task of the secondary school

Against a background of the over-all task of education, the particular responsibility of the elementary school, and some indication of the nature of the pupil seeking admission to the secondary school, it is important to see the specific place of secondary education in the total educational picture. One of the most graphic statements of the nature and function of secondary education the author has found is that given by the Committee on the Orientation of Secondary Education of the Department of Secondary School Principals. They defined secondary education thus:

> "Secondary education" denotes the education provided by schools for the purpose of guiding and promoting the development of normal individuals for whom on the one hand the elementary school no longer constitutes a satisfactory environment, and who on the other hand are either not yet prepared to participate effectively in society unguided by the school, or are not ready for the specialized work of the professional schools or the upper division of the liberal arts college.[10]

[10] Committee on the Orientation of Secondary Education. *Issues of Secondary Education.* Page 22, Bulletin No. 59. Department of Secondary School Principals. Chicago: National Education Association, January, 1936.

This definition is a much more significant pronouncement than at first glance it may appear to be. *First,* the period comprising secondary education is stated entirely in terms of function. The secondary school has a clearly defined task in relation to the assigned responsibility of the elementary school which precedes it. The secondary school assumes responsibility for the education of the learner when he reaches that stage in his development that the "elementary school no longer constitutes a satisfactory environment." At the upper limits the secondary school has discharged its responsibility for the learner when certain competencies have been acquired.

Second, there are no mechanically imposed lines of demarcation that separate the elementary from the secondary school. No age- or grade-level standards are imposed. The passing of certain critical scores on one or more standardized tests does not indicate the child is ready for the school above. The time has come for a change for each child when he reaches that stage of biological, social, and intellectual maturity where he finds he is no longer interested in the things that are of primary concern to childhood. For a given individual this time may arrive while he is in the typical fifth grade, and for another not before he has reached the traditional eighth- or ninth-grade age-level.[11]

Third, no arbitrarily rigid standards determine when the work of the secondary school has been completed. The completion of a prescribed number of years or the acquisition of a given number of school credits, now the usual practice, will not be accepted as a basis of graduation from the secondary school. Two criteria are set for the determination of when a person has reached the place where he should no longer continue in the secondary school. Either (1) he has achieved such competencies that he is "prepared to participate effectively in society unguided by the school," or (2) is competent to carry on "the specialized work of the professional schools or the upper division of the liberal arts colleges." These criteria would clearly indicate that when youth has developed those competencies recognized as essential for successful adult life he no longer belongs in the secondary school.

---

[11] For data on the variation in individuals of the onset of puberty see Cole, Luella, *Psychology of Adolescence,* Third Edition, chapter IV. New York: Rinehart and Company, 1948; also "Growth and Development," *Review of Educational Research,* vol. XX, no. 5, pp. 393–402 (December, 1950).

Fourth, the task of the secondary school is definitely implied in this definition. The secondary school has the specific responsibility of "guiding and promoting the development of normal individuals" between the elementary school period and the time when he has achieved competencies essential to the assumption of the responsibilities of adulthood. The period in the life of the individual thus spanned by the secondary school somewhat roughly corresponds to the period of the emergence and maturing of the sex function — the time of adolescence. The biological characteristic of the learner in the elementary school is that of a child. The elementary school is therefore the school of childhood. When puberty begins, the school of childhood no longer provides a satisfactory environment for the emerging adolescent. The early phase of secondary education must be concerned with the continued development of the competencies partially acquired in the elementary school, and the orientation of the individual into a world constantly unfolding with new meanings and new problems of adjustment. As the adolescent matures he must begin to think of himself in a larger role as a developing citizen with the necessity of achieving those needed competencies essential for adult life, such as assumption of larger family and home responsibilities, full civic community participation, the selection of a vocation and the development of some degree of salable skills therein.

It should be evident to the careful student that the conception of the purposes of secondary education outlined above involves the constant effective adjustment of the individual to his environment through consistent changes in his behavioral patterns as he progresses through the elementary and secondary schools. When he is judged ready to accept the mantle of full adulthood he has, through the wealth of experiences provided by the secondary schools, become fully oriented intellectually and emotionally toward his role in society, and, in maximal degree consistent with his maturity, has accepted and developed those personal, social, and vocational skills in his daily living that give assurance of their continuance and further development in his enlarged role as an adult.

Objectives of the secondary school

In addition to the list of general objectives applicable to both elementary and secondary education presented by the Educational Policies Commission of the National Education Association, previously mentioned,[12] those concerned with secondary school teaching should be familiar with at least one additional list of objectives, formulated specifically for secondary education by the National Association of Secondary School Principals. These objectives are stated in terms of the basic needs of youth which it is the duty of the secondary school to help them attain. They are listed below:

THE IMPERATIVE NEEDS OF YOUTH OF SECONDARY-SCHOOL AGE [13]

Imperative Need Number 1 — All youth needs to develop salable skills and those understandings and attitudes that make the worker an intelligent and productive participant in economic life. To this end, most youth need supervised work experience as well as education in the skills and knowledge of their occupations.

Imperative Need Number 2 — All youth need to develop and maintain good health and physical fitness.

Imperative Need Number 3 — All youth need to understand the rights and duties of a citizen of a democratic society, and to be diligent and competent in the performance of their obligations as members of the community and citizens of the state and nation and of the world.

Imperative Need Number 4 — All youth need to understand the significance of the family for the individual and society and the conditions conducive to successful family life.

Imperative Need Number 5 — All youth need to know how to purchase and use goods and services intelligently, understanding both the values received by the consumer and the economic consequences of their acts.

Imperative Need Number 6 — All youth need to understand the methods of science, the influence of science on human life, and the main scientific facts concerning the nature of the world and of man.

Imperative Need Number 7 — All youth need opportunities to develop their capacities to appreciate beauty in literature, art, music and nature.

Imperative Need Number 8 — All youth need to be able to use their leisure time well and to budget it wisely, balancing activities that yield satisfactions to the individual with those that are socially useful.

Imperative Need Number 9 — All youth need to develop respect for

[12] See pp. 16–18. Attention is again called to *Principles of Secondary Education* written by the author, chapters X and XI; also to Alexander, W. M., and Saylor, J. G., *Secondary Education*, chapter IV. New York: Rinehart and Company, Inc., 1950.

[13] *The Imperative Needs of Youth of Secondary School Age*, Bulletin No. 145, The National Association of Secondary-School Principals, Washington, D.C. (March 1947). The entire bulletin is devoted to an analysis of the ten imperative needs listed.

other persons, to grow in their insight into ethical values and principles, and to be able to live and work cooperatively with others.

Imperative Need Number 10 — All youth need to grow in their ability to think rationally, to express their thoughts clearly and to read and listen with understanding.

QUESTIONS AND PROBLEMS

1. Trace the development of the secondary school in America, and explain why the major institutional changes have marked its evolution.

2. (*a*) In what respects is the high school of today different from the high school of 1850?

   (*b*) Explain the lack of uniformity in purpose and curriculum among many high schools of today.

3. Discuss the effect upon the character of our present secondary institution of the rapid growth of our high school population since 1900.

4. Explain the lack of uniformity in our secondary school organization.

5. How do you distinguish between the functions of the elementary and secondary schools?

6. Critically evaluate the following as a definition of education: "Whatever else we may say about it, then, education is a process of growth, it means liberation of capacity."

7. Explain why adolescence is considered such an important phase of the individual's life.

8. How does the school share with other agencies the responsibilities of the youth's education?

9. What do you understand by the term "adjustment function" of the secondary school? Criticize the phrase.

10. Criticize the functions of secondary education as discussed by the author. What changes would you propose?

11. Criticize the following definition of adolescence: "That period in the life of the boy or girl which extends from the beginning of puberty through the maturation of the reproductive function."

12. Critically evaluate the conception of the function of the secondary school as "preparation for adult life."

SELECTED BIBLIOGRAPHY

Adolescence. Forty-Third Year Book, Part I, National Society for the Study of Education. Chicago: University of Chicago Press, 1944.

Anderson, John E. *The Psychology of Development and Personal Adjustment.* New York: Henry Holt and Company, 1949.

Anderson, V. E., Grim, P. R. and Gruhn, W. T. *Principles and Practices of Secondary Education.* New York: The Ronald Press Company, 1951.

Anderson, W. M. and Saylor, J. G. *Secondary Education,* Chapter IV. New York: Rinehart and Company, 1950.

Blair, Arthur W. and Burton, William H. *Growth and Development of the Preadolescent.* New York: Appleton-Century-Crofts, Inc., 1951.

Bogue, J. P. *The Community College.* New York: McGraw-Hill Book Company, Inc., 1950.

Bossing, Nelson L. *Principles of Secondary Education.* New York: Prentice-Hall, Inc., 1949.

Brameld, Theodore. *Patterns of Educational Philosophy.* New York: World Book Company, 1950.

Briggs, T. H., Leonard, J. P. and Justman, J. *Secondary Education.* New York: The Macmillan Company, 1950.

Brubacher, John S. *Modern Philosophies of Education.* New York: McGraw-Hill Book Company, 1939.

Bryson, Lyman, Finkelstein, Louis, and Maciver, R. M. *Goals For American Education.* New York: Harper and Brothers, 1950.

Cardinal Principles of Secondary Education, Office of Education Bulletin, No. 35, 1918. Washington, D.C.: Government Printing Office.

Caswell, H. L. et al. *The American High School,* Eighth Yearbook of the John Dewey Society. New York: Harper and Brothers, 1946.

Cole, Luella. *Psychology of Adolescence.* New York: Rinehart and Company, 1948.

Douglass, A. A. *The American School System,* Revised Edition. New York: Farrar & Rinehart, Inc., 1940.

Eby, F. and Arrowood, C. F. *History and Philosophy of Education.* New York: Prentice-Hall, Inc., 1940.

Faunce, Roland C., and Bossing, Nelson L. *Developing the Core Curriculum.* New York: Prentice-Hall, Inc., 1951.

"Functions of Secondary Education," *Bulletin of the Department of Secondary School Principals,* vol. 21, no. 64 (January 1937). Washington, D.C.: Committee on the Orientation of Secondary Education, Department of Secondary School Principals, National Education Association.

Garrison, K. C. *Psychology of Adolescence,* Fourth Edition. New York: Prentice-Hall, Inc., 1951.

"Growth and Development," *Review of Educational Research,* vol. XX, no. 5 (December, 1950). Washington, D.C.: American Educational Research Association, National Education Association.

Havighurst, R. J., and Taba, H. *Adolescent Character and Personality.* New York: John Wiley and Sons, Inc., 1949.

Horrocks, John E. *The Psychology of Adolescence.* Boston: Houghton Mifflin Company, 1951.

Hurlock, E. B. *Adolescent Development.* New York: McGraw-Hill Book Company, Inc., 1949.

"Issues of Secondary Education," *Bulletin of the Department of Secondary School Principals,* vol. 20, no. 59 (January, 1936). Washington, D.C.: Committee on the Orientation of Secondary Education, Department of Secondary School Principals, National Education Association.

Monroe, Paul. *Founding of the American Public School System,* vol. I. New York: The Macmillan Company, 1940.

Mulhern, James. *A History of Education.* New York: The Ronald Press Company, 1946.

Philosophies of Education. Forty-first Yearbook, Part I, National Society for the Study of Education. Chicago: University of Chicago Press, 1942.

Spears, Harold. *Secondary Education in American Life.* New York: American Book Company, 1941.

The Purposes of Education in American Democracy, Educational Policies Commission. Washington, D.C.: National Education Association and the American Association of School Administrators, 1938.

The Unique Function of Education in American Democracy, Educational Policies Commission. Washington, D.C.: National Education Association and the Department of Superintendents, 1937.

Umstattd, J. C. *Secondary School Teaching,* chapter II. Boston: Ginn and Company, 1944.

Wahlquist, J. T. *Introduction to American Education.* New York: The Ronald Press Company, 1950.

Wiley, George M. *The Redirection of Secondary Education.* New York: The Macmillan Company, 1940.

Williams, L. A. *Secondary Schools for American Youth.* New York: American Book Company, 1944.

Part

II

ORGANIZATION OF CURRICULUM

MATERIALS FOR INSTRUCTION

2

How Shall the Curriculum Be Organized?

Until very recently a consideration of the curriculum, such as is the concern of this chapter, would not have appeared in a conventional textbook on the methods of teaching. *Curriculum* and *methods* were distinctly separate. The *curriculum* was regarded as the special province of the administration whereas *methods* became the obvious domain of the teacher.

Our modern psychological approach to learning envisaged in the Gestalt-Organismic-Field theories of learning, closely intertwine the larger aspects of the *curriculum* with *methods* in the total process of learning. In this chapter enough attention will be given to the general curriculum to enable the teacher to understand and utilize its interrelationship with methods more effectively in guiding the learning activities of youth.

1. Why a Problem?

Too many teachers have assumed that basically the curriculum was set in its format and content. To be sure some minor variations were to be found, and there existed some controversy over certain phases of the curriculum, but these all too often have been considered of relatively minor importance. On the other hand there has been a growing awareness and confused concern that all was not well with the curriculum.

31

Curriculum in confusion

Possibly at no time in our educational history have we been in greater disagreement about the curriculum. In spite of the centuries devoted to the determination of the content and organization of the curriculum it will not remain static. Especially has the curriculum become greatly unsettled since the turn of the century. As a science of education in America began to develop, the curriculum became one of the first and has remained one of the major areas of critical educational concern. No part of it has been exempt from critical educational study. At first the adequacy of the informational content of the curriculum for education was the dominant point of attack. Later, even the relevancy of the conception of informational content as the major concern in curriculum organization for education came into question.

Curriculum gaps

It is a long cry from the early fifth century when the *Trivium* and *Quadrivium* of the Seven Liberal Arts — consisting of rhetoric, grammar, dialectic (logic), arithmetic, geometry, astronomy, and music — could be accepted as the basis and largely the circumference of existing knowledge. Even a little over three hundred years ago the great educator Comenius thought it was feasible to compress all essential existent knowledge between the covers of one book.

That day has passed. By the middle of the last century the question of what to teach in the schools was becoming a problem. Within the past fifty years it has assumed the proportions of a major insoluble problem for those, particularly, who cling to the outmoded theory of learning as the acquisition of encyclopaedic information. A recent radio commentator made the statement that within the past ten years alone more new knowledge was discovered than it would be possible for one person to assimilate within a lifetime. A recent study revealed that more courses were offered in one of America's major universities than it would be possible for a person to cover in 400 years at the regular rate of progress through the courses now customarily accepted as a reasonable student course load.

Even back in the twenties the problem of serious "gaps" in the curriculum assumed the proportions of an educational crisis. How

to insure that a properly balanced selection from the rapidly mounting and accumulating mass of information could be made available
to pupils within their capability of mastery and at the same time
avoid glaring informational gaps in the education of the child, became the absorbing problem of curriculum makers.

Controversies raged as to whether one needed to know all the
combinations of the four fundamentals in arithmetic, or whether
100 or 200 combinations in each would be sufficient for competency
in these fundamental operations. The same debate was under way
in the field of spelling. Obviously one could not learn to spell all
the words of his use vocabulary. How could serious gaps in one's
spelling competency be avoided? These were the days of the "One
Thousand Most Commonly Used Words," the "One Hundred Word
Demons" and the "five" and "ten" thousand most commonly used
word lists. It was the period of intense research as to what geographical or historical facts it was thought all should know of the
myriad such facts extant. It was the period of frantic effort, still
continuing in abated tension, to discover so-called "minimum
essentials" in the traditional fields of knowledge.[1]

A more serious issue, hotly debated at the secondary school
level, centered around what areas of knowledge, and what courses
therein, should be made a requirement for all students. It was becoming increasingly clear that the world of informational knowledge had become too voluminous and too diversified for it to be
practical for the school to attempt to teach it all, or even to include
all the important definitive areas into which knowledge was emerging. For example, high school students are generally required to
elect one or two courses in science. If only one is taken, and that
let us say is biology, it means that for that student, except for his
out-of-school contacts, the entire world of physics, chemistry,
geology and astronomy, remains largely closed.

Uniformity in courses lacking

For many critics of modern curriculum development, it is a
somewhat startling discovery to learn that their vociferous condemnation of possible gaps in the newer curriculum forms are much
more pertinent with respect to the older curriculum. It is almost

[1] For a vivid picture of the stress placed upon research of this nature see the
second to sixth Yearbooks inclusive, of the Department of Superintendents,
National Education Association. Washington, D.C., 1924–1928.

impossible to find two textbooks or two courses of study in any given subject where the content is identical. In many situations a student might with profit repeat a course with the same title, but following in the second course the outline of content of a widely divergent textbook or course of study.

This probability has come to be so generally recognized by alert teachers and administrators that schools desirous of overcoming the large gaps present in the use of a single textbook or rigid course of study, and without adequate library facilities, have resorted to a novel device of textbook usage. Instead of providing identical textbooks for every member of a class, several titles of textbooks appropriate for the course are selected, and five or six copies of each title are purchased. Thus, for a class of thirty pupils, duplicates for five or six titles, representative of the varied viewpoints and emphasis of that many different authors, would be available. This would assure to the student a wealth of factual material, and the inclusion of a wide range of topics calculated to reduce the existing gaps in courses, and to some extent between courses.

2. What is Basis of Modern Curriculum?

There is a growing conviction among curriculum workers that the organizational problems of the curriculum cannot be satisfactorily met by an attempt to close the gaps in the traditional informational (subject matter) type of curriculum. Within a world of continuously accelerated tempo and consequent mounting accumulation of informational data, it becomes increasingly difficult, if not impossible, to avoid large and serious gaps in one's knowledge of his world. With each passing year the gaps become greater, one's knowledge of his world necessarily more fragmentary in its nature, and the problems of the curriculum become more acute.

Functional curriculum

Recent changes in educational theory have contributed to a more functional approach to curriculum problems. The older conception of education placed primary emphasis upon memory processes and the acquisition of knowledge. The basic assumption underlying this theory of learning and education was that the acquired knowledge, or information, would, per se, transmit itself into appropriate action patterns when the need for such arose.

The concept of education now commonly held in theory, if not yet translated into general practice, is that learning is the process of changing behavior patterns through appropriate experience situations. Education is concerned that these changes in behavior patterns be such as to insure that the learner will acquire those general types of behavior competencies necessary for effectively living in his contemporary environment and which will give promise of increased effectiveness as the demand upon him becomes greater in the larger activities of the adult citizen.

The focus of attention is thus shifted from the selection and organization of inert bodies of informational materials to the development of a dynamic curriculum of experience-situations that is always concerned with the extent to which the experience-situations set up for learning actually result in changed and appropriately functioning behavior. Its continued functionality must constantly be evaluated in terms of the degree to which the learner evinces progressive effectiveness in wholesome adjustments to the total of his living environment.

Flexible curriculum

Such a functionally conceived curriculum must be highly flexible in content and organization. The behavior patterns of boys and girls in rural and urban communities are somewhat different. The kind of behavior competencies necessary in a rural farm community where the planting and harvesting of crops, the care of livestock, familiarity with and ability to use different kinds of farm machinery, and a dozen and one other types of competencies necessary for successful adjustments peculiar to the farm, are not necessarily appropriate to the behavior competencies most needed by urban youth. The latter may live in large crowded apartment dwellings, in densely populated surroundings, where the pressing behavior adjustment problems for these youths involve the development of skills in living happily and successfully together under constant restrictions upon individual freedom of action, skills in creatively utilizing leisure time wholesomely, as well as the development of other behavior patterns appropriate to radically different environments from that of their rural cousins. Variations in climatic conditions, cultural differences, and differences in occupational activities require flexibility in the curriculum to meet markedly different community environments.

Our knowledge of the complexity of and the range of individual differences, within each individual, between individuals, and in the living environment of each, suggests that the functional curriculum must have great flexibility. This means some adjustment of the curriculum to meet the needs of each individual within a class group, for different classes, even for each school within a community, and among communities.

Furthermore, the rapidity of change in the manner of life of all suggests that the curriculum must be subject to constant change. A world in a continual and accelerated state of flux must have a very fluid curriculum to meet the needs of boys and girls who must learn to adjust and readjust to keep pace with a world that so rapidly outmodes present conditions.

Basic curriculum pattern

Some extremists impressed with the necessity of flexibility in the curriculum to keep it functional have too hastily concluded that any organized curriculum pattern was out of order. Since it could not be set and fixed it must remain a creature of the moment.

At least two considerations suggest that in the midst of need for curriculum diversity there remains the basis for broad curriculum patterns. The studies made of children do suggest that in the presence of tremendous differences in their growth and development there are some indices of similarities in the way growth takes place and roughly in the time sequence of these developments. They might be called stages except that there appear to be no pauses in the growth process. For example, there are periods of infancy, early and later childhood, early and later adolescence in the somewhat broadly characteristic similarities for these designated periods in the lives of children and adolescents with rough time sequences or age groupings for each of the so-called stages of development. These [2] are definitely related to the physiological, mental, emotional and social growth and maturation of the individual. Comparison of individual with individual will show wide differences in development at the same age-level, but compared in

---

[2] For more extended discussions of this problem see Blair, A. W. and Burton, W. H. *Growth and Development of the Preadolescent.* New York: Appleton-Century-Crofts, Inc., 1951; Jenkins, G. G., Schacter, H. and Bauer, W. W. *These Are Your Children.* Chicago: Scott, Foresman and Company, 1949; Dunn, Fannie W. *The Child in the Rural Environment.* Washington D.C., Department of Rural Education, N.E.A., 1951.; and any standard text on child or adolescent psychology.

large groups there is a rough norm of development or maturation in the large group divisions enumerated above. It is possible to assume very broadly the growth level of a large number of children at these various age groupings, if it is remembered that these are but segments in a continuum of development, somewhat artificially designated for the convenience of educational workers who must deal with children at all ages.

A second basis for the assumption of a broad over-all curriculum pattern to guide the school is the fact that at all levels of development of the learner there are basic needs common to all within our democratic culture irrespective of community or individual differences. Whether one lives on the Atlantic or Pacific coast, in a large city or farm in the Middle West, he must have developed those communication skills of reading, writing, spelling, and listening essential to carrying on social intercourse with others within our culture. In spite of some variations, the basic *mores* and conventions governing the institutions of the home, church, school, the other social agencies of society, and the general patterns of acceptable social conduct are much the same in America. To be a successful consumer or producer he must have developed competencies in quantitative thinking and skills in the manipulation of at least the rudiments of the monetary system which is a part of our society. Likewise to get along he must understand and be able to efficiently utilize many skills necessary for adjustment to our system of government and structure of living, such as competency to live and work cooperatively with others, the development of salable skills, and the acceptance and discharge of the many responsibilities of citizenship necessary within our democracy.

Inasmuch as the nature and progress of growth and development is broadly the same for all individuals, their basic needs much alike, and the structure of our culture fundamentally the same to which all must learn to adjust, there appear large common factors in the education of youth that will suggest the possibility of the organization of the curriculum at least in general over-all patterns.

3. How Has Curriculum Changed?

Modification of subject curriculum

Ever since educators became seriously aware of the disparity between the rapidly accumulating body of knowledge and the avowed purpose of the school to make this available to the learner, some effort has been made to correct this discrepancy between intent and practice. At first there was a reluctant admission to the curriculum of areas of knowledge that had developed since the early formulation of the content and structure of the curriculum. This was the period sometimes characterized as "curriculum-making by additions." Subjects were added to the existing curriculum which, as far as possible, was left undisturbed. This urge to modify the curriculum [3] by the addition of new areas of knowledge reached a point where in 1921–22, in Chicago, there existed twenty-nine distinct curriculums from which the student entering high school theoretically might choose; fourteen of these were four-year curriculums and fifteen were two-year curriculums. Fortunately, not all of these were offered in each high school of the city, which restricted the problem of student selection. This made obvious the serious existence of gaps in knowledge. It was the logical and absurd outgrowth of the older theory of education.

Recent efforts at modification of the subject curriculum have involved the attempt to determine what important selections of subject matter from major areas of knowledge might be representative of the whole, and provide something of an "aura" or "halo" effect of understanding of the larger area. Many who have been influenced in part by current theories of learning have tried to maintain the subject basis of the curriculum while at the same time applying some modern principles of learning to curriculum organization. Correlation of various subject fields, even some effort at fusing two or more subjects have become popular. To care for individual differences in ability, social background, and interest, differentiation and gradation of subject matter have been attempted. The practice of organizing subjects around "units" for instructional purposes has become widespread.

Early drastic innovations

Efforts to modify the curriculum as described above are typically a part of the normal and seemingly necessary process involved in any healthy form of social evolution. Many educators, however, saw quite clearly that these modifications of the curriculum, though highly desirable, were but palliatives and did not meet the needs

---

[3] For a more detailed picture of curriculum development before 1925 see *Curriculum-Making: Past and Present*, Twenty-Sixth Yearbook of the National Society for the Study of Education, Part I. Bloomington, Illinois: Public School Publishing Company, 1926.

of the educational principles involved. Accepting the more recent concepts of learning, and what they understood to be their implications for education and the curriculum, some of these educators pioneered a radical change in curriculum making.

Two of these innovations that have come to be accepted as typical of these pioneering efforts are the curriculum programs developed in the states of Virginia and Mississippi. In over-all form they have stimulated the general direction of much of curriculum reorganization for the past two decades.

They began by accepting the concept that learning is the change in behavior that comes through experience. Education is thus concerned with the direction of the learning processes involved in experiences, so that desirable observable behavior conduct results. Experiences then became the focal point of the curriculum: the school curriculum was defined as consisting of those experiences children had under the direction of the school.

There are a number of implications in this conception of learning, education, and the curriculum, which contrast sharply with the old. Whereas learning is here thought of as a process of changing behavior that comes out of an experience-situation which confronts the learner and through which he tries to evolve some satisfactory adjustment in his mode of reaction, the older point of view thought of learning as a simple process of memorization whereby certain information was fixed in memory. In the conception of learning implied in the newer approach the school is concerned with the kinds of experiences the learner should have in order to insure appropriate change in behavior patterns. Experiences become the vehicle by which desirable learning takes place and thus become the essence of the curriculum. The focus of attention is now placed upon what kinds of experiences should the learner have, while in the older conception of education, informational data became the end product of learning and subject matter became the curriculum.[4]

---

[4] Throughout this discussion of the differences between the newer educational-curriculum ideas and the old, to avoid confusions that arise with recent tendencies to modify older practices in the direction of the newer, the more primitive characteristics of the old are held up for comparison in order to see clearly the educational implications of the old memory-knowledge theory of education by contrast. Muscular skills are now taught in laboratory situations under the so-called subject-matter curriculum. It must be remembered that fifty years ago mechanical skills had practically no place in the school curriculum except as it was thought that they could be intellectualized.

If "experiences" rather than "information" now became the curriculum it required a new approach to curriculum organization. The organization of the old curriculum in its beginning was achieved in somewhat this general way. All existing or essential knowledge data was assembled, classified into subject divisions on some principle of group characteristics — as for example, all knowledge data of quantitative or numerical characteristics were grouped together as mathematics, while all knowledge data about man's activities related essentially to time sequence were brought together as history. The various subject-matter fields thus developed became the curriculum of the school. When this subject-matter data became more voluminous the problem of setting up some principles of selection arose as discussed earlier in this chapter.

Under the conception of the curriculum as consisting of experiences a much different form of curriculum formulation was required. The Virginia and Mississippi state curriculums represent very similar organizational patterns with minor differences so will be considered together.

The plan of organization followed gives recognition to the fact that in experience learning it is not possible for pupils to have experiences paralleling every conceivable type of situation they will in the future encounter. Nor do these plans assume such is at all necessary. Experience learning is essentially learning how to meet problem-situations effectively, and thereby developing appropriate behavior skills in problem solving. While problems are recognized to be of many kinds, yet there are characteristics that are common or universal in all problem-situations, however uniquely different a given problem-situation may at first appear to be. The student can thus be trained to analyze every problem-situation, to discover the characteristics therein common to all problem-solving situations as well as the new factors involved, and develop those behavior skills of over-all problem attack that will enable him to skillfully solve a wide range of different problem-situations as they are met.

Under these circumstances it is necessary only to determine the milieu in which vital problem-situations arise for the learner and into what possible categories of general similarities these problem-situations can be classified. If this can be done then it is necessary only to insure that each pupil have a rich and varied assortment of experiences in meeting problem-situations in all the areas previously determined.

This was done in the two state curriculums. In Virginia it was decided that the milieu in which vital life problems occurred represented the total range of man's Social Living. Mississippi decided that there were many vital activities of life that could not be designed as social in character, therefore, designated a milieu in which vital problems were met as the total range of Human Activities.[5] They then explored the possibilities of discovering some basis for grouping problem-situations that occur into categories or classifications with respect to characteristics of problem similarities. Virginia adopted eleven such categories and designated them "Major *Functions* of Social Life." Mississippi arrived at a somewhat different though similar classification and labelled them "Major *Areas* of Human Activities." The two classifications are listed below in parallel columns for easy comparison.

VIRGINIA	MISSISSIPPI
Major Functions of Social Life	*Major Areas of Human Activities*
1. Protection and Conservation of Life, Property, and Natural Resources	1. Protecting Life and Health
	2. Making a Home
2. Production of Goods and Services and Distribution of the Returns of Production	3. Conserving and Improving Material Conditions
	4. Cooperating in Social and Civic Action
3. Consumption of Goods and Services	5. Getting a Living
4. Communication and Transportation of Goods and People	6. Securing an Education
	7. Expressing Religious Impulses
5. Recreation	8. Expressing Aesthetic Impulses
6. Expression of Aesthetic Impulses	9. Engaging in Recreation
7. Expression of Religious Impulses	
8. Education	
9. Extension of Freedom	
10. Integration of the Individual	
11. Exploration	

[5] *Tentative Course of Study for the Core Curriculum of Virginia Secondary Schools, Grade VIII*, p. 18. Richmond, Va.: Virginia State Board of Education, 1934; and *Mississippi Program for the Improvement of Instruction,* Curriculum Reorganization in Secondary Schools, Grades 7–12, p. 28. Jackson, Miss.: State Board of Education, 1939.

In modern curriculum parlance, the total milieu or matrix in which problem-situations occur and experiences are to take place is known as the "Scope" of the curriculum. Since the curriculum here is interpreted to consist of experiences, the "Scope" of the curriculum represents the total living environment in which the learner faces problem-situations and consequently has learning experiences. In the traditional curriculum the "Scope" would consist of the total range of subject matter the learner was to master. When an effort is made to break down the "Scope" of the curriculum into some natural divisions based upon some grouping characteristics inherent within the kind of curriculum envisaged, these divisions are now commonly called "Areas" as is applied in the Mississippi classification of nine areas. The Virginia plan of organization is the same, except that "Areas" are technically labelled "Functions." In a subject curriculum the parallel divisions are familiar to the reader in such categories as mathematics, science, English, or social studies.

After the *Scope* of the curriculum had been established it was necessary to consider the problem of organizing the curriculum on some sequential basis. Obviously the traditional basis of sequence in the order of subject matter could not be used. Experiences occur only in vital problem-situations and these happen normally in the natural environment of the learner. Still maintaining the idea of Grades in sequence planning, the Virginia plan set up what was called "Centers of Interest" for each grade to conform to what was thought of as the natural environment of the learner at a given level of his activities and maturity. For children of Grade 1, for example, it was thought that the major problem-situations which would arise for experience learning would center around the environment of the home and the school. Therefore, *Home and School Life* became the "Center of Interest" for this grade. It was thought that the problem areas of living in Grade II would likely shift more to the larger considerations of community understanding and adjustment so the "Center of Interest" for this grade was designated as *Community Life*. "Centers of Interest" are set up for all grades through the high school. That the reader may see schematically this plan the organization for the first three grades and the first three Functions of "Scope" of the Virginia curriculum are here reproduced.[6]

[6] It should be noted that the Virginia and Mississippi curriculum plans out-

Scope of Work of the Core Curriculum for Virginia Public Schools

Major Functions of Social Life	Grade I HOME AND SCHOOL LIFE (Center of Interest)	Grade II COMMUNITY LIFE (Center of Interest)	Grade III ADAPTION OF LIFE TO ENVIRONMENTAL FORCES OF NATURE (Center of Interest)
	ASPECT OF CENTER OF INTEREST SELECTED FOR EMPHASIS		
Protection and conservation of life, property, and natural resources	How do we protect and maintain life and health in our homes and school?	How do we in the community protect our life, health, and property? How do animal and plant life help people in our community and how are they protected?	How do people, plants, and animals in communities with physical environments markedly different from ours protect themselves from forces of nature?
Production of goods and services and distribution of the returns of production	How do the things we make and grow help us?	What do we in our community do to produce goods and services?	How do environmental forces of nature affect the goods produced in different communities?
Consumption of goods and services	How does our family provide itself with food, clothing, and shelter?	How do we use the goods and services provided in our community?	Why can communities markedly different from ours furnish us with goods we cannot produce?

Tentative Course of Study for the Core Curriculum of Virginia Secondary Schools, Grade VIII, p. 16. Richmond, Virginia: Virginia State Board of Education, 1934.

Recent curriculum development

In the years that have passed since the pioneer work of Virginia lined thus far apply only to what is called the Core Curriculum when the secondary-school grades are reached. There is a definite flare back to, or compromise with, the traditional form of the curriculum at the high-school level outside the Core Curriculum.

and Mississippi in curriculum reorganization, many schools have tried to carry the major ideas inherent in these curriculum innovations into the total organization of the curriculum throughout the elementary and secondary school. There have been many adaptations of these plans and many modified schemes for curriculum improvement suggested. For example, an interesting attack in the problem of *Scope* of the curriculum accepts the principle that learning takes place through experiences which occur in vital life situations. The Scope of the curriculum then becomes *Persistent Life Situations.* These are classified into three [7] principal areas; namely, (1) Growth in Individual Capacities, (2) Growth in Social Participation, (3) Growth in Dealing with Environmental Factors and Forces. Each in turn is subdivided into smaller groupings of "persistent life situations."

Possibly the major directions of curriculum development within recent years have been the emphasis placed upon problem-situational curriculum content, the development of "units" as a means of facilitating curriculum organization around problem-situations for instructional purposes, and the constant effort to completely unify and integrate the curriculum evidenced in the growing emphasis upon the organization of the core curriculum; with the core program as an integral part of the total curriculum experiences of the learner. The Educational Policies Commission of the National Educational Association has given strong impetus to the developing core-curriculum idea. It has graphically presented a basic point of view with respect to the organization of the curriculum presented below. There seems to be every reason to accept the broad point of view of the Commission as the general direction which curriculum development in the future will take.[8]

4. How Organize the Modern Curriculum?

Many problems involved in the organization of the curriculum have been in evidence as we have seen the pattern of the curriculum undergo change. Other important phases of curriculum devel-

[7] For a more detailed discussion of this approach see Stratemeyer, Florence, et al. *Developing a Curriculum for Modern Living,* chapter V. New York: Teachers College, Columbia University, 1947.

[8] For a more detailed discussion of the Core Curriculum see Faunce, Roland C. and Bossing, Nelson L., *Developing the Core Curriculum.* New York: Prentice-Hall, Inc., 1951.

	HIGH SCHOOL			COMMUNITY INSTITUTE	
GRADES	X	XI	XII	XIII	XIV

1	*Individual Interests* (Elected by the student, under guidance, in fields of avocational, cultural, or intellectual interest.)

- *

2	*Vocational Preparation* (Includes education for industrial, commercial, homemaking, service, and other occupations leading to employment, apprenticeship, or homemaking at the end of grade XII, XIII, or XIV; education for technical and semiprofessional occupations in community institute; and the study of sciences, mathematics, social studies, literature, and foreign languages in preparation for advanced study in community institute, college, or university. May include a period of productive work under employment conditions, supervised by the school staff. Related to the study of economics and industrial and labor relations in "common learnings.")

Science

3	Methods, principles, and facts needed by all students

4	*Common Learnings* (A continuous course for all, planned to help students grow in competence as citizens of the community and the nation; in understanding of economic processes and their roles as producers and consumers; in cooperative living in family, school, and community; in appreciation of literature and the arts; and in the use of the English language. Guidance of individual students is a chief responsibility of "common learnings" teachers.)

**

5	
6	*Health and Physical Education* (Includes instruction in personal health and hygiene; health examinations and follow-up; games, sports, and other activities to promote physical fitness. Related to study of community health in "common learnings.")

* Broken line indicates flexibility of scheduling.

** Heavy line marks the division between "differential studies" (above) and "common studies" (below).

Curriculum Organization Pattern in American City

Educational Policies Commission, *Education for All American Youth*. Washington: National Education Association, 1944, p. 244.

opment have been somewhat obscured by the more spectacular aspects of the changes considered. At this point the teacher may well see these problems in their total relation to a well-planned and organized curriculum. For in the development of the modern curriculum the teacher shares with others in its formulation. Whether the teacher participates directly in the making of the over-all school curriculum or is restricted to his own course planning the problems faced are essentially the same.

Determining principles

Before the teacher attempts to determine the program to be carried on in the school, it is essential that he be clear with respect to those basic principles which give validity and consistent direction to his efforts. Curriculum workers are quite generally agreed that these principles derive broadly from our accepted psychology of learning and social philosophy.

If the point of view expressed in the opening chapter of this book be accepted then the philosophy that guides the organization of the instructional activities of the school must be democratic in character. We visualize a democratic society. The basic function of the school must be to so educate youth that it may participate effectively in a democratically operative society.

The acceptance of the democratic nature of the educational ideal carries with it the recognition of certain basic principles of learning which must determine in part the validity of the instructional aims. Obviously, such an aim as "the development of unquestioned obedience to authority" would be psychologically unsound. It would not develop that intelligent critical evaluation of governmental policy and regulation best calculated either to safeguard the rights of the citizen or to prepare youth to participate in adulthood in the wise formulation of governmental policy so essential in a democracy.

Every school does or should have a carefully formulated statement of these basic principles which should become the point of orientation for its instructional activities. Many such statements of principles have been developed. The following list of principles prepared by the writer for a state curriculum handbook is suggestive of such a statement.[9]

[9] *Handbook on Curriculum Study,* Curriculum Series, Bulletin No. 1, pp. 75–82. State of Oregon, Department of Education, December, 1937.

1. The curriculum will be effective to the degree that it accurately mirrors the dynamic nature of environment and the "inevitability of social change."
2. Basic social change is in the direction of increasing social complexity and of cooperative endeavor.
3. For purposes of curriculum development society is here conceived as a democracy in which the growth and welfare of the individual and of the social group is regarded as of transcendent importance.
4. The school is one of the agencies of society for the continuation and recreation of itself.
5. Experience is the fundamental basis of learning.
6. Growth processes in individuals and in society are resultants of continuing interaction between individuals and society.
7. There is a wide range of differentiation among individuals in interests, understandings, appreciations, abilities, ability to learn.
8. Effective curriculum development must be comprehensive and continuous.
9. Curriculum making is a democratic process and should provide for inclusive participation.

Determining aims

The teacher should recognize that there are two major concepts of the nature of aims and objectives. One point of view regards aims as somewhat discrete and specific in character. Typical aims of this kind are:

To develop the habit of brushing the teeth at least once each day.
To develop the habit of visiting the dentist at least once a year.
To acquire the ability to read in large word groups.
To learn to use the gerund correctly.

This approach to the development of aims leads to the amassing of hundreds of minute objectives for a curriculum area such as health, or of a given subject such as English. In the twenties this type of detail analysis of objectives was most popular. Basic to this approach was the thought that learning is additive in nature. Therefore, aims could be arranged in some scheme of ascending order and learned one by one. The stimulus-response bond theory of psychology aided and abetted this concept of the nature of objectives.

The point of view rapidly gaining credence in educational thinking now looks upon "aims" as broad characterizations of behavior patterns which should be exemplified by the ideal citizen. Aims are not minute and discrete but large patterns of ability, understandings, or conduct comprehensive and interrelated. Aspects of the whole may be especially emphasized in a given grade or curricular area but these aspects must be recognized as a continuing part of the whole which constantly develops as the total educational process continues.

Two representative examples of this newer concept of the nature of aims are found in the statements of aims by the state of Virginia and the Educational Policies Commission of the National Education Association. An added reason for the importance of the Virginia statement is the widespread acceptance of the underlying concept implicit in the form of the statement. The aims of education are given in three categories of (1) Emotionalized Attitudes, (2) Generalizations, (3) Special Abilities. One example is given from each category.[10]

(1) EMOTIONALIZED ATTITUDES

The Attitude of Self-Integrity.
   The disposition to accept responsibility for the consequences of one's acts.
   Freedom from fear, worry, and the sense of inferiority.
   The disposition to maintain emotional balance in the face of difficulty or defeat.
   The belief in the worth of one's personality.
   The tendency to face reality squarely.
   The desire to be faithful to promises.
   The tendency to accept criticism cheerfully.
   Willingness to assume the obligations of leadership.
   The urge to do all work efficiently and honestly.
   The tendency to do one's full duty.
   The determination to be happy.

(2) GENERALIZATIONS

The Understanding of the Interdependence of All Forms of Life.
   Individuals are dependent upon other individuals and have responsibilities to them.
   Individuals are dependent upon social groups and have responsibilities to social groups.

[10] *Tentative Course of Study for the Core Curriculum of Virginia Secondary Schools, Grade VII,* pp. 2–14. Virginia State Board of Education, 1934. Reprinted by permission.

All types of groups are dependent upon one another and have responsibilities to each other.

Man's thinking grows out of his experience with individuals, groups, and nature.

People are dependent upon the wise use of plants and animals.

Personal liberty is decreased as man increases his control of nature and society.

Opportunities for exploitation increase as interdependence grows.

(3) SPECIAL ABILITIES

The Ability to Read.
The ability to use the mechanics needed in reading.
The ability to analyze, interpret, and evaluate reading materials.
The ability to use reference books.
The ability to interpret thought in oral reading.
The ability to use silent reading as recreation.

The second example, drawn from the Educational Policies Commission statements, is cast in a somewhat different framework. The uniqueness of the Commission's statement is that the emphasis upon objectives as the end product of learning, expressed in terms of demonstrably achieved active behavior patterns rather than potentials, is here more sharply brought into the foreground of our thinking. Four groups of objectives are given with the following explanation: [11]

To recapitulate, four aspects of educational purpose have been identified. These aspects center around the person himself, his relationships to others in home and community, the creation and use of material wealth, and socio-civic activities. The first area calls for a description of the educated person; the second, for a description of the educated member of the family and community group; the third, of the educated producer or consumer; the fourth, of the educated citizen. The four great groups of objectives thus defined are:

1. The Objectives of Self-Realization
2. The Objectives of Human Relationships
3. The Objectives of Economic Efficiency
4. The Objectives of Civic Responsibility.

[11] *The Purposes of Education in American Democracy,* Educational Policies Commission of the National Education Association, pp. 47, 50. Washington, D.C.: National Education Association, 1938. Reprinted by permission. See Chapter 1 for the complete list of these objectives. This section is repeated here for convenience of comparison.

The first of these groups will be produced in detail to illustrate the procedures followed.

(1) THE OBJECTIVES OF SELF-REALIZATION

The Inquiring Mind. The educated person has an appetite for learning.
Speech. The educated person can speak the mother tongue clearly.
Reading. The educated person reads the mother tongue efficiently.
Writing. The educated person writes the mother tongue effectively.
Number. The educated person solves his problems of counting and calculating.
Sight and Hearing. The educated person is skilled in listening and observing.
Health Knowledge. The educated person understands the basic facts concerning health and disease.
Health Habits. The educated person protects his own health and that of his dependents.
Public Health. The educated person works to improve the health of the community.
Recreation. The educated person is participant and spectator in many sports and other pastimes.
Intellectual Interests. The educated person has mental resources for the use of leisure.
Aesthetic Interests. The educated person appreciates beauty.
Character. The educated person gives responsible direction to his own life.

Determining scope

The formulation of a body of aims in conformity with an accepted set of basic or guiding principles is an important achievement in curriculum and course planning. Now some limiting device must be adopted to provide inclusiveness and direction to the learning experience. In many schools the textbook has served as the determiner of the center and circumference of the educative task. In others dominated by the doctrine of interest, the sole limitation of the curriculum and course is determined by the vagaries of chance interests which may be aroused.

To many educational leaders the very nature of the educative task when thought of in the perspective of successful participation in a democratic society requires the instructional program to be as broad as the life demands of that society. Too, it has seemed highly desirable that the instructional program be related as closely as possible to the activities and problems which compose the normal processes of living in a democracy.

As assurance that the curriculum of the school should admit of no serious gaps in the range of activities, studied efforts have been made to discover the major areas of these activities. As previously seen, in the Virginia Course of Study there have been identified eleven of these called "Major Functions of Social Life." In the Mississippi curriculum program these areas are given as nine in number designated "Major Areas of Human Activity." In the Stratemeyer list there are three such areas called "Persistent Life Situations." Similar lists have been developed by other groups of interested curriculum workers. Area captions vary often but a comparison of the lists shows how strikingly the total of the one is basically inclusive of the other.

The teacher should think of the scope of the curriculum in terms of some such broad plan as is given above. The limits of his own instructional program should be set by orientation to some phase or area of activities which it is desired to emphasize. These limits insure for the teacher's work a high degree of functionality. The aims which are to be focal in the program will suggest a natural affinity to one or more of these areas. That there will be a natural carry-over from the periphery of one area to another in the learning experience should be expected. The organization of the instructional program should be such that these interrelationships will be facilitated.

Determining sequence

The question of how to determine sequence in the curriculum has come to be a burning issue in contemporary education. It is inextricably a part of the development of the immediate instructional program, as well as of the larger organizational aspects of the curriculum. The farther the educational worker moves in the direction of modern educational thinking, the more critical the issue becomes. The nature of the issue, however, may be clarified by looking at the two extreme points of view with respect to "sequence" in the curriculum and within the more immediate instructional program of the classroom.

The extreme right wing insist upon the logical form of organization. The traditionalists have ever been the protagonists of logical development in subject matter. For example, they have argued

that a foreign language should be learned in logical sequence —
alphabet, vocabulary, verb form, sentence, paragraph, story. The
logicians in organizing mathematics and science have insisted upon
a mastery of plus (+) and minus (−) signs before a serious
study of mathematical problems involving the use of these symbols; and in science the study of the simplest form of single-cell life
before a consideration of complex animal organisms. In other
words, the fetish of "simple to complex" in the development of the
curriculum or of a course has been the prime emphasis of this
group, irrespective of the consequent remoteness of the curriculum
or course-content to the conscious experience of the students. This,
in spite of the cumulative evidence that language students seldom
achieve facility in language usage by this route, or science students
achieve interest in or significant functional value from science so
organized and taught.

The extreme left, on the other hand, have scorned emphasis upon
the logical development or sequential arrangement of curriculum
or courses. They have made central, sometimes exclusively so, the
doctrine of interest. The extreme manifestations of this point of
view have been more in evidence in elementary education. The
secondary school has been too much a victim of traditionalism to
show a too-ready response to innovations in educational theory and
practice. The elementary "activity schools" have been most productive of the extremes to which the emphasis upon the psychological
organization — particularly that of interest — may lead. The now
threadbare story that has gone the rounds of educational circles
well illustrates this point of view carried to absurdity. The story
is told of the "activity school" teacher who, according to her usual
morning custom, asked the children what they wanted to do for
the day. It chanced that on the way to school some of the children
had observed with interest a funeral procession. It was suggested
that the class play funeral. The idea caught the fancy of the rest
of the children. The teacher consented, and a most exciting day
was spent in the activities imitative of a funeral. In fact, so well did
the day succeed that the children urged a continuance of the activity the second day. The story goes that an entire week was given
over to this intensely fascinating so-called educational activity on
the part of the children.

The more moderate advocates of the psychological basis for
organization contend that interest is more fundamental than "simple

to complex" in learning. They argue, for instance, that to learn a language the psychological way would be to begin reading and speaking the language, at first in simple form to be sure, with the immediate urge to convey interesting ideas to others or to secure such ideas from the printed page. They would say that the study of biology around the motive of the control of body disease would be far more productive of vital learning than to begin by the laborious and deadening process of the study of remote single-celled life through and into the complexities of the human organism.

It would be unfair to accept the extremes as characteristic of the two schools of thought just described. They represent points of emphasis, rather than clear-cut segregation of practice. The third type of possible organization, known as the pedagogical, gives emphasis to an *eclectic* point of view. Many of those who emphasize the psychological contend that the last two are one and the same. The writer is convinced that failure to differentiate between these two types of organization leads to confusion. The pedagogical organization gives due emphasis to the natural-sequence or logical-development type of learning, as well as to the psychological elements inherent in certain areas or subjects. For example, the writer, as a high school and college student, was subjected to the rigorous logical organization of language and science studies. He studied a language for four years intensively in logical fashion but never achieved by the process an easy reading knowledge of the language.

After being subjected to this form of language study, it was a matter of keen interest to meet a young lady who had traveled extensively in Europe and resided briefly in Germany. Incidentally, she had acquired both a fluent speaking and an easy reading knowledge of German. She was then enrolled in a course in German in college. The writer chanced to compliment her on her accomplishment, and to express some wonder that she should be studying German in college. She replied that she had more difficulty than the other members of the class, for, while she could read German almost as easily as she did English, she knew nothing about grammatical construction. This young lady had learned German by the psychological method, and subsequently was refining her understanding of German through a critical study of the language structure.

Many advanced schools try to arouse interest in and secure

facility in the use of a language by organizing on the psychological basis, while at the same time directing attention to the language structure in developmental form as it contributes to the understanding and effective use of the language itself. This plan would represent the pedagogical type of course organization.

The same idea is present in the modern functional concept of the teaching of English composition. The pedagogical form of organization would recognize "centers of interest," at the same time so organizing the course that development and progression would be assured, while a felt need would naturally be aroused for an understanding of those structural elements of the language that would insure increased facility in oral and written expression.

That the experience curriculum requires a radically different conception of "sequence" than has been practiced in the subject curriculum appears to be generally accepted. It is evident in the sharp break with the old, found in the reorganized curriculum programs of Virginia and Mississipi, discussed at some length earlier in this chapter, along with many other curriculum innovations of more recent date.

As yet, no satisfactory "sequence" plan has been devised. The clear logic of the experience conception of learning would suggest that psychologically "sequence" must depend upon the maturity and development of each individual as well as upon the nature of the behavior skills to be acquired. In that sense the curriculum cannot be mass patterned and lock stepped, except in the broadest terms, but must be individually patterned for every learner. Even the alert teachers, still trying to hold to the subject curriculum, have been forced, in the light of the now generally accepted principles of learning and of individual differences, to modify the older strait-jacket curriculum form into a semi-streamlined individualized curriculum.

There is a noticeable trend in the direction of more individualization of the curriculum for pupils, schools, and communities. Many schools engage in extensive periodic planning of the over-all curriculum, some have week by week planning, with modifications made to provide better sequence of learning experiences for the local school with much freedom for teachers to determine the sequence of learning activities.

In many states and cities, the old Courses of Study with their fixed content and sequence have given way to general Curriculum

Guides. These Guides represent the best thinking of educational leaders with reference to the over-all curriculum pattern but are suggestive only of major curriculum ideas. Each school and each teacher is left to apply and modify to meet local and individual needs.

In order to facilitate more latitude for teachers to develop a better curriculum "sequence" for each pupil, a number of devices are coming into use. Instead of setting up a curriculum sequence by grade-levels, as traditionally done, many schools are developing general curriculum patterns for larger groupings; such as early childhood, later childhood, early adolescence, later adolescence. Stratemeyer develops such a suggested curriculum "sequence" for the divisions: Early Childhood, Later Childhood, Youth, Adulthood.[12] Another device is to let the teacher stay with a group of pupils for longer periods of time, often through one of similar intervals mentioned above as Grades 1–3, 4–6, junior or senior high school. This enables the teacher to know each pupil and his learning needs more fully, and thus, the better to individualize the curriculum.

Determining source materials

For most teachers of the subject curriculum the source material for instructional use derives from the mass of accumulated informational knowledge. In general, this means the familiar collection of this informational mass brought together in the time-honored textbooks covering the area of the curriculum in question whether it be the area of Mathematics, English, Science, or some other. In addition related collections of organized bodies of subject matter in the several subject areas are usually available in the school library. As alert teachers take a more liberal view of the nature of subject matter they have cautiously reached out to include materials not traditionally a part of the subject curriculum.

The teacher who accepts the experience curriculum point of view finds the matter of source materials for instruction much more extensive, varied, and difficult to organize properly for instructional purposes. Paraphrasing the religious leader who said, "the world is my parish," the teacher of the experience curriculum might well say "the world is the source material of my curriculum." It in-

[12] See Stratemeyer, Florence B., et al. *Developing A Curriculum for Modern Living*, pp. 126 ff. New York: Teachers College, Columbia University, 1947.

cludes all the knowledge found in books, and much more beside. For the experience curriculum involves all of the complex environment of the learner, which the teacher must wisely draw upon to organize into vital life problem-situations whereby appropriate experience learning may result under the wise guidance of the teacher.

Much of these source materials, probably most of it we may some day recognize, is not capable of being assembled within the four walls of a school room, or even within a school building. The market place, the halls of government, industry, the home, all that does or should touch the life of the learner becomes grist to the mill of the teacher for educational purposes. We have only begun to explore these larger reservoirs of source materials lying outside the physical limits of the school. It is imperative that somehow greater use of these be made.

5. Who Makes the Curriculum?

Subject curriculum

Major responsibility for the development of the subject curriculum has fallen to the subject expert. He is the one who has written the textbooks which until recent years have in effect determined the curriculum; and it is he who has done the voluminous research, referred to earlier, that has provided the basis for the selection of content from the mass of knowledge available. The school administrator has until recently shared responsibility for curriculum making. As the educational leader of the school he has determined the extent of curriculum offerings to be made available in his school. And in an earlier day, he selected the textbooks to be used.

As states developed educational leadership and legal controls of the school, they shared in the determination of the general outlines of the curriculum; and where the state assumes authority to select uniform textbooks for the schools, they still exercise that function. There is a growing practice, however, to utilize local teacher committees to cooperatively determine the school curriculum, select the textbooks, and serve on state committees to prepare Courses of Study and Curriculum Guides.

Experience curriculum

By the very nature of the "experience curriculum" it is impossible, for experts, administrators, or State Departments of Education, to formulate the school curriculum. They may be very helpful in sharing their more extended experience in the study of technical curriculum problems. At the state level it may be most helpful with the cooperation of the rich experience of administrators, curriculum experts, and teachers to set up suggestive curriculum guides to help the less well-trained teacher and to provide for all teachers helpful lists of resource materials and suggested methods that have been proved successful by master teachers.

However, the teacher occupies a unique place where the modern experience curriculum is used. The previous discussion has indicated clearly the central place the individual teacher holds in modern curriculum implementation. In a real sense the teacher *must* carry the major responsibility in curriculum making for the learner.

Curriculum making for the modern school is a cooperative task. It involves the administrative staff, the teachers, the community and even the pupils. Now that experience learning is recognized as embracing the total environment of the learner, planning adequately the kind of learning experiences that he should have requires the participation of representative members of the community, parents particularly. Since learning to live successfully in a democratic society involves active participation of the learner in the solution of vital problems of group life, good curriculum practice suggests that the educand be brought in to those phases of curriculum planning that involve his cooperative participation.

QUESTIONS AND PROBLEMS

1. Have a class discussion on the question: "To what extent should the curriculum be planned?"
2. Have a class or panel discussion on the question: "Who should plan the curriculum?"
3. Why do we have a curriculum problem today?
4. Discuss the various phases of this problem as these have developed over the past fifty years.
5. How would you go about reorganizing the curriculum?
6. What are some of the problems with which one is confronted in the determination of the Scope in the subject curriculum? In the experience curriculum? Two class committees might make a thorough study of each of these questions and present their findings to the class for discussion.

58

Curriculum Organization

7. A class or panel discussion might be most profitable on the question: "To what extent should the Sequence of the curriculum be pre-determined?"

8. Have class committees make an evaluation of major lists of objectives formulated within the past century as to the theory of learning they appear to represent, and their educational implications for the curriculum.

9. Criticize the following two statements of objectives from an educational point of view: (1) "The student with a good attitude toward the school and his classmates increasingly makes and keeps friends." (2) "To know the difference between a verb and an adverb."

10. Have a debate on the question: "Should the State adopt uniform textbooks to be used in the schools of the State?"

11. Have studies made of methods used in the selection of textbooks for schools throughout the United States for the past twenty-five years, showing trends, if any, and apparent reason for the various methods employed.

12. What evidence is there, if any, of a trend away from the use of the single textbook in classes?

13. If the class agrees that there is such a tendency, committees might investigate for class report and discussion such questions as: (1) What are the arguments pro and con for the use of single textbooks in a course? (2) What are the alternatives to the use of the single textbook in a course and their relative advantages? (3) In what ways, if any, does the use of a subject curriculum or an experience curriculum have a bearing upon the use of the single textbook or other alternatives?

SELECTED BIBLIOGRAPHY

Alberty, Harold. Reorganizing the High School Curriculum, chapters IV–VII, XV. New York: The Macmillan Company, 1947.

Blair, Arthur W. and Burton, William H. Growth and Development of the Preadolescent. New York: Appleton-Century-Crofts, Inc., 1951.

Burton, William H. The Guidance of Learning Activities, chapter VIII. New York: Appleton-Century-Crofts, Inc., 1944.

Douglass, H. R. et al. The High School Curriculum, chapters II, III, VII, X, XV. New York: The Ronald Press Company, 1947.

Douglass, H. R. and Mills, H. H. Teaching in the High School, chapter III. New York: The Ronald Press Company, 1948.

Educational Policies Commission, Education for All American Youth. Washington: National Education Association, 1944.

Faunce, Roland C. and Bossing, Nelson L. Developing the Core Curriculum. New York: Prentice-Hall, Inc., 1951.

Goetting, M. L. *Teaching in the Secondary School,* chapter V. New York: Prentice-Hall, Inc., 1942.

Leonard, J. Paul. *Developing the Secondary School Curriculum,* chapters IX–XII, XVI. New York: Rinehart and Company, 1946.

Mudd, Dorothy, *A Core Program Grows.* Bel Air, Maryland: Board of Education of Harford County, 1949.

Noar, Gertrude. *Freedom to Live and Learn.* Philadelphia: Franklin Publishing and Supply Company, 1948.

Pierce, Paul R. *Developing a High-School Curriculum.* New York: American Book Company, 1942.

Rivlin, Harry N. *Teaching Adolescents in Secondary Schools,* chapters II, XIII. New York: Appleton-Century-Crofts, Inc., 1948.

Sands, Lester B. *An Introduction to Teaching in Secondary Schools,* chapter IX. New York: Harper and Brothers, 1949.

Smith, B. O., Stanley, W. O., and Shores, J. H. *Fundamentals of Curriculum Development,* chapters XVI–XX. New York: World Book Company, 1950.

Stratemeyer, Florence B. et al. *Developing a Curriculum for Modern Living.* New York: Bureau of Publications, Teachers College, Columbia University, 1947.

"The Curriculum: Learning and Teaching," *Review of Educational Research,* vol. XXI, no. 3, (June, 1951). Washington, D.C.: American Educational Research Association.

Thut, I. N. and Gerberich, J. R. *Foundations of Method for Secondary Schools,* chapter IV. New York: McGraw-Hill Book Company, Inc., 1949.

3

How Develop Units?

1. How Define the Teaching Unit?

Unit idea gaining prominence

A careful perusal of educational magazines, new courses of study and recent elementary and secondary textbooks reveals that the unit idea is gaining general acceptance in educational circles. The discussion in the previous chapter of the organization of the modern curriculum pointed clearly to the need for a change in the time-honored approach to the organization of the curriculum for instructional purposes.

The underlying concept of the unit is not new even though the current terminology is of recent origin. Students conversant with the genesis of developing educational ideas will recognize that the germinal basis of the unit goes back at least as far as Herbart. The Herbartian "formal steps" in learning, particularly as developed by the American Herbartians, implied unity in the learning situation from the first to the last step. The early "Project" both in manual training and agriculture assumed a unitary situation as the basis of learning. "The "Project" as refined by Kilpatrick, Collings, and others, and the "Unit" associated with the "Mastery" concept and the "Cycle Plan of Teaching" as developed by Morrison, have more nearly conformed to modern conceptions of learning. Consequently, they have been most influential in popularizing the development of and the widespread use of units within the past twenty-five years.[1]

[1] For a more detailed discussion of the Herbartian Steps, the Project and

At this point the teacher should understand clearly the basis in the theory of learning of the shift to the "Unit" form of curriculum organization for instructional purposes. The older atomistic conception of the way we learn made learning a matter of adding one small item of knowledge to another, bit by bit. It was somewhat like stringing pearls on a chain. Each pearl was self-contained, independent, but with enough strung together they could make a necklace or bracelet largely dependent upon how many separate pearls were so used and how they were finally manipulated into a pattern. Learning by this theory became simply an additive process, a matter of adding separate items of knowledge or skills until enough of these had been acquired when they could be brought together into some over-all pattern. This atomistic conception of learning was implicit in the old "mind storage" and the "S – R Bond" notions of the way we learn. As a result, much of our educational activities in the past were carried on through assignment of segments of subject-matter-to-be-learned without particular reference to the relationships of similar segments of subject matter previously learned, or, in the future to-be-learned. It was exemplified in the daily assignment of spelling-book lists of words to be memorized, so many pages in advance in a history text, and the endless practice of scales on the piano before these were brought together into a complete composition, however simple.

The basic reason underlying the popular growth of the "unit" idea lies in the rapidly growing acceptance of the Gestalt-Organismic-Field theories of learning with their emphasis upon the "wholeness" or the "unitary" nature of learning. Contrary to the atomistic concept of learning, this newer approach is based upon the assumption that effective learning — if, indeed, there can be any other learning possible — must take place in an environment in which the goals of learning are clearly perceived, and every phase of the operational procedure is viewed as a relational part of the total learning situation. Thus, the learner reacts to the

Morrison's unit idea as they are related to learning theory, see Chapter 4, "How Can Problem Solving Be Used?" Those interested in the historical development of the unit idea should consult the more extensive discussions found in such sources as: Gwynn, M. J. *Curriculum Principles and Social Trends*, chapter VII. New York: The Macmillan Company, 1950; Alberty, Harold. *Reorganizing the High-School Curriculum*, chapter VIII. New York: The Macmillan Company, 1947; Umstattd, J. G. *Secondary School Teaching*, chapter VI. Boston: Ginn and Company, 1942.

problem-situation as a whole, and not to parts in isolation. He understands that it involves an effort to make modifications in his total behavior in such ways as to achieve the goal; he must make effective adjustments to the problem-situation at hand. Throughout his efforts to achieve, he will examine every phase of his progress toward the goal, and continuously make those modifications in his general behavior he deems most likely to overcome the obstacles in the way of his success. Instead of running isolated music scales that have no immediate purposive significance for the learner, as in the additive theory of learning referred to above, the learner starts with a desire to play a specific single composition. After seeing it as a whole, he tries to discover the relational skills necessary for its production, then tries to modify his behavior in such ways as to achieve the pattern of behavior skills needed to play the composition. Along the learning continuum, as he reacts to the composition as a whole, no doubt there will occur points at which particularly difficult and recognized obstacles will have to be given special attention, and further effort to overcome them made.

Definition of a unit

Few terms in modern educational usage have been more extensively used with as much disagreement as to meaning as has the term "unit." Much of the difficulty seems to find its genesis in the conflicting ideas of learning held by educational workers, the hesitancy of many to move too far afield from traditional ways of doing things, and the obvious failure of many to see clearly the full implications of newer concepts of learning which they profess to accept.

However, more recent writers in the fields of curriculum and methods are bridging the gap between the extremes of earlier differences. In many instances it appears to be a matter of relative emphasis rather than of basic differences in educational concept. Some of these apparent shades of differences may be chargeable to semantics.

In the statement which follows the writer has endeavored to present a definition of the unit giving recognition to the inclusive nature of learning in conformity with best modern educational thought. *A unit consists of a comprehensive series of related and meaningful activities so developed as to achieve pupil purposes, provide significant educational experiences, and result in appro-*

priate behavioral changes. There are at least four major aspects of modern learning connoted in this definition. *First,* learning is accepted as an active rather than passive process involving emphasis upon pupil behavior; *second,* the "wholeness" or "unitary" nature of learning is recognized in the complete continuum of interrelated activities toward the achievement of purposes or goals; *third,* the place of purpose in learning is integrally a part of the unit concept; and fourth, experience learning is fully recognized as the heart of the unit idea.

Types of teaching units. Although many classifications of types of units have been suggested by curriculum specialists, there are two major classifications which find more general acceptance, namely: "subject-matter" and "experience" units.[2] The usual explanation of the distinction assumed to exist between the two is that the first focuses attention upon large bodies of information or subject-matter to be acquired and understood. The second directs attention to the learner and the experiences it is desired he should have as the result of certain life situations (problem-situations) with which he may be confronted and to which he fully reacts.

Even these two classifications may be open to serious question. If the Organismic-Field theory of learning be accepted, then the implications of major difference in the twofold classification of "subject-matter" and "experience" types of units may not be found defensible. If all learning is the resultant of the interaction of the learner with an environmental problem-situation in which some satisfactory adjustment of the learner to the situations in question involves modifications in his basic behavior patterns, then it is beside the point to talk about two inferentially different types of units. There can be only one basic kind of learning, namely: learning through experience that has as its end product change in behavior. By this same token there can be only one kind of unit possible for this conception of learning, and that is the "experience" unit.

[2] For further detailed discussion on unit types see Caswell, H. L. and Campbell, D. S. *Curriculum Development,* pp. 402–427. New York: American Book Company, 1935; for other forms of classification not generally accepted but of interest see Smith, B. O., Stanley, W. O. and Shores, J. H. *Fundamentals of Curriculum Development,* pp. 555–558. Yonkers, N.Y.: World Book Company, 1950; Goetting, M. L., *Teaching in the Secondary School,* pp. 310–314. New York: Prentice-Hall, Inc., 1942.

As the teacher tries to develop functional instructional situations, it may be desirable at times to have clearly in mind that the material drawn upon for a given unit may be predominantly limited to so-called subject-matter sources. When that is so, the unit may require somewhat different handling than will a unit which naturally draws upon a predominance of source material of a less abstract verbal nature. But it is a dubious procedure to attempt to draw an artificial distinction between the traditionally organized bodies of knowledge familiarly labelled "subjects" and all the other sources used to create learning situations. Such a sharply drawn dichotomy between types of source materials for instructional purposes should not, and in reality does not, exist.

Much harm has been done modern education by the false impression often inadvertently given by those who try to emphasize the more inclusive use of all the wealth of source data available for enriching the learning experiences of youth. All that is known in whatever form is grist for instructional purposes to the mill of the good teacher. It is grist, however, in whatever form the source is found, as a means and not as an end in itself. Throughout this chapter it is assumed there is only one kind of unit which will conform to the Organismic-Field theory of learning, namely: the "experience" unit based upon the concept of experience learning.

2. What Constitutes a Good Teaching Unit?

A general discussion or definition of the unit often implies many things which at first reading escape detection. A more specific statement of the characteristics of the unit, followed by sample teaching units, should assist the teacher to understand more clearly the instructional significance of the unit.

Characteristics of a good unit

1. *The unit is unified.* Unlike the segmental and fragmentary type of lesson common in earlier teaching, and too frequently still in use, the unit with its emphasis upon a "series of related and meaningful activities" suggests *wholeness* in organization. The student is perforce conscious of a definite relationship between one activity and another which may be involved in the achievement of a purpose or goal. That relationship is natural and inherent, not artificial. To fulfill the requirements of the unit idea there must be a natural cohesion and coherence in the unit organization.

2. *The unit is organized around purposes of the learner.* The most significant developments in teaching methods for the past fifty years have emphasized the importance of pupil purposes in the learning activity. Herbart recognized the importance of the pupil understanding at least the direction or goal of the immediate learning activities. Morrison emphasized the importance of the pupil seeing clearly the goal of his learning quest, and gave much greater stress to the need of a desire on the part of the learner to seek this clearly discerned objective. These are definitely a part of Morrison's "Unit" idea, and provided for in the first two steps of his "Cycle Plan of Teaching." John Dewey has made "purpose" or "goal-seeking" a sine qua non of learning, and a primary concern of teaching. Kilpatrick and others have given it more explicit form in a framework of instructional procedures by making "Pupil Purposing" the first and key step of the "Project" method of teaching.

If it is true that learning takes place only as one tries to make satisfactory adjustments to a problem-situation which challenges him, then the importance of "purpose" in the unit is clear. In this connection the teacher should keep in mind the twofold nature of "purpose." It is not enough to feel disturbance or irritation in a given situation; the learner also must recognize somewhat clearly the goal or object, which, if reached, will relieve the disturbance or irritation felt and substitute therein a sense of relief or satisfaction. Learning as one psychologist has defined it is "activity under tension toward a goal." Purpose, then, has dual aspects, namely: *first,* a stimulation or desire (motive) for a modification of an existing unsatisfactory condition involving the learner, and *second,* a recognition of what appears to be a feasible goal which will bring about a satisfactory adjustment of the situation and thus provide relief or satisfaction. Many people have a sense of irritation or dissatisfaction with an existing condition or situation which may even reach a point of serious physical and mental disturbance; at the same time they do nothing about it because they do not see a feasible objective or goal which they recognize would provide welcome relief. It is when these two important factors are brought together that a basis for learning is provided — *purpose.*

For teaching effectiveness the teacher should see the operation of "purposes" in reverse. Education has sometimes been defined as the creation in the individual of a divine discontent. That is, there are many corrections or improvements in the behavior patterns of the learner which the teacher realizes should take place if the learner is to progressively assume more effective participation in the democratic way of life. The learner has no such awareness of his shortcomings, and if his insensitiveness to the general state of affairs continues no improvement in his action patterns will result. It will be only as the teacher helps to create "purposes" within him that improvement can occur. The significance of the unit organization around "purposes" is thus seen to be crucial.

3. *The unit provides a place of beginning and ending.* The unit organization will suggest to the learner, and to the alert teacher, where he should begin and clearly indicate the point at which he might reasonably conclude his efforts. This is a characteristic of the unit emphasized even by its earlier protagonists. This is one reason why the use of topics such as "The Second World War," "Transportation," "Food," or "Production," cannot be accepted as true units. They violate every principle of the concept of units involved in the definition of units accepted in this book, and of the principles of learning underlying the unit concept there implied.

There is no problem-situation involved in such topics, and therefore they cannot represent pupil purposes. Where, for example, should we begin in an attack upon the topic "Transportation"? It presents no point of departure for study. What should one wish to know about "Transportation"? The alert teacher can think of dozens of problem-situations involving transportation. Until some aspect of "Transportation" is cast into a genuine problem-situation for the learner, it remains for him a somewhat nebulous thing of no personal concern. He can be challenged with some phase of the broad topic when it becomes specific for him and identified with some vital personal concern.

A young lad, obviously not at first hand familiar with transportation beyond the immediate community limits, was observed to approach the window of the station agent somewhat timidly and anxiously to find out how he could get from where he was to another distant place apparently not very accessible. For almost forty minutes the agent struggled with the boy's direct question: "How can I get from here to ——?" Whatever the driving force back of the lad's concern, it was perfectly clear to him that he wanted to reach a certain goal, and the problem centered around the best means by which he could reach his purposed destination. The eavesdroppers learned that there were several combinations of travel modes open to the lad. He must choose from among about three combined means of travel to reach his destination. The notes made by the agent concerning the possible travel plans were carefully pocketed by the lad as he left the station for further study of the route most desirable for him to take. Until it was important for him to go to this place the relevance of transportation to this spot did not occur to him. The newspaper and radio carried the story of an old pioneer in the community who was taking a plane trip back to his childhood home which he left as a young man by ox cart to find greater opportunity in the then undeveloped West. Mention was made in the newscasts of the change in transportation this plane trip of the old pioneer highlighted. It became a matter of interest and discussion in several classes in the local school. Such questions as: "Why couldn't he travel by train?" "Why didn't he take a stagecoach?" "When did the railroads come into existence?" "Were there other ways of traveling at that time?" Out of these questions emerged a general interest problem for one high school class, namely: "How have changes in transportation since pioneer days affected the way we live in this community?" A fourth-grade class finally set up its problem concern around this question: "What changes in transportation have occurred since the first white man came to this community?"

In each of these problem-situations only a small phase of the topic "Transportation" is attacked. In each the problem-situation is cast into the form of a question. In each question there is a clear delimitation of the problem. The pupil sees clearly at what point his attack upon the problem is to begin, and by the same token knows when his goal is reached. This is one of the reasons it is suggested that unit titles be formulated into question form or clearly implied questions. It is only by such a device that purposive goal seeking can be most sharply set up as definite problem-situations.

4. *The learning activities of the unit are educationally significant.* The teacher must constantly evaluate the activities involved in the development of the unit with respect to their own worth and the extent to which activities are significantly interrelated. As educationally sound as was the Activity Movement of a couple of decades ago, it suffered from many of its well-meaning but misguided followers. Many caught the form without the understanding, with the result that all too frequently teachers emphasized activity for its own sake. When its excesses were at their worst, the extreme

manifestations of activity misuse were reported by a district supervisor who was called to a two-room school in a rural community. One teacher had caught the idea that activity per se had educational value, and that the greater the activity, the greater the assurance education was taking place. The Supervisor reported that as he reached the school pandemonium seemed to hold sway in one room. When he questioned the teacher as to what was going on, she proudly informed him they were engaged in an activity program. For her, undirected bodily activity with a heavy accent upon rigorous movement was assumed to be evidence in itself of learning.

Good teachers realize that activity for its own sake may have very dubious educational value. The value of an activity must be appraised in terms of the socially desirable behavior it develops. Uncontrolled or undirected activities may create bullies and boors with antisocial characteristics, as well as persons of responsive, self-controlled, cooperative tendencies desirable in good citizenship. Likewise, the more effective the activity is educationally, the more it will be responsibly meshed with other activities toward the realization of the unit purpose or goal.

Activities to be educationally significant must be those which pupils recognize will contribute to the goals they seek. Pupils quickly tire of activities which they do not see lead to the achievement of desired ends. Pupils, too, should learn to carefully evaluate each activity in terms of its relevance to the achievement of their purposes. They should see that, even admitting the worth-while-ness of certain activities at times, there are others that will more economically and more effectively aid the pupils in realizing their purposes.

Again, some activities are worth while but more appropriate to a different age group. The teacher must judge activities in terms of the ability of certain individuals or groups to use them effectively. Studies have shown that many activities favored for certain age levels are inappropriate because of the maturity level of the student. For example, it is not as effective for seventh-grade girls to engage in mature household management problems as it is for twelfth-graders who are thinking seriously of a home of their own, and for whom the skills in home management begin to assume greater meaning and importance. There are activities of varying difficulty, all of which may be essential to the realization of the unit purposes. When committees are formed to engage in these various activities, the wise teacher must evaluate them in terms of the competency of particular pupils to handle them.

5. *The unit is comprehensive.* It is possible to think of a learning experience situation unified and relatively complete in itself which would require not more than one or two class periods. The type of learning skills with which the school is concerned are best achieved in a larger problem situation. Too, there is grave danger of discreteness and fragmentation in such short learning situations. One of the distinct values attributed to the unit organization by its many advocates is that the focusing of attention upon a relatively large unified learning situation tends to insure unitariness in the total learning experience of the pupil. The teacher, too, in his planning is much more likely to see large units relationally, than when many small learning situations are used.

6. *The unit is practicable for pupil attack.* This story is reported from one of the major state curriculum reorganization programs of a few years ago. A coastal community with a lighthouse as a conspicious part of the nearby coastline and with others not far distant, led to a very interesting unit on "lighthouses" which involved a study of different lighthouses, their types, location, and function in the community. This was a vital practicable unit in this community where the lighthouse occupied so prominent a place in the lives of the community, and particularly for many families with members and relatives dependent upon the lighthouse for personal safety when at sea. A fascinating and pedagogically well-developed unit concerning the lighthouse was taught; on account of its organization it was publicized throughout the state as a sample of good unit organization and teaching. Unfortunately units on lighthouses began to appear in remote hamlets of the state far from the ocean, where lighthouses would have only a minimum of concern to the pupils, and where vital phases of the development of the original unit situation — such as a first-hand study of lighthouses — was impossible.

Often the teaching of certain types of units practicable in one community situation may not be practicable in another, either because of the relevancy of the matter to be considered for the learning experiences of the pupils in question, or the mechanical difficulties involved. Units of learning which are educationally significant and practical for development in a rural community may have little value and be wholly impractical for carrying through in a metropolitan center, and vice versa.

7. *The unit provides for a variety of activities.* Both within a given unit and in the use of several units there should be a wide variety of activities to facilitate all forms of learning. One of the advantages claimed for the unit has been that it provided for individual differences within the class, in a way that was not true of traditional subject-matter forms of instruction. A properly organized and conducted unit will provide a wide range of interest challenges to the members of the group through a variety of individual and committee activities on various phases of the unit problem-situation. These same individual and committee activities generally represent a gradation in difficulty levels to challenge the corresponding levels of abilities represented in the group.

Over a period of time units studied by a group should cover the major areas of the curriculum, to insure a well-balanced development of the individual in those areas of living in which essential competencies are necessary. Unless this is carefully safeguarded, serious blind spots in the scope of the pupil's education will result.

8. *The unit involves full teacher-pupil cooperation.* As indicated earlier in this chapter, the development of the unit idea has steadily given greater emphasis to the place of pupil purposing in learning. This in turn has been reflected in the larger place given to teacher-pupil planning of the unit and in the various steps of the unit development. It is the ideal of modern unit teaching that every phase of the unit process should represent cooperative planning by teacher and pupils in the realization of pupil purposes. The teacher as the guide of youth in learning thus identifies himself with the pupil purposes of the unit. This is a cardinal characteristic of all good unit organization and unit teaching.

9. *The unit provides the basis for its evaluation.* The teacher and pupil should recognize in the unit itself the basis for evaluating the success with which the goal of the unit may be achieved. A good unit will be so clear in its statement of a goal that the pupil and teacher can set up in advance the broad criteria of successful achievement. This does not mean of course, that achievement in every situation can be known in any absolute sense. A problem-situation in a community where a large number of the people appear to suffer from typhus infection led to a unit in school on

"How can we eliminate the source of typhus infection in this community?" This unit was capable of evaluation by specific criteria inherent in the unit. The study of the unit led to the discovery of the source of infection, recommendations for its removal, and the actual elimination of the source of infection by the carrying out of the recommendations. On the other hand, for a unit drawing heavily on so-called subject-matter sources, such as: "What were the causes of the first World War?" it would be easy to set up broad criteria of success in achieving the goal implied in the unit. Obviously when the learner could list all the "causes" he would have attained his goal. But it is not possible to compile a list of "causes" with full assurance that one or several have not been overlooked. In this instance, therefore, we should set up criteria which take into account a reasonable canvass of the literature of the outstanding writers on the subject as a basis for assuming that all the important "causes" have been discovered. Some such qualified criteria of evaluating achievement is necessary for many learning goals.

10. *A good unit stimulates further action.* Although this criteria should be operative in general, occasionally a unit is found to have recognized educational value which does not lead the group to other problem-situations. A vital problem-situation, when attacked, should bring other related problems into the foreground for pupil consideration. It is the experience of most teachers engaged in unit teaching that a good unit suggests to pupils more leads for further profitable study than can be used.

Samples of teaching units

The two units presented below represent quite different approaches to unit teaching. The first example presented grew out of the desire of the teacher to maintain the subject-matter emphasis and at the same time provide as near as possible a vital problem-situation challenge to the learner. It is a unit selected from among several others which comprised an experimental attempt in a specific school situation to develop a fusion course in chemistry and physics. It represents a high level of effort to utilize the basic unit problem-situation within the framework of an accepted subject-matter course. Since many teachers must begin unit teaching within a somewhat traditional subject-matter curriculum set-up, this example may prove suggestive of a way by which transition can be effected.

A UNIT OUTLINE:

How Can Comfort Be Increased by Air Conditioning? [3]

By Shailer A. Peterson

Sub-units:

A. What is there about air to be conditioned?

B. How do we use chemical abbreviations to describe our heating plants?

C. Is there a better way of heating your home?

D. What would it cost to air condition your home in summer?

Time Required for This Unit.

This unit will require approximately six weeks to complete.

Terms and Concepts (merely mentioned here — explained in later units).

Electrical circuit, large Calorie, linear measure, mass, matter, percentage composition, volume measure, weight.

Terms and Concepts (introduced earlier — amplified here).

Except for "introductory chapter," this is the first unit; therefore we may consider all terms to be introduced for the first time.

Terms and Concepts (introduced here — only mentioned later).

Bunsen burner, comfort zones, compressor-type refrigerator, dew point, "Electrolux" type (gas) refrigerator, Fahrenheit, fire extinguishers, fuels, heating plants, heat exchange, hot air heating, hot water heating, humidostats, kindling point, kindling temperature, liquid thermometers, moist air heating, refrigeration, relative humidity.

Terms and Concepts (introduced here — amplified later).

Absorption of heat, bi-metal thermometers, binary compound, boiling, boiling point, B t u, burning, calorie, Centigrade, chemical change, chemical property, circulation, coefficient of explosion, combustion, compounds, conduction convection, elements, equation, evaporation,

---

[3] This unit plan is for II A. in outline for *Physics and Chemistry Fusion Course.* Prepared by Shailer A. Peterson while head, Science Department, University of Minnesota High School.

explosion, English system, flame, food temperatures, freezing point, gas, gas thermometers, heat, heat of conductivity, heat of fusion, heat of vaporization, heat values, humidity, inert elements, liquid, melting, melting point, metals, metric system, mixtures, naming binary compounds, non-metals, oxidation, physical change, physical property, radiation, reflection of heat, solid, states of matter, symbols, temperature, thermometers, thermostats, valence, valence numbers.

Sub-Units:

A. What is there about air to be conditioned?

1. Refer to previous introductory unit by mentioning a few topics that will be included in this unit and draw attention to the fact that both chemistry and physics contribute.

2. Introduce the five factors of air conditioning, (1) temperature control, (2) humidity control, (3) circulation, (4) cleansing, and (5) replenishing fresh air.

3. Describe how people through the ages have endeavored to make themselves comfortable by some sort of air conditioning devices. Compare these attempts to the five factors mentioned above. Mention the importance of air conditioning to the various industries with which the pupils are more or less familiar.

4. Introduce element, compound, and mixture through a discussion of the analysis of air showing it to include oxygen, nitrogen, argon, and carbon dioxide. (Show percentage composition by volume.)

5. Describe the part that elements play in forming compounds. Compare this with the rôle that the letters of the alphabet play in forming different words.

6. Elaborate upon the difference between elements, compounds, and mixtures by demonstrations to show the influence of chemical changes and physical changes upon both chemical and physical properties. (Use common names and also a few chemical names here.)

7. Remind the pupils of the importance of air to human life by comparing the composition of inhaled and exhaled air and describe the conditioning necessary to make the air usable again.

8. Introduce the meaning of the humidity by discussing water, its three states, solid, liquid, and gas, as well as the importance of water vapor in the air.

B. How do we use chemical abbreviations to describe our heating plants?

1. Refer back to the previous section and the analogy of elements and the alphabet building blocks. Compare the way in which letters change the meaning of words and show how the different elements and their amounts change the characteristics of the substance.

2. Describe the burning of wood or coal by a word equation. Use demonstrations to show the significance of these equations and introduce the use of chemical abbreviations, symbols and formulas.

3. Mention the significance of equations and formulas in terms of atoms and molecules. (Not too completely, for this must not confuse the present issue and then too, it will be discussed later in detail.)

4. Show how classification of elements into metals, non-metals, and inert elements helps to simplify the writing and understanding of formulas and equations.

5. Introduce the naming of simple binary compounds by showing that all end in -ide.

6. Introduce the concept of valence. Use the analogy of "lugs and cogs" by which to show visually how the elements combine to form compounds. (This concept leads directly to the electron theory in Unit IV and Unit VI.)

7. Merely mention the fact that a complete equation also specifies whether heat is produced or absorbed. (Topics such as these are to be thrown in as interesting side-lights instead of as new, vital material.)

8. Show short-cut method of writing formulas with valence numbers by crossing the valence number of one element over and making it the subscript number of the other element in the binary compound. (Give only a small amount of drill in writing equations for this should be saved until the next and following sections.)

C. Is there a better way of heating your home?

1. Introduce the topic by a discussion of the heat supplied by the chemical action of burning.

2. Distinguish briefly at this point between heat and temperature by drawing an analogy between heating a cup full of water or heating a bathtub full of water to the same temperature. (Demonstrate with match, thimble, beaker, and thermometer.)

3. Discuss the problem of heating in terms of first: (1) the nature of the reaction substance (to be burned), and (2) the amount of the reacting substance. Second: (1) the nature of the sub-

stance to be heated (such as water, air in room, or steel pipes), (2) the amount of the substance to be heated, and (3) the temperature that one wishes the substance to attain.

4. Introduce the terms "heat value" and B t u and show how the consumer makes use of the advertised heat values to determine the best buy.

5. Explain the significance of specific heat and give practice in solving various kinds of heat problems that are practical to air conditioning and common around the house or school. (Work with English system: B t u's, Fahrenheit, pounds, etc.)

6. Continue the heat problems introducing the concept of exchange of heat showing its importance in all heating systems.

7. Explain methods of transferring heat: (1) conduction, (2) radiation, and (3) convection.

8. Elaborate further upon the difference between heat and temperature and explain the process of burning in detail giving the temperature of the various flame zones of candle or Bunsen burner.

9. Introduce the "kinetic theory" concept (but *without its name*) and explain the lighting of fires, kindling points, kindling temperatures, and the three ways of extinguishing a flame: (1) cooling below its kindling temperature, (2) smothering, and (3) removing materials of combustion. Explain types of extinguishers. (Use demonstrations to explain principles.)

10. By charts and local data collected by pupils compare the cost of heat units depending upon the grade of coal, oil, or wood, or whether gas or electricity is employed for heating. It should be pointed out that these comparisons directly assume all furnaces and heaters to be equally efficient.

11. Describe and discuss fully the steam, hot air, and hot water heating systems. Show by illustrations and demonstrations the advantages and disadvantages of each in terms of the factors involved in air conditioning. (Constantly refer to heat exchange here.)

12. Introduce heat conductivities and show their importance to heating and radiating systems and then show their importance in insulating a house or room against heat loss.

13. Discuss ways, other than conduction, by which a house or a room loses heat, and discuss ways of correcting these conditions.

D. What would it cost to air condition your home in summer?

1. Introduce this section by a review of temperature. Discuss the

advantages of one type of thermometer over another and explain what factors are desirable for a satisfactory liquid, gas, bi-metal, or other type of thermometer. The pupils should discuss what liquids are more desirable than mercury or alcohol and also whether large or small bulb thermometers are most desirable, etc.

2. Explain the applications of coefficients of expansion in places other than thermometry.

3. Show simplified method of converting Fahrenheit temperature to Centigrade temperature scale.

4. Explain usefulness and conveniences of the metric system and how conversions may be made easier with it than with the English system. Use chart to make the concept graphic and show the similarity that exists for all measures whether they be volume, weight, or linear measures.

5. Compare the Btu with the calorie and barely mention the large Calorie that some of the pupils may remember from their biology, general science, or "diet" literature.

6. Give the pupils plenty of practice in using the metric units in the various types of problems that they have had.

7. Review the states of matter and explain the transition that takes place. Make use of this to introduce the heat of fusion and the heat of vaporization. Give numerous examples and review concept of exchange of heat with demonstrations.

8. Review exchange of heat to explain how well water may be used for cooling homes in summer and using hot underground spring water to heat homes in winter.

9. Review evaporation and the heat of vaporization in order to introduce the explanation of the compressor type refrigerator. Compare the different refrigerants and the advantages and disadvantages of each as indicated by its properties.

10. Draw a rough comparison of the costs of installation of the various types of cooling systems and show how the cost of operation compares with the cost of installation. Explain the "Electrolux" type of refrigerating system.

11. Explain the importance of refrigeration in cold storage and give some information about the temperatures at which different foods should be stored. Explain briefly the action of thermostats in terms of thermometers. (Leave discussion of electrical circuits, etc., till Units III and IV.)

12. Explain the cost of operating a refrigerator at lower tempera-

tures than necessary. Compare this with heating a house to higher temperatures than are healthful or wise.

13. Explain the function of a refrigerating unit in dehumidifying a refrigerator or in dehumidifying a home.

14. Show the importance in maintaining the correct humidity for utmost comfort. Explain dew point, relative humidity, fog and rain in terms of refrigerating units and comfort.

15. Summarize the whole problem of air conditioning by discussing the multitude of problems that must confront a builder or a consumer when it comes to deciding upon the equipment to be used and then how it must be operated for greatest economy and usefulness. Take this opportunity also to point out the various contributions that both chemistry and physics have made to this whole problem.

16. Wind up unit with a view toward the unit which follows on "Building."

Evaluation:

The pretest and the final achievement examinations for the course are comprehensive tests that have been divided into "areas" or "units." The gross or total score of a test is not as useful as the scores from the various test units when it comes to analyzing and interpreting pupil achievement and also when the teacher wants to determine where his own teaching should be modified. These test unit scores form an achievement "profile" and they also prove useful in comparing the class achievement with that of other sections as well as with other physical science classes for which this test is intended. The test units include: (1) Apparatus and its uses; (2) Periodic chart and concepts relating to atoms and molecules; (3) Recognizing chemical abbreviations and their meaning; (4) Problems dealing with weight, volume, energy, and force; (5) Associations of common names and formulas; (6) Chemists and physicists; (7) Metric system and mathematical constants; (8) Practical problems that use physics and chemistry; (9) Scientific reasoning and using the scientific method; (10) Writing and balancing chemical equations; (11) Miscellaneous analytical tests; (12) Laboratory procedures; and (13) Ionization, electrolysis, and electricity.

As far as is convenient, the daily and unit tests are also divided into the various areas toward which each contributes. The small number of items does not allow any set of profile scores for each little test, but all scores contribute toward a profile that may be compiled at the completion of the unit. Pupils keep records of these scores so that they may see how they are progressing but to keep the bookkeeping simple, there are frequently a few "miscellaneous" items as well as some that are included into a test unit called, "the consumer."

The tests given during the unit may be listed as:

1. Short daily tests
   Time: about 10 minutes
   Frequency: about 2 each week
2. Mid-Unit test
   Time: one full period
   Frequency: one, part-way through the unit
3. Final-Unit test
   Time: one full period
   Frequency: one, at the completion of the unit
4. This teaching unit contributes to all of the test units with the exception of No. 13 on electricity, etc.

The unit above typifies the teaching unit planned in advance. It was organized in much detail as one in a series, which was to be taught in serial order and approximately as planned. This is characteristic of the way the unit idea is generally adapted to a subject-matter curriculum concept.

The next unit plan to be described represents in essence the true experience unit. It was written up after it had been taught. As it stands it has been amplified in suggestions and source references to make it a better suggestion guide for other teachers who might find it desirable as a teaching unit. The unit outline approximately fifty pages in length is here given in abbreviated form. It is typical of the units developed in the public schools, elementary and secondary, of Long Beach, California. It was prepared by Hilda Peterson, Classroom Teacher, John G. Whittier School, Long Beach, California, with the assistance of other teachers in 1946.

A SIXTH GRADE UNIT:

How Changes in Communication Affect People's Lives
Introduction

"The Long Beach Public Schools accept the theory that the purposes of education in the elementary schools can be achieved best through integrated activity units. From the rich and varied experience which integrated activity units afford, the children gain skill in using the techniques of democratic living and a will to live democratically. . . .

The integrated activity unit insures a clearer understanding and better mastery of the '3 R's'. . . . "

The scope of the curriculum is defined in terms of "sixteen broad social functions," into which are classified the needs of children. These are repeated in all units developed within the school system.

1. Conserving human resources
2. Conserving material and natural resources
3. Securing raw material
4. Producing commodities
5. Transporting and exchanging goods
6. Consuming goods
7. Rendering and utilizing services
8. Communicating
9. Cooperating in social and civic action
10. Securing an education
11. Expressing and satisfying aesthetic needs
12. Expressing and satisfying spiritual needs
13. Discovery and developing new knowledge
14. Enjoying recreation
15. Living in the home
16. Getting a living

Objectives

Anticipated growths in the child

Physical (samples)

He increases in muscular control and coordination.

He maintains an interest in play activities.

Social (samples)

He shares his work and findings more willingly.

He cooperates in group projects.

Intellectual Knowledges (samples)

He understands the major types of communication that have affected man's social and economic progress and understands the basic influences of each.

— Habits (sample)

He organizes his work before starting it.

— Skills (sample)

He expresses himself more fluently and more pointedly.

Emotional (sample)

He acquires self confidence through success.

Spiritual (sample)

He shows reverence for the sacredness of life.

Generalizations. As a result of this study children should show a growth in, and understanding of, the following social concepts: (samples) [4]

The use of electricity increases the necessity for safety measures. (1)
Organization and democratic regulation further group work. (9)
Radio broadcasting has contributed to the oneness of the world. (4, 8, 9, 12)

Overview

Description of the class

I.Q. range: 83–118 (56% of the class were between 96–105)
Age range: 10.2–12.7
Reading range: 4.0–11.0
Race represented: Anglo-American

Initiation — An arranged environment (here are listed the materials used in the room display to arouse pupil interest in possible unit)

Pictures — (lists)
Books — (lists)
Realia — (lists)

Responses to environmental stimuli (excerpts from comments and reactions of pupils to the materials displayed above)

"I didn't know what a telephone looked like inside," one boy admitted. Harvey asked if he might bring his telegraph key, sounder and transformer that he made in the Hamilton Summer School.

Subsequent Activities
(Several pages of activities listed)

Needs and Desires (samples)	*Experiences Involved* (samples)
To learn more about how and why aerials are grounded	Listening to what Charles thought he knew
To learn the telegraphic code	Consulting adults (parents or neighbors)
To learn how sound travels	Reading about telegraphic codes; discussing them and their uses
	Listening to recordings of lessons on the code
	Tapping different substances in environment to find which carries sound the best

[4] The numbers in parentheses refer to the social functions listed on page 79 and show how this unit contributes to an understanding of these social functions.

Additional Opportunities Within this Area of Experience

"This unit offers many opportunities for the intensive study of other aspects of communication other than those described in the overview. A few of these opportunities are explored on the following pages." (Here follow four pages of suggestive activities not taken up in this unit as it was studied.)

Illustrative and Informational Materials

Music References (lists)
  Songs
  Records
  Songs for radio programs in rooms
  Reference books on music

Audio-Visual Materials (lists)
  Charts
  Exhibits
  Film strips
  Glass slides
  Motion pictures
  Stereographs
  Study prints
  Transcriptions

Bibliography

(Here follow several pages of bibliographical materials under special captions showing where they are available.)
Available in Textbook Room
Available in School Library
Available in School Library and Public Library
Available in Public Library
Available in Music Office and Teachers Library
Available by request: Federal Security Agency, U.S. Office of Education, Washington, D.C. (free)

The major weakness of this unit is its failure to provide a section on "Evaluation" which is a vital part of unit development, and is generally a part of the unit plans used by the Long Beach Schools.

3. How Preplan a Teaching Unit?

Frequently the uninformed critics of modern education charge that teachers in so-called modernistic schools do not plan what they are to teach. They characterize the teacher as coming before the class with the question: "Now, class, what shall we do?" From that point on what is done is the likely happenstance of the first suggestion that catches the fancy of a majority of the group. Superficially, there is a sense in which this may appear to be true in unit teaching — but it is true only when most superficially considered.

The basic concept of learning accepted in this book and the definition of the unit given in the earlier part of this chapter, preclude complete and inflexible preplanning. There must be a readiness for adaptation to the exigencies of the immediate situation. Otherwise, the concept of "purposive" learning becomes meaninglessly academic. Even so, the wise teacher does extensive planning before coming before the class group.

The first step in preplanning is selection of a possible unit. The teacher may well make two or three alternative plans for a series of units thought desirable and possible of challenge to the group. In doing this the teacher should carefully study the social and educational background of each member of the group. Unless the teacher has had the group before, the cumulative records of each pupil should be canvassed to find out what has been studied, the indications of individual needs, and where it is thought possible that group could reasonably be expected to begin. All this should be checked against the scope of the curriculum to discover any evident educational gaps in areas of the over-all curriculum.

It is important for the teacher to set up objectives toward which the group, collectively and as individuals, should be led to reach. A list of general objectives such as those outlined by the Educational Policies Commission, given in Chapter 1, should be accepted, and those general behavior characteristics to which the needs of the class particularly point should be designated. The teacher should realize that reaching objectives is a gradual and continuing process, and thus a matter of continual emphasis with stress at points where weaknesses appear noticeable. The teacher should keep in mind that his objectives for the education of the learner may not parallel those of the pupil. The teacher should be concerned that the purposes of the learner, in fact, realize the objectives of the teacher.

The teacher is then ready to set up some tentative problem-situations for unit organization. This was done by a teacher who had spent a summer working on such a series of units for a year's work with a tenth-grade group she was to start with the following

September. At the close of the summer's work her attention was called to the nature of learning and the possibility that some of the units prepared might not be used if pupil-purposing were genuinely respected. Although a couple of the units were subsequently used in modified form, at Christmas the teacher reported she had not found use for any unit prepared that summer. This she thought was due to the development in the war situation and the definite shift in pupil concerns by the time school opened. Another teacher who carefully planned a tentative program for the year, then spent a couple of days "thinking things through" with the group, found the pupils purposing many of the problem-situations the teacher had anticipated.

The teacher who is beforehand in preplanning will check carefully the available resource data important for satisfactory study of the unit or units. What may, for educational reasons, appear to be desirable units for study may not have sufficient resources available to warrant their study.

With proper resources available for certain units, the teacher should plan how the units may be set up and organized for instructional purposes. Here is where information about each member of the group becomes valuable as the teacher thinks of the different facets of the unit, and the way each pupil should be challenged to a task in keeping with his needs and abilities. The possible range of activities that are necessary or which might contribute to the enrichment of the unit study should be carefully listed.

Even though the good teacher does appear to come before the class with considerable flexibility to plan with the class the immediate problem-situation to be studied, in reality, much planning has been done and stage-setting arranged by the imaginative teacher to subtly suggest to the group the direction of their purposing. Although the group movement may seem to go obliquely to that anticipated in the unit planned, the chances are that the unit finally selected will have greater educational significance because it has some learning relationship to the one planned by the teacher.

4. How Shall the Teacher Guide the Unit Activities?

After the teacher has made a careful study of the pupils in the class and has gone through the exercise in preplanning, he is ready to try his 'hand at guiding the development of a unit problem in the class. There are at least four major procedural steps generally recognized in the development of a unit.[5]

1. *Initiating the unit.* There is no cut and dried way in which unit learning may be introduced, as teachers experienced with unit teaching know. One teacher, wishing to capitalize upon a serious strike situation that had paralyzed transportation in the community, sought through a study of this strike to help her pupils better understand the complex nature of the economic structure in the community. From day to day she posted the lead articles and editorials from the local papers and trade journals on the strike upon the bulletin board in the classroom. As the strike continued, articles from magazines of national repute which attempted to deal with the issues more objectively and dispassionately found their place on the bulletin board, which was fast becoming overcrowded.

At first only a few curious pupils read the materials displayed while most of the class glanced hastily at the bold captions to the articles and passed on. Gradually more interest in the articles became evident, and the pros and cons of the strike became a topic of discussion interest among the pupils. Finally, the interest became so great members of the class wanted to know why they could not spend some time studying the reasons for such a strike and ways in which future strikes of the kind could be avoided. The teacher encouraged a discussion of why the pupils thought such a problem was important for them to consider in the class. All the reasons given were carefully listed on the blackboard. Throughout the preliminary discussion it became clear there were many aspects of the problem in which pupils revealed varying degrees of interest. This led to the formulation of the statement of the problem inclusive enough to cover most of the subsidiary questions the class deemed important.

Another teacher who was teaching within the framework of the old subject curriculum with a textbook as the basis of class work,

[5] At this point the reader should study the steps outlined by Kilpatrick, Collings, and others for the study of "projects." It will be seen that the four steps in "project" development parallel closely the development stages outlined here, and by such writers as Burton, Goetting, Lee and Lee, Rivlin and others, listed in the Selected Bibiliography at the end of this chapter. For a clear statement of the over-all steps in problem-solving which the teacher can use in this phase of unit teaching see "Problem-Solving Techniques" in Bossing, Nelson L. and Martin, Robert R. *Youth Faces its Problems*, pp. 6–16. Chicago: Laidlaw Brothers, 1950.

was encouraged by her principal to experiment with the experience unit approach. Somewhat cautiously she waited until the class discussion of a topic in the textbook led off somewhat tangentially to a problem-situation which was vital for the class but which was not treated adequately in the text. Some time was spent exploring the issues involved until the teacher was satisfied the class was really interested, and that the problem would make a worth-while unit study. She then asked whether the class thought the problem important enough to consider apart from the textbook. The class was enthusiastic and anxious to begin the study. The wise teacher suggested that she did not know the answer or whether it was possible to find a solution to the problem, but agreed that the problem was important, and that she would gladly cooperate with the class in an effort to find a possible solution.

The alert teacher who has developed experience in initiating such units is seldom at a loss for vital problem-situations that challenge group attack. The environment, be it school, local or the large world community, provides a wealth of problem-situations with which pupils are being constantly challenged, or which provide a ready basis for such challenge. It is well to remember that pupils are associated with adults in the home, relatives and friends, who are grappling with real problems daily that baffle and distress them. Youth often vicariously enters into these problem-situations. They frequently identify themselves with the issues as they recognize their pertinence for themselves, and how these affect them now or threaten their future security.

The young teacher just beginning, or the older teacher in a stage of transition from more formal teaching procedures to the unit, may well begin as the teacher in the second illustration above did. Until the teacher has established full assurance of his ability to utilize the modern educational approach completely, it is well to feel the security of a safe anchorage in some more or less set course of study, textbook, or adopted series of so-called prepared units.

2. *Planning the unit study.* This is one of the most vital phases of unit development. It should not be done hastily, because the success and the expeditiousness with which the work of solving the problem is carried out will depend in large measure on the thoroughness of the planning done. The things to be considered during this phase of the unit study are not necessarily considered in the order that need be followed, but broadly represent the logi-

cal procedures in good planning. It is of the utmost importance for the pupils to have a real part in this phase of the unit development. It cannot be too often repeated or too strongly urged that it is not the solution of the problem that is the goal of unit teaching, important as that may be in given cases. The goal is primarily the development of skill in sensing and formulating problems, skills in planning a valid attack, and the general skill and habit of carrying through to a successful conclusion all the processes involved in unit learning.

After the problem for attack has been clearly formulated it is desirable to see clearly all the facets of the problem that need to be subjected to further study. Pupils under the subtle guidance of the skilled teacher soon learn to discover these, and to arrange them, when necessary, in some logical order of sequential development. Many pupils, then, see quickly the general mode of attack necessary on the major facets of the problem. Some may require library research, other community visitation, and some even manual construction activities. It is essential that the principal lines of attack upon the several aspects of the problem be recognized before the next phase of the planning is undertaken.

By the time the third phase of planning has been reached many pupils have in mind those aspects of the problem about which they are most concerned. As an educational device the committee plan of organizing the members of the group for active study of the problem is most practicable. In a few cases it may be desirable for one pupil to work alone on some important aspect of the problem, but in most cases where large classes, particularly, are involved, it is pedagogically better to have committees work on the several parts of the problem previously determined. It is at this point that the teacher can exercise real leadership in getting the proverbial square peg in a square hole. Teachers who use the unit extensively in teaching, generally agree that in setting up committees individual differences can be best provided for. Committee work usually provides for a variety of activities of different levels of difficulty and of interest. Voluntary pupil selection of committees tends to conform to the level of pupil ability, for the obvious reason that a phase of the problem-situation (sub-problem) which is far beyond their depth of competency, psychologically speaking, is not likely to challenge them. If the teacher sees that a serious error in selection is likely to take place, timely suggestion may lead to a proper committee choice. To safeguard congenial and successful committee work the teacher must be alert to prevent the possibility of clashing personalities coming together in committee work.

Good planning, too, involves a careful study of the source data for each committee. While each committee should be left to work out many of the details of its activities, there should be an over-all awareness of the major materials with which each committee will work. This phase of committee planning is closely associated with the fifth phase, which must be concerned with the physical locale of committee work. In many units the work is of such nature that it can be done within the classroom. The use of other available rooms helps to eliminate noise and confusion as the committees plan their own work. One teacher in a classroom of thirty-seven had seven committees working effectively in groups within the room. Some committee work must be carried on largely outside the school building, some in the art room or shops. All this should be foreseen and planned for.

Two other phases of planning need to be cared for if the unit work is to function smoothly. The sixth concern of the planners must be an agreement upon some devices for periodic total group checking and interrelating the progress of individuals and committees toward the solution of the problem. All good planning takes into account a possible final or seventh step, namely: setting up an estimated over-all allotment of time for the completion of the unit, and for the various phases outlined above. Such planning gives a sense of direction and urgency to the total unit activity and approximates the conditions of normal life activities outside the school.

3. *Guiding the work activities.* In the over-all planning period the large group has had valuable experiences in the art of group dynamics, where each has tried to find opportunity to express himself, to convince others, and to think with others toward a common goal. This becomes a more varied and valuable type of experience where, as a member of a small group, there is greater opportunity for interchange of ideas, compromise, agreement, and assumption of individual responsibility for one's share of the load, in brief, learning the art of successfully working with others — the basis of successful living within a democracy. For the teacher it is a test of leadership and management ability.

This is the phase in which the committees further plan the details of their work, collect whatever data is essential to their accepted responsibilities, where they accept or reject data proposed, classify and organize materials and activities considered germane to their purposes, and prepare the form of reports which the nature of their materials and the nature of the unit suggest as most appropriate. It is the major phase of the unit and should require the lion's share of the time alloted to it.

The teacher will find that this period is likely to be the most difficult phase of unit activity. Instead of one group to keep functioning together there are several groups to keep unified in their activities. This is greatly accentuated when groups do part of their work in different physical locations where direct supervision is not always possible.

One important factor in the teacher's success in guiding the activities of the groups is to see that each committee is clear with respect to its particular task, and the elements of successful group participation. A visitor to a successful unit teacher entered the classroom a few minutes before the class was to convene. As the bell rang the teacher excused herself for a moment, turned to the class and said: "Are all committee chairmen present? What has each committee mapped out for itself to do today?" After each committee chairman had outlined satisfactorily what his committee had on that day's agenda, the teacher then asked: "Now what is the function of a good chairman? What are the rules we have agreed upon for successful committee work?" After three or four simple rules for group behavior, which evidently had been agreed upon previously, were suggested by members of the class, the teacher said: "All right, go ahead with your work." With this she turned to the visitor and continued her explanation of the unit the class was then studying. The committees in business-like manner got together and were quickly at work.

Burton [6] has offered a list of pertinent suggestions to aid the teacher in the guidance of the work period. The teacher will do well to check the list carefully.

1. Guide the group during the planning period to develop plans which are so definite and so clear that all know what to do and how to do it.

[6] Burton, W. H. *The Guidance of Learning Activities*, pp. 292–293. New York: Appleton-Century-Crofts, Inc., 1944.

2. Check with individuals and committees before they disperse for work to see that the more detailed plans are definite and clear.

3. Anticipate difficulties in carrying out plans as made and be ready to call a group conference when the difficulty occurs and before discouragement and work stoppage can result in disorder.

4. Guide during the planning period so that sufficient work is outlined to keep all individuals and groups busy over a reasonably long period of time. Replanning will keep the sequence going so that lack of work does not cause disorder.

5. Call for replanning conferences as work develops unevenly. Workers may be reassigned and activities redistributed.

6. Keep in touch with the varied activities by moving from group to group, by participation, by asking questions, by making suggestions, thus exercising both guidance and control.

7. Foresee certain common opportunities for disorder and forestall them by developing with the pupils regular routines:

   a. For having all materials, tools, and supplies ready before need for them arises

   b. For distributing materials, tools, supplies, books, papers, quickly and in an orderly manner

   c. For using reference materials, particularly when many pupils wish to consult an inadequate number of references

   d. For holding conferences with individual children who ask for help

   e. For using as helpers any individuals who may for any reason be unoccupied for a time

   f. For moving groups, for observing as groups, without crowding or jostling

8. Introduce new activities to small groups directly concerned so that tryout will be without the confusion which might result from misunderstandings within a large group and from too many persons trying a new process without sufficient guidance

9. Give constantly, directly and indirectly, training in the conventions and routines of group work: taking turns, not interrupting, turning to some other aspect of one's work instead of standing around waiting for tools or materials in use elsewhere, signing in and out for tools and materials, etc.

10. Develop with the pupils flexible plans for their own activities: budgeting time, scheduling group conferences, announcing times for individual conferences, etc.

11. Develop constantly, directly and indirectly, the understanding

that freedom carries responsibility, and that self-control and co-operation are advantageous to the pupils themselves and not something required by the school

Many types of units naturally lead to some more or less dramatic form of concluding activity. Units of a construction type which involve manipulative skills usually associated with the making of objects, such as furniture, play apparatus, clothing, foods, or those activities that anticipate an audience situation, such as art, displays, musical renditions, and literary performances, often add to their interest and educational values by some form of display of group achievement, whether these be within the class, open to the school, or for full community observation. These are known as "culminating" activities. Occasionally, units which by their nature suggest the desirability of a "culminating" type of activity should be so featured. There are definite educational values inherent in this form of unit conclusion for the pupils participating and for those observing.

As each unit comes to a close the teacher and pupils should be alert to possible leads to other units that have arisen as work on the unit has proceeded. Few genuine problems that confront us are truly found in complete isolation from the continuum of our lives. They are but a part of the total pattern (Gestalt) of our living and necessarily infringe upon other aspects of our lives. Consequently, the exploration of a unit problem-situation should and usually does suggest other vital and related problems that may be important to study.

4. *Evaluating unit success.* There are two important though interrelated aspects of evaluation of the success of any unit. The first is concerned with the general organizational and procedural efficiency of the unit development. That one's hindsight is usually better than one's foresight few, if any, would deny. As the teacher looks back critically over the progress of the unit, generally there are many things noted that might have been improved to have made the unit click better. The teacher should review each of the steps, painstakingly noting possible weakness in his guidance at each phase of the unit's development that might account for some of the difficulties that later appeared, or for suggestive changes that would have expedited progress through the unit processes. Such critical review of each unit taught should enable the teacher to guide the next unit more effectively.

In part the organizational and procedural success contributes to the second aspect of the success of the unit. The real worth of the unit, of course, must be evaluated in terms of how much the unit resulted in an observable change in the behavior patterns of the learners. These must be related clearly to the objectives (outcomes) set up for the unit. Here the teacher must apply the best that is known in modern evaluation procedures. These will need to be related to the kinds of behavior skills that unit was designed to achieve. Pencil and paper tests may contribute some data for evaluation purposes. The pupils themselves can likely contribute much to a real evaluation of the unit. Since whatever skills the teacher had in mind as the possible outcomes of the unit must be related to the pupil purposes that ultimately decided the unit studied, evaluation must include the cooperation of the group in carefully re-examining the purposes for the unit accepted by the pupils and an appraisal of the extent to which they judge their purposes to have been realized. It is desirable that at this point the teacher help the group to see more fully the larger educational objectives that should have been achieved in the unit study. It is at this point that the crucial factors in the carry-over of the learning experience to new problem-situations can be made clear and their realization cooperatively evaluated. Too, it must be remembered that an important educational accomplishment of the pupil is his competency to evaluate constructively his own and the group's activities — the extent to which he and they have succeeded in the realization of the unit purposes, the factors which have contributed to, and those which possibly have prevented, complete success; and what modifications, if any, might have been made in the procedures followed that suggest promise of greater success. This competency to evaluate one's activities critically and constructively is a sine qua non of successful living.

What actual instruments and procedures may be used in various phases of evaluating the learning success of a particular unit are varied. In general they are those commonly used in evaluating desirable forms of learning. These are discussed at length in Chapter 9, "How Can Pupil Progress Be Evaluated and Reported?"

5. How are "Resource Units" Developed?

Thus far the "teaching" unit only has been considered. Whatever may be the disagreement as to the possible types of "teaching" units, curriculum workers are agreed that units should be given a twofold classification with respect to function.

Distinction between "teaching" and "resource" unit

Strictly interpreted on the psychological basis of the experience form of unit recognized in the early discussion of this chapter, *a "teaching" unit is one planned for a specific group of pupils, in a particular school, and for a definite time.* As in the example of the Long Beach unit, such a unit can be written up only subsequent to its use, as it must represent the joint planning and activities of the teachers and pupils in their efforts to resolve a vital problem-situation.

This does not preclude the teacher anticipating a specific situation and preplanning the possible organization of a unit it is hoped the given class will accept as their own for study. This type of preparation is evident in the careful preplanning of the teacher described in the section of the Long Beach unit captioned "Initiation — An Arranged Environment," described above as well as the data collected on the characteristics of the members of the class.

On the other hand, *a resource unit is concerned with a large general problem-situation that may be present in many places under varying forms of specific emphasis, for which the major problems, issues, activities, bibliographies, evaluation techniques, and other resource data have been brought together and organized in the general pattern of a unit so that teachers may draw upon it for partial data in developing teaching units.*

Form of resource unit

So-called resource units of all kinds and descriptions are available. Some of them keep the essential characteristics of the true unit while others are little more than topic areas with extensive lists of bibliographies and other source data. A good resource unit has a close resemblance to a good teaching unit in its general format. In fact many excellent resource units represent teaching units that have been somewhat broadened in scope and extensively developed with a wealth of suggestions for possible wider use. Such a resource unit is presented in general outline from the public schools of Long Beach, California. This one is chosen especially so that the differences between "teaching" and "resource" units may be clearly outlined as conceived by the Long Beach schools. The two outlines, the "teaching" unit presented above and the "resource" unit presented below, should be studied carefully to see their similarities and differences. This resource unit presented below, too, was developed in 1946. It is presented in very brief outline. The total unit form is quite extensive with sections covering twenty or more pages of outline suggestions. At points the word (sample) follows a major section with one or two items listed to give the reader an idea of what might be found there.

A RESOURCE UNIT FOR SEVENTH GRADE SOCIAL LIVING CLASSES
How the School Environment Provides for the Needs of Pupils

Preface

Here the scope of the curriculum is discussed and sixteen "broad social functions" of the curriculum are given. Since these were listed in the "teaching" unit outlined previously the reader should consult the unit in question.

General Objectives

The list of general objectives for seventh grade social living are here given in a form that represents active behavior as in the "teaching" unit.

I. *Introduction*

II. *Anticipated Outcomes*
    A. In terms of Pupil Behavior
    B. In terms of Generalizations (samples)
        1. Education is a continuous process of self improvement. (10) [7]
        4. Knowledge gained and resulting behaviors are more important than the marks received. (10, 13)
       13. Good manners are founded on kindness to and consideration for others. (1)

III. *Suggested Problems* (samples)
    A. How can we make the best adjustment to our new school environment?
    B. How can the school meet our needs most satisfactorily?

IV. *Analysis of the Unit — How the School Environment Provides for the Needs of Pupils*
    A. How can I become a Good Junior High School Citizen? (samples)
        1. How can I find my way around the school?
        2. What rules and regulations must I know?
        3. What does the student body government do?
        4. Why are schools necessary?

[7] The numbers in parentheses refer to the activities listed in the "Preface" which define the scope of the social education curriculum of the Long Beach Public Schools, and show the relationship between this unit and the total program.

B. How Can I Learn to Study Better? (samples)
    1. Of what use are books and other equipment in the room?
    2. What is there for me to use in the library?
C. How Can I Make My Life in Junior High School a Happy One? (samples)
    1. How can I make and keep friends?
    2. Why should I have a code of ideals to follow?
D. How Can I Grow Up Strong and Healthy? (samples)
    2. What health rules should I follow to do my best in school?
    5. How can I learn to choose a good, well-balanced lunch in the cafeteria?

V. *Suggested Activities*
  A. Initiatory Activities
  B. Development Activities (16 pages devoted to this section)
  C. Culminating Activities

VI. *Evaluation*
  A. Skill Tests
  B. Personality and Interest Tests
  C. Attitude Tests
  D. Examples of Kinds of Tests and Check Lists Teachers Can Make.
  E. Check Lists. (See Appendix II–E)

VII. *Bibliography* (11 pages of classified references given)
  Appendix   I: Audio-Visual Aids
  Appendix II: Tests and Evaluation Devices (21 pages devoted to this section)
  Appendix III: Vocabulary Lists
  Appendix IV: Suggestions to Teachers (13 pages devoted to this section)
  Appendix V: Data on Long Beach Public Schools

Who makes resource units?

Many times individual teachers, after teaching a unit, rework the unit outline to correct faults found during the progress of the unit development with the class. Various parts are amplified to provide extensive suggestions which might aid that teacher or others who later may teach a closely related unit. Teachers often have anticipated a possible need for a teaching unit in a general problem area and have developed resource units as a precaution.

The resource unit outlined above appears to represent a unit worked out in a summer workshop period by some fifteen or more teachers mutually interested in the development of resource data for possible teaching units. It has been a favored and profitable practice for groups of teachers to work together marshalling the source data pertinent to a problem-situation area which they recognize as a fertile area for teaching units. Extensive use of summer workshops sponsored by institutions of higher learning has been made by schools and teachers where groups could have both the guidance of specialists in the curriculum and the larger library sources there available.

It has become a rather widespread practice for school systems where many good resource units are developed to make them available in mimeographed form at a nominal price. This has made possible the sharing of efforts in the preparation of resource data with large numbers of teachers and schools. Unfortunately, many poor units, and some not truly units, have been published. Teachers should be very discriminating in the use of published resource units.

One of the reasons for the hesitancy of many teachers in the past to use the unit plan of teaching has been the lack of such resource data available to them. This shortcoming is rapidly being overcome. Some commercial and non-profit organizations have given considerable attention to the preparation of resource units. Among the non-profit type organization teachers should be familiar with the work of The National Association of Secondary School Principals, and The National Council for the Social Studies Program. The well-known series of resource units entitled "Problem in American Life Series," is typical of such resource units.

QUESTIONS AND PROBLEMS

1. (a) From books on "Curriculum" and "Methods" have the class collect the definitions given of the "teaching unit."

    (b) Have the class classify these definitions from the educational points of view implied in the various definitions given.

    (c) Have the class decide which definition or definitions it thinks to be educationally defensible.

2. The class may then consider the question: "In the light of the definition of the teaching unit accepted by the class, how may units be classified as to types?"

3. In what ways would you add to, disagree with, or modify the "Characteristics of a good unit" as presented in the text?

4. (*a*) Have the class evaluate the two teaching units given in the text against the "Characteristics of a good unit" given in the text, or which the class agreed upon in item 3, above.

   (*b*) Have members of the class select teaching units found in the library and evaluate these units against the class or textbook list of "Characteristics of a good unit."

5. Have a panel discussion of the question: "Can a teaching unit be planned in advance?"

6. Have the class compare the procedures outlined in section 4 of this chapter with those presented by other writers who discuss procedures involved in "guiding the unit activities."

7. Have a group or panel discussion on the question: "In what ways are evaluation techniques used in experience unit learning different from those used in evaluating traditional teaching?"

8. Have each member of the class prepare the major outlines of a teaching unit.

9. What is the difference between a "teaching" and "resource" unit?

10. Have the members of the class compare resource units found in the library with the one prepared by teachers of Long Beach, California, outlined in the text. In what respects are they inferior or better than the resource unit described in the text?

SELECTED BIBLIOGRAPHY

A Primer for Common Learnings. Minneapolis, Minnesota: Minneapolis Public Schools, 1948.

Alberty, Harold, *Reorganizing the High School Curriculum,* chapters VIII–XI. New York: The Macmillan Company, 1947.

Biddick, Mildred L. *The Preparation and Use of Resource Units.* New York: Progressive Education Association.

Burton, W. H. *The Guidance of Learning Activities,* chapters IX–X. New York: Appleton-Century-Crofts, Inc., 1944.

Butler, Frank A. *The Improvement of Teaching in Secondary Schools,* Revised Edition, chapter X. Chicago: University of Chicago Press, 1946.

Consumer Education Series. Washington, D.C.: Consumer Education Study, National Association of Secondary School Principals, N.E.A., 1946.

Douglass, H. R. and Mills, H. H. *Teaching in High School,* chapter XI. New York: The Ronald Press Company, 1948.

Giles, H. H. *Teacher-Pupil Planning.* New York: Harper and Brothers, 1941.

Goetting, M. L. *Teaching in the Secondary School,* chapters XV–XX. New York: Prentice-Hall, Inc., 1942.

Group Planning in Education, 1945 Yearbook. Washington, D.C.: Department of Supervision and Curriculum Development, 1945.

Gwynn, J. Minor. *Curriculum Principles and Social Trends,* Revised Edition, chapter VII. New York: The Macmillan Company, 1950.

Hopkins, L. T. *Interaction: The Democratic Process,* chapter VII. Boston: D. C. Heath and Company, 1941.

Jackson, D. D. and Irvin, W. B. *The Unit Method of Learning and Teaching.* Lubbock, Texas: Texas Technological College Book Store, 1942.

Jones, A. J., Grizzell, E. D. and Grinstead, W. J. *Principles of Unit Construction.* New York: McGraw-Hill Book Company, Inc., 1939.

Krug, E. A. *Curriculum Planning,* chapter V. New York: Harper and Brothers, 1950.

Lee, J. M. and Lee, D. M. *The Child and His Curriculum,* Second Edition, chapter VII. New York: Appleton-Century-Crofts, Inc., 1950.

Leonard, J. Paul. *Secondary School Curriculum,* chapters XIII–XIV. New York: Rinehart and Company, 1946.

Noar, Gertrude. *Freedom to Live and Learn.* Philadelphia: Franklin Publishing and Supply Company, 1948.

Quillen, James. *Using a Resource Unit.* Washington, D.C.: National Association of Secondary School Principals, 1942.

Risk, T. M. *Principles and Practices of Teaching in Secondary Schools,* Second Edition, chapters XIV–XV. New York: American Book Company, 1947.

Rivlin, Harry N. *Teaching Adolescents in Secondary Schools,* chapter V. New York: Appleton-Century-Crofts, Inc., 1948.

Schorling, Raleigh. *Student Teaching,* Second Edition, pp. 140–146. New York: McGraw-Hill Book Company, Inc., 1949.

Smith, B. O., Stanley, W. O. and Shores, J. H. *Fundamentals of Curriculum Development,* chapter XXIII. Yonkers, N.Y.: World Book Company, 1950.

Stratemeyer, Florence B. et al. *Developing a Curriculum for Modern Living,* chapter VI. New York: Teachers College, Columbia University, 1947.

Strickland, R. G. *How to Build a Unit of Work,* Bulletin No. 5. Washington, D.C.: Office of Education, 1946.

"The Curriculum: Learning and Teaching," *Review of Educational Research,* vol. XXI, no. 3, chapter IV (June 1951). Washington, D.C.: American Educational Research Association.

Thut, I. N. and Gerberich, J. R. *Foundations of Method for Secondary Schools,* chapters IX–XIV. New York: McGraw-Hill Book Company, Inc., 1949.

Umstattd, J. G. *Secondary School Teaching,* Second Edition, chapters VI–IX. Boston: Ginn and Company, 1944.

Part

III

THE PROBLEM OF METHOD

4

How Can Problem Solving Be Used?

1. Why Is Problem Solving Important?

Importance for life

Says Averill: [1]

> The only worth-while life is a life which contains its problems; to live without any longings and ambitions is to live only half-way.

Averill might have gone further and said that a normal individual could not possibly live his life without facing problems and finding some sort of solution for them. Facing problems is of the nature of life itself. Even the most elementary existence is filled with problems of finding the physical satisfactions of food, shelter, and safety. Dewey echoes something of this primacy of the problem-solving aspects of life when he refers to their place in childhood: [2]

> The child's primary problem is mastery of his body as a tool of securing comfortable and effective adjustments to his surroundings, physical and social. The child has to learn to do almost everything: to see, to hear, to reach, to handle, to balance the body, to creep, to walk, and so on. These operations of conscious selection and arrangement constitute thinking, though of a rudimentary type.

These adjustments to which Dewey refers must be made throughout life. As the problems involved grow increasingly complex, the

[1] Averill, L. A. *Elements of Educational Psychology*, p. 218. Boston: Houghton Mifflin Company, 1924.
[2] Dewey, John. *How We Think*, pp. 157–158. Boston: D. C. Heath and Company, 1910.

101

thought necessary to their solution must become correspondingly less elementary and more reflective. With the coming of adolescence there appear problems of larger implication in social adjustments: mastery of the school curriculum; the choice of a career and preparation for it; and later the adult problems of home, family, business, and social, and political life. Parker has summarized this well, in these words: [3]

> The practical inventor and the innovator in the work of applied science furnish striking examples of the social importance of reflective thought. With them rank the great originators of social reforms, the men and women who furnish the ideas that more mediocre thinkers copy and put into execution. From these great problem-solvers we may pass by gradual steps to common everyday men or women with their domestic and economic problems and perplexities, such as whether to feed the baby cow's milk or some prepared food; whether to whip the youngster or to overlook his misdeeds; whether to eat all the meat one desires or to be a vegetarian; whether to let a cold run its course or to consult a physician; whether to pay rent or buy a home in the building association, etc. Many persons whose vocational activities are highly routinized are confronted only by such problems as these. In the lives of all people, however, they play a very important part, and schools are beginning to realize this and to provide training that looks toward efficiency in dealing with the problems of common everyday life.

If the solution of problems constitutes one of the important aspects of human existence, as thoughtful writers agree, then it is incumbent upon the school to give large place to a method of training that will enable the individual to increase his power of problem solving.

Relation to learning and the curriculum

Throughout the discussion in this text thus far there has been a constant emphasis upon the peculiar relationship of "education" and "learning" to problem solving. Learning, it will be recalled, has been defined as the changes in behavior that result from the persistent efforts of the learner to make some adequate adjustment to an important problem situation. In fact so central is this idea in the modern conception of learning that problem solution has been considered the basic milieu of learning.

---

[3] Parker, S. C. *Methods of Teaching in High Schools*, Revised Edition, p. 177. Boston: Ginn and Company, 1920.

It is this fundamental conception of the nature of learning that has led to the present radical readjustment of our thinking about the curriculum. The concept of the "experience" curriculum is based upon the premise that learning basically grows out of problem-situations, and that the curriculum, therefore, should have its focus in problem-situations. This notion of learning and the curriculum as discussed in the previous chapter has given validity to and popularized the unit form of curriculum organization for teaching and learning.

Quite obviously, then, good teaching must make central the significance of all that is involved in good methods of problem solving for all other aspects of learning. Likewise, in whatever way the teacher can contribute to the better effectiveness of pupils in the development of their skills in problem solving, the greater assurance the teacher can have of the greatest educational service to the learner.

2. What Is Nature of Problem Solving?

The nature of thinking

There are those who assert very little "thinking" takes place on the part of average folk. Among those who deprecate the lack of mental effort put forth by the ordinary person are many of our psychologists who insist that much that passes for thinking is in reality nothing of the sort. Much in this vein were the remarks of Bernard Shaw, made on one of his visits to this country. To the press he suggested that the reason he was famous while most people were not was because he did some thinking at least twice a week. These remarks, uttered rather facetiously, suggest the meaning given the word "thinking" by some reputable present-day psychologists.

Four types of thinking

Dewey has endeavored to classify thought processes into four types, beginning with the most rudimentary phases of mental activity and extending to the most complex forms of intellectual behavior. He would include, within the meaning of thought at its lowest level, idle fancy, day dreaming, or anything that flitted across the mind without continuity or particular sequence.

The *second* stage of thought applies to things not associated with the usual five senses. Imaginative stories and incidents that have continuity, but are not acceptable as fact or truth, are included in this classification.

A *third* stage of thinking is belief, for which little or no proof has been demanded or is possible. Some of these beliefs have been accepted without much question, perhaps because they are assumed to have been proved. The individual who holds the belief has not carefully examined the nature of the evidence that may support it. Our prejudices and superstitions, for example, may grow out of tradition or instruction through which we come to accept uncritically certain beliefs.

The *fourth* type of thinking is reflective thought. At this stage a critical inquiry into the nature and correctness of our beliefs constitutes the highest form of thought process. As Dewey concludes: [4] "Active, persistent, and careful consideration of any belief or supposed form of knowledge in the light of the grounds that support it, and the further conclusions to which it tends, constitutes reflective thought."

It is clear that those who have been critical of the capacity for and the habit of thinking on the part of human nature, have identified reflective thought with thinking, and have ignored the lesser forms which Dewey classifies as elemental thought. Whatever claims these lower forms of mental activity have upon us as "thinking," they are not universally so recognized. For the purposes of this chapter "reflective thinking" of the highest order is our concern.

Characteristics of reflective thought

That reflection is commonly regarded as the highest form of thought, there is no question. By some it is considered the only form of mental activity that can claim the distinction of being thought in any real sense. There are certain well-defined characteristics of reflective thinking that the teacher should have clearly in mind. Possibly the most widely recognized is the classic quotation from Dewey, frequently cited in educational literature. Though written more than two decades ago it is as pertinent now as then. With slight alterations and paragraph headings, as used by Parker and others who have appropriated this famous passage, the characterization of reflective thinking by Dewey [5] is given:

[4] Dewey, John, *op. cit.*, pp. 2–6.   [5] *Ibid*, pp. 12–13.

Origin in some perplexity. We may recapitulate by saying that the origin of thinking is some perplexity, confusion, or doubt. Thinking is not a case of spontaneous combustion; it does not occur just on "general principles." There is something specific which occasions and evokes it. General appeals to a child (or to a grown-up) to think, irrespective of the existence in his own experience of some difficulty that troubles him and disturbs his equilibrium, are as futile as advice to lift himself by his boot straps.

Form a tentative plan based on past experience and prior knowledge. Given a difficulty, the next step is suggestion of some way out — the formation of some tentative plan or project, the entertaining of some theory which will account for the peculiarities in question, the consideration of some solution for the problem. The data at hand cannot supply the solution; they can only suggest it. What, then, are the sources of the suggestion? Clearly past experience and prior knowledge. If the person has had some acquaintance with similar situations, if he has dealt with material of the same sort before, suggestions more or less apt or helpful are likely to arise. But unless there has been experience in some degree analogous, which may now be represented in imagination, confusion remains mere confusion. There is nothing upon which to draw in order to clarify it. Even when a child (or grownup) has a problem, to urge him to think when he has no prior experiences involving some of the same conditions is wholly futile.

Plan not accepted until carefully examined and criticized. If the suggestion that occurs is at once accepted, we have uncritical thinking, the minimum of reflection. To turn the thing over in mind, to reflect, means to hunt for additional evidence, for new data, that will develop the suggestion and will either, as we say, bear it out or else make obvious its absurdity and irrelevance. Given a genuine difficulty and a reasonable amount of analogous experience to draw upon, the difference, par excellence, between good and bad thinking is found at this point. The easiest way is to accept any suggestion that seems plausible and thereby bring to an end the condition of mental uneasiness. Reflective thinking is always more or less troublesome, because it involves overcoming the inertia that inclines one to accept suggestions at their face value; it involves willingness to endure a condition of mental unrest and disturbance. Reflective thinking, in short, means judgment suspended during the inquiry, and suspense is likely to be somewhat painful. . . . The most important factor in the training of good mental habits consists in acquiring the attitudes of suspended conclusion and in mastering the various methods of searching for new materials to corroborate or to refute the first suggestions that occur.

To maintain the state of doubt and to carry on systematic and protracted inquiry — these are the essentials of thinking.

Essential characteristics of good thinking

From these comments, as well as from other sources, it may be
well to adduce for the teacher a list of the most essential characteristics of good thinking.

1. *Ability to sense the presence of a perplexing problem.* While
this may be considered as basic to all thinking, it is always a characteristic of good thinking. Unless a genuinely baffling perplexity
exists to spur on mental endeavor, the rigorous form of mental
activity which is the essence of reflective thinking will not take
place.

2. *Ability to recognize clearly the nature of the problem.* Unless
the individual sees clearly the nature of his problem and can
formulate it concisely, there is little chance to make a frontal
attack upon it. Many people are only vaguely and uncomfortably
aware that a perplexity exists; they are unable to bring it out into
the open and define it clearly. Continued mental confusion must
characterize the efforts of such people to think.

3. *Ability to hold problem in mind as it is studied.* It is easy to
become side-tracked into blind alleys and by-paths in the effort
to solve a problem. It is one of the constant dangers in the classroom discussion. It is no less a problem of adult deliberative
groups. Some chance remark in the discussion leads to a comment
that in turn directs attention to a topic quite irrelevant to the
subject under consideration. When the enthusiasm engendered by
the chance remark has died down, the group awakes to a sheepish
realization that they were beside the point and the main problem
still remains unsolved.

4. *Ability and readiness to venture a bold guess or hypothesis.*
Few of the great scientific achievements and discoveries that bless
mankind would have been possible had there not been those who
dared to think boldly and to suggest answers to questions often
revolutionary in character. Galileo and Copernicus, to mention
two, dared, even at the price of possible physical violence and the
certain disapproval of the social leadership of their day, to suggest
possible solutions to problems that had long baffled mankind.
Experimenters and researchers are frank to admit the value of
"hunches" in discovery. Often the so-called hunch is a reasoned

guess with only a few leads to warrant the hypothesis. Where more promising solutions do not seem in evidence, these should be followed. Indeed, no less an authority than John Dewey, sensing the importance of adventurous thinking, voices a plea for boldness and the flight of imagination in the search for truth: [6]

> As far as any plea is implicit in what has been said, it is, then, a plea for the casting off of that intellectual timidity which hampers the wings of imagination, a plea for speculative audacity, for more faith in ideas, sloughing off a cowardly reliance upon those partial ideas to which we are wont to give the name of facts.

5. *Ability to formulate possible hypothesis or solution.* The fertile mind is a mind full of suggestions and capable of drawing up a well-reasoned plan of attack. After all, the ability to formulate a careful statement of the problem is a matter of training and intellectual endowment. The fact should not be overlooked, however, that the power of imagination and the spirit of bold venturesomeness referred to above are phases of training and endowment important in the formulation of an hypothesis.

6. *Ability to examine critically proposed solutions.* This is the acid test of thinking. Can the individual evaluate critically all the factors involved, and analyze and synthesize until, as a result of this critical study, there comes a definite conclusion? As will be seen later, there are complete systems or techniques of thought necessary to the critical study of hypothesis. To evaluate successfully, special devices must be set up as standards to test the relevancy of the factors that enter into the proposed solution.

7. *Ability and readiness to cast aside hypothesis found not valid.* Here the thinker often finds the integrity of his motives tested. Thinking implies objectivity and singleness of purpose. One hypothesis must be no better than another when it has been critically examined and found wanting, but to cast it aside may take courage. Hours, days, even weeks and months, and sometimes years are involved in the effort to solve problems. It is difficult at times to prevent what one has perhaps unconsciously come to expect or hope would be the outcome from coloring the results. A research professor remarked recently to the writer that he was becoming dubious of the spectacular things some experimentalists in his field seemed to find. His own experiments had not come out

---

[6] Dewey, John. *Philosophy and Civilization*, p. 12. New York: Minton, Balch and Company, 1931.

as he had reason to expect they would. He frankly wondered if results were not often influenced by what investigators hoped to find. Objectivity in critical thought is a crucial thing and exceedingly difficult to achieve, because much of our reflection takes its hue from the subjective values that pervade all our thinking. Complete objectivity should, however, characterize rigorous thinking, and there should be no hesitation in casting aside hypotheses or proposed solutions when they are found invalid.

8. *Ability to maintain attitude of suspended judgment.* This is closely akin to the characteristic just mentioned. All scientifically minded folk, which means all good thinkers, must hold judgment in abeyance until all the facts are gathered, weighed, sifted, and evaluated. This is very important if correct results are to be obtained. It is difficult to judge impartially when the hypothesis has already been prejudiced. Prejudices will enter in spite of the individual. It is far less of a strain to jump at conclusions and remove suspense. As Dewey points out in the lengthy quotation above, "suspense is likely to be somewhat painful," although "the most important factor in the training of good mental habits consists in acquiring the attitude of suspended conclusion."

9. *Ability and readiness to recheck conclusions to test their validity.* This is frequently referred to as the process of verification in deductive reasoning. It is highly important to retrace the steps taken to reach the conclusion, and to be sure nothing was overlooked, and that errors in thought were not inadvertently allowed to escape detection. Even the child in arithmetic is taught the importance of rechecking his work to be sure there were no errors of calculation or method.

If these characteristics of good thinking could be made to characterize the product of our schools, the evils of our political and social life would be radically reduced and the level of our social thought would be greatly raised and our civilization considerably advanced. Inability to think vigorously, unwillingness to think intensely and the indisposition to think honestly in large areas of human relationships — these are hindrances to human progress.

Reflective thinking and problem solving

By this time it must be perfectly clear to the teacher that when we speak of thinking, particularly when reflective thinking is mentioned, problem solving is the process we have in mind. A mental perplexity has been recognized as essential to reflective thought. That problem solving is inextricably interwoven into the very woof and warp of reflective thinking is frankly recognized by Dewey in his classic discussion on "thinking" referred to above. He says: [7] "Whatever — no matter how slight and commonplace in character — perplexes and challenges the mind so that it makes belief at all uncertain, there is a genuine problem." He further ties problem solving to reflective thinking in these words: "The problem fixes the end of thought and the end controls the process of thinking." Another writer has defined the problem thus: "A problem exists for an individual when he has a definite goal that he cannot reach by the behavior patterns which he already has available." [8]

There are two aspects of problem solving the student must grapple with which the teacher should keep clearly in mind. Frequently, both are considered together in a classroom situation.

The *first* is the solution of problems commonly accepted as problems. New situations are met for which new modes of attack must be discovered. This means a careful search for new ways of dealing with the problem, and the formulation and testing of techniques that are adequate for the purpose. In this realm much of our mental effort is expended, both in and out of school.

The *second* aspect of problem solving takes the student a step beyond the simpler solution of a problem near at hand, and attempts to discover principles and general meanings of an abstract character. Here several problem-solving situations may lead to the formulation of a principle or abstract concept. Strictly speaking the processes are not greatly different. The second may be superimposed upon the first. For example, I may work out a solution for a problem that involves reduction of a fraction to its lowest terms. If a number of such problems have been correctly solved, the student is ready to begin the solution of another problem superimposed upon the first, but more abstract in nature; namely, the discovery of a general rule for the expeditious solution of problems that involve reduction of fractions. Similarly, to develop a basis for the abstract concept of justice, it may be desirable to proceed through a number of problems familiar to the experience of the student, and from these move on to the acquiring of an

[7] Dewey, John, *op. cit.*, pp. 9, 12.
[8] Gates, A. I. et al., *Educational Psychology*, Third Edition, p. 449. New York: The Macmillan Company, 1949.

abstract idea of the word "justice." Both aspects of problem solving are important for the school; both are frequently interwoven in the same effort at problem solution.

3. What Are the Techniques of Problem Solving?

General approach to problem solving

Broadly speaking, there are two general approaches to the solution of any problem. A problem given in the Terman Revision of the Binet Scale for the measurement of intelligence, known as the "ball-and-field test," is designed to illustrate either or both of the approaches. The person to be tested is told that a ball has been lost in a large circular field. He does not know from which direction the ball may have come, or whether it was thrown or carried into the field. In short, nothing is known except that the ball is there. He is then asked to indicate how he could proceed to locate the ball. When the writer wanders rather aimlessly about a section of the golf course in search of a lost ball, this test invariably comes to mind. The candidate who traces a jagged course hither and yon over the area of the circular field, without any suggestion of plan, is making his attack on the problem by the time honored trial-and-error method — if method it may be called. At once it is labeled for what it is — an unintelligent procedure in the solution of problems. It is akin to the reported study habits of the boy who, when asked how he would proceed to study a lesson, replied that "he just hopped to it till he got it." This approach of trial and error is the method of animal learning and of the untutored. There is a real sense in which men never escape it. To set up an hypothesis is basically to guess at a solution of a problem and is, in essence, trial and error. It was this fact that led the late William Jennings Bryan to misjudge the theory of evolution as nothing more than a random guess. The degree to which the guess is bolstered up by reasoned judgment differentiates it from the trial-and-error approach of the person who traces the path of search in the field-and-ball test without an apparent plan, except a vague general one to cover the field.

The other general approach is indicated by the person who, in the test referred to above, pencils a systematized course over the field, designed to cover every bit of it with the minimum of lost motion. The student who organizes a definite plan of attack when confronted with a problem is using a systematic organized plan to achieve his purpose. It is this last method that concerns us. To be able to perfect an intelligent systematic attack on the myriad of problems that the individual meets in and out of school is indeed an accomplishment.

Two systematic types of problem solving

The systematic approach involves two generally recognized procedures. The inductive procedure means that thinking moves from the particular to the general. That is exemplified when one faces a question such as might well be asked in a social-science class, "Have all depressions in the United States had a similar cause?" The student would begin by studying every depression through which this country has passed, endeavoring to discover the apparent reason for each. With the reasons carefully noted, he would be able to compare the causes so discovered and if they were similar, the conclusion or generalization could be drawn. This would be a pure form of inductive problem solving.

On the other hand, deductive procedure moves from the general to the particular. Some time ago when a group was discussing causation of social political movements, one member asserted economics was the primary determiner of social-political change. Immediately this hypothesis was subjected to critical examination. Movement after movement was called up to discover whether it could be explained on the theory of economics as a determiner. Other hypotheses were suggested and subjected to the same critical review. This is generally considered a deductive form of approach.

It is clear that in the latter example, when recourse was had to particular cases as a means of verifying or disproving the hypothesis, there was an interrelation evident between deduction and induction. Because of this interplay of the one or the other in normal thought situations, some treat the procedures of thought as one general process. Dewey, in his discussion of induction and deduction in his book, *How We Think*, presents quite convincingly the case for the double movement of thought. In ordinary life situations, he holds, thinking may start inductively, but it is likely to move quickly to an hypothesis and then back to induction through verification or rejection of the hypothesis. Possibly as splendid an example as may be found of this interplay of the inductive and deductive procedures may be observed in the tireless researches of Pasteur to discover the action of fermentation, given in graphic narrative by De Kruif.[9]

"Here are little gray specks sticking to the walls of the bottle. . . . What can that mean," he pondered. . . . "No yeast globes here, no, but something different, something strange he had never seen before, great tangled dancing masses of tiny rodlike things. . . . Those little rods in the juice of the sick vats are alive, and it is they that make the acid of sour milk — the rods fight with the yeast perhaps, and get the upper hand. They are the ferment of the sour-milk acid just as the yeast must be the ferment of the alcohol!"

It was only a guess, but there was something inside him that whispered to him that it was surely true. There was nothing uncanny about the rightness of his guess; Pasteur made thousands of guesses about the thousand strange events of nature that met his shortsighted jeerings. Many of these guesses were wrong — but when he did hit the right one, how he did test it and prove it and sniff along after it and chase it and throw himself on it and bring it to earth! . . .

"I can't study these rods that I think are alive in this mixed-up mess of the juice of the beet pulp from the vats," Pasteur pondered. "I shall have to invent some kind of clear soup for them so that I can see what goes on — I'll have to invent this special food for them and then see if they multiply, if they have young. . . ." He tried putting some of the grayish specks from the sick vats into pure sugar water. They refused to grow in it. "The rods need a richer food," he meditated, and after many failures he devised a strange soup. . . . Then on the point of a fine needle he picked up one of the gray specks from some juice of a sick fermentation. Carefully he sowed this speck in his new clear soup — and put the bottle into an incubating oven — and waited. . . .

He put a drop from the bottle before his microscope. Eureka! The field of the lens swarmed and vibrated with shimmying millions of the tiny rods. "They multiply! They are alive!" he whispered to himself. . . .

Time and again in the days that followed he did the same experiment, putting a tiny drop from a flask that swarmed with rods into a fresh clear flask of yeast soup that had none at all — and every time the rods appeared in billions and each time they made new quantities of the acid of sour milk. . . . Here was the one important fact: *It is the living things, sub-visible living beings that are the real cause of fermentation!*

[9] De Kruif, Paul. *Microbe Hunters,* Text Edition, chapter III. New York: Harcourt, Brace and Company, 1932.

Throughout the search of Pasteur for the answer to the cause of fermentation, the double movement referred to by Dewey is in evidence. Pure induction, if this were possible, would assume no hypothesis but a study of particular cases and then a general conclusion. Pasteur, on a "guess" which had been arrived at by numerous incidents of experience that led to an hypothesis, began the test of his hypothesis. Finally, after casting aside many hypotheses, and after carefully verifying the one that seemed to yield results, he was able to generalize his conclusion, which is stated in the concluding sentence of a much abstracted description of his procedures.

Steps in the deductive procedure

In spite of the fact that much of our attack in reflective thinking represents a mixed approach, there is much of problem solving within the school and out where the deductive method is necessary. There are four steps usually given to guide deductive procedure.

The first step is the clear recognition of the problem. This, as we have seen, is a universal characteristic of good problem attack. The nature of the problem must be clearly understood. Often the problem is not sharply defined, and cannot therefore "properly control the process of thinking." At this point deduction and induction have properties alike. Note, however, that a different manner of stating the problem may make a different method of solution more appropriate. Instead of, "Have all depressions in the United States had a similar cause?" substitute, "War has been the primary cause of all depressions in the United States." Here a problem has been so stated that "the end controls the process of thinking" in a different direction: the statement of the problem has in itself set up the second step in deductive thought.

The second step is the search for tentative hypotheses for the solution of the problem. The first statement of the question in the foregoing paragraph left it optional with the individual whether to make an attack *via* a careful analysis of the cause of each depression before drawing a conclusion, or to set up an hypothesis and then test the guess. The latter would, of course, be a clumsy long-drawn-out way to attack the problem, but it might be done. Choice of procedure is predetermined by the nature of the second statement. The two problems in reality are not identical. The first seeks the one underlying cause of depressions if such exists; the second, rigidly interpreted, demands only that "war" as a cause of all depressions be proved or disproved. When this has been done, the first question may or may not have been answered. In the second step an hypothesis has already been set up as the point of departure in the problem attack. When this is true, the second step is omitted and the third merely assented to. Usually, however, in any attempt to solve problems where the range of possibilities is great, the tendency is to cast about in experience, reason, and observation for data that will give some hopeful clue. Otherwise interminable time might be spent in running down clues, which careful examination on the basis of experience and observation would have quickly rejected as non-probable leads. This step was clearly the one used by Pasteur to arrive at a tentative hypothesis.

The third step in deductive procedure is the formulation of a tentative hypothesis that appears to have promise as a probable or possible solution of the problem. Where the problem has been so stated as to set up the hypothesis, acceptance of it is all that is necessary as a point of departure. If we go back to the question, "Have all depressions in the United States had a similar cause?" since there are so few cases to cover, it might be simpler to examine the separate depressions for their causes without an hypothesis. Were the question one that admitted of almost unlimited conjecture, then the desirable thing to do would be to search for and to formulate a tentative hypothesis or reason that seemed plausible. The student of logic can find some aid in syllogistic reasoning. If the major premises seem to hold up in the chain of reasoning involved, it is a possible hypothesis to accept.

The fourth step in the deductive approach is that of verification. This is, of course, the crux of the deductive procedure. Here a careful examination of the factors that entered into the setting up of the hypothesis must be meticulously made. Where the problem involves possible recourse to documentary sources, the student must consult the evidence for or against. If the problem is of the nature which requires experimental procedures, as in the case of Pasteur quoted above, then the testing must take place in the atmosphere of test tubes and the laboratory. Much of the technique of the traditional school science laboratory experiment is nothing but a verification technique of a low order. In some phases of problem solving this verification by repetition is impossible as well as costly in time. The last is not a justifiable basis for the omission of this important phase of training in problem solving. There are far too many people, both in school and out of it, ready to go off half-cocked without subjecting their apparent findings to the most rigid scrutiny. Often the nature of the problem is such that a retracing of steps for verification is impossible. Many of the experiments that throw light on our social problems, for example, are not readily subject to repetition. Another form of verification, then, is to check the hypothesis against known facts or accepted standards of procedure to determine its validity. This is a short-cut form of verification technique quite widely employed. Incidentally it explains in part the researchers' practice of reporting meticulously the technique of research employed, with the results of each stage of development of the study carefully recorded. The correctness of the technique, judged by accepted standards of procedure, and the legitimacy of the inferences and conclusions drawn from the data adduced can thus be carefully examined and verified or rejected.

Steps in the inductive procedure

The inductive procedure in modified form is possibly the most commonly used in problem-solving school work. There are certain problems that demand this approach. It should be recognized by the teacher that two procedures are clearly available, each with a distinct advantage. On the other hand, the teacher should know that many problems confront us psychologically and should be attacked on that basis, though the intertwining of two logical procedures may be involved. If Dewey be followed, it may be considered more natural for overlapping to occur.

The first step in the inductive procedure is the clear recognition of the problem. It is identical with that of the deductive procedure, and need not be explained further.

The second step in the inductive procedure is the search for data. In the question previously used as an example of simple induction, "Have all depressions in the United States had a similar cause?" the second step would involve a study of the history of the United States and a gathering together, from all historical or interpretative economic sources, of the evidence about each depression. It is true that in every one of the cases studied the full cycle of inductive procedure would probably be employed on each depression in the process of the collection of data for the larger question raised. In any event the data assembled would include all pertinent evidence of the cause of each depression period.

The third step requires the careful sifting, comparing, and abstracting of the significant data collected. In the actual assembling of data no such airtight compartments in mental processes would be likely to obtain. The student would be sifting, comparing, and abstracting relevant from irrelevant materials, though the actual comparison and abstraction of pertinent facts on the main problem might not take place until all data had been collected. The normal expectation would be that steps two and three would move along, in part, simultaneously. In this step rigorous thinking is required. Keen analysis and a sense of the pertinence of data are important.

The fourth step is generalization. Again this phase of mental activity in problem solving no doubt parallels in some measure step three. It is difficult for the active mind to carry forward the steps of procedure in such complete isolation. At best these procedures indicate only the principal phases in the order of their predominance, rather than any isolated elements in mental behavior. Generalization has two phases to it. The first consists of the organization of data in such a way as to permit a view of its main outlines and points of convergence. The second involves the drawing of necessary conclusions or inferences from all data so collected, compared, and organized. Either there has been discovered an underlying uniform cause for recurring depressions in American history, or no uniform cause was found to exist. It is almost certain that actually much more was learned than the immediate answer to the question, for the concomitant learning of most frequent causes, if such exists, would have resulted from the quest of the answer to the original question.

4. What Are Some Problem-Solving Methods?

The Herbartian "Formal Steps" an inductive procedure

The nearly forgotten once famous Herbartian Formal Steps in teaching represent one of the early efforts to develop the inductive procedure into a teaching formula. If the later abuse of the basic idea through misuse of the formula is forgotten, there is much that is still helpful in the underlying ideas of Herbart. There is no reason why teachers may not modify the teaching technique of a basically sound form of learning into a modern pedagogical form of directing pupil learning.

1. *Preparation.* The first formal step of Herbart was preparation. In this phase there was to be aroused in the mind of the student a conscious need to solve a problem, and to lead the student to a clear recognition and understanding of the nature of the problem. In this connection past experience was recalled to give meaning and vitality to the problem about to be attacked. In terms of modern pedagogy, this step serves to provide the motivation and understanding of the problem so fully stressed. In the language of the old colored man, it provided the "rousements." It is thoroughly psychological in that the establishment of a genuine perplexity is both a characteristic of good thinking and a primary purpose of this step.

2. *Presentation.* The second formal step, presentation, paralleled the inductive step — the collection of data. In this step Herbart carried forward the actual presentation to the students of the new materials to be learned. Inasmuch as the Herbartian theory presupposed the teacher rather than the student as the actor the data was given in lecture form. If the student's interest had been thoroughly aroused as contemplated in step one, then he would be alert to all the data presented. The teacher marshaled before the students the examples, incidents, and pertinent facts necessary for the solution of the problem outlined in step one, and the teacher of course was the judge of the completeness and relevancy of the data offered in the class.

3. *Comparison and abstraction.* The third step involved the effort to analyze the data presented and to organize it into significant relationships. The discussion applicable to step three of the inductive procedure may be used here also, except that in the Herbartian scheme the actual responsibility for the demonstration rested with the teacher, the students following with rapt attention and occasional questions.

4. *Generalization.* The fourth and final step, in the Herbartian formal steps, meant the summary of the critical and careful evaluation of the preceding step into a general conclusion or statement of a principle, as the case might warrant.

5. *Application.* This was the fifth step added by Herbart's followers. They recognized the fact that although inductive reasoning actually completed its cycle and the problem was solved in

the four steps Herbart had developed, yet for practical pedagogical purposes the student had not always clearly in mind the salient features in the lesson. It was important to be able to apply this knowledge or understanding to new situations and thereby to fix these ideas more firmly in mind. The teacher, or sometimes the students, therefore applied the new generalization arrived at in the fourth step to many new particulars. This had an additional pedagogical value, in that it insured the abstraction of the conclusion or principle from association with the original framework of the problem. In this the followers of Herbart were on psychologically firm ground. This step is, of course, deductive in nature, and usually a desirable one to follow after a purely inductive procedure has been completed.

It should be obvious that in the Herbartian Five Formal Steps the teacher has at hand a problem-solving technique of no mean worth. The fact that it has been made unpopular, through misuse by teachers who have taken over its form without a full appreciation of its spirit, should not relegate it to the limbo of forbidden methods. Rejuvenated in the light of modern psychological theory and educational thought, the Herbartian five steps can be effectively utilized as a problem-solving method. For example, there is no reason why the burden of effort should not be transferred to the shoulders of the student instead of being carried by the teacher. The classroom situation can be so organized that the student assumes direct attack upon the problem under the teacher's general guidance. The attack may be made, and broadly developed through the steps laid down by Herbart, with the student in the role of chief executor of the attack as general and buck private, and the teacher in the role of technical adviser. There is no reason why the Herbartian formal steps reconstructed to conform to our best educational ideals may not at times be applied to the lecture or recitation methods.

The Morrisonian "Teaching Cycle and Problem-Solving"

Closely akin to the Herbartian formal steps is the *cycle plan of teaching* as applied by Morrison to what he calls the science type learning. It may be taken to represent what was spoken of in the last chapter as a reconstruction of the Herbartian formal steps. While the processes are somewhat similar, there are radical differences which only a detailed study will fully reveal. It is not in place here to enter into a comparison of similarities and differences. Sufficient to say both are based upon the inductive procedure, and as such represent two teaching methods that are applicable to problem solving. The cycle plan is admirably adapted as a problem-solving technique. A brief statement of the central idea in each of the five steps will serve to show the utility of Morrison's plan for problem solving.

1. *Exploration,* Morrison says, has three main purposes; namely: economy, the establishment of an apperceptive base, and orientation. It serves to eliminate needless repetitions of phases of work previously studied by acquainting the teacher with the student's background for the unit to be studied. It serves also to tie up the experiences of the student with the problem to be studied and thus motivates him. Oral questions, discussion, and occasional written tests are used to orient the teacher into the preparation of the class for what is to follow.

2. In *presentation* the teacher gives to the class, by lecture or demonstration, the essential understanding of the unit. Details are omitted. The ideas are presented in a simple straightforward manner calculated further to arouse interest and give focus to the more detailed study ahead for the student. A presentation test is then given to determine which of the students have not understood. If exploration and presentation are taken together, they may very roughly be paralleled with the first step of the inductive procedure previously discussed.

3. The *assimilation* phase plunges the student into the details of the understanding he seeks to acquire. Here he learns to collect the data of that understanding from sources which the teacher has made available to him in the form of lists of reference books, mimeographed sheets, etc. The ideal arrangement demands that these sources be readily available in the classroom where the student in a laboratory or directed-study situation gathers together the pertinent data of the understandings sought. Again, this step parallels roughly the second and to some extent the third steps of the inductive procedure.

4. The *organization* step carries forward the work of the last phase into a coherent logical statement of conclusions, or the essential basis for the understandings that have culminated from the study. This is the acid test of his understanding or, speaking in problem-solving terms, his solution of the problem. This step cor-

responds closely to the fourth step in the inductive procedure, though overlapping the third step somewhat.

5. The final step, *recitation*, does not contribute to the further understanding or solution of the problem except as an attempt to convey the results of one's study to others fixes the understandings more firmly or gives final clarity to one's thinking. In this phase some students present orally the results of their organization and understanding, while the rest of the class offer written summaries of their work. Following the "floor talks" a period of questioning and comment may take place over the reports given.

The strong similarity between the first four steps of the Morrisonian "Cycle Plan" of teaching for the science type units and the inductive procedure becomes quite evident as each step is studied and the relations noted. They do not parallel each other exactly, as might well be expected when a procedure for developmental reasoning is compared with a definitely refined technique of teaching method built upon this developmental process in thinking.

The project method

Originally the "project" had reference to a method of problem solving largely associated with practical problem-situations of a manipulative or constructive nature in manual arts or agriculture. As problem-solving procedures became accepted as educationally more important, the techniques of the "project" were recognized as having broad application value in all types of problem-solving situations. Particularly has this been true as the emphasis has shifted from primary responsibility of the teacher to that of the pupil in the actual process of learning. Pedagogically the method is fundamentally sound and contemporary in applicability to *problem-solving learning*. All authorities on method accept four steps in the project-method procedure and agree on the nomenclature of those steps. These steps are: Purposing, Planning, Executing, Judging. These will be seen to approximate closely the steps suggested for problem solving.

1. *Purposing.* Throughout the whole of modern methodology is heard the note of emphasis upon motivation. It was stressed particularly in the consideration of the problem method. It is returned to here. A special virtue of the problem is that it arouses mental perplexity that leads naturally to a desire to find relief from

the mental disturbance thus engendered. Because of its practical problematic nature, the project should enlist the wholehearted cooperation of the student even more effectively. Ideally, as all admit, in cases where the project originates with the pupil the fullest measure of genuine purposing is achieved. It is his own. There is a definite urge present to carry it out to completion. As far as possible, the students should be encouraged to originate projects. There are difficulties of a very real nature, however, in undirected, pupil-initiated projects. The all-absorbing thing that the student may be emotionally set to do, possibly has little educative value. Or, it may have educative value for another time and place, but little value in contributing to the immediate needs of the student in the particular learning stage which he may have reached at the moment. Continuity and next steps may, indeed probably will, have much to do with the determination of the appropriateness of a given project at a particular time. The grave danger of over-emphasis upon student initiative in the selection of projects lies just here. The projects are likely to be devoid of educative value on the one hand, or, if valuable educationally, they may be badly misplaced, with the result that they benefit the student very little. The good teacher knows that the average student is readily sus-ceptible to suggestion. It is usually not difficult to lead the student to desire or purpose to do the things which the teacher's larger perspective and knowledge indicate should be done. The imma-turity of the student, as contrasted with the maturity of the teacher, dictates the wisdom of the teacher's selecting the projects that best meet the educational needs of the student, and then challenging the student's acceptance of these projects.

It should be borne in mind that the genius of the project lies in the wholehearted enlistment of the student in the doing of it. If this is not secured, the project has little more value than any other method. In one sense it is no more a project than the problem is a problem when no true perplexity exists. The motions of project performance may be discharged, but the significant values, the peculiar virtues resident in the method, will not be realized.

2. *Planning.* Once the project has been wholeheartedly accepted, the students usually are eager to get the task under way. Impetu-ous youth may be more eager to "do" than to "plan." None the less, the crux of the project method is in the planning. It is the important phase of the problem-solving aspect of the project. The

success of the project depends upon the care with which the details of procedure in the undertaking have been worked out. The student should carry the chief responsibility for planning. He cannot achieve vicariously the power of good planning. The strategy of good planning comes only by constant intelligent planning, with some errors; but with the errors, comes wisdom. Too often learning is acquired only at the expense of costly mistakes. The school seeks to reduce the need for such expensive learning to a minimum. For this reason, the teacher will not permit errors of too serious a nature to occur. Subtle guidance will steer the student past the most serious pitfalls, but the wise teacher will probably allow a certain number of minor errors to occur so as to make the student conscious of the need for alertness, and for the most critical examination of every proposed step in the carrying forward of the project. The competent teacher will guide the activity by subtle questions that direct the student's attention to problems of procedure, force a careful appraisal of a given step in the development of a plan of action, and in consequence lead the student to an habitually critical study of a plan before the plan is adopted. A written statement drawing up the details for the execution of the project gives the student excellent training. It forces him to think exactly instead of in the vague way in which one is too likely to think when he has not forced himself to commit his cogitations to objective statement. More than that, he can examine deliberately and critically every proposed step for the accomplishment of the project. When group acceptance of a common project has taken place, the teacher may act as discussion leader to draw from the group a desirable plan for the execution of the project.

3. *Executing.* The execution of the project is the most interesting phase of project teaching. In the eager mind of the student this is the most vital part of the project procedure. He finds here that activity and the doing of things of a tangible nature, in which are developed immediate interests of a most challenging sort. It will be relatively easy for the student to become lost in things he is doing and to overlook the original purpose of his activity. Every phase of the activity should be directed toward the realization of the objective that brought the project into being.

As far as possible, the teacher should see that necessary materials are readily available. As in the problem method, the student should be able to keep attention and energy centered on the educative aspects of the project, and not allow time and effort to be dissipated in fruitless bypaths. If too much effort is given to nonessentials, the focus of attention will be diverted from the project, and interest will lag as well.

The student may prove to be "all thumbs and no fingers" in the execution phase. It may require excessive time to do things the teacher realizes he could do in but a fraction of the period allowed the student. Teachers, at times, to escape the discomfort of slow clumsiness, are prone to want to do things for the student. They must curb their impatience, and realize that this is a vital part of the youth's training. Anyone doing things for the first time is likely to be slow and awkward. It is to be expected of the student. This is his royal road to learning. It cannot be short-circuited without loss to the individual. When excessive slowness tends to hold back a class, it may be necessary to speed up the work of the individual for the benefit of the group. Not only will project work seem slow to the mature teacher, but the product of the work may be very crude. Even so, the value or need of the project might be in question if the work bore evidence of too much finish. It is the training that counts when the best efforts of the students have been put forth.

The teacher needs to observe closely the progress made while the execution phase is in progress. Plans should be followed carefully. The student should be trained to follow plans as carefully as he is trained to make them, and at the same time he should be taught to maintain a critical attitude toward those plans. He should be taught to be critical of every phase of the execution technique. Auto-criticism was a factor in Binet's judgment of mental ability. Certainly it is indispensable to the student who wishes to profit by his experience. This is essentially a supervised-study phase of teaching, and the teacher should adopt much the same attitude and technique as that which applies to supervised study. There are times when an appropriate suggestion will be in order. It may be that in some constructive phases, where mechanical skill is necessary, the teacher at times may well give discriminating assistance. The teacher must at all times act in the rôle of friendly stimulator, lest enthusiasm falter in difficult or non-spectacular phases of the project's execution. Projects should not be abandoned partly finished. The student should be taught the practical values of seeing a thing through to completion, at whatever cost.

4. *Judging.* The final stage in project learning is the passing of judgment upon the finished product. The student who has completed the task set before him has achieved something. What is the worth of that achievement? "By our mistakes we learn," someone has said. This is true, of course, if we have been made aware of our mistakes, and further, if we have had some constructive suggestions as to ways in which improvement might be made either in the finished product or in the techniques to be used in a similar project undertaking.

Here again the tendency of the teacher will be to act as judge and jury without reference to the students. The procedure here must be conditioned by the circumstances. If the project is individual, the student should become as far as possible his own best critic. The teacher should equip him with the necessary standards of evaluation and guide him in his use of them. As occasion may demand, the teacher may become judge, but only when student judgment proves inadequate. The student receives a most valuable training in self-criticism. Psychologically it is a well-established fact that self-criticism will be received more gracefully than will suggestions from others.

Where group activity is involved, student judging is most desirable. It is the student who needs to develop powers of critical analysis and the ability to offer constructive suggestions. It has a wholesome effect on the morale of the group to be given the responsibility of evaluating their own project work. A student is more likely to receive seriously the judgments of his peers than he would those of the teacher. The average student is much more concerned with the opinions of those of his own age or set than with any others. The teacher should take advantage of this additional spur to student incentive. Collings suggests [10] four procedures in student judging that deserve the careful study of the teacher.

> *First,* suggestions for changes either in what has been done, by additions, eliminations, modifications, etc., or completion of phases of the plan which for some reason may have been neglected.

[10] Collings, Ellsworth. *Progressive Teaching in Secondary Schools,* p. 60. Indianapolis: The Bobbs-Merrill Company, 1931.

Second, evaluation of the improvement; how it might be done; whether it is now feasible or desirable to do it.

Third, the opportunity to express a judgment for or against suggested improvements.

Fourth, the actual execution of the improvements where such are deemed necessary.

Suggested method

A more general approach to a problem-solving attack is offered than the methods given above suggest. The broad procedural steps for problem solving are given, followed by their application to a problem-situation which it is hoped may be helpful both to teachers and students. The technique illustrated is particularly pertinent to unit teaching.

STEPS IN PROBLEM-SOLVING TECHNIQUE [11]

I. Recognize the difficulty (problem)
  A. Locate the source of the difficulty.
  B. Discover the particular aspects that are disturbing.
  C. Decide in what area this difficulty falls.
    1. Determine whether the difficulty is purely personal, about which a principal, counselor, or teacher should be consulted.
    2. Determine whether the difficulty is of a nature that its solution requires the cooperative effort of a number of others, such as the class, a club, or similar group.
  D. Decide whether the difficulty is of real or vital concern.
II. State the difficulty as a problem
  A. Determine clearly the nature of the difficulty.
  B. Be able to formulate this difficulty as a problem.
  C. Decide whether this is a major problem in itself or only a part of another problem.
  D. Determine whether related problems should be considered in the solution of this problem.
  E. Discover whether there are facilities available with which to attack this problem.
  F. Decide whether it is possible to set up tentative hypotheses as a guide for attacking this problem.
III. Attack the problem
  A. Collect the data.

[11] From Bossing, Nelson L. and Martin, Robert R. *Youth Faces Its Problems,* pp. 7–9. Chicago: Laidlaw Brothers, 1950.

1. Outline what you already know about the problem.
2. Find out what others have done toward the solution of this problem.
   a. Build a bibiliography, examine the literature, talk with other people in the community.
3. Decide whether additional information is necessary.
   a. Collect necessary data or information from the library, from reading, personal interviews, questionnaires, or experimentation.

B. Organize the data
   1. Decide what mechanics are involved in recording this material conveniently: loose-leaf notes, cards, snapshots, original drawings, charts, containers for bulk material, indexes of library materials.
   2. Decide how the data collected may be organized most advantageously for study.

C. Analyze the data
   1. Decide upon the relevance of the material collected to the problem involved.
   2. Decide what weight should be given to the various items collected for purposes of interpretation.
      a. Determine whether all data collected have equal value for testing the hypotheses.
      b. Determine why some evidence is rejected as invalid and other evidence accepted as valid.

IV. Draw conclusions
   A. Determine what conclusions appear possible in the light of an analysis of the data available.
   B. Decide what conclusion appears to be most adequately supported by the evidence.
   C. Decide whether the weight of evidence appears to be final and conclusive for any single conclusion or group of conclusions.

V. Implement the conclusion
   A. Decide whether the conclusion suggests further action.
      1. Consider whether an individual or group should carry out the conclusion.
   B. Determine the types of action implied in the conclusion.
   C. Decide what must be done to put the conclusion into effect. Consider whether a community project is involved.
   D. Determine whether additional related problems need further study.

That teachers and students may see graphically how this problem-solving technique can be applied in a specific problem-situation, a problem of a general nature has been selected for an example. A general problem formulated from a local incident of pupil concern is attacked according to the method of problem solution outlined above.

APPLICATION OF THE TECHNIQUE IN A
PROBLEMATIC SITUATION

Problem 4, included at the end of Unit 1, Area 1, of this book,[12] reads: *Many women have been leaders in the struggle for women's rights. Why have these women devoted so much time and attention to the issue of women's rights?*

This is closely tied in with an incident which occurred recently in a certain community. A popular teacher was married before school started in September, and her resignation was demanded because her husband was employed at a good salary. This aroused the school, and the graduating class in particular. At once many questions arose relative to the rights of women:

Why do women, not men, have to give up their maiden name in marriage?

Are women discriminated against in employment opportunities?

Can women expect equal pay with men for equal work?

Will the girls have an opportunity to compete on equal terms with the boys for jobs after the class graduates in June?

Is it possible for girls to compete with boys in their professional aspirations?

The boys raised the question of the possibility of marrying early and maintaining the standards of living if women were to be denied the right to work after marriage. Many boys knew of incidents of discrimination that had affected mothers, sisters, and other relatives.

I. Recognizing the difficulty (problem)
    A. Teacher and pupil discussion and planning brought out the following general agreements:
        1. Several students had had real difficulty over the question of women's rights.
        2. Several points at which real questions have arisen over the issue of women's rights were recognized:
            a. Some students felt that their sisters, mothers, and women relatives were discriminated against in a number of ways.

[12] From Bossing, Nelson L. and Martin, Robert R. *Youth Faces Its Problems,* pp. 11–15. Chicago: Laidlaw Brothers, 1950.

b. Some girls were greatly concerned about the matter of competing with boys in the class for jobs upon graduation.

c. Several girls with professional aspirations found certain fields apparently closed to them.

d. Most girls anticipating the possibility of marriage were agitated over what they believed to be the loss of legal freedoms, even loss of certain legal protection, in the event of marriage.

e. Many boys were concerned about maintaining their living standards if the girls they married lost their positions as the result of marriage.

f. The class was concerned that men and women might be able to participate equally in political activities.

3. The issue of women's rights was sufficiently broad to involve the interest of all: for most of the members of this class, personal and large-scale implications of this issue seemed vital to personal happiness, to community welfare, and to democracy as a way of life.

II. Stating the difficulty as a problem

A. At first several boys made the point that it looked to them as though some of the girls were actually concerned about "superior" rights to men. Quickly it became clear that the real difficulties arose over the belief of the girls that women were in fact accorded "inferior" status with men. All agreed that the heart of the difficulty could be clarified in the form of major questions:

1. Why have women believed there were rights accorded to men which they did not share?

2. What is the nature of these rights which women believed they did not have?

3. What evidence is there that women still believe they are not accorded equal rights with men?

a. The class cited the recent legislative proposals before the 81st Congress of the United States to accord to women further equality of rights.

b. They pointed out the current widespread agitation among women for equal employment opportunities.

4. Are there fundamental ability differences between the sexes?

5. Would not the continuance of this feeling of unequal rights on the part of women create disharmony between men and women?

6. Does not inequality of women's rights violate democratic ideas?

7. May not the fact that women feel strongly that they do not have equal rights with men lead to serious emotional maladjustments?

B. After considerable discussion, the class finally set up their problem in a twofold form:

1. To what extent does there exist an inequality of rights between men and women?

2. What stand should this class take on the question of women's rights?

C. To further clarify thinking on the many aspects of the issue, the following hypotheses were set up to be tested by the evidence collected by various committees:

1. The problem arises out of biological differences between the sexes, and nothing can be done about it.

2. The problem is one of inequality between men and women under the law, and legislative action will be required to solve it.

3. Discrimination between men and women is inherently traditional, and the only solution is to change social traditions.

4. This is a pseudo-problem because, although men and women have been granted the franchise, a majority of them fail to exercise it.

5. There is really no problem, because men and women are accorded equal rights at the present time.

6. The problem arises out of a situation that is largely economic and social and must be solved through appropriate economic-social reform.

III. Attacking the problem.

A. Collecting the data

1. Each committee chose the particular hypothesis on which the members wished to work, and collected data accordingly.

2. Classroom activities involved preparing bibliographies, looking up references in the school library, preparing maps, charts, tables, and graphs, drawing up questionnaires, and schedules, planning interviews, arranging talks by community leaders.

3. Activities outside of class involved interviewing persons, distributing and collecting questionnaires, taking pictures, making field trips, observing.

B. Organizing the data

1. This involved the marshaling of data largely from printed and written sources, from personal interviews, and from questionnaires. The class committees, therefore, felt that a

uniform plan of recording should be followed. It was decided that most of the data could advantageously be recorded upon separate cards or sheets of paper of uniform size. Certain suggestions were agreed upon:

    a. One major idea should appear on each separate card or piece of paper.

    b. The idea should be conspicuously captioned at the top of each sheet or card.

    c. Each card should be fully documented as to the source of the idea recorded on it.

    d. The cards or sheets of paper should be carried in a small folder or container while information was being collected: from time to time they should be transferred to a more permanent type of container which would facilitate classification and indexing.

    e. The material gathered on this particular problem should be classified with respect to the major ideas involved: definition of equality, definition of rights, sex differences, nature of democracy.

C. Analyzing the data

    1. After collecting the data, the committees turned their attention to the possible significance of the material. To set up some bases for evaluation and classification of the data, the following questions were formulated:

        a. Is each recorded item related to some aspect of the hypothesis being tested?

        b. What is the relative importance of each item for the hypothesis to which it applies?

        c. Does the data analyzed provide an adequate basis for testing the particular hypothesis?

        d. If the data appears inadequate to test the particular hypothesis, what can the committee or the class do to provide the additional data needed?

IV. Drawing the conclusion

A. After analyzing the data with respect to the hypothesis, each committee tried to determine the extent to which the evidence supported the hypothesis being tested. The various committees then reported in turn to the entire class. The members of the class checked with equal care the possible relevance of the data supporting each hypothesis. As a group they finally agreed upon certain conclusions.

V. Implementing the conclusion

A. After careful study the class agreed that hypotheses 2, 3, and 6 were in part true: as a group they determined the most effective solution. Some action was felt to be beyond the ability of the class; other phases it was felt that the class, and members as individuals, could do something about. The ways and means of such action became a project engaging their attention.

5. What Special Considerations Are Involved in Problem Approach?

Criteria for selection of problems

The practical nature of problems is in large measure accountable for the special considerations that govern their selection. Every problem should be scrutinized carefully, with the following criteria in mind:

1. *It should have definite educational values.* The problem's educative significance should be readily apparent not in generalities but in particular relation to the student's needs. A unit of activity might conceivably have great educational value in one situation, and in another comparatively little. It is easy, too, to mistake the trappings surrounding some problem-projects for the essential worth they are erroneously assumed to possess.

2. *It should be adapted to the needs of the situation.* Two considerations need to be kept in mind at this point. The maturity of the student socially and intellectually may determine at once the worth of a problem. A problem splendidly adapted to the social background of a city youth may have no challenge for him, or it may contribute little to his environmental needs or understanding. The frequent efforts of many teachers in metropolitan centers to develop agricultural projects in an urbanized environment may be well meaning, but they show no educational discrimination.

3. *Availability of materials should be fully considered.* Many worth-while problems are impossible because the materials needed cannot be secured. This applies as well to situations. There is little purpose in launching a project to construct a baseball diamond in a city school in the heart of a thickly populated area where there is only enough room for a narrow strip of lawn, if any, between building and sidewalks.

4. *The time consumed must be commensurate with the values that accrue from execution of the problem project.* This is very important. After all, sufficient time for the adequate education of our youth is at a premium. The time element cannot be totally

neglected. The worth of the problem method as compared with other methods must be decided in part by the economy of time involved. The teacher should constantly ask, "Does the additional educational return justify the extra time involved?" It should be remembered, however, that time is a minor factor to be considered in the selection of a problem for study.

5. *The adaptability of problem performance to the regimentation of the school should be carefully considered.* The teacher is not the administrator, and he must adapt his classroom work to the exigencies of the situation. Many problem-situations require adjustments in the school program and class schedule. Increasingly schools are adopting a more flexible organization of the school program to meet the needs of problem teaching. Even so, it is not possible in a large school to become flexible enough to meet all needs. Seldom should schedules be modified greatly for the convenience of one section of the school. Only in the rarest of situations should the teacher presume to ask for special dispensations for his work. If a contemplated problem cannot be made to "fit in," it should be rejected.

6. *Cost of materials often proves the determining factor in the selection of problem projects.* The critical financial condition of the schools in recent years has accentuated this factor in problem selection. The unfavorable attitude toward school costs revealed under the stress of rising economic pressures of taxes and inflation, is likely to persist for many years. Even under most favorable circumstances costs of materials have been and will continue to be a major consideration which teachers must face in the selection of projects.

7. *A problem should be capable of completion within the time limits set by the course.* This means that only those problems which can be completed within a single semester should be undertaken in a single semester course. The fact that the four steps in project procedure are to be carried through under the guidance of the teacher, necessarily puts time limits particularly on the project. A project would lose much of its value if part of the execution and all of the judging were done without benefit of teacher or class reaction to the finished product. This criterion further means that each proposed problem should be evaluated in terms of the time allotted to the course for other activities that give cohesion and significance to the complete section of learning contemplated in the course.

Teacher guidance in problem solving

Although the teacher may not appear to occupy the center of attention in some aspects of the problem method, yet the teacher is an important cog in the machinery of this method. The tendency is to individualism in problem solution. Whatever the direct approach, the degree to which the teacher himself is a master of problem solving will bear a somewhat direct relation to the effectiveness of his direction of others in this process. A teacher who has the ability to see problems clearly, the power to analyze with a keen discernment, and the facility to synthesize and draw conclusions with an uncanny accuracy, will be a rare help to the students in their mastery of the difficult technique of problem attack. Guidance in problem solving is in reality training in "how to study," and, it might be added, in "how to think." The essential items the teacher must focus attention upon in the direction of students in the act of problem solving were given under the caption "Characteristics of Reflective Thought."

Relation of problem method to other methods

For those methods which have for their primary purpose the development of mental skills, concepts, attitudes, and ideals, the problem is somewhat basic, particularly for those which deal with general ideas. These do involve reflective thought. Some methods, such as the lecture or recitation, may serve other educational purposes besides the development of mental skills. They may, at times, legitimately center upon perceptual, memory, or associational learning. At other times their use can be justified only when they are adapted to problem solving in some form. The problem and project methods are the newer methods developed to train students specifically in the solution of problems. They are not readily usable in perceptual or associational learning, except as these become by-products of problem-solving effort. The more individualistic methods, such as the Morrisonian, Contract, Wisconsin, and Supervised Study are closely identified with the problem method, since problem solving or the development of reflective thinking is an important factor in their *raison d'être*.

QUESTIONS AND PROBLEMS

1. What is a problem?
2. Why is the problem and its solution such an important factor in our lives?
3. What is Dewey's classification of types of thought? Which is the most important type? Which type do we use the most?
4. Define reflective thinking.
5. What are the most essential characteristics of good thinking?
6. What relation exists between problem solving and reflective thinking?
7. What are the distinguishing characteristics of deductive and inductive thinking?
8. Select a typical problem of everyday life and apply the steps of deductive reasoning to its solution.
9. How does Morrison's "Cycle Plan of Teaching" differ from the Herbartian "Five Formal Steps"?
10. What are the factors that influence the success of the problem method?
11. How does the problem method contribute to the development of mental skills, concepts and attitudes?
12. Trace the origin of the term "project" in educational activities.
13. Plan a problem-project which will involve drawing upon the content sources of several time-honored school subjects.
14. How would you determine the success of a completed problem-project?

SELECTED BIBLIOGRAPHY

Bayles, Ernest E. *The Theory and Practice of Teaching.* New York: Harper and Brothers, 1950.

Bode, Boyd H. *How We Learn,* chapters X, XIII, XV. Boston: D. C. Heath and Company, 1940.

Bossing, Nelson L. and Martin, Robert R. *Youth Faces Its Problems,* pp. 6–16. Chicago: Laidlaw Brothers, 1950.

Dewey, John. *How We Think.* Boston: D. C. Heath and Company, 1933.

Gates, A. I. et al. *Educational Psychology,* Third Edition, chapters X–XIV. New York: The Macmillan Company, 1949.

Goetting, M. L. *Teaching in the Secondary School,* chapter IX. New York: Prentice-Hall, Inc., 1942.

Kingsley, Howard L. *The Nature and Conditions of Learning,* chapters II, VII, XV. New York: Prentice-Hall, Inc., 1946.

Mursel, James L. *Developmental Teaching,* chapters VII–IX. New York: McGraw-Hill Book Company, Inc., 1949.

Risk, Thomas M. *Principles and Practices of Teaching in Secondary Schools,* Second Edition, chapter XX. New York: American Book Company, 1947.

Schorling, Raleigh. *Student Teaching,* Second Edition, chapter VII. New York: McGraw-Hill Book Company, Inc., 1949.

Wertheimer, Max. *Productive Thinking.* New York: Harper and Brothers, 1947.

5

How Can the Lecture Be Used?

The past thirty years have witnessed a revolutionary change in educational theory with respect to methods of teaching. The time-honored lecture and recitation have surrendered first place to problem-solving methods. Even these older methods have undergone modifications in emphasis to contribute in greater degree to problem-solving learning. This is rightly so. Practice, however, has lagged far behind theory. As has been made clear in our earlier discussions, rapidly changing conditions, modern understanding of the learning process, and the needs of a complex democratic society better understood today, have rightly focused attention upon the primary need of problem-solving learning. This has necessitated a change in emphasis upon teaching methods, as well as some adjustment of the older methods to fit modern needs.

1. What Is the Significance of the Lecture?

Nature of the lecture

The lecture is given larger interpretation in this chapter than the term popularly indicates. Practically all writers in the discussion of methods agree that lecturing and telling, while basically different, are alike in nature and use and may be considered together.

It is well at the outset to recognize that lecturing and telling are not identical, though telling may often be a part of the lecture. The lecture is a method of exposition, while telling is essentially one of narration. As used in education, the "lecture method" refers to the teaching procedure involved in the clarification or explanation to the student of some major idea that has been cast into the form of a question or problem. The technique is, therefore, that of exposition. Exposition, while its purpose is "to explain something," none the less makes extensive use of narrative and description. Telling, on the other hand, is an effort to supply the student with information about events, incidents, and simple facts; it makes great use of the story. The narrative is the form in which telling is cast, since its purpose is not to explain something but rather to present to the mind a series of events or facts that may inform or become the basis for the solution of a problem. Often telling serves only to entertain. Exposition is frequently used in the story form in order to arrest attention or to stimulate imagination. This has been particularly true of the platform lecturer, who finds it necessary to resort to such a device to sustain the attention of the audience until he has put his ideas across.

The lecture in teaching

Modern education has given little place to the lecture in the high school. Some declare that it has no place in the college or university, its time-honored strongholds. Few textbooks on secondary methods within recent years acknowledge that it is sufficiently important to devote a chapter to the lecture, while some ignore it entirely. The trend has been undeniably in the direction of other forms of classroom methods, with the increased emphasis upon student activity in learning. An effort has been made to develop a methodology which gives maximum opportunity for self-expression. Further, the philosophy that lay back of the lecture method no longer exists for the high school. The older ideas of education made the school teacher-centered. Its activities were centered upon the teacher. The student was considered an empty vessel into which could be poured the wisdom gathered by advanced study, age, and experience. This philosophy of education involved a passive, not an active, concept of learning. The idea that education is knowledge-acquisition is implicit in the older notions of education and is reflected in the traditional methods. In the opening chapter of this book, place was given to knowledge in education, but only to the end that it might become the vehicle for broad understanding, problem solution, or that it might result in emotional sets — appreciations and attitudes.

It is an open question whether the proponents of the newer

methods have not too hastily condemned the lecture. It is the writer's contention that every method has some virtues and some weaknesses. It is, therefore, desirable to have students come in contact with a variety of methods. It is inconceivable that all knowledge and skills necessary in life are to be gained, for example, by the "problem" or the "socialized-recitation" methods, valuable as these methods are. Life outside the schoolroom is not cast exclusively in the peculiar mold of any one classroom method. The affairs of life impinge upon the mind of the individual in myriad forms, and not the least of these is the impact of ideas upon the mind through the medium of the lecture. Then there are many classroom situations where monotony may be overcome through the presentation of a vivid story or description; or, where some problems may become instantly clear through a few minutes' exposition. It must be remembered that the great example of effective teaching held up as an example to the American teacher has been the classroom teaching of Germany. No one can doubt German schoolroom efficiency. The lecture has been the time-honored method of the German schoolroom, even in elementary schools.

Special usefulness of the lecture

If the teacher visualizes normal classroom situations, there appear times when it would seem that resort to the lecture would be the most effective and economical method of presenting some ideas to the minds of the students. In certain forms of appreciational learning the lecture offers a most advantageous way to establish the best mind-sets and to arouse adequate emotional toning for the appreciations it is hoped to develop. Again, here and there, a few minutes devoted to explanation to the entire class seems desirable if not imperative. Often just a bit of information given the class will enable it to hurdle a serious obstacle to learning. The technique of exposition or narration, if used for ten or even twenty minutes, approximates the same care of details as does the more formal lecture. Experience with teachers in the classroom reveals all too plainly the effects of ignoring this method. Exposition poorly prepared and delivered, telling so ineffective that little good can result — these are the frequent reminders that this phase of teaching deserves more attention than recent educators have been willing to accord it.

Another consideration that modern writers in education seem to have lost sight of is the responsibility of the school for the training of good listeners. The American public is increasingly subjected to influence through radio address. A recent editorial in one of our more thoughtful weekly journals laments the fact that the present tendency of the government, from the President down, has been to resort to the radio as a means of appeal for public approval. It has become a widespread device of the advertiser and the politician. The editorial raises the timely inquiry as to what the significance of this may be, since people have been taught to show some discrimination when reading press material but they do not as yet have the ability to listen critically. One writer has said, "Training in the art of listening is therefore an important part of exposition." While student reports, debates, etc., can be used effectively for this purpose, the teacher may well ask what part he should assume in personal example. Whatever the emphasis given to this phase of the problem, which should probably not be overstressed, the lecture in its broader meaning cannot safely be eliminated as an educational method. It has its peculiar values that should not be ignored. In general, it may be agreed that the lecture should never be used extensively at the secondary level.

2. What Is Desirable Technique of the Lecture?

When to use the lecture

It is never possible to say with positiveness just when one method should be used in preference to another. The extreme protagonists of the various methods often see little place for any method other than their own, and individual teachers show wide variation in their ability to handle different methods. Some teachers who are most effective with the "project" have little ability to use the lecture. Conditions in specific classroom situations bear definitely upon the value of a given method at a given time.

Laying these considerations aside, some general suggestions may be offered to guide the teacher in the use of the lecture:

1. When information can be given through the lecture more effectively than through any other means, both with respect to the learner's understanding and to the retention and the economy of time and effort involved, it should be used. If learning through the use of the lecture is just as effective for the purpose required, then there is little object in the acquisition of necessary informa-

tion by more laborious means. The time thus saved can be utilized to advantage in other ways. The use of the lecture-demonstration method is a case in point. If information is the purpose of teaching science, then it is a waste of time and money to work in the laboratory to learn imperfectly in two or three hours what may be gained in one when the teacher demonstrates his lecture. Experimental research has shown quite conclusively the relative merits of lecture-demonstration over the laboratory method.

2. Whenever the teacher has available desirable data, not easily obtainable by the class, common sense would dictate the obligation on his part of presenting this to the class in the most effective manner possible. Some form of the lecture would normally appear to be the technique to employ. It is assumed that adequately trained high school teachers have a much more intensive training in the subject-matter fields than is available to the student through the limited resources of the average school library. Further, the general cultural background in related fields or in the social experience of the teacher ought to provide a wealth of data available to the students only through some process of telling or exposition.

3. When the time comes to introduce a new topic or unit, or to conclude the same, an introduction or summary carefully prepared by the teacher can be most valuable. In general, some form of the lecture should be employed, even though it be supplemental to the class summary of a segment of work completed. In the case of some topics or units, when little connection exists with the immediate past, the lecture is the only effective way to properly provide an apperceptive basis for the new work.

4. Where a proper mind-set towards a phase of work is desired, or where general enthusiasm is to be aroused, there is no substitute for the alert, dynamic teacher who, by an interesting narrative or incident, can inspire the class with eager joy and curiosity. This is one of the very effective uses of the lecture; also, it is one of the most difficult to pigeonhole and say "use here — and here." The teacher must often be sensitive to the mood of the class. The writer recalls a teacher in a very difficult subject who seemed to have the knack of sensing when the class was most discouraged. He always brought the class back to a state of enthusiasm for the course just when all felt ready to admit defeat. Sometimes it was accomplished through a story, some challenging thing about the subject, or just through the buoyancy of his attitude toward the subject.

Preparation of the lecture

As in every other teaching method, the care given to the preparation of the lecture determines in no small measure its success. There are definite considerations entering into the preparation of the lecture that demand more careful preparation than do other forms of teaching, since major responsibility throughout rests squarely upon the teacher.

1. *Lecture preparation and lesson planning hold much in common.* One writer has asserted the lecture to be "nothing more than a topical recitation by the teacher." This is not strictly true. The psychology of the two situations is vastly different, and the technique required in the lecture is at points sharply divergent from that demanded of the recitation. Many aspects of preparation for the two, however, are similar, as is true in respect to every method. The lecture, as said of the daily lesson plan, is essentially an experience in anticipatory teaching, and as such must reflect the characteristics of anticipation required in the preparation of any good lesson.[1] The lecturer must visualize the next day's situation and with that definite picture in mind prepare the lecture. The laws of learning that govern lesson planning must be recognized in the preparation of the lecture.

2. *Preparation must keep objectives clearly in mind.* This, it would seem, requires no extended discussion here. The objectives of education and the particular objective of the lecture should be clear to the teacher. The issue or problem of the lecture must be kept obvious to the class at every step in the lecture.

3. *The lecture must be clearly outlined.* The teacher should guard this phase of the preparation with unusual care. Upon it depends much of the success of the lecture. Where telling is the mode used, the artistry of hiding the outline from the class is desirable when emotional reactions and appreciations are the results desired. When exposition is the method employed to clarify an issue or develop the stages in the solution of a problem, then it is important that the outline steps should stand out clearly.

4. *All pertinent illustrative devices should be carefully prepared.* It is not safe to expect, on the inspiration of the moment, to find the exact illustration to fit a point in the lecture. The illustration has too many possibilities for misinterpretation to be used without the utmost care in its selection. When concrete devices are employed,

[1] For discussion of anticipatory teaching see pp. 284–289.

every detail should be carefully prepared so that maximum class attention may be focused upon the idea illustrated, and not upon the devices employed.

5. *The lecture should capitalize the apperceptive experience of the class.* This should be done in the selection of the illustrations, in adapting the lecture as far as possible to the known interests of the class and to the level of experience the students represent. The extended discussion of apperception in relation to lesson planning should be reread at this point.

6. *When the lecture is expository in nature, the general principles of induction-deduction should be used.* The wise teacher will make every possible adaptation of these development procedures to the principle of psychological approach. The logical procedures cannot be ignored as a technique of problem solving, although they may be robbed by the ingenious teacher of some of their deadening formalism if combined with a psychological approach. For all practical purposes, preparation for exposition may well follow some adaptations of the general outline of induction made famous by the Americanized Herbartian "Five Formal Steps," namely:

a. Preparation. This has a twofold function: (1) To present clearly to the student the purpose of the lesson — if a problem, to define clearly what is the nature of the problem and the purpose of the attack upon it. (2) To bring into perspective whatever experience the student may have that will aid him in understanding. It may be necessary to build up a proper apperceptive basis before an attack on the problem can be made.

b. Presentation. Here the data germane to the problem are made available to the student.

c. Comparison — abstraction. At this point the data are carefully compared and analyzed to show relationships that can subsequently be used to discover implications.

d. Generalization. Here the elements of similarity and dissimilarity are brought together to enable definite implications to be adduced, and from these, more inclusive conclusions can be drawn about the issue or problem under consideration.

e. Application. Here the conclusions are applied to various situations to make clear the significance of the conclusions previously reached. The last step is in reality deduction.

7. *Where the lecture involves narration or description, simple clarity and interest are the features preparation must seek to as-*

sure. The simple facts of narration or description must be so well in hand and so coordinated as to present continuity and arouse interest. Many devices are available to the narrator to create the interest factor, and these should be carefully studied in advance and the appropriate ones chosen to meet the needs of the occasion. Story telling is an art, and the price of effectiveness in any of its phases is painstaking preparation.

Procedures in effective lecture technique

Much has been written on the artistry of the lecture. It is an art the good teacher should covet. The procedures in its use are varied and complex. In spite of the best preparation, no teacher can adequately anticipate the exact procedures to follow. Some general suggestions can be offered, however, to guide the teacher in effective lecture technique. These must be adapted to the peculiar type of lecture employed, its purposes, and its length. For use in the secondary school no better list of suggestions seems more appropriate than the one given by Douglass,[2] and reproduced here.

1. Where talks are to consume more than a few minutes, they should be outlined and clearly thought through. Impromptu talks, like impromptu teaching, are apt to be loosely organized and ineffective.

2. Illustrations should be provided, if practical, in the way of charts and diagrams.

3. Begin, if possible, by arousing in the minds of the class a problem, a question upon which you propose to throw light.

4. As much as possible, keep the class in a problematic and expectant attitude. Point out problems and questions along the way.

5. Be careful as to pace. Speakers generally talk too rapidly. Allow time for thought — for mental supplementation. Adjust pace to difficulties of the material presented and to the ability of the class to take notes, if notes should be taken.

6. Occasionally check up on your audience to see that it is following you. Be careful not to fall into the fallacy of assuming that what you say is as clear to your hearers as it is to you.

7. Use interested, earnest conversational tones and a personal con-

[2] Douglass, Harl R. *Modern Methods in High School Teaching*, pp. 9–10. Boston: Houghton Mifflin Company, 1926. For an elaborated list of these suggestions see Douglass, Harl R. and Mills, Hubert H. *Teaching in High School*, pp. 234–236. New York: The Ronald Press Company, 1948.

versational manner. Look into the face of your hearers and talk to your pupils; do not lecture to your class.

8. Pause occasionally for reactions. Break up the long stretches. Occasionally intersperse discussion.

9. On occasions it is wise to furnish the class with an outline of your talk in advance. This may be in the form of hectographed copies, or written on the blackboard. Outlines of this sort serve as a constant summary, and relieve the class of what may be a distraction — the note taking. A very good device to use when you are thoroughly familiar with what you expect to say, is to outline your talk on the board as you proceed.

10. Exhibit a sense of humor in some other way than using funny stories as illustrations. Phrase your remarks where possible in an attractive way. Do not be self-conscious and sensitive while you are talking. Beginning teachers are too inclined to regard all deviations from obvious attention as personal matters or affronts; experienced lecturers learn to regard such things objectively.

11. Cultivate a good time sense. The time usually seems much longer to your hearers than to you. Avoid digressions. They often serve as distractions rather than illustrations.

12. In some subjects pupils should be trained to take intelligent and useful notes. Illustrate occasionally by taking notes on your own talk on the board. Encourage the pupils to "write up" notes at the conclusion of the talk, and allow time for such an exercise. A good device is to permit students to work in pairs, or to consult each other while writing.

13. Hold your pupils definitely responsible for the content of talks and lectures.

14. Check what the pupils have learned from your talks, as a means of diagnosis and as an aid in remedial teaching. A short test at the close of the lecture, or at the beginning of the next period, may be used for this purpose, and may serve also as an inducement to careful attention.

3. What Additional Factors Contribute to the Success of the Lecture?

Teacher personality

Factors of teacher personality play an important part in the method, whatever its nature, but no method places greater values on certain phases of teacher personality than does the lecture. A good voice is essential for effective speaking. It should be well-modulated, resonant, colorful, and vigorous. A monotonous voice lacks stimulation and does not have the power to arouse interest. Good enunciation is essential to understanding. Students should be able to hear words clearly and distinctly. Teachers with vocal peculiarities should use the lecture sparingly. Seldom, if ever, should they attempt extended telling. Most teachers can overcome the majority of these limitations through constant effort. Teachers would do well to take a course or two in public speaking while in the training school. Since teachers generally have public responsibilities, such training would aid them both in and out of the classroom.

The manner of the teacher while speaking has much to do with the effect of the lecture. Teachers who know how to smile while speaking, how to avoid an overseriousness about the subject, and who have a sympathetic, pleasing, engaging manner, will find the students eager to listen. The teacher must appear enthusiastic, though not overeffusive, about the topic discussed. The lecture must be given an importance by the eager manner of the teacher. The student will be inclined to take his cue of values from the manner of the teacher while discussing the subject. The art of the speaker should be carefully studied, and wise use made of the devices that create and sustain interest. Usually the teacher should stand before the class and in poised, animated, conversational style, talk directly to the students. Looking at the ceiling or out of the window does not enable the teacher to strike fire with the students. He should look directly at the students, for the eyes have a peculiar power to transmit the mood of the teacher to the pupil. Too, the facial expression of the student should be most revealing to the teacher as a barometer of the student's interest and understanding.

Responsibility of the teacher in the lecture

In a peculiar sense, the teacher occupies a very responsible position before the class when the lecture is used. More than is true in other methods, the teacher guides, if not determines, the thought of the student. The latter, however, the teacher should make every effort to avoid, except where appreciation or emotional sets are the objects sought. Nevertheless, it is exceedingly difficult to avoid tingeing the lecture with the coloring of one's own thought. This the bright students are quick to detect. Usually the favorable position of the teacher in the eyes of the student tends to prejudice the mind of the student in favor of the teacher's attitude or point of view. Where exposition with some conclusion is involved, the teacher has a real opportunity to present a case, so that debatable issues are approached with a tentative attitude, or, at least, so that the possibilities of other conclusions are frankly recognized. This approach is particularly important in social-science fields.

An admirable case in point was observed in a class in economics conducted by a student teacher. The class discussion revealed considerable confusion as to the implications of certain theories of taxation. The teacher undertook to set forth the basic ideas of each theory, such as the single tax, sales tax, income tax, etc., with the claims of each for popular support. A very searching analysis was made, and the strong and weak features of each were given. The observer watched carefully to detect any personal bias in the exposition, and went from the class with a sense of the clearest, most succinctly given and well-balanced exposition of each theory he had ever listened to. Only by an indirection not available to the class was it possible even to suspect which theory met the favor of the teacher. While there is some debate as to the legitimacy of propagandizing in the school, it is certainly contrary to a democratic theory of education to attempt to influence student thought on matters of debatable policy. The teacher in American schools carries the major responsibility, then, of conducting the exposition type of lecture in such a manner as to challenge thought, but, where conclusions cannot be accepted as final, of refusing to reveal to the class a personal commitment to any one conclusion.

Under the lecture technique the teacher carries almost solely the responsibility for motivation. In other methods it can be assumed that, with a proper mind-set established, much of the motivation of the class can come through subsequent activities or sheer interest in the text materials. Not so the lecture. Throughout, student interest depends largely upon the teacher. The manner in which the subject is presented determines, quite as much as the nature of the subject, what the reaction of the class will be.

Again, the ability of the class to gain maximum value from the lecture depends upon the way it is handled. If very carefully organized, so that main points and subsidiary ones are easily recognized as logical in sequence, it will be comparatively easy for the student to follow. If the teacher uses the blackboard to outline the main points and important subpoints, note taking as well as understanding will be facilitated. The teacher should seldom, if ever, expect the student to carry in mind the development of his thought. Too, the teacher can utilize this form of blackboard outline to teach the class correct methods of organizing class notes.

To safeguard against difficulties of comprehension the teacher should have recourse to at least two approaches.

First, where careful analysis of the problem indicates more than usual difficulty, special care should be taken to insure understanding. Repetition, approach from another angle of thought, and special emphasis upon that particular phase of the lecture, may serve to eliminate confusion.

The *second* very important agency for the removal of centers of difficulty is the wise use of verbal and concrete illustration. Often a parallel situation more easily understood may serve for comparative study. Where the lecture involves exposition of complicated relationship, as in mechanical fields, miniature devices, such as a model steam engine cut down the middle to show the steam channels, valves, etc., can be most helpful. The teacher should make large use of verbal and concrete illustration in the lecture, not alone to illuminate difficult points, but to add to the interest of the lecture generally. An abstract lecture at the adolescent level is almost always doomed to failure.

QUESTIONS AND PROBLEMS

1. What are the distinguishing characteristics of the lecture?
2. Give the reasons why educators have discouraged the lecture method in secondary education.
3. When can the lecture be used to the best advantage?
4. What are the chief weaknesses attributed to the lecture method and how may they be eliminated?
5. What are the essential elements in the lecture technique?
6. If you were preparing a lecture, what procedure would you use to help insure its being an educational success?
7. Have the class check one or two lectures given in the assembly or community by some visiting speaker. Compare the points of agreement and disagreement with respect to the understanding of what the speaker said.
8. What traits should a teacher possess to make the lecture method an educational success?
9. How may you determine whether or not your lecture is a success?
10. What are the teacher's responsibilities when using the lecture technique in a classroom?

SELECTED BIBLIOGRAPHY

Douglass, Harl R. and Mills, Hubert H. *Teaching in High Schools,* chapter XII. New York: The Ronald Press Company, 1948.

Goetting, M. L. *Teaching in the Secondary School,* chapter VIII. New York: Prentice-Hall, Inc., 1942.

Ise, John. "The Lecture System," *The Education Digest,* 8:8–10, (February, 1943). •

Jayne, Clarence D. "Teaching by Lecture and Silent Film," *The Education Digest,* 10:24–25 (January, 1945).

Mursell, James L. *Successful Teaching,* pp. 21–22, 172–173. New York: McGraw-Hill Book Company, Inc., 1946.

Muse, Maude B. *Guiding Learning Experiences,* chapter X. New York: The Macmillan Company, 1950.

Risk, T. M. *Principles and Practices of Teaching in Secondary Schools,* Second Edition, pp. 378–385. New York: American Book Company, 1947.

Stiles, Lindley J. and Dorsey, Mattie F. *Democratic Teaching in Secondary Schools,* pp. 80–82. Chicago: J. B. Lippincott Company, 1950.

Wesley, Edgar B. *Teaching in Social Studies,* chapter XXVII. Boston: D. C. Heath and Company, 1942.

6

How Can Socialized Class Procedures Be Used?

1. How Is Concept of Recitation Changing?

The recitation in transition

An arresting book has been published entitled, *The Passing of the Recitation*.[1] The title of this book, as well as the tenor of the author's comments, suggests that the time-honored recitation is soon to be numbered among our educational relics. A further indication of the way the educational wind is blowing is found in the tendency of recent writers of general textbooks in secondary methods to omit chapters on the recitation. They confine their attention to the socialized recitation, or they word the heading of the chapter so as to imply no relationship between the procedures discussed and the older recitation method. Some educators have become so antagonistic to the idea of the recitation that they find no place for it in modern theories of method.

The older views of the recitation

From time immemorial "lesson hearing" has been a prominent characteristic of the recitation. From the catechetical schools of the early Christian era until recent times, "lesson hearing" in some form has characterized much of educational procedure. Until the

---

[1] Thayer, V. T. *The Passing of the Recitation*. Boston: D. C. Heath and Company, 1928.

149

turn of the century, the "lesson hearing" recitation and the lecture divided honors as the two principal methods of instruction. "Lesson hearing" implies that the teacher listens to the parrotlike repetition of an assigned quantity of factual materials, committed to memory by the student. The form this process has followed has been a question-and-answer procedure. Often the paragraph heading given in the older textbooks in bold type was read and then the student was asked to recite on this paragraph. The student was expected to repeat from memory, as fully as possible, the content of the paragraph.

An etymological study of the word recitation clearly indicates the connection between the "lesson hearing" procedure and the nomenclature historically associated with it. Citation means "the act of quoting or citing a passage from a book, or the words of another; enumeration." The technical use of the word in connection with legal procedures where the law is cited conforms to its simple meaning. "Re" means "back," "again." To be assigned material to learn and then give it back is exactly what the traditional recitation did. In more graphic if less elegant language, the recitation was but a regurgitation in the recitation period of facts, dates, and passages committed to memory. The things memorized may have been understood or not — frequently not — but so long as the materials could be reproduced from memory the principal requirements of the recitation were met.

Newer view of the recitation

Among responsible writers in the field of secondary school methods the re-citation concept of the recitation has been *passé* for the past twenty-five years. Parker,[2] one of the two most influential writers on secondary school methods, as far back as 1915 criticized severely the older recitation practices, and made the following definite suggestions for a recitation of a different character:

> The common practice of using the class period for mere repetition of material learned in the textbooks is one of the most pernicious sources of waste and lack of interest to be found in schools. . . . Instead of such recitations the teacher should raise questions which keep the pupils actively thinking because they involve (1) interpretation,

[2] Parker, S. C. *Methods of Teaching in High Schools*, pp. 424–425. Boston: Ginn and Company, 1915.

(2) criticism, (3) supplementing, or (4) application along the lines studied in the assignment.

Such a conception of the recitation in practice sweeps away the objections raised against the "lesson hearing" idea of class procedure. This picture of the ideal recitation is quite in keeping with the best thought of present-day educators. Still another characterization of the recitation by a later writer will serve to show how completely the old ideas of the recitation have been rejected by those who have attempted to direct the thought of the newer generation of teachers over approximately a thirty-year period. Foster declared: [3]

> Discarding any thought of it as a mechanical repetition by the student of memorized facts or phrases, the recitation is taken as the rethinking in the class exercise of the experience of the student, acquired as a set exercise previously assigned by the teacher.

The ideas of the recitation held by these writers, neither of whom wrote later than thirty years ago, reveal how completely the traditional view of the recitation has been set aside for a newer conception that conforms in large measure to the demands of the most ardent critic of the old. Reflective thinking, cooperation, initiative and creative expression, interest and favorable attitudes toward school work and the ideals of social living, group responsibility and respect for individual differences, are all envisaged as the conception of the recitation maintained by these writers.

With such a modern conception of the recitation there is little disagreement. For a recitation technique based upon this point of view there is a large place in modern education. There is a place for this form of discussion and class evaluation of data used in problem-solving and unit procedures.

2. What Are the Techniques of the Recitation?

Purpose of the recitation

The statement of the newer view of the recitation sets forth in general the legitimate objectives attributed to the recitation. These objectives are not of equal value, and in the following list no

[3] Foster, H. H. *Principles of Teaching in Secondary Education*, p. 74. New York: Charles Scribner's Sons, 1921.

attempt has been made to enumerate them so as to suggest the relative importance of each.

1. To stimulate reflective thinking.
2. To stimulate interest in learning activities.
3. To fix in mind essential facts or ways of thinking.
4. To train the student in the technique of problem attack.
5. To supplement knowledge acquired or data necessary for understanding.
6. To train the student in the power of critical evaluation.
7. To guide the further study of the student.
8. To stimulate and develop creative expression.
9. To develop wholesome social attitudes.
10. To train the student in cooperative effort.
11. To train the student in the organization and expression of ideas.
12. To train the student to do group thinking.

Procedure in the recitation

No one procedure can be recommended for the conduct of the recitation. Rather, the plan adopted must vary widely with the subject and with the approach which the teacher, or the teacher and the class, may elect to make. There are some general suggestions that the teacher should observe, however, especially if the recitation occupies any considerable part of the class period. The beginning teacher, especially, should remember that practically every method that may be used will involve, at some point, elements of the lecture or the recitation. These phases may last for a few minutes as incidental to the major procedures employed, or, they may be the dominant mode of the hour. It is important, therefore, to recognize the flexible nature of the recitation and the manner of its conduct.

1. *Teacher directly responsible for the establishment of favorable attitudes.* Unless the teacher can win the interest and cooperation of the class in the beginning, the recitation must be judged by modern standards a failure. There are too many of the purposes of the recitation which cannot be achieved in an atmosphere other than that of keen interest and a ready spirit to enter wholeheartedly into the work of the hour. Interest and cooperation can be secured in a number of ways. A direct and effective procedure is to create a problematic situation in which students eagerly enter the search for the answer. Often a student can be induced to present some

item of interest to the class from his experience or from sources provided by the teacher. Sometimes a story or incident connected with the topic of the lesson, told by the teacher or by a class member, or a direct question from the teacher that challenges, may be all that is necessary. Visual aids in many subjects provide the desired materials to awaken interests or arouse curiosity. Favorable attitudes should be established both by means of the previous assignment and by the approach adopted by the teacher at the beginning of the class hour. An attitude of alert eagerness on the part of the teacher is likely to arouse a similar attitude in the class.

2. *The recitation should be well planned.* In the conduct of the recitation, movement from phase to phase should take place with precision and naturalness. This is necessary to keep the spirit of interest. Uncertainty and drag will kill any recitation. The vacillating teacher soon transmits to the alert student the uncertainty of his own mind. To the slowing up of the pace of the class must be added the distraction of attention from the main theme of the hour and the tendency to digression. As suggested in a previous chapter, the teacher should be sensitized to the needs and mood of the class and should be ready to throw aside the prepared work whenever the situation seems to make its continuance inadvisable. There are times when to proceed with the lesson, in the face of unexpected situations, is to achieve the undesired results the teacher sought to avoid.

3. *Discover the adequacy of the preparation of the class.* There is little value in continuing a discussion when there is little background for intelligent participation. When the preparation has been insufficient, immediate steps should be taken to correct the deficiencies. The teacher may supplement through a brief lecture; a student or students may be asked to contribute to the class needs from their better preparation; or, under some circumstances, it may seem desirable to refer the class to supplementary sources and let it make up its own deficiencies before the recitation continues.

4. *All should participate in discussion.* The attitude of the class should be such that all are eager to contribute something toward the common purpose of the class, whatever it may be for the day. The members of the class should be made to feel a genuine responsibility for the work of the period. Every effort should be put forth to draw the attention of the students away from the teacher and toward themselves as the agency of class success or failure. A

suggestion that certain data be the responsibility of particular individuals or groups of three or four is an effective way to get those
naturally reticent to participate. Some students are always ready
on the trigger and, unless devices are employed to correct their
tendency to monopolize the class time, others will resign the class
to them — if not physically, at least in spirit.

5. *Students should carry the major responsibility for participation.* The most frequent criticism of classroom procedure in the
recitation is of the tendency of the teacher to do the talking. The
effort to overcome this weakness may result in several desirable
class outcomes. The teacher tends to ask questions of broad searching significance which will require extended response, and provoke
a number of subsidiary questions and comments from the class.
This effort will, furthermore, focus the attention of the teacher on
those devices most likely to bring the student into the forefront.
To secure spontaneity and eagerness to participate, the student
must have his own classmates, rather than the teacher, in the center
of his consciousness; unless the teacher has that rare ability of making the student forget the traditional teacher-student relationship
and accept the teacher as one of the group.

6. *Encourage students to talk to each other.* The criticism hurled
at the recitation as individualistic, rather than social in nature,
grows out of the tendency of the teacher to ask questions and
receive answers direct from the student. While this is necessary
and desirable in certain phases of the recitation, generally the best
educational ideals are achieved when students think of the teacher
as counselor and source of reference in discussion. The give-and-
take in the clash of opinion with their peers is a most wholesome
type of socialization. The student learns that different plausible
conclusions from the same data, are possible. Group evaluation of
data, and the attempt to arrive jointly at acceptable conclusions,
require a give and take in discussion, courtesy as an indispensable
means of group progress in thought, and open-mindedness toward
the ideas of others. When these conditions exist, many of the
defects of the recitation have been removed.

7. *Students' cooperation should be sought in the planning of the
recitation.* This can be done without adbication of the prerogatives
of the teacher to use his mature judgment in the determination
of the general nature of the course of study. Even the advocates of
full determination by students of the activities they are to engage
in, do not feel at liberty to defer completely to immaturity in such

matters. It has been unfortunate that the wholesale condemnation of teacher-determined curriculum has given the impression that the protagonists of a new education sponsor for students "free license to do as you please." Such a position, of course, would be educationally untenable. The degree to which the teacher encourages participation in planning must depend upon a number of factors. These have been discussed at length in earlier chapters, to which the class should refer.[4]

3. How Is the Recitation Being Modernized?

Thus far the traditional recitation has been considered in relation to those modifications in its purpose and conduct that make it conform to modern educational thinking. Its further modernization has, in fact, transformed the recitation into something beyond what it has conventionally been conceived to be. It is probably correct to speak of these more streamlined forms rather as types of socialized class procedures.

The great objective of the socialization of class procedures is to provide a classroom situation where normal socialization can take place. Thayer has indicated this [5] as one of the basic reasons for the emergence of the so-called socialized recitation. Tracing the development of our changing democratic ideal, he says:

> This conception of democracy as an organization which promotes cooperation on the basis of mutual recognition of interests, requires for its realization an educational program which aims directly at the socialization of the individual; and it requires the organization of the school in such a way that the child develops traits of initiative and responsibility within a group membership and in harmony with group interests.

Those elements of socialization necessary for successful participation in a democratic society are the qualities it is assumed the classroom should foster. "Training children for democracy by giving them training in democracy," is, one writer declares, the all-

---

[4] For practical suggestions concerning pupil cooperation in planning both in the immediate class situation and in the larger relationships of the school, see the following references: Giles, H. H. *Teacher-Pupil Planning*, New York: Harper and Brothers, 1941; *Group Planning in Education*, Washington, D.C.: Association for Supervision and Curriculum Development, 1945; *Planning and Working Together*, Bulletin No. 337. Lansing, Michigan: State of Michigan Department of Education, 1945; *Toward Better Teaching*, Washington, D.C.: Association for Supervision and Curriculum Development, 1949.

[5] Thayer, V. T., *op. cit.*, p. 219.

absorbing purpose of socialized class procedures. Cooperative endeavor is the keynote of the method. A sentiment of "oneness" in
the class enterprise is essential to its success. When this spirit
dominates the class, goodwill is an immediate by-product, with all
students working with a will. It is easy under these conditions to
establish effective student responsibility for the work of the group,
and also a sense of mutual interdependence. No longer will the
observer find present the attitude of antagonism between student
and teacher so characteristic of the old recitation and bitterly cen-
sured by its critics. Students, rather than holding themselves consciously aloof, will be wholeheartedly intent upon the issues under
consideration. In any socialized situation "thinking" will take place.
Initiative and creative activity will flow naturally from reflective
thought stimulated and encouraged under these conditions. There
must inevitably be the spirited, spontaneous easy give-and-take of
normal discussion. One has only to watch a group of adolescents,
or children for that matter, eagerly exchanging ideas within their
own informal groups to understand the socialization values sought
by the transfer of that general atmosphere to the classroom, where
the topics of discussion can be projected within definitely coordinated educational channels. The problem of the socialized class
procedure, in brief, is to capture and reproduce in the controlled
environs of the classroom the spirit spontaneously generated,
though often misdirected, within the out-of-school social situations
natural to adolescent youth. All that was set up as the ideal of the
recitation is envisaged here, and more.

Formal and socialized class procedures contrasted

A graphic way of presenting the differences between the ideas
that lie behind socialized procedures and the older traditional recitation is to offer in parallel columns the generally accepted characteristics of each. The characterization, with some modification,
might apply to several of the newer methods as well as to the
recitation. Then, too, the caution may again be offered that the
traditional picture of the formal recitation has nowhere been accepted by educational writers of the past twenty-five years, who
have given it a legitimate place in their repertoire of classroom
methods. They have rather emphasized for the recitation those
qualities attributed to socialized class procedures by the new school
of methods writers. The characteristics of the formal recitation,
therefore, have been outmoded in theory for nearly three decades,

but are still prevalent in classroom practice. It is an interesting commentary on the reluctance of lagging practice to keep pace with advancing educational theory.

CHART SHOWING CONTRAST BETWEEN SOCIALIZED CLASS PROCEDURES AND FORMAL RECITATION

Pupil

Socialized School Work	Formal School Work
Natural interests	Artificial interests
Natural activities	Unmotivated tasks
Critical attitude	Passive attitude
Social conduct	Non-social conduct
Effort	Strain
Thinking	Memorizing
Expressing thoughts	Reciting information
Independence	Dependence
Self-control	Imposed control
Cognizance of values	Ignorance of values

Teacher

Creating natural environment	Making artificial setting
Utilizing child activities	Imposing teacher purposes
Guiding natural activities	Dictating artificial tasks
Student with pupils	Teacher all wisdom
Interest primarily in children	Interest in subject matter
Attention on desirable ends	Attention on subject matter

The Education Process

Aim of social efficiency	Aim of unknown future readiness
Taking into account present needs	Consideration of possible future needs
Natural student environment	Formalized schoolroom environment
Normal adjustment	
Real life experiences	Formal learning
Normal natural activities	Artificial exposures
Reference books	Abnormal lifeless tasks
Subject matter as means	Textbooks
Including concomitant learning	Subject matter as end
Discussion	Emphasizing primary learning
Unification of effort	Recitation
Psychological order	Division of effort
Attitudes, skills, habits, knowledge	Logical order
	Subject matter, information, skills

4. What Are the Techniques of Socialized Class Procedures?

Types of socialized class procedures

There are many forms into which socialized class procedures have been cast. The previous discussion of the recitation has recognized the presence of a very elemental study-recite type of recitation procedure all too prevalent in practice. At the same time it was evident that educational leaders in the field of methodology for a generation past have advocated a form of the recitation designed to call forth a high degree of cooperative, creative thinking. This has been popularly known as the socialized recitation.

Efforts to create a more vital form of learning situation with the classroom as a starting point, have led to the development of many procedures that involve social interaction as groups grapple with critical problem-situations. These procedures are recognized as aspects of the forms of group behavior typical of democratic action, for which the youthful citizen should acquire requisite skills. At least five major types of such socialized class procedures are recognized. There are some not easily classified, and there are omissions of many variants of those described.

1. *Informal group discussion — pupil leader.* To develop leadership competencies so necessary in myriad situations within a democracy, alert teachers often have a pupil assume the place of the teacher before the class in charge of discussion activities. Where pupils have developed skill in discussion group leadership it serves the additional purpose of removing whatever hesitancy pupils may feel to express a point of view when the teacher leads the discussion. Peer leadership often provides for an easier development of a "we" feeling within the class group, so essential to a thoroughgoing give-and-take critical thinking experience.

The teacher who is a good leader of a group discussion often finds it difficult to manage this form of class procedure. Like so many skilled workmen, he may be an effective group discussion leader but lack the ability to help others develop these skills. However, it is an important aspect of modern teaching, since our democratic processes require competent leaders who can handle group considerations of many important problems that arise. It is not alone a matter of singling out the youth with marked leadership ability for special training; every citizen should be capable of competent group leadership in many smaller community or sub-community situations. Most important of all, every one should understand the rudiments of group processes and how to participate most effectively in group procedures.

To successfully conduct such a class the teacher must carefully plan with the pupil leader the general procedures of the class hour. The pupil should have clearly in mind the general steps the discussion should take if it is to develop any significant learning for the group. He must be prepared to meet contingencies that might arise in the group discussion. The wise, alert teacher will be ready with lead questions which will help keep the discussion on the track, or make sure important issues pertinent to the discussion are not overlooked.

2. *Formalized group discussion.* While visiting a high school in a distant city, the writer happened to step into a room where a young woman sat at the teacher's desk. A glance over the class revealed at the rear of the room a more mature young woman seated, quietly observing, and evidently very much interested in what took place. The class was engaged in a discussion of certain literary characters connected with the story just previously studied. There were reports on important phases of the production by members of the class. Following these reports two critics for the day came to the front of the class and commented upon the nature of the reports offered, with corrections of grammatical errors, style of presentation, and suggestions for improving their content. Other members of the class were then free to add their comments and enter into a discussion of the general subject of the lesson. Near the close of the hour, the lesson committee reported to the class the work for the next day, with the special responsibilities this committee had assigned various members in the preparation of the lesson. After their report the chairman for the day called for nominations for the chairmanship for the succeeding day. This was promptly settled by the class, according to correct parliamentary procedure. The chairman had timed the discussion to give just time for the routine of lesson assignment and election of the chairman before the bell rang at the end of the period. The teacher had participated only three or four times, and then only to ask questions that guided the students back into the main road when the discussion tended to wander into by-paths. On two or three occasions the chairman had appealed to the teacher for help on some moot point which the class obviously could not settle for lack of necessary

information, or which was apparently not covered in the lesson, or at least not understood by any one. In conversation with the teacher, following the class period, it was learned that the teacher sat with the committee on the program and worked out the lesson for next day in some detail. The students were encouraged to suggest ideas and plans, but the teacher knew before the class assembled exactly what was to be done during the hour as well as what the assignment was to be for the succeeding lesson.

There is a somewhat different kind of formalized discussion group procedure coming into popular adult use with which secondary school pupils should become familiar. It keeps the characteristics of the total group discussion but provides more highly specialized functions for certain members of the group. It is coming into extensive use in large conferences where the activities of small discussion groups, in a greater or lesser degree, contribute ultimately to the thinking of the total group.

This discussion group consists of a discussion leader, and in addition to the usual discussion participants, several resource members who represent special skills or specialized knowledge essential to the problem the group is discussing, and a recorder. It is the function of the leader to carry on the usual responsibilities of the good discussion leader. He must keep clearly in mind his leadership functions, which remain fundamentally the same in all forms of face-to-face group discussion. They are: (1) to aid the group select and define the problem or problems for discussion; (2) to maintain group morale; (3) to see that the discussion is kept keyed to the problem under consideration and not permitted to digress; (4) to maintain an atmosphere of fairness and insure that the democratic process is operative, so that all members of the group have an opportunity and are encouraged to participate, and that all aspects of the problem are fully explored; (5) at intervals to summarize or clarify the discussion when he senses confusion is likely; (6) to help the group arrive, where possible, at definite conclusions and determine such implementation as these conclusions imply.

It is assumed that all group participants have a background knowledge of the essential facts basic to the discussion. However, a feature of this form of discussion group is the presence of so-called experts or those who are especially familiar with the issues, facts, and skills important to the final resolution of aspects of the problem under discussion. These resource members are available to the leader or members of the group much as a library would be. They participate in the discussion, and volunteer from time to time those resource data the group may need for an intelligent solution of their problem.

The recorder is charged with the responsibility of recording the general direction of the discussion, pertinent facts brought out, and decisions made by the group. Should the leader or group wish to check back on the development of the discussion, to refresh memories of significant facts, arguments, or decisions made, the recorder is presumed to be ready at any time to provide such information.

More recently, as discussion groups have become more interested in the processes of group procedures, as well as in the pertinency of the discussions, another functionary has been added. He is known as the observer. There may be more than one observer. It is the business of the observer, who is particularly skilled in group processes — or "group dynamics" as it is now called — to study the processes of group interaction. At times, usually at the close of a discussion session, he helps the group "see itself as others see it." That is, he helps the members see the forces operative in the discussion to advance the group movement, to delay, or thwart movement, to force clarification of issues, and the like.

3. *"Panel" or "Round Table" discussions.* Over the radio it has become popular to broadcast "panel" or "round table" discussions of some vital and current problem of public interest. It has become a popular device of conferences, institutes, and workshop groups.

The teacher and pupils should understand clearly the differences between the "panel" or "round table" discussion technique in contradistinction with the face-to-face discussion group organizational forms previously considered. It is somewhat amusing at times to see a small group of fifteen or twenty decide to have a "panel" discussion by selecting, more or less at random, four or five of their number to participate. Obviously they wish to be up-to-date in the use of discussion devices without a knowledge of the specific function of the device.

The major function of the "panel" is to conserve the advantages of a discussion group in a large audience situation where the group size does not make practicable total group participation. In a sense it provides for the large group the benefits of vicarious participation in a discussion situation carried on by a few selected participants.

By the very nature of the discussion technique only a limited number can profitably engage in it. The processes of thinking must be such that while several minds bring out all the issues and important relevant facts, these must not be so profuse or unrelated as to greatly retard or inhibit logical progression of the discussion. When a group becomes too large for face-to-face discussion, the participants are likely to be limited to fragmentary, often disjointed, comments that distract from a progressive developmental sequence of ideas that move toward a satisfactory conclusion.

In setting up a "panel" or "round table" it is customary to select a small group of a half dozen or so members, representative of several points of view with respect to the problem under consideration, and each well qualified in background knowledge to make a contribution to the discussion. In large conferences it is the practice to select expert participants, unusually well prepared by experience and knowledge to make a contribution to group thinking. It is assumed that these discussants in the usual process of group discussion will bring out all of the salient facts and arguments pertinent to the problem. The audience thus vicariously shares in the "give-and-take" exploration of the problem that goes on in the progressive development of the panel discussion.

While there are modifications of the "panel" procedure as described above, it should be kept clearly in mind that the "panel" is a device by which the advantages of a small face-to-face discussion group is made available to a larger group situation where group size would make impractical face-to-face discussion. It is the function of the chairman to see that the problem is clearly stated and to keep the discussion going as in the small group. It is likewise important to understand that speech-making by participants in the panel is not a part of this procedure. The panel represents the free give-and-take of the usual small unrehearsed discussion group. For panel discussants to make formal speeches, long or short, is a violation of the purpose of the "panel."

4. *Symposium — lecture discussion.* These two discussion devices, while slightly different, are basically of the same mold. The "symposium discussion" differs from the "panel discussion" in that each of the participants is expected to present a well reasoned argument or point of view with respect to the problem being discussed. Each participant is presumed to present a somewhat different point of view. By this device the audience is expected to be confronted with the major points of difference and the supporting arguments

with reference to the problem under consideration. These presentations may vary from five to twenty minutes depending upon the number of participants and the length of the session, usually predetermined.

After the formal presentations it is customary to have audience participation either through questions or comments. Generally such questions or comments are directed at members of the symposium group. Consequently, the discussion takes place largely between members of the audience and individual members of the symposium group. Each symposium member is assumed to be an expert in his field, and his background of specialization to have recognized relevance to the problem being discussed. Possibly such radio programs as Town Hall of the Air would be fairly representative of the symposium discussion.

In planning such a discussion program it is important that the members of the symposium be selected with care to insure that a real difference of opinion exists between them. A visit some time ago to a highly advertised symposium discussion meeting proved very disappointing. A large, expectant audience came prepared for a lively clash of thinking on an important controversial problem. When the speakers were through it was obvious no clash of thinking worth-while had taken place. The last speaker, with a sense of embarrassment, suggested that he found himself in general agreement with his colleagues, therefore, saw no point in repeating what had already been said. With this statement he sat down. The efforts of the chairman to create a controversial situation failed. The audience quickly began to disperse; the purpose of the "symposium-discussion" meeting had fallen quite flat.

The "lecture-discussion" is conducted much as is the "symposium-discussion." One speaker with a twenty- to thirty-minute formal presentation is then subjected to questions and comment from the audience. The function of the "lecture-discussion" is sharply divergent from that of the "symposium-discussion." Here attention is called to one position quite fully explained. To the extent that the lecture involved a controversial issue the focus of attention is upon the nature of the position held and the cogency of the argument presented. Often such a lecture is not controversial but explanatory or the presentation of an interesting thesis. Consequently, the questions and observations from the audience are essentially keyed to gain a better understanding of the speaker's ideas.

There is much to be said for this form of group procedure. The problem of semantics is increasingly being recognized as a primary barrier to understanding. The opportunity for the audience to raise questions often reveals serious misunderstandings of the point of view of the speaker, and the need for amplification or correction. Not long ago the writer was speaking to a luncheon group of businessmen on the "Core Curriculum." As we left the luncheon a graduate student who had gone to the luncheon remarked that after the luncheon the man seated next to him had commented: "I am not sure I understood what the Doctor was talking about. He frequently used a word I am not sure about. Do you spell that word "C-o-r-e" or "C-o-r-p-s"? Obviously the lecture was wasted as far as that businessman was concerned.

5. *Institutional forms of socialized procedures.* It has become popular to cast the class or group activity into one of the many forms of social organizations that exist in the community. Setting up civic patterns, such as city councils, legislative assemblies, party conventions, courts, and lesser organizational groups, to demonstrate procedures and get the feel of our democratic institutions at work is worth while.

Once a social science instructor invited the writer to visit a moot court then in session in his high school classroom. The court sat for several days. The jury had already been sworn in and the taking of testimony was in progress. It was a most pleasant and profitable hour. Interest was intense — so much so that many students in related courses who had study hall at this period had been permitted to attend. To provide a proper audience-situation for critical study of the procedures, the opposing sides had kept an air of secrecy about some of their witnesses and the development of their cases. The class had studied briefly the general theory and organization of legal jurisprudence. Those members who participated actively as judge, counsel, bailiff, and jury foreman had consulted legal talent, and were unusually well versed in the simpler aspects of court procedure. This experiment dramatized the place of our courts and legal machinery in a democratic society as no amount of reading could have done.

It is a common expedient in social science classes, during the excitement of presidential elections, to set up mock nominating conventions. Often these have been broadened out into an after-school-hours event to permit the entire student body, and even their parents, to attend. When general interest is aroused, as in an election period, it is easy to generate intense interest in rather un-usually difficult forms of class organization. On occasion such spec-tacular organizational forms may be warranted on the larger grounds of general school morale, even if the classroom values might not wholly justify it.

Usually the less involved types of social organization are em-ployed. An English class in journalism may set up a newspaper staff organization. This is flexible and permits easy adjustment to the needs of the class. Literary clubs, or even simple reading of parts of plays by students, may produce much of the dramatic effect without elaborate organization. The use of simple parliamen-tary forms with only a chairman to referee discussion is very effec-tive. Debating clubs and even temporary debate procedures are frequently employed with great success. At the junior high school level, students may be encouraged to organize into simple com-petitive groups, choosing sides with leaders and checkers to keep scores, while the teacher, or some member of the group, announces the drill exercises. The plan is useful whether a quick recall of important arithmetical processes, spelling, necessary applications of correct usage in English, or other data are the objectives in question. This device is simple and, if properly motivated, effective. The effective use of variations of this plan has been observed fre-quently.

Certain principles to be remembered

A *first principle* of all formal types of organization is to cast the form of organization in as simple a mold as possible. In an effort to get creaky machinery to work smoothly, it is easy to get lost in the web of complicated machinery, with consequent loss of valuable time. Furthermore, there is ever increasing danger that, as the complexity of organizational machinery increases, the atten-tion of the class will be diverted from its primary objective to the novelty of the machinery itself. One of the dangers of all organiza-tional efforts to gain facility in the attainment of desired goals is just this tendency to become involved in the meshes of complicated machinery. Teachers who desire to use the formal type of recita-tion will be surprised at the variety of simple forms such organiza-tion may take.

A *second principle* of conducting the formal-type class is that the form employed should be adapted to the needs of the group. It is questionable whether the formal class organization will facilitate every need of the class. In many situations no doubt formal organization hinders rather than helps. The teacher must be guided in the selection of form by several considerations.

1. Does the form truly exemplify the ideas the lesson is to convey to the student? Obviously the moot court can be valuable only as it reveals principles of legal justice of the type common to local civic needs. Imitations of Supreme Courts, etc., are not valuable forms of training. To apply a literary organizational form to science classes would be clearly non-applicable to the needs of the subject.

2. Classroom situations differ widely, and the form that would apply to one would be ill-advised in another. Often the level of ability of a class will be the determining factor in the selection of the form the activity should take. Experienced teachers can visualize classrooms in social science where an attempt to hold a moot court would be doomed to failure at the start, because of the lack of students qualified to act the parts adequately. Again, a highly involved legislative assembly, with many committees, etc., is out of place in a class of ten or fifteen students. Since the smaller high schools average very limited class enrollments, a corresponding limitation is placed upon their use of a number of the more spectacular forms.

3. The acquaintance of students with community organizational activities will play no small part in the wise selection of the device. Unless the device contains within itself some of the elements of learning desired, instruction in its use may be a waste of valuable time. Particularly is this true when there are available other forms for class organization which are so familiar to the student that no time need be wasted in showing pupils how the device is to function.

4. There are some phases of learning that it is highly desirable for the teacher to guide. Where the teacher, for example, has the resources not available to the class, it would be most wasteful to coach certain members of the class for the sake of full student control of the class hour.

A *third principle* of organization would dictate that organizational officers should be few, and that they should be changed frequently. This is highly desirable, and for much the same reason pretentious organizations should be shunned. The policy of using only the officers who will actually contribute to the smooth operation of the form of recitation employed enables the teacher to give more concentrated attention to the few. No plan will operate of itself. Students must be guided and encouraged constantly. The teacher who can focus attention and effort upon the work of a few student leaders at one time will be able to secure a better quality of work than when attention must be dissipated over a wider area. Since the purpose of institutionalized procedures is to democratize educational consciousness on the part of the students, it is also necessary to avoid any idea of monopolies on the part of favorite students. Moreover, the training in group leadership, while something of a by-product, is an important value of this form of procedure. No rule of thumb suggestion can be offered to govern the frequency of change in class leadership. The nature of the procedural form employed must determine in part the frequency of rotation of responsibility. Some forms would have their effectiveness destroyed or seriously marred by "swapping horses in midstream." A moot court would be a good example in point. The size of the class and the consequent opportunity for participation in responsible positions must be a factor considered. Smaller classes need not change as often as large ones.

A *fourth principle* is that the teacher maintain a vital control of the class as guide and counselor, even though visible control at times be delegated. This will assert itself in at least two important directions.

First, when the plan to be used and the students to be chosen as leaders must be decided, the teacher should quietly though firmly keep a steady hand on the "ark" lest it founder. The adroit teacher, however, will exercise control with a minimum of obviousness to the class. Students are easily carried away in their enthusiasm for the spectacular forms which may be wholly unsuited to the immediate educational purpose; or, the form favored by the students may be impossible because of inadequate facilities or personnel. The teacher may well suggest to the class a form he thinks appropriate to use. A teacher with personality usually can win the students to wholehearted acceptance of the idea he favors. Later, the teacher may welcome suggestions from the students, and depend upon his ability to lead them to see the impracticality or dubious wisdom of using certain forms. In the last resort the teacher should not shrink from the exercises of a firm but kindly veto power where it is evident the proposed plans will defeat the purpose for which they are intended. The selection of the personnel to direct the new plan is of equal importance. To allow some students to be selected by their confreres for key positions for which they are manifestly unfit, can seldom be justified. In the initial use of institutionalized procedures, the teacher should exercise considerable authority when it is necessary to insure efficient leadership. If the teacher tacitly assumes this power, there will be little question raised on the part of the class. The maxim, "Delegation of power as students evince ability and disposition to use it wisely" should guide the teacher in the degree of self-determination allowed.

Second, the direction in which this principle will assert itself will be in the relationship of the teacher to the class while the form adopted is executed. The teacher needs to keep certain factors of the larger teacher-student relationship clearly in mind. He cannot be true to his position and abdicate his leadership of the class. He represents mature wisdom and technical training in the midst of immaturity and need for guidance. The attitude of some teachers that socialized procedures means freedom of the students to manage the class largely without close supervision is educationally untenable. The teacher is always responsible for the success of the educational processes that take place. Thus the rôle of guide and counselor must be aggressive and positive, not insipid and negative. He should have his finger on all planning of committees, and have some assurance of the significance of their recommendations. He must refrain from such domination as to make students "rubber stamps" of the teacher. Genuine planning should belong to the students. The teacher should content himself with questions that stimulate the students to creative activity, and as far as possible he should use questions that lead students to a searching evaluation of their tentative conclusions which will enable them to locate weaknesses and rectify them. The power of absolute veto must be the teacher's prerogative, though the resourceful teacher will function in the rôle of guide and counselor without resort to it, except on rare occasion.

A final word of caution needs to be added lest the too-enthusiastic teacher accept the form as identical with the spirit it is supposed to generate. There is no assurance that the adoption of the mechanics of institutionalized procedures will eventuate in a democratic consciousness and cooperative spirit among the students.

Without a spirit of socialization permeating it, a formal procedure can be, of all things, most lifeless. Let the teacher never for a moment forget that devices are but means to an end, and never in themselves guarantee the end's being realized. The writer has observed some formal situations that could scarcely be exceeded in lifelessness by the traditional recitation at its worst.

Conduct of the informal class procedure

There is more of the natural in the informal class. No pretentious machinery is set up, and one visiting an informal class procedure might easily identify it with the traditonal form. The teacher may be in front of the room asking questions and the pupils answering them. This all-important difference between the traditional and the socialized informal class would be noted by the discerning observer, however: the socialized class would be alert, eagerly asking as well as answering questions, and more often directing these to each other than to the teacher. An exhilarating atmosphere of interest and a keen exchange of verbal blows, as ideas clash in the search for truth, would be in evidence. A complete lack of a sense of teacher compulsion or teacher restraint would characterize the proceedings. In fact, a thoughtful visitor would not fail to notice a group consciousness, and an acceptance of the teacher as one of the group, not characteristic of the traditional recitation where the teacher asked the questions and the pupils answered directly to the teacher.

It is not easy at all times to detect just when a truly socialized class procedure is in progress. The transition from the teacher domination to the consciousness of "we-ness," referred to as a distinguishing characteristic of the socialized class procedure, is so gradual and the twilight zone between the two so attenuated that it is not always easy to say "this is," or, "is not" a socialized class. Nor should the teacher be greatly concerned when this twilight zone is reached. A class that can be guided into such a condition is not "far from the kingdom." It will sooner or later, probably sooner, come into the full possession of this coveted spirit. For, as has been said repeatedly, the socialized recitation is not a matter of mechanics but of spirit, and no amount of mechanization can be substituted for it.

Let us hasten to say, however, that mechanics can be of inestimable value in the hands of a skilled teacher in unlocking the gates that will release the spirit. To put it in another way, there are very well-understood techniques which more naturally create conditions that induce the spirit sought. In the use of some of these the teacher should develop skill. One of the first suggestions involves the physical aspects of class seating. As will be suggested in Chapter 17 on "How Can the Learning Environment be Improved?" the common seating arrangements found in schoolrooms is a flareback to an older theory of education, which conceived of the student as an open vessel into which might be poured the golden wisdom possessed by the teacher. Thus the student faced the teacher. The traditional recitation necessitated the same seating arrangement since the teacher remained the center of attention, and the question-answer procedure was between teacher and student. To accentuate the centrality of the teacher in the psychology of the classroom situation, often a raised dais was provided him. To eliminate the teacher as far as possible as central in the student consciousness, it is good psychology to arrange the students in a circle or around tables, when the class is small enough, with the teacher seated in the circle. While the teacher retains definite leadership of the class in this informal arrangement he is not set apart from the students, but assumes a position of "oneness" or "we-ness" with the group. The teacher is no more in the class than any other member. This leads to a forgetfulness of the dominance of the teacher, and to an easy give and take discussion within the group.

In large classes, of course, this seminar or discussion-group plan of seating arrangement is not generally feasible. The teacher must then depend upon his personality, with a few devices from his bag of tricks to create the desirable atmosphere. An unassuming, eager, buoyant manner may be contagious, leading students to forget the teacher in the all-absorbing question or problem before them. The teacher must develop the delicate power of asking questions or creating situations that draw out the student and eventuate in a ready clash of opinion or search for facts which become so absorbing that the teacher ceases to become focal in class consciousness. Another approach is through a student report so staged as to draw out questions and arouse discussion. The discussion form is one of the simplest and most adaptable means of socializing the class activity.

Group dynamics

Basic to all that has been considered in the socialization of class procedures has been the recognition of the need for increased competency of individuals and groups to function collectively in our democratic society. Democracy is dependent upon the intelligent effectiveness of group action and reaction. These competencies do not just occur. The school must provide the necessary environment and teach youth the social skills necessary to make democracy as a way of life work. The discharge of this responsibility on the part of the school is facilitated in part by organizational devices discussed above. Important though they are, these alone are not enough.

In a large degree the development of such skills is made possible by careful study and understanding of those subtle nuances of individual and group relationships that make group processes tick. This effort to discover what these processes are that govern member interaction within the group is now known as *group dynamics*. Within the past ten years, particularly, intensive study and research have been made into those interactive personality forces that make for successful group action, or tend to frustrate and paralyze it. The teacher will do well to acquaint himself with the findings of this rapidly growing field: the nature of the complex interactions within the group and how these may be influenced, and the instruments, such as sociometry and sociodrama, that are available to the teacher with which to guide pupils into more vital group activity.

QUESTIONS AND PROBLEMS

1. Explain the old and new meanings applied to the term "recitation." In what ways do the older and newer uses of the term "recitation" differ?
2. Have a group discussion on the relative merits of the "recitation" as an educational method.
3. Have a "panel" discussion of the values of a teacher-led versus a pupil-led class discussion.
4. Have the members of the class recall both a "good" and a "poor" recitation in which they participated as individuals while in high school, and write up descriptions of each with the reasons why they judged each to be good or bad.

5. Have a class discussion on the question: "Why are socialized class procedures more in harmony with the needs of democracy than the traditional recitation procedures?"

6. In one class period have a member of the class describe the nature and use of the "sociogram" in not more than thirty minutes and then have the remainder of the period devoted to questions, with a recorder keeping a record of who participated and how often. Have another recorder keep a record of the questions asked. If possible, have the question period tape-recorded. During the next class hour have the class discuss their experience as an example of the "lecture-discussion" procedure.

7. In a "symposium-discussion" procedure have three or four of the students present the advantages of several socialized class procedures.

8. In what ways does the leadership responsibility of the teacher change from the use of the face-to-face discussion class and the institutionalized group procedure?

9. What factors must be considered by the teacher in planning and conducting the informal socialized class procedure?

10. What factors should be considered in determining the type of socialized class procedure to be used to the best advantage in a classroom?

11. After a class discussion of the meaning of sociodrama have a section of the class demonstrate the principles of sociodrama as an audience situation.

12. A single, or series of class discussion situations with the secret aid of a few members of the class might be set up to demonstrate to the class the principles of group dynamics.

SELECTED BIBLIOGRAPHY

Auer, J. J. and Ewbank, H. L. *Handbook for Discussion Leaders.* New York: Harper and Brothers, 1947.

Bales, Robert F. *Interaction Process Analysis.* Cambridge, Mass.: Addison-Wesley Press, Inc., 1950.

Bradford, Leland P. and French, John R. P., Jr. (Editors), "The Dynamics of the Discussion Group," *The Journal of Social Issues,* vol. 4, No. 2 (Spring, 1948).

Burton, William H. *The Guidance of Learning Activities,* chapter XIII. New York: Appleton-Century-Crofts, Inc., 1944.

Cooper, A. M. *How to Conduct Conferences.* New York: McGraw-Hill Book Company, Inc., 1942.

Dale, Edgar and Raths, Louis. "Discussion in the Secondary Schools," *Educational Research Bulletin,* 24: 1–6 (January 17, 1947).

Douglass, Harl R. and Mills, Hubert H. *Teaching in High School,* chapter X. New York: The Ronald Press Company, 1948.

Educator's Washington Dispatch, *Two Lessons of Group Dynamics.* New York: The Publisher, 1948.

Elliott, Harrison S. *Process of Group Thinking.* New York: Association Press, 1932.

Goetting, M. L. *Teaching in the Secondary School,* pp. 161–166, 174–178. New York: Prentice-Hall, Inc., 1942.

Haiman, Franklyn S. *Group Leadership and Democratic Action.* Boston: Houghton Mifflin Company, 1951.

Jennings, Helen H. *Sociometry in Group Relations.* Washington, D.C.: American Council of Education, 1948.

Konopka, Gisela. *Therapeutic Group Work with Children.* Minneapolis: University of Minnesota Press, 1949.

Maaske, R. J. "Symposium Method in High School Teaching," *School Review,* 57: 217–222 (April, 1949).

Muse, Maude B. *Guiding Learning Experience,* chapters XII–XIII. New York: The Macmillan Company, 1950.

Raths, Louis. "Improving Classroom Discussion," *Educational Research Bulletin,* 24: 6–13 (January 17, 1945).

Risk, Thomas M. *Principles and Practices of Teaching in Secondary Schools,* Second Edition, chapter XVII. New York: American Book Company, 1947.

Schnepp, G. J. "Panel Discussions in the Classroom," *Catholic Education Review,* 46: 490–496 (October, 1948).

Stiles, Lindley J. and Dorsey, Mattie F. *Democratic Teaching in Secondary Schools,* chapter XV. Chicago: J. B. Lippincott Company, 1950.

Wagner, Russel H. and Arnold, Carroll C. *Handbook of Group Discussion.* Boston: Houghton Mifflin Company, 1950.

Walser, Frank. *The Art of Conference.* New York: Harper and Brothers, 1938.

7

How Can Good Study Methods
Be Taught?

1. Why Be Concerned with Study Improvement?

Modern education makes good study methods essential

The simplicity of primitive life made educational procedures
simple. The learning of the few meager skills necessary could be
achieved largely by imitation, and the few rules of the road needful
to be kept in mind did not involve a serious tax on memory. This,
plus the fact that little was known about the learning process, re-
tarded the development of study skills.

The preceding chapters have indicated quite clearly the complex
nature of adjustment necessary to live successfully in modern
society, and particularly within our democracy. It requires a high
degree of problem-solving skills to meet the complexity of problem-
situations which now confront the learner. Simple imitation and
the memorization of a few facts are not enough. We know, too,
that learning is not the simple thing we once thought it to be; even
memory is a complex function.

Today we recognize that complex problem-solving skills are not
automatically acquired. They must be taught. And since modern
education stresses the generalized carry-over of processes rather
than facts in learning, attention is increasingly being focused upon
the development of good study (learning) procedures by the pupil.

Problem of school failures

When education was restricted to the few, and these somewhat

selected, there was little consciousness of peculiar learning difficulties. As the democratic conception of education began to crowd
our elementary and secondary schools with youth of every sort, attention was called to the disparity in learning achievement and the
excessive attendance mortality among the students who started in
school but finally dropped by the wayside. One of the most significant revelations of the maladjustments prevalent in our schools, and
the heavy ratio of failure to success among students, came as a
result of the extended study made by Ayres [1] through a subvention
from the Russell Sage Foundation. He found an average retarda-
tion of 33 per cent for all cities studied. This did not include
eliminations, which A. S. Draper, Commissioner of Education of
New York State in 1908, estimated to be from 60 to 70 per cent for
those entering school to the completion of the eighth grade. A
recent Report of the United States Commissioner of Education's
office reveals that of one hundred children who complete the fifth
grade only thirty-four complete the freshman year in high school,
and of these but thirteen complete the senior year. Not all of these
eliminations are due to scholastic failures, though a heavy percentage is the result of inability to carry the load successfully.
Extensive studies of student failures in high schools and colleges
have shown an appalling amount of dropping by the wayside, even
among students whose general scholastic record is average or
above. With increased attention to the study habits of these students, it has been found that large numbers of these failures are
due to poor study techniques, rather than to lack of mental endowment. The degree of success that has followed special efforts to
correct the study difficulties of individual cases has emphasized
the need for special attention to correct study habits.

Technique of study a new development

By 1900, it became quite generally recognized among our foremost psychologists and educators that learning was a very complex
activity, and that the capacity to learn varied greatly with different individuals. Along with the discovery of this important characteristic about learning have come most painstaking efforts to
analyze the elements in these complex learning activities. With this
analysis has come the development of general and specific tech-

[1] Ayres, L. P. *Laggards in Our Schools.* New York: The Charities Publication Committee, 1909.

niques of study to harness efficiently these principles of learning
for the ready use of the learner. It is these factors that have sharp-
ened the realization of the need of proper study habits, and the
demand that these newly developed techniques of study be made
available to the student.

In spite of these facts, it has been only within comparatively
recent years that the idea has taken form that the teacher had some
definite responsibility for the way students went about the preparation of the advance work. For several years it was the duty of
the writer to lecture each autumn to some three hundred college
freshmen on *How to Study*. Each year these incoming freshmen
were asked the question: "How many recall definite instruction by a
teacher on how to study a lesson, either in high school or elementary school?" Never were there more than a half dozen in any
incoming class of freshmen who could recall specific instruction in
effective study methods. So rapid has been the growing emphasis
on study guidance within the past few years, that it is doubtful
whether a college freshmen class could now be found in which a
large percentage would not indicate very definite awareness of
specific directed study while in the high school.

Possibly the pioneer book to find a firm place in the educational
literature on the subject was that of McMurry,[2] published in 1909.
Within the past twenty years the number of texts on study methods
has increased rapidly.

2. What Are Some Prerequisites of Effective Study?

A single chapter on study methods in a general text cannot enter
into a detailed explicit consideration of the techniques of study
essential to the pupil or to the teacher. There is scarcely a phase
of the total problem of study the teacher can afford to neglect. In
a field where many books have been written, little more can be
done in a few pages than to call attention to the most important
factors that contribute to good study. The teacher must supplement this with a most extensive and rigorous study of the best that
modern students of the subject have contributed.

Four essentials of effective study

The student who wishes to succeed in study must give diligent

2 McMurry, F. M. *How to Study and Teaching How to Study*. Boston:
Houghton Mifflin Company, 1909.

attention to those factors which make for success. There is no royal road, or any easy short cut, to true study efficiency. The wise teacher will keep this patent truth constantly before the mind of the learner. Nor can the teacher forget to be guided by the implications of these four prerequisites as the task of supervised study is envisaged. Particularly is this so, since three of these the teacher must recognize as keystones in the success of any plan of study guidance he may undertake.

1. *Ability.* Without a foundation upon which to build, success in mastering the difficult art of effective study is impossible. The student is handicapped when natural endowment is low. The teacher cannot expect a high quality of achievement where mental ability of a high order is not present. Happily, even at the high school level, there is little room for the fatalistic attitude that too often has pronounced the student hopelessly dumb. Very often, the difficulty with those who appear to possess a low mental capacity is traceable to causes that are subject to correction. There is much less determinism in the attitude of modern educators toward the evidence of low mentality or natural capacity than characterized educational thought a few years ago. Careful diagnosis of individual cases has revealed an astonishing number of difficulties of an acquired rather than inherited nature, such as: bad mechanics of reading, removable physical defects, snarled emotions with numerous resultant inhibitions, etc. Today, before admitting a genuine lack of ability, every effort is put forth by enlightened school administrators and teachers to discover if the difficulties are not due to removable causes. Frequently, only the teacher thoroughly trained in clinical psychology and the corrective-study methods can discover the true nature of the student's difficulty. The writer has often seen elementary, high school, and college students who were considered deficient in natural ability, placed in the hands of an expert clinician in educational psychology who diagnosed their difficulties, discovered they had superior ability, put them under corrective training, and within a few months had the students back in their classes doing normal to superior work. So frequent has been the experience of the writer with such students who seek admission to his university classes, that now, low-scholarship students, found to be chronically so, are quite generally referred to a colleague, a clinical specialist, for careful diagnosis before they are assumed to be actually deficient in potential ability.

Further, it should be remembered that there is less willingness at present than formerly to assume the static nature of the I.Q. Too much evidence has been adduced showing the I.Q. amenable to environmental factors to accept it as a perfect index of the student's native and unmodifiable capacity. There is much to encourage the teacher to believe students of apparently low ability can, through training, be brought to a very much higher standard of intellectual achievement. There will always remain, however, a significant relation between power to do and the true potential capacity of the student.

2. *Purpose.* A vital purpose is fundamental to successful study. It is virtually impossible for one to pursue a continuous, persistent direction against odds without a driving purpose. Human nature seems to be so constituted that it cannot continue sustained effort of any kind without a purpose. The purpose may be immediate, or it may be remote. It matters not, so long as there is some *end-desire* that goads the organism on to its fulfillment. In a vacant lot near by some little boys have been at work for days, as school duties and family interference have given time. From everywhere in the neighborhood, it seems, discarded Christmas trees have been converging upon this lot; little folks have been struggling and toiling to drag big trees for three and four blocks — a task not small for those twice their age. They have wielded spade and rake to dig a big hole and collect large quantities of dead grass. Aching muscles, even blistered hands, have not daunted. But why this sustained strenuous effort? Children would have thought it most inconsiderate to have been asked by parents to gather these trees on the vacant lot just to convenience adults. Parents would have been quick to question any other parent imposing on tender age in this fashion. Yet the children were impatient of all obstacles that kept them from their task. Why? They were making a fort! Their faces plainly mirrored surprise that anyone should question the significance of the thing they were doing. We work and often count not the cost when purposes are dominant enough. Read the fascinating accounts of the work of great discoverers, and note the driving power of purpose that made a Pasteur virtually a slave of his test tubes and microbes; or that stimulated an Edison to deny himself the ordinary satisfactions of hunger, so intent did he become at times in some experiment.

A driving purpose means concentration.[3] Thinking cannot take place without deep concentration — that is, sustained difficult thinking. Study requires concentration; the degree of concentration depends upon the difficulty of the thinking involved in the study. We are gradually pushed back upon a hierarchy of satisfactions quite universally recognized by psychologists. Unless there are satisfactions to be achieved as the result of effort, this is likely to be desultory, if it does not cease entirely. Our purposes may involve satisfactions immediate or remote, but there must be present some conviction of the attainability of the purpose, and the consequent enjoyment of the satisfactions cherished. The teacher must give to the student not only a sense of confidence and assurance that the objective can be realized, but also an attractive driving purpose that will challenge him to sustained concentrated effort. It has been found repeatedly, both with high school and college students, that a purpose for study was an essential bulwark to success. Students who are in school, they know not why, have revealed little inclination toward serious scholarship. They have no driving purpose, therefore no real power of concentration to make effective study possible. As one writer has said: [4] "The *sine qua non* for genuine concentration is a vital purpose. Without purpose no cencentration is possible. With purpose all concentration is possible."

This same author offers five practical suggestions by which to achieve concentration, in addition to purposiveness. These may prove suggestive to the teacher when restated to meet the study needs of high school students. As paraphrased they read:

1. Impress upon students the need to avoid all distractions; remove or avoid distractions as far as possible within the classroom.
2. Teach the student to work under pressure.
3. Impress upon the student the importance of starting study with vigorous initiative.

[3] At this point consult Mursell, James L. *Using Your Mind Effectively*, pp. 185–190. New York: McGraw-Hill Book Company, Inc., 1951.

[4] Headley, Leal A. *How to Study in College*, p. 56. New York: Henry Holt and Company, 1926. While Chapter III, "How to Concentrate," is written for college students, as the title of the book suggests, the teacher will find much in the broad discussion of principles which is applicable to the high school student as well.

4. Impress upon the student the need to keep physically alert, and teach him how this may be achieved.
5. Impress upon the student the need to respond actively to subject matter and situations that comprise the object of study.

3. *Knowledge.* It is one thing to have potential ability to study effectively, and another to be sufficiently challenged to devote one's best effort to attain a desired goal. But it is quite as necessary to know the most expeditious ways of moving surely, step by step, in the direction of the coveted objective. The somewhat naïve assumption in the past has been that, if one possessed real ability and a driving purpose, he would work out his own salvation — develop a method of attack that would ultimately lead him to attain the goal set before him. It is true that one with plenty of native capacity will eventually evolve, through a long painful trial-and-error method, a workable plan which in a goodly percentage of cases will result in some measure of success. This idea, however, is now *passé.* We know the trial-and-error method does not always culminate in good study procedure. There is no reason why the cumulative experience of careful students of study techniques should not be made available to youth at the earliest possible moment. It should be the ideal to establish correct study habits in the elementary grades; then study methods in the high school might be devoted to perfecting a technique fundamentally correct, but still in the rough, and to the correction of maladjustments where the elementary school had failed to do a perfect work.

Educators are becoming increasingly concerned that study be begun right, and that correct habits be established which need not be torn down and new ones built up. It is a costly expenditure of time and energy to undo and rebuild habits. To correct wrong habits is difficult. Many teachers have found it most discouraging to students to try to break down old habits and substitute new ones. It is much easier to start right than to try to retrace steps and begin again. The writer recalls a college friend who became quite a proficient player of the clarinet. A later decision to take special training under most competent instructors took him to Chicago. There he discovered his first task was to undo some bad habits of technique. Six months later he could not be persuaded to play at a public function as of yore, and, much more serious, he was on the verge of giving up his purposed musical career, for he discovered, after these months, his old-time skill gone, so that on the surface at least, the latter state of the man was worse than the first. This is the normal experience where complex habits are subjected to correction. Old habits also have an embarrassing way of rising up to mock us. A student in music who has learned to play the piano by ear, with correspondingly bad technique in finger movements, etc., will find it exceedingly difficult to learn by note and to escape the chains of bad habits fastened upon him. Frequent lapses into the old are likely to occur. Under strain or intense momentary excitement, old habits are likely to flare up in patterns originally learned.

4. *Practice.* Little need be said to emphasize the necessity of constant practice to build up correct habits of study. No amount of instructional knowledge of *how to study* will make a good student. Effective study can come only by the rigorous practice of those techniques which the student knows to be of value in successful study. Efficient habits of study, like playing the piano or solving problems in Euclid, can never be attained vicariously. Practice alone makes perfect.

Mechanics of reading

Few aspects of study technique appear to relate themselves more directly to study efficiency than does reading. In the past, educators and teachers have assumed reading to be a somewhat simple skill. It is only within the last three decades that reading has received serious attention by American educators as a complex technique. Indeed, the beginnings of widespread interest in the subject among American educational leaders came after World War I. More studies of a scientific nature on the subject of reading were published in 1923 than in the period 1880–1916. Almost coincident with this surge of interest came a recognition of the complexity of the problem of reading, and the serious defects in reading mechanics prevalent in our schools.[5] Good readers are

[5] For more complete discussions of the various aspects of "reading" mechanics, see *Reading in the High School*, Part II, Forty-Seventh Yearbook, National Society for the Study of Education. Chicago: University of Chicago Press, 1948; Gladfelter, M. E. *Changes in Reading Ability of 474 Students During the Freshman Year in College.* Philadelphia: University of Pennsylvania Press, 1945; Strang, Ruth et al, *Problems in the Improvement of Reading in High School and College.* Lancaster, Pa.: Science Press Printing Company, 1940; Gray, W. S., editor. *Basic Instruction in Reading in Elementary and High Schools,* Supplementary Edition, Monographs No. 65. Chicago: University of Chicago Press, 1948.

generally the most successful students. Correct reading mechanics are essential to scholastic success. Until very recently it was assumed a poor student lacked genuine ability. Now the tendency is to investigate for possible reading difficulties as the first cause of poor scholarship, as well as of low scores on mental tests.

One of the sources of great difficulty in reading has been the mechanics of the eye movements across the page. The correct mechanics of reading require, among the most important essentials, well-spaced eye fixations, rhythmic movement from one fixation to another, automatic return-sweeps from the end of one line to another, few regressive eye movements, and good tempo as reading progresses. The good reader tends to cover the words in a line with only a few shifts of the eyes, including in each eye-pause a large and significant phrase. On ordinary reading material the good reader will average from three to six fixations per line, while the slow may double or treble that number with correspondingly less phrase reading. The tendency to pause, hesitate, and start over again from some point in the line to pick up connecting threads of meaning is due to frequent fixations, with meaningless segments of words or partial words in unrelated connection. To avoid regressive eye movements, students should be taught to read by phrase, which requires in turn few fixations per line. Good readers usually reveal a rapid tempo, which is in part achieved by rhythmic movements of the eye from one fixation point to the next. It is generally conceded, as a result of experimentation, that maximum rapidity of reading can be achieved through silent reading only. Rapidity of reading orally, or through the use of lips, is limited by the slow reaction time required for muscular coordination. When reading is done silently, only the obstacle discussed above interferes, as visual-mental reaction time is most rapid.

Unfortunately, it is not possible for the student to analyze his own difficulty without help. He may be cautioned against regressive eye movements, but that will avail little if he does not tend to take in phrases or whole words in each fixation. The teacher should watch students who are slow readers, and at least call attention to correct mechanics. Headley [6] suggests a simple device by which alert teachers may discover the more flagrant difficulties of eye movement. The reader, seated at a table with a book open before him, should place a mirror on the page opposite the one

[6] Headley, L. A., *op. cit.*, p. 261.

from which he is reading. The teacher may sit across the table directly opposite the reader and follow the movements of the student's eyes as he reads. Where clinic specialists on reading and study problems are not available, as they are not in most of the smaller schools, every teacher should be prepared to aid the correction of the more obvious faults of reading mechanics. Efforts to correct these difficulties by other than specialists probably should center around efforts to speed up reading through longer phrase reading, silent reading, and shortening the pauses between fixations.

There is a significant relation between rapid reading and comprehension. This may be clear when it is recognized that there appears to be a very definite relationship between a large perceptual span and comprehension on the one hand, and comprehension and memory span on the other. Psychologically, we might reasonably expect such to be the case. A large perceptual span means familiar groupings of words into phrases and clauses, rather than individual words or syllables. Reading rate is determined more by the perceptual span than by attempts to shorten fixation time. If this be true, then it is clear why a definite relation exists between memory span and perceptual span as they affect comprehension. The more successfully one can crowd into memory span a large unit of material, the more will he have available for a single interpretation.

The teacher needs to bear in mind that speed, valuable as it is, is not all. The type of material read, the student's familiarity with the general ideas contained therein, as well as the purpose of the reading, will affect materially the desirable rate of reading. Novel reading for the most part may be rapid, as thought is not closely knit and words generally are familiar. Textbooks with compact meaning or unfamiliar vocabulary must slow up one's reading pace. Unless time is taken to acquaint oneself with new words and exact meanings, the results may be superficial. As Ruskin once declared, it were better to read "one page with our understanding than ten thousand pages without." Photographic studies of eye movements show a sharp change, both in the number of fixations per line and the duration of pauses, when reading material for the main ideas or for details; or when various subjects were compared, such as fiction, algebra, history, or Latin.

3. What Are Some General Techniques of Study?

Intelligent reading techniques

The teacher can make a distinct contribution to the student by directing his attention to a few simple suggestions that will apply to some phase of the reading required as part of the supervised-study period.

1. *Strive for mastery of words.* Rapidity of reading is greatly impeded where a limited vocabulary requires repeated pause to search for meaning. Naturally a comprehension or reading vocabulary should be more extensive than a usage vocabulary. There is a natural relationship between the two, but every high school student should seek, without being offensive or affected in manner, to use an extensive vocabulary based upon his rapidly enlarging comprehension vocabulary. To the extent that words can be made thoroughly familiar can reading become rapid. The student should be encouraged to use the dictionary freely — to establish the dictionary habit. The student should be taught to make extensive use of contextual interpretation of word meaning and breadth of application. Many words, difficult to define in isolation, become perfectly clear in context. Further, the broad significance of words can add greatly to the student's comprehension vocabulary if he develops a habit of careful observation of word usage.

2. *Adapt reading rate to the character of reading materials.* Intelligent reading requires that the student adjust his reading to the nature of the material and to the purpose of the reading. Many students defeat their possible effectiveness in reading by not making distinctions in what is required of various types of materials, or the purpose for which the reading is done. A student who is reading a bit of fiction may well race along rapidly, getting the main thread of the story. When he turns his attention to history, the pace must be slackened if he is not to miss important factors of cause or effect, or fail to give due weight to certain facts in the possible sequence of events. Again, the grammar or algebra studied may require much more minute weighing of every sentence, even of words and phrases. As Bacon has said: "Some books are to be tasted, others to be swallowed, and some few to be chewed and digested."

When a student is gathering data on a topic where extensive reading is necessary to cover all possible phases of the problem,

he adopts a browsing method. The first source should no doubt
be read with care. As each subsequent source is read the tendency of the intelligent reader will be to skim quickly over the
material. Ideas previously met, and events similarly treated, can
be detected quickly and passed by with but scant attention. Two
or three minutes given to a hasty perusal of the paragraphs in a
chapter may be sufficient to reveal no contribution from that source
to the topic in hand. This is an achievement all students should
covet. It is not easy to do, and takes extended practice to accomplish, but it becomes increasingly important as the extensive use
of sources, other than the textbook, is popularized. In more progressive schools there is a distinct tendency for the textbook to give
way to an extended use of numerous sources from the library.
Teachers, therefore, should give special attention to student training in the art of skimming. It is as important for the student to
learn what not to read as it is for him to learn what not to skip.

Much of the reading assigned to the student may be quickly
skimmed,[7] and, if important sections are found that need rereading,
the student may do so after the preliminary rapid survey has given
a bird's-eye view of the treatment of the topic. For this form of
reading, five suggestions may be offered the student:

1. Read headings and captions.
2. Read by paragraphs, scanning the opening sentence, and possibly
   a sentence near the middle and end of the paragraph when its
   value is doubtful.
3. Give important paragraphs, such as the first and last paragraphs
   of a chapter, special attention. Usually they state the theme and
   the summary of the discussion.
4. Look for signpost paragraphs important in directing the thought
   of a section of the topic.
5. Where possible, read by parts that are larger than the paragraph.
   Often a glance at a line or two on a page will reveal no new ideas
   of importance are presented.

3. *Study the habits and point of view of the author.* Very often
the most illuminating thing about an author is his general point
of view. Given that, his conclusions on a given subject are reasonably obvious. This, of course, can come only when the student
has become somewhat familiar with an author and his fundamental

[7] See Mursell, James L. *Using Your Mind Effectively*, pp. 223–224. New
York: McGraw-Hill Book Company, Inc., 1951.

point of view. The teacher can do much to help the students acquire a larger acquaintance with the outlook and philosophy of the author. A teacher was observed making an assignment of a topic on World War I, estimated to cover approximately two weeks. Various books on his desk were taken up, one by one, as he referred the class to the source material for the unit of study. The general point of view of each was given if there was evidence of a distinct bias influencing the writers, as there was in at least two books written openly in support of a definite thesis as to who was responsible for the War. Something of the personal history of each author was given that would aid in understanding his undercurrent of thought. The student was thus prepared to read each source in the light of the intimate background given. A good approach is to study the preface, where most writers reveal what they tried to do in the book. Taken in conjunction with the table of contents, the general organization of the book is often thrown into sharp perspective. In textbooks, summaries, either preceding or following the chapter, frequently serve to give its highlights. Students should be taught to use these as an indication of what to expect in the chapter.

Each writer has a definite style of writing and a vocabulary peculiarly his own. The reader should be taught to watch for these. Man is more a creature of habit than he cares to admit. The informed student will take advantage of this fact. For example, every writer has a definite plan for the use of the topic sentence. A few cast it into a summary sentence at the close of a paragraph. Some embody it in the heart of the paragraph, while the vast majority make it the springboard of the paragraph. Two or three pages of any book will be sufficient to discover the predilection of the writer in this regard. Once this has been discovered, skimming is easy where this type of reading is desirable.

4. *Ask questions about a topic.* One of the most effective ways to study is to ask questions about the topic. Every chapter heading and every title to a book can be subjected to a battery of questions. The more pertinent the title to the discussion that follows, the more valuable the method. This is so simple that every student can become quite adept in asking significant questions implicit in the topic. It has several distinct advantages.

First, it serves to sharpen the student's thinking as to the full scope of such a topic.

Second, it focuses attention upon those items which the chapter or source should illuminate, if it measures up to its reasonable obligations in the discussion of the topic. This serves to direct the study of the student. He will read with these questions in mind, throw aside irrelevant comment and almost unerringly single out his answers as they appear.

The *third* advantage comes through the close scrutiny which the data irrelevant to his immediate search receives, since this may reveal significant answers to questions not thought of in the original questioning of the topic or chapter heading. To cast aside data as not bearing upon a battery of questions previously formulated, must by indirection sharpen the attention to the importance of data overlooked. When the source has been read the student can easily check the results of his reading. He is prepared to ask what the answers were to each question. If some were not answered, he is in a better position to re-examine the topic to determine the validity of his questions. Then, too, the additional data revealed enable the student to reorganize his concept of the topic, after he has found what others legitimately interpret it to include. McMurry voices his conviction [8] of the worth of this method of reading in the following quotation from Morley and Gibbon:

"Some great men — Gibbon was one and Daniel Webster was another and the great Lord Strafford was a third — always, before reading a book, made a short, rough analysis of the questions which they expected to be answered in it, the additions to be made to their knowledge, and whither it would take them. I have sometimes tried that way of studying and guiding attention; I have never done so without advantage, and I commend it to you." Says Gibbon, "After glancing my eye over the design and order of a new book, I suspended the perusal until I had finished the task of self-examination; till I had resolved, in a solitary walk, all that I knew or believed or had thought on the subject of the whole work or of some particular chapter; I was then qualified to discern how much the author added to my original stock; and, if I was sometimes satisfied with the agreement, I was sometimes armed by the opposition of our ideas."

5. *Practice self-recitation.* Similar to the formulation of questions is the recitation to oneself of the significant things read in the source or sources. Questions would not be very significant if a

[8] McMurry, F. M., *op. cit.,* p. 31. Also see Mursell, James L. *op. cit.,* chapter II.

summary of the answers secured were not undertaken at the end of the reading. However, it is not inherent in the former that the recitation take place, nor is it necessary in the self-recitation plan that questions be formulated in advance of the reading. This may be done at the end. Such is not recommended here, however. The ideal is to combine the advance questioning with the concluding self-recitation. This has not only the advantage of directing the study instead of permitting a hazy pointless reading, but also of clinching the answers to the questions.

In a recent experiment university students were instructed to read an assignment through rapidly, then to reread carefully a section of the assignment, with special attention to the main ideas or facts discussed. The students were then asked to try to formulate questions the answers to which would require a brief summary of the thought of the section read. Even when this was done the testimony of the students was overwhelmingly in favor of the self-recitation method. Of one hundred and thirty-nine students enrolled in the "How to Study" classes where this method was employed, seventy could recognize no disadvantages in the method. Only three disadvantages were recorded for the plan, as over against nine advantages claimed for it.[9]

6. *Definitely react to what is read.* Possibly no better practice for the student could be suggested than the example of Gibbon in the quotation above. At the high school level the student may have little background to contribute to his reading, but such as he has should be used. In the nature of the case this must be done in some measure, for his interpretation of the meaning of what is read must be contingent upon his apperceptive preparation for that reading. The backgrounds of writer and of reader are different. The student must put forth effort to understand. Most textbooks merely suggest ideas, leaving opportunity for imagination to fill in the gaps. Good literature is valued more for what it leaves to the imagination than for what the explicit statement offers. It would lose its charm and, in large measure, cease to be good literature, if every idea were laboriously elucidated. The average textbook can but suggest ideas that must be fully clothed by imaginative thinking. The reason many subjects are *dry* to students is that the students give nothing to their reading. That Columbus dis-

[9] Bird, Charles. *Effective Study Habits,* pp. 68–78, 87–93. New York: The Century Company, 1931.

covered America in 1492 is a most prosaic historical fact. To visualize its human meaning for Columbus, as the poet saw it in the poem, "Sail On, Sail On," or to let the imagination bear upon its significance for subsequent history, provides it with thrill and romance — but only for those who give imagination to the fact. Statements should not be supinely accepted, but critically evaluated for accuracy and for validity of conclusion. One should always ask, "What are the implications for us, if these are the facts, and the conclusions drawn from them are warranted?" The teacher himself should constantly react, and stimulate students to react, to whatever is read.

Importance of note taking

Few students have ever been taught to take notes properly. Even in colleges and universities, students have been left largely to the trial-and-error method of formulating a satisfactory technique by which to understand the lectures given or reading done and preserve some records for later consultation. Yet it is one of the very important accomplishments every adult and every high school student should possess. It is an ability needed through life. There are important occasions when the individual desires to take in outline or summary form something read or the remarks of some speaker. Memory is short and the power of forgetting great. We do not retain long in memory those things not fixed there by repetition or by special attention. Note taking tends to fix items and ideas in mind because it requires both repetition and special attention. The power to analyze keenly an article or editorial or an address heard, is of inestimable value. Intelligent citizenship requires it. Demagogy in a democracy is possible only when people are unable to analyze the speciousness of a demagogue's high-sounding phrases.

The first prerequisite of such an ability is the developed power of attention. It is generally conceded that few adults have the power to give undivided attention to an address. One of the objections raised against the lecture at the secondary level has been that adolescents are able to attend to a lecture continuously for only thirty to forty-five minutes. There are psychological reasons for part of this inability, but the process of taking notes forces attention of a very rigorous order. If there is any value in the transfer of training, there should be a direct transfer to later maturity of the ability to attend to a lecture at the adolescent level. Learning is active, not passive. Note taking forces an active attention that goes far to remove the objection of passivity commonly attributed to a lecture situation.

Further, the student who has mastered the art of intelligent note taking has also acquired the power of critical analysis of what he hears or reads. To condense what the speaker or writer is saying into much briefer form with only the outstanding ideas reduced to writing requires the power of analysis to a very high degree. Critics are not wanting who insist that this is an ability beyond the power of high school students to achieve. The weight of proof must rest with those who make the assertion. Association with junior-senior high school students leaves little doubt of their ability to acquire unusual facility in analysis of what they read and see.

Note taking, too, develops in the student an ability to organize and to recognize organization as few other processes will. The acid test of his ability to understand is his power to organize the principal ideas of a writer or speaker into a coherent whole presenting an easily inferred conclusion. Unfortunately, the student will find at times that the document or lecture is itself not well organized. Even to discover this fact is often to reinforce the student's sense of the importance of organized address.

An additional value frequently claimed for note taking is that, to reduce the writer's or speaker's ideas, lengthily expressed, into the essence of his thought, requires that the student recast these ideas into his own words. This demands a thorough understanding that the mere copying of words does not. Thus the notes so taken force upon the student a clear recognition of the degree to which full understanding has taken place. A student's best test of his own understanding of the thought of another is his ability to give intelligent expression, in his own words, through writing or verbal report, of the ideas that have come to him through visual or auditory channels.

The student in the high school will be called upon to record at least three types of notes. Many things given in oral or lecture form by the teacher may need to be written down for future reference. The giving of student reports in class often necessitates some bolstering of the memory through summaries or more detailed outlines of the reports themselves. Many students find it very helpful to jot down important points from their textbooks, or even to sketch the main ideas in the lesson assigned. Where the long unit with extended study periods is employed, the student is usually required to consult many sources for the data necessary to throw light upon his topic. Note taking of a very exacting nature is demanded under these circumstances, for no student can carry in memory important data from numerous sources which it is necessary to weld later into a unified statement of the problem, findings, and conclusions.

Suggestions for taking notes

Many books have been written within the past few years on effective methods of study. Most of these devote a chapter or a section to the technique of note taking. The teacher should regard these more complete treatments of the subject as supplemental to the suggestions offered here. It is possible, in a book of this nature, only to call attention to the general and most important factors that contribute to effective note taking.

1. *Notes should be taken in accordance with some definite outline form.* There are in use many approved forms of outline. Some use numerals, begin the main headings with Roman numerals, follow with Arabic numerals, and, when the outline becomes too minute, resort to the use of the alphabet. Others reverse the procedure and begin with the alphabet and end with numerals. The important thing for the student is to adopt some system that permits an orderly arrangement of notes, and then to be consistent in its use. The power of habit can be of the utmost assistance here. The mechanics of recording should be made automatic, otherwise valuable time that should be given over to mental evaluation and organization of the writer's or speaker's remarks must be devoted to mechanics of outline form.

2. *Notes should be brief, yet detailed enough to give a balanced picture.* One of the frequent faults of note taking is overcompleteness. Many college students troubled with a course have been called into the office for conference over the difficulty, which is usually with their notes. Sometimes it is evident that the student has tried to copy indiscriminately everything the professor said. This proved impossible, and the class notes in consequence represented a jumbled confusion of sentences, half-sentences, and mere phrases. The student, frantically attempting the impossible, did not have time to listen and evaluate, but only to copy with a growing sense of futile desperation.

The student should spend more time in listening or reading than in note taking. He needs to learn the writer's or speaker's style. He needs to discover when a new idea is presented, and to distinguish between a topic sentence and explanatory data. He is concerned particularly with the new ideas and the topic sentences, and their bearing upon one another. As much of the explanatory material may be recorded as seems necessary to clarify the meaning of the ideas expressed. These data should be kept at a minimum. Individuals differ as to the amount of notes necessary for intelligent understanding. The student can learn this only through trial and error. One of the keenest students the writer knows never took a note in his graduate classes. He gave undivided attention to the speaker, but the moment the lecture was over he jotted down on a card the half-dozen main points in the lecture. From these he could reproduce much of the detail. Students of such ability are the exceptions, however. There is as grave a danger that the student will attempt to get along with a modicum of outline, with the result that he finds that points he has recorded are meaningless within a few days after they are written. Again, students will find that books and lectures vary greatly in compactness of ideas as against filler — detail and illustration. With experience the student will learn to reduce to a minimum the amount of notes consistent with full intelligibility.

3. *Notes should be phrased in the student's own words.* When the main points are given in brevity with such clarity as to render the meaning unmistakable, it is desirable to use the writer's or speaker's language. The student should learn to recognize almost instantly the appropriateness of the main points for copy. Every device that facilitates economy of time and effort should be utilized. Often the language of the writer or speaker, though brief and striking, does not convey clear meaning to the student. Under these circumstances the statement should be rephrased. Practice is the royal road to efficiency in both the recognition of statements that can be accepted verbatim and the power to recast the statements into language that conveys identical meaning. At first the student need not be surprised to find that his rephrasing of the writer's or speaker's language has not resulted in identical meaning. The final achievement of the ability to restate another's thought is well worth the temporary inconvenience of the inaccuracies that result from early efforts.

There are many items that should be taken down verbatim. Often quotations closely knit in thought and expression should be copied as given. The teacher, when lecturing, should indicate to the student when such seem to be of sufficient value to merit exact reproduction.

4. *Students should be taught to study peculiarities of the writer's or speaker's methods.* No two persons use exactly the same devices for transition from one point to another. Teachers should help pupils study different writers until the pupils develop competence in detecting the literary devices authors use for this purpose. The teacher may well demonstrate through class lecture or telling how to detect a speaker's use of transition devices.

5. *Students should learn to take notes in such form that they need not be recopied.* There are exceptions to every rule. In general, it is a serious loss of time and waste of energy to take notes in the rough and recopy later. Some learning values may be claimed in support of recopied notes. The time thus consumed from other learning would seem to offset the added thoroughness of the student's mastery of the materials of the lecture. It is doubtful whether the notes of the average high school class have enough permanent value to justify the extra effort required to recopy. The objectives of high school education are not concerned primarily with knowledge that may be locked up in classroom notes. Most of the data of secondary school experience are of transitory value. It is the concomitant learning, of which the data are but the medium or vehicle, that counts most. The process is the important end product of this form of learning. This learning cannot be reduced to notes. The notes should be so well-organized and so clear in the first draft that they suffice for immediate needs. Further, it is questionable educational psychology to suggest anything less than the student's best the first time. Consciousness that notes are to be recopied leads to carelessness in first impressions. Students should learn to do things well the first time. When additions or corrections are found necessary, they should be made. As students move up the ladder of years, they will find it a costly habit to do over work that should have been done well in the beginning. Moreover, the inestimable worth to the student and to the adult of the ability to listen to a speaker or read a book and take accurate, intelligent notes, is a consideration not to be overlooked. This facility can come only through practice in accordance with

an ideal. With these considerations in mind the student should carefully determine the form of note system to be used, whether notebook or cards, the style of outline form to use, and should then accustom himself to think of the notes taken in the stress of the school situation, for all practical purposes, as final.

6. *Students should be encouraged to practice constant note taking.* Since good notes are the result of long rigorous training, the student should utilize every means available to practice note taking. When the student listens to an assembly speaker, hears a sermon, or attends a lecture under community auspices, it is exceedingly good practice to take notebook and pencil, and, as inconspicuously as possible, try to outline the address. Soon the student will discover, when listening to a speaker, how easily he can analyze and organize the outline of the address. For this student, subsequent lectures of whatever kind will be better understood and appreciated. Moreover, since there is a direct transfer of the training in classroom note taking to adult situations, the concomitant values for classroom efficiency in taking notes will become apparent.

The use of books and the library

Very few high schools have as yet introduced specific courses in study methods. Every teacher, therefore, should assume it a personal responsibility to teach students the simple ways to discover quickly what is in a book, a preliminary estimate of its worth, and the general procedure necessary to find what one wants in an ordinary library. Even where such courses are offered, the student needs constant guidance to insure facility in this accomplishment.

Every student should be trained to notice at least six things about the book he reads. The acumen developed in the use of these will depend considerably upon the guidance given by the teacher. As the student learns to generalize his ideas gleaned from many experiences, he will acquire power to evaluate his sources with a deft sureness possible only when clearly recognized, sharply defined evaluation standards are employed.

The *first* thing the student should note is the copyright date of the source. Recency of copyright imprint does not always insure a corresponding recency in data used, or modernity of point of view. A competent teacher of history once remarked in casual reference to a text just published by an historian of recognized scholarship, who had written a similar text some thirty years previous, "Dr. B wrote his new textbook from the same point of view from which his first book was written." The modern emphasis in the writing of history had changed quite radically in those thirty years. Whereas older historians wrote compendiums of information of political events, modern history emphasizes the socio-economic aspects of man's historic development. In many sources, one might safely say in most sources, recency of copyright determines in large measure its value. In many fields, such as science, economics, education, and sociology, rapid changes have been taking place that render many of the facts of yesterday untrue today. Within the past few months a teacher asked the advice of the writer as to the wisdom of purchasing a set of nature-study books which could be procured at a bargain. The teacher was asked two questions — first, the copyright date, and second, the importance of recency in its effect upon the development of the phase of the subject treated in these books. The teacher thought the books were not too old because the publication date was 1925. When the teacher was asked to check on the copyright date for each volume, and thus incidentally learned the difference between publication and copyright dates, he found the set practically useless because the volumes were originally written between 1885 and 1901, without subsequent revision. Even in those fields assumed least subject to change, namely, literature and foreign languages, the attractiveness of book printing, and devices to facilitate understanding are frequently of great value.

The *second* concern of the student should be to read the Preface, where an entire book or significant section is to be read. It tells what the author intended to do in the book, and it frequently indicates something of his point of view.

The *third* step is the perusal of the Table of Contents. This provides a bird's-eye view of the total panorama or the high lights of the author's thought on the subject. The table of contents is often significant for what it omits, as well as for what it includes.

Fourth, where the source admits of reference to the work of others, the student should cultivate the habit of a quick check on the author's documentation. The recency of sources in the references, as well as the nature of these references, should constitute the next item of information the student should seek.

The *fifth* standard by which the text should receive a preliminary estimate of worth, is found in the evidence of judicious open-mindedness with which the writer approaches his subject. Dogmatism and superlatives are the marks of bias and the absence of a tempered judicious perspective. Indications of polemical writing, particularly, should place the student on guard against a too ready acceptance of the point of view registered by the author.

Sixth, the Index is an important part of a book students should be quick to use when in search of minute data. Many students scarcely know what an index is, or what its purpose is. It contributes little to them because they do not know how to use it. Suppose I have a book in the field of method but find no chapter on supervised study. A hasty check down the alphabetical list of the index may reveal no notation, "Supervised Study." A glance at that point in the index where "Directed Study" or "Study" should be, may reveal extensive sections or paragraphs devoted to the subject. The student should understand his tools. These devices in a textbook are there definitely to assist the student. They have value only when properly used.

Even among college students one is amazed at the too general inability of students to use the library intelligently. Many students are permitted to graduate from high school with little or no knowledge of the purpose of a library card or an index system, or of the use of trays. An unpardonably large number of students do not know how to use available library sources to locate material for a report or term paper on current problems. In small communities library facilities may be quite limited, but schools are developing libraries, and access may be had to public libraries in near-by towns or cities. Where possible, students should be taught the use of the card-index trays, *Readers' Guide,* special guides, encyclopedias, etc. No competency in the original search for data, and the ability to answer an important question dependent upon library sources, can be built up without training and practice. The teacher should feel a personal obligation to satisfy himself that all students under his care are able to use the library effectively, and to marshal the data necessary for a satisfactory solution to a problem, the source material of which could be obtained only from the library. The supervised-study period provides ideal conditions under which situations may be produced to necessitate the use of the library, and thereby give opportunity for such training.

Wise use of time

Few people have developed a real sense of the importance of time. Even fewer people have developed the ability to organize and use their time efficiently. Yet, to a much greater degree than most people realize, it is the key to success or failure.

Students are notoriously lacking in both a recognition of the importance of time, or the ability to wisely organize their time for study. It is a serious contributor to their failures or unsatisfactory work in school. A few suggestions are offered to help the pupil organize the major features of his study.

1. *Develop a plan for the day.* The teacher in training may well begin by "practicing what he later expects to preach." The pupil in the secondary school, traditionally, has been more circumscribed than the college student. He starts the day with a bell, shifts at specified intervals during the day at the sound of the bell, and in many ways appears to have had his time carefully programmed for him. This is more apparent than true. With the shift to larger blocks of class time more freedom is given the student to exercise his judgment.

Let us begin with the day's schedule. Pupils come to school tardy, nervously wrought up with last minute frantic efforts to beat the bell. Why? They have not planned their time. How much time does it take to bathe, dress, eat, and cover the distance to school? If pupils would check the time required to perform these necessities with dispatch but without a sense of "rush," they could determine when to get up in the morning, thereafter proceeding in an unhurried but businesslike manner with the routine according to schedule. They would conserve energy for the day's work often dissipated in nervous tension and exhaustion because of lack of planning and scheduling.

The school day usually calls for a certain schedule of classes, possibly library or study-hall periods, or part of the class period for study. The pupil should analyze the work required and plan specific time schedules for doing specific tasks. This planning should involve both in-school and out-of-school time as the tasks may require. In general there should be a definite time in the day set aside for certain tasks.

2. *Develop a plan for a week or for large periods.* Some assign-

ments, for example, may require reports, papers, written work of one kind or another to be completed at given dates. If a report requires library or other forms of activity to collect necessary data, the pupil should plan when these are to be secured, when the report is to be written, all with a margin of time to care for the unexpected, yet have the report ready on time.

3. *Reserve time for emergencies.* In all planning the pupil should reserve time for emergencies, to insure a few extra minutes between tasks for reflection, and to keep perspective for the rest of his schedule. As all good businesses maintain a "contingent fund" against the unexpected, so pupils should have a reserve of time. It is not possible always to plan work within the exact minutes required.

4. *Post study schedule.* The wise pupil will post his schedule so that it will be a constant reminder of the tasks to be done, the order in which they are to be done, as well as the approximate time limits for each phase of the schedule. At times it may be found desirable to shift the schedule. The fact that one has a schedule safeguards the time for the tasks involved in the shift.

5. *Rigorous observance of schedule.* The pupil should rigorously hold to this schedule and permit no exceptions until he has become habituated to thinking in terms of the routinization of his time and activities.

6. *Flexibility in use of spare time.* When the pupil has planned his work carefully he will feel a strange sense of relief from the pressure of time. He will discover that he has time for all his activities and time to spare. The wise pupil will utilize this time either to take up slack in the schedule to cover other portions which may be too closely timed, or may use this time to reflect on the total picture of his work. The writer once listened to a stimulating lecture on the subject "What do you do when you have nothing to do?" The lecturer dealt with the importance of wisely using the free time we have for doing better those things we have to do, or doing many of the worth-while things our free time makes possible.

7. *A definite place for study.* The pupil should visualize a definite place for the carrying out of each phase of his program. If, for example, he has the second period free, he may well assign this regularly to the preparation for the fourth-period class, or whatever portion of it is needed. He should think in terms of the kind of work and the functional relation to a possible place of study. Ob-

viously, the library is the place to do assigned reading or the collection of data for most reports, or the art room for work that requires the use of such facilities. If possible, some place at home should be reserved for quiet study and this made part of the schedule. It should be remembered that an habitual place for certain forms of study is as important as the setting aside of a definite time for a specific type of study.

4. What Are Some Special Techniques of Study?

As the pupil or teacher approaches the problem of study, three special aspects of study must be considered in addition to the general ones mentioned above. Unless careful attention is given to these, learning during study may be ineffective.

Recognition of types of learning

Few students understand that there are different types of learning or that these require, in part, different modes of study. Unfortunately, too many teachers only vaguely recognize differences in learning types, and seldom is a distinct technique of study recognized as essential to each. As a result, students too frequently apply a memory technique to all but the sensory-motor type of learning. Their test of learning success is the ability to reproduce. For example, a student confronted with the Geometric Theorem, *Vertical Angles Are Equal,* may simply memorize the statements of proof without an understanding of the fundamental reasons why the statements are so, just as he would probably memorize a list of dates in history, or bits of poetry in literature, with the idea of giving them back later in the anticipated examination. The student would be little aware that the theorem might involve logical reasoning, or that historical dates had significance for socio-political understanding of human events, or that literature had possible values as a source of appreciation of human aspirations.

While psychologically there is unity in all learning, and much interplay and overlapping of one type with another, at least four distinct types of learning are commonly recognized, with the implications of each type for the guidance of study.[10] These are:

[10] The teacher should familiarize himself with discussions of the various types of learning such as are found in Trow, W. C., *Educational Psychology,* Second Edition, chapter X. Boston: Houghton Mifflin Company, 1950; Reed, Homer B., *Psychology and Teaching of Secondary School.* New York: Prentice-

1. Sensory-motor, related to perception and motor skills.
2. Associative learning or memory.
3. Problem solving or reflective reasoning.
4. Appreciation, or the training of the affective nature-development of attitudes and ideals.

The failure to recognize that associative learning on the one hand, and appreciation learning on the other, require quite radically different teaching and study procedures, has been largely responsible for the generally recognized failure of the teaching of appreciation in literature and art — in literature especially.

Psychological differentiation within subject fields

It is well for the pupil and the teacher to recognize that while learning differentiates itself into types, as the secondary school is now organized and bids fair to remain for some time, there is an additional learning problem associated with the psychological differentiation between subject fields. It has been generally, though somewhat vaguely, recognized for many years that mathematics involves somewhat different mental reactions than do history and languages, for example, but the exact differences were not clearly understood. Studies have shown in general that ability to succeed in one subject leads to success in another, yet these same studies have shown that noticeable differences do exist between subjects. A student may be good in mathematics but mediocre in history or the biological sciences, and vice versa. Even within given fields there appear differences, as between arithmetic, algebra and geometry, or between composition and literature in English. Suggestive examples alone must suffice to reveal the significance of the problem to the teacher who would intelligently guide the student in his study. Arithmetic involves simple concepts of quantitative relationships or comparisons arbitrarily determined. Algebra, on the other hand, involves highly abstract symbolic relational concepts of a most difficult sort — difficult because most of the student's experience has been of a concrete nature. Very close abstract analytical reasoning is required. Geometry, in contrast, is concerned with spatial perceptions. There is a definite relational

Hall, Inc., 1939; and Mursell, James L., *The Psychology of Secondary School Teaching*. New York: W. W. Norton and Company, 1939. Each classifies learning types somewhat differently yet the basic types suggested above are to be found in each.

imagery in geometry common to everyday experience. The student from childhood has dealt with form and spatial concepts of distance, which are peculiar to the science of geometry and differentiate it from both arithmetic and algebra. "Arithmetic, algebra, and geometry each represent some form of mental activity not included in the others. No one can make a psychological analysis of these sciences without recognizing the distinctive character of the mental processes involved." [11]

History projects the student into a difficult perception of time relationships with emphasis upon a "proper judgment of time and the sequence of events in time." Judgment and imagination must be exercised to a high degree to visualize historic events, situations, and personages to make them live for the student. To be sure, all of these subjects require extensive reflective thought in their applications, but are cast in somewhat differing psychological molds as the mental processes are called into play.

Purpose for which subject is studied

The purpose for which a subject is studied should, and, if intelligently understood, would determine the mode of study attack to be employed. Too much of teaching and study is done on the basis of uncritical imitation of ways that have been in popular vogue. Whether the methods pursued square with the results desired is not too closely scrutinized. For example, modern languages in high school and university are at once the poorest and possibly the best taught subjects in the curriculum, depending upon the purpose one attributes to the teaching. If knowledge of grammatical form or an etymological study of language has been the prime purpose of linguistic study, then it would seem necessary to concede that modern-language teaching has been exceedingly well-done. If, on the other hand, the main objective of modern-language teaching has been to give the student easy facility in reading or speaking the language, then the conclusion is unavoidable that no subject in the curriculum has been more atrociously taught or studied. This has been because teachers have not forced themselves and their students to square their methods critically with a clear-cut purpose. Language teaching with primary emphasis upon grammar can result only in mastery of the niceties of grammatical

[11] Judd, C. H. *Psychology of High School Subjects*, p. 129. Boston: Ginn and Company, 1915.

forms. Ease in reading and speaking are psychologically inhibited by the method. Not inapplicable is the homely story of the centipede who managed his many legs very efficiently until asked how he performed such a feat; whereupon he landed paralyzed in a ditch beside the road, unable, consciously, to get his legs to act in easy coordination. There is only one royal road to a speaking use of a language and that is to speak it, just as the only sure route to an easy reading knowledge of a language is to read it. Attention to grammar should be incidental, if not omitted entirely, until facility in speaking or reading the language has been acquired. What is true of language instruction is also true of every other subject taught. The teacher should clearly define the purpose of the subject, both to himself and to the students, and then guide the students in the use of the most efficient study techniques to achieve the goals thus set before them.

QUESTIONS AND PROBLEMS

1. List some rules for effective note taking of the three types mentioned.
2. Explain what is meant by "definitely react to what is said" in reading.
3. Have the class outline a technique for rapid comprehensive reading.
4. Have the class recall and outline their method of reading for comprehension some assignment for the day. Have them check their procedures against those suggested in this chapter.
5. As a class exercise, have the students explain the six things referred to in this chapter which a student should notice about a book before reading it. Apply these items to a textbook they are now using. Notice how this procedure affects your reaction to the textbooks so studied.
6. Have the class name at least four types of learning and give the essentials of each. How would the student's method of study differ for each type of learning?
7. How do physical conditions affect study efficiency?
8. What are the essentials of an intelligent reading technique?
9. What is the significance for reading of recasting major headings in a book into question form?
10. Have the class enumerate the essentials of effective study, and justify the importance of each; then apply these essentials to specific instances which they describe in some detail.
11. Have the members of the class develop a schedule for study of the program they are carrying in school.

SELECTED BIBLIOGRAPHY

Adler, Mortimer. *How to Read a Book.* New York: Simon and Schuster, Inc., 1940.

Bond, Guy L. and Bond, Eva. *Developing Reading in High School.* New York: The Macmillan Company, 1941.

Burton, William H. *The Guidance of Learning Activities,* chapter XII. New York: Appleton-Century-Crofts, Inc., 1944.

Butler, Frank A. *The Improvement of Teaching in Secondary Schools,* Revised Edition, chapter XII. Chicago: University of Chicago Press, 1946.

Eells, H. *Learning to Study,* Fourth Edition. Yellow Springs, Ohio: Antioch Press, 1948.

Harris, A. J. *How to Increase Reading Ability,* Revised Edition. New York: Longmans, Green and Company, 1947.

Katona, G. *Organizing and Memorizing.* New York: Columbia University Press, 1940.

Kelley, V. H. and Greene, H. A. *Better Reading and Study Habits.* Yonkers, N.Y.: World Book Company, 1947.

Mursell, James L. *Using Your Mind Effectively.* New York: McGraw-Hill Book Company, Inc., 1951.

Reading in the High School and College, Forty-Seventh Yearbook of the National Society for the Study of Education, Part II. Chicago: University of Chicago Press, 1948.

Risk, Thomas M. *Principles and Practices of Teaching in Secondary Schools,* Second Edition, chapter XXIV. New York: American Book Company, 1947.

Rivlin, Harry N. *Teaching Adolescents in Secondary Schools,* chapter IX. New York: Appleton-Century-Crofts, Inc., 1948.

Robinson, Francis F. *Effective Study.* New York: Harper and Brothers, 1946.

Tibbitts, F. L. *Streamline Your Study Habits.* Fullerton, California: Mission Press and Lithograph Company, 1947.

Wrenn, C. G. *Practical Study Aids.* Stanford: Stanford University Press, 1946.

—— *Study Hints for High School Students.* Stanford: Stanford University Press, 1947.

8

How Can Appreciation Be Taught?

1. Why Is Education of Emotions Necessary?

Introduction

For some time students of education have sensed a serious short-coming in the effectiveness of our educational program. As suggested in Chapter 1, the possession of factual knowledge does not give assurance that such knowledge will translate itself into functional relationships. Even the potential ability to attack problems effectively, of such vital concern to the individual and society, gives little certainty that the abilities thus possessed will be utilized. One may know much about the laws of health and still persist in living unhygienically; or be fully aware of the intellectual implications of citizenship in a democracy and yet fail completely to exercise the rights and duties of a desirable citizen. The early failures of the agencies of church and government through "book learning" to educate the Indian of our reservations in the accepted ways of living and modes of thought of the white man is a case in point. This failure reveals clearly the potency of other forces to nullify knowledge and even to supersede it as a controlling power over attitudes and conduct.

Throughout this text the place of emotional direction as expressed in mind-sets, attitudes, and ideals is accepted as vital in education. The education of the emotions is frankly acknowledged as of equal, if not of greater importance in the educational program of the secondary school than the acquisition of factual knowledge, or the development of the potential ability to attack and resolve problem situations. These three phases of the educational program of the high school are not, however, separate entities wholly unrelated to one another. On the contrary they are but aspects of a larger integrated unitary concept and program of education. The distinction between these aspects of an integrated educational program is largely one of emphasis. For convenience they are generally treated somewhat as separate segments, but this is done to secure facility in emphasizing the peculiar characteristics of each, and the specal treatment each should receive if they are to be effectively interrelated.

Thus far, major attention has been given: (1) to understanding, and (2) to the power of attack in the solution of problem situations. Nevertheless, constant emphasis has been placed upon the importance of motivation, and the development of correct procedures to insure the media of emotional toning essential to a satisfactory learning situation.

The problem of this chapter

The particular emphasis of this chapter is upon the third major factor in an integrated educational program at the secondary school level; namely, the direction of the student in the acquisition of those emotional dynamics — mind-sets, attitudes, and ideals — that give vitality and force to the whole of life. While there are some educational writers who agree that the emotional nature of the adolescent, and of the adult as well, is a more potent influence in the direction of his life than any accumulation of formal book knowledge or acquired skills, the curriculum remains heavily freighted with informational content, and only minor attention is given to the problem of the emotional adjustment of the individual to his world. No teacher is prepared to grapple with the education of the adolescent until he has some satisfactory answer to such questions as the following:

1. How do emotions operate to provide integration and directive force to one's life?
2. To what extent are mind-sets, attitudes, ideals, and tastes determined or influenced by emotional or intellectual considerations?
3. What procedures seem most effective and feasible for the teacher to use to insure the development of desirable mind-sets, attitudes, ideals, and appreciations?

To the answers to questions such as these the considerations of this chapter are devoted.

2. Why Are Emotional Controls Important?

In the opening chapter of this book, approval was given the quotation of Briggs to the effect that "Our intellect is a mere speck afloat on a sea of feeling." To the observant teacher it must become evident that "we feel more, both quantitatively and qualitatively, than we think." If not, the anomalies of human conduct become wholly inexplicable. Nowhere does the effect of emotional control over man's activities, his likes and dislikes, become more apparent and convincing than in a consideration of the influence of the *mores*, or social custom, upon the conduct patterns of the individual.

The nature of the mores

In his now classic monograph, *Folkways*, Sumner [1] gives a descriptive definition of the *mores*. He says:

> The *mores* are the ways of doing things, which are current in a society, to satisfy human needs and desires, together with the faiths, notions, codes, and standards of well-living which inhere in those ways, having a genetic connection with them.

According to this definition, the *mores* in primitive and civilized society find their genesis in the performance or observation of certain practices assumed to have social value for the group. For the most part, the assumption of value for these accepted practices was, and is, based upon very uncritical thinking.

It is highly important, nevertheless, to recognize that the *mores* have their origin in customs thought by the group that gave original assent to them to have peculiar merit toward the realization of cherished social values.

Time gives these customs and practices special sanction with the masses. The majority of those who live by the established *mores* are unable to give an intelligent reason for the practices which they so slavishly follow. "As time goes on, the folkways become more and more arbitrary, positive, and imperative." Men tend to act from force of habit and not from the dictates of clear

[1] Sumner, W. G. *Folkways*, p. 59. Boston: Ginn and Company, 1906.

reason. If the man of the street were asked why he acted in certain ways, he would probably answer that he did so because it was customary to act that way. Or, possibly, in some obvious embarrassment at the query, he would attempt unsuccessfully to rationalize his behavior.

The reason for this unquestioned, somewhat slavish acceptance by the individual of the established *mores* of the group is further clarified when the mode by which the individual is inducted into group life is considered. Sumner suggests [2] that "the process by which *mores* are developed and established is ritual. . . . Ritual is something to be done, not something to be thought or felt." He then continues with this trenchant comment, "We are led by suggestion and association to believe that there must be wisdom and utility in what we do." Modern society has not provided for this induction of the youth into the *mores* of the group with the conscious attention given to these matters by primitive peoples. Among primitive folk there were definite ritual ceremonies established for the induction of the youth into the conscious group life of the tribe or clan. These ritual ceremonies were usually set to take place at the pubertal or adolescent age. They were elaborate, highly emotional in character and, by the setting of the initiation rites, planned to doubly reinforce the emotional tone of the ritualistic exercises that transferred the youth into the conscious privileges and duties of the adult group. These ceremonies of induction were designed not so much to give to the initiate a reasoned basis for his future behavior and attitudes, as to impart to him the accepted ideals and behavior patterns of the group. These patterns he was expected to accept and follow thereafter without deviation. The ritual served further to imbue the youth thoroughly with the spirit of kinship with the tribe.[3] The process employed by modern society for the fusion of the individual into its group life does not depend upon specific ritualistic ceremonies. The procedures, however, are not fundamentally different from those of primitive groups, though they are less obvious and less carefully planned. In his home life it is expected that the child will be taught the common *mores* regarding property rights, the accepted etiquette and proprieties of the

[2] Sumner, W. G., *op. cit.*, pp. 60–62. See also Murphy, Gardner, *Personality*, pp. 778–783. New York: Harper and Brothers, 1947.

[3] See Uhl, W. L., *Secondary School Curricula*, chapters I–II, New York: The Macmillan Company, 1927, for an extended account of the nature of these initiatory ceremonies.

group, family loyalties, etc. At school, through class and school membership, flag-raising ceremonies, etc., he is brought to accept approved ways of group behavior and group loyalties with concomitant emotional conditioning.

There are those who insist that the nature of the *mores* requires their almost unquestioned acceptance by the masses, if their perpetuation and usefulness are to be sustained. Hartmann, a German writer in this field, declares: [4]

The mores (*Sitten*) are, before any beginning of reflection, the regulators of the political, social, and religious behavior of the individual. Conscious reflection is the worst enemy of the mores, because mores begin unconsciously and pursue unconscious purposes, which are recognized by reflection often only after long and circuitous processes, and because their expediency often depends on the assumption that they will have general acceptance and currency, un-interfered with by reflection.

The contention that "reflection is the worst enemy of the *mores*" is, of course, true to the extent that the *mores* in question have no validity in fact or reason. Students of social problems agree that many of our *mores* have long outlived their usefulness and, in fact, are serious obstacles to progress. In a fast evolving social order, this is to be expected in the very nature of the *mores* and of human nature. Yet there are many customs and practices accepted today that have validity in reason. The goal of education, which it must be admitted is not accepted wholeheartedly by some influential elements in our population, is to make conduct-control subject to rationality as far as possible. *Mores* that no longer have validity should, through reflection and education, be subject to elimination, and more desirable ones substituted where needed. James Russell Lowell, the poet, expressed this need for rational change in these words: "New occasions teach new duties; Time makes ancient good uncouth." Whatever our wishes to the contrary, certainly it must be agreed that in common practice little, if any, thinking is done by the masses with respect to the *mores* that dominate them. If any of the accepted *mores* are challenged by thoughtful students of social custom, the reaction to this challenge on the part of those who accept these *mores* is likely to be emo-

[4] Quoted in Sumner, W. G., *op. cit.*, pp. 59–60. See also Pendell, Elmer, editor, *Society Under Analysis*, pp. 224f. Lancaster, Pa.: The Jaques Cattell Press, 1942.

tional rather than intellectual. It is this powerful emotional resistance to change that makes the arts of the demagogue and unscrupulous politician so dangerous and inimical to the welfare of society.

Influence of the mores on thought and conduct

The influence and power of the *mores* [5] as the regulators of human conduct are generally admitted by students of social phenomena. No part of our lives escapes the strong currents of influence set up by the *mores*.[6]

They pervade and control the ways of thinking in all the exigencies of life. . . . The *mores* are social ritual in which we all participate unconsciously. The current habits as to hours of labor, meal hours, family life, the social intercourse of the sexes, propriety, amusements, travel, holidays, education, the use of periodicals and libraries, innumerable other details of life fall under this ritual. Each does as everybody does. For the great mass of mankind as to all things, and for all of us for a great many things, the rule to do as all do suffices.

The oft-quoted statement attributed to the wise churchman, "Give me the child until he is seven and I care not what you may do with him thereafter," is extreme, but contains too much truth in it to be ignored. Modern psychology has tended to emphasize the importance of childhood and youth as the formative years for the inculcation of mind-sets, attitudes, tastes, and ideals. "No creed, no moral code, and no scientific demonstration can ever win the same hold upon men and women as habits of action, with associated sentiments and states of mind, drilled in from childhood." [7] Psychologists and educators agree that the earlier these habits of action and general mind-sets are firmly established, the better. In the matter of attitudes, tastes, and ideals, there is much opportunity for education peculiarly appropriate to the adolescent age. The physiological changes, with their concomitant psychological effects, and the larger social outlook of this age, make the adolescent period an important one in which to cultivate certain social atti-

[5] The term *mores* as used in this chapter is applied in a broad nontechnical sense to include customs and conventions that have come to have general acceptance by a large group of society, whether these customs or conventions have rationality or not.

[6] Sumner, W. G., *op. cit.*, pp. 59–62.

[7] *Ibid.*, p. 61.

tudes and ideals with respect to the relations of the sexes, the family, the community, and the larger interrelations of society, both national and international. The majority of adults will not stray far from the accepted patterns of conduct and sentiment firmly established in childhood and youth.

Personal and social significance of the mores

When the potency of the *mores* in the control of human conduct and the predominance of the emotional over the intellectual factor in their nature and persistence is granted, we may recognize clearly the significance of the *mores* in the education of the emotions. The teacher should think of their importance in relation to the education of the emotions in at least five particulars.

1. *The mores provide a means of integration.* "Integration, the most important characteristic of the wholesome individual personality, is also the most significant characteristic of the normal social group." [8] Integration can take place only around a commonality of ideas and purposes. Social customs, as has been seen, provide the means of commonality of group purpose inasmuch as they become the common means by which the group strives, consciously or unconsciously, to achieve desired goals or satisfactions. Where the individual or the group finds conflicts in purpose or action, emotional tensions and a sense of personal and group frustration result. A sense of frustration, felt either by the individual or the group, leads to a sense of discouragement or futility and a consequent paralysis of the power of action. The highest degree of satisfaction is felt by the individual members of the group when all seem to be working in unison or harmony. Likewise, the highest degree of individual and group power is evidenced under conditions of complete integration. "United we stand; divided we fall," or "In union there is strength," are maxims that express this truth neatly. "Morale" is the term used most commonly to express the effect of integration in marked degree. Educationally the value of the *mores* as an agency of integration cannot be ignored by the school without serious consequences to the effectiveness of its own program and to the welfare of society.

2. *The mores provide a means of social control.* If man is to an extraordinary degree the follower of the fashions of the group,

[8] Burnham, W. H. *The Wholesome Personality,* p. 488. New York: D. Appleton and Company, 1932.

these customs become in turn the powerful directive controls of his attitudes and conduct. Those who can mold the customs of the group are, by the same token, to that degree the masters of the individual's conduct. It is seldom possible to decree a fashion by fiat, though often modes of conduct, successfully established in this manner, have with time emerged into the full status of binding *mores*. In matters of etiquette, dress, and social intercourse, a few influential leaders, particularly in the middle and upper social classes, often determine the social *mores* for the masses. The weightier social customs are not so susceptible to the direct influence of a few leaders. However, they are subject to creation and modification by the consistent and persistent efforts of a few, through whose efforts converts are won to the new modes of thought and behavior until a formidable array of recognized leaders and prominent members of the group have accepted the new customs. Then, as by magic, the rank and file accept the change, and new *mores* are established. The school can exercise tremendous power through adult and student leaders in setting fashions that soon become traditions of the school — traditions which may become rigid and inflexible controls of the group. The importance within the school of wisely stimulating desirable fashions of conduct will be discussed in the chapter on discipline. Desirable group life will be experienced, both within the school and without, to the extent that there are prevailing fashions to which the groups concerned subscribe, and to the extent to which these dominant *mores* are socially desirable.

3. *The mores provide a means of conserving energy.* In his well-known discussion of the significance of "Habit" in human economy, William James laid particular stress on the conservation of time and energy as the great boon of reducing as many activities as possible to automatic routine. The excessive drain on one's mental and emotional life, when one is constantly confronted with the pros and cons of the next act, was vividly pictured by this great psychologist. In much the same vein Sumner declares: [9]

> The great mass of the folkways give us discipline and the support of routine and habit. If we had to form judgments as to all these

[9] Sumner, W. G., *op. cit.*, p. 62. Also see Thorpe, Louis P., *Psychological Foundations of Personality*, pp. 228–279. New York: McGraw-Hill Book Company, 1938.

cases before we could act in them, and were forced always to act rationally, the burden would be unendurable.

A recent advocate of the inclusion of the teaching of the *mores* as an integral part of the high-school curriculum comments thus: [10]

> When educators realize that all men ordinarily substitute quick, automatic reactions without disaster for expensive and unnecessary thought, they will realize the responsibility for laying more emphasis in the curricular program on good habits and on the sound *mores*. Habits and *mores* are economical, then, in that they free time for important reflection and rational thinking in the extreme crises of life.

4. *The mores provide a means of directing wholesome leisure-time activities.* To the extent that the *mores* governing the recreational activities of the group are wholesome, they serve to govern indirectly the type of leisure-time activities in which members of the group engage. Further, to the extent that the general *mores* of the group are strongly conditioned emotionally by ideals and uncompromising attitudes favorable to personal and group conduct of a superior type, the individual will seek to conform to those standards in the selection of leisure-time activities which bring subjective and social approbation. Teachers need to be reminded frequently that leisure-time activities will tend to reflect the conduct patterns of the approved general *mores* of the group.

5. *The mores serve to inhibit social change.* This fact is both an asset and a liability. The inertia of the group to change its *mores* is of inestimable worth when those *mores* are basically good and their acceptance is intellectually reasoned as well as emotionally conditioned. The inhibitions against change in those *mores* whose *raison d'etre* is understood can more easily be broken down when the conditions that gave them worth for a given time or place no longer obtain. However, when strong emotional conditioning is the primary basis for support of *mores* that have ceased to have group value, the natural tendency of social customs to resist change is intensified, and they then become a menace.

Emotions essential to development of mores

Obviously the teacher who studies the educational implications of the folkways must be impressed with the extent to which they

[10] Briggs, T. H. *Secondary Education*, p. 457. New York: The Macmillan Company, 1933.

affect the life of the individual at nearly every point of his social relations. Too, it must be equally obvious to the teacher that social customs are influenced by the emotional life of the individual to a much greater degree than by his intellect. Clearly the relation of the folkways to emotional controls lies predominantly in the feeling of satisfaction or discomfort that arises when the individual conforms or fails to conform to the accepted standards of the group with which he desires to be identified. The intensity of these emotional reactions will in part depend upon the inflexibility of the group *mores* in question, and in part upon the degree of reasoned or unquestioned loyalty the individual gives to them.

If the secondary school is to be charged with the responsibility of educating youth to seek and to formulate better ways of living than those which now obtain in society, and this book has maintained throughout that that is a primary obligation of the school, then we must face the drastic modification and change of many existing customs and conventions. We must be constantly prepared to undertake modifications and changes of social conventions as changing conditions may require. No program of education will be adequate for this task which does not take full cognizance of the emotions as essential factors in conditioning the members of the social group, both to instigate desired changes in the existing *mores* and to accept with fervor new patterns of social behavior when these have been rationally determined.

3. What Is the Nature of Appreciation?

Appreciation a recognition of values

In the acquisition of motor skills, memory skills, factual knowledge, or the power to solve problems, primary concern is with mastery in these learning processes. In the appreciation type of learning we deal with values assumed to exist in a given situation or in a given experience.[11] It is this recognition of value that sets appreciative learning somewhat apart from pure motor or pure ideational learning. Knowledge or skills possess no value within themselves, and they may be pursued quite independently of any recognized values which may accrue from their mastery.

Recently the writer was in conversation with a group of men,

[11] Morrison, H. C. *The Practice of Teaching in the Secondary School*, p. 339. Chicago: University of Chicago Press, 1931.

among whom was a scientist who had just received considerable
newspaper publicity in connection with an experiment being conducted under his direction. The conversation drifted to the nature
of the experiment. When the scientist had explained the details, a
layman present immediately ventured the query, "Of what use will
the experiment be when it is completed?" After a moment's hesitation the scientist replied that he did not know that it had any
value. However, he went on to explain that most of the valuable
scientific discoveries of history had no immediate worth, and that
it was only after years had elapsed that men found that some of
these early discoveries had practical value. The terms *applied
science* and *pure science* have been used to distinguish the scientific
knowledge that was recognized to have utilitarian value and the
scientific knowledge considered at the moment to have no value
within itself.

Here it is necessary to repeat what has been suggested often
in this book; namely, that the most effective learning does not take
place apart from motivation. Motivation arises out of situations
wherein are sensed values of worth to the individual, which either
inhere directly within the situation or indirectly through goals that
are relational in character. To the scientist the relational values
may be very remote, but they are sufficient to motivate and direct
his effort. Unfortunately, the mass of our adult population and immature adolescents need more positive assurances of immediate
values for adequate motivation.

Frequently, however, the individual is not confronted with the
determination of the presence or absence of values, or the discovery of new values. Rather, in numerous situations, values exist for
the individual in many degrees and varieties. One may find it
pleasant to engage in certain types of activities and not in others.
In fact, one frequently confronts the necessity of choosing between two or more activities, each attractive in itself. It may be
that a choice between the theater and the lecture is necessary.
Perhaps one finds on a visit to a near-by city that a Shakespearean
play, a popular moving picture, and a lecture by an authority long
admired are scheduled for the same hour. Or, again, one may have
to choose between engaging in an immediate enjoyable activity or
foregoing it for some other in which the enjoyment and values are
deferred. A hierarchy of values thus confronts the individual and
forces a choice of the greater as over against the lesser values as

they exist for him. It is part of appreciational training, therefore, so to condition the individual as to insure the proper reaction, not only to values as such but to values in hierarchical relationships. Under these circumstances, and in a very restricted sense, appreciation may be thought of as "the *evaluation of the values* which . . . present themselves for our acceptance, and which are sometimes mutually incompatible."

Appreciation a matter of emotion

The teacher might infer that the recognition of values in appreciation made it an essentially intellectual procedure. This is quite contrary to fact, much as it might be desired that values could be more coldly and objectively appraised. In reality, values are not so discovered. It is emotion that colors thinking, and to a large degree acts as a co-determiner of values. As William James pointedly remarked,[12] "If your heart does not want a world of moral reality, your head will assuredly never make you believe in one." This fact is clearly recognized by Coffin [13] in these words:

> The appreciation of "value" is not an intellectual process alone; "value" appeals and attracts; the characteristic element in appreciation is affection-feeling tone, rather than cognition. Feeling is as basic a mental process as thinking, and furnishes the motive not only for overt reaction, but for all of the intellectual processes as well.

Another writer,[14] recognizing the nature of attitudes and ideals in the determination of values, says:

> The development of an ideal is both an emotional and an intellectual process, but the *emotional element is by far the more important*. Ideals that lack emotional coloring are simply intellectual propositions, and have little directive force upon conduct.

Nor can we think of appreciation in its "affective glow" as wholly positive. Implicit in the favorable attitudes toward certain values are the probabilities that there are other elements in the total situation toward which negative reactions have been made simultaneously. After all, values generally grow out of contrasts, and when

---

[12] James, William. *The Will to Believe*, p. 23. New York: Longmans Green and Company, 1896.
[13] Coffin, J. H. *Personality in the Making*, p. 85. Boston: Houghton Mifflin Company, 1923.
[14] Bagley, W. C. *The Educative Process*, p. 223. New York: The Macmillan Company, 1905.

intense emotion or feeling-color obtains toward a given set of values, it is probably accompanied by negative attitudes toward elements in the situation which bid for favor but were rejected as being of lesser or false value. "The feeling-tone strain in appreciation need not be a pleasant one. The statement, 'I appreciate your position but still feel constrained to reject the manuscript,' implies that the speaker has arrived at an intellectual evaluation of the situation but that the feeling-tone is negative." [15] These negative and positive factors combine to insure in appreciation strong emotional feeling-tones. In part, *appreciation, therefore, may be said to consist of the emotional disposition to choose those values in life conceived to be of greatest ultimate significance to the individual and society.*

Appreciation and the mores related

A close affinity is observed to exist between *appreciation* and *mores*. Both are concerned with a sense of values inherent in a situation. Both are heavily freighted with emotional feeling-tones which predispose the individual to a certain type of response. Both are subject to education through creation, development, and direction. Both are subject to similar educational procedures which will predispose the individual to react in conformity with definite appreciational patterns, or to react in conformity with definite patterns of social conduct. The *mores* may be said to be an aspect of appreciation, inasmuch as the *mores* concern the acceptance of values as these values relate themselves to conduct patterns assumed to have value for the group, and for the individual in his relations to the group. Hence, the further consideration of the creation and development of desirable *mores*, and the predisposing of the individual to participation in the wholesome *mores* of the group, will be treated as an aspect of ethical-social appreciation.

Types of appreciation

Among writers on appreciation there appears little agreement on the matter of the classification of types of appreciation. This naturally follows from the lack of agreement as to the exact nature of appreciation. If *appreciation* is limited to mean *sheer enjoyment* as it is by some writers, then no further classification is possible.

[15] Powers, F. F. and Uhl, W. L. *Psychological Principles of Education,* p. 287. New York: The Century Company, 1933.

Some writers classify appreciation as *aesthetic, ethical,* and *intellectual,* while others follow a twofold classification of *technical* and *aesthetic.* To attempt such a classification implies a rigorous separation of the emotional and intellectual elements in appreciation, quite at variance with a psychologically sound concept. Coffin [16] who calls appreciation "sentiment at work," suggests a fourfold classification in which the emotional and intellectual elements are recognized in each of the four types enumerated, thus: "the *intellectual* sentiment is a feeling-attitude toward questions of truth; the *aesthetic,* to the question of beauty; the *moral,* to the question of goodness; and the *religious,* to God."

It would seem more in accordance with the nature of appreciation to give to it a twofold classification; namely, *aesthetic* and *ethical-social.* The objection that the concept of appreciation still remains somewhat inexact as applied in a specific situation is in part true. It cannot be known in a given case whether the appreciation is predominantly emotional in content or highly intellectual. The presence of both influences in some degree, however, is necessary in the very nature of appreciation as defined in this chapter. This composite nature of the appreciational experience is accepted by Zane,[17] who says: "An *appreciation experience* is the composite produced when one places sensory, feeling, emotional, and intellectual evaluations upon any experience."

Aesthetic appreciation may be defined as the satisfactions that result from experiencing the beautiful in a situation — harmony of color and sound, symmetry of shape, rhythm of motion. For the novice, beauty in a given situation may be general, diffused, vague, yet none the less real. Aesthetic appreciation may even be the result of the conscious or unconscious association of a given situation or object with an experience definitely pleasurable or an idea definitely appealing in its nature. The strains of a musical selection incidental to, but associated with, the experience of a mellow moonlight night, a canoe on a placid lake, and romance, may thereafter, for the participants in this experience, clothe a very commonplace musical selection with rare beauty, charm, and the subtle power to stir the emotions deeply. Two lines or bars crossed in a given rela-

16 Coffin, J. H., *op. cit.,* pp. 92–93.
17 Mueller, John H., and others. *Studies in Appreciation of Art,* p. 54. Studies in College Teaching, Bulletin 3. Eugene, Oregon: University of Oregon, 1934.

tion may produce a plus sign with no appreciational significance for the individual, but let these lines or bars be so arranged and proportioned as to make the form of the cross, and immediately this figure takes on symbolic significance capable of arousing the most profound emotional responses of reverence or adoration on the part of devoted followers of the religion of which it is the symbol. This simple figure of the cross is clothed with aesthetic qualities for most peoples of Western nations, due wholly to its ideational and historical associations.

In aesthetic appreciation there may be a decided predominance of the feeling-tone as one is emotionally stirred by the music to which he is listening. He may know little about the technical aspects of the composition or the skill of the player. However, these intellectual aspects of appreciation cannot be wholly lacking. Normally, the greater the recognition of the presence of these qualities within the situation, the greater the concomitant emotional reaction, and the greater the total appreciation that results. It is possible for one to be fully cognizant of the technical skill present in the situation, and at the same time to find his emotional response minimal, though this is not likely to be the case.

Ethical-social appreciation may be defined as the satisfactions that result from the recognition of the social or moral qualities of goodness and truth present in a given situation. These qualities may be poorly defined or quite vaguely sensed, rather than clearly understood. It is even possible to attribute to a situation or activity certain qualities which in reality it does not possess, such as has frequently happened with respect to many *mores* of society. Here again it may be difficult to determine the degree to which the emotional and the intellectual predominate in the appreciational mood. A display of loyalty to the team by a seriously hurt player on the football field, who continues to play at the price of jeopardy to health, may arouse a veritable paroxysm of joy and admiration among the less thoughtful spectators on the bleachers; but the same exhibition of loyalty may cause a more thoughtful member of the group, who understands the seriousness to the player of such misguided loyalty, to find his emotional ardor greatly inhibited by his intellectual understanding of the situation. Furthermore, one who stands in the presence of a great truth just discovered, might vaguely recognize the elements of its social significance with but a trace of emotion, while another with a much fuller understanding and a greater imagination might recognize much more clearly and vividly the far-reaching social significance of the discovery; with the result that the concomitant surge of emotion aroused might become so intense as to make speech momentarily impossible.

Education for appreciation important

The discussion of the importance of emotional conditioning in relation to the development of mind-sets, attitudes, and ideals with respect to the *mores*, need but be recalled to emphasize the value of appreciational development for efficient social participation and group control. The development of worth-while interests and aesthetic appreciations for wholesome leisure-time activity and enjoyment is fast becoming a consideration of first importance. With the rapid development of technology more leisure time is available to the individual. Labor organizations and many thoughtful students of social-economic problems have demanded that the hours for labor in industry be restricted to thirty per week. It is contended that the production of all goods necessary for the use of society is possible with a labor schedule of less than thirty hours per week. There are social engineers who claim that a planned economy would reduce the actual labor necessary to provide the material needs of society to from two to three hours per day. In any event, the future is likely to allow the individual a large part of the day for leisure activities. Possibly no greater responsibility rests upon society, and through it upon the school in the future, than that of the development of those appreciations which will enable people to use their leisure time in a way that is personally wholesome and socially profitable.

Emotional-appreciational education requires differentiated technique

Most educators recognize that a different technique is needed to educate for appreciation from that used to teach skills and knowledge. Unfortunately, educational practice in the past has too often failed to distinguish appreciational learning from other types of learning, with the result that the same methods which were found to be very effective in the teaching of skills and factual knowledge were applied to the teaching of appreciation. The school has consequently failed to inculcate effectively a love for the beautiful, and to develop favorable attitudes toward the most desirable forms of conduct.

Educational leaders have long since learned that most satisfactory learning takes place under conditions of pleasure and satisfaction. The tendency of educational method, therefore, is distinctly away from threat and compulsion in learning, even where pure motor or memory learning is involved. The effort to escape as far as possible the deadening effect of a sense of compulsion in learning has been stressed in the consideration of every method thus far discussed in this book. If, as has been said, "appreciation is an affective state attached to a concrete experience," then appreciation can be developed principally as pleasant feeling-tones are associated with the learning experience. For the most part, appreciation cannot be taught under threat or compulsion. The incongruity of such efforts is thus strikingly portrayed by Kilpatrick.[18]

> Some other things cannot be assigned at all under penalty, for example, appreciations and attitudes. . . . Imagine a teacher's saying, "You boys are deficient in your appreciation of Nicholas Nickleby. You must stay in this afternoon and raise your appreciation to 70 or above." Or imagine the principal's saying, "If you boys don't like your teacher any better by next Monday I'll have to punish you till you do."

There is little likelihood that pleasurable responses will attach themselves to situations with which are associated only unpleasant experiences.

It is this fact that makes training in appreciation unusually difficult. The teacher cannot drive the student to experience pleasurable reactions to situations. It is a matter of leadership that awakens these desirable responses. The teacher can assign the memorization of a poem, and, by setting up a series of unpleasant consequences which greatly offset the particular unpleasantness that may surround the ordeal of memorizing the poem, force the student to master the assignment. Since memorization involves a form of learning over which the student has control, the learning can take place irrespective of the fact that such learning is distasteful. The teacher, too, can set up the tests that determine mastery of the verbal repetition of the poem, and to some degree the student's understanding of the poem. The teacher cannot, however, determine the feeling-tone that envelops the activity. No devices are yet available by means of which this can be done

18 Kilpatrick, W. H. *Foundations of Method*, p. 288. New York: The Macmillan Company, 1925.

adequately. Furthermore, the student does not exercise complete control over his emotional responses. The very nature of the organism itself predisposes it to follow certain patterns of response. Under extremely adverse situations the student could not, no matter how hard he tried, immediately overcome an aversion acquired for a given situation or object as the result of some particularly unpleasant experience associated with it. In some situations the negative feeling-tone has been so strongly emotionalized and the attitudes so firmly set, that it is virtually impossible ever completely to overcome such aversions. The emotional conditioning in childhood against darkness and snakes is an example in point. Many adults are never able to reason away the emotional conditioning received in childhood toward similar situations or objects, no matter how hard they try.

4. How Is Ethical-Social Appreciation Developed?

Elements of appreciation involved

It is not possible to draw hard and fast lines between *ethical-social* forms of appreciation and *aesthetic* forms. The aesthete would be quick to resent the implication that *aesthetics* did not contribute to social values or social well-being. Arbitrarily, therefore, the consideration of *ethical-social* appreciation will emphasize the development of those interests, attitudes, ideals, and *mores* that contribute most directly to the social welfare, and to the wholesome enjoyments and pleasures of the individual within the social milieu. In each of these appreciational forms, emotion and intellect play a part. "Wholesome enjoyment and pleasure" may require but a minimum of the intellectual element and a maximum of the emotional; while ideals may carry the individual to the opposite extreme of maximal thinking and minimal feeling, though this is not likely to be true.

Technique of developing ethical-social appreciations

No complete set of suggestions can be offered for the development of ethical-social appreciations that would apply in every situation or with every individual. The cultivation of an attitude may vary considerably from that of the development of an ideal, the establishment of desirable *mores*, or the winning of loyal conformity to existing social customs. Besides, as has been suggested previously in this chapter, there is less positively known about the most effective means of developing interests, attitudes, ideals, or the establishment of *mores* than is known about the successful direction of the other types of learning. The suggestions offered here are among those usually considered effective in the development of ethical-social appreciations.

1. *The teacher can best teach the attitudes he himself shares.* The personality of the teacher plays a more important part in the teaching of appreciation than in any other phase of teaching. In the very nature of the teacher-student relationship, and the strategic place of the school in the community life, the ideas and attitudes of the teacher are potent influences in shaping the thinking of the student. No teacher can successfully lead the student to acquire attitudes he himself does not share. Sham and hypocrisy are generally anathema to people, and to adolescents in particular. It is hard to give lip service to an attitude one does not genuinely feel. The ring of insincerity is likely to be detected in the voice or facial expression. This is true because attitudes and ideals are heavily freighted with emotion, and genuine emotional tone is extremely hard to simulate when it is not present. This inability readily to imitate feeling-color that does not exist is due in large measure to the fact that objective analysis of the expression of emotion when one is within its grip does not take place. Indeed, it is an open question whether objective analysis is fully possible. Emotional feeling-tone is so subtle that it is likely to fade away and elude the one who attempts to hold it for analysis. For the most part analysis of emotional states must take place subsequent to the experiencing of the emotion one desires to study.

The reaction of the student to an assumed enthusiasm is likely to be one of contempt for the teacher, and positive antagonism to the interest, attitude, or ideal the teacher wishes the student to adopt. If the teacher accepts, but does not feel strongly concerning a desirable attitude or ideal, little effort should be made to conjure up a pretended enthusiasm for the benefit of the class.

2. *The teacher should exemplify the ideals he teaches.* There is close kinship here with the above suggestion. The old adage, "What you are speaks so loudly I cannot hear what you say," expresses the idea concisely. It is possible to feel strongly the value of certain attitudes and ideals, yet seldom if ever act upon them. Sooner or later the students who have opportunity to become somewhat in-

timately acquainted with the social activities of their teachers, as many do in the smaller schools and communities, begin to compare the teachers' conduct with the ideals professed. It is of the utmost importance that the teacher "practice what he preaches." No teacher can justify his right to teach who encourages attitudes or permits ideas to become current which are inimical to the social life of the school or to society. It is incumbent upon the teacher to live ideals, irrespective of whether he specifically sets them before the students in words. It is the total situation as it concerns the teacher to which the student reacts. The teacher of physical education — athletic coach in most schools — occupies an enviable position in his influence over high school boys. If he proclaims strongly ideals of fair play, honesty, and truthfulness, but plays ineligible boys where he can "get by," he not only loses the respect of the students and forfeits his opportunity for leadership in developing proper attitudes and ideals, but tends as well to nullify the social value of ideals in the minds of these students.

3. *Precepts may be effectively used.* The power of *precepts* in the control of personal behavior, the formulation of attitudes and ideals, and the establishment of *mores* are too often underestimated by the teacher. The strength of precepts and slogans lies in the condensation into a striking catch phrase, jingle, or rhyme, of an idea of general interest or worth dogmatically asserted. Precepts and slogans grip the imagination, and often enough and generally enough repeated, come to have a powerful influence over the thought and social behavior of people. From childhood years most adults have heard such precepts repeated as: "The early bird catches the worm," "Honor thy father and thy mother that thy days may be long," "Pride comes before a fall," or

> Early to bed,
> Early to rise
> Makes a man healthy,
> Wealthy, and wise.

Slogans are closely akin to precepts as effective determiners of attitudes and social controls. "America for Americans" is one type of slogan that produces a glow of emotion and blind prejudice, but results in little intellectual activity. It is very effective, however, in building up a strong nationalistic sentiment. The power of slogans to control attitudes and conduct is still vivid in the memory of those adults who participated in World War I. Such slogans as "He kept us out of War" elected a man to the presidency of the United States, just as the slogans coined by that same man — "The War to end Wars," and "Make the world safe for democracy," led those same voters to become possessed with an unshakable conviction, born of emotion, that they were embarked upon a most holy crusade in behalf of human liberties. In World War II, "Remember Pearl Harbor" was one of the few slogans which made an impression on the public. While "slogans and maxims are usually quoted and accepted with little intellectual consideration," [19] they are powerful instruments of emotional conditioning toward attitudes, ideals, and group *mores*, which the school can ill afford to ignore.

Those who believe that the school should stress only an intellectual basis for conduct insist that all instruction should be directed toward providing the student with full information and the technique of problem solution as a guide to every behavior situation. They challenge the pedagogical wisdom or right of the school to inculcate attitudes, or to be instrumental in the establishment of social-behavior patterns not fully intellectualized for the student. Such a point of view ignores realities and the practical social situation of which the school is inextricably a part. Academically, all must admit the desirability and responsibility of the school to make the attitudes, ideals, and *mores* of society as intelligent as possible to the individual members of the group. Practically, the school must sense the actualities of the social situation and recognize the educational responsibilities of the school, implicit in the nature of society. As Briggs points out: [20] "But when the feelings are dominant, however occasionally, should we not be concerned that they are the right feelings directed toward good objectives?"

4. *Ethical-social instruction, both direct and incidental, should be utilized.* Some writers advocate the incidental teaching of appreciation only. They contend that you cannot teach ethical-social appreciation as you teach algebra or chemistry. That is quite true. The objective of algebra and chemistry teaching has been largely to acquire factual knowledge and problem-solving skill. The objective for the teaching of ethical-social appreciation is the development of interests, attitudes, and ideals, which includes the recognition of values within desirable social patterns and the emotionalizing of the acceptance of these values by the student. To the extent

[19] Briggs, T. H., *op. cit.*, p. 429.   [20] Briggs, T. H., *op. cit.*, p. 429.

that the intellectual element is involved in social appreciation direct instruction would seem pertinent. The school should lead the student to a rational discovery of those attitudes, ideals, and *mores* worthy of acceptance and emulation, and of those that need to be established to achieve more readily the desirable goals of the individual and society. Indeed, it would seem quite imperative for the student to discover the reasons why a certain form of behavior is considered either inimical to or beneficial to the best interests of society or the individual. The student should be made cognizant of specific social qualities which racial-social experience has led to quite universal acceptance as desirable or undesirable. These qualities should be generalized in the mind of the student through the use of numerous concrete situations brought to his attention, in which the effects of the operation of the social qualities in question are unmistakably discernible. To a much greater extent than is generally assumed, ethical-social appreciation *can be directly taught*. It is the aim of education to remove conduct as far as possible from blind subservience to group *mores*. Such teaching involves strong emphasis upon the intellectual elements without neglecting the emotional concomitants that should accompany the intellectualization of attitudes, ideals, and loyalties to existing or desired group *mores*. The direct teaching of the evil effects of alcohol for a generation preceding the advent of prohibition is a case in point where both the intellectual and emotional aspects of the situation were stressed with telling effect.

However, the incidental or indirect teaching of appreciation is of vital importance. It is said of the late William Rainey Harper, President of the University of Chicago, that "he taught Hebrew as a series of hairbreadth escapes." It would scarcely be inferred that he did not teach the language facts of Hebrew as well as many contemporary teachers of Hebrew. Rather, it is fair to assume that these language facts were taught as well by President Harper as they were taught by contemporaries, if not better. Indeed, through his enthusiasm, his attitudes, his manner, and his methods he vitalized — emotionalized — the learning of Hebrew with a warmth of feeling-tone that awakened interest in and aroused enthusiasm for the study of the language. From the standpoint of the teacher the teaching both of facts and attitudes was directly done by the use of specific techniques, though the student was little conscious of other than the direct method employed.

Some of the most effective teaching of ethical-social appreciation has been carried forward by indirect methods. It is generally conceded that Harriet Beecher Stowe's *Uncle Tom's Cabin* played a significant part in educating public opinion to the evils of the deeply rooted social-economic convention of slavery in American life. More than a generation later, T. S. Arthur's *Ten Nights in a Barroom* had no small part in crystallizing public sentiment against the evils of the saloon. In both of the examples cited, the pedagogical strategy in developing attitudes was to attach the opprobrium of generally recognized, undesirable social qualities to a social situation and practice. Enough facts were introduced clearly to identify universally repugnant social qualities with each form of social practice, then, through the incidental medium of a human-interest story, mind-sets were very strongly emotionalized against these specific social customs, even to the point of arousing intense hatred against everything associated with these practices.

5. *At times pressure may be employed to establish or teach respect for, and conformity to, the mores.* There is an inexorableness about conformity to the *mores* of the group. Wherever possible, the positive factors in the determination of attitudes that conform to group practice should be stressed. However, there are occasions when emotional conditioning favorable to some of the dominant group *mores* seems impossible without resort to the use of the fear of the unpleasant, properly to condition the mind-set of the individual toward acceptance of the *mores* in question. The use of social approval and disapproval in positive fashion should be utilized under these conditions to secure conformity, until more desirable conditioning factors can be made to operate. Realism, substituted for fanciful wishing, must force the teacher to recognize that in normal life-situations the machinery of social control often tends to operate relentlessly, often with cold impersonality, as it maims or destroys those who get in the way or who attempt to defy its operation. The rigorousness, the inexorableness at times, of the operation of the *mores* should be made a reality to the student through fact and experience. The child soon learns through a few experiences the consequences of touching a hot stove, or of getting too close to a flame. As a result of these experiences he acquires very definite attitudes toward fire, emotionally conditioned, in direct ratio to the intensity or vividness of his experiences. The school would fail of its complete duty to youth were it to neglect

the negative aspects of appreciational training through a mistaken sentimentalism in behalf of the positive — the pleasurable.

6. *Provision should be made for the expression of the desired interest, attitude, or ideal.* Teachers of physical education know that the best way to develop genuine interest in a given form of sport is to get the subject to participate successfully in the sport. The proverbial fascination of golf for the devotee of this sport, with the equally well-known concomitant suffusion of emotion that envelops the participants, can never be obtained vicariously. To enjoy the full exhilarating effect of the emotional warmth of the game one must be a participant. To the prosaic observer, nothing could appear more stupid and uninteresting than for the mature man deliberately to hit a diminutive rubber ball, carefully replace his club in the golf bag, in company with one or two companions nonchalantly walk to where the ball stopped, slowly, deliberately, choose a club and repeat the previous performance, not once more, but repeatedly as he and his companions advance up hill and down for the space of an hour or more. It becomes a decidedly different situation when the observer assumes the status of full participant.

To give expression to acts of kindness, generosity, and other desirable social qualities tends to strengthen attitudes and ideals because of the pleasurable feeling-tone engendered by intellectual satisfactions which result, or by the conscious approval of others whose good opinions are valued. The Boy Scouts of America has proved itself to be one of the most effective character-building agencies for youth. The scout is conditioned toward the loyal acceptance of desirable attitudes, ideals, and social patterns of behavior in two very definite ways.

First, the scout is led to recognize and accept certain desirable social attitudes, ideals, and conduct-patterns through positive instruction in the ways a good scout thinks and acts. The initiate is committed to the ideals and practice of scouting through the scout oath. The scout oath is taken in a ritualistic setting designed to impress the tenderfoot scout with the importance of scout ideals, and to condition emotionally his acceptance of these ideals.

The *second* way in which the scout is led to the acceptance and practice of social ideals is through his pledge "to do a good turn every day." Participation, practice of his scout ideals, provides for the satisfactions that arise from translating ideals into concrete accomplishments. The evidences of appreciation from the recipients of the "good turns," the definite social approval of companions and elders of the community that attend acts of thoughtfulness, the obvious approval of scout master and fellow scouts, and not least of all the sense of personal achievement and of personal approbation for duty well done, are factors that strongly condition the youth toward socially desirable ideals and behavior. It suffuses his whole being with a strong feeling-tone of satisfaction. Necessarily, the attempt to fulfill the obligation of "a good turn every day" leads to the discovery and appropriation of new social ideals and practices. Social appreciations are thus extended and developed, with the recognition and acceptance of new social values as these are identified with new situations.

It is this significant factor of self-expression in the development of social appreciation that gives point to the demand of modern educators for the reorganization of the curriculum and methods of the school to provide for activities — projects — of a life-situation type through which attitudes, ideals, and desirable patterns of social behavior may better be developed.

It should not be inferred that direct participation is the only means of providing expression for desirable interests, attitudes, and ideals. Many valuable ethical-social attitudes and ideals can be established or greatly strengthened through vicarious experience. It is this fact that makes biography and literature valuable as agencies of ethical-social appreciation. Literature of noble theme enables the student to live in imagination with the characters, identify himself with the activities of the participants, and develop strong sentiments favorable to worthy motives, ideals of social justice, etc., as portrayed in the incidents and in the thoughts and acts of favorite characters. Literature usually has its villains and ignoble characters who provided definite contrasts to the characters which the authors desire the readers to accept as heroes. The specific acts of each group are associated with undesirable or desirable attitudes and conduct that tend to establish emotionalized mind-sets for and against the attitude or conduct-traits of the two character groups. Biographies of great men and women who have won general approbation because of the sterling qualities of character and the nobility of their attitudes and ideals, expressed in concrete social situations, have given ample proof of the vitality of these materials, when used as a means of vicarious expression of attitudes and ideals by youth. Agencies devoted to character building have long recognized the potency of 'literature and biography as media through which to develop new appreciational values for worthy conduct patterns and to strengthen worthy attitudes and ideals already present with the student.

7. *Ritual may be effectively used to provide adequate emotional conditioning.* In the section on "the nature of the *mores*," the importance of ritual in the emotional conditioning of social attitudes and social conduct was stressed. "The process," says Sumner,[21] "by which mores are developed and established is ritual." Since much of ethical-social appreciation, as reflected in the *mores*, is predominantly emotional rather than intellectual, ritual becomes particularly effective as a means of establishing predispositions toward socially desirable forms of conduct. The rituals of organizations such as the Boy Scouts, Girl Scouts, Camp Fire Girls, Order of DeMolays, Rainbow Girls, Hi-Y Clubs, etc., are powerful directive and controlling forces in developing attitudes, ideals, and social practices. Through undervaluation of ritual the schools, and, indeed, civilized society as a whole, have neglected one of the most potent forces available for the development of ethical-social appreciation.

5. How Is Aesthetic Appreciation Developed?

Aesthetic appreciation defined

Aesthetic appreciation has been defined in this chapter as the *satisfactions that result from experiencing the beautiful in a situation — harmony of color and sound, symmetry of shape, rhythm of motion, etc.* We think of beauty not only as it is related to art, music, rhythmic movements; but in its relation to ideas, and to the arrangement of words as the symbol of ideas and sequences of ideas in written or spoken forms. The artistry of the composition of words as the expression of ideas by lip or pen is a cherished form of beauty. Aesthetic appreciation, like ethical-social appreciation, involves both emotional and intellectual qualities. In one instance or with one individual the surge of emotion may be the characteristic appreciation tone; while in another situation or with another person the intellectual element in appreciation may predominate.

[21] Sumner, W. G., *op. cit.*, p. 60.

Disagreement as to standards of beauty a problem

Mueller [22] deplores the lack of agreement as to what is art, thus:

It is, however, extremely disheartening to embark on the task of selecting, from the motley confusion of aesthetic principles the precise vocabulary which is most plausible and convenient for one's purposes. Indeed, so diametric are the contradictions that it has moved one liberal commentator to assert that "rival critics begin, it would appear, by inverting the cardinal doctrines of their competitors."

So we find that to many, art is incomprehensible by logic or science, but conceivable only through intuition, while to others, the fine arts are quite as accessible to the logical mind as is the practical world. According to one point of view, art is an improvement over nature, more real than physical reality, and more acceptable, but to others, art portrays nature not as it ought to be but as it is. While Matthew Arnold condemns *Anna Karenina* because it is a piece of life, Scott-James, a contemporary English critic of eminence, exalts the piece for the same reason. Such disagreements in evaluation of merits are by no means uncommon. To Hanslick, Beethoven's Ninth Symphony was an aesthetic monstrosity, while Wagner's judgment of the same work placed it at the pinnacle of artistic achievement.

The teacher who has tried to grapple with the problems of teaching aesthetic appreciation has found that the establishment of tangible standards by which to distinguish real beauty from pseudo forms, is a source of great difficulty. Students, however, are quick to demand definite criteria by which to judge beauty.

If the teacher pauses to reflect on the psychological nature of beauty, some reason for the confusion among writers as to what beauty *is* will become obvious, and the problem thereby will become less formidable. Strictly speaking, beauty does not reside in the *object* of appreciation. It is the reaction of the individual to the object that determines for him the presence of the qualities of beauty or ugliness. Beauty is, then, in part, the product of the past experience of the individual in relation to the object, or elements recognized in, or associated with, a situation in which beauty is present. If this experience has been pleasurable there is a ten-

[22] Mueller, John H., and others, *op. cit.*, p. 7. For further discussion of this problem see Kellett, E. E., *The Whirligig of Taste*. New York: Harcourt, Brace and Company, 1929; Chambers, Frank, *Cycles of Taste*. Cambridge: Harvard University Press, 1928; and Babbitt, Irving, *On Being Creative*. Boston: Houghton Mifflin Company, 1932.

dency toward appreciative response, both emotional and intellectual. If the apperceptive experience has elements of annoyance or unusual unpleasantness that are now associated with the new object or situation, the emotional reaction is likely to be negative. The naturalist, or the person who from childhood has made pets of snakes, sees much in them of beauty in color, form, and grace of movement. To the person who has been taught from earliest recollection to think of snakes as loathsome, poisonous, sneaky, crafty things — the usual symbol in literature and religion of evil, and the antithesis of the good and lovely — this much-maligned creature of nature has power to provoke only unpleasantness and loathing. Again, a sunset will not mean the same thing to a painter that it does to a poet, though there may be much in common between the two persons in the nature of the aesthetic experiencing that takes place. The fact of experience, as a conditioning factor in appreciation, explains many of the apparent contradictions among people as to what constitutes beauty and art in their various manifestations. A natural corollary would be the expectation of wide legitimate variation in appreciational reaction, as the teacher undertakes to develop moods and standards of aesthetic appreciation with the class.

The technique of teaching aesthetic appreciation

The teacher of aesthetic appreciation must intelligently face the fact that there is much divergence in the apperceptive experiences possessed by his pupils. It is assumed that there are aesthetic values which are made up of qualities that can be recognized, and that can become the basis of standards by which to determine, within latitude, the presence of beauty in a given instance. The teaching of aesthetic appreciation, therefore, is not greatly unlike the teaching of certain phases of ethical-social appreciation. The following factors appear to have most significance in the technique of developing aesthetic appreciation.

1. *The teacher must genuinely appreciate that which he wishes others to enjoy.* Just as the teacher will find it difficult to teach ethical-social appreciations he does not share, so will the teacher find aesthetic appreciation difficult to teach when he does not himself sincerely share that appreciation. At least two factors contribute to the great difficulty in teaching an appreciation of the beautiful which one does not himself experience.

First, there is far less unanimity as to the elements that constitute beauty than there is as to those qualities that make up socially desirable behavior. It is much easier to establish attitudes and mind-sets toward conduct patterns quite generally accepted, and for which there can be adduced obviously cogent reasons for the observance.

Second, beauty is less tangible than goodness, when the latter is ethically-socially conceived. To a much greater extent than goodness, beauty results from the fusion of elements that inhere in a specific pattern. Aesthetics depends more upon the total effect of the synthesis of qualities which produce an emotional feeling reaction than upon intellectual understanding. Appreciational teaching, therefore, must undertake to a large extent to transmit to the student the feeling-tone which the teacher experiences in the presence of the beautiful. All that has been said with reference to the teacher's sharing genuine appreciational experiences with the student in ethical-social appreciation applies with even greater force to aesthetic appreciation.

2. *The appreciation lesson should be so presented as to stimulate the student to further activity.* Often an animated telling of some of the most interesting scenes in the literature the teacher wishes the student to read will be sufficient to stimulate the student to read appreciatively. Similarly, the recounting of the unusual incident or situation that led to or surrounded the creation of a poem, story, or work of art, as for example, Longfellow's *Evangeline,* Whittier's *Ichabod,* Lew Wallace's *Ben Hur,* Handel's *Messiah,* or the traditional account of the composition of Beethoven's *Moonlight Sonata,* will whet the student's appetite for new aesthetic adventures. To call attention to the year's best seller or the Nobel prize novel produces interest and favorable anticipation for an appreciative reading. The psychology of suggestion implies that what everybody else agrees is good must be; therefore the reader is not only anxious to read the book but is predisposed to find something to enjoy in it.

A classic portrayal of the way in which curiosity may be used to stimulate interest and possible appreciation of good literature is strikingly shown in the oft-quoted address of Professor Scott, delivered before a meeting of the North Central Association of Colleges and Secondary Schools. Alluding to the well-known failure of most teaching of the appreciation of good literature, he said, in part: [23]

> If I were not engaged in this inferior business of teaching in a university, and my time were not all taken up with it, I should like to go into a high school where these formal prescriptions had been put aside and take charge of a class in English. I think I should talk to the pupils in some such way as this:
>
> "The classes of former years have been reading this prescribed set of books — a pretty poor sort of literature, in my opinion, and not proper for young people to read. You are very fortunate in being able to get rid of them. They are mostly very dull and uninteresting. There is the Iliad, for example, full of fighting and blood and the killing of men, and of armies clashing with one another in desperate conflicts where all the elementary and violent human passions are set free. Horrible! The International Peace Society cannot approve of anything of that sort. We will put this book aside, and I hope none of you will touch it. Then there is the 'Faerie Queene,' all about giants and maidens in distress, magic and mystery of all sorts — perfectly useless, a futile, silly thing, nearly as bad as the Arabian Nights. Don't go near it. I trust, also, that no one will attempt to read 'As You Like It,' which has a wrestling match in the very beginning (these minor athletics ought not to be allowed in literature) and tells about a girl who ran off into the forest in boys' dress — a most improper performance on her part. I am sure we ought not to talk about those things in this class. And even worse, perhaps, is Tennyson's 'Princess,' where a prince, who ought to know better, disguises himself in woman's clothing and gains admission to a girls' academy. A scandalous thing! No gentleman would act in that way. In short, these books are all harmful and ought to be destroyed. For the present I will put them on the top shelf of the closet here, and just as soon as the janitor is at liberty we will have them burned."

3. *For general appreciation, analysis should be restricted to those essentials directly contributory to understanding.* The teacher should always bear in mind that the greater the intellectual bases for understanding, the greater the potential possibilities for appreciation. For the literary specialist, appreciation is enhanced by painstaking technical analysis for figures of speech, allusion, plot,

[23] Scott, F. N. "Discussion of High School English Uninfluenced by College Entrance Requirements" in *Proceedings of the North Central Association of Colleges and Secondary Schools*, 1912, pp. 70–72.

structure, rhyme scheme, etc. Unfortunately college teaching of literature has seldom differentiated between the student of specialized and general interest in the subject. The student of specialized interest in an appreciational field already has his interest in that field established. Thereafter it is wholly a matter of expanding his intellectual understandings in this field to enhance the possibilities of greater appreciation. For the neophyte no such appreciational interests are established.

The teacher's primary task, therefore, is to establish this interest which may become the basis for later development. The same lack of discrimination has characterized much of the teaching of literature in the high school. Colvin cites an incident [24] in which a junior high school literature class devoted one hundred and eighty minutes to the study of *Julius Caesar*. Most of the questions concerned the meaning of words, historical facts, syntax, outline of story, rhetoric, prosody, mythology, plot, and but six questions "connected with present life." The teaching of other appreciational subjects has not been greatly different from that of the teaching of literature. Experience has revealed clearly the deadening effect upon appreciational learning of too much analysis for those whose interests have not been fully established. Scott, in an imaginary classroom situation,[25] describes vividly how literature should not be taught; and brings out very clearly the disastrous effects on appreciational learning of the overanalytical method so prevalent in the traditional teaching of literature. He says:

"And now we are going to take up some books which I know you will enjoy. I want you to be just as enthusiastic as you can about them, for we are going to study them and study them hard, and you will get a great deal of profit out of them, and all will be greatly improved. For the boys we will take Captain Mayne Reid's 'Afloat in a Forest.' We are going to read that book a paragraph at a time and examine carefully every allusion in it. It is about some people who floated down the river Amazon. First we will draw a map of South America, locating the course of the river, and then we will ascertain how wide the Amazon is at various points and how fast the current moves. Finally we will determine the amount of silt which is deposited by the river at its mouth. Captain Mayne Reid, by the way, makes a mistake. He has three people float down in a much

[24] Colvin, S. S. *An Introduction to High School Teaching*, p. 312. New York: The Macmillan Company, 1924.
[25] Scott, F. N., *op. cit.*, pp. 70–72.

shorter time than they possibly could. You will see that this is so
when we discover the exact relationship between the flow of the
stream and their rate of progress. We shall go into these details with
the utmost care, and after a little while you will write some nice
little essays about them.

"For the benefit of the girls we will read in the same careful and
scholarly way Robert Chambers' 'Heart Throbs of a Multimillionaire.'
We will determine just how many times the heart throbs when two
hearts are in unison, and learn about the two kinds of blood corpuscles,
and so on, and there will be essays on all these things also.

"But this is not all. Two years from now, when you are seniors,
we will take these books up again and go over them and over them
and over them until you know the answers to every last question in
regard to all these mathematical, biological, chemical, and topograph-
ical things, and that will be absolutely delightful."

I think we can all prophesy what would be the result of such an
experiment. If the room were not locked or the closet door locked,
after two or three weeks those classics which were put on the top
shelf would have to be rebound, and as regards the other books, when
their very names were mentioned, I think the pupils would fly shriek-
ing. They would never want to see the "Heart Throbs of a Multimillionaire" again, or even "Afloat in a Forest," good as that book is.

4. *Whatever is offered for appreciation should be presented in
as striking a manner as possible.* Effective speakers and the press
know the value of dressing up facts and ideas in such spectacular
or graphic form as to arrest attention, grip the imagination, and
engender emotions of awe, wonder, fear, or enthusiasm appropriate
to the situation. Teachers have been too prone to present facts or
ideas in a commonplace manner or in abstract form and then to
wonder why definite appreciational responses were not secured.
Examples of concepts of space and time, strikingly presented, will
suffice to illustrate this point. Sir James Jeans, in a truly thrilling
account of our universe, makes effective use of the graphic to
develop an appreciation of the innumerable stars that course
through the heavens and the immensity of space, thus: [26]

And the total number of stars in the universe is probably something
like the total number of grains of sand on all the sea-shores of the
world. . . . This vast multitude of stars are wandering about in space.
A few form groups which journey in company, but the majority are

[26] Jeans, Sir James. *The Mysterious Universe,* pp. 1–2. New York: The
Macmillan Company, 1930.

solitary travelers. And they travel through a universe so spacious that it is an event of almost unimaginable rarity for the star to come anywhere near to another star. For the most part each voyages in splendid isolation, like a ship on an empty ocean. In a scale model in which the stars are ships, the average ship will be well over a million miles from its nearest neighbor, whence it is easy to understand why a ship seldom finds another within hailing distance.

Of similar import is an example of an effort to give an appreciation of events in relation to time in vivid narrative style: [27]

The whole existence of mankind is generally assumed to have lasted not less than 240,000 years. . . . If this period is represented by a day of twelve hours, then each hour would represent 20,000 years, each minute 333⅓ years. If we imagine that we of the present are living at noon on that protracted day, the startling fact comes out that *for over eleven and a half hours there is nothing to record.* At twenty minutes before twelve the earliest vestiges of Egyptian and Babylonian civilizations begin to appear. Greek literature is seven minutes old. At one minute before twelve the *Advancement of Learning* makes its appearance. The steam engine is only a half minute old. From this we get a vivid idea of two facts; first, the enormous period during which there was no progress record, and secondly, the exceedingly rapid progress during the final stages.

5. *Appreciational teaching should be governed by the appropriateness of the situation.* Teachers of science, particularly of biology and botany, know through necessity the importance of adjusting their teaching of certain phases of their work to appropriate seasons when it is possible to go afield in search of specimens of plant, flower, insect, or living matter germane to their study. Literature and art have their moods for the seasons, the days, and special circumstances. These should be carefully observed to capitalize the opportunities for the most appropriate situations in which to develop the desired appreciations. Paintings of snow and bleak winter scenes can be most effectively used in winter, while harvest and Indian summer scenes can be appreciated more fully in autumn. As one writer aptly observes, the attempt to secure the "appreciation of the *Psalm of Life* in the afternoon with the junior 'prom' to be held in the evening," is as likely to meet with failure

[27] Adams, John. *The Evolution of Educational Theory,* p. 86. New York: The Macmillan Company, 1912.

as is the effort to develop an appreciation for *The Moonlight Sonata* before a jazz entertainment.

6. *The materials for appreciation should be within the range of the student's understanding.* This principle of learning has been so thoroughly stressed throughout this book that it needs only to be recalled in connection with appreciational teaching. Possible exception to this principle may at times be taken, especially in connection with poetry. Although a student may lack full understanding of a poem, the meaning that he does get combined with the lilt and rhythm of the poem often makes the reading pleasurable. This initial acquaintance with a poem often leads to a fuller appreciation of the poem when he is mature enough to understand it. Where the thought looms large as the basis for appreciation, great care should be exercised. Fortunately for the teacher of literature, helpful studies are available to guide him in the selection of appropriate materials for high school grade and age levels.

7. *Memorization is often an effective means of teaching appreciation.* Very little memory work should be required of the student in literature or music — the two fields of appreciational teaching where memorization is customarily practiced. The assignment procedure is likely to arouse antagonisms rather than to develop appreciations. An effective practice is for the teacher to motivate memorization by calling attention to beautiful passages customarily learned and quoted by adults, by offering special credit inducements for memorization, or by arranging for special attention to those who successfully memorize passages of poetry or who play or sing from memory before the class, school, or assemblies. The chance to exhibit achievement and the opportunity to feel the thrill of social approval are often sufficient motivation to cause many students to undertake extended memorization of gems from literature and music. If the teacher sees to it that efforts at memorization are followed by pleasurable experiences he is likely to get good results in his teaching of appreciation.

8. *Participation and expression a very effective means of developing appreciation.* The old principle that "we learn by doing" applies to the teaching of appreciation. The application of this principle to outdoor recreational forms of social appreciation was discussed in the previous section on the techniques of developing ethical-social appreciation. It is no less appropriate to the development of aesthetic appreciation. The one who can paint or model,

even though his work be crudely done, gets distinct satisfaction from his efforts and enters more fully into the labors of the artists whose work he studies. The same is true of the one who can express his aspirations and emotions in music. The writer has observed high school students thrill with the opportunity to participate in the dramatization of a passage from great literary masterpieces, or to read feelingly from similar passages suited to such expression. Briggs cites [28] an example which most experienced teachers could similarly duplicate:

> Benito was an Italian youth poorly prepared, uninterested, and failing in literature. . . . An ingenious teacher kept him after school one day and asked him to prepare to read to the class "Mia Carlotta" because, she said, he could do it better than anyone else. After careful coaching he read the poem with such success that he pleaded for other opportunities. After he had had similar success with "Da Leetla Boy" and "Da Boy from Rome" his attitude was so changed that there was little difficulty in getting from him more satisfactory work on the selections provided in the course.

QUESTIONS AND PROBLEMS

1. What evidence can you deduce to support the thesis that education is not fully effective if it emphasizes information and problem solving and neglects training of the emotions?
2. Either defend or refute the assertion that "Our intellect is a mere speck afloat on a sea of feeling."
3. Draw up a list of the *mores* in our society which you think are capable of defense on rational grounds. Draw up a similar list of those *mores* which you believe cannot be defended on a rational basis.
4. Contrast the modes of ancient and modern societies in perpetuating their group *mores*. Write a paper of 700 to 1000 words in length in presenting this contrast.
5. How would you support or challenge the statement: "Reflection is the worst enemy of the *mores*"?
6. What is meant by the statement, "The *mores* are social ritual"?
7. To what extent do you think the high school should attempt to establish "school traditions"?
8. It is generally agreed that politicians and demagogues have frequently utilized the cherished *mores* of society against the best

[28] Briggs, T. H., *op. cit.*, p. 434.

interests of society. In what way or ways can the school assist to reduce the evil effects of attempted misuse of group *mores*?

9. (a) In what way or ways are the emotions and *mores* related?

(b) In what way or ways are emotions and appreciations related?

10. Can you show that the *mores* and "social appreciation" are closely related? Be explicit.

11. (a) To what extent, if any, do you think the secondary school can be used to develop desirable social *mores* for the community and society?

(b) If you believe that the school can become a vital force in the development of socially desirable *mores,* what methods could the school employ to develop these desirable *mores*?

12. To what extent, if any, may negative stimuli be employed to develop social appreciation?

13. How would you distinguish between the teaching of appreciation and the teaching of information or problem solving?

14. Why is it considered so difficult to teach "aesthetic appreciation"?

SELECTED BIBLIOGRAPHY

Ash, S. E. "The Doctrine of Suggestion Prestige and Imitation in Social Psychology," *Psychological Review,* 55: 250–276 (September, 1948).

Bobbitt, J. Franklin. *The Curriculum of Modern Education,* chapter IX. New York: McGraw-Hill Book Company, Inc., 1941.

Briggs, Thomas H., Leonard, J. Paul and Justman, Joseph. *Secondary Education,* chapters XI–XVII. New York: The Macmillan Company, 1950.

Brogan, Denis W. *The American Character.* New York: Alfred A. Knopf, Inc., 1944.

Coffin, J. H. *Visual Outline of The Psychology of Personality.* New York: Longmans, Green and Company, 1940.

Cole, Luella. *Attaining Maturity.* New York: Farrar and Rinehart, Inc., 1944.

Hartman, George W. *Educational Psychology,* chapters VIII, XII. New York: American Book Company, 1941.

Kingsley, Howard L. *The Nature and Conditions of Learning,* chapters XVI, XVII. New York: Prentice-Hall, Inc., 1946.

Lowie, Robert H. *An Introduction to Cultural Anthropology.* New York: Farrar and Rinehart, Inc., 1940.

Lund, Frederick H. *Emotions: Their Psychological, Physiological and Educative Implications.* New York: The Ronald Press Company, 1939.

Murphy, Gardner. *Personality.* New York: Harper and Brothers, 1947.

Murphy, Lois B. and Ladd, Henry. *Emotional Factors in Learning.* New York: Columbia University Press, 1941.

Mursell, James L. *Developmental Teaching*, chapter X. New York: McGraw-Hill Book Company, Inc., 1949.

—— *The Psychology of Secondary School Teaching*, chapter VIII. New York: W. W. Norton and Company, Inc., 1939.

Prescott, Daniel A. *Emotion and the Educative Process.* Washington, D.C.: American Council on Education, 1938.

Risk, Thomas M. *Principles and Practices of Teaching in Secondary Schools,* Second Edition, chapter XII. New York: American Book Company, 1947.

Sumner, William G. *Folkways.* Boston: Ginn and Company, 1906.

Thorpe, Louis P. *Psychological Foundations of Personality.* New York: McGraw-Hill Book Company, Inc., 1938.

Tuttle, Harold S. *Dynamic Psychology and Conduct.* New York: Harper and Brothers, 1949.

9

How Can Pupil Progress Be Evaluated
and Reported?

---

1. What Is the Problem of Measurement?

Someone has said that examinations find their origin in antiquity. Whenever man has tried to think critically about the relative success of his activities, some form of evaluation of these activities has taken place. For the most part this evaluation has been highly subjective and, where conscious standards have been accepted as the basis for judgment, they have been crude and in general poorly defined.

With the rapid development of education, within the past few decades, and particularly since the turn of the century, the demand for some satisfactory evidence of the success of the work of the public school has become insistent. It has been part and parcel of the larger demand of society that all agencies of social progress justify the increasing financial burden which their support imposes upon a tax-conscious public. A highly competitive world has developed highly refined objective instruments by which to evaluate efficiency within the sphere of its industrial and business activities. It has been but natural that the same relative ability to determine the efficiency of the work of the school should be expected by this same society.

When one considers the attention given at present to the problem of the evaluation of the results of teaching, particularly their measurement, it is difficult to appreciate the recency of this emphasis. It is less than sixty years since Dr. Rice presented to the Department of Superintendence, then in session in Indianapolis, the results of his efforts to evaluate teaching success through a refined instrument of measurement. At this time the educational leaders of the country looked askance at the idea that the product of the school could be evaluated through the measurement of pupil achievement. To the members present at this meeting it seemed little short of an absurdity that anyone should seriously suggest the possibility of measuring the work of the school, yet at the meeting of this same Department of Superintendence in St. Louis, in 1912, just fifteen years later, a complete reversal of judgment had taken place, for at this meeting forty-eight addresses were devoted to the problem of evaluating the results of teaching. What these speakers, in reality, were saying was that evaluation of teaching success in the past had been based largely upon subjective judgment. Now it was considered possible to use measuring instruments which would provide objective data with which to measure the quantitative achievement of pupils and thus provide a better basis for evaluating teaching success. From that time forward a major emphasis has been given in educational circles to this subject. An extended and constantly growing literature of books and magazine articles is now available on almost every phase of educational measurement. This has led to the extensive development of instruments of measurement and their widespread use.

2. What Is the Purpose of Evaluating the Results of Teaching?

At this point the teacher should understand the difference between evaluation and measurement. Though different in function they are closely related in use. Evaluation involves an effort to make a considered judgment on the basis of evidence of the relative success of our educational endeavors, whatever they may be. In this chapter we will be concerned with ways of determining how successful we may be in helping youth learn to be good citizens.

Measurement is concerned with the instruments and processes by which achievement in a given area has been made. It gives us a "quantitative description of observable phenomena."[1] Stated

[1] See Ross, C. C., *Measurement in Today's Schools,* chapter XVII, "Evaluation." New York: Prentice-Hall, Inc., 1947. See also Anderson, V. E.,

another way, measurement instruments are the "means by which quantitative aspects of human behavior are observed with greater accuracy." [2] Measurement then becomes a vehicle in any modern effort to evaluate instructional success. While measurement does not evaluate, it is a most essential aid to any adequate attempt to evaluate the success of the school program.

Measurement of pupil ability

With the advent of the Terman Revision of the Binet Scale for the measurement of intelligence, just on the eve of America's participation in World War I, the efforts of educators to evaluate pupil-capacity, or ability to succeed in the school, suddenly found an effective instrument at hand. Immediate prestige was afforded the idea and the device, since the idea was applied to the selection and placement of army personnel, with modification of the device to make it applicable to group usage. Prior to that time the rank and file of teachers and parents had assumed that failure to succeed in school was due to sheer indolence on the part of the pupil or to inefficiency in instruction. Now, for the first time, a reasonably dependable measurement might be made of the relative ability of the pupil to carry forward successfully the work of the school.

The measurement of general pupil-ability has enabled the school to gauge the possible progress of the pupil under normal conditions. It has enabled the school, further, to formulate differentiated standards to care for varied abilities within the class when sectioning did not seem feasible or desirable. This is all the more significant since ability-differences are generally found to be both quantitative and qualitative in nature.

In addition to the measurement of general ability, now common, it is also possible to measure roughly the degree of special ability possessed by different students. Within recent years much research has been done on this problem, and many measuring devices have been created to evaluate the presence of special abilities, or aptitudes. These measuring devices have been used extensively, both for educational and for vocational guidance. Tests have been used

Grim, P. R. and Gruhn, W. T., *Principles and Practices of Secondary Education,* chapter XII, "Evaluating and Reporting Pupil Progress." New York: The Ronald Press Company, 1951.

[2] Lindquist, E. F. (editor). *Educational Measurement,* p. 3. Washington, D.C.: American Council on Education, 1951. A valuable treatment of the field of measurement.

to aid the student in making vocational choices. Again, many prognosis tests of the students' special ability in mathematics, language, music, etc., have been used to encourage or discourage individual students in the study of certain curricular subjects.

Measurement of pupil achievement

The time-honored purpose for which most efforts at evaluation have been put forth is the measurement of achievement. It must remain an important purpose though measurement of achievement is not now as narrowly interpreted as in the past. Until recently, evidence of achievement was utilized almost exclusively for the assignment of school marks. Today, achievement tests are used as well to determine the relative achievement of classes, schools, and school systems. This has been made easily possible by extensive use of exhaustive achievement tests in schools throughout the country, so that the average of achievement for pupils in grades and subjects for the nation at large might be established. Against these grades and standards, often national in extent, superintendents, principals, and teachers have been able to compare the local achievements of their pupils.

Modern education now frowns on the extensive use of achievement measurement for these purposes. Achievement scores alone are not sufficient data with which to evaluate the accomplishment of pupils. There are many other factors that need to be considered for each pupil. Further, the whole matter of comparison use of pupil achievement data is coming into question. Such procedures carry the implicit, if not explicit assumption that the curriculum is everywhere uniform, which it is not; and that conditions everywhere are the same, or justify the application of uniformity of standards, which is equally untenable. It may be politic to use achievement comparison somewhat broadly between schools and communities of similar educational-socio-economic background to answer critics of modern education. It has dubious pedagogical or educational justification.

As the educational process is recognized to be highly complex and uneven in development within the individual, and as attention is focused more upon behavioral changes which must be individual in character, the use of achievement measurement is seen to be primarily a means of providing data for evaluation of the further instructional needs of pupils.

Diagnosis of pupil weaknesses

The use of evaluation-procedures to diagnose pupil weaknesses has come to be accepted as one of the most valuable purposes of examinations. As the doctor recognizes a correct diagnosis of the patient as the first prerequisite to a possible cure, so teachers have come to consider a proper diagnosis of the pupil's learning difficulties essential to any effective corrective procedure they may apply. With the better understanding of the complex nature of learning that now obtains, educationalists have given greater attention to the problem of analysis of learning difficulties. It is possible, through properly constructed evaluation devices, to determine both class and individual student weaknesses in many particulars. When a class fails in a given test, the difficulty, for example, may be traceable to the lack of an adequate apperceptive basis for the new learning required. Often a new teacher finds, upon thorough testing of the class, that the pupils have not sufficient background to do the work expected of them. It may be that the entire class, or the individuals within the class, are not sufficiently automatic in certain forms of responses to do the work with the requisite speed expected of advanced students. Where this weakness appears, the remedial procedures are easily determined. Again, a student may reveal in the test evidences of incorrect habits of study: he does not realize that some things should be memorized, whereas others should be reasoned out, if understanding is to result rather than an accumulation of meaningless word symbols that have been committed to memory. This difficulty often occurs where rules and principles may be memorized, rather than understood. Evidences of carelessness or inaccurate attention to details may come to light, together with repeated indications that the student has wrongly interpreted statements in his reading. Inability of students to evaluate properly, to pick out the relevant from the irrelevant, to analyze, synthesize, and abstract the essentials in a problem-situation, may come to light through properly formulated evaluation procedures. The weaknesses of the student in the sheer mechanics of reading may be detected in part by the alert teacher who studies examination papers carefully. To assist the teacher, specially prepared evaluation devices for this purpose are available.

Diagnosis of teaching effectiveness

Of interest to teachers and school officials alike are the two approaches to this problem. The older emphasis has concerned the relative merit of the teacher. Ever since teachers have been subject to employment, the evaluation of teaching efficiency has been an issue of prime concern to employing officials. Good teachers should be retained and merit rewarded. Highly inefficient teachers should not be permitted to handicap the educational opportunities of youth. The past twenty-five years have witnessed a steadily rising emphasis upon evaluating devices that would single out the efficient from the inefficient teachers. Some factors that enter into this problem will be considered in Chapter 21.

For too long, measurement of teaching success has been used for the purpose of promoting, hiring, and firing teachers. From a purely pedagogical standpoint, measurement of teaching effectiveness finds its greatest value in the possibilities it offers for the improvement of teaching. It is not enough to diagnose student difficulties. Many so-called student weaknesses are the result of poor teaching procedures. The teacher should recognize that an examination, properly prepared, may function as a two-edged sword. It reveals the weaknesses of the pupils, and lays bare the shortcomings of the teacher. The examination, if improperly prepared, may reveal in its make-up a lack of any true grasp of the subject taught, the failure to separate the relevant from the irrelevant, an overemphasis on the trivial, a lack of coherence and progression in development, and the predominance of questions which call for a good memory rather than those which are thought-provoking. Often an analysis of an examination presents a fair picture of the mental distortions of the teacher with respect to the subject taught.

On the other hand a well-prepared, well-balanced examination will reveal much of significance concerning teaching effectiveness itself. If a reasonably large proportion of the class, including both good and poor students, fails on a given question, the teacher may well accept responsibility for the failure and begin to search for the source of difficulty within the teaching techniques or procedures employed. For example, an analysis of the results of an examination given by a teacher disclosed a 70 per cent failure to answer one question correctly. A careful study of the question showed that it was well stated and could not possibly have been misinterpreted.

Further, a careful study of the emphasis of the course clearly demonstrated that the ability to answer the question was essential to an understanding of the unit of work completed as a basis of this examination. The only possible conclusion that could be reached was that the teaching had been inadequate. More than that, a mastery of the next unit required as a prerequisite the understandings implied in the question missed by such a large proportion of the class. There was nothing for the teacher to do but attack the problem through another approach.

In a college class in general psychology, the procedure employed by the instructor had been the study of principles, and then the marshaling of examples to illustrate the application of the principles. The students had been taught the behavioristic law "that for every stimulus there must be an appropriate and adequate response." In the examination the problem situation was so established that the answer to the question required the converse statement of the law they had assumedly learned, namely, "that for every response there must be an appropriate and adequate stimulus." When a majority of the students failed the question outright, the baffled instructor began a careful search for the difficulty. It finally dawned upon him that the difficulty was one of teaching technique. A retest of the class revealed almost a one hundred per cent ability to state the law as the class had learned it. Without question the error lay at the door of the instructor. The use of evaluation procedures to disclose instructional weaknesses has proved to be one of the most valuable ways by which to improve teaching effectiveness.

The direction of effective study

This use of the examination to train the student in correct study methods has been utilized but little. Educators are just becoming aware of the potential value of the examination as a means of guiding the student into correct study habits. If the teacher calls attention to this function of the examination, the effectiveness of the procedure will be greatly enhanced. A teacher may well spend some time after each major test analyzing the structure of the examination and the technique of study which it presupposes if it is to be passed successfully. If students know that an examination will be so constructed as to emphasize a knowledge of important elements in the unit studied, that it will call for a careful evaluation synthesis, and the abstraction of significant conclusions from the work of the course and appropriate behavioral skills as the teacher understands these to be inherent in the unit, then these students will become critical of the study methods which they use in attacking this unit. Possibly at no point in the learning experience of the student can a painstaking effort to master the art of good study technique be so effectively motivated as in the eagerness of the student to do well in examinations. Psychologically, much could be achieved incidentally to create a different attitude toward the proverbially despised examination, if the student could be led to look upon it as a means of developing his power to study effectively.

3. What Are Older Types of Evaluation Procedures?

Various forms of evaluation devices have been employed in the school, both as a measure of the effectiveness of instruction and as a means of improving instruction. Of the most common procedures used, at least five deserve special consideration:

1. The oral quiz
2. The essay examination
3. Themes, reports, notebooks
4. Standardized tests
5. The new type, or teacher-created objective examination .

The oral quiz

This has been one of the most commonly used evaluation devices, if the oral question in all its evaluation usages is considered. Classes are sometimes examined orally instead of by a written examination. The time that would have been devoted to a written examination has been spent by the teacher in asking questions of various members of a class, somewhat after the manner of the old-fashioned "spell down" so prevalent in the elementary school of a generation ago. In a small class of a half dozen to a dozen students this method has much to commend it still. An oral examination makes possible a correctional function at the time the false judgment is made, and before a possible mind-set becomes fixed. When a student misses the question and it is passed on to another for answer, the psychology of the situation is likely to fix firmly in the mind of the erring student the correct answer. This is much more likely to happen under these circumstances than in a written examination, where the embarrassment occasioned by the fact that classmates witness the deficiency is not present. It is well known that in practice only the better, more conscientious teachers utilize the results of written examinations for purposes of remedial instruction. This remedial teaching is inherent in the oral quiz situation. It cannot be escaped when the question is passed on to others until a satisfactory answer is given. If the teacher will permit limited questioning, or offer a comment or two when necessary to make the answer clear to all, this virtue of the oral quiz becomes enhanced. If a correct question-technique is employed, each student will carry through the formulation of a tentative answer for each question asked lest he be called upon for the answer. In this way all the class participates in the answer to each question, even though one student is singled out for the response. Thus each student becomes critical of the answer, and, though not called upon, benefits by the possible correction to his own thinking through the correction of his fellow students. As a variant in the use of evaluation techniques teachers should not overlook the use of the oral quiz with small classes.

This type of evaluation procedure is subject to the limitations of any oral procedure. The answers must be evaluated on the spur of the moment, with no time for a deliberate estimate of worth. The possibility of obtaining a true sample of the student's understanding of the unit tested is limited, since each student may have not more than three or four opportunities out of the total quiz with which to demonstrate his ability. If, by chance, the three or four questions asked of him were the most difficult, or included the one or two questions the student could not answer, his showing may be all out of proportion to the actual knowledge he possesses. Had he been asked three or four questions that chanced to fall to the lot of any of four or five others in the class, his record might have carried a perfect score for the quiz. It is obvious that questions requiring careful reflection and extended intricate response are not convenient in examinations of this character. Further, students cannot or will not be given adequate time in which to formulate reasoned answers. The tendency, therefore, is for these examinations to become highly factual in nature. It should be borne in mind, however, that against these limitations is the fact that students need training in oral response which will be the dominant form of out-of-school activity and later adulthood.

The place of the oral question in the recitation has been considered in Chapter 6, where its legitimate function has been carefully appraised. Its use as an evaluation device, the sense in which it is treated in this chapter, seems unjustified. Happily the old use of the recitation question as a means of obtaining data for class marks is now taboo, and rapidly passing into the deserved limbo of discarded teaching arts.

Essay examinations

With essay examinations we are all familiar. For many years it has been the dominant means used to evaluate student progress and teaching efficiency. It is still the principal device used to measure the product of the classroom, although it has had to withstand a withering broadside of criticism and condemnation within recent years. Through the years 1920 to 1930 extremists tended to deny the essay examination much value. Many critics recognized the values of expression and organization inherent in true essay forms, but they were quick to suggest that these educational values might more legitimately be obtained by other devices, employed under more favorable conditions than were normally provided under the circumstances of tension so characteristic of examination periods. The chief limitations of the essay examination are found in the subjectivity involved in the evaluation of the student responses; the difficulty of utilizing the results of such examinations for comparative purposes — one class with another, or one community with another; the possibility for bluffing; the difficulty of diagnosis of either pupil or teacher weaknesses; and the likelihood that through the use of only a few questions in an examination only a fragmentary picture would be gained of the student's grasp or knowledge of a subject. These limitations will be considered in more detail later in the chapter as they affect, as well, other non-objective evaluation devices.[3]

When, toward the middle of the last century, there were forced upon the Boston School Committee the practical considerations of mass evaluation of teaching in the school as an administrative device, the essay examination was hailed as the harbinger of a new day in educational efficiency. The former committees had followed

---

[3] For a discussion of the essay examination in connection with other types, see Marshall, Max S. *Two Sides To a Teacher's Desk*, chapter V, "Evaluation." New York: The Macmillan Company, 1951.

a time-honored custom of visiting the school and examining the pupils orally on the content of the curriculum. The rapid expansion of the schools soon made the practice a burdensome one. In consequence of efforts to cope with the situation, the Boston School Committee, through its sub-committee, in 1845 began the formulation of a series of written examinations to be given to all students in the grammar divisions. These questions, formulated and printed, were given by members of the committee simultaneously and unannounced in the several Boston schools. Horace Mann, then Secretary of the Massachusetts State Board of Education, wrote enthusiastically of this innovation in educational measurement in the Boston schools. The advantages he enumerated in behalf of the written as compared with the oral examination may be cited as representative of the legitimate claims that may still be offered in their behalf. As will be seen later, many of these claims are subject to much qualification in the absolute, though they all have relative merit. The advantages claimed are summarized, as follows:

1. It (the written examination) is impartial. It gives the same questions to all the pupils of a class and, where several schools are concerned, to the same grade in each.

2. It is just to the pupils. An hour written examination gives the pupil a chance to answer every question whereas sixty questions asked of thirty pupils by the oral method would give but two questions to each pupil.

3. It is more thorough. Sixty questions will provide the examiner with a better idea of the knowledge of the student, just as the same number of questions will enable the student to present to the examiner a better picture of his attainments.

4. It prevents officious interference of the teacher. The pupil has an opportunity to answer the questions without frequent interruption from the teacher who may seek to give the student aid.

5. It provides an adequate measure of teaching efficiency. Such an examination "determines, beyond appeal, or gainsaying whether the pupils have been faithfully and competently taught."

6. It removes the possibility of favoritism. The same questions are given to all.

7. It makes the results of the examination available to all. In the oral examination only those present could judge of the merits of the test. With written questions and answers kept as a matter of record, all who wish may read them.

8. It is possible to determine which are the easy and which the hard questions by a study of the questions, and a further study of the ones passed or failed by the students.

Status of the essay examination

For almost two decades the essay examination has been the storm center for much adverse criticism. The most ardent critics have been unwilling to concede it much place in evaluation procedures of the future.

In contrast are the conclusions of some who have given considerable attention to both the objective and non-objective type of examinations. Weidemann,[4] as a result of extensive study of the new-type tests and essay forms, inclines to the conclusion that objective types are more useful in the lower grades and very simple essay examinations may be used with value there, while the reverse is true in the "upper and graduate years of college." Careful studies of improved forms of the essay examination, with improved objective types, indicate that "the overlapping of mental functions measured under actual classroom conditions drops to approximately 60 per cent." He further concludes that the forms of the essay examination, compared with certain of the new-type tests, definitely indicate that each measures functions not measured by the other, and he therefore claims a place for the written examination in comprehensive examinations at the college level. If evidence can be adduced to show that the essay examination is indispensable to any complete evaluation program at the college level, it would seem logical to infer some values for it in the secondary school, since the learning in the upper grades of the high school is not greatly dissimilar from the type of learning that takes place during the first two years of the traditional college course, and certainly not totally different from that of the "upper and graduate years." Leighton,[5] after several years' study of methods to improve both

---

[4] Weidemann, C. C. "Written Examination Procedures," in the *Phi Delta Kappan*, volume 16, pp. 78–83 (October, 1933). For discussion of development of essay examination, see Lindquist, E. F. (editor). *Educational Measurement*, chapter XIII. Washington, D.C.: American Council on Education, 1951; Ross, C. C. *Measurement in Today's Schools*, chapter VI. New York: Prentice-Hall, Inc., 1947.

[5] Leighton, R. W. *Trends in the Development of Comprehensive Examinations*. Unpublished report to the Social Science Division of the University of Oregon, October, 1933; also by the same author, "Improvement of the Essay Type Examination" in *Research in Higher Education*, Washington, D.C., Office of Education, Bulletin No. 12. 1931, pp. 15–20.

the new-type and essay examination, agrees that the essay examination has a definite place in evaluation procedures at the college level, and indicates a definite trend toward the greater use of the essay form in comprehensive examinations for colleges. It seems safe to conclude, therefore, that in spite of the evident weakness of the essay examination it possesses distinct value as an instrument of evaluation. Studies thus far made give a firm basis for the belief that essay forms can be improved, and that there is every reason to expect the development of better techniques for the construction of essay examinations paralleling the refinement of new-type tests.

Suggestions for improvement of the essay examination

The standards for good test construction do not vary greatly between the new-type and the essay-examination forms. The same care applied to the construction of an essay examination as that which is recognized as essential in making a new-type test would greatly strengthen the quality of the essay examination. The difficulty has been the readiness of the teacher to write out hurriedly a few questions, almost as they flash into mind, without the careful study which is given to the new-type form. Attention to suggestions offered will do much to improve the quality of the written examination.

1. *The teacher should study carefully the criteria of a good evaluation instrument.* The essay examination should be made to conform to the basic criteria of good examinations. There seems to be no reason why essay examinations should not be as valid as any other form of test, if care is exercised to make them so. They have some functions distinctly different from objective forms. If a careful outline of the unit to be examined is made, it should be as easy to select significant data for the essay form with reference to the purpose of the examination as for the new-type tests. An outline will aid the teacher to select more intelligently materials and procedures based upon the purpose of the examination whether it be to test for memory of facts, for reasoning power, for attitudes, for understandings, for organization, for expression, or for some other abilities.

Reliability is more difficult to achieve in an essay examination because sampling is much more restricted than with the new-type test if the same time limits are maintained. Where fewer questions are asked, they must be more carefully formulated and their significance must be more rigorously determined. A careful outline of the unit would serve to focus attention upon the relatively significant data for the test. Certainly it would show the absurdity of a question which the author encountered on a test on Kansas history in his high school days. The question was: "How did Kansas acquire the nickname, *Jayhawker*?" The test was supposed to cover the entire history of Kansas, yet it consisted of only five questions and this one so inconsequential that only a footnote was given to it in the book which the class had been using as a text. In spite of their immaturity the members of the high school class easily recognized the trivial nature of this question, and naturally resented such disproportionate emphasis in an examination of this character.

2. *The teacher should study carefully the discussion on the topic, "Construction of new-type tests."* Some of this discussion is applicable only to new-type tests, but most of it has direct application to the improvement of the essay examination as well. The emphasis upon the curriculum as the basis for examination, the selection of items to be tested, the formation of question-forms, the arrangement of questions, etc., are as important in the essay as in other types of tests. Adaptations are necessary to fit the discussion to the needs of the mechanics of essay-test construction, but the principles are sound for each of the major forms of test.

3. *The teacher should study carefully the discussion on "Types of questions," and "Characteristics of good questions," in Chapter 12.* Since the type of questions used in the essay form varies considerably from those of the new-type tests, it is desirable for the teacher to study the classification of questions peculiarly adapted to the essay examination. Weidemann is convinced that the essay-examination question or statement is as varied and complex as the new-type test forms, if not more so. Significant is his working hypothesis that "the difference between objective-test types and essay-test types is one of degree, and continues on a scale from *objectivity* to that of *subjectivity*." [6] Weidemann's discussion reveals rather clearly the intricate nature of the essay form of question or statement. He lists 194 specific commands or queries used to introduce essay questions or statements. The variation in interpretation possible, as well as the different forms of reaction demanded, makes this a problem of most fruitful study.

4. *The teacher should give special attention to definite standards*

6 Weidemann, C. C., *op. cit.*, pp. 78–83.

for the evaluation of student responses. Unlike the scoring of the thoroughly objective new-type tests, where a single predetermined response can be established as the one and only correct answer, and this so arranged that a simple mark may designate the correctness of that response, the response to an essay-test item is generally involved, complex, and exceedingly varied. Many elements must be evaluated in determining the degree of correctness of the response. It has been this inherent difficulty in scoring an essay examination that has caused its value as a measuring device to be seriously questioned.

There are a number of ways in which the scoring can be made more uniform and objective. Many teachers write out in advance an acceptable answer to an essay-test question. If the question may be answered in two or three different ways, the teacher prepares the two or three answers which would be acceptable. A list of important ideas that should be found in the answer, with acceptable procedures and processes involved, will prove an excellent guide to more uniform scoring of tests. Such a plan not only tends to narrow the elements of subjectivity in scoring, but may also reveal weaknesses in the form of the question and thus enable the teacher to restate the question satisfactorily or eliminate it entirely. Another device is to draw up specifications to govern the grading of questions in general, and specific criteria for particular items in the test. General specifications, such as neatness, use of the correct principle, accuracy, organization, spelling, punctuation, grammatical forms, etc., should be settled in advance, and students made cognizant of the part each is to play in the scores assigned.

The correct use, the misuse, or the omission of technical terms in subjects in which the ability to use such terms intelligently is a reasonable index of the student's grasp of the subject, should form a part of the criteria of accomplishment. The importance to be given to criteria of this sort should be carefully determined, and the students taking the examination should be informed of it. A further means of securing uniformity in scoring is to score one question at a time until all papers have been scored on this question, then to turn to the second, and so on through the examination. These are but a few of the many ways of improving the scoring results of essay examinations. The value of the essay examination depends quite as much upon the care exercised in scoring the results as in the formulation of the examination.

Themes, reports, notebooks

Themes, reports, notebooks, *et cetera,* are widely used forms of evaluation devices. Witness any educational gathering where products of the school are displayed in an array of reports and notebook forms. They have been accepted as an integral part of our teaching procedures. The theme, report, or notebook may become very valuable both as an educational tool and as an evaluation device. The emphasis should be placed upon the educative function of these devices, rather than upon their use as measuring rods of pupil growth or achievement. Themes and reports should be written because the student has something to say. They should be critically studied by the teacher, primarily as a means of improving the student's power of organization and expression. Incidentally, some evaluation of the product in terms of the goal of fluent expression no doubt should be made. The student should have his attention focused, however, not upon this evaluation but rather upon those elements in which improvement is possible. It is in these forms of activity that the student has an opportunity to reveal his power of expression, analysis, organization, and generalization. The power to observe, evaluate, and express are the major educative values that justify the use of these devices. Through these instrumentalities the teacher can observe closely the change in behavorial skills in expression and organization.

Standardized tests

By standardized tests is meant those tests primarily objective in form for which norms have been established. A test is generally considered standard when it has been given to a sufficiently large number of individuals to indicate what may be expected of other pupils of a given age or grade who might be given the test. Such tests are usually developed by those especially well trained in the making of examinatons, and in accordance with the best principles recognized as essential to proper test construction. The development of standardized testing in America has been phenomenal. The standardized test movement is slightly more than forty years old. Certainly its rapid development postdates World War I. At the height of the movement, on the eve of the depression, it is estimated that between forty and fifty million copies of standardized tests were sold in a single year.

The standardized test, while generally assumed to apply to educational tests, covers a wide field. The earlier efforts at standardization were applied to tests of intelligence. At the present time, however, many standardized tests have been prepared to measure qualities other than intelligence or school achievement. These include aptitude tests of various kinds, such as mechanical-aptitude tests, musical-aptitude tests, teaching-aptitude tests, and science-aptitude tests; prognosis tests in algebra, Latin, modern-language and other subjects; basic-interest tests; personality tests; and the Civic Attitude Test, among many.

The standardized test has made a unique contribution to the problem of the evaluation of the results of teaching. It has made available to the teaching profession a variety of examination forms of merit other than achievement tests. It has also served to focus the attention of teachers and administrators on better techniques of test construction.

It may not be amiss to repeat at this point the word of caution about the present attitude toward standardized tests made earlier in this chapter. Modern educational theory finds little justification for the use of standardized achievement tests. Even the use of other forms of standardized tests should be preceded by a critical study of their limited functions.

The Non-Standardized Objective Examination

The Non-Standardized Objective Examination, sometimes called the New Type or Teacher-Created Objective Type Examination, is the outgrowth of the popularity of the standardized test movement. The phenomenal development of standardized tests has brought into sharp relief the improved techniques employed in the construction of these tests, in contrast with the crude manner in which the ordinary classroom examinations were made. Furthermore, the efforts to develop standardized tests worthy of extensive use have focused attention upon the necessity of the refinement of the techniques of test construction to give them recognized value. In consequence of this, some of the best technically trained minds in education and psychology, with large financial subsidies for their researches, have devoted their energies to this task. From the laboratory of this experimental effort has emerged a body of accepted principles of good test construction, and definite procedures in the technique of test building.

Because of obvious limitations to the extended use of standardized tests, there has been a widespread attempt to make available to the classroom teacher the principles and refined techniques of the expert for use in the improvement of the ordinary classroom examination. Teachers and educational leaders have been quick to sense the significance of this trend in educational measurements, so that today there is available to the teacher a wealth of literature, couched in non-technical language which the non-specialist can understand, with specific directions for the application of scientific principles in test construction. The best of our teacher training schools have, for several years past, offered courses on the newer approach to the improvement of the written examination. It is with this effort to improve the classroom examination that the teacher should be most concerned. Particularly, the teacher should be aware of recent educational thinking about this form of examination.

Construction of new-type tests

Each type of examination varies somewhat in its construction. In the limited discussion of the techniques of test construction possible here, only the general procedures that apply to all can be given.[7] These are given and discussed in the approximate sequence they would logically be considered.

1. *Determine the purpose of the test.* Obviously this is the first step in test construction. All that follows bears a direct relationship to this. The validity of the test will be determined with reference to the purpose for which it is created. In a narrow sense this will involve an inquiry into whether the thing desired is an evaluation of information acquired, of the powers of reasoning developed, of the diagnosis of particular weaknesses, or of other relevant data that might be gleaned from an examination of a class. In a broader sense the value of the test must depend upon its appropriateness to the curricular content to which the class has been subjected. This the teacher should safeguard through a clear and definite formulation of the purpose of the test, in conformity with the curriculum taught.

---

[7] In each case it is recommended that the teacher consult some of the specialized textbooks on the test construction. Special attention is called to Ross, C. C. *Measurement in Today's Schools*, chapters IV–V. New York: Prentice-Hall, Inc., 1947; Lindquist, E. F. (editor). *Educational Measurement*, chapters V–X. Washington, D.C.: American Council on Education, 1951; and Travers, Robert M. W. *How to Make Achievement Tests*. New York: The Odyssey Press, Inc., 1950.

2. *Select the items of the curriculum for testing.* This is an important step. The fundamental worth of the test is determined by this and the first step mentioned above. The reliability of the test, as well as its validity, is involved in the care with which the items that make up the test are selected. Every effort should be made to select those items germane to the curriculum as taught, and to the purpose of the test. If a diagnostic test of limited or specific nature is desired, then the curricular content of the course should be surveyed carefully for those elements that would serve as the basis for such a test. When a survey test is contemplated, sampling of content should be general.

It may be taken as axiomatic that the greater the care exercised in the selection of test items, the greater the worth of the resultant test. Numerous devices have been employed to facilitate this step. If the unit to be tested is extended, an outline of the unit, in some detail, will provide the framework for the test items. If items from each section are labeled in some form, then each item from a given section may always be identified as it passes through the process of sifting. Twenty-five to fifty per cent more items should be marked for test purposes than one expects to use. If the unit is large enough, it is frequently desirable to select enough significant items to make two or three test forms covering the unit.

3. *Cast items into test form.* The nature of the items or the purposes of the test often have much to do with the mold into which the item is cast. The teacher must determine whether the true-false, multiple-choice, completion, simple-recall, sequence, or other type best fits the nature of the test or of the items involved. Growth of reasoning ability or the recognition of relationships could not be tested by the use of simple recall-type objective tests; whereas sequence or multiple-choice types would be splendidly adapted to the evaluation purpose sought. It is generally recommended that items cast into test form be written out on separate uniform slips of paper and properly identified for filing and sifting. When a large number of items are available, this is of distinct advantage. A careful selection of those of most value can then be made for the test. Usually each item can be cast into several test forms. One interesting device employed by many teachers is to recast a multiple-choice test into a true-false type, and *vice versa.*

After the forms have been decided upon, it is important to scrutinize the statement or question to avoid possible ambiguity. It is well to study Chapter 12, on the use of the question in teaching, for pertinent suggestions on this point, since the language in which the statement is couched will have bearing upon its value in the test.

4. *Determine the length of the test.* The length of the test will be determined by several factors. First, the purpose of the test, in many instances, will be a deciding factor. If the test is of a comprehensive survey nature, it must be long enough to cover the significant items in the field in the section of subject matter upon which it is based. This aspect of the test is particularly important if the reliability of the test is to be assured. When a limited diagnosis is the dominant motive, a short test may suffice. Another factor of moment, in the determination of the length of the test, is the length and complexity of the unit to be tested. Where a few days' work is to be evaluated, even by an information test, it need not be long to cover salient points. Again, in general, experts in test construction assume that a direct ratio exists between reliability and the length of the test. The longer the test the greater the reliability that may be expected to result from the use of the test. The obviousness of this principle is at once apparent. Sampling at best is subject to many chance errors. When tests are lengthened, the element of chance errors in sampling is reduced, and the probable reliability of the test is increased. There are, of course, limitations to the operation of this principle. It is a safe policy, however, for the teacher to exercise unusual care when short tests are used.

5. *Plan arrangement of items in test.* Many authorities argue for a chance order in the arrangement of items in the test. They insist that the student should find easy and difficult questions interspersed throughout the examination and that chance order be applied also to the sequence of items so that they will not appear in the natural order in which they were studied. If history has been studied according to a chronological sequence of events, then to have the examination items so arranged provides a large element of aid to the student through recall by association. The purpose of the test must be the ultimate criterion by which the arrangement of items is determined. A power or difficulty test must of necessity have the items arranged in ascending order of difficulty. Otherwise, chance arrangement may be considered a better plan to follow, with a few of the easier items definitely placed at the beginning of the test for their favorable psychological effect upon the student.

Most authorities discourage the omnibus test, or the arrangement of different-type test items in chance order. To avoid possible confusion for the student it is best to segregate all true-false, completion, multiple-choice, and other forms used in a single test. This further facilitates directions for each type of test employed, especially where students are not familiar with the different forms, or where unusually complex types are used.

Whenever possible, different types should be utilized. Variety is as welcome here as in teaching method. Then, too, except where a limited purpose is served by the test, a greater range of learning is evaluated. Each type of test has its peculiar virtues and emphasizes some phase of learning, such as memory, discrimination, reasoning, etc., more than does another form. At least over a semester or year a wide variety of forms should be employed, though in a single examination it may be found desirable to use but one type of item.

6. *Where possible prepare alternate forms.* When units of six to nine weeks or a semester are made the basis of a general test, it is possible and highly desirable to formulate two or more tests of approximately equal length, difficulty, and reliability. When 200 to 300 significant items can be found for test purposes, it is easy to arrange them, both in order of assumed difficulty and as they cover phases of the unit. Odd and even numbered items could be selected for alternate test forms. With careful study, over a period of time, items could be interchanged and new ones added to supplant poor ones until two comparable forms of relatively high reliability were developed.

7. *Use care in the preparation of general test form.* The care exercised in the mechanical makeup of the examination as a whole will have much to do with the effectiveness of the examination and the ease of its administration. If the test can be prepared in mimeographed or hectographed form, the problem is much simplified. The paper should have a uniform place for the test title in the upper center of the page, and provision for the name of student and date of examination most conveniently placed at the upper right hand corner of the test paper. Either below or in the left upper corner should be a place for the score and grade. Many teachers have found an additional space for median score desirable, as it enables students to judge their individual performance in relation to the class. Then for the answer to the test items either a right or left page margin should be provided. The form should be so aligned that a scoring key, usually a dummy clipped from a test

form, can be placed side by side with the test for rapid, convenient scoring. In completion tests, the blank spaces should appear before the statements as well as in the appropriate places in the sentences. The same principle should apply to all test forms. Directions should be prepared with the utmost care to make them clear and concise. These should be specific for each test form, and should appear directly before each type of item used in the examination. When dictation is used, the teacher should insist upon uniform-sized paper, and a definite scheme for writing responses should be suggested to the class to facilitate grading.

8. *Prepare an answer key.* The key to the test should be prepared while the test is under construction, not after the examination has been given and the teacher is ready to grade the papers. Answers should be determined at the time the test-form for each item is made. Often the preparation of answers at the moment of selecting the test-form the item is to take will reveal a weakness in the statement as formulated. In the free completion test it may be necessary in some instances to change an answer here and there by adding one or more possible answers, as a study of students' responses is made. The free completion test cannot be made rigidly objective unless confined to informational-type data. Synonyms are the chief sources of difficulty in the use of the free completion test.

9. *Formulate rules for scoring.* Present trends are definitely away from weighted scores for different questions. While all will agree that some items in a test are relatively of much greater importance than others, experimental evidence seems to warrant the conclusion that the increased accuracy gained is not justified by the extra time involved in a careful effort to weight each item in a test. The accepted practice is to give one point for each correct response. For example, a correctly answered true-false statement would count one point, as would a completion-test statement with one blank to fill. Where two or more blanks occur in a single completion statement, a point should be awarded for each blank in which the student has written a correct response.

When the type of test used provides a possibility for *guessing*, the practice has been to penalize the student on the assumption that guessing has taken place. Not all writers favor the use of a correction formula, since it is easy to show hypothetical absurdities as the result of its use. When class grades are based upon a distribution of scores, rather than on the relative sum of scores, for

ordinary practical purposes the attempt to use a correction formula
seems unnecessary.

4. What Are Some Newer Evaluation Procedures?

Experience versus subject matter appraisal

There are two sharply divergent approaches to the problem of
measurement and evaluation. The conventional approach has assumed that appraisal should be considered largely in terms of the
extent of knowledge content or subject matter the learner has
acquired. Measurement devices, therefore, have been constructed
to determine as accurately as possible the range of information-
knowledge the pupil possesses. Under this conventional conception
of learning, periodic measurement of acquired knowledge becomes
the index of pupil educational progress.

In contrast is the conception of learning now coming into acceptance; namely, that learning consists of the changes in the behavior
patterns of the learner, brought about through experience; this concept requires a radical shift of emphasis in measurement and evaluation. Attention, in this form of learning, is focused upon the actual
changes that occur in the individual's behavior as a result of his
learning experiences. It does not neglect testing of knowledge, for
despite the misinterpretation of a few, it is recognized that learning
does not take place in a vacuum. Instead of being an end in itself,
however, information-knowledge becomes one of the several important means of creating situations through which desirable learning experiences may be had. The emphasis upon the development
of successful behavior patterns that will insure the learner's competency to meet successfully the complete range of his living activities places an enlarged responsibility upon measurement and evaluation. Every aspect of the behavior activities of the learner becomes
a matter of great importance to the educator, and an area for
appropriate descriminating measurement and appraisal.[8]

Objectives and evaluation

Earlier in the book attention was called to the change in the
statement of educational objectives from the older form of potential

[8] At this point the earlier chapters should be reread to recapture the difference between "subject-matter" and "experience learning," as well as the more
extended discussions of the shift in the approach to objectives.

competencies to the newer emphasis upon actual behavorial changes. For example, under the knowledge concept of learning a satisfactory objective might be stated: "To know the difference between the present and past tense of a verb"; following the experience concept of learning the objective would be stated in the form of a behavorial outcome, thus: "In speaking he uses the present and past tenses of verbs correctly." Evaluation, in experience learning, is primarily concerned with the evidence of appropriate behavioral change observable under normal living conditions. Measurement finds its chief concern with the formulation of techniques by which the existence of changes in behavior, the recognized outcomes of learning, can be shown to exist.

The objectives of the Educational Policies Commission of the National Education Association, given in Chapter 1, illustrate the statement of objectives cast in the form of behavior outcomes required in experience learning. The objective, "The educated person reads the mother tongue efficiently," is stated in an active behavioral form. It represents an efficient behavior achievement. To make it useful, however, for teaching or evaluation purposes, it must be made more specific. Reading is complex, and involves many forms of behavior activities that are aspects of the total reading competency, and as it is stated represents an integrated behavior outcome. A few sample behavior skills characteristic of the efficient reader might be stated as follows:

A. He analyzes sentences and paragraphs effectively.
B. He reads rapidly.
C. He understands the vocabulary he reads.
D. He adapts his style of reading to the nature and purpose of the content read.

Development of evaluative instruments

When reading was regarded as the mastery of the simple mechanics of pronouncing words in their order on the printed page, tests of reading ability were simple. It could be done by asking the pupil to read, and checking carefully the mechanics of his reading. The evaluation of the competency of the learner in respect to the items listed under efficient reading characteristics, might be done exclusively by observing pupil behavior in the process of reading and the explanation of what he read; in A, B, and C, pencil-and-paper tests might suffice to reveal what he knew about good reading techniques. Even in D, a well-devised evaluative measurement might provide sufficient data for an intelligent judgment. It might show what the learner knew he should do in each situation, but would not reveal satisfactorily whether in practice he utilized the skills he knew. The acid test must be the extent to which these behavioral patterns are present in the reading habits of the pupil. Measurement of "experience" learning, therefore, ideally should reveal both behavior practice and its possible relation to knowledge where behavior skills are deficient.

The task of developing evaluation instruments in experience learning is essentially that of setting up or discovering appropriate situations, in which the pupil will reveal both the extent to which he possesses the desired types of behavior skills and utilizes them in normal practice. This is an exceedingly difficult requirement to meet. It cannot be met satisfactorily by the older measurement devices. As shown above they can provide significant help, but a new form of evaluation technique must be employed to reveal both the presence of the behavior competency and its habitual use.[9]

Observational evaluation instruments

Many of the evaluation instruments previously discussed will find some use in the evaluation of experience learning. Many newer forms of evaluation instruments are being developed which attempt to provide a better index of actual achievement of behavioral skill and its habitual practical use.

1. *Log or diary.* The ship's log or the personal diary may well convey the essential idea of this evaluation device. It represents the day-by-day notations of significant events in the life of the learner. Over a period of time it may reveal significant changes in many aspects of pupil behavior. Taken as a whole the record may reveal noticeable changes in the behavior of the learner not evident over a period of several days or a few weeks. Many teachers and pupils in core classes keep a form of cumulative record in which the activities and experiences of each day are listed along with samples of things done. Teachers and pupils separately, or together, may keep such a record. Its value depends upon its completeness.

2. *Anecdotal records.* A visitor to a primary classroom chanced to inquire of the teacher how she kept evaluative records of the learning which took place in her class, particularly in matters of

---

[9] For a newer approach to this form of measurement, see Smith, E. R. and Tyler, R. W. *Appraising and Recording Student Progress.* New York: Harper and Brothers, 1942.

group-living behavior skills. Unexpectedly, she took from under her arm a chart on which was each child's name and the day of the week, with plenty of space after each name for comments. She showed the visitor the record for the first three days of that week. While several children had no notation after their names, most of them had one or more comments listed. When a child, weak in a given social skill, did something to indicate improvement in thoughtfulness or courtesy for another it was briefly noted. Apparent lapses from behavioral practices were also noted. The teacher found it convenient to keep the chart under her arm as she worked along with the children, thus finding it easy to jot down an occasional comment as such appeared important. At the close of the year this anecdotal record would be invaluable in appraising pupil behavioral changes.

Teachers in many secondary schools keep a small record book handy to note occasional incidents that mark significant behavior development on behalf of pupils. Where the traditional pattern of many classes a day is in vogue some teachers have made use of anecdotal records of their homeroom pupils particularly, as the behavior of these become observable from time to time in corridors, and student activities apart from the classroom. Modern education places great emphasis upon a closer pupil-teacher relationship. The methods best designed for the experience type of curriculum bring the teacher and the pupil into closer working relationship, and thus provide to the alert teacher a wealth of opportunity for anecdotal incidents.[10]

3. *Interview and conferences.* The good teacher provides opportunities, mostly informal, for conferences and interviews with his pupils. The experience curriculum with its emphasis upon unit teaching provides many opportunities for pupil conferences, occasionally long, but usually short ones, generally informal in character. The newer conception of teaching also stresses the general guidance function of the teacher. It is all the more important that teachers look upon their relationships with pupils as involving myriad personal problems of pupil adjustment. These can best be handled through conferences and interviews.

More often than many traditional subject-matter teachers suspect, the source of much school difficulty, apparent disinterest, and fail-

[10] The anecdotal record is treated fully in Jarvie, L. L. and Ellingson, M. A. *Handbook on the Anecdotal Behavior Journal.* Chicago: University of Chicago Press, 1940.

ure is due to personal out-of-school problems. Informal conferences might do much to locate the nature of the behavior difficulties and give the teacher a chance to help as well as obesrve the
development of proper behavior skills and habits.

4. *Pupil self-appraisal.* Contrary to the opinion of many, pupils
can be very helpful to the teacher in evaluating pupil progress and
behavioral proficiency. Some oppose these devices because pupils
are said to be too immature to know what their objectives should
be, or the degree to which they are achieving them. All this in part
may be granted. It is not assumed that pupils can render competent judgment in all areas of learning. This would be to make the
oft-repeated mistake of assuming that one instrument was equally
effective for every purpose. It would be to put adult heads on
young shoulders.

The good teacher who helps youth to set up behavioral goals
carefully and definitely, with clearly indicated characteristics of
progressive changes in behavior, can expect real assistance in evaluating pupil progress. In many areas no one can know better than
the pupil how well he is achieving consistent behavior progress.
If together pupil and teacher have carefully set up the behavior
outcomes of learning, the pupil on many phases of learning can
report reasonably accurately to the teacher the degree of his success and failure. In fact, this method is becoming one of the accepted devices by which to help pupils learn.

5. *Pupil reports.* The teacher who has pupils make many and
varied reports on many subjects, can get a very good estimate of
the pupil's general knowledge, his expanding vocabulary, his growing ability to collect facts, organize and express ideas, discriminate
between good and dubious sources, and other ideas. These reports
will give a much better basis for evaluating changing behavioral
skills than is possible in the usual test devices customarily employed. If the teacher encourages the pupils to file many out-of-
school or non-class written forms, a valuable addition can be made
to the data at hand for sound evaluating.

5. How Can Pupil Progress Be Recorded and Reported?

No discussion of the evaluation of the results of teaching would
be complete without a consideration of the real significance of
measurement scores once they have been obtained. The same critical appraisal of test forms that led to the present effort to

strengthen the instrument of measurement also cast suspicion on the older practices of interpretation of the results of these tests translated into grades. In this discussion, the value of some form of symbols showing gradation in achievement is not questioned.

Grading by the percentage plan

Until recent years school achievement quite generally was graded on a scale of 100 points. It was not uncommon to hear the announcement at the time of graduation that the Valedictorian had won by a margin from close competitors. His nearest competitor had something like a grade of 97%, while the victor edged out his rival by a flat 98 per cent grade. In consequence, the naïve assumption has prevailed that the Valedictorian in reality was the undoubted intellectual superior of his class.

One reason for the disfavor into which this system of grading has fallen is the theoretical assumption, implicit in the plan, that school accomplishment can be measured in minute degrees from complete absence of accomplishment to perfection. A grade of 95 in the first year of high school biology cannot mean that the student lacks just 5 per cent of complete knowledge of biology, or even of perfect knowledge of the first-year course. The further weakness of the assumption of an absolute scale is the evidence from experience and experimentation that when an arbitrary passing mark is set, say at 70 or 75, it consciously affects the grades given a class. The teacher tends to pass about the same number of students, whether the passing mark be placed arbitrarily at 60 or 75.

Another serious objection to the percentage plan is the inability of the teacher to measure with such refinement assumed by the 100 per cent scale. It is a generally accepted fact among students of the subject that man's ability to shade differences in categories of judgment is very limited, and normally does not exceed a range of over ten divisions — a range of five is most widely approved.

Grading by the Missouri Plan

In contrast to the use of an absolute standard such as the percentage scale, nearly all students of measurement have looked with favor upon some scheme of relative grading. The use of the normal probability curve in educational measurement, known as the Missouri Plan, appears to provide the most satisfactory basis for this idea. Two factors of observation and experience give weight to the proposal to grade upon a normal-curve-of-distribution basis. The first is the mathematical law of chance. If several coins are tossed several hundred or a thousand times, the frequency with which certain combinations appear will tend to describe a curve not unlike that made by the outline of a bell. Most of the frequencies tend to cluster about the center, gradually spreading out with decreasing frequencies in equal ratios on either side of the center of greatest combination frequency.

The second factor, the observation of the actual operation of this normal probability curve in the field of biological variation, gives support to the plan. Thus far in the study of biology, where definite factors have not entered to influence development abnormally, the emergence of variation in characteristics has very closely approximated the normal probability curve. Teachers are familiar with variations in mental ability which follow the normal probability curve in striking fashion.

Applications of normal curve to class grades

If this plan of grading is applied to test scores, it avoids the doubtful procedure of attempting to use absolute standards in the measurement of achievement. The measurement will be relative and the implications less readily misunderstood. There have been many suggestions for the application of the normal curve to grades. If a fivefold grading system is employed, what percentage of the class should receive each of the five grades under the application of the normal probability curve? This can be determined through the use of the binomial theorem. If the binomial is expanded to the fourth power we have an approximate distribution as follows: 6–24–40–24–6. Restated with letter-grade symbols this gives: A's for 6 per cent, B's for 24 per cent, C's for 40 per cent, D's for 24 per cent, E's or F's for 6 per cent. The exact percentage allotted to each grade is not a matter of common agreement. Below are a few of the many forms of this general-curve theory, applied to grade distribution.

A	B	C	D	E
3	22	50	22	3
3	23	48	23	3
4	24	44	24	4
5	20	50	20	5
6	24	40	24	6
10	20	40	20	10

•

Most teachers seldom have class enrollments in excess of fifty students; therefore, when such a plan is followed it is much better to allow for considerable flexibility in the distribution of grade ranges. At times no A's should be recorded; at other times no failures should be given. At no time should the teacher forget that the Missouri Plan involves at least two important assumptions seldom present in the classroom situation. The one assumption is that the normal probability curve freely operates in the classroom situation without the interference of selective factors that would vitiate it. The other assumption is that the normal probabiliy curve is reliably achieved only with infinite numbers. Obviously, in a given classroom situation the possibilities of the influence of chance factors are extremely great.

Changing attitudes toward marking systems

There has been mounting evidence of a growing dissatisfaction with school marks as traditionally derived and administered. At first criticism was directed at the lack of uniformity in the standards used in determining grades or marks, as indicated in the preceding pages. Lately more fundamental objections have been raised against time-honored marking systems.

Foremost among these objections leveled at traditional school marks is that they are based too narrowly upon informational or factual acquisition. Education represents much more than the amassing of information, valuable though that may be. The percentage system and later the Missouri Plan assumedly revealed the pupil's achievement in understanding and even in attitudes; but in reality the marks given represented for the giver as well as for the interpreter very narrow academic achievement.

School marks based upon the Missouri Plan and similar marking systems face a serious objection from the modern educator because they usually imply a man-to-man comparison; that is, the mark represents relative achievement between one student and a group. Education is made highly competitive. It tacitly assumes that our educational philosophy affirms rigorous selectivity in our school population. Too frequently, marks thus achieved do not represent the actual achievement of the student but become an index of relational speed between members of the group tested. The practical operation of such marking systems has the effect of eliminating the less able or less quick reaction students from the educational opportunities provided in the public schools. Possibly a more serious by-product of such marking schemes is the terrific nerve strain placed upon the students with its comcomitants of undesirable attitudes and warped personalities.

Again, objection is offered that the prevalent A, B, C, D, E, or I, II, III, IV, V type of grades in themselves have little meaning. They are not definite. What does an A in English mean? Does it stand for complete achievement? Does it mean that the recipient of this grade has complete knowledge of the subject or only of a segment of it? If a segment is implied, then how extensive is this segment and what is its relative importance to the entire subject and to the needs of the student who received the A? Or, does the mark mean that the recipient possesses more information, or more skill, or more understanding, or more appreciation, or more of all of these, than any other member of the class with whom he has been compared? It may mean only that for the particular segment of English composition or literature for which the mark is given, this student is able to do more than his fellow students on the test forms employed in the limited time permitted the class for reaction. In which case the A stands for a comparison of the reaction speed of the individual with the members of the class. Here again it tells us little, since we do not know whether this class was above average or below the speed levels of other classes. Besides, we do not know what if any value to place on speed in this given subject.

Basic to all the objections thus far raised against the traditional type of school marks is the radical change taking place in our philosophy of education. For the past score years particularly there has been a growing emphasis upon a functional conception of education in contrast with encyclopedic informational learning. Hence, whatever the student studies must have some functional significance both for and to him. Henry C. Morrison became the dominant exponent of a "mastery" conception of learning, based in part upon this educational point of view, in which marks had definite connotation but always with reference to the individual learner. Functional learning must result in some phase of adaptation of personality. This could be possible only when "understanding" or some "ability" or "skill" had been achieved. Such "mastery" could not be expressed comparatively nor could it be expressed in relative degrees. For Morrison a mark could express either the possession of or non-possession of a given phase of learning. Only two symbols were necessary, one to express possession or "mastery" and the other to express non-possession. These symbols could have significance only as applied to a given individual.

A further development of the functional conception of education has been the increasing emphasis upon the social-citizenship significance of education for youth within a democracy. Coupled with the general acceptance of the psychological principle that learning is change in behavior through experience, there is required a new orientation with respect to the nature and function of school marks.

A marking system should reflect an inclusive evaluation plan so effectively devised that it will reveal broadly the degree of social-citizenship development of the student in general and with respect to important aspects of social-civic orientation. Such a marking system should give due consideration to acceptable patterns of social behavior, individual ability and background of opportunity, and the degree of effective orientation that should be expected at various maturity levels. School marks of this kind will be individual, not comparative, based upon definite if somewhat broad standards.

Efforts to develop new recording and reporting systems

The attempt to develop a recording and reporting system in harmony with a modern philosophy of education has revealed both ingenuity and variety. Three general types of plans will be mentioned as suggestive of newer and varied efforts being made to bring school evaluation into conformity with modern educational thought.

Variants of the first type emphasize the individual nature of this system of marking. Marks are still given but with reference only to the actual achievement of the student equated in terms of his ability to achieve. A sample of this type of marking is shown on page 273.

The second type of marking system attempts to give a general estimate of the pupil's work based upon his total reaction in the school in terms of a number of qualities assumed to characterize the good citizen in a democratic society. Again, the estimate is based upon the pupil's ability and generally accepted personal qualities of good citizenship. Each degree of variance from the ideal standard is descriptively characterized. A sample of this form of report is shown on page 275.

Report of	HENRY JONES				Grade 9

Subjects in Course of Study	First Sem.		Second Sem.		Teacher's Comment
	Sub.	Att.	Sub.	Att.	First Semester
Social Living	S	S	S	E	Noticeable improvement in attitude — still needs to watch conduct. L.B.C.
Science	S	E	E	E	
Industrial Arts	E	S	E	E	
Mathematics	S	E	S	S	Very fine attitude. Could work harder. Needs to concentrate. — H.S.P.
Home Economics Mathematics					
Art					Excellent in his music work. Wholesome attitude. — E.B.
Drawing					
Crafts	E	E	E	E	
Music	E	E	E	E	Not doing his best. Not enthusiastically interested. — D.N.
Language					
French					
General Lang.	S	S	S	E	Second Semester
Library	S	S	S	E	Doing very good work in science. — H.S.P.
Band	E	E	E	E	
Drama	E	E	E	S	Very fine student. — E.B.

E — Exceptional ⎫	At times very thoughtless of others in class. Some improvement. — L.B.C.
S — Satisfactory ⎬ In relation to the pupil's own ability	
U — Unsatisfactory ⎭	Attitude toward work shows marked improvement. Needs to develop better study habits. — D.N.

Accompanying the subject (Sub.) mark is an attitude (Att.) mark. Based on the judgment of the teacher. A pupil's attitude is made up of such characteristics as application, cooperation, sportsmanship, cheerfulness, reliability, self-reliance, etc.

The third type of marking system, illustrated on page 276, is in the nature of a progress evaluation report. Usually in this type, grades or evaluative marks are abandoned. An effort is made to indicate descriptively aspects of progress made in all phases of personal development within the school. Definite evidences of improvement in academic fields, personal trait development, and social maturation or adjustment are noted. To collect these data various devices are employed, such as achievement graphs, anecdotal records, logs, case histories, student self-evaluation reports, general impressions, and so forth.[11] Some schools have invited the

[11] An interesting and suggestive account of the way data are collected for such progress evaluation reports is to be found in a sixty-four page mimeographed document produced by the Santa Barbara, California, schools, entitled *The Development of Curriculum, Report of Progress.* Evaluation Com-

parents to the office and then discussed with them the evidences of progress of their children. Other schools have tried to report these data to parents by letter, often enclosing with the letter a copy of a personal progress evaluation paper prepared by the pupil. Copies of these data and letters and/or reports of interviews are made part of the administrative permanent record file of the student.

Teacher-parent conference

Teacher-parent conferences have grown rapidly both in use and popularity. This development is the logical outgrowth of the effort to create evaluative devices in harmony with "experience" learning. It is difficult to reduce characteristic qualitative-behavioral changes to brief A, B, C, D, E types of categories.

It has been found even more difficult to report briefly but satisfactorily to parents on the nature of those behavioral changes in the boy or girl, judged to be of good or undesirable citizenship qualities. Behavior is usually symptomatic of springs to action that lie deep within the individual and his environment. It would not be feasible or politic to attempt to include any consideration of these factors in written reports to parents. What is more significant, the probabilities are that the teacher does not have all the facts at hand necessary to a reasonably complete picture of the behavior of the learner, and what it is that makes him behave as he does.

The new approach to reporting involves a reciprocal one of parents and teachers reporting in turn to each other. The mutual evaluation by teacher and parent together on the basis of a joint sharing of data concerning the child represents the logic of modern education. The school, through the teacher, is not in the dubious position of passing judgment on the child. It is rather in the position of cooperatively sharing the responsibility with the parents of exploring the reactions of the child within his total environment. This united effort is carried on to discover cause and effect relationships in the child's behavior, and in what way it is possible for the home and school, hand in hand, to set about creating a better learning environment.

Where schools utilize this form of reporting, the teachers plan a

mittee, June, 1940. Santa Barbara City Schools, Progress Report No. 2. Santa Barbara, California.

Student.............................. Subject.............. Teacher..............

CITIZENSHIP QUALITIES

Quality	Grade 1	2	3	4	5-Failure
Obedience	Voluntarily cooperates to maintain a good school morale	Promptly and cheerfully responds to suggestions	Careless and indifferent to request of authority	Unwilling to cooperate in securing order except under compulsion	Deliberately obstructs; insubordinate
Industry	Works to full extent of capacity as nearly as can be measured	Does more than average but does not work up to full capacity	Does ordinary assignments of his own accord	Aims to get by with as little efforts as possible	Seldom prepared
Responsibility in performance of group obligations, such as: punctuality, routine requirements, class and student activities	Performs faithfully and without reminder such duties	Willing, but requires occasional reminders	Willing, but thoughtless and needs frequent prodding	Careless and unwilling to assume such responsibility without urging	Utterly irresponsible
Property responsibility, care of building, furniture, books, materials	Careful regard for his own and public property	Occasional carelessness	Frequently careless and wasteful and occasionally defaces property	Destroys and wastes his own material and (or) defaces school property	Deliberately destroys and wastes his own and other property
Self-reliance	Relies entirely on his own efforts to accomplish his work	Occasionally calls on teacher or students for work which he could do for himself	Depends frequently on others for assistance	Habitually depends on others for class exercises	Copies, cheats, and so plagiarizes
Courtesy	Always considerate of others in classroom, halls, and assembly	Considerate but interrupts others to express his own ideas	Frequently disregards courtesy in classroom, hall, and assembly	Habitually noisy and rude in classroom, hall, and assembly	Deliberately rude and discourteous
Cooperation	Cheerfully works with others for the best interests of the group in classroom and student activities without detriment to his own progress	Works – but not consistently for the welfare of the group	Indifferent to activities tending toward the welfare of group	Fails to participate in activities which do not contribute directly to his own personal interest	Selfish, disloyal, willfully obstructs group activity

A check (✓) in one of the squares opposite a "Quality" indicates the teacher's judgment of the student's attainment with respect to that Citizenship Quality.

FINAL REPORT TO PARENTS

DATE _____

NEXT YEAR _____ WILL BE IN _____ GRADE

TEACHER'S COMMENTS:

DAYS PRESENT _____ DAYS ABSENT _____ SIGNATURE OF PARENT OR GUARDIAN _____

TEACHER'S REPORT TO PARENTS

TO PARENTS:

The purpose of education is to help each child to become a desirable, useful, and happy citizen. Such an individual must have not only skill in the fundamental tools of learning — reading, writing, and arithmetic, but also the ability to maintain maximum health, a firm sense of responsibility, and personal ideals and traits of a high order. This is what parents as well as teachers desire in children.

Because of their common interest in the child, parents and teachers have a natural partnership. This partnership can be served best by the teacher and parent planning together for the child in an atmosphere of mutual trust. In an effort to plan with parents of each child, one or more of three written report cards will be replaced by individual conferences as far as possible.

There are three reports to parents each year. The first report will be in the form of a conference wherever possible. If the teacher cannot arrange a conference with the parent a written report will be used. The second report will be a conference in some cases and in others a written report. The third report at the end of the school year will always be a written report.

This form will be used by all teachers and will be used both as a record of conferences held and for written reports.

Superintendent of Schools

SCHOOL _____ TEACHER _____ PRINCIPAL _____

minimum of two to three 30–60 minute conferences with each parental unit. The use of the Core Curriculum or homeroom organization ideally provides a total of 40–70 pupils per teacher for such conferences. Problem cases require more frequent teacher-parent contacts. It is the practice in many schools to free the time of teachers from class work for these conference periods.

QUESTIONS AND PROBLEMS

1. Why has it become desirable to measure the efficiency of education mathematically?
2. In what ways are teacher effectiveness and pupil achievement related?
3. Under what circumstances may the essay type of examination be used to better advantage than any other?
4. From the teacher's standpoint, what are the particular advantages and disadvantages of the standardized test over the teacher-created test?
5. Prepare a short objective test for any subject and apply the criteria of a good evaluation instrument to it.
6. As a class project study educational magazines and other sources as a basis of collecting samples of newer forms of reporting devices.
7. Why has there been a growing tendency to discount norms?
8. Why is diagnosis assuming greater importance in teaching?
9. Would you base your entire guidance procedure on the results of a standardized test? Explain your answer in some detail.
10. What are the advantages of equivalent forms of an examination?
11. What are the chief reasons for using teacher-created objective tests?
12. Prepare objective tests for three of any of those types mentioned in this chapter, for the materials covered in the chapter.
13. Why is it advisable to prepare answer keys and scoring instructions for standardized tests?
14. What means could be employed to make the scoring of essay examinations more uniform?
15. Discuss the relative merits of the percentage and Missouri plans of grading.
16. How would you solve the problem of grading ability section? Justify your answer.
17. Have a class debate on the proposition: "The older objective achievement tests are better instruments to measure pupil efficiency than are the new measurement devices discussed in this chapter."

SELECTED BIBLIOGRAPHY

Bell, John E. *Projective Techniques.* New York: Longmans, Green and Company, 1948.

Burton, William H. *The Guidance of Learning Activities,* chapters XVII, XIX. New York: Appleton-Century-Crofts, Inc., 1944.

Butler, Frank A. *Improvement of Teaching in Secondary Schools,* Revised Edition, chapter XVII. Chicago: University of Chicago Press, 1946.

Douglass, Harl R. and Mills, Hubert H. *Teaching in High School,* chapters XX–XXI. New York: The Ronald Press Company, 1948.

Goetting, M. L. *Teaching in the Secondary School,* chapters XIV, XIX. New York: Prentice-Hall, Inc., 1942.

Jarvie, L. L. and Ellingson, M. *A Handbook on the Anecdotal Behavior Journal.* Chicago: University of Chicago Press, 1940.

Lindquist, E. F. (Editor) *Educational Measurement.* Washington, D.C.: American Council on Education, 1951.

Marshall, Max X. *Two Sides To A Teacher's Desk,* chapter V. New York: The Macmillan Company, 1951.

Mursell, James L. *Successful Teaching,* chapters XIV–XVI. New York: McGraw-Hill Book Company, Inc., 1946.

Risk, Thomas M. *Principles and Practices of Teaching in Secondary Schools,* Revised Edition, chapters XXVII–XXVIII. New York: American Book Company, 1947.

Rivlin, Harry N. *Teaching Adolescents in Secondary Schools,* chapter XIV. New York: Appleton-Century-Crofts, Inc., 1948.

Ross, C. C. *Measurement in Today's Schools,* Second Edition, chapters IV–VI, XVII. New York: Prentice-Hall, Inc., 1947.

Smith, E. R. and Tyler, R. W. *Appraising and Recording Student Progress.* New York: Harper and Brothers, 1942.

The Measurement of Understanding. Forty-fifth Yearbook, Part I, National Society for the Study of Education. Chicago: University of Chicago Press, 1946.

Thut, I. N. and Gerberich, J. R. *Foundations of Method for Secondary Schools,* chapters V, VIII, XI, XIV. New York: McGraw-Hill Book Company, Inc., 1949.

Toward Better Teaching. Washington, D.C.: Association for Supervision and Curriculum Development, 1949.

Travers, Robert M. W. *How to Make Achievement Tests.* New York: The Odyssey Press, 1950.

Traxler, A. E. *The Nature and Use of Anecdotal Records.* Educational Records Supplementary Bulletin D (Revised). New York: Education Records Bureau, 1940.

Wood, Ben D. and Haefner, Ralph. *Measuring and Guiding Individual Growth*. New York: Silver Burdett Company, 1948.

Wrightstone, J. Wayne. *Appraisal of Experimental High School Practices*. New York: Teachers College Bureau of Publications, Columbia University, 1936.

————. *Appraisal of Newer Elementary School Practices*. New York: Teachers College Bureau of Publications, Columbia University, 1938.

Wrinkle, William L. *Improving Marking and Reporting Practices*. New York: Rinehart and Company, 1947.

Part

IV

TEACHING TECHNIQUES

OF THE CLASS PERIOD

10

How Improve Daily Planning?

1. Why Plan the Daily Work?

Definition

Whether the teacher employs the unit as the basis of instructional planning or follows the pattern of the older daily lesson plan, some day-by-day planning is required. The most ardent disciples of the unit idea on occasion, for a phase of a unit or some specific and limited learning situation, will approximate the technique of the daily lesson plan. The *lesson plan,* in all probability, will continue to be an important instructional device.

Unfortunately many definitions of the term *lesson plan* focus attention upon the teacher rather than the pupil as central in the daily classroom situation. It emphasizes teacher activity rather than pupil activity in a learning situation. The writer proposes the following definition to overcome a possible misplacement of emphasis: *Lesson Plan is the title given to a statement of the achievements to be realized and the specific means by which these are to be attained as a result of the activities engaged in day by day under the guidance of the teacher.* This definition tends to focus the teacher's attention upon: (1) outcomes or results in terms of the pupil; (2) definite processes and procedures with a recognition of activity as the basis of learning; (3) the pupil in the foreground and the teacher in the background as guide and director only of the learning activity.

Value of daily lesson plan

Daily lesson planning is just as essential as planning the general course. Indeed, the teacher should think of planning for the day's lesson as one phase of the larger problem of instructional planning which requires complete coordination and integration with the work of the planning of the course. When the course has been carefully planned, many important aspects of lesson planning already have been anticipated. The major aspects of objectives, content, and sequence will have been broadly determined. Even the general procedures for the attack on the units of learning will have been forecast, to a greater or lesser degree, for the guidance of the teacher in the particular lesson situation. Specific daily lesson planning is, therefore, dependent upon good course planning. At almost every step in the formation of the lesson plan, it is necessary for the teacher to keep clearly in perspective the total learning contemplated in the course, if the day's lesson is to contribute in maximum degree toward the achievement of the objectives of the course.

2. What Is Good Lesson Planning?

Nature of lesson planning

Lesson planning is essentially an experience in anticipatory teaching. It is living through in advance, mentally and emotionally, the classroom experience as the teacher visualizes it. The eager faces, the questions that will arise, the difficulties the pupils will encounter, the way these difficulties are to be met — all these will the teacher experience in imagination. This is the first essential of good teaching. It is here that the teacher can bring into play the subtle power of a well-developed imagination. The more vivid the better, so long as it is fully tinged with realism. To the degree that the teacher can imaginatively anticipate the actual classroom situation can the lesson plan provide for the needs of the class. This first step in learning to teach requires, as a basis for an effective anticipatory experience of the actual class hour, four major prerequisites.

First, the teacher should possess a broad understanding of the subject matter, materials, and activities that will provide the nucleus for the classroom experiences. This understanding will enable the teacher to anticipate probable difficulties inherent in the materials, and plan for them should they actually arise.

Second, a teacher needs to have an intimate knowledge of the environmental forces that have played upon the life of the class, collectively and individually. These have a vital relation to the apperceptive approach each pupil makes to a situation and his consequent reactions.

Third, a thorough comprehension of the psychology of the mental processes, with an understanding of the relation of the laws of learning to the anticipated classroom stiuation, is imperative. Every form of leadership and salesmanship today recognizes the importance of knowing the laws that govern learning and human behavior. If this knowledge is important for those who wish to capitalize it for personal aggrandizement, it is exceedingly important that the teacher be master of it as a basis for anticipating pupil reactions and wisely planning lessons to meet and direct them.

Fourth, the teacher must know the most approved teaching techniques to meet the general and the specific needs of a learning situation. These must not be known superficially; only a fundamental understanding of them and their psychological validations will prove efficient.

Kinds of lesson planning

Two kinds of lesson planning are recognized — the memorized, and the written. The first visualizes the expected activities of the classroom, and plans for the situations as it is believed they will arise. Nothing is committed to visible form, but the problems are met, questions are asked or considered as anticipated from the class, and the details of the lesson are formulated. The teacher trusts his memory to follow the course of his protracted thought upon the anticipated experience. The second kind of lesson planning requires the same vivid imagery and vigorous reflection as does the first. It does not, however, depend upon memory to be the sole repository for lesson plans, but commits these reflections to writing in the form of a well-organized plan.

There are distinct advantages for the memorized lesson plan, as it requires a minimum of time to prepare and is not subject to misplacement. However, its weaknesses are apparent in the advantages obviously belonging to the written lesson plan. It is of value to review the most important advantages attributed to the written form. These are:

1. *Definiteness in thinking.* Thinking, the results of which are not committed to graphic form, is likely to be hazy and vague. No doubt the reader has found, in his own experience, that efforts at

careful thinking which he believed clear and lucid were decidedly nebulous when an attempt was made to commit them to
writing. An eminent scholar once said to his class, "If you want to
test your understanding of something you believe you comprehend,
try to convey that understanding to others either in speech or
writing. Frequently you will find your thinking has been exceedingly vague." The experience of many has been that it was necessary to resort to writing to clarify their thinking. One is enabled,
when his thoughts have been committed to written forms, to stand
off, as it were, and coldly appraise them. The spans of memory
and attention make appraisal of unexpressed thought exceedingly
difficult.

2. *Orderliness and development in thinking.* The span of memory is too short, and the span of attention is too brief, to permit
extended abstract thought to be carried on in rigorous, orderly, and
developmental fashion such as is required in lesson planning. Too
many possibilities must be taken into account in the anticipatory
stage of teaching. Only as planning is committed to written form,
and opportunity provided for revision and supplementation, can
the teacher be sure of proper sequence in the lesson plan.

3. *Protection against forgetting.* Memory is not infallible. Under
the stress of the give-and-take of the classroom, it is a rare teacher,
indeed, who can remember all the important items that were to
play a part in the class exercise. Even when the written lesson plan
is briefed in extended form, there are few occasions when faulty
memory has not tricked the teacher at one point or another.

4. *Freedom in teaching.* The mental processes tend to move as
it were in grooves. This tendency psychology recognizes when it
uses the phrase "mental pathways" in its approved terminology.
This tendency has a concomitant danger. When the teacher would
digress from the beaten path of anticipated classroom procedure,
there is danger of being unable to retrace his steps to the point of
digression. This fear tends to make the teacher a slave to his preparation, unless that preparation is in written form to act as a signpost when unexpected developments in the class make digression
from the planned way desirable or imperative. With a written
lesson plan before him the teacher is master of the lesson plan, not
the lesson plan of him.

5. *Plans for later improvement.* Most teachers reteach the courses
assigned them, from year to year. When that is true it is a costly

expenditure of time and energy to build new lesson plans each time the course is taught. The wise teacher will not rely upon a lesson plan once made, nor will he consign it to the wastebasket once its immediate use has passed. Instead, the wise teacher will make notations on it of weaknesses and inadequacies discovered, and suggestions for improvement and then file the lesson plan for future revision as another occasion for its use arises. A successful speaker once remarked to the writer that he considered an address once created and delivered just at the initial stage of its development. Thereafter, he was in a position to do his best work upon it. In this way the teacher should value his written lesson plans.

Essential elements of a good lesson plan

Many teachers recognize the need for some form of guide during the progress of the lesson. Especially is this true of the new teacher who finds the class hour an extremely difficult and complicated performance. Too often the inexperienced teacher does not suspect that the difficulties of the class hour are due as much to an inadequate lesson plan as to the absence of one. Many times the writer has found student teachers in the training school in trouble because of a faulty lesson plan. It is pertinent, therefore, to consider the essentials of a good lesson plan. The six elements enumerated are those most universally recognized as essential to any complete lesson plan.

1. *The plan should evince a clear understanding of the outcomes to be achieved.* This involves a recognition, both of the immediate results of the lesson and of the relation of the immediate to the more remote inclusive objectives of the course. If the teacher's objective for the lesson is different from that of the pupil, the lesson plan should reveal this.

2. *The plan should definitely relate the lesson to the previous work of the course.* Many new teachers, particularly, are prone to think of each lesson as an isolated experience. The consequences are that each day's activities of the pupil stand out as independent experiences. Those who use the unit plan of teaching avoid this difficulty. The pupil's experiences do not provide him proper perspective, nor is he able to take advantage of yesterday's experience in the interpretation of new situations confronted today. Unless the teacher provides for this conscious recognition of the connection between past and present experiences, pupil progress will be im-

peded. The teacher should remember that even under the unit plan pupils need day-by-day reminders of the interrelations of the problem situation they are working with over a period of time.

3. *The plan should provide for the selection and organization of subject matter, materials, and activities.* Materials of some form are necessary for every lesson or unit phase. These may involve subject matter as found in textbooks, library references, the experience gleaned from others, or apparatus and equipment of various sorts. While modern education lays less stress than formerly upon factual materials as the *sine qua non* of education, yet factual data are indispensable as the basis of intelligent learning. Activity, too, is increasingly being recognized as an effective medium of education. These materials require very careful consideration by the teacher if the most appropriate are to be selected. The way in which they are organized for use, too, has much to do with their effectiveness.

4. *The plan should indicate the application of appropriate teaching procedures to the lesson.* Within recent years we have learned much about the learning process. We know that there are different types of learning. We know, also, that they require different techniques for efficient development. While there is much need for extensive experimental study of the best techniques to employ with a given type of learning, yet enough is known to make broad adaptation of methods to learning types an inescapable responsibility of the teacher. The lesson plan should reveal discernment in analysis of the learning types involved and the application of approved teaching techniques to each.

5. *The plan should provide for the proper evaluation of success in the realization of the objectives.* How successful has the lesson been? That is, how well have the outcomes sought been achieved? If the objective has been reached but partially, what still remains to be done? At what point has there been ineffectiveness in the procedures employed, or possibly inappropriateness of materials and activities used? These are some of the questions that legitimately demand an answer. All but the last question may be answered by appropriate evaluation techniques. The trained critical teacher will have some suggestions in answer to the last question. Intelligent teaching requires such evaluation. The lesson plan is defective if it does not provide for it.

6. *The plan should project today's lesson into tomorrow's situ-*

ation. When the lesson activities for today are over, the pupil should have his attention focused upon the next step. In fact, he should be prepared for that step. Unless this has been definitely provided for in the lesson plan, it is likely to be poorly planned and executed. A lesson plan without an assignment, even though it be little more than calling attention to the immediate phase of the unit to be attacked on the morrow, is scarcely conceivable of the successful teacher.

Some writers omit numbers 2 and 6 in the preceding list; others include even more. Lessons are not all alike, and some require additional elements. It is difficult to conceive of any learning activity for which these six elements would not be necessary as a part of the teacher's plan for its successful direction.

At the risk of repetition the writer wishes to stress, in summary fashion, certain features that in general should be observed in lesson planning and should be embodied in the parts. They are:

1. Well-formulated aim.
2. Good assignment.
3. Good summary.
4. Provision for individual differences.
5. Inclusion of pivotal questions.
6. Inclusion of important illustrations.
7. Review.
8. Content materials.
9. Motivation techniques.
10. Evaluation techniques.
11. Rough allocation of time to each phase of the lesson.
12. Attention to apperceptive learning — new related to the old.

3. How Use Lesson Planning?

Cautions to be observed in making lesson plans

Important as lesson planning is, there are dangers besetting the novice which must be guarded against in the construction of lesson plans. These are set forth here as things to be avoided.

1. *Avoid overcompleteness.* A lesson plan that attempts to cover every detail of the lesson is apt to prove more confusing than helpful. It is similar to the taking of notes. It may become so extensive that the trees cannot be separated from the forest. The main items should be present in the plan, together with whatever details may

be necessary to insure proper development of the lesson. This difficulty is likely to overtake the timid, inexperienced teacher who is afraid to trust himself before the class.

2. *Avoid too fragmentary a plan.* The writer recalls a very vivid experience with a student teacher who trusted the barest outline of the lesson to aid her before the class. After several visits to the classroom of this teacher, where a uniformly poor lesson was witnessed, the observer thought he detected the source of the difficulty. When the student came for a conference the daily lesson plan was requested. In large Roman numerals the development of the lesson was indicated in five major points. Under the first were two questions supposed to lead the students' discussion into the heart of the problem. The second major division had but one minor point under it, and the remaining sections had no suggestive notations under them. When the student was given specific directions for lesson planning and the adequacy of her plans checked, she immediately overcame her difficulties and within two weeks was doing highly creditable teaching. The beginner, particularly, should work out lesson plans in considerable detail, even though it is found best to brief them before use in the class.

3. *Avoid sameness in plans.* One of the principles of motivation is the use of variety in classroom technique. Provide an air of expectancy on the part of the class through the use of the unexpected. The teacher has a rare opportunity to reveal creative genius in teaching, and nowhere else is it so productive of fruitful results as in lesson planning.

4. *Avoid undue reverence for the printed text.* The teacher is prone to accept anything that appears in the text as law and gospel. The fact that it appears in the textbook is no guarantee that the statement is correct, nor that the organization of the material there has uncanny merit. The competent teacher will exercise the utmost freedom consonant with the administrative limitations placed upon him in the choice of textbook material and in the reorganization of content for better teaching purposes.

5. *Avoid the tendency to too ambitious a program.* The attempt to cover too much ground in the lesson plan is a common fault. This is likely to be again the fault of the beginner. Learning is a comparatively slow and deliberate process. It is well to remember that old, but still pertinent, precept — "Line upon line, precept upon precept, here a little and there a little." Sometimes "haste

makes waste." It is better to have done well a lesser program than to cover more ground imperfectly.

Constructive use of the lesson plan

The new teacher should keep at least six suggestions in mind for the intelligent use of the lesson plan.

First, use the lesson plan as a guide, not a crutch. The latter may seem necessary for the first few days of teaching. In fact, it has been the policy of the writer to advise student teachers in the training school to lean heavily upon their lesson plans for the first few days, if they find this reassuring. The teacher should, however, be ready very early to depart from the lesson plan slightly in the interest of seizing an opportunity to improve a learning situation. Certainly, as confidence and ease come to the teacher in the classroom, the lesson plan should more and more be looked upon as a guide to stimulate thought and not as something to be slavishly followed. Indeed, at times good teaching demands the complete shelving of the lesson plan to meet an emergency. Too often the experienced supervisor has seen golden opportunities for vitalizing a teaching situation missed because the teacher seemed to be irrevocably committed to what was in the lesson plan only. Even in college and university an occasional instructor is found who is utterly confused before a class without his manuscript, though he may have grown gray in the service. This danger of becoming a slave, not a master, of the lesson plan can be side-stepped only by constant alertness for opportunities to supplement or modify the lesson plan while teaching. We are more or less creatures of habit. Developed habits of independence of the lesson plan may be formed almost as readily as those of subservience to it.

The *second* suggestion is that the plan, once used, should become the basis for extended development. There is a real danger that the indolent teacher will place undue dependence upon a lesson plan once carefully prepared. In spite of the fact that most teachers reteach one or more courses in successive years, the personnel of the classes change, advances are generally recorded in content or methodology or both, and even environment shades off from year to year. A college lecturer once was heard to remark before a class in which he had referred to some statistical data about life-insurance companies: "At least these were the facts twenty years ago when I gathered them, and I doubt not but they represent the situation today." The class had serious misgivings of the applicability of twenty-year-old data to the present. Even though the use of the plan in outline can be repeated, no plan is ever perfect and the teacher, to be at his best, must again live through the class hour in anticipation shortly before the class convenes. For the teacher using the true unit plan these cautions have no relevancy.

The *third* suggestion for the use of lesson plans is that one should use rather detailed plans at first, but as experience is gained a briefer form may be employed.

Fourth, in any wide-awake classroom it is impossible to predict the line of development the lesson will take. The more freedom one attempts to use in teaching, the greater the possibilities of divergence from the plan formulated. Since omniscience or clairvoyance seems not vouchsafed to man, readiness for the unexpected is the part of good planning. The teacher may have flashes of insight under the stimulus of the classroom situation not present before. These may lead far astray from the plotted course. Yet the good teacher will risk the adventure; perchance rich treasure may be the reward.

Fifth, it cannot be repeated too often that no two pupils react exactly alike. Even the day-by-day reactions to the same apparent stimulation may vary widely. None the less, the general patterns of behavior reactions in a given situation generally have elements of similarity. It then becomes obvious that the full assortment of questions and illustrative material needed cannot be prepared in advance. Outside of pivotal questions and some illustrative data, there must be a readiness to capitalize the opportunity of the moment with a repertoire, as it were, of well-selected questions and illustrative materials. When these are not applicable, necessity should become the mother of invention. The more thorough the preparation, however, the less need there will be for improvised aids generally imperfect at best.

Sixth, it is a rare teacher, indeed, who can estimate the exact time required to complete the task laid out in a daily plan. This would be difficult even if every aspect of the classroom situation could be calculated. With the uncertain factors that enter in, time approximations only can be determined. If, however, these are carefully estimated and checked for accuracy through subsequent · experience, and a record kept of time consumed by each major phase of the lesson or unit, the teacher can become quite proficient in estimating the time required for the work to be done.

Proposed Outline for Daily Lesson Plan

Date......... Class.............. School...............

Problem or Topic:

Objectives:

(Here teacher should distinguish those major objectives to which this lesson is expected to contribute. The more limited and immediate goals of the lesson should be clearly indicated.)

Major Outline of Problem or Topic Development: **Methods of Attack**

              How initiate lesson:

              Materials to be used:

              Possible activities:

              How provide for individual differences:

              Key questions and illustrations:

              Culminating Activities or Summary and Conclusions:

              How evaluate lesson:

              Assignments or leads for next day:

              Approximate time various phases:

Note: The student should consult the previous chapters which considered the unit form of organization for instruction and the various methods of teaching. Lesson plans must be adapted to the purpose and method employed.

QUESTIONS AND PROBLEMS

1. What do you understand by the term "lesson plan"?
2. Give at least ten important reasons why a daily lesson plan improves the process of teaching.
3. Have a class discussion on the question of the differences in daily planning involved in the use of various methods of teaching.

4. Have a debate on the "advantages" versus the "disadvantages" of daily planning in experience unit teaching.
5. Have a class discussion on the merits of the memorized and the written lesson plan.
6. Outline and defend each item of the good lesson plan.
7. Make a daily lesson plan of some topic in which you are interested. Then evaluate it according to the textbook discussion of an ideal lesson plan.
8. Have the class take a teaching unit and show how daily planning would be involved. Have the class compare daily planning in unit teaching with daily lesson planning in more traditional forms of teaching.
9. Have class discussion of the factors the teacher must take into account if the lesson plans are to be used most effectively.
10. In what ways will daily planning be different where the lesson considered is one with major dependence upon textbook and one of a project nature with many activities necessary outside the classroom and school building?
11. Could a case be made for the contention that lesson planning as thought of twenty years ago is now outmoded?
12. As applied to modern educational thinking would it be more accurate to speak of "daily planning" rather than "lesson planning"?

SELECTED BIBLIOGRAPHY

Burton, William H. *The Guidance of Learning Activities,* chapter XV. New York: Appleton-Century-Crofts, Inc., 1944.

Butler, Frank A. *The Improvement of Teaching in The Secondary School,* chapter XVIII. Chicago: University of Chicago Press, 1946.

Cook, Luella B. "What Kind of Lesson Plan is Best Suited to Language Development." *English Journal* XXXII: 135–142 (March, 1943).

Douglass, Harl R. and Mills, H. H. *Teaching in High School,* pp. 128–138. New York: The Ronald Press Company, 1948.

Giles, H. H. *Teacher-Pupil Planning.* New York: Harper and Brothers, 1941.

Goetting, M. L. *Teaching in the Secondary School,* chapter XI. New York: Prentice-Hall, Inc., 1942.

Risk, Thomas M. *Principles and Practices of Teaching in Secondary Schools,* Second Edition, chapter XVI. New York: American Book Company, 1947.

Rivlin, Harry N. *Teaching Adolescents in Secondary Schools,* chapter VI. New York: Appleton-Century-Crofts, Inc., 1948.

Sands, Lester B. *An Introduction to Teaching in Secondary Schools,* chapter X. New York: Harper and Brothers, 1949.

Schorling, Raleigh. *Student Teaching,* Second Edition, chapter VI. New York: McGraw-Hill Book Company, Inc., 1949.

Stiles, L. J. and Dorsey, M. F. *Democratic Teaching in Secondary Schools,* chapter XIII. Chicago: J. B. Lippincott Company, 1950.

Thut, I. N. and Gerberich, J. R. *Foundations of Method for Secondary Schools,* chapter VII. New York: McGraw-Hill Book Company, Inc., 1949.

11

How Can Assignments Be Used?

1. What Is the Nature of the Assignment?

The assignment defined

Recent writers tend to play down the use of the word "assignment." Both in the general connotation of the word and in its historical educational usage it has had about it a bad flavor of authoritarianism. It has implied to most readers the ideal of the imposition of a task without necessarily securing first the willing consent of the one to whom the assignment has been made. Certainly the older connotation associated with the word has little place in modern educational theory or practice. Rather, *the assignment applies to that part of the instructional activity devoted to the clear recognition and acceptance by the pupil of the next unit of learning to take place and of the processes by which this learning may be achieved most effectively.* Such a definition recognizes four factors as implicit in the concept of the assignment: (1) laying out a task to be done; (2) fitting to the task an appropriate procedure for accomplishment; (3) teacher direction but pupil acceptance of task and procedure; and (4) assumption that the most effective learning is the product of pupil activity self-imposed.

Importance of the assignment

The central position of the assignment in the technique of teaching has remained unquestioned. Betts,[1] in an earlier book on

[1] Betts, G. H. *The Recitation*, p. 107. Boston: Houghton Mifflin Company, 1911.

The Recitation, asserts that "upon the proper assignment of the lesson depends much of the success of the recitation, and also much of the pupil's progress in learning how to study." Another writer [2] later suggested that "teachers generally do not appreciate the importance of the assignment, and the work of the pupils probably suffers as much from hasty or careless assignment as from any other single cause." A more recent book [3] on secondary school methods that has come to the writer's desk continues the unbroken emphasis upon the assignment when he says: "The assignment represents one of the most important phases of teaching." The writers go on to suggest that the assignment should be recognized "as an aspect of teaching instead of just as a preparatory step to teaching."

While little objective data can be advanced to support the unanimous belief of educational writers in the value of the assignment, there is some corroborative evidence of its essential significance. Charters and Waples,[4] in a very elaborate investigation, studied, by recourse to "competent judges," the value of each of a large number of teacher activities. Thirteen groups, each including twenty-five judges representative of every major division of educational leadership in teaching, from the kindergarten-primary teachers to college instructors, evaluated 1001 teacher activities. These evaluations were given in decile rank order. A total of eleven of the thirteen groups placed the assignment activities in fourth rank or above. The following table of the assignment activities rated, and the median ranks given by each of the groups immediately concerned with secondary education, will show how important "competent judges" assume the assignment phase to be on the high school level.

These ratings reveal how overwhelmingly those most concerned with classroom problems agree that the assignment is of major importance in the technique of teaching. It is worthy of note that only two rankings are below third place, and the lowest comes from the group least vitally in touch with the teaching problems of the classroom.

Another study, made by a committee of Chicago school princi-

2 Drum, W. N. *A Preview of Teaching,* p. 237. Boston: Ginn and Company, 1928.
3 Douglass, Harl R. and Mills, Hubert H. *Teaching in High School,* p. 149. New York: The Ronald Press Company, 1948.
4 Charters, W. W. and Waples, D. *The Commonwealth Teacher-Training Study,* Part II, "The Findings." Chicago: University of Chicago Press, 1929.

TABLE 1. *Decile Ranks of Activities as Rated for Importance by Representatives of Secondary School Groups* *

Activities from Check List Assigning Work	Univ. of Chicago graduates (H.S.)	City H.S. principals	Supervisors of practice teaching secondary grades	College instructors Secondary Education	City Junior High School Teachers	High School English Teachers	High School Mathematics Teachers	High School Science Teachers
1. Selecting Group Assignments	2	8	2	1	3	2	3	4
2. Presenting directions for doing work	1	8	2	5	1	2	1	2
3. Checking pupils' understanding of work to be done	3	9	6	4	6	5	2	2
4. Adapting assignments to the abilities and needs of the class	1	3	3	1	1	2	3	1
5. Adapting assignments to the needs of individual pupils	2	2	4	3	2	2	6	4
6. Following up assignments	1	6	4	3	1	1	3	2
Median of ranks given by each group to the six activities	1.5	7	3.5	3	1.5	2	3	2

* Data adapted from Charters and Waples, pp. 567 and 623. The deciles are numbered from 1 to 10. The figure 1 represents highest decile while 10 indicates the lowest decile.

pals, attempted to discover the presence or absence of certain teaching skills among teachers rated "superior" or "just satisfactory." Data were secured from 120 Chicago principals, who were asked to pick from their schools two teachers, one rated "superior" and another considered "just satisfactory." These principals were then asked to indicate the presence or absence of 216 characteristics in each of the teachers rated. It was found that 97 per cent of the superior teachers possessed skill in making assignments, and 68 per cent of these were judged unusually skilled in the use of the assignment technique. Only 8 per cent of the "just satisfactory" group were considered exceptionally skillful in making assignments, while the principals rated 50 per cent of this group as deficient in assignment skill.

2. What Are the Properties of the Assignment?

Criteria governing effective assignment [5]

It is impossible to state a set of criteria or governing principles that would apply to all assignments. The situations vary under

[5] In connection with this set of criteria the reader should compare the "Characteristics of Good Assignments" given by Burton, pp. 231–233, in *Learn-*

which assignments are made. The essential factors in a particular case may suggest the presence or absence of certain accepted elements in an assignment if that specific assignment is to be judged good or bad. The teacher must bear in mind, therefore, that the treatment of the criteria enumerated and discussed assumes general applicability to normal classroom conditions. It is a wise teacher, indeed, who has a fundamental grasp of the significance of each of the criteria suggested, and can thereby apply them intelligently in a given classroom situation.

This is the more necessary since a careful study of the literature on assignment reveals a general though not complete agreement among educational writers as to what criteria should be accepted as governing a good assignment. Two lists of assignment criteria, gleaned from two extensive studies on this subject, are given as typical. Yoakam[6] reports a study of the criteria of the assignment as given by eighteen writers of books on methods of teaching. He lists the ten qualities of an assignment mentioned most frequently by these writers, as the following:

1. Definiteness
2. Clearness
3. Interest
4. Stimulation
5. Inspiration
6. Exposition
7. Preparation
8. Direction
9. Discrimination
10. Individualization

Yoakam further gives a list of seventy-four terms used to characterize the assignment by forty writers on the subject. Seventeen of these describe qualities of the assignment. He thinks the seventeen may be compressed, however, into the ten qualities gleaned from the eighteen textbook writers on method. Another slightly larger and more detailed list is given by Carr and Waage [7] under the caption: "Thirteen Assignment Principles."

A comparison of these two somewhat typical lists will suggest

ing and Instruction, Forty-Ninth Yearbook of the National Society for the Study of Education. Chicago: University of Chicago Press, 1950.

[6] Yoakam, G. A. *The Improvement of the Assignment,* pp. 89–91. New York: The Macmillan Company, 1932.

[7] Carr, W. G., and Waage, John. *The Lesson Assignment,* pp. 71–72. Stanford: Stanford University Press, 1931.

some differences, though a study of the fuller discussion of each by the authors reveals these writers to be in approximate agreement. When so many radically different methods of teaching are prevalent as in secondary education today, no set of criteria could be drawn up which would be applicable at every point to all methods. In the light of the functions given for the assignment, the following criteria are suggested as essential for most assignments:

1. *The assignment should be clear and definite.* Definiteness of the assignment is of primary importance. Much of student failure to prepare properly the advance lessons may be laid at the door of the teacher's indefiniteness in outlining the work to be done.

The pupil must see clearly some reason for the task assigned him. To the same extent that objectives are essential for the teacher in giving direction and definiteness to his lesson plans, so objectives for the pupil give direction and definiteness to his thought and activities. The assignment should enable the student to see a purpose for his study, and some definite values to be attained or objective to be reached as a result of his execution of the assignment. In a study [8] of the reasons why high school students lose interest in their work, 12.75 per cent of the 651 college students who served as the basis of the investigation reported that it was because of lack of clear explanation on the part of the teachers. This percentage, coupled with the replies of 28.9 per cent that their lack of interest was due to their failure to see the need for the subject studied, suggests the necessity for a clearly and concisely defined task. While an immediate assignment might be clear-cut and yet the ultimate worth of the subject unconvincing to the student, it may be safely assumed that a clearly defined task will tend to focus the student's attention upon an immediate goal that for him becomes a challenge.

Further, a well-defined assignment reduces to a minimum the probabilities that students will fritter away their time and energies in meaningless or fruitless activity. Recently, the writer stepped into the classroom of a student-teacher, where the preparation for the day evidenced general confusion on the part of the class as to the meaning of the previous day's assignment. As a possible clue to the cause of the present confusion and obvious dissatisfaction on the part of the students, that phase of the class work devoted to the assignment for the following day was carefully appraised.

[8] Young, Florence M. "Causes for Loss of Interest in High School" in *Journal of Educational Research*, vol. 26, pp. 110–116 (February, 1932).

When the next day's assignment was placed on the board the observer noted that it was so indefinite and confusing that at least two distinctly different types of preparation might be inferred on the part of the students. Indeed, it was not until the observer had an opportunity to discuss the assignment with the student-teacher that he himself understood what preparation was intended in the assignment attempted. Such lack of definiteness in the assignment technique can lead only to diffused and wasted energy, with consequent bad study and learning habits, let alone antagonistic mental sets developed toward the school.

Still another consideration of this function of the assignment is the general dependence of class progress upon assigned tasks, clearly defined and understood. Particularly is this true where promotion is based upon class achievement, rather than upon the progress of the individual pupil. It is an accepted truism in teaching, where group instruction is the vogue, that class progress must be paced by the ability of any considerable minority within the class to advance. Upon the degree of clarity with which the assignment designates definite goals to be attained and carefully delimits the outlines of the task depends the ability of the class to perform its work intelligently.

Several factors enter into the formulation of a clear and definite assignment.

First, there must be sufficient detail clearly to delimit the task. For example, it lacks much in clarity and definiteness to say to a class in English literature: "We shall now begin the study of *Evangeline*. You will find this poem in your textbook beginning on page 167. Read to the end of part one. Study the footnotes carefully, and be prepared to answer questions tomorrow." Unfortunately, many studies and observations compel the admission that many assignments are not even as specific as is this one. To a certain point the task is clearly delimited. The student knows where he begins reading and where he is to stop. He must read the footnotes. He must answer questions — assumedly about the poem and the footnotes. He knows where to find the poem. He does not know what to look for in the poem. It is not clear what emphasis is to be placed upon the footnotes *vs.* the poem — whether his study should emphasize historical allusions, mere outline of the story, elements of poetic quality, or a dozen other things that might become the basis for questioning on the morrow is not indicated. A detailed list of guide questions might well be used to clarify further and to render this assignment more definite. Free use of problems, exercises, questions, directions, etc., may be used to insure definiteness in the assignment.

Secondly, an assignment might be definite to a fault and yet remain misunderstood because the language used was not suited to the age and experience of the class. This is a frequent fault of the beginning teacher just out of the training school. It is a fault of the over-brilliant teacher as well. This can be avoided only by the utmost care in the use of simple language in the classroom, and a frequent check upon the difficulties of students to see that these do not originate in unfamiliar teacher vocabulary.

A *third* factor in clarifying an assignment is the resort to the concrete to explain an abstract principle. We tend to explain abstract ideas by the use of equally abstract terminology. A copious use of concrete illustrations, reference to the experiences of the class, and, where possible, the use of physical materials, will enable the teacher to remove most of this type of difficulty.

2. *The assignment should be concise but sufficiently detailed to enable each student to understand the task assigned.* No arbitrary rule can be set down governing this point. The elaborateness of any assignment depends upon three factors: (1) the extent of the unit of work involved; (2) the learning difficulty of the unit; and (3) the degree of homogeneity of ability and common background of the individuals within the class. What may be thoroughly understood by one student may not be by another. No two students approach any situation with identical preparation for the new experiences involved. It is necessary to remember that a simple, brief, inclusive statement may suffice for a part of the class. For most of the class amplification will be imperative. It is a good plan for the teacher to pick out the slower members of the class and satisfy himself that the assignment is understood by them. A little experience will enable the teacher to both plan and make the assignment in the briefest form consistent with definiteness and an assured understanding of what is expected by each member of the class. Economy of time, avoidance of confusion by making points of emphasis stand out in sharp perspective, and the sustained interest of the class are factors that demand conciseness and reasonable brevity in the assignment.

3. *The assignment should anticipate special difficulties in the ad-*

vance work, and suggest ways to overcome them. Every new unit of learning assumes new elements to be mastered. The presence of unfamiliar difficulties offers a stumbling-block to the uninitiated student. They likewise offer to the teacher an opportunity and a definite responsibility. The assignment is wholly inadequate that does not equip the student both with a knowledge of these difficulties and with some suggestions by which they may be overcome. To say: "Take ten problems in advance," and then to assume no further responsibility even though the problems require a new type of attack on distinctly unfamiliar elements, is to fail utterly in an appreciation of the significance of the assignment.

A supervisor observed a young teacher make an assignment in a class in geometry. The successful solution of the problems in the next day's lesson involved the application of new principles, which the teacher overlooked in an otherwise carefully assigned lesson. The supervisor recognized the nature of the difficulty, and with as little embarrassment to the teacher as possible asked the privilege of asking a question or two of the class. Adroitly the supervisor led the class to see the implications and use of the new principles to problems similar to those just assigned. The alert teacher saw her error; the class, unconscious of the real purpose of the supervisor's questions, was saved from certain failure and the teacher from the embarrassment of a poorly prepared class the next day.

4. *The assignment should definitely relate the new unit to past experiences.* The principle of apperceptive learning has been previously discussed; it is too well recognized to need further amplification here. Our concern at this point is with the application of this principle of learning to the assignment. Two problems are involved in this issue: namely, the degree to which the advance unit of work requires a definite recognition of the elements in the learning experience of the previous assignment, and the degree to which a new unit may demand recourse to previously unrelated social experience. Examples of these two problems may be found in a course in mathematics, as contrasted with one in the social sciences. In a course in trigonometry as usually organized, constant reference must be made to the theorems, axioms, and principles learned in plane geometry as well as to the principles learned in the previous unit of work. It is, therefore, only necessary for the teacher, for purposes of connecting the old with the new, to satisfy himself

that the students recognize those particular data previously learned which apply to the new unit.

On the other hand a teacher of a course in "modern social problems," now rapidly coming into vogue in our high schools, faces no such simple task. The teacher must draw heavily upon the experiences of the students in their social environment, as well as upon a less unified set of learned data from previous classroom study. Since high school students represent a widely varied reservoir of social experience, this phase of the assignment technique becomes increasingly important and difficult for the teacher. At the same time the varied background provides a wealth of resource from which the alert teacher may draw to clarify and vitalize the advance work.

5. *Students should understand the importance of the assignment.* As Carr and Waage aptly suggest,[9] unless motivation passes beyond the ephemeral to a recognition of the genuine merits of the advance work, interest will lag and positive antagonism to the assignment may result. On the other hand, human nature is so constituted that when the individual is convinced of the worthwhileness of the thing to be done, he is not likely to be deterred by the drudgery entailed. This is an important fact for the teacher to remember. The major reason for the student's lack of enthusiasm for his work is his inability to understand the personal value of his school work.

The teacher is confronted with two unfortunate premises in the situation. The one is that, as courses and school work are often constituted, it is exceedingly difficult for the teacher to see a valid reason for the study of a given course. Particularly is this the case in languages and mathematics, where the original disciplinary values especially assumed to inhere in them are now seriously questioned by educational psychologists. In such a situation the teacher must find new values of genuine worth in the course, revise the content and method of teaching the course to insure the presence of real values, or frankly acknowledge that while real worth may be there it is difficult to reveal it. The other premise is that while values are present, they are frequently so remote or intangible that the immature mind of the adolescent has difficulty in perceiving them.

The more evident are the immediate and utilitarian values of

9 Carr, W. G., and Waage, John, *op. cit.*, pp. 49–50.

the work assigned, the more readily the student will attack it with avidity. Through the assignment the teacher should attempt to challenge the student with the true purpose and worth of the unit to be studied. These values, however, may be so remote that the teacher must employ an immediate goal that challenges the student, while as teacher he recognizes the true purpose of the assignment to be quite different.

6. *The assignment should arouse an interest in the advance work.* Motivation is a definite function of the assignment. To require a student to do something without regard to his interest or enthusiasm in the enterprise is generally frowned upon by contemporary educators. The reasons for this are, moreover, threefold.

First, modern psychology has discovered that the student does not learn as readily when he has no interest in the thing to be learned. The problem is then a question of increased learning efficiency through adequate motivation.

Secondly, the effective development of habits and attitudes is directly related to the problem of motivation in learning. If, while learning is taking place in a particular situation, it is accompanied by a lively interest and enthusiasm, a favorable attitude toward that type of activity may be awakened. For example, if the student studies the English classics under circumstances that are pleasant and engaging, he is likely to develop an abiding interest in this literature and through this interest to establish a habit of reading for enjoyment books of accepted literary merit. While many desirable habits and even some desirable attitudes are developed within an unpleasant atmosphere of force or threat — negative stimulation — they do not flourish readily under these conditions; dependence upon the unpleasant as a device for motivation is at best precarious.

The *third* reason for this emphasis upon motivation is less fundamental though important. It is natural for the student when interested to be on his good behavior. Unpleasant conduct and disciplinary problems are reduced to a minimum when the students reflect a pleasurable reaction to the total school situation. Not only does such a condition relieve the unpleasant nervous strain upon the teacher, but the major energies and attention of the teacher can then be focused upon the educational needs of the students. The students, as well, find distractions within the class fewer and attention less diverted. Under such favorable surroundings the highest degree of learning efficiency can be attained.

Frequently other interest-stimuli which are supplemental to and sometimes actually in lieu of a genuine purpose must be used. Among some of the most effective devices that may be employed to create immediate interest in advance work are:

(*a*) *Dramatization.* This has been a popular device, particularly with literature classes in English. Junior high school students respond to it eagerly, although it has proved quite effective with students of the senior high school.

(*b*) *Scrapbooks and notebooks.* A common use of this means of creating interest, for example, is in the study of language. Some excellent studies of word derivation from the Latin and French languages, as gleaned from the advertisements in newspapers and especially from magazines, have been observed. A striking example of the effective use of the scrapbook noted by the writer was the graphic presentation of the evolution of transportation in pictorial form arranged from clippings. These have both educational and interest value that may be adapted to assignments of units of considerable length and often as supplementary devices.

(*c*) *The problem.* This is the most direct and simple means of stimulating interest. The problem may be presented by means of questions, or by the use of blackboard, maps, or other visual aids. A high school teacher was observed, near the close of the class hour, to place on his desk a device, later discovered by the students to be an electroscope. As part of the assignment for the next day he called attention to two thin strips of gold leaf suspended in the jar. Every time he brought a pointed instrument near the round knob on the top of the jar, the thin strips were observed to separate and spread until they touched the sides of the jar. When the curiosity of the students had been aroused to a high pitch, the teacher explained that the phenomena just observed had an important bearing upon a principle of electricity they were about to study. For the next day they were to find out all they could about this jar, and the reason the suspended strips of gold leaf behaved as they did when the pointed instrument was brought close to the top of the jar. The eagerness with which the class entered upon a study of the advance assignment can be easily imagined, as well as the vivid fixing in memory of an important principle in physics achieved by this means of motivation through the use of a problem.

(*d*) *Manual work.* Students normally respond to assignments that call forth genuine creative activity. Adolescents enjoy "doing." In recognition of this psychological factor "activity curriculums," "activity schools," and "activity programs" are catch phrases now quite familiar in educational literature. It is a wise teacher, indeed, who understands the significance of motor activity in learning, and utilizes this type of activity intelligently for the motivation of school work. Effective use has been made of this form of motivation to quicken interest in subjects of which the immediate value to the student seemed quite remote. The construction of models of Cæsar's bridge, or the making of Roman fasces, to motivate class assignments in Latin, are examples in point. These devices, if properly used, may not only foster interest in the subject but provide significant educational values within themselves.

(e) *Use of suspense.* Suspense is a simple, economical device, very effective when properly used. It has the advantage of ready adaptability to almost any situation. No agency has made greater and more effective use of this device than the motion picture industry in the segmented previews of "coming pictures." Small sections of a forthcoming attraction that depict scenes of intense interest, are thrown on the screen and leave the "movie fan" eager to learn the sequence of events. The wide-awake teacher will capitalize freely this same psychological principle to motivate future study. Strebel and Morehart [10] give two examples, among others, of the use of suspense in the assignment which are worthy of wide dissemination as illustrative of this form of motivation.

A teacher of history was observed who used suspense in making an assignment on Burgoyne's invasion in the American Revolution. She said, "We have reached the most important part of the war for we are now at its turning point. Burgoyne had determined to cut New York State from the New England and southern colonies." At this point she stimulated a short but well-pointed discussion on the probable effects of such isolation. She then continued, "St. Leger was to proceed to Albany by way of the St. Lawrence River and the Mohawk Valley; Burgoyne had the same objective, going by way of Lake Champlain, and Howe was to come up to Albany by way of the Hudson. The colonists' cause was now in great danger for these generals were of England's best. A life and death struggle was at hand. This story is one of the most interesting we can find." By this time the children were agog with interest. The teacher then announced that the conclusion of this interesting story could be found on a certain

[10] Strebel, R. F., and Morehart, G. C. *The Nature and Meaning of Teaching,* pp. 145–146. New York: McGraw-Hill Book Company, Inc., 1929.

page in their textbooks. Indeed no coercion was needed to induce the class to "finish the story" for they were *ready* to do so.

A teacher of biology showed the class an amœba which he had located under a microscope, and then told them that this was a one-celled animal so small that it was indiscernible to the naked eye. He asked them if they thought that this infinitesimal bit of proto-plasm could carry on all of the same life processes as does man, including feeding, digestion, excretion, respiration, reproduction, and the others. Some thought that it could, but the greatest number thought not. A short discussion followed which was concluded as soon as it became most interesting. He then told the class that they could find an alluring account of this very subject in their textbooks, giving them the specific page reference.

7. *The assignment should provide for differences in the ability and interests of students.* Another commonly accepted function of the assignment is the recognition of individual differences. Psycho-logically, no two individuals react in identical fashion to a given stimulus. While general patterns of response can be assumed for groups within an average class when a cross section of all students is considered, yet even then extremes in individual cases are likely to be present. All studies in mental measurements agree that among people there exist vast differences in intelligence, aptitudes, and temperament. Even the interests of students are found to be widely divergent. By the time the secondary period is reached these in-terests oftentimes have become very sharply defined.

In the discussion of motivation the importance of aroused in-terest in the facilitation of learning was strongly emphasized. Possibly nothing brings greater dissatisfaction to the student than to be assigned tasks far beyond his mental ability to comprehend or accomplish. His reaction is that of discouragement, followed by dislike. Psychologists have also found that for people to labor at tasks far below their ability leads to loss of interest, often to the extreme of antipathy and repugnance for their work. Certainly all of us work with far more vigor, ease, and pleasure when the things we do are in conformity with our natural interests. It is, therefore, exceedingly important that the assignment, so far as possible, pro-vide for these varied interests, aptitudes, and abilities resident within a class of high school students.

If students do not bring to the class the same level of mental ability it is necessary that the program of work be differentiated to provide less arduous requirements for the less capable; or require the same amount of work from all members of the class, but recognize a difference in the quality of work done in approximation of the ability of each; or insist that the same amount and quality of work be done but follow the familiar plan of differentiating the length of time permitted for each student to complete the assignment. Broadly speaking, one of these three methods or modifications of them should be recognized in every assignment. In unit teaching the first plan obviously is the one most appropriate to use.

No less should differentiation in interests present within the group be recognized. Wherever these can be discovered the wise teacher will do well to utilize them. An extreme example may serve best to illustrate this factor in the assignment. While visiting classes of a junior high school, under the direction of the principal, a classic illustration of this point was discovered. Upon entering the classroom of a teacher of history, the writer noticed, displayed on a shelf behind the teacher's desk, interesting models of the Santa Maria and sister ships of Columbus's westward voyage to the new world. They were models of workmanship and almost exact replicas in miniature of the originals. It was suggested to the writer that a comment to the teacher on these models would draw from her a very interesting story. Her story, verified by the principal, centered around two boys who were judged incorrigible by practically every teacher in the school, and who were on the point of expulsion when a happy incident changed entirely the future course of events. By accident, in conversation with the boys, the teacher discovered that they were keenly interested in "making things." A check with the manual training teacher revealed that in this work the boys excelled and were interested. Thereupon the teacher suggested to the history class in early American history the value of models of ships used by Columbus. She further proposed that if these boys would make such models for the class she would gladly release them from her history class for a period of time to work at this project in the manual training room. They accepted the proposition with alacrity. The first thing the boys did was to study specifications for sailing vessels of the period of Columbus. Their interest led to a study of ships of various kinds and historical periods. When the boys were done with their project the teacher affirmed they knew almost everything that was to be known about ships of that period, and incidentally the boys had acquired as much, if not more, general

310 *Use of Assignments*

historical knowledge than the other members of the class. Most valuable of all — they became intensely interested in their school work and were rated among the school's most industrious and dependable students.

8. *The assignment should be motivated chiefly by the hope of worthwhile achievements, rather than scholastic reward or the fear of punishment.* Carr and Waage [11] stress this idea among their "Thirteen Assignment Principles." Motivation of school work by dangling scholastic rewards before the students as tempting bait is at best among the less desirable means of stimulating the interest of the student. It also has doubtful value for the arousal of permanent functional interests beyond school days. The student whose interests have been challenged by something of fundamental worth is the greater beneficiary thereby. The stimulus of scholarship reward likewise carries with it overconsciousness of competition. In our social democracy, at least, and even in our industrial world the competitive motive is recognized as possessive of much that is positively inimical to the highest welfare of society, even granting at once its many values. While wholesome use can and should be made of scholastic rewards the assignment conforms to the highest educational requirements when it makes its appeal through more fundamental interests. Much the same strictures can be marshaled against any form of extraneous reward for student effort.

Theoretically, fear of punishment should have little place in motivating learning. Psychologically we respond to the pleasurable, and find our learning efforts inhibited by the disagreeable. This fact has led some pedagogues to advocate the elimination of the fear of punishment entirely in education. This extreme position is indefensible. At times, in our complex and artificial civilization, it may become necessary to resort to the fear of punishment as our last recourse to stimulate essential learning. It should be used sparingly, and as a last resort. The comment of Kilpatrick [12] at this point deserves careful study.

> There are some things we can easily assign for learning under penalty, such as the simpler skills and the memorizing of printed matter. Both of these mainly rely on simple repetition. These we can assign precisely and test easily. Some other things cannot be assigned

[11] Carr, W. G., and Waage, John, *op. cit.*, p. 72.
[12] Kilpatrick, W. H. *Foundations of Method*, p. 288. New York: The Macmillan Company, 1925.

at all under penalty, for example, appreciations and attitudes. . . . Imagine a teacher's saying, "You boys are deficient in your appreciation of Nicholas Nickleby. You must stay in this afternoon and raise your appreciation to 70 or above." Or imagine the principal's saying, "If you boys don't like your teacher any better by next Monday, I'll have to punish you till you do."

9. *The assignment should stimulate thought.* Some types of learning require the development of motor skills, others demand a maximum of memoriter learning, while still others require a mastery of complex ideational learning. Assignments for the first two involve a maximum of simple practice to assure fixity, or skill, or both, with a minimum of thought effort required. In secondary education ideational learning should predominate, with rigorous demands upon the student's ability to think. It should be noted that emphasis upon facts is rapidly decreasing, while insistence upon one's ability to do something with facts as the vehicle of thought steadily gains favor in modern education. A series of good assignments, therefore, should reflect this newer emphasis.

10. *The assignment should provide necessary and specific directions for the study of the lesson.* In the opening statements of this chapter, the definition accepted for "the assignment" presupposed this phase of teaching as essentially a major aspect of directing learning. As will be seen in a later chapter, the assignment is thought of by many to be closely identified with the concept of supervised study. Practically all recent authorities consider the chief function of the assignment to be the giving of specific and sufficiently detailed directions to enable the student to attack intelligently the problem or problems of the advance unit. This criterion, then, becomes the principal measuring rod by which to judge the worth of an assignment. It is one of the chief sources of weakness in the teaching practice of the average teacher. A decade ago little was available for the teacher in the way of a treatise on methods of study. Within the last few years, volume after volume has appeared analyzing the peculiar types of learning demanded of various subject fields, and offering suggestions for the most efficient acquisition of the learning in question. Whether the assignment covers a short or a long unit of work, it should show clearly that the teacher has asked and satisfactorily answered three questions: *First,* "What are the new elements of learning in this unit?" *Second,* "What types of learning do these elements involve?" *Third,* "What

definite suggestions do the students need to equip them with adequate techniques for an effective attack upon the elements of learning present in this unit?" Few assignments can be justified that do not give evidence of these questions having been asked and intelligently answered.

11. *The assignment should be adjusted to the time and opportunity of the class.* Most high school students carry four basic courses; some carry five. Under these circumstances it is comparatively easy to determine the amount of time students should devote to the preparation of lessons. Where the Core Curriculum and unit method are in use, of course, the problem of the time to be devoted to the assignment is very different. Each teacher should make every possible effort to insure an assignment that will require a proportionate share of the total time the student is expected to devote to preparation. The assignment that requires more time than this of the average student is indefensible. Skill perfected by careful study, observation, and experience are necessary to determine how extensive an assignment should be. One writer has suggested that the teacher work out a number of assignments given and check the length of time required to fulfill them. A weakness of this plan is the achieved skill the teacher brings to the assignment. Thus the teacher-student comparison is scarcely comparable. It is much better to make an analysis of the nature of the assignment, a rough approximation of probable time required, and a check on the actual time consumed. The experienced teacher who has observed carefully can approximate the time factor. Still another element in the situation that may need to be considered is the availability of materials with which to work. The teacher should be sure that reference works are handy or laboratory equipment available and in usable condition. Often students find but one or two source books available for a class of twenty-five or thirty. Under such circumstances it is but fair that the assignment take this fact into account. It is often true that the necessary use of a source is so infrequent as to make the purchase of additional duplicate materials unjustifiable.

12. *Materials of the assignment should be varied, and adaptable to the needs and interests of the students.* The old proverb: "Variety is the spice of life," is especially applicable in the classroom. Students become surfeited with the monotony of sameness. It is an alert teacher, yes, a marked one, who has learned the art of diver-

sification of his work. The introduction of new materials, or using old materials in different ways, arouses interest. An ingenious teacher will stamp the assignment on the mind of the student by the unaccustomed ways in which the assignments are handled. "No three assignments in succession alike" might well be an ideal of the younger teacher, until variation becomes something of a habit. The teacher who can do this will have his students looking forward with interest to "what's next?"

The most practical demonstration of adapting a course of study to the needs of the students came in the report of a high school principal of the way in which he vitalized his assignments in a course in physics. In an isolated rural community he found that the school had not only little physics equipment, but that it was also ill adapted to the needs and background of his students. Through the co-operation of the members of the class a collection was made of all discarded mechanical contrivances from the farms that were not too cumbersome for use. The girls brought egg-beaters, mechanical can openers, etc., while the boys brought cast-off radios, electrical appliances, mechanical tools and one, a cream separator. The cream separator proved most valuable for the demonstration of many principles of physics. Students in the midst of farm chores had repeatedly wondered, for example, why cream could be separated from milk in a rapidly revolving container, and why a handle slowly turned should result in the excessive speed of the cylinder that separated the cream from the milk. No extra effort was required to stimulate an interest in mechanical principles when the assignment was motivated by the use of such materials. The young instructor found the lack of equipment that appeared at first to be a liability, actually to be a blessing in disguise.

These criteria, as indicated, are not to be considered as complete. Nor should they be considered as applicable to every assignment. Only those criteria are included, however, in this list that appear to have quite universal applicability. Every teacher might well place these beside the prepared assignment and candidly scrutinize any failure of the assignment to meet the criteria.

Evaluation of the assignment

As suggested in the last paragraph, it is a good policy for the teacher to set the criteria given for a good assignment beside the actual assignment for critical comparison. A device that proposes

Questions	Place check in the proper column after each question			
	Always	Frequently	Seldom	Never
SELF-IMPROVEMENT OUTLINE FOR CHECKING ASSIGNMENTS				
1. Do your assignments definitely contribute to the development of your pupils?......				
2. Are your assignments well suited to the age and grade of your classes as a whole?				
3. Are your assignments adapted to the varying abilities of the pupils?.........				
4. Are your assignments varied so as to satisfy the individual interests of your pupils?				
5. Are your assignments adapted to the varying social, vocational, and educational needs of your pupils?...........				
6. Do you make the purpose of your assignments clear to your pupils?...........				
7. Do your assignments seem important in themselves to your pupils?...........				
8. Does the learning involved in your assignments have immediate utility to your pupils?......				
9. Do your pupils participate in developing assignments?..................				
10. Do your pupils help to state all or parts of the assignment?...............				
11. Do you clearly subordinate grades and marks as motives for doing assignments? .				
12. Do you allow adequate time for complete development of your assignments?......				
13. Do you show the relation of each assignment to the knowledge already acquired?				
14. Do you plan assignments in the light of what your pupils already know or can do?				
15. Do you organize the work of the course so that assignments are in terms of large units?.......				
16. If you assign work on a large unit basis, do you provide frequent brief oral or written reminders?.......				
17. Are your assignments clear and definite to you and to the pupils?...............				
18. Do you show your pupils how to prepare assignments?...............				
19. Do you suggest ways by which pupils may tell when they have prepared their assignments?...............				
20. Do you plan for assignments so that you can check up on their accomplishment?				

to evaluate the assignment should be more complete, though not too extensive, and couched in language different from that of the criterion itself; however, it should cover the requirement set up in the criterion. The literature on the subject abounds in various devices evolved for the purpose. The check list is the form used most frequently for purposes of evaluation. A sample of a shorter form, usable by supervisor or teacher, is given by Carr and Waage.[13] This form is based upon the "Thirteen Assignment Principles," and further illustrates the interrelation that should exist between criteria and the check list.

A careful study of this check list suggests its particular applicability to the daily lesson, though it may be applied to a longer unit-assignment as well. A number of check lists devised tend to be exhaustive. While it is true that the device which makes the more detail obtainable for a judgment in general, will give a more complete picture, it is equally true that many devices tend to defeat themselves by their very elaborateness. That is, the busy teacher or supervisor is not likely to employ a cumbersome, time-consuming instrument. The maximum of accuracy with the minimum of detail is the ideal of the busy teacher.

3. What Is Technique of the Assignment?

When to make the assignment

This is a widely debated issue. There are protagonists for the placement of the assignment at the beginning of the class hour. Others insist the time to make the assignment should be governed solely by the arrival of the psychological moment, whether that be at the beginning, at the end of the class hour, or somewhere in between.[14] By "psychological moment" they mean the place in the development of the lesson that naturally leads to a question as to the nature of the advance work. This does not always come at the close of the class hour. Indeed, it is conceivable that the question might be uppermost in the minds of the students when the class first assembles. If the lesson did not require development before the next assignment could be made, the "psychological moment" would be deemed to have arrived. The trend of recent writers on the subject is to suggest flexibility in assignment practice, with a sensitiveness to the readiness of the class for the assignment irrespective of the part of the period when this occurs.

Those who argue for the close of the hour, with the appearance of logic suggest that in a developmental lesson the advance work

---

13 Carr, W. G., and Waage, John, *op. cit.*, pp. 75–76.

14 The discerning reader will sense at once that much of this discussion centers about the more traditional forms of teaching. It has little relevance to the newer unit approach to teaching emphasized in the earlier sections of this book.

necessarily must wait until the conclusions have been reached, inasmuch as they may have direct bearing on the intelligibility of the next assignment. They further argue that in such procedures as the socialized recitation it is impossible for the average teacher to predict with certainty how far the lesson will develop before the close of the hour. Another argument advanced is that psychologically last impressions are least subject to confusion. If directions are left until the last of the hour the student approaches the new work with these final instructions still ringing in his ears.

It is safe to say no one plan should be followed to the exclusion of the others. The lesson situation should be the criterion determining when the assignment should be made. The personal equation of the teacher should be a factor considered. If the teacher has a predilection toward cramping the time of the assignment if left to the close of the hour, then in fairness to the class he should make the assignment earlier. Logic as well as the psychological factors involved would suggest the end of the hour as the usual opportune time for the assignment. When a unit covering several days to a month or six weeks is the basis of the assignment, then the previous discussion is not in point. Obviously, for such units the only feasible time for the assignment is at the close of one unit of work and the beginning of another, irrespective of the part of the class period when this transition comes.

Time devoted to the assignment

On this point there is no general agreement among authorities. Some early writers have suggested one fifth to one third of the hour might profitably be spent in the assignment. General observation and the results of objective studies have revealed a lamentable tendency to skimp the assignment phase. Extensive studies summarized by Carr and Waage,[15] involving more than 1300 recitations, showed that the assignment had been omitted from 5 to 15 per cent of these recitations. A study of 343 recitations revealed [16] the average time devoted to the assignment to be slightly in excess of five minutes, or approximately eleven per cent of the recitation period.

[15] Carr, W. G., and Waage, John, *op. cit.*, pp. 30–31.
[16] Koos, L. V., and Troxel, Oliver L. "A Comparison of Teaching Procedures in Short and Long Class Periods" in *School Review*, vol. 35, pp. 342–343 (May, 1927).

The length of time given to the assignment must be determined by many contributing factors. Obviously an assignment to cover the work for one day in advance should be assumed to require a much shorter part of the class hour than an assignment given to prepare the class for a unit to cover an entire week. Where the long unit is used, one to two days might be spent most profitably in the assignment phase. The nature of the subject or problem and the relative difficulty of the advance work would also have much to do with the length of the assignment. It might not be amiss to suggest to the average teacher that the criteria laid down for the assignment imply this as an important phase of the class hour. Therefore, where daily assignments are the rule, it would be wise to question the adequacy of an assignment that did not require 10 to 15 minutes of a 60-minute class period. Adequacy, based on criteria, rather than length *per se,* must be the ultimate determiner of the time devoted to the assignment.

Technique of the assignment

As the teacher approaches the actual task of making assignments, the answer to two major questions will offer fruitful suggestions for guidance in this important phase of teaching. The first question is, "What are the sources of difficulty in making effective assignments?" The second questions is, "How can an effective assignment be made?"

1. *Assignment difficulties.* "To be forewarned is to be forearmed." This adage applies with unusual force here. If difficulties of the assignment can be anticipated, the pitfalls incident to them can be largely avoided. Fortunately some studies have made available the collective judgments of experienced teachers on this problem. One of the most complete and suggestive of these has been reported by Fleming and Woodring.[17] These writers secured from 230 junior and senior high school teachers a list of important assignment-difficulties experienced by these teachers. Fleming and Woodring have tabulated from these reports a list of seventeen such difficulties, which are reproduced here. The alert teacher will study these with care.

[17] Fleming, Cecile White, and Woodring, Maxie N. "Problems in Directing Study of High School Pupils" in *Teachers College Record,* vol. 29, pp. 322–323 (January, 1928).

1. Insufficient thought and preparation in planning the arrangement.
2. Inability to obtain an acceptance by the pupil of a worthy purpose for performance of the task.
3. Stimulation of preparation of the assignments by appealing to the interests of adolescents and by providing for real needs growing out of pupil experience.
4. Prevention of loss of interest due to too long lapse of time between the assignment and preparation.
5. Avoidance of assignments so long that successful accomplishment is impossible in the time available for preparation, with consequent loss of interest.
6. Guarding against too many and too varied activities, resulting in dividing interests with consequent bad habits of work, and unsatisfactory accomplishments.
7. Difficulty in presenting work to be done so that it is clearly understood by the pupils; also, the difficulty of ascertaining whether *every* pupil understands.
8. Gauging the difficulty of work so that success is possible for each pupil.
9. Determining essential requirements, and differentiation of assignments to suit the various levels and types of ability existing in the class.
10. Inclusion of challenges to mental exploration by the pupil, thereby stimulating real thinking.
11. Provision for continuity of work by presenting new problems as a continuation of previous experience and anticipation of future problems.
12. Correlating with other subjects and outside activities.
13. Focusing attention on important elements in the new problem or task, and directing the attack in such a way as to increase interest rather than lessen it, to stimulate effort, and to overcome seemingly insuperable obstacles to accomplishment.
14. Providing the necessary tools for preparation by training in study procedures and techniques, and in selection, organization, and use of material, thereby developing effective habits of independent work.
15. Giving to pupils devices for checking the mastery and performance of work undertaken.
16. Evaluating the effectiveness of an assignment by the quality of response during the presentation of the assignment, and by the adequacy of pupil preparation.
17. Providing sufficient time for adequate consideration of the assignment and determining the psychological moment for its presentation.

2. *Suggested assignment procedure.* While no rule-of-thumb plan can be given in answer to the question, "How can an effective assignment be made?" a general procedure may be suggested. These suggestions are not necessarily given in the sequential order the assignment technique would follow, but where sequence is implied the natural order has been followed.

1. Analyze the nature of the learning process required in the advance unit. This is without exception the first step in a good assignment procedure. Much of what follows in any good assignment depends upon this analysis.
2. Study the various types of assignments available and select the one, or modified form of it, that appears to fit best the learning situation. Some assignment types are admirably adapted to one form of learning or teaching but not to others.
3. Provide the essential background for the advance work where uncertainty exists that such background obtains. At this point too many teachers are likely to assume the adequacy of this background when in fact it may not exist. Scarcely can one emphasize too strongly the apperceptive preparation for the new.
4. Whether this is the next step in the assignment procedure or not, it is obvious that very early in the assignment phase the teacher must throw out a challenge to the student that will enlist his interest and maximum effort in the new unit.
5. Outline in sufficient detail the advance unit to be studied.
6. Suggest some plan of attack upon the new unit. It is well to remember one caution — do not do for the student that which he may be led to do for himself. This suggests the desirability of leading the class in a cooperative discovery of desirable leads for the general attack upon the new.
7. Where reference to source material other than the textbooks is necessary, this should be made specific. The most satisfactory plan in the large unit assignment is to provide the select list of available sources in mimeographed or hectographed form with chapter or inclusive page references given. Some points of interest concerning the author, the authoritative or popular nature of the reference may give the student valuable hints on the proper evaluation of the sources used. The writer once listened to a teacher of history as she gave just such a personality touch to each reference in a mimeographed list in a long unit assignment. He was so impressed that he determined then and there to read two of the sources described by the teacher and felt a genuine regret that time forbade browsing among two or three other references in which the teacher had aroused a keen interest in a seemingly incidental fashion.

8. It is desirable in the long unit assignment especially to indicate the approximate length of time that may properly be devoted to various phases of the assignment. For example, in an assignment following the Morrisonian unit and cycle plan, the teacher incidentally remarked that of the ten days given to the study of the unit the students might well spend four days in the collection and evaluation of data from the mimeographed list of sources just given them. Possibly three days should be set aside for organization. The teacher thought they might find it profitable to spend a day or a day and a half discussing the results of their study followed by a short mastery test.

9. The final step in any assignment procedure is the check upon the students' grasp of the work ahead. Many devices are available for this. Pivotal questions about the assignment may detect any lack of a fundamental grasp of the advance work. Or a pupil apparently uncertain of the significance of the assignment may be asked to summarize the main points of the assignment for the class. Many teachers safeguard against misunderstanding or forgetfulness by requiring a supplemental notebook in which the student notes explanations and amplifications of any mimeographed outlines or written directions passed out to the class.

10. A suggested technique for the assignment procedure that deserves much more extensive use than it now receives is the use of the blackboard. Re-enforcement of the ear through the eye is sound psychology. Its application to an assignment procedure is equally sound pedagogy.

Type of assignment

A survey of the literature of assignment fails to reveal any two identical classifications of types. Furthermore, except in the most recent efforts in this direction, no common point of departure has been recognized for such a classification.[18] A practical classification on a single principle, and suggestive of more recent efforts to reveal a wealth of possibilities to teachers, is formulated below. It will be observed that some types overlap. So many variations are possible to the ingenious teacher that the classification is suggestive and not offered as complete.

1. *Page or paragraph assignment.* Often thought of as the textbook assignment. Unfortunately, this method is still widely used as recent studies have revealed.

[18] For examples of a form of unit assignment see Billett, Roy O., *Fundamentals of Secondary-School Teaching*, chapters XVII–XVIII. Boston: Houghton Mifflin Company, 1940.

2. *Chapter assignment.* Another form of the textbook assignment though vastly different from the page or paragraph form. Chapters usually are of a unitary nature and involve some elements of completeness within themselves.

3. *Topical assignment.* This type may or may not center about a single chapter in a textbook. It has a wealth of possibilities in the social sciences particularly.

4. *Problem assignment.* Where an arbitrary distinction is set up between a problem and a project as is done in later chapters of this book, the type becomes a very valuable form of assignment.

5. *Project assignment.* Adapted especially to the workshop, natural sciences, and in some measure to the social sciences. Its special appeal is through the natural motor activity required.

6. *Exercises.* Most frequently used in mathematics. It represents the old traditional approach to teaching although if used in combination with other types, this form can be used very effectively.

7. *Individual or group report assignment.* Used extensively as a device to supplement other types and to provide for individual differences in interests and capacities within the class, very effective.

8. *Unit assignment.* It may apply to any extensive segment of classroom activity that presents factors of cohesion and a relatively complete ideational element around which the unit may resolve itself as a core. A rather pretentious problem may serve as this unitary core.

9. *Experimental assignment.* This is a form of the problem and project types characteristic of the science laboratory. Too often in practice it does not represent either an experiment of a problem in the true sense. It can be made a vital instrument of educational training if properly used.

10. *Practice assignment.* This type represents an assignment of repetitions of activities designed to produce mental or motor skills. Mastery of the simple combinations in arithmetic, memorization of a poem, or practice in speed on the typewriter are example of this type of assignment.

QUESTIONS AND PROBLEMS

1. Define the modern concept of the assignment and discuss the difference between it and the older view.

2. How can the assignment be made to help develop in the student effective habits of study?

3. What evidence do we have to support the assumption of the importance of the assignment?

4. In what ways does motivation enter as an important aspect of the daily assignment?

5. Evaluate the importance of each of the ten qualities of an assignment given in the text.
6. Criticize an assignment you have observed being made to a class in high school in the light of the recognized qualities of a good assignment.
7. What are the major things that the student should know with reference to the advance work at the close of the assignment?
8. By means of the check list given in this chapter for evaluating an assignment test the assignment phase of the lesson plan as constructed under item No. 7 of Questions and Problems for the previous chapter.
9. At what place in the class period should the assignment be made? Discuss this problem in detail.
10. Indicate some of the most common causes of assignment difficulties and the best means of avoiding or overcoming them.
11. For the assignment used in item 8 draw up an assignment procedure and check it with the one in the book to see if it contains the essential elements. How could you justify any change in order of the procedure steps as given in this chapter?
12. Which of the different types of assignments enumerated do you regard as most in harmony with our modern conception of education? Under what circumstances would each be most applicable?
13. What are the important advantages and disadvantages of the longer units in assignments?
14. An instructor, who carries a very heavy teaching load in high school biology for sophomores, has the unit system of making assignments. Each asisgnment is to be worked out in supervised study from given references and the text. These units consist of four or five blocks requiring four days — on the average — of the students' time. Many students are rushed and therefore work out many of the individual mimeographed blocks at home, without proper study guidance and reference material. Tell what particular problems will undoubtedly arise and discuss some specific remedies in each case.
15. Prepare an assignment for a modern type of unit such as the "teaching unit" outlined from the Long Beach Schools and quoted in Chapter III.

SELECTED BIBLIOGRAPHY

Brink, William G. *Directing Study Activities in Secondary Schools*, chapter IV. New York: Odyssey Press, 1937.
Burton, William H. *The Guidance of Learning Activities*, chapter XI. New York: Appleton-Century-Crofts, Inc., 1944.
Butler, Frank A. *The Improvement of Teaching in Secondary Schools*,

Second Edition, chapter IX. Chicago: University of Chicago Press, 1946.

Douglass, Harl R. and Mills, Robert H. *Teaching in High School,* pp. 149–155, 398–403, 223–224. New York: The Ronald Press Company, 1948.

Learning and Instruction, pp. 226–233. Forty-ninth Yearbook, Part I. The National Society for the Study of Education. Chicago: University of Chicago Press, 1950.

Risk, Thomas M. *Principles and Practices of Teaching in Secondary Schools,* Second Edition, pp. 306–402. New York: American Book Company, 1947.

Rivlin, Harry N. *Teaching Adolescents in Secondary Schools,* pp. 175–187. New York: Appleton-Century-Crofts, Inc., 1948.

Thut, I. N. and Gerberich, J. R. *Foundations of Method for Secondary Schools,* Chapter VII. New York: McGraw-Hill Book Company, Inc., 1949.

Umstattd, J. G. *Secondary School Teaching,* New Edition, pp. 270–273. Boston: Ginn and Company, 1944.

Yoakam, Gerald A. *The Improvement of the Assignment.* New York: The Macmillan Company, 1932.

12

How Use Questions in Teaching?

1. What Is the Nature and Function of the Question?

Importance of the question

Few teachers have appreciated fully the true significance of the question. It is fundamental to any adequate conception of learning. The question, silently or vocally expressed, is among the first stimuli to the mental life of the child; and it remains throughout life the major mainspring to mental activity. Into a "blooming, buzzing world of confusion" the child is born, declared William James, and as the child grows older his world becomes steadily more perplexing. Wonder, surprise, curiosity, and doubt are of the essence of the question. These are the principal mental incentives to learning. The modern emphasis in the teaching approach is on the twofold process of stimulation and direction of the learning activity. The question is one of the best stimuli and it is readily available to the teacher. Its importance has been recognized by the great teachers of method for a generation past. Colvin,[1] one of the most eminent of these earlier ones, gave recognition to this fact in these words:

> The efficiency of instruction is measured in a large degree by the nature of the questions that are asked and the care with which they are framed. No teacher of elementary or secondary subjects can succeed in his instruction who has not a fair mastery of the art of questioning.

[1] Colvin, S. S. An Introduction to High School Teaching, p. 310. New York: The Macmillan Company, 1917.

A recent writer on secondary methods [2] continues in somewhat the same vein: "The question remains one of the major educative forces of early childhood," and the questions asked by later adolescents, "seem few and superficial" in comparison. A complete understanding of its nature and possibilities, as well as skill in using it effectively, therefore, becomes one of the most valuable articles of equipment with which the teacher can assume the responsibilities of the classroom.

Difficulties inherent in question technique

While much of the discussion in this chapter is appropriate to both the written and the oral question the writer has had in mind particularly the give-and-take of the classroom situation. The question technique was difficult enough in a day when most teachers regarded the purpose of classroom recitations as that of pupil regurgitation of previously assigned and memorized facts from a textbook. The technique is infinitely more complex now that primary emphasis is no longer upon facts memorized, but upon the ability of the student to analyze, critically evaluate, and generalize in constructive fashion from the text or the data collected in connection with a class problem-situation. Perhaps twenty or thirty students are engaged in the process of doing something about the material at hand. Such a group will not be content merely to answer questions propounded by the teacher. They, too, have questions to ask. The teacher must not only be prepared to follow up effectively the answer to a question she has asked, thinking several steps ahead of the class; she must also be able to analyze quickly an unexpected response, see its implications, and with lightning-flash rapidity formulate a question procedure calculated to meet this unexpected situation and tie it back into the original train of thought. At the same time a watchful eye must detect any signs of mental confusion on the part of less forward members of the class, determine how best to meet such a difficulty, note problems of inattention, select for consideration from a barrage of questions propounded by members of the class those germane to the lesson, and constantly adapt the procedure to individual differences. These are but a few of the many factors that enter a normal learning-situation in a modern class period. Simultaneously, of course, the

[2] Rivlin, Harry B. *Teaching Adolescents in Secondary Schools*, pp. 190, 193. New York: Appleton-Century-Crofts, Inc., 1948.

teacher must keep the class moving steadily and progressively in the direction of its ultimate goal and, if possible, toward the realization of its immediate objective. There are occasions when the alert teacher will realize that the class must, for the time being, move obliquely toward the goal, if the larger values of education are to be realized.

Teacher prerequisites to successful class questioning

To meet the difficulties inherent in the use of the question under classroom conditions requires some personal equipment on the part of the teacher beyond a technical knowledge of the approved mechanics of questioning. Four skills need be enumerated which the earnest teacher should regard as basic to all good question technique.

The *first*, "clear and rapid thinking," may be regarded as the first ability of the successful teacher. Clarity involves mastery of subject matter and the power and habit of logical thinking. Unless the teacher is master of the content of the field under consideration, there is little likelihood that the inferences and implications of the questions asked will be understood. Commenting on this point, a writer suggests that, "When we say that a teacher's questions are poor, we actually mean that her knowledge and thinking are weak."[3] In addition to this intimate acquaintance with the content of the field the good teacher should also have a power of analysis, and the ability to make comparisons and generalizations. Only long arduous schooling in rigorous habits of thought will develop this power. Unless the teacher achieves this power his effectiveness in class questioning will be seriously handicapped. If, in addition to an inability to think logically, there is natural slowness in mental reaction, successful questioning under the most trying of classroom conditions is unlikely.

The *second*, "a keen sense of relative values," is essential if the teacher is to handle questions and responses of the class to the best advantage. It is not only important to determine the value of a given question or response to the development of the immediate problem under consideration. Some questions may well be ignored or passed by lightly. Others offer genuine leads for the progression of the class discussion. Furthermore, the timeliness of a question

[3] Butler, Frank A. *The Improvement of Teaching in Secondary Schools,* p. 211. Chicago: University of Chicago Press, 1946.

for the larger and possibly more remote, purposes of education may bring a coveted opportunity — indeed, may even demand the class venture afield for treasure trove quite apart from the lesson in hand. Again, the question or response of the student may reveal quite unexpectedly serious deficiencies that must be corrected before the immediate learning phase can advance. This ability to sense the implications of student question or response requires alertness and thorough appreciation of the relative significance of the question.

The *third*, "skill in wording questions," is subject to much more direct approach than the two prerequisites previously discussed. The teacher might be ever so much a master of content, he might be schooled in habits of logical thinking, quick in mental reaction, and possess almost uncanny power to distinguish between essentials and non-essentials in the give-and-take of class discussion, and yet fail through his inability to frame questions skillfully. There are four distinct difficulties in the formulation of questions, which the writer has observed particularly in working with young teachers in training.

The young teacher tends to think and speak on a vocabulary level quite beyond the apperceptive experience of the class. It is difficult for the young teacher, a senior or a recent graduate from the university, to realize that a considerable gulf separates the levels of thought and vocabulary usage of a junior or senior high school student from those of a college senior. Questions, therefore, are likely to be pitched to a level of abstraction quite beyond the ability of the pupils; or a vocabulary of technical nature often foreign to the common usage and, therefore, to the understanding of the students, is used. A student of history and sociology was observed teaching a social science class of junior high school pupils. Repeatedly the observer noted the vague expression on the faces of members of the class as the teacher asked questions none could answer because of the terminology employed. When referring to the social habits of peoples, for example, instead of using such words as customs, standards of conduct, rules of conduct, etc., familiar to the student, the teacher employed the term "mores," a common enough word for a college class in sociology, but unknown to the average junior high school student.

Closely akin is the tendency of the brilliant beginner to telescope several steps in the formulation of a question. He is particularly liable to error where step-by-step development of a process is necessary, as in mathematics. Brilliant students are the chief sinners in this respect. Unconsciously they leap across several steps in one mental process, and then wonder why pupils cannot follow what appears to them to be a single step. It is important, furthermore, to say in a question exactly what one means, and not always easier for the experienced teacher than for the beginner. This difficulty grows out of the very nature of language, which is but the symbol of ideas. Care in the exact use of words to express specific meaning, and in the selection of words which have the same experiential content for both teacher and student, is essential.

A *fourth* prerequisite that might well be offered is "self-confidence." Frequently teachers who have brilliant records as students, and who could meet all the requirements thus far mentioned in conversation with a small informal group of friends, find themselves ill at ease and their flow of thought seriously inhibited when standing before a class of thirty or forty high school students. It may be a temporary stage fright, but frequently the cause is more fundamental and difficult to overcome. In rare cases the causes may be so deep-seated as to prejudice the teacher's chances of ever gaining the requisite self-confidence to meet the exigencies of the classroom. Until self-confidence is achieved, clarity and rapidity of thought before a class is impossible.

Function of the question

No complete statement of the functions of questioning can readily be made. The author, therefore, suggests those he regards as most important. Many of these might easily be broken down to compose a much more extensive list, should the individual teacher feel that a more detailed statement of purpose would aid him to grasp this phase of the subject. The following statement, while not complete, covers the essentials of the problem.

1. *To test student achievement.* Unfortunately, class questioning in the past has overstressed the memorizing of factual data, often to the exclusion of any other purpose. The most extensive study of classroom questions thus far reported through the use of stenographic notes is that of Miss Stevens.[4] In spite of the fact that the

[4] Stevens, Romiett. *The Question as a Measure of Efficiency in Instruction,* p. 47. Teachers College, Columbia University Contributions to Education, No. 48. Eighth Impression, March, 1927. New York: Bureau of Publications, Teachers College, Columbia University, 1912.

study is not a recent one, the data are still pertinent for illustrative purposes, and the table given below has been adapted from her study.

TABLE 2. *The Number of Memory and Thought Questions in Two Groups of Classes Observed*

	Group I			Group II	
Subject	Total Number Questions	Number Memory Questions	Subject	Total Number Questions	Number Memory Questions
1. History	41	29	1. History	90	75
2. "	66	60	2. "	94	74
3. English	69	39	3. "	125	87
4. "	70	26	4. "	142	103
5. "	73	33	5. English	94	26
6. "	74	61	6. "	129	65
7. Science	86	58	7. Science	122	92
			8. Latin	105	89
			9. Mod. Lang.	196	196

An analysis of some of these class exercises reveals them to be little more than memory tests. Rightly conceived and correctly carried out, the test of mastery of essential facts basic to the consideration of an important problem-situation should be significant, though it should require a minor part of the class hour. Thinking can take place only when there are sufficient factual pegs upon which to hang thought. It is incumbent upon the teacher, however, to determine what are the essential facts necessary for intelligent and profitable class discussion.

2. *To aid the student to relate pertinent experiences to the lesson.* Most students have read, traveled, and had other experiences that may have an important bearing upon the understanding of a given lesson. It is a wise teacher who will use the question to draw upon this valuable reservoir to supplement and interpret data already before the class. When developmental lessons are used, a few deft questions that recall to the student important principles previously learned may quickly clarify an otherwise difficult point.

3. *To stimulate interest.* The third function of a question is to arouse curiosity and create true intellectual interests. Curiosity is the best stimulus to learning that can be capitalized by the teacher. Curiosity means the presence of a strong desire to explore and know the answer or solution to a baffling problem. At the heart of every problem is a question. A few well-directed questions about

a lesson or situation may change an indifferent student into one fully alert and eager to seek the answer to the perplexity presented to his mind.

4. *To provide drill.* Retention is facilitated by frequent recall, and if a fact is to continue to stimulate thought, it must be fixed in the memory. Furthermore, for certain types of efficiency it is necessary to pass far beyond the threshold of memory and achieve a condition of automatic response. Such attainment, for example, is required in language response.

5. *To stimulate thought.* It has been said above that at the heart of every problem there is a question. It is almost equally true that at the heart of every question there is a problem. At certain stages in learning for some individuals, even the most simple memory questions will evoke thought. With factual knowledge accepted for the most part as only incidental to learning, we may assume that in modern education the primary function of the question is the stimulation of thought.

6. *To develop the power and habit of evaluation.* Evaluation is one phase of true thinking, though more prominent in some types of thought than in others. We are constantly called upon to evaluate the merits of this fact or that statement, over against other facts or statements, as the basis for intelligent generalization. The habit of careful evaluation is especially important in a social milieu where much that is asserted, and all too often passes for fact, is in reality false.

7. *To insure proper organization and interpretation of materials and experience.* It is not enough to be capable of rigorous evaluation. The student as well as the adult must be able to take the data evaluated and organize it into a form that makes larger generalization possible. Many who are skilled in the analysis and evaluation of minutiae find it exceedingly difficult to bring these more or less isolated items into a unity and cohesion that renders larger interpretation possible. It is the opportunity of the teacher to formulate questions that will lead the student to see the relation of one fact to another, and the possible effect of that relationship upon broader interpretation and conclusion.

8. *To direct attention to significant elements in the lesson.* To aid the student to achieve the ends set forth in purposes 6 and 7 above, it is advantageous for the teacher frankly to direct the attention of the class to important items in the lesson through questions.

9. *To obtain individual or class attention.* If wisely used, the question is very effective as a challenge to attention. In a class growing listless, a stimulating question will sometimes arouse intense interest. Even though it may be, at the moment, somewhat off the line of thought-development, such a question is justified if it is germane to the lesson. Moreover, to ask a student a question when he is "mentally wool gathering," or giving attention to matters other than the lesson, may bring him back to the items before the class.

10. *To discover interests and establish rapport with students.* Wide-awake teachers will recognize that education is concerned with a lesson only as a means to an end. A real opportunity awaits the teacher who can so win the confidence of students that fundamental interests and aspirations are made known to him. The teacher can then utilize this knowledge to broaden and quicken interests found worth while. These discoveries can best be made by understanding questions and a sympathetic interest in the eager questions of the student. A natural outcome is a rapport between teacher and students, psychologically most ideal for learning.

11. *To develop appreciation.* In the opening chapter of this book, training of the affective nature of man was noted as an important phase of education. If the question can be used to "stimulate thinking" and "to create intellectual interests," certainly it can also be used to draw out, for encouragement or discouragement, likes and dislikes. A well-directed series of questions may even awaken a certain type of response to a given situation. Subtle suggestion in the form of the question itself, or the manner of asking it, may tend to color student attitude toward certain situations, and condition the response thereafter toward similar ideas or modes of behavior. Wherever an appeal to the intellectual is possible in developing appreciations, it should be used. Questions that bring these elements to the fore should be stressed.

2. What Is the Technique of the Question?

Characteristics of good questions

The following qualities are important:

1. *Questions should be concisely stated.* The span of attention and memory is short. Auditory memory, particularly, is limited. It is only fair to the student to word a question so briefly that its

meaning can be quickly grasped and the entire statement held in mind as he endeavors to formulate an answer.

2. *Questions should require thought.* There are exceptions, of course. When the purpose of questioning is drill, the question should be cast into recall or memory form. Unless the lesson is avowedly a drill or memory type, it should contain a predominance of thought-type questions.

3. *Questions should not be ambiguous.* Those who have had extensive experience as teachers know how hard it is to make a question mean just what they intended it should, and nothing else. When a question is capable of two or three interpretations, its value is lost. The utmost care in the choice of words and the phrasing of sentences is necessary to insure that ideas are clearly conveyed from teacher to student, and *vice versa.* This is a constant problem even with the most skilled and experienced teachers, because words are but the symbol of ideas. Ideas are the result of experiences, and no two people have had absolutely identical experiences. It is natural, therefore, for words to vary in exact meaning.

4. *Questions should be adapted to age and ability of students.* There is a marked difference between the general level of ability of children at the beginning of the junior high school and that of the senior high school student. Teachers shifted from classes of one age to another are likely to overestimate or underestimate the capacity of their students. Often wide variation is found within an age-grade itself. Homes of culture, opportunity for travel, and extensive contacts add greatly to qualitative difference. The alert teacher will gauge his questions to the ability of his students as the circumstances of age, mental alertness, and environmental opportunity point the need.

5. *Questions should require extended response.* When drill is the purpose of questioning, limited response is desirable and generally necessary if speed in reaction, an essential in most phases of drill, is to be obtained. The criteria enumerated for good questions, however, assume that thought is a desirable result. Questions that admit of single-word or phrase answers tend to become the simple recall type. Extended analysis, synthesis, and organization of response are the more probable results where the student is forced to cast his answer in sentence or paragraph form.

6. *The form of the question should not suggest the answer.* It is easy for the teacher to be tricked into a betrayal of the answer by

his statement of the question. The question that uses a negative and requires a single-word response is especially open to this criticism. "Did not Washington become the first President of the United States?" is an example.

7. *Questions should avoid "yes" or "no" response.* In addition to being a limited-response type of question, questions calling for either "yes" or "no" have the further defect of introducing a large element of guessing into the classroom situation. Either response nets the guesser a 50–50 chance of being correct, even though the student knows nothing about the matter under consideration. Moreover, it is difficult to frame this form of question without a tendency to suggest the answer.

8. *Questions should involve single ideas.* So-called double-barreled questions are confusing and difficult to keep in mind. Their use generally ends in the teacher's re-casting the ideas into separate questions for the convenience of the student, after embarrassment and delay for both teacher and class. Such a question as, "Would you, please, name and locate the digestive juices of the body, and then explain in some detail the action of one of these in the intestines?" would probably end with the name and location of each digestive juice. The last part would need re-asking. In all probability the student called upon for a response would legitimately ask that the question be repeated before he began even on the first half.

9. *Questions should reflect a definite purpose.* A question has no value unless it has a definite purpose to fulfill. To the teacher, the observer, and generally to the student, the question should reveal a direct relation to the objectives of the course and lesson. Questions that lead nowhere soon kill the spirit of the class.

10. *Questions should avoid phraseology of the textbook.* Recourse to the wording of the textbook in phrasing questions puts a premium on memorizing textbook phrases verbatim. Furthermore, there is a danger both for student and for teacher that parrot-like repetition of language may deceive both into an assumption of understanding that in reality does not exist. The best way for one to be sure he understands is to formulate his thought in non-textbook language.

Teacher technique of class questioning

No hard and fast rules to govern the use of the question before the class can be given. All suggestions offered are subject to exception. An understanding of the reasons lying behind the suggestion will free the teacher to take "French leave" of the rule when the educational values in the situation require it.

1. *Address questions to class before designating one to respond.* This method of class questioning has three distinct educational values.

First, it has the advantage of securing general attention to class procedure. Students whose attention is in danger of being lured away by momentary distractions tend to give attention lest they be asked to answer the question.

Second, the method gives all members of the class an opportunity to formulate a tentative answer in their minds. If Harry had been called by name and then asked the question, the attitude of most of the class would almost unconsciously have been — "Let Harry do it." As a consequence, only a few of the most interested students would have troubled to arrive at an independent answer.

The *third* value of this procedure is that it serves to bring the critical attention of the class to the answer given. All have some kind of an answer formulated. At what points does the answer given agree with or differ from those of the class? Where differences appear, student attack is likely to occur. Rigorous thinking in the clash of opinion results.

2. *Distribute questions as far as possible to members of class evenly.* It is a not uncommon experience to observe a class and note that most of the questions are being asked of a few students. Several students are asked possibly one question each, a few bear the brunt of fifty per cent of the questioning, while still another minority group neither volunteer nor are called upon during the entire hour. Unless they are on guard, teachers tend to ask questions of those from whom they have reason to believe an intelligent response is probable. Educationally, they may be least in need of the experience that classroom participation gives.

The modern teacher does not use the class hour for "taking grades"; this practice not only wastes time, but it also gives the student an exaggerated idea of the importance of marks. He does see to it, however, that all students have an opportunity to take part in the class activities and reap the educational benefits of such participation. General participation should be achieved by the most effective but least obvious devices possible. It is not always desirable that every student should participate each day, especially in large classes, nor that each student should mechanically be assigned the same number of questions. Other considerations, such as the appropriateness of the question to the ability of the student, and the value of developing sequential thinking on the part of a student, should be among the factors determining when and of whom particular questions are to be asked. Mechanical devices rigorously applied tend to defeat the fullest recognition of these factors.

3. *Allow sufficient time for the formulation of answers.* The old simple explanation of the lifting power of a vacuum chamber, such as used in well pumps, was that "nature abhorred a vacuum." The statement might be paraphrased for the teacher-question situation by saying that "teachers abhor silence in the classroom." The general experience of competent observers is that teachers are too impatient of delayed response to questions. The teacher is prone to overlook the fact that while he has a tentative answer in mind before the question is put, the student must pause to redefine for himself the meaning of the question, marshal from memory the appropriate experiences significant to the problem raised, evaluate, form a conclusion, and choose the correct words with which to clothe his response. Even when the student has his materials well in hand and his mental processes move rapidly, time must be permitted for a reasoned response.

This tendency to rapid pacing of question and answer in the classroom is graphically revealed in the study of the question by Miss Stevens.[5] A study of classes throughout a full day was made at different grade-levels for 10 days. A stenographic account of the class activities was kept. The study below is adapted from her report.

Miss Stevens found in this study the average number of questions for a day's activity to be 395. If proper time is allowed for assignment, etc., the rate of questioning can readily be imagined. Miller, in a study of rapidity of class questioning and its relation to the ability of students to react, concluded that the tempo at which thought questions were asked in the average class was too rapid, and adapted to the ability of the best ten students in one hundred. In other words, only the upper 10 per cent of a normal class is adjusted to the question-pace set by the teacher. Through experi-

[5] Stevens, Romiett, *op. cit.*, pp. 12–15.

TABLE 3. *The Questioning Activity of Particular Classes Throughout an Entire School Day*

Grade	No. Classes Observed	Length Class Period	No. of Questions	No. of Answers
1st year H. S.	5	45 min.	516	516
2nd year H. S.	5	45 "	372	372
1st year H. S.	6	45 "	348	348
7th grade	5	30 "	411	411
1st year H. S.	5	45 "	372	372
1st year H. S.	5	30 "	338	338
2nd year H. S.	5	30 "	417	417
2nd year H. S.	5	45 "	483	483
1st year H. S.	5	45 "	370	370
8th grade	4	40 "	321	321

mental studies Miller [6] found that freshman high school students required an average of fourteen seconds in which to see simple relations in analogy tests.

It would be well for a teacher, when alone in his room, frequently to ask a question and note the extended period of silence while his watch ticked off fourteen seconds, the minimum of time that should be allowed a bright student to answer a thought question. Where drill is the objective with memory questions, then speed is desirable to render recall automatic. The teacher must determine the purpose and nature of the question, and then gauge the time appropriate to the need.

4. *Ask questions in such manner as not to suggest the answer.* A question may be so worded as not to portray the answer, but the inflection of the voice, or the context out of which the question arises, immediately gives a clue to the answer. For instance, to ask this question, "Did President Wilson favor entering the World War at the time of his re-election?" in a natural tone of voice as though you did not know the answer yourself, would give no lead to its possible answer. However, if the question were asked with a rising inflection upon "did" and "time," it would be obvious to the class that the teacher thought the answer was, "No."

5. *Assume student to be correct when he indicates inability to answer question.* A most embarrassing situation is often created for the student concerned, and the class time is wasted when the

[6] Miller, W. S. *The Administrative Use of Intelligence Tests in High School. Twenty-First Yearbook* of the Society for the Study of Education, Part II, p. 207. Bloomington, Illinois: Public School Publishing Co., 1923.

student indicates he does not know the answer to the question asked. To say, "Now, Henry, I am sure you know that. Just think!" (heard all too often in a classroom) only adds confusion to a sensitive student. It is better to direct attention elsewhere in the class immediately.

6. *Organize questions around pivotal ideas.* Instead of covering scattered, unrelated facts, however valuable in themselves, questions should serve to re-enforce other questions and progressively develop a main idea or thesis. If the teacher will give attention to the organization of questions to insure cohesion and development, he will be agreeably surprised to observe how the continuity of idea in his questions reacts on the general interest and motivation of the class.

7. *As a rule, do not repeat questions.* If the class knows the question will be repeated, on demand, there is a tendency for students to give less strict attention to the discussion. Demand undivided attention, and when a student has failed to get the question, pass on to another. By the teacher's manner, more than by anything he says, the student will feel a definite rebuke in the presence of the class for his inattention. Such a policy will do much to stimulate full attention.

8. *As a rule, do not repeat answers.* Here, again, attention of the class should be insisted upon while others as well as the teacher are speaking. The response is a valuable part of the class hour. The answer merits the careful critical evaluation of the class. Then, too, students should be trained as a matter of courtesy to speak loudly and distinctly enough for all to hear without too much effort. A student conscious of his obligations to an audience-situation will try to formulate what he says with greater care. Again there are exceptions to the rule which the discerning teacher will recognize. A short time ago the writer, after a discussion of the technique of the question with a university class in Methods, accompanied part of the class to observe a supervisor conducting a review recitation. In the conference period with the students that followed the observation, the instructor was interested in their reactions to the question technique of the supervisor. During the recitation, which fully met the criteria set up in the chapter on "Review," the supervisor had occasionally repeated significant answers of students. As was to be expected, some of the class in Methods, who remembered the rule but not its meaning, called attention to

his procedure and quoted this rule as evidence of bad technique. When they took into consideration that this was a review lesson, that the review had for one of its purposes the fixing of important ideas about the unit reviewed, and that the supervisor had repeated only very important answers that he desired to fix in the minds of the class by repetition, the critical students realized that a broad principle had been given them and not a rule of thumb.

9. *Occasionally ask questions of the inattentive.* This method, as indicated in listing purposes of the question, is a good device to handle some disciplinary situations of inattention. When so used the question serves only indirectly a legitimate educational function. Such questions should have another more valid function so that when answered they will have real significance for the lesson and class.

10. *Questions should be asked in easy confident manner.* "Of course you are able to answer the question," should be the confident manner in which the question is directed to the student. It may be an unwarranted assumption; but even so, if the student half knows the answer, there is likelihood that he will say what he can. He is under challenge not to disappoint the teacher. Psychologically, the stage is all set for him to utilize his latent powers to the maximum.

11. *The teacher should show adaptability in questioning.* As suggested earlier in the chapter, no teacher can anticipate fully the classroom situation as it will be. Well-thought-out questions may need to be cast aside and new ones formulated as the exigencies demand. The teacher should show such close rapport with the class and such mastery of the subject that questions will appear fresh blown for the moment, and perfectly at point.

Teacher reaction to student questions

The attitude and response of the teacher to questions asked by students also has an important bearing on teacher success. The following suggestions will prove valuable:

1. *Student questions should be encouraged.* Education is not a pouring in or a pumping out process, though our emphasis upon the teacher's questioning technique might warrant that inference. The more teachers can bring students to think and question, the more certain they can be that education is taking place. The teacher, therefore, should use every possible means to get students to participate through questions.

2. *Insist that questions be significant.* While questions are encouraged, it is necessary to guard against trivial and insincere questions that do not reflect thought, or that are designed to sidetrack the lesson into bypaths. Trivial questions are frequent, and indicate immaturity or superficial preparation of the student. It is but fair to acknowledge, however, that it is very difficult always to distinguish between trivial and important, and between sincere and baiting questions — particularly the latter.

3. *Require courtesy in questioning.* The occasional eagerness of students to ask questions leads at times to several questions being propounded to the teacher simultaneously. It is a splendid opportunity for the teacher to show the class how courtesy and self-restraint often make both for speed and for the realization of desires, too. Failure to insist upon one question at a time from the class inevitably leads to confusion, and later to bad disciplinary problems.

4. *Recognize the timeliness of questions.* It is in meeting this requirement that item two in this list of suggestions approaches a real difficulty. Often questions quite apart from the lesson in hand, but suggested by phases of the lesson, appear. These questions may have more educational value than the lesson itself. If they are significant for the entire class, it is well to pause then and there and consider them.

5. *Grant earnest student right to question your position.* Students should be encouraged to ask questions that indicate a sincere disagreement with the teacher. No real thinking that represents a clash of opinion will take place if the teacher frowns upon any disagreement with positions he has taken. He has no right to set himself before the class as infallible. The teacher should encourage the student to think for himself, not to accept unquestioningly the point of view of the teacher. This attitude is fundamental in secondary education.

6. *When teacher cannot answer questions, frankly say so.* The teacher has nothing to gain by bluffing but loss of student respect. Students are quick to detect when a teacher is "putting up a front." On the other hand, a frank admission as a matter of course that the teacher is not an oracle of all wisdom will be accepted with increased respect for the teacher. A teacher cannot afford to be too often put in a position where lack of essential knowledge must be admitted. A classroom veteran of twenty-five years explains that at times he has thought of a problem likely to arise

just before entering the classroom. If the issue can be safely avoided, he steers around it until he has leisure to inform himself on the point. If, before the class, he is forced to face a question he cannot answer, he frankly, in a matter-of-fact manner, admits his ignorance, then adopts one of three ways out of the difficulty. He may promise to check on the question before the next class meeting and report, which he is careful to do; he may make the problem the basis of a student assignment for report to the class; or, if the question appears unimportant, he simply dismisses it.

Teacher reaction to student's response

The attitude of the teacher toward the response of the students, and his handling of the response, will have much to do with the success of the class.

1. *Show appreciative attitude toward student response.* It is just as essential to encourage a response to a question as it is to elicit a question from the student. If the teacher is sympathetic when an effort at response is made, students will feel free to venture participation at times though they are in some doubt as to the correctness of their comments. When it is necessary to check sincere efforts at participation, the checking should be done appreciatively and delicately to avoid quenching the spirit completely. This may be the unfortunate result with sensitive students unless care is used.

2. *Interpret sincere response to advantage of student.* The author will always remember one of his teachers for his artful acceptance of student responses. The answer might be seriously deficient, but it was given full value for its content; then, beginning with a characteristic sentence, "Yes, that is correct . . . except that these additional factors need to be considered," he would go on explaining and supply the data necessary to make the answer complete. He had a further trait worthy of emulation. He always gave the student the benefit of the doubt and interpreted his response in the direction of the correct answer, even though it seemed dubious to the class at times whether the student really meant what the teacher assumed him to imply. The effect on the morale of the class was exceedingly wholesome. Neither student nor class, however, was ever left with less than a complete and accurate notion of what the ideal response should have been, so carefully was the response analyzed.

3. *At times desirable to get class evaluation of partially correct*

responses. When the most approved question technique has been employed, the class is ready for a critical constructive evaluation of the answer given. The teacher will do well to employ this form of correction liberally, so long as the sensitive student is safeguarded against harsh criticism. Class evaluation provides splendid training in courteous impersonal comments on another's effort, both to the class and to the individuals whose efforts are thus subject to analysis.

4. *As a rule, students should not be assisted in response.* Let the student make his own contribution unassisted. Kindly efforts at assistance often prove more of a hindrance than a help. Besides, he needs to be trained to reply on his own resources without friendly assistance.

5. *Responses should be couched in complete thought units and be correct grammatically.* There has been a widespread attitude on the part of teachers that only those responsible for courses in English composition and literature should be concerned with correct expression. Modern education insists that correct English usage is as much a matter of habit as of knowledge of correct grammatical form, if not more. If this statement is true, it is incumbent upon all teachers, whether of English composition, history, science, or any other subject, rigorously to insist upon those correct forms of expression in order that they may become habitual to the student before he quits the secondary school.

QUESTIONS AND PROBLEMS

1. Why is the technique of questioning considered more difficult in the light of modern methods of teaching?
2. Why is the questioning technique so much more difficult and important when the teaching emphasis is not so much on the facts as on the analysis and evaluation of the facts?
3. Enumerate and define the primary qualities a teacher must possess to conduct class questioning successfully.
4. Which of the functions suggested in the text for class questions particularly stress and fulfill the requirements of the modern concept of educational purpose?
5. Psychologically, what are the most important uses of the question in class work? Substantiate your answer.
6. What is the most prevalent yet least important use of the question? What evidence have you to support your answer?

7. Why are thought questions so important pedagogically? Prepare a classified list of at least ten types of thought questions. Give examples of each of your own formulation.

8. Take six thought questions asked by professors in your classes and analyze them according to the ten characteristics of a good question given in the text.

9. Give the characteristics of a *good* questioning technique; justify these in accordance with modern principles of education and pedagogy.

10. How and why should questions be distributed among the members of a class during an individual class period?

11. What psychological and physiological facts determine the character of questions and the rapidity with which they may be asked?

12. Of what value are the student's questions to the teacher; to himself; and to the class?

13. What should a teacher's attitude be toward the questions of the students?

14. Show by examples how the art of questioning may be used to stimulate definite intellectual interests.

15. What type of questions is most valuable to the student? Substantiate your answer.

SELECTED BIBLIOGRAPHY

Burton, William H. *The Guidance of Learning Activities,* chapter XIV. New York: Appleton-Century-Crofts, Inc., 1944.

Butler, Frank A. *The Improvement of Teaching in Secondary Schools,* Revised Edition, chapter XI. Chicago: University of Chicago Press, 1946.

Crawford, C. C. *How to Teach,* chapter XV. Los Angeles: Southern California School Book Depository, 1938.

Douglass, Harl R. and Mills, Hubert H. *Teaching in High School,* chapter XIV. New York: The Ronald Press Company, 1948.

Frederich, R. W., Ragsdale, C. E., and Salisbury, R. *Directing Learning,* chapter VIII. New York: Appleton-Century-Crofts, Inc., 1938.

Hall, J. W. *The Question as a Factor in Teaching.* Boston: Houghton Mifflin Company, 1916.

Heer, A. L. *Steps to Better Teaching,* chapter XIX. New York: W. W. Norton and Company, Inc., 1937.

Lancelot, W. H. *Permanent Learning,* chapter XVII. New York: John Wiley and Sons, Inc., 1944.

Muse, Maude B. *Guiding Learning,* pp. 322–333. New York: The Macmillan Company, 1950.

Risk, Thomas M. *Principles and Practices of Teaching in Secondary Schools,* Revised Edition, chapter XXIII. New York: American Book Company, 1947.

Rivlin, Harry N. *Teaching Adolescents in Secondary Schools,* chapter VII. New York: Appleton-Century-Crofts, Inc., 1948.

Struck, F. T. *Creative Teaching,* chapter IX. New York: John Wiley and Sons, Inc., 1938.

13

How Can Review and Practice

Be Used?

1. What Is the Nature and Purpose of the Review?

The nature of review

Much confusion still exists in popular thought about the review. The average person of traditional training remembers the *review* as a tiresome, dull retracing of work previously covered in the class or in the textbook. The essential difference between the traditional type of review and the older practice of the recitation was largely one of time. A segment of work covered by class recitation in six weeks might be covered in a two days' review. Since the older recitation practice emphasized factual learning, almost to the exclusion of any other form of learning, the review became a repetition of the major factual materials in the unit of work concerned. While the principle of apperception was implied in the Herbartian formal step, "preparation," in applying it to the daily recitation few teachers carried it beyond a brief reminder of the outstanding factual data of the previous lesson. Traces of that early practice are still evident in the point of view expressed by a few recent writers on methodology.

Further confusion exists because some tend to use the term *review* to cover the process of *drill*. Repetition in any form does carry with it an element of drill, but to think of the terms as having the same meaning is to confuse entirely two fundamentally different educational processes. Drill has for its purpose the making of set responses, rapid and, to a large extent, automatic.

The term review connotes not a mere repetition of facts to fix them more firmly in mind, but rather a new view of these facts in a different setting that results in new understandings, changed attitudes, or different behavior patterns. With this conception of the review, most recent writers are in general agreement. Rivlin thinks of the review as "deepening the student's insight into the problem or . . . increasing his appreciation of its ramifications." [1] The total educational process, from understanding through changed attitudes to modified behavior, should be envisaged in the review. The more extensive the review involved, the more completely these attributes of the review should be realized. Obviously a review of a few minutes' duration could not achieve much more than a new understanding of the data under consideration, while an extensive review might, with justification, be expected to affect in some degree attitudes and behavior.

Importance of the review

The review as contemplated in the above definition is raised at once to a position of importance in educational method. It is equally true that if its significance is measured by the space devoted to its consideration in textbooks on secondary school method, the review has not received the attention that its true importance for education warrants. While some recent writers devote a chapter to the review, others dismiss it with a paragraph or two. There appears to be a significant relationship, however, between the attention given the review and the extent to which the writers are removed from the traditional conception of it. The use of the unit plan of organizing instruction along with problem method actually involves the review function in the final stages of these procedures Consequently, these phases of the newer methods are not commonly thought of as fulfilling in part the review concept associated with the more traditional forms of instruction.

It is generally recognized that while understanding, attitudes, and behavior are the results sought in education, these cannot be achieved without a foundation of information. As pointed out earlier, we must have factual data as pegs upon which to hang our

[1] Rivlin, Harry N. *Teaching Adolescents in Secondary Schools*, p. 309. New York: Appleton-Century-Crofts, Inc., 1948.

thinking. On the other hand, the human mind cannot with profit continue to amass these factual data without relating them in some meaningful form; nor can we continue activities in uncritical fashion and expect progress. Only as we evaluate previous actions are we able to find an intelligent basis for future behavior. For example, to continue shooting at a mark at one hundred yards will not contribute to marksmanship unless the neophyte critically evaluates the results of his shooting. One segment of his practice may have been devoted to a discovery of the effect of gravity upon the bullet at that distance, another to wind pressure and its influence upon the path of the projectile, and still another to the gauging of the sights for correction of these error tendencies. To achieve satisfactory results, the marksman must have available a mass of factual data. It is of equal importance, however, that he relate these data in some unified, meaningful fashion. He must recall essential facts and appraisals of segments of experience in a final summary that actually involves a new view, and a new understanding, and provides a basis for changed behavior. This is a major reason for the fact that new problem-solving methods and the unit plan are rapidly taking precedence over time-honored instructional practices.

Purpose of the review

While we have tried to catch the larger significance of the review through a consideration of its essential nature and importance, a more thorough understanding and appreciation of it may be gained by an analytical statement of its purpose from the point of view of the teacher and the student. The more important purposes of the review are summarized below.

1. *To fix in mind activities or materials learned.* As previously mentioned, the review in earlier practice was associated largely with the concept of drill. Although this aspect of the review has now assumed a position of minor purpose, it still has value. The psychological principle of over-learning insures greater retention with the repetition involved in review. Any repetition will tend to fix materials previously studied more firmly in mind. This is a valuable concomitant of the larger results to be obtained by the review. Since not skills, but ideational data, are the forms of fixations desired in review learning, fixation as a by-product of repetition can be secured through recall that is related to different and more extended associational patterns.

2. *To organize the materials and experiences into larger units for understanding.* School work, whether organized on the daily recitation plan or larger unit basis, cannot avoid an impression of choppiness or fragmentariness. Each day's work tends to stand apart in some isolation from what has preceded and what follows. At best this difficulty will always be present. The span of memory is limited, as is also the span of attention. Memory-span and attention-span are closely interrelated. As a result, it is necessary to put forth every effort to prevent the experiences of each day from becoming isolated. Since elements in a total situation — if that total situation be extensive — must be learned somewhat piecemeal, each new segment must be related to its immediate past, and later all the elements must be brought into a larger unity for interpretative purposes. For example, a class in social sciences is engaged in the study of American history, and the unit under consideration is America's Immigration Policy. To understand that policy will require a study of a number of phases of American history that may seem to the student quite remote. He will want to know the early policy of "open arms to immigrants," and why these peoples were so welcome to young America. He will study the changing trends in the source of supply of these immigrants, from early days to the present time. The oriental problem will necessarily require attention. Our industrial and economic development will, of course, enter into the picture. Other related problems will need careful study as well. Each will demand the acquisition of factual data and interpretation. In spite of the effort to have the student see the relation of every part to the larger problem, each will have an element of isolation from the rest. Only as the major items of interpretation from each are brought together and focused upon the main topic under consideration can the fuller interpretation, the more complete understanding, take place. This function, whether small or large segments are involved, the review fulfills most admirably.

3. *To enable the student to gain perspective.* When the materials and experiences have been organized into larger units, the student can gain a perspective not possible while fragments of the whole were in considerable isolation. A day-by-day study of a series of topics, all part of a larger unit, tends to leave the student with the impression that all the topics are of equal worth. It is only when an evaluation has been undertaken that the student can begin to give each item of fact or experience its proper place and

weight in the total unit. It is not unlike the experience one has
when in a valley and later on the mountain peak. When one is in
the valley it is difficult to get a perspective of the relative heights
of certain mountains and their relation to each other. From the
vantage point of a mountain summit it is possible to see the terrain
in its true proportions, and to note the proper relation of each ridge
and canyon to the section of the mountain range in question.

It is necessary for the student to stand apart, as it were, from his
task and take a panoramic view of the unit studied. The trees will
begin to separate themselves from the forest. Main and subsidiary
items will begin to take their place in true value and correct relationship. New understandings will appear. It should not be inferred that this transformation will take place in some magic
fashion. It will not. Painstaking analysis, careful evaluation, and
discerning synthesis are the price one must pay for the perspective
of the review. The student will often find, however, that after toil-
some and seeming fruitless effort, this perspective may dawn upon
him almost unawares. Psychological processes have been at work.
With apparent startlingness relationships appear and perspective
is gained.

An incident in point was related to the writer while he was a
student by a now distinguished educator who had done his post
graduate work in philosophy. Said he:

> My first year as a student of philosophy will remain a vivid though
> unpleasant memory. It seemed that I had a mass of unrelated knowl-
> edge without any significant meaning. The second year was little
> better, although I felt more familiar with the great philosophers and
> their views. The third year it seemed as though the fog suddenly
> rolled away, and I felt the thrill of seeing these various philosophies
> as they developed out of and related themselves to each other. Now
> I can understand how a certain philosopher has found the genesis of
> his ideas in the thoughts of earlier philosophers.

An analysis of this man's experience reveals this process; the first
two years were spent largely in a mastery of the ideas of individual
philosophers, and only progressively was serious effort put forth
to relate them. The last year was largely devoted to synthesis. It
was in this period of his study, characteristically a review phase,
that perspective was gained with seeming suddenness and the thrill
of understanding attained.

4. *To provide for desirable expansion and supplementation of*

materials and experiences. In any study of a topic or unit it is seldom possible to include all the worth-while materials or experiences that appertain to the subject. The review offers opportunity to supplement where such supplementation is found desirable or necessary to render understanding complete. Moreover, while in the review unexpected expansion of the topic or unit may seem advisable for completeness, the alert teacher will never assume that the lesson plan or assignment is perfect. The review will be regarded as the opportune time to make up any deficiencies that appear. Sometimes an added word of explanation, a further reference that needs to be consulted, or even an extensive marshaling of additional data *via* the lecture route may be the best means of clarifying a confused point in the review.

5. *To provide an apperceptive basis for future study.* If the class is about to take up another segment of work in which certain principles derived in the unit just studied will find application, then the review becomes merged with the apperceptive function of the assignment. It is highly desirable that the essential properties of the principle to be invoked are clearly recognized in the review. Then the students should be led to realize possible applications of the principle in the direction of the next lesson. New understandings are thus assured and the review made functional. This use of review applies particularly to such subjects as mathematics and the sciences.

The larger-unit review should not ordinarily be satisfied even with a "new view," unless that new view projects the students into a consideration of the application to new situations of the conclusions reached. In a field such as history, the full value of any unit of study that does not lead the student to ask the possible implication, for future periods of history, of the historical data just mastered might well be questioned. The teacher who uses the review in this way will produce a realization on the part of the student that historical events are in the main not accidental, but have their roots deep in the past. Likewise the student will be keenly aware that the history of tomorrow will be the child of the events of today. The sense of fragmentariness so often associated with classroom activities will largely disappear.

6. *To diagnose student weakness in preparation and understanding.* Students are likely to show deficiencies in two particulars. The first is at the point of inadequate preparation. This is not always

the result of indifferent study. Too often it is due to paucity of experience or available sources of information. Whichever its cause, a good review should reveal it. The second, a weakness in ability to analyze and generalize when sufficient information is at hand, is more serious, and cannot as readily be overcome. It is more difficult to detect this weakness because the teacher must be satisfied the preparation has been adequate before probing for the second.

7. *To diagnose teacher weakness.* Frequently the weakness of the student is in reality the weakness of the teacher. Failure to insure the student's contact with sufficient materials or experiences of the right kind may be brought to light quickly through the review. Again, directions in the assignment may have been open to misunderstanding, or possibly the objectives of the lesson were not made sufficiently clear. At any rate, the teacher should look upon the review as more of an index of his own shortcomings than those of the students. At least he should maintain this attitude until careful evaluation convinces him of those difficulties he may rightfully charge to the students.

8. *To create new interest in old materials.* The fragmentary nature of our teaching has tended to leave the student with the mental reaction to the completion of a segment of work — "Well, this is over. I'll not have to bother my brain with this stuff any longer." Because it seems to have value but for the moment, the knowledge gained arouses little or no enthusiasm. The teacher who can utilize the review as a means of drawing into the immediate picture data from previous units studied will bring life and vitality to the classroom. For the student to realize that knowledge gained today may prove most effective in the understanding of problems to be studied months later will stimulate interests not possible when the lesson is assumed to have only transitory significance. It must bring real satisfaction to the student who is engaged in the study of our Civil Service system, for example, to discover as a definite connection with its growth the appearance of the "Spoils System" under President Jackson, and the continued insistence upon the use of our postal department as the spoils of political patronage through the appointment of postmasters by the political party in power. The action of President Taft, at the close of his administration, in removing this glaring evil by placing postmasters under Civil Service, and the immediate reversal of this act when

Wilson became president, will be better understood when brought into perspective with the large problem of Civil Service. Or the class in literature may be studying historical novels, such as those of Gilbert Parker. Early colonial history will take on much more interest and significance when recalled and viewed through the lenses of human impulses and the emotions associated with literature. In the review the teacher has a rare opportunity to vitalize his work by levying tribute on what has gone before. Incidents that may have been studied as part of other units will suddenly appear to have new meaning in the review under the direction of a skilled teacher.

2. What Is the Technique of Review?

Planning the review

The review should be most carefully planned. It is a difficult phase of teaching, because no two situations are alike. Skill is required because the most difficult of mental tasks is that of critical evaluation, synthesis, and interpretation, and these are of the essence of the review. It is only by the most rigid planning that a review procedure can be formulated to fit the specific purpose desired by the review. Care must be used in the selection of the type of review to be employed. For example, a review that might fit a daily lesson in foreign language or English composition would be ill adapted to a course in Social Problems. The selection of problems that actually draw out all that is fundamental in a unit of work, demands thoughtful preparation.

When to review

Where long units are used, the review generally comes at the completion of the unit of study; or when the daily recitation is employed for materials not closely interrelated, it should come at the close of the recitation. Where the recitation involves continuity of theme in developmental progression, the review comes at the end of the recitation and, in very abbreviated form, may appear at the beginning of the next day's lesson. The intelligent experienced teacher is the best judge of when the review should be used.

Length of the review

No set time-limits for a review can be given. It is obvious that

352 *Using Review and Practice*

the purpose to be realized, as well as the difficulty and extent of the unit covered, must in part determine the time. The daily recitation review should not be permitted to usurp more than a very few minutes. Even this statement must be qualified, for the cumulative review may, toward the last of a unit of study, justify a reasonable part of the hour. Two or three days may profitably be devoted to an extended and complicated unit.

3. What Is the Nature of Practice?

Importance of practice in learning

Few, indeed, there are who would question the desirability of committing as many as possible of our routine activities to habit reaction. More than a half century ago William James in *The Principles of Psychology* wrote his now famous chapter on "Habit." He stated the case well for relegating much routine behavior to habit reaction in these words: [2]

> The great thing, then, in all education, is to *make our nervous system our ally instead of our enemy*. It is to fund and capitalize our acquisitions, and live at ease upon the interest of the fund. *For this we must make automatic and habitual, as early as possible, as many useful actions as we can,* and guard against the growing into ways that are likely to be disadvantageous to us, as we should guard against the plague. The more of the details of our daily life we can hand over to the effortless custody of automatism, the more our higher powers of mind will be set free for their proper work.

The case for the development of habits has never been stated more clearly. Do I wish to read? Then the extent to which I have made habitual certain mechanical movements of the eye across the printed page, the extent to which I have made instant recognition of the meaning of words practically automatic, along with other mechanics involved in reading, can I read easily, rapidly, and with pleasure. Do I wish to play the piano? Then the degree to which the sight of the score on the music sheet almost automatically transmits itself to the appropriate fingers, and in turn they to the appropriate places on the keyboard, am I able to reproduce in delicacy of sound the music of the score. All this, of course, can be said of the skills needed in walking, speaking, sports, most of the labors

[2] James, William. *The Principles of Psychology*, vol. I, p. 122. New York: Henry Holt and Company, 1890.

of one's calling, particularly those involving mechanical competencies, to mention a few areas of living only.

James recognized then as we recognize now, that habits are formed through rigorous *practice*. There is no other royal road to habit formation. Simple observation indicated that in many areas of human activity responses became automatic through repeated efforts to react in a certain way.

Meaning of practice

Unfortunately, there has been much confusion in recent years over the question of drill and repetition. The older conception of drill as a means of habituating behavior reaction, assumed an exact duplication of a pattern of behavior until such behavior pattern became automatic. The past generation, schooled in the stimulus-response-bond (S-R bond) theory of learning, has held that learning was a matter of repeated stimulus of a specific sensory neuron, which carried the stimulus to a series of connecting neurons in the central nervous system, which in turn carried the stimulus to a motor neuron where it produced an appropriate action response. Stated in another way, they explained that an S-R bond connection was made automatic by means of creating a neural pathway for the stimulus by constant repetition of a specific stimulus until a given response was made certain. This constant repetition of an exact stimulus was known as drill.

Experimental evidence brought the validity of this theory into question. The widespread acceptance of the Organismic-Field theories of learning with the notion that the whole organism reacted to stimuli rather than a single sensory neuron on a S-R bond circuit, led to a general discrediting of the older idea of the value of repetition and drill. Many superficially rejected all ideas of practice as a legitimate aspect of learning. This because practice was considered synonomous with the older discredited notion of drill and repetition. To avoid the possibility of confusion, *practice* is used here instead of the older terms *drill* and *repetition*, so long associated with an outmoded theory of learning.

Practice, however, under modern conceptions of the learning process, remains an important aspect of learning. If learning is defined as the change in behavior which occurs as the learner makes repeated efforts to react in the most effective way possible to successive situations with which he is confronted, then practice is recognized as an integral part of learning.[3] The concept of learning in this definition implies that one does not make a fully satisfactory behavior adjustment to a situation at his first effort. It requires repeated efforts before the most economical and efficient behavior pattern is achieved in the learner's reaction to a situation. The efforts of the individual to react repeatedly to a situation may be expressed graphically thus:

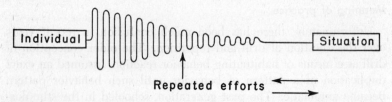

The significant differences in the conception of practice in the learning process here conceived in contrast to the older notions of drill or repetition in S-R learning, is that practice does not assume repeating the same identical activity. According to this theory of learning, with each effort to react to the situation there is some modification in the total behavior pattern of the learner, however great or minimal. At each successive effort at reaction a consequent change in the behavior pattern results. Under this theory of learning, the learner, in fact, during the process of learning, never repeats his reaction twice exactly alike. At each effort at adjustment the learner begins a new approach based upon the consolidation of his previous efforts. He, in fact, makes a new and modified effort at adjustment. Therefore, repetition (drill) as formerly conceived in the learning process does not take place, and is not to be confused with the conception of practice in learning here presented.[4]

[3] This definition is similar to one found in Gates, et al., *Educational Psychology*, Second Edition, p. 299. New York: The Macmillan Company, 1942. At this point the student should review those portions of Chapters 2, 3 and 4 where learning is discussed. The modern concepts of Organismic-Field theories of learning should be restudied in such sources as Hartmann, George W. *Educational Psychology*. New York: American Book Company, 1941; Hilgard, Ernest R. *Theories of Learning*, New York: Appleton-Century-Crofts, Inc., 1948; and Kingsley, Howard L. *The Nature and Conditions of Learning*. New York: Prentice-Hall, Inc., 1946.

[4] See discussion of this point in Kingsley, Howard L. *The Nature and Conditions of Learning*, chapter V, "Repetition," and chapter XI "The Development of Motor Skills." New York: Prentice-Hall, Inc., 1946.

4. What Principles Should Govern Practice?

1. *Practice should be emphasized where responses are to be automatic.* If the modern theory of learning — which assumes learning is the modification of behavior through the process of experience — be correct, then the need of some practice in all learning is probable. Those complex behavior responses which need to be fixed and made automatic require extended practice. Special attention to the problem of appropriate practice should be given where skill learning is involved.

2. *Practice must be purposeful to the learner.* Purposiveness is assumed to be a prerequisite of learning. Where it is necessary to make repeated efforts to achieve skill in adjustment to situations a strong desire to develop such skill is essential. Practice without the motivation of a strong desire to learn on the part of the educand has been found to be uninteresting, boring, and ineffective. When the pupil rather than the teacher determines to "practice to make perfect," the experiences involved are challenging and pleasant. More than that, practice under these conditions assures a critical awareness of the nature of the goal sought, and provides a basis for an intelligent understanding of the modification of the procedural steps involved in the acquisition of the desired skill.

3. *Practice is more effective under mild emotional stimulus.* Experimental studies have shown that certain types of automatic or near-automatic skill responses are achieved more quickly under the stimulus of certain forms of rhythmic music. The use of simple rhythmic melodies has long been practiced in facilitating the acquisition of automatic responses and speed in typewriting. Rhythm tends to relax muscles and aids muscular coordination.

Rhythm, like most other aids to learning, must be used discriminatingly. In many forms of learning rhythm may prove a hindrance rather than an asset in the early stages of efforts at adjustment. To use a metronome in the teaching of the piano before the pupil has learned the position of the keys on the keyboard is likely to inhibit learning. The same can be said for the use of music in beginning typewriting before the location of the keys has been learned. Again, after a class has reached a fair speed on the typewriter, it will be necessary to vary the speed of the music or timing used to take care of varying rates of speed acquired by different individuals within the class.

4. *Where a group engages as a unit in practice, attention also must be given to the practice needs of individuals.* It is possible to invlove all the members of a class in practice in the acquisition of a given skill. However, no two learners will respond in the same way in their efforts to acquire a skill. The alert teacher should help each to make his own approach in developing the skill in question, as each applies general principles of adaptation to the learning situation. After the gross aspects of the skills have been achieved by the class, in all probability increasing attention will need to be given to the practice procedures of individuals.

5. *Practice is more effective where the learner is aware of his progress.* Experimental evidence supports our common sense conclusions that one learns more expeditiously when he is conscious of his successes. The old saw, "Nothing creates success like success," has considerable merit. When behavior patterns are assumed to be modified with each effort at adjustment to a situation, a critical evaluation of the rightness of each effort, and any intelligent modification of each of the successive efforts, must be conditioned upon some knowledge of the degree of success of each preceding effort, and the possible source of incorrectness of the responses made.

6. *For complex skills a combination of wholes and part methods in practice may be more effective.* In simple learning situations it it now advised that we try to learn by wholes instead of adding a series of parts. This is consistent with the Gestalt or Organismic theory of seeing and reacting to a total situation. The evidence, too, seems to favor this approach in learning through practice of the complete process of adjustment. However, in complex or difficult learning situations, psychologists generally recommend that after some practice in the over-all response to fix the entire gross sweep of the response, attention be given to those sections where additional practice is necessary. It would seem a waste of time to practice all parts of a total complex skill just to master a few difficult spots. It is important, though, after mastery of the parts to incorporate these difficult special parts into the whole in practice so that they become consolidated into the entire smooth-flowing skill process.

7. *Practice should be carried on energetically.* The establishment of a skill is most efficiently achieved when practice is done vigorously. To attack a learning situation with zest in all probability carries with it a concomitant raptness of attention and enthusiasm,

so essential to efficient learning. It means a complete focus of attention on the matter in hand. Such alertness creates within itself an exclusion of ordinary distractions, and a critical sense of awareness of the possible weaknesses and strengths of the responses made. This is important for evaluation and projecting a reasoned modified response into each successive effort to adjust satisfactorily to the situation.

8. *Practice should be carried on under conditions similar to those in which the skill will be used.* This has become an important principle of learning. Studying skills out of context with their normal usage has not been found effective. For example, compositional skills are not learned by memorizing rules of grammar. Even the composition of traditional type essays does not provide as efficient skills in the formulation of reports for civic groups as practice in the formulation of reports in a real or somewhat analogous situation does. It has been found that learning vocational skills apart from the conditions of the vocation is not as efficient as when the skills are acquired under conditions approximating their normal use. This has forced the schools, as far as reasonably possible, to develop skill learning under simulated conditions to those where the skill is used naturally.

9. *For most economical use practice periods should be short and liberally spaced.* Considerable research has been done on the problem of practice. Because conditions under which learning takes place are so varied, exact answers to the question of length and frequency of practice periods cannot be given. In general, the simpler the learning and the younger the learner the shorter the period. However, it appears to be generally agreed that approximately thirty minutes may be the best length of practice period. For most learning, practice periods below fifteen minutes, except for children, were not long enough, while periods much in excess of an hour were wasteful of time. In general long periods should be avoided.

Specific data is even less conclusive on the question of spaced practice periods. Mass practice — that is, continuous practice — until the skill is learned, is not economical. There should be liberal time lapses between practices. The length of these intervals depends upon the difficulty and complexity of the learning involved. In difficult learning several hours to a day may prove to be satisfactory spacing periods.

Many believe that time intervals are necessary between practice periods to permit some unknown processes involved in learning to take place, which in effect consolidates the learning of previous practice periods.

It is not the province of this book to enter into speculation as to why spacing of practice periods appears to be conducive to efficient learning. It is important only that we recognize maximum learning of skills takes place normally with practice periods relatively short in duration, and these spaced with several hours of rest between the periods.

10. *Where skills are not to be used soon or often after learning, overlearning or occasional practice periods may be provided.* At times it seems justifiable for the schools to teach youth skills they may not use for some time following their acquisition or which they may use only infrequently. To insure continuance of the skill in maximum retention, it is possible to practice the skill to a point far beyond normal efficiency. This is known as overlearning. The skill thus learned will not deteriorate as rapidly as when learned just to the threshold of efficiency or automotization. Rather than utilize the tremendous amount of time and energy required to overlearn a given skill, it may be more economical of effort to plan occasional practice periods in order to maintain the skill at a reasonably high level.

QUESTIONS AND PROBLEMS

1. What is the accepted definition of review as used in this chapter? How does this definition contrast with the older, popular conception of review?
2. How does review differ from drill? How are reviews and drills related?
3. How does the present treatment of review fit in with the newer educational point of view? Be explicit.
4. Select one unit of a given subject in your special field of teacher preparation for review and show how the review can fulfill at least three of the purposes enumerated in this chapter.
5. Why is organization of material and experiences into larger units desirable?
6. Show how "gaining perspective" from a history review can be achieved. Be explicit.
7. Of what value is the review as a means of diagnosing weaknesses in teaching?
8. Select a topic or unit from each of three traditional subject fields of

the high school and determine a desirable method of review for each.

9. How could we use the problem review in relation to experience units?
10. List some points of guidance by which to determine when to review in certain areas.
11. How can the teacher determine the adequacy of a review?
12. Suggest motivation for a review in a specific foreign language unit in one of the subject fields for which you are preparing to teach.
13. Make a plan for review in any unit of your teaching subject, using one of the methods suggested in this chapter.
14. How may the review be used to create wholesome attitudes toward school work?
15. How would you describe changing ideas with respect to drill, repetition, practice?
16. Have a panel discuss the question: "What is the significance for the teaching of "practice" of the change from the S–R bond to the Organismic-Field theories of learning?"

SELECTED BIBLIOGRAPHY

Burton, William H. *The Guidance of Learning Activities,* chapter XIV. New York: Appleton-Century-Crofts, Inc., 1944.

Douglass, Harl R. and Mills, Hubert H. *Teaching in High School,* chapter XIII. New York: The Ronald Press Company, 1948.

Frederick, R. W., Ragsdale, C. E. and Salisbury, R. *Directing Learning,* chapter X. New York: Appleton-Century-Crofts, Inc., 1938.

Hartmann, George W. *Educational Psychology.* New York: American Book Company, 1941.

Hilgard, Ernest R. *Theories of Learning.* New York: Appleton-Century-Crofts, Inc., 1948.

Hopkins, Thomas L. *Interaction: The Democratic Process,* chapter VIII. Boston: Ginn and Company, 1941.

Kingsley, Howard L. *The Nature and Conditions of Learning,* chapters II, V, XI, XIII. New York: Prentice-Hall, Inc., 1946.

Macomber, F. G. *Guiding Child Development in the Elementary School,* chapter VIII. New York: American Book Company, 1941.

Mursell, James. *Developmental Teaching,* pp. 70–71, 118–119, 208–210. New York: McGraw-Hill Book Company, Inc., 1949.

Muse, Maude B. *Guiding Learning Experiences,* pp. 329–333. New York: The Macmillan Company, 1950.

Risk, Thomas M. *Principles and Practices of Teaching in Secondary Schools,* Second Edition, chapter X and pp. 386–390. New York: American Book Company, 1947.

360 *Using Review and Practice*

Rivlin, Harry N. *Teaching Adolescents in Secondary Schools,* chapter X. New York: Appleton-Century-Crofts, Inc., 1948.

Schorling, Raleigh, *Student Teaching*, Second Edition, pp. 234–241. New York: McGraw-Hill Book Company, Inc., 1949.

The Psychology of Learning, chapter X. Forty-first Yearbook, Part II. National Society for the Study of Education. Chicago: University of Chicago Press, 1941.

Umstattd, J. G. *Secondary School Teaching*, Second Edition, pp. 280–284. Boston: Ginn and Company, 1944.

Wrinkle, William L. *The New High School in the Making,* chapter XIV. New York: American Book Company, 1938.

14

How Use Verbal Illustrations
in Teaching?

1. What Is the Nature of Verbal Illustration?

Meaning of illustration

Some of the recent writers on visual education and authors of treatises on method have tacitly, at least, given a very limited interpretation to the problem this subject involves. For many the alternative for pure abstraction in learning and teaching appears to be such concrete materials as the student may see, feel, and manipulate. If this implication were true it would be most unfortunate for education, since much of learning and teaching must and should necessarily remain on a non-visual basis. Most schools could not afford to provide a concrete basis for all ideational activity, even though it were possible or desirable.

The problem must be considered from the vantage point of a larger perspective. While a dictionary definition should not be accepted as final in a technical application to current usage, within specialized fields, it may shed some light on the basis of that technical use. "To make clear, intelligible, or apprehensible; to elucidate, explain, or exemplify, as by means of figures, comparisons, and examples" — "To make clear or intelligible by concrete examples; explain by comparison or examples," are quotations from the verb form of the subject of this chapter. They comprehend the total field of mental imagery, whether stimulated by word pictures or recourse to physical materials.

It is obvious from these definitions that visual materials supply but one form of aid to understanding. Any adequate treatment of the learning process and teaching technique must recognize two main forms of aid to the clarification of thought. Roughly, these may be classified as word symbolism and concrete materials. Anecdotes, stories, descriptions, word pictures that stimulate the imagination, or recall of incidents of student experience may serve to provide the mental imagery necessary to clarify an abstract idea or principle in learning. The older educators depended upon this form of illustration almost exclusively. In recent years concrete materials — visual aids — have received extensive consideration, and have led some writers in methods to ignore or treat very incidentally what possibly should be considered still the larger aspect of illustration.

Importance of illustration

The ability to think abstractly is one of the most difficult of human accomplishments. The philosopher is popularly supposed to have achieved, to a very marked degree, the power of sustained abstract thought. It no doubt accounts in part for the reason philosophy has never been a popular pastime of the masses. Books of a noticeably abstract character seldom achieve popular acclaim. The eminent English playwright, George Bernard Shaw, on a visit to America rather facetiously remarked during an interview that the reason he was famous, while others were not, lay in the simple fact that he did some thinking at least twice a week. Psychologists have been wont to assert that real thinking was done very infrequently by the average person. By that assertion they meant that few people engaged extensively in pure reason — abstract thinking unsupported by definite imagery.

Much of what is accepted in common parlance as thinking is closely associated with mental imagery. Most people find it exceedingly difficult to carry on ideational activity, apart from the crutch of vivid mental imagery, to give significance and color to the idea. Effective public speakers have long recognized the importance of clothing their thought in rich mental imagery if they expected to get ideas across to the listeners. It is a recognized art of public address carefully to select pertinent mental imagery to clarify ideas. The student of public speaking is thoroughly drilled in the importance of imagery, and the wise selection and use of vivid word pictures, incidents, or stories as a prerequisite of convincing address.

For the past quarter of a century professors of speech have never failed to direct the attention of youthful aspirants for platform power to the vivid imagery of the justly famous Cross of Gold speech of the late William Jennings Bryan, delivered at the Democratic National Convention in 1896. For thirty years following that famous political speech the Great Commoner had no peer on the American platform. The secret of the power that drew thousands of people to his addresses, as it were by a magnet, many of them traveling fifty to one hundred miles and sitting or standing in all kinds of weather to listen for two hours to that golden flow of words, can be found in part by a careful study of the Cross of Gold speech. It is replete with striking vivid imagery. The closing words of the address: "You shall not press down upon the brow of labor this crown of thorns; you shall not crucify mankind upon a cross of gold!" while no doubt the most vivid and telling imagery of the address, are characteristic of both that convention speech and the art of public address that made Bryan famous on the platform. It is equally true that the great ministers of pulpit fame have owed much of their power to the wealth and vividness of the mental imagery with which they clothed their thought. It must not be forgotten, however, that some of the world's greatest thinkers have not been facile in the use of illustration to give clarity to their thought. The reason most people respond to those who use imagery freely to give tangibility to their ideas is that they themselves do most of their thinking through such media.

Visual and mental imagery

In the evolution of human thought the tendency has been more and more in the direction of the abstraction of ideas from the framework of various forms of imagery. Primitive man found it difficult to think apart from definite imagery. He found it equally difficult to convey ideas abstractly. Pictographic writing — the conveyance of ideas to others by means of pictures — is the earliest beginning of modern writing of which man has record. A hunter of a primitive people observes a herd of wild game moving off on the horizon. He cannot describe in word language what he sees, or his plan of action. He must resort to a picture drawn on a piece of bark or a rock to transmit his ideas to members of the tribe who might pass that way. He tries to draw a picture that resembles the animal in question — a rough sketch of the landscape to point the direction where the herd was seen, and some pictorial representation of what he plans to do about it. The hieroglyphic writing of the Egyptians was a distinct advance upon the pictograph, because ideas began to be transmitted in part through symbols that did not in themselves give a clear visual reproduction of the imagery or idea the symbol tried to call forth. The Chinese character language is but a few stages removed from the earliest pictograph.

The early North American Indian provides a splendid example of the reliance upon visual and mental imagery to aid thought.[1] For example: "The Omaha Indians reckoned time by 'sleeps.' If an Omaha were asked how long a journey he had taken, he would say that it had taken so many 'sleeps.' A Kiowa Indian, if asked the same question, would say that it had taken so many 'darks.' . . . When, at length, a unit of time larger than a few days was needed, the time from new moon to new moon served very well. This measure of the time was the moon or month." After language of a highly abstract symbolical form had been invented it was possible to eliminate definite visual imagery through pictographs and gesticulations to convey ideas. Even then, among peoples of early times, we find "word pictures" used as a substitution. These continue to be used extensively today, even among those considered highly educated.

If, in the childhood of the race, excessive dependence was placed upon visual and mental imagery, it is to be expected that childhood and youth will lean heavily upon visual and mental imagery as the framework of ideas. Childhood, and to a lesser degree youth, lack the mastery of highly inflected language symbols for ideational thought and expression. Modern language symbols are highly complex, artificial, and extremely abstract. Further, experience adds a wealth of imagery that becomes the basis for the abstraction of ideas and concepts. It seems necessary to have this accumulation of data from experience to build up adequate ideas, as well as to correct erroneous ones. A child whose acquaintance with dogs is limited to the family pet, a black poodle, may acquire an entirely erroneous idea of dogs. If later he were to see a massive, light-brown St. Bernard, there would be a violent clash of imagery

---

[1] *The Story of Our Calendar*, pp. 4–5. Prepared under the auspices of the Committee on Materials of Instruction of the American Council of Education, Washington, American Council of Education, Achievement of Civilization, No. 4, 1933.

and the resultant concept of a dog would be vastly different from the one hitherto accepted.

While the value of training in abstract thinking is desirable and should form a larger part of adult experience, it is necessary to recognize that immature youth, by habit and by limitation of ability, has utilized imagery as the framework of thought and the accumulation of ideas. Indeed, it is imperative that education shall provide the child and youth with a wealth of imagery experience so that he may the better abstract the essential ideational elements for accurate thought procedures. Indeed, few adults find it satisfactory or feasible to do much abstract thinking. Psychologically, it is doubtful if man ever will.

Problem of verbalism in teaching

Quite unmindful of the evident need of rich imagery for adolescent learning, much of our teaching tends to rely on word symbols through which to express ideas. A brief study of high school textbooks of the past twenty-five years will reveal how abstruse they have been. The teacher who followed the trend of the textbook in his teaching method led the student to acquire a vocabulary of many words, but often without much understanding. Former United States Commissioner of Education Tigert never tired of telling an experience he had in a school in the Blue Ridge Mountains of North Carolina. While visiting a school nestled back in these mountains, he asked a number of questions of a bright girl about geography. She, parrot-like, described the mountain chains of North America, locating the Appalachian Mountains and describing them in some detail. Then Mr. Tigert asked if she had ever seen the Appalachian Mountains. With the perfect assurance of innocence she informed him that she never had. This astonishing declaration, when at that moment she stood in the very heart of them! In English composition we have too generally assumed that the mastery of definitions insured correct expression. Recently, an old school purist, interviewing candidates for a position on his high school staff, became very much agitated because some of the candidates could not give the rules for the use of predicate nominatives, among others, nor could they too readily recognize the rules that applied in certain examples submitted to them for analysis. The fact that the chief offender had had several years of very successful teaching experience, and had more than ordinary facility in language usage, mattered not at all.

The author remembers vividly a county teachers' institute where a round table discussion was in progress over the results of an objective examination given to seventh- and eighth-grade pupils throughout the county. One section of the examination, devoted to composition and grammar, contained two questions on the sentence that were illuminating in the responses pupils had given. Statement 1 read: "A sentence is a group of words expressing a complete thought." True-False. Statement 2: "This is a sentence: A bushel of apples." True-False. When the results of the examination tabulation for these questions were consulted, it was found that every pupil had checked correctly statement 1; but almost 50 per cent of these same pupils had declared statement 2 correct. The results were disillusioning, and very much of a shock to the English teachers present. It was a classic example of the way teachers in most subjects for a generation past have taught words to their classes with a naïve belief that parrot-like repetition of words and understanding were synonymous.

The crux of the difficulty has been the failure of both teachers and textbook writers consciously to recognize that language is but the symbol of ideas; and words are but the accepted combination of artificial figures called letters, to which arbitrary meaning has been assigned. A highly inflected language, such as most modern peoples employ, has none of the imagery inherently associated with Egyptian hieroglyphics or Chinese characters. Hence, the arbitrary meaning of words must be taught.[2] Our words sun, moon, mountains, have no pictorial interpretations but rely upon the arbitrary assignment of meanings, while these same words in

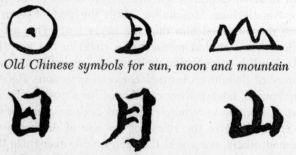

Old Chinese symbols for sun, moon and mountain

Chinese characters of sun, moon, and mountain

[2] See, for interesting discussion of this problem, *The Story of Writing*, Committee on Materials of Instruction of the American Council on Education, Achievements of Civilization, No. 1, Washington, D.C., 1932.

Chinese carry suggestive imagery in the character formations themselves, as may be seen from the illustrations on page 366, taken from *The Story of Writing,* which show the evolution of the character formations from the ancient Chinese pictographic language.

Language symbolic of ideas

Two subsidiary problems for student and teacher immediately come to the fore with a recognition of modern language as arbitrarily symbolic of ideas. The first concerns the relation of adequate apperceptive background to the correct ideational content of word symbols. If arbitrary meanings must be given words, then the nature of the experience one brings to a word must determine for him its ideational symbolism. A teacher of long experience had a son nearing graduation from the university. Suddenly one day she discovered, through a chance remark, that through the years they had used the same words for colors with totally different ideational content. He was color-blind. It has frequently been said that many a bitter argument would have been avoided had the parties concerned first assured themselves that words had the same meaning for both. The way differences of apperceptive approach to the symbolism of words may bring to naught the best efforts of the teacher, unless carefully watched, is recounted by Professor C. H. Ward.[3] He vouches for the authenticity of this incident that occurred in a class which was beginning the study of Scott's *The Lady of the Lake.*

The class had wrestled with that harp that moldering long had hung and was trying to visualize the scene in the opening stanzas. Scott took pains to make a picture full of vivid details, so that a reader might start with a definite impression of the setting. You may recall some of the lines:

> The stag at eve had drunk his fill
> Where danced the moon on Monan's rill;
> And deep his midnight lair had made
> In lone Glenartney's hazel shade.
>
> .   .   .   .
>
> Tossed his beamed frontlet to the sky.
>
> .   .   .   .
>
> A moment sniffed the tainted gale
>
> .   .   .   .
>
> With one brave bound the copse he cleared.

[3] Ward, C. H. *What is English?*, pp. 444–445. Chicago: Scott, Foresman and Company, 1925.

The teacher detected something peculiar in an answer to a very commonplace question about this setting of the poem. Fortunately for him and for that portion of the world that likes a funny story, his mind was not keyed to "an affection that springs from delight," but was curious to find out what mental picture was in the mind of this boy who answered so oddly. He directed his probe with a genius that will always excite my admiration and that should inspire the rest of us to emulation. He inquired, "What is a stag?" Remember, else you will lose the point of this section, that the boy's answer was not taken from *Judge* or *Life*, but was given in an actual classroom. He replied, "Why-uh, a stag is — is when a fellow hasn't got any girl." (Laughter.)

You laugh at the "limited vocabulary." Stop laughing and think of what a certain notable passage of literature had meant to that boy. It was this sort of stag who had "drunk his fill" — not improbably he had been drinking at Monan's Grill. It was this sort of stag who made a "lair" at midnight. What the beacon red was, or the warder call, or the beamed frontlet, will never be known, but we can guess at "the tainted gale" — it was natural for a stag who had been at Monan's until midnight. We know about the copse. The boy had pictured this kind of stag, after this kind of night, as having the vitality to leap over several cops.

It is of the utmost importance that the apperceptive basis for the pointing of word meaning be assured, or provided in its absence, by the teacher. It is often disastrous to assume the commonality of the word meaning that does not exist between teacher and different members of the class.

Closely akin to the difficulty suggested in the incident above is another that does not result mainly from provincial usage, but principally from the accepted differences in word meanings. For example, the word "run" has totally different meanings and calls forth varied mental imagery, dependent upon the context in which it is used; for example: The lady has a run in her stocking; the boy runs a race; the motor runs smoothly; there was a run on the bank; he runs a saw mill; the conversation runs on interminably; the engineer's run is a long one; the store runs an ad in the paper; a beautiful love theme runs through the story, etc. Or again, the use of the word "fire" may carry totally different meanings, as a few examples will illustrate: The fire is hot; I saw him fire the shot; he must fire several employees. The teacher can add almost indefinitely to the varied meanings these words and scores of others have in accepted usage.

Dale, in a study of the Thorndike Word List,[4] makes this pertinent observation on the frequency of homographs in current usage: "The number of homographs, unfortunately, is far greater in the words of high frequency than in the words of low frequency." The word "run," cited above as an example, appears in the first five hundred most frequently used words. It is necessary, therefore, to insure wide acquaintance on the part of the student with the many possible interpretations a word may have. Not to know the possible meanings of a word under the varied circumstances of usage is to condemn the student to miss many ideas others may wish to convey. Worse still, he may even seriously misinterpret the expressed intent of others. An added difficulty of language symbolism at once becomes evident. Where words legitimately carry so many and such divergent meanings, it is essential to the teacher to assure himself that the proper mental imagery appropriate to the situation is called up with the use of a word. The danger of false concepts as a result of teaching abstractly is thus all the more apparent.

2. How Can Word Symbolism Be Used Effectively?

Purpose of non-visual illustration

No one can doubt the importance of non-visual illustration in teaching. No one can question the problems incident to the use of a highly inflected language so abstract that mental imagery must result from an artificially assigned significance meaning given to a word. At least two major considerations confront the teacher who would use word symbolism effectively; namely, purpose and correct usage. Correct usage, however, is dependent upon a full understanding of what are the specific purposes served by non-visual illustrations. While those given below apply in general to visual as well as to non-visual illustrations, there are purposes served by word symbolism not aided by the imagery awakened through the use of visual illustration.

1. *To attract attention.* Good teachers know the value of a striking incident, a gripping story, or a humorous anecdote to bring to attention a class growing listless through too continuous an effort to do abstract thinking unrelieved by much mental imagery. The teacher who has a repertoire of good illustrations at hand usually maintains full class attention.

---

[4] Dale, Edgar. *Evaluating Thorndike's Word List*, p. 454. Educational Research Bulletin, Ohio State University, vol. 10, No. 17 (November 25, 1931).

2. *To facilitate reasoning and understanding.* The most cogent reason for the use of illustrations is to aid understanding. Oftentimes an incident, a story, or an explanation through comparison of the elements of similarity of the problem in hand with another the student knows, will lead the students to a flash of understanding. So many aspects of normal experience have elements of commonality with new problems being attacked, that to awaken a mental imagery of these elements of similarity enables a baffled student to see the relationship and then to abstract the idea or ideas involved. For example, a student in physics is having some trouble understanding the application of principles in the fulcrum. A recall of the vivid imagery associated with childhood experiences in balancing teeter-totters may illuminate a most difficult problem that purely abstract mental activity had not solved. The value of a homely story to provide a mental imagery that strikingly portrays relationships is well known but too seldom used in the classroom. Abraham Lincoln was a master of the use of the story to arouse imagery directly applicable to an obtuse point that made the logical answer to the problem obvious. Teachers too often have acted as though they felt such a procedure to aid understanding beneath the dignity of the classroom. So thought the colleagues and political associates of Lincoln; yet he managed, through the story and anecdote, to aid others to get at the essence of a troublesome problem where the proponents of a high plan of abstract thinking often failed. Most people can think better if they tie their thinking to some definite mental imagery — the recall of incidents, stories, comparisons of things experienced, or events observed — that contains significant elements applicable to the problem at hand. Many require this mental imagery as the vehicle of thought through which they abstract ideas and carry on creative thought.

3. *To vivify realization or experience.* A student may know a fact, an axiom or principle, or some conclusion, but it has not impressed him much. It is therefore likely to have been forgotten quickly. Or, while he may know that something is very important, he has not sensed its true importance. A well-chosen incident or story may make its significance so vivid that it will not soon be forgotten, or the student will recognize how valuable this experience or fact may be for the solution of future problems or interpretations of subsequent experiences. A high school teacher of biology, while discussing an important phase of metabolism, re-

marked to the class that in a recent examination given a class in biology in the university, the same question he had asked them the day before was asked in this university class. The teacher asked his class why they thought such a question should be repeated in an advanced university class in biology. The incident was deftly used to make vivid to the class the importance of facts just learned for any advance study in this field.

4. *To stimulate the imagination and provide incentive for action.* The propagandist knows full well the power of word picture, story, and incident to fire the imagination, arouse the emotions, and incite to action. It may be the quack or high-pressure advertisement with its lurid word picture of miraculous cure-alls for ailing folk, or the marvelous short cuts to power or riches grippingly depicted, that robs the ailing of millions each year and accounts for the responsible estimates of over twenty-five millions annually pouring into the coffers of the gold-brick artists. The demagogue knows the power of word pictures to excite the mob to a state of frenzy, as exemplified in the recrudescence of the K.K.K. movement following World War I. The vivid imagery of word picture stimulating the imagination can be used as well to lift individuals or groups into realms of sublime ecstasy and resolution to worth-while action. Unfortunately, in our emphasis upon cool, rational mental processes as the *sine qua non* of ideal academic procedure, we have seriously cramped the larger possibilities of intellectual development of the adolescent through the failure of adequate stimulation of the imagination and the will to intellectual activity. We have also sadly neglected the third function of adolescent education laid down in the opening chapter of this book, namely, the education of the affective nature of youth. No more powerful instrumentality lies at hand to the teacher for the development of attitudes and ideals than the use of the vivid imagery of word symbolism to stimulate the imagination and, through it, the affective life of the individual.

How to use non-visual illustrations

To make the use of the illustration most effective, certain prerequisites must be observed. The standards suggested do not apply with equal force in every situation. Obviously, the purpose of the illustration must condition certain factors in its usage.

1. *Use illustrations common to student experience.* The real test of the wide-awake teacher lies in his ability to apply illustrations

from student experience. It is easy to assume identity of student background with that of the teacher. If examples from everyday practice are used, care must be exercised that the examples are from the practices of the community where used. Some years ago the author spoke to a group of young people in Chicago. To illustrate his points, frequent reference was made to farming practices with which he was familiar in the Middle West. It was a matter of embarrassment and chagrin, after what the speaker had considered an effective address, to have young people come at the close of the session to inquire the meaning of certain references. It was evident some important ideas at least had not been clarified by the illustrations used. A professor of English recently complained that most of the Biblical allusions of the old classical writers were lost upon the majority of the present generation of college students. The heterogeneity of social and educational background of present high school students makes the use of illustrations common to the experience of the class exceedingly difficult.

2. *Use simple illustrations the meaning of which is obvious.* The illustration may be within the range of student experience, but so complex or involved as to render its meaning difficult to grasp. Long, cumbersome stories, incidents encrusted in much detail, or subtle allusions are likely to miss the mark, except for a few of the brighter students. Subtle allusions, particularly, are undesirable in most classroom situations. The problem of understanding is not likely to be troublesome with the brighter section of the class, and the true value of the illustration lies in its effectiveness for the comprehension of the slower, weaker members.

3. *Use illustration that actually illumines the idea.* There is nothing so pointless as an illustration that does not illustrate. The least of its evils is the waste of time. Bewilderment, misinterpretation, disgust — one or all may result. A story, incident, allusion, or comparison should have one central idea that applies to the situation. Often one thinks he has a good illustration when a little analysis reveals the application as most superficial, and reflection on the part of the student is likely to lead to erroneous deductions.

4. *Use illustration that does not permit the framework to detract from the idea it clothes.* Unusual language should be avoided since it attracts attention to itself and consequently the essential idea is lost. For example, the dialect in which an idea is clothed may become focal in attention, as the imitation of the peculiar racial char-

acteristics — Irish, Negro, etc. Striking, excessively vivid word pictures are subject to this misdirection of attention, as are descriptions that warp the resultant imagery out of normal proportions. If, to give some idea of the depth of the ocean, one were to suggest that all the houses in a named village, placed one on top of each other, would not reach to the bottom of the ocean, the chances are the students' attention would be focused upon the contemplated picture of house piled upon house and miss the appreciation of depth. Again, the student might become greatly troubled to understand how you knew the combined height of the houses in question.

5. *Use illustrations approximately accurate.* The accuracy of elements in the illustration should be accepted without question. A teacher was describing a certain geographical spot of interest in a foreign country which she had not visited. For all practical purposes the description served its purpose, but one student, who had visited this place, immediately called attention to a minor inaccuracy in the description. For that student, and probably for most of the class, the purpose of the reference was lost in the focusing of attention on an inconsequential inaccuracy of description.

6. *Use sufficient illustrations to insure abstraction of essential idea.* One writer warns against too many illustrations; another insists that danger lies in the use of too few. Judged in the light of extended observation, the danger would seem to lie in under- rather than over-use. The besetting sin of the inexperienced teacher is the impatience to cover ground. What is obvious to the modern teacher, with a major or minor preparation in the fields taught, is not obvious to the immature high school beginner in the subject. The patient, careful guidance of the student, with many illustrations where needed to illumine trouble spots in his development of thought, is the teaching situation to be devoutly sought. Very few have been observed to have achieved it. Most teachers teach in an environment of excessive abstraction. Progress in learning is not to be considered synonymous with the coverage of pages in the textbook, nor the absence of illustrative aid given. The extent to which illustrative aid should be given must remain a matter of discretion on the part of the teacher. Whether the student is dull or bright, the class a fast- or slow-section group, the relative difficulty of the subject, whether predominantly thought or memory in nature, are factors the teacher must keep in mind.

7. *Use illustrations at times vivid and realistic.* Vivid and realis-

tic imagery should be evoked with care. None the less, for purposes of attracting attention, to impress an important point in memory, or to arouse such emotional response as to lead to activity or the formation of attitudes, this form of illustration is most valuable. Who will soon forget the vivid picture of the chariot race in *Ben Hur?* A score of years have passed since it was read, but vivid mental imagery still remains. Similarly, indelibly stamped on memory is one tense scene in Cooper's *The Red Rover,* where the pirate ship, unknown to the crew of the fleeing vessel, and incidentally also to the reader, has fastened a cable to the ship in flight so that, in spite of desperate efforts to elude the pursuer, no appreciable gain can be observed in the attempted escape. Of this graphic scene it is said that the great Dana agitatedly paced the floor as he read it. Every teacher can recall word pictures that have left behind vivid mental imagery; some pleasant to recall, others unpleasant; some that have produced lasting values in attitudes established, while others would be better forgotten, if it were possible. A keen-edged scalpel is a dangerous weapon in irresponsible or unskilled hands; a benefaction to mankind in the hands of a skilled surgeon motivated to helpfulness. The competent, socially minded teacher can make telling use of vivid imagery.

8. *Use illustrations for the most part prepared in advance.* The same reasons for using questions which have been carefully thought out in advance, discussed in the previous chapter, apply with even greater force to word symbolism. Illustrations are more complex and subtle. All too frequently they do not illustrate because the mental imagery aroused does not coincide with the idea it is expected to clarify. Careful scrutiny of the word pictures to be employed at crucial points in the lesson will greatly insure their applicability. As in the use of the question, many illustrations will necessarily be required where unexpected. If careful preparation has been made against possible contingencies, the chances that inappropriate mental imagery will be aroused are reduced to a minimum.

9. *Illustrations should be varied.* A constant diet of stories soon palls, no matter how appropriate. The possibilities in story, incident, anecdote, description, comparison, etc., offer almost unlimited opportunity for variety. Individual differences in the mental reactions of students will best be served by a wide range of illustrative forms.

10. *Use sparingly illustrations of personal-experience type.* It is natural that one's personal experience should be most vivid and replete in mental imagery. It is most natural that recall should bring to the fore appropriate experiences to fit a given situation. Frequently, if used judiciously, it is a most valuable form to use. The danger lies in the impression of egotism that may be left as an unwholesome aftereffect. No hard and fast rule can be laid down. The effectiveness of personal experience as the source for illustrative data differs with different teacher personalities. The safest rule to follow is to use sparingly personal reference for illustrative purposes. When it is used, avoid as far as possible the first personal pronoun.

QUESTIONS AND PROBLEMS

1. Define the word illustration as it is technically used in education.
2. What are the two main forms of aid used for the clarification of thought?
3. List as many means as possible by which abstract ideas and principles may be clarified in teaching.
4. Why is word imagery so effective in transmitting ideas?
5. Notice how much imagery your minister uses in his sermons. Why does he use it so much?
6. What is abstract thinking and how do we achieve the ability to do abstract thinking?
7. What is the most important relation that must exist between the teacher's word symbolism and the student's background of experience?
8. Name the primary educational values that visual illustration may provide which pure word symbolism does not have for the adolescent.
9. List and discuss the importance of the characteristics of good non-visual illustrations.
10. What preparation should the teacher make for the use of non-visual illustrations?
11. What are the senses we rely on largely for the transfer of ideas, and what are their limitations in educational work?
12. From your own experience as a student, give concise reasons why particular illustrations were most valuable to you.

SELECTED BIBLIOGRAPHY

Billett, Roy O. *Fundamentals of Secondary School Teaching*, pp. 141–148. Boston: Houghton Mifflin Company, 1940.

Burton, William. *The Guidance of the Learning Activities,* pp. 42–49, 67–69, 89–94. New York: Appleton-Century-Crofts, Inc., 1944.

Gates, A. I., et al. *Educational Psychology,* Third Edition, chapters VI, XIII. New York: The Macmillan Company, 1948.

Hayakawa, S, I. *Language in Action.* New York: Harcourt, Brace and Company, 1941.

Horn, E. "Language and Meaning," chapter XI, in *The Psychology of Learning,* Forty-first Yearbook, Part II. The National Society for the Study of Education. Chicago: University of Chicago Press, 1942.

Jones, H. E. and Conrad, H. S. "Mental Development in Adolescence," chapter VIII, in *Adolescence,* Forty-third Yearbook, Part I. The National Society for the Study of Education. Chicago: University of Chicago Press, 1944.

Kingsley, Howard L. *The Nature and Conditions of Learning,* chapter XIV. New York: Prentice-Hall, Inc., 1946.

Rivlin, Harry N. *Teaching Adolescents in Secondary Schools,* pp. 261–263. New York: Appleton-Century-Crofts, Inc., 1948.

Shoemaker, F. "Communication through Symbols in Literature." *English Journal* 37:235–240 (May 1948).

The Story of Our Calender, Achievements of Civilization, No. 4. Washington, D.C.: American Council of Education, 1933.

The Story of Writing, Achievements of Civilization, No. 1. Washington, D.C.: American Council on Education, 1932.

15

How Use Effectively the Concrete Illustration in Teaching?

1. What Is the Nature of the Concrete Illustration?

Need for concrete materials as illustrative devices

Recently an educator remarked that it was somewhat embarrassing for one in his position to be the father of an adolescent boy of superior ability, who was, however, so auditory-minded he could not pass a good written examination at school. Yet this boy was thoroughly informed, and if subjected to an oral examination over his general knowledge could acquit himself with honor.

While it has long been recognized that we learn through the traditional five senses, with the resultant imagery visual, auditory, tactile, etc., the school has restricted itself largely to the auditory and the visual. As pointed out in the previous chapter, abstract word symbols rather than concrete aids to learning have been most extensively used by the teacher.

Psychologists have long recognized that some people are able to think abstractly, while others are more dependent upon concrete materials as aids to thought. It has been generally recognized that the more brilliant the individual, the greater his power of abstract thought; and conversely, the lower the mentality, the greater the dependence upon visual imagery as a vehicle of thought. This is not always true, however. Some very capable individuals seem to react more effectively in the environment of visual imagery.

There is practical agreement, however, that many of the normal experiences one has are associated with visual imagery. We can dismiss, for what it is worth, the exaggerated claims of the protagonists of visual education that 90 per cent of all sensory impression is visual, and still grant the obvious fact that a significant part of experience results from visual imagery. If so, a sound basis is laid for the demand that secondary education give a much larger place to visual aids than heretofore.

One may build up very erroneous mental imagery when dependent upon word symbolism for his ideas of a definite place or thing. In spite of an elaborate word picture of a modern telephone transmitter, if a youth had never seen one, he might easily fail to recognize it when casually brought into its presence. The mental imagery set up as a result of description might bear but little resemblance to the visual imagery the thing itself produced.

The author will not soon forget the shock that resulted from his visit to the famous Gettysburg battlegrounds. From the descriptions of the battles contained in the American histories studied in the secondary school, a very definite mental picture had resulted of the terrain and of Pickett's charge across the valley and up the slopes, to be turned back at the crest of the mountain time after time in what proved to be the "high water mark" of the rebellion. When the party reached this particular spot, the guide said, "Here is where Pickett made his famous charge, leading his troops from that road you see about a quarter of a mile distant. Here is the monument that marks the farthest point Pickett's men were able to penetrate the Union lines." The author stood in blank astonishment at the picture as it was. Instead of a long, steep, mountainside at an angle of at least 45°, the party looked out over a relatively flat terrain with but a suggestion of a knoll, that gradually rose, so it seemed under the shock of disillusionment, not over twenty or twenty-five feet above the level of the road from which the charge began. The difficulty here clearly arose from the different imagery aroused by words. No doubt the word "slope," if actually used by the historian, whose description led to the grossly exaggerated imagery of a mountain, did not have the same connotation for the reader as it did for the historian.

When one describes to another a beautiful flower, its shape, color, size, etc., the resultant imagery will be vastly different from the imagery obtained from seeing the flower with one's own eyes. It may be described as red— but what shade of red? It may be said to be round — but the term is used so loosely that the quality or degree of roundness is still subject to vastly different imagery depending upon the experience of the listener. It was this impossibility of transferring to the mind of another identical imagery through word symbols that caused Rousseau to voice this dictum: "In general, never substitute a sign for the thing itself." Kinder has suggested the sources of learning might be listed in the following descending order of their effectiveness: [1]

1. Things one experiences directly.
2. Seeing something through media of pictures, films, or models.
3. Hearing about it from someone who has experienced it at first hand.
4. Reading about it — least effective.

Types of visual materials

The number of visual materials available to the teacher is already large, and growing in both number and refinement. No classification of these materials could be made that would not be subject to some adjustments as the teacher considers their uses. Broadly, these materials can be classified into two categories considered from the standpoint of usage — those available in the confines of the classroom or at least within the school, and those by nature separated from the school building and classroom.

I. *Classroom visual aids.*
1. Pictures — photographs, art pictures, lantern slides, film slides, motion pictures, television, stereopticons, opaque projectors.
2. Semi-pictorial devices — maps, charts, diagrams, graphs, blackboards, bulletin boards or display boards.
3. Objects — globes, models, specimens, small aquariums, science laboratory equipment.
4. Demonstration — dramatization and laboratory demonstration.
II. *Field and excursion visual aids.* Nature-study trips to field and park, factory and commercial establishments, museums, governmental and civic institutions, places of scenic and historic interest.

Principles governing selection of concrete materials

Unless the teacher uses wisdom in the selection of concrete materials, excessive waste of pupil-teacher energy will result and the

[1] Kinder, James S. *Audio-Visual Materials and Techniques,* p. 51. New York: American Book Company, 1950.

school will become involved in unnecessary costs for questionable materials. A few standards set up to guide in the selection of visual aids, if faithfully adhered to, will help the teacher avoid many pitfalls in their use.

1. *Need for visual aid.* Not all types of learning could profit by concrete aids. Visual aids for memorized learning would be of doubtful assistance. Simple types of learning may not justify the effort which the selection of such aids would entail. It is well to determine first that a real need exists in the learning situation itself before visual aids are employed.

2. *Cost of materials.* The cost of materials is a variable factor in the selection of visual aids. It depends upon a number of contingencies other than the absolute value of the article itself. The general value of a motion-picture machine may be granted at once and its desirability acknowledged, yet it may be that the limited budget of the school would mean the denial to the school of every other form of concrete material for the year. On the other hand, in a school whose budget amply provided for large outlays for material devices, the cost probably would be considered nominal in consideration of the added values the machine would bring to the teaching effectiveness of the school.

3. *Availability of materials.* The stage of the auditorium may be desired for the dramatization of some special work in the literature class. It is not essential to the understanding of the drama under consideration, but it would enliven interest in it and bring out more clearly elements for appreciation. However, the stage is all set for a senior-class play and would require considerable adjustment to make it available for the other activity. For all practical purposes the auditorium is not readily available. Again, the class is studying civil institutions and would profit considerably from a visit to a juvenile court. The nearest one, a good one, is in a city some thirty miles distant. The question the teacher must consider is whether the importance of the experience, adjustment of schedules to make a Saturday visit feasible, etc., make this juvenile court available or not.

4. *Economy of time in use of visual aids.* Sometimes a device may have value, but to use it means to sacrifice other important elements of the subject. When these alternatives arise, it would seem that visual aid must justify its use beyond question or be rejected as wasteful of time.

5. *Effectiveness of visual materials.*[2] Another criterion that needs critical application is the real value of the visual material as an educational device. Not all so-called visual aids actually aid learning. Experimental evidence, for instance, seems to show beyond doubt that still life is not effectively portrayed by motion pictures. The wise teacher will study types of visual materials in the light of available experimental data and personal observations before adopting them for teaching purposes. A weakness in some forms of materials is that the novelty of the material devices so detracts from their functional significance that the effectiveness is lost or greatly impaired.

6. *Adaptability of materials.* "Can the materials used in this situation be used in others?" is an important question to consider in the selection of visual aids. The purchase of an article that can be used to illustrate a number of ideas in the coures of the year is obviously of more worth than one half as costly which can be used to illustrate but one thing in the course. A physics teacher reported that the most valuable piece of equipment to be had was an old mechanical cream separator, since it could be used to illustrate so many principles of mechanics.

7. *Permanence of materials.* Materials that do not outlive their initial cost may be considered a questionable acquisition. Visual aids of flimsy materials easily perishable should be scrutinized carefully as to their worth before being purchased. In the long run, materials that cost slightly more, but have wearing qualities, are cheaper in the end. On the other hand, to spend hours drawing elaborate designs on the blackboard that are usable but for a day or two, may represent a waste of time. The purchase of a few visual materials with provision for their careful preservation may mean, in reality, a large variety of materials to work with over a period of time.

2. What Are the Techniques of Visual Instruction?

General suggestions for the use of visual aids [3]

While specific comments need to be offered in the case of many

---

[2] At this point the reader should consult sources on the evidence of the effectiveness of these materials, such as may be found in "Research on Audio-Visual Materials," chapter XII, *Audio-Visual Materials of Instruction*, Part I, Forty-Eighth Yearbook, The National Society for the Study of Education. Chicago: University of Chicago Press, 1949.

[3] The student will find helpful suggestions in the more extensive treatment

of the visual materials suggested for use, there are general observations that should be offered the teacher to guide his use of all concrete materials.

1. *The routine for the use of visual aids should be well planned.* If the doctrine of generalized transfer of training has any merit, this idea should be literally seared into the consciousness of the teacher or aspiring teacher who has studied this book thus far. Routine is so important to the success of the teacher and the student that it bears repetition. The teacher needs to have all visual aids properly classified and ready for instant use. Where mechanisms are involved, these should be carefully checked to insure that they are in perfect working order before use. When a number of materials are to be used, they should be arranged in order so that each will be used in proper turn. If reseating of the class is desired, this should be planned. No detail that would detract from the effective use of the visual aids should be overlooked.

2. *Students should receive preparation before exposure to visual materials.* The extent to which the student is cautioned about the particular things for which he should be on the lookout will depend upon the extent and complexity of the materials used. A few pictures, a model, or a graph may need but a suggestion or two, while a film may require considerable detail in advance. If there are novel aspects to the material in question, these should be incidentally mentioned so that the keen edge of attention may quickly pass to the essentials for which the material is presented. Some teachers follow the technique of alluding to these singular features, pausing for curiosity to satisfy itself when the device is shown, and then proceeding to the heart of the issue. Often students lose the significance of the visual illustration because they have not been warned concerning the things to look for. Lectures, reports, and assigned readings may be used singly or together in this preparation.

3. *Visual aids should serve some vital purpose well established in advance.* The temptation to use visual aids in a vague assurance that they will be helpful too often accomplishes nothing but a waste of time. The teacher should see clearly a real need for visual as-

of this topic in McKown, Harry C. and Roberts, Alvin B. *Audio-Visual Aids to Instruction,* Second Edition, chapter III. New York: McGraw-Hill Book Company, Inc., 1949; and Kinder, James S. *Audio-Visual Materials and Techniques,* chapter IV. New York: American Book Company, 1950.

sistance, and then select a concrete device that will actually assist the student to overcome his difficulty.

4. *The teacher should be sure visual aids are what he has assumed them to be.* It is disconcerting, to say the least, to find out too late that the materials used did not fit the need. This, of course, is more likely to happen in the case of films, slides, etc., secured through advertisements but not carefully reviewed before use.

5. *The teacher should use visual aids judiciously.* "Too many cooks spoil the broth" may have its application here. Too many materials used may confuse rather than enlighten. While it was suggested that verbal symbolism was not likely to be overdone, there is danger that concrete materials may be used too profusely. However, a word of warning needs to be offered. If, for example, only one model is to be used, the teacher should take care that the idea is correctly abstracted. To confront a student with a rectangular form such as this, and not to make clear to him its essential

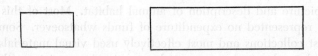

characteristics so that if he saw the figure he would instantly recognize the essential likeness, would be to misuse the visual aid. Rather, it would be better to use several models in such a situation. It is better to risk over-use than under-use in clarifying an idea. The greatest danger lies in a profuse use of concrete materials in and out of season without due regard to actual needs.

6. *The teacher should require student reaction to visual materials.* Learning is a matter of active response to a situation. What "I attend to" arouses mental activity. There is danger that students will comfortably "settle back" during a motion picture or the showing of a set of prints, without the stimulation of mental activity. If the student knows he is to be accountable in some form for what he has seen, he is not likely to accept passively the presence of visual materials.

7. *The teacher should be sure visual materials are visible to all the class.* A very real danger in the use of many forms of concrete materials is that they are not made sufficiently visible to all students to be of value. Teachers who use models, graphs, and pictures are likely to err in this respect. A small model on the teacher's desk

is not clearly visible to students in the rear of the room. Pictures and graphs held up before a class are likely to be distinguishable only to those near the teacher.

8. *Varied types of visual aids should be used.* As in other aspects of teaching, variety reduces monotony to a minimum, and here the teacher has unlimited opportunity for choice. Fortunately, for many forms very little money is necessary. The wealth of illustrative materials that may be had for the asking, such as pictures taken from home magazines by students, or the collection at the school of certain magazines from families who do not care to preserve copies after reading, may prove a revelation to the teacher. Not long ago the author visited the room of an experienced junior high school teacher during an "activity" period. The subject under consideration was "Animals and Their Habits." The visitor marveled when the teacher stepped to her supply closet and brought out dozens of *National Geographic Magazines* with page after page of lithographed colored animal pictures, scientifically accurate both as to picture and description of animal habitat. Most of this collection represented no expenditure of funds whatsoever. Some of the best collections and most effectively used visual materials the author has observed represented an extensive variety gathered together by resourceful teachers at little cost.[4]

Consideration of specific types of visual aids

Quite a variety of types of visual aids are available for school use, the more important of which are:

1. PICTURES

A. *Flat pictures.* In this category are included photographs and prints of all kinds. These are the most numerous and readily accessible to the teacher because many are available without financial outlay and those that must be purchased are for the most part procurable at nominal price. Photography has become so universal an art that good pictures are obtainable for almost any purpose. They are accessible through textbooks, books on special subjects such

[4] For sources of materials free and purchasable, see McKown, Harry C. and Roberts, Alvin B. *Audio-Visual Aids to Instruction*, Second Edition, chapter XXI. New York: McGraw-Hill Book Company, Inc., 1949. This chapter is given over entirely to a classified listing of available materials.

as nature, architecture, art, geography, etc.; magazines devoted to special subjects profusely and accurately illustrated, as the *National Geographic Magazine, Nature Magazine,* and *Popular Mechanics;* magazines of a popular nature more and more given over to pictures of high quality; advertising circulars of travel and commodities; newspapers, advertisements and pictorial sections of Sunday editions; and inexpensive post cards and picture prints.

Pictures have a distinct advantage as visual aids inasmuch as they may be easily secured to meet almost any topic of classroom interest, are easily handled, and can be compactly filed and stored. If special cabinets are not available, cheap manila folders may be used for the purpose. Also, students can be encouraged to collect very significant pictures from newspapers and magazines to visualize graphically phases of social development, custom, mechanical invention, etc. One alert student in social science brought together prints and clippings from newspapers and magazines, and so organized them in a notebook that modes of travel for almost every stage of development since the beginning of the Christian Era were made vivid to the class.

Certain cautions need to be observed in the use of pictures. All pictures should be carefully checked for accuracy. Created pictures are very likely to prove faulty in this respect. Veronese's "Marriage at Cana" may be taken as a case in point. Here a sixteenth-century painter garbs his subjects of a first-century period in the styles of his contemporaries. Even photographs can be guilty of distortions, portraying the unusual rather than the commonplace. To show actual pictures taken under ideal circumstances, and tacitly representing these as typical of conditions in the situation depicted, is a familiar practice of unscrupulous groups, sometimes even well-meaning public-spirited community groups not escaping this pitfall. Incorrectly labeled pictures give misleading information and impressions. Sensitive Oregonians, for example, are frequently exercised to maintain such beauty spots as Multnomah Falls and Crater Lake among their justly prized possessions.

Again, pictures should be large enough and sufficiently clear-cut to bring out detail. Another consideration of detail that needs to be watched is that the picture contain familiar items as standards of comparison with items that are new to the experience of the observer. A picture that endeavors to present some idea of the size of an African pigmy should contain some object of whose size the observer has a definite mental imagery built up as a criterion by which to measure the pigmy's size. A normal-sized man by his side is most desirable as it provides similar elements for comparison. A picture of a pigmy standing alone without any familiar objects near for mental comparison can give the student only the remotest idea of his actual size.

B. *Projection pictures.* In this group are considered slides, film slides, stereographs, and moving pictures. Frequent objection is raised to the picture as a visual aid because it is so small that members of the class have unequal advantage when the teacher holds it up for class inspection. Passing the picture distracts attention, and by the time it is viewed individually by the class the point for which it was used may be forgotten or the class may be wrestling with another problem.

1. *Slides.* The refinement of the stereopticon and any similar projection apparatus makes them readily acceptable for ordinary classroom use. Some relatively inexpensive projectors, capable of reflecting pictures from books and prints of ordinary size, are now on the market. Since a darkened classroom is no longer necessary for projection, these projectors become a ready help to the teacher. Some projectors use only slides. Large school systems have built up extensive collections of slides on various subjects and have carefully catalogued them for ready reference. Similar collections are to be found in most of our large universities and colleges today and in some State Departments of Education, so that smaller schools can secure for a nominal rental fee slides in carefully sorted collections. Projectors are often available as well. In large cities, art institutes and museums of natural science generally stand ready to co-operate with the schools in the use of their lantern slides.

2. *Film slides.* Glass slides are cumbersome, easily broken, and expensive. The film slide overcomes some of these difficulties. Pictures are printed on regular motion-picture film, generally of noninflammable material. Each roll, in small spool or capsule form, may contain any number of pictures that the subject featured may require. A film strip of one hundred pictures will occupy but a few feet of film. They are compact, durable, and easily handled. The cost of these film slides ranges from approximately five to twenty-five cents per picture, depending upon whether the film is standard size or the smaller size especially adapted to school usage, and upon the number of slides per roll, the quality of coloring, etc.

Another advantage of the film slide is the relatively inexpensive, simply operated, special projection apparatus available for these slides. Or, if the school already has a projector for glass slides, a small attachment is available to fit certain types of projectors which permits the additional use of film slides with little trouble or cost.

A disadvantage of the film slide is that the teacher may not want to use all slides on a given film, and the particular picture desired may not be readily located in a film roll. Neither is it easy to classify these slides, since they may not be filed separately as in the case of individual glass slides.

3. *Stereograph.* Another very real objection to the flat picture, film or slide, is that it does not give the impression of depth or third dimension. This difficulty is mitigated considerably for the high school student through his years of experience gauging such pictures. The stereograph, two pictures of the same object taken simultaneously by a double camera, gives most of the values of the flat picture plus third dimension. The handicap of this type of projection is that only one student can look at the picture at a time, since a binocular instrument, called a stereoscope, must be used. Experience with the stereograph has led most teachers to consider it unsuited for class use. It can best be used by students working on individual problems or as a reference source.

4. *Motion pictures.* The moving picture is the "greatest achievement" in picture projection. Much of human activity is physical motion. If visual aids are to stimulate equivalent mental imagery, they must faithfully reproduce the impression of motion. More than that, motion pictures may combine some of the advantages of still pictures with action in rapid sequence to give the student a sense of narrative or story. Much of history can be dramatized before the eyes of the student through the "movie." Since motion pictures have been perfected to so slow down the movements of the action observed that the minutest detail of movement may be carefully scrutinized, it has become invaluable as an aid to learning. Students of typing, for example, may watch the correct finger touch, etc., of an expert typist, and have accurately visualized for them the mental imagery the teacher has struggled ineffectually to obtain by verbal means. Physical education has given a large place to the motion picture, both to analyze the exact movements, successful and unsuccessful, of athletes as a basis for a correct teaching methodology, and also to visualize for the student correct proce-

dures. Experimental and research studies [5] seem to show beyond question the value of motion pictures in depicting movement and making vivid narratives of history, travel, etc. Normal experience with the community motion-picture theater leaves little doubt of the effectiveness of the "movie" as a purveyor of ideas, wholesome or otherwise, and of its interest appeal to youth and adult alike.[6]

In recent years rapid progress has been made in perfecting motion-picture apparatus serviceable for schools. The development of portable sound tracks has made possible the combination of sight and sound in the same experience. This has added immeasurably to the value of the motion picture in the school. Machines have been simplified in both operation and construction. Instead of some massive apparatus that needed specially built and equipped projection rooms, we now have compact, lightweight forms that may be conveniently carried in medium-sized portable cases. By the use of 500- to 1000-watt electric bulbs and noninflammable film, it is possible to attach the projector to an ordinary electric-light socket and improvise a stand for it in any schoolroom, with complete safety and a minimum of effort. Now that these projectors may be used under daylight or semi-daylight conditions, they are all the more available. The costs, therefore, have been so reduced that schools of ordinary size may afford such equipment.

II. Semi-pictorial Devices

A. *Maps, charts, graphs.* Closely related to pictures may be considered maps, charts, and graphs. Often charts are really pictures in very enlarged form, as a likeness of the human body in a physiology chart or a lifelike colored representation of some flower in a botany chart.

Maps are among the most useful visual aids for geographical or historical subjects. The pictorial map has become a highly developed art. There are maps of various colors, organized primarily to show the boundaries of different countries with the principal mountain and river systems and usually the principal cities, maps of the

---

[5] See previous reference to the Forty-Eighth Yearbook, Part I, chapter XII, of The National Society for the Study of Education.

[6] Dale has dealt somewhat exhaustively with the use of the motion picture in the school. The student will find his discussion at this point most profitable. Dale, Edgar. *Audio-Visual Methods in Teaching,* chapters VII–VIII. New York: The Dryden Press, Inc., 1946.

same color but varying from light to heavy shades to show differences in rainfall, density of population, etc., maps of varied color, usually green to heavy shades of brown, showing the physical contours of continents, road maps, and relief maps. These are but a few of the many ways in which maps have made useful information graphic to the eye and mind. Because of the extensive use of maps and the universality of codes for map interpretation, map reading becomes an early accomplishment of the student. Maps are relatively easy to read, easy to handle and, when it is necessary to use other than textbook maps, they can be purchased in individual or collection form with convenient racks or stands for class use. Large maps of durable construction are still somewhat expensive, but no single form of visual aid is more indispensable to the school than good maps.

Charts are much on the order of maps and, as previously suggested, may be collections of pictures on large sheets of heavy paper or cloth, manipulated much as are large maps. Often they represent large diagrams, such as chronological tables, and enlarged graphs of population areas, etc. In the secondary school they are probably most widely used in the science courses. Their possibilities in other fields have never been fully explored.

Graphs are beginning to have an increasing place in education. Much of an adult's reading today requires a graph-reading ability. In governmental bulletins, and in magazines of a serious nature which are related to business, economic, and social life, we find an extensive use of all sorts of graphs and diagrams — bar graphs, step graphs, frequency polygons, segmented circles, pictograms. These are all intended to give the reader a vivid mental image of comparative data. Institutions and various groups desirous of catching the public notice and drawing attention to their messages are more and more alert to the effectiveness of the graph as an educational device. Graphic representation, while it may be effective, may likewise be deceptive. The school, therefore, has an obligation not only to use graphic aids for creating vivid mental imagery for learning, but also to teach students to read them intelligently.

A distinct value of the graph lies in the power of the teacher to create his own, as well as to use those made by others. The student should be encouraged to make them to express ideas to others and to vivify his own thought.

B. *Blackboards and bulletin boards.* These adjuncts of visual materials are included here, for although not in themselves visual aids, they form a very essential part of any teacher's equipment for visual instruction. Bulletin boards are arbitrarily interpreted here to include all forms of display boards, whether used for written materials, graphs, or pictures of one form or another. Every classroom should be provided with some means of displaying interesting pictorial materials of varied forms. Where schools have not made such provision in classroom construction, an inexpensive device is to stretch burlap, or any color desired to harmonize with the color scheme of the room, over excess blackboard space or wall space. This can be neatly done, and if a manual-training department of the school is available, attractive bulletin-board effects can be secured at trifling cost. Burlap provides a very serviceable material on which to pin pictures, drawings, graphs, etc. It is a point of never-failing interest to enter a teacher's classroom and observe the ingenuity revealed in the use of bulletin boards for display purposes. Some teachers assign space to various classes for interesting displays of their work. Many schools use corridor bulletin boards in the same way, as an important source of educational interest to the entire school.

Every classroom has a large area devoted to blackboards, yet it is astonishing at times to see how little use the average teacher makes of this important visual education adjunct. The graphic portrayal of the work of the class is limited only by the imagination of the teacher and his power to depict that imagery in sketch and diagram. The ability of an artist is not required. Too much detail of an artistic nature may detract from the essential idea. One of the most effective uses of the blackboard ever experienced by the author as a student was made by an instructor who invariably resorted to four lines on a blackboard to visualize an abstruse point to a class. These lines were capable of more vivid imagery than now seems possible. The ability shown by the instructor in making four simple lines convey so much vivid imagery occasioned continual comment within the class. Such restriction of graphic power is not recommended, but is given to illustrate what the ungifted teacher in drawing may do at the blackboard with a few simple lines. If, added to this, colored chalk is used the lines can be made much more significant. Even the mere outlining of the points in a lesson is a more valuable visual aid to memory than expecting students to hold in mind the points made in a lesson's unfoldment.

The use of the blackboard by students should not be overlooked, although the tendency today is away from excessive use of the blackboard by students en masse. Modern methods of teaching frown upon the old mass methods and frequent waste of time represented in blackboard drills. The blackboard, when judiciously used, is still a valuable aid to class teaching. If, instead of mass use of the blackboard, individuals or groups of students, who have data that should be shared with the class in visual form, were encouraged to graph, diagram, or outline such material on the board, the value of the blackboard would be greatly enhanced educationally.

Frequently what might have been a very beneficial use of the blackboard has been seriously jeopardized by failure to observe some very elemental considerations. Among the most important should be mentioned:

1. Due care should be given to light reflection upon the board at certain angles, and to the seating of students at such angles to the writing as to make distinguishable the written work.
2. There is an occasional tendency to use blackboard space at the sides of and in the rear of the class. This produces confusion and discomfort if students must turn in fixed seats to read and make notations.
3. Some teachers, when using a blackboard to outline the development of the lesson, so encumber the board as to make the result more confusing than had the blackboard been left blank.
4. Another frequent error is to visualize an incorrect form, and then beside it place the correct form. This misuse of suggestion is frequently observed by the classroom visitor.
5. There is an all too prevalent practice of filling the blackboard from top to bottom, so that students in the rear are with difficulty able to see what is on the lower part of the board. Many learning difficulties arise from inability to see clearly all data on the blackboard.

III. Objects

A. *Globes, models.* Two kinds of globes are commonly used to supplement the maps used in geography and history. The smooth-surface map, placed on a sphere to show more vividly and accurately location and relationships of parts than is possible with a flat map, constitutes one form. All the characteristics of the map forms considered under the topic "Maps" are possible on the sphere. The other form is the base-relief map, which tends to show by raised portions and depressions the surface contour of the world. The chief value of the globe is the added correction to the students' imagery of our world as a sphere. Pictures or pictorial materials are never capable of producing accurate imagery of the thing depicted. Models of squares, triangles, etc., in mathematics, of buildings, etc., in literature, and of various machines, plants, or bodily organs in science, aid very materially the understanding of various cultures, of properties, of mechanical principles of operation, etc., that would be less vivid, if not more difficult to understand, by description or explanation through word symbols only. Since in complicated mechanisms complete detail cannot always be included, care must be exercised to avoid wrong conceptions through incompleteness or the miniature nature of the models.

B. *Specimens — laboratory equipment.* Here is opened up a large field which is growing more important in the school. Specimens range from live animals, and plant and insect life, to preserved forms of the same. Geological collections of rocks and minerals are valuable additions to the curriculum of the school. Increasing emphasis on flowers and pets in the school enable the student to study at firsthand the life habits and care of these forms of life. It is invaluable to the student to visualize many life processes of the human through a study of other animals. Further, a genuine appreciation of nature is inculcated in the student through association. In our large cities museums cooperate with the schools to make available preserved specimens of every kind from the insect to the mounted bird. Aquariums, too, offer their facilities to the school for the study of animal life under conditions approximating their normal habitats.

Laboratory equipment has been found of especial value in the sciences. Many of the material aids thus far discussed have made up part of the assorted equipment of the laboratory. Firsthand acquaintance with chemicals, mechanical devices in physics, life forms in biology and botany, rock forms in geology and geography, has received almost universal recognition as an educational aid. In some of the sciences, however, there is noticed a definite tendency to avoid the more complex and novel type of material in favor of simpler, more commonly used equipment. If familiar mechanical objects are used, interest in the principles of operation is more likely to be aroused than if a novel object is used. Many teachers have discovered that materials found in the community are more serviceable than purchased equipment from laboratory concerns. Students evince a natural interest in why things work as they do, for the question has been an oft-recurring one as they have manipulated or have observed others handle tools or mechanical contrivances of one kind or another.

IV. Other Forms of Visual Aids

A. *Demonstration.* The two most common forms of demonstration are dramatization and teacher-demonstration, sometimes called lecture-demonstration. Dramatization and pageantry are especially popular in literature and the social sciences. To dramatize an act or scene from Shakespeare, or an especially vivid section of a poem or novel, provides a wholesome emotional experience and a mental imagery of the scene the writer has endeavored to portray. If attention is paid to stage setting, dress, etc., much valuable information concerning the environment of the period presented will be gained. It is one of the most valuable means of quickening interest in class, and of awakening immediate and permanent interests in literature. The same values hold for historical episodes that are dramatized or depicted in pageant.

The results of experimental studies have thrown much light on the effectiveness of lecture-demonstration for learning. In the past, laboratory experiment was regarded as the principal way students could profit by exposure to processes that were to be visualized. A cumulative body of data indicates that the teacher-demonstration is more economical of time and as effective, if not more so, for immediate learning and retention. Much economy in duplication of materials incident to the laboratory is thus possible. Time spent by students in the laboratory may thus be curtailed, with the added assurance that accuracy of performance will be possible if the demonstration is made by the teacher. It is well occasionally to have students rather than the teacher conduct the demonstration before the class. Pupil training in performance before an audience is not to be overlooked.

B. *Field trips.* Field trips and excursions have become very popular and valuable visual aids in education. These range from elementary school nature-study hikes to parks and near-by fields, to extended field trips into the hinterland by geological and botanical classes from a university, which often consist of groups who may spend months on such trips. For the secondary school, late-afternoon or Saturday trips are feasible and their use quite general. Among the various kinds of field or excursion trips the following are typical:

1. *Nature and science study trips.* Science classes have long incorporated into their curriculum visits afield. Visits are made to study flowers, trees, and various forms of vegetation. The students are enabled to see vegetation as it grows naturally, and to watch growth and development periodically. Field trips to acquaint the student with the geologic formations of his community, to study various forms of rocks, and through these to learn to read earth's story told in rock and terrain, is both thrilling and worth while. To learn to appreciate nature through direct contact and understanding is a consummation greatly to be desired. It cannot be gained in any adequate way except by direct observational contact.

2. *Visits to factories and commercial emporiums.* Economics, business, and manufacture are now matters of absorbing interest to high school students and even to elementary pupils. Well-coordinated courses in schools include visits, when such are feasible, to industrial and business centers. In most of our larger cities responsible concerns welcome and plan special facilities through the use of which students may inspect and observe routine processes of business or manufacture. Trips to printing presses, department stores, factories, flour mills, and steel mills are common. It is instructive to watch manufacturing processes, and to appreciate the careful organization necessary to the smooth dispatch of business.

3. *Museums.* Museums have been alluded to before; suffice it but to reiterate the splendid educational opportunities awaiting the visits of classes to museums of art, natural history, botany, and zoology. Most of our large cities have one or more of these, and fortunately most museums regard cooperation with the schools as one of their major opportunities and responsibilities. A liberal education can be had through frequent visits to these places.

4. *Governmental and civic institutions.* In this group may be

mentioned juvenile courts, county or district courts, penal institutions, city councils, state legislatures, and eleemosynary institutions, such as orphanages and old-people's homes. Much of the internal organization of government may be better understood, a wholesome respect aroused for the many problems of government, and a sense of civic pride and responsibility fostered by such visits. Every year in the state where the author resides social-science classes from schools as far away as a hundred miles persuade willing friends or parents of class members to take them to the state capitol to watch the legislature in session. No more vital experience could be given as a part of education.

5. *Visits to places of historic interest.* A person from the West, traveling through the many historic scenes of the East, is tempted to envy the schools there for their many opportunities to visit historical spots and places made famous through association with great men and women or with great deeds of heroism and sacrifice. To visit the haunts familiar to Longfellow, Emerson, Poe, Louisa M. Alcott, Washington, Jefferson, and Franklin, and memorable places such as Bunker Hill, Yorktown, Mount Vernon, Valley Forge, and Gettysburg, to mention but a few, are privileges not as available to newer portions of the country. Historic and literary appreciation are possibilities not to be overlooked in the educational life of youth so accessible to these shrines of famous men and great deeds.

While field trips and excursions as valuable forms of educational experience should be utilized to visualize and vitalize education more than is done in most schools, the technique of conducting them is not without its problems. Many teachers shrink from their use because the difficulties appear too numerous. It should be remembered that only those schools most favored by location can take advantage of most of the varied forms of field trips and excursions. Schools located in large metropolitan centers will find the museums, business and manufacturing establishments, civic institutions, and park facilities available for excursions. It will no doubt be hard to organize convenient field trips to localities suitable for the study of geological or physical phenomena of nature. Some small isolated communities may find field trips of every kind prohibited by distance. Today, with good roads and the automobile, these barriers are less and less an obstacle to the energetic teacher.

Special problems

Some of the greatest problems in the conduct of successful field trips and excursions are:

1. To coordinate the curriculum properly so that the natural period for the consideration of phases of botany, physical geography, etc., coincides with the season of the year most profitable for the study. To have important phases of botanical study come in midwinter would make supplementary study through field trips obviously impossible.

2. To fit field trips and excursions into the regular school program without too seriously disrupting other classes demands patience, tact, and the full cooperation of all members of the school staff. It can be done, for it is constantly being done in our better schools without serious inconvenience to others.

3. To secure proper transportation facilities may prove impractical in some instances. For most schools a little careful planning and selling of the idea to parents will meet with hearty response. Most parents are willing to inconvenience themselves considerably if they believe their children will receive comparable benefits in return.

4. To organize and conduct the class so that it will act as a unit under perfect disciplinary control is the crucial test of any teacher's fitness to conduct field trips and excursions. It is at this point that most teachers hesitate. If the class is properly organized, with leaders responsible for definite sections of the class and these in turn made to realize their responsibility to the teacher, and if detailed instructions have been worked out and explained to class and leaders, these difficulties are likely to be more formidable in anticipation than in realization.

5. To derive value from the trip, the class should be drilled in points to observe and the meaning of these observations. Ruskin once said: "Some men travel from Dan to Beersheba and find all wilderness." It is quite apropos here. If the class has been carefully coached in what to look for, how to recognize the things looked for when confronted by them, how to interpret their meaning, etc., the trip will in all likelihood prove a most profitable educational venture.

6. To clarify mooted points in the visit, students should be instructed to take notes, and a discussion of the visit, with a careful appraisal of the significance of things observed, should follow as soon after the visit as is practicable.

QUESTIONS AND PROBLEMS

1. How important is visual imagery in secondary education? Give reasons.
2. Discuss the relative efficiency of visual and word imagery for different types of students.
3. What visual aids would you consider particularly beneficial to the learning process for a class in English, history, civics, or mathematics?
4. In the preparation of a course, what principles should govern your selection of visual aids?
5. What is the general plan that should be followed by the teacher in the use of visual aids that will result in the most benefit to students?
6. Outline a plan by which you would determine the best visual aids to use in a specific course, and how these visual aids might be secured most economically.
7. Make a list of the commonly used visual aids in teaching.
8. What facts should be considered in the selection of an educational moving picture?
9. What are the educational possibilities of television?
10. Of what importance are graphs as visual aids in learning and education?
11. Give the precautions a teacher should observe when using the blackboard in the classroom.
12. Give the arguments and evidence for and against the laboratory-demonstration method of teaching science.
13. (a) What trips can a class make in an urban community and what are the special benefits to the students?
    (b) How does the idea apply to a rural community?
14. List the precautions a teacher must bear in mind and the preparation that must be made when planning field trips and visits of the class to places of particular interest.
15. Compare the use of motion pictures with other types of visual instruction.
16. From your own experience as a student, give concise reasons why particular illustrations were most valuable to you.

SELECTED BIBLIOGRAPHY

American Council on Education, Committee on Motion Pictures in Education.
——— *Projecting Motion Pictures in the Classroom,* 1940.
——— *The School Uses Motion Pictures,* 1940.
——— *Motion Pictures in the Modern Curriculum,* 1941
Washington, D.C.: American Council on Education.

Audio-Visual Materials and Methods in the Social Studies, Eighteenth Yearbook. Washington, D.C.: National Council for the Social Studies, N.E.A. 1948.

Audio-Visual Materials of Instruction, Forty-eighth Yearbook, Part I. National Society for the Study of Education. Chicago: University of Chicago Press, 1949.

Chandler, Ann C. and Cyher, Irene F. *Audio-Visual Techniques.* New York: Noble and Noble, Inc., 1948.

Dale, Edgar. *Audio-Visual Methods in Teaching.* New York: The Dryden Press, Inc., 1946.

Dale, Edgar, et al. *How to Teach with Pictures.* Grand Rapids, Michigan: Informative Classroom Picture Publishers, 1947.

Dent, Ellsworth C. *The Audio-Visual Handbook.* Chicago: Society for Visual Education, 1949.

Douglass, Harl R. and Mills, Hubert H. *Teaching in High School,* chapter XVI. New York: The Ronald Press Company, 1948.

Educational Film Guide. New York: H. W. Wilson Company (Annual).

Elliot, Godfrey M. (Editor) *Film and Education.* New York: Philosophical Library, 1948.

Fattu, N. A. and Blain, B. B. *Selected Films for Teacher Education.* Bloomington: The University of Indiana Press, 1950.

Goetting, M. L. *Teaching in the Secondary School,* chapter XII. New York: Prentice-Hall, Inc., 1942.

Haas, K. B. and Packer, H. Q. *Preparation and Use of Visual Aids.* New York: Prentice-Hall, Inc., 1946.

Hampel, Margaret, et al. *Films Interpreting Children and Youth.* Washington, D.C.: The Association of Childhood, 1949.

Hoban, Charles F., Jr. *Movies That Teach.* New York: The Dryden Press, Inc., 1946.

Hogben, Lancelot. *From Cave Painting to Comic Strip.* New York: Chanticleer Press, 1949.

Kinder, James S. *Audio-Visual Materials and Techniques.* New York: American Book Company, 1950.

McKown, Harry C. and Roberts, Alvin B. *Audio-Visual Aids in Instruction,* Second Edition. New York: McGraw-Hill Book Company, Inc., 1949.

National Education Association of the United States, "Audio-Visual Education in City School Systems," *Research Bulletin,* vol. 24: no. 4. (December, 1946).

Risk, Thomas M. *Principles and Practices of Teaching in Secondary Schools,* Second Edition, chapter XXV. New York: American Book Company, 1947.

Rivlin, Harry N. *Teaching Adolescents in Secondary Schools,* chapter VIII. New York: Appleton-Century-Crofts, Inc., 1948.

Thut, I. N. and Gerberich, J. R. *Foundations of Method for Secondary Schools,* chapter XIX. New York: McGraw-Hill Book Company, Inc., 1949.

Umstattd, J. G. *Secondary School Teaching,* Second Edition, chapter XII. Boston: Ginn and Company, 1944.

Weaver, G. G. and Bollinger, E. W. *Visual Aids Their Construction and Use.* New York: D. Van Nostrand Company, Inc., 1949.

Wesley, Edgar B. *Teaching the Social Studies,* chapter XVIII. Boston: D. C. Heath and Company, 1942.

Wittich, Walter A. and Fowlkes, John G. *Audio-Visual Paths to Learning.* New York: Harper and Brothers, 1946.

16

How Can Radio and Television
Be Used?

1. How Important Are Radio and Television?

The phenomenal development of radio

Possibly no single achievement in the realm of science within this generation holds more actual and potential significance for education than the development of radio, unless it be radio's twin sister television. Less than thirty years ago, in the "crystal set and earphones" era of radio, few people made use of the radio equipment available. Today, more than 40,000,000 radio sets are to be found in American homes, shops, and offices. Between 85 and 90 per cent of the homes in the United States have radio sets. American homes have more radios than telephones. Automobiles are wired for radio installation. Broadcasting stations are so numerous and so powerful that the remotest community need not be without the benefit of radio. Moreover, the technical development of radio has made a high quality of reception possible through mechanically refined precision receiving sets and through greatly improved broadcasting techniques and equipment.

The development of television promises to be as phenomenal as that of the radio. Authorized on a commercial basis just before Pearl Harbor at the end of World War II, there were at that time six television stations in operation and 7000 receiving sets in America. Early in 1950 there were ninety-eight stations on the air and more than four million receiving sets in the country. In May, 1949, the Chairman of the FCC prophesied that within five years there would be between 600 and 800 stations on the air. The Commissioner of the FCC the next month predicted that by 1955 there would be over 20,000,000 sets in use, serving over half the homes in America.[1]

The services made available through radio are varied and extensive. The possibilities through the media of television appear to be equally significant. The listener may hear the best of symphonic music or dial in his favorite swing band; he may enjoy a wide variety of light entertainment or serious lectures or forum discussions of a political, religious, or educational nature, all the while observing on the television screen many of the entertainers or speakers. Important news from all parts of the world is broadcast within a few minutes after the event. News analysts, national leaders, diplomats, from home and foreign capitols, speak frequently. There seems to be no limit to the range and wealth of attractions made available by means of radio and television. The educational possibilities inherent in radio and television programs are obvious. The responsibilities of the school are equally clear.

Development of radio and television in education

A cursory look over the field of radio activity might suggest that we were making small use of our educational opportunities. We have scarcely begun to comprehend fully, certainly not to utilize adequately, the possibilities of radio. An experienced worker in radio education has given the following explanation for the delay: "Radio came so quickly; people were so busy with their old established interests and duties; and it took hold of people so rapidly that not even to this day have we caught up with its implications."[2]

When we realize that technical developments did not make extensive educational use of radio practicable much before 1930, it is encouraging to note that as early as 1928 or 1929 groups of parents were listening to educational broadcasts from Ohio State University and adult education by radio was having its beginnings. Since that time radio has become such a significant factor in adult

[1] Siepmann, Charles A. *Radio, Television and Society,* p. 318. New York: Oxford University Press, 1950.

[2] Darrow, B. H. "Classroom Radio — Its Origin, Present Status, and Probable Future," in Herzberg, Max J., et al. *Radio and English Teaching,* p. 53. New York: D. Appleton-Century Company, 1941. Reprinted by permission.

education that organized adult groups called "listening groups" now number upwards of twenty thousand in the United States, with from 300,000 to 500,000 members. These groups meet regularly to listen to certain types of programs. Usually they study and actively discuss the subject of the broadcast. The subjects represent a wide range of interests, as may be noted from the following types of programs around which "listening groups" have been formed: *Family Life Radio Forum, Homemakers Forum, America's Town Meeting of the Air, Radio Garden Club.*

From the period of radio's infancy, educational leaders who have seen educational possibilities of radio in the school have not been wanting. Haaren High School in New York City in 1923, and the schools of Oakland, California, in 1924 were among the pioneers in the use of radio to broadcast lessons to the classroom. By the end of the twenties and the early part of the thirties a number of significant ventures with the radio broadcast in schools were under way. In 1929 the Ohio School of the Air began broadcasting for classroom purposes during school hours. Within a relatively short time it "reached a registered audience of 300,000 school children." [3] Courses in Art Appreciation, Civics, Music, Current Events, and Geography were among a wide range of offerings made available to the schools through the Ohio School of the Air.

At present radio is an important factor in the educational program of our schools. Practically every large school system makes extensive and varied use of the radio. Even in the small rural school the radio is becoming standard equipment.

As yet television has not become a real factor in our educational program. Already some schools in the centers of dense population are experimenting. New school plants are being wired for television. For example, the new laboratory school at the University of Minnesota is being equipped for televising in connection with the University's teacher education program. When it becomes possible to complement hearing with sight as we utilize contemporary events in the classroom, the school will have one more medium to facilitate the education of youth. [4]

[3] Darrow, B. H., *op. cit.* To date this source is one of the best condensed but graphic narratives of the development of radio education in America before 1940.

[4] The educator should be aware, however, of some of the possible limitations that confront the use of television not limiting the use of radio. Some of these limitations are considered by Siepmann, Charles A. *Radio, Television and Society,* pp. 348–358. New York: Oxford University Press, 1950.

2. What Are the Uses of Radio and Television in Adult Education?

The radio and television in adult life

From the foregoing discussion and the general acquaintance of the educational worker with the habits of adults, it is evident that the radio is an important adjunct of adult living.[5] The fact that upwards of 90 per cent of our American homes possess radios is indicative of the value placed upon them. The New York Regents' Inquiry study of educational conditions among its youth found that of out-of-school youth many more listened to the radio than read books or magazines. Only 4 per cent of the young people could be classified as non-users of radio. The 96 per cent used the radio extensively. The boys listened on the average eleven hours per week while the girls listened on the average fifteen hours per week.[6]

In those areas where television has become available, school leaders are already showing much concern over the tendency of children and youth to stay up late at night to see television programs to the point where the exhaustion of youth in school affects the quality of work done in the classroom. This will no doubt tend to correct itself as the novelty of television wears off. It does bespeak the potential of a media of educational interest.

The quality of the radio and television programs listened to, however, is a matter of some concern. Studies made of the types of radio programs listened to indicated that the programs of a lighter vein were the most popular. Adult radio tastes seem to parallel quite closely adult reading tastes. However, it is estimated that almost one quarter of all programs broadcast may be classified as educational. Broadcasting stations are anxious to put on the type of program which is likely to reach large numbers. Particularly is this true where commercial companies sponsor programs as a medium of advertising. The substantial group who respond to "quality" programs should both encourage and challenge educational leaders with the possibilities of radio education for adults.[7]

[5] In this chapter the term "adult" is interpreted non-technically to include all persons not regularly enrolled in our public and private secondary schools.
[6] Spaulding, F. T. *High School and Life*, pp. 45–46. The Regents Inquiry. New York: The McGraw-Hill Book Company, Inc., 1938.
[7] The reader may be interested in the extensive survey of the kinds of programs listened to and preferred by adults reported by Lazarsfeld, Paul F. and Kendall, Patricia L. *Radio Listening in America*. New York: Prentice-Hall, Inc., 1948.

School-sponsored programs for adults

Rapidly the educational program of the school is being expanded to include a varied service to adults. Educational leaders generally accept the dictum that the services of the school should be available to all ages; that in a world of rapidly accelerating change it is necessary that the school serve as a medium of constant reorientation of the adult to changing conditions.

While responsibility for leisure time entertainment has been considered the province of agencies other than the school, this assumption cannot longer be justified. The school must not only carry its share of responsibility for developing leisure-time tastes for individuals in school, but it must recognize its obligation to arrange leisure-time activities for adults. Music, drama, and a wide range of literary offerings are possible through talent from local schools or other centers, or through recordings.

The socio-civic area is another in which the school can render signal service. Through sponsorship of debates, forums, and addresses by those competent to speak upon social, economic, or political issues of the moment, an educational service may be rendered the citizen and the country. As more school systems develop their own broadcasting facilities greater opportunity for this kind of educational broadcasting will be possible.

No school system, particularly one which cannot afford broadcasting equipment or which does not have access to a commercial studio, should overlook the wealth of programs available in the broadcasts from other centers. At present commercial stations and the stations of institutions of higher learning offer a surprisingly varied program of superior talent drawn from every section of our political, economic, and social life.

The school as a civic agency might well become the community center for many of the "listening groups" now meeting in private homes. It should seek to encourage and give leadership to these groups. The school should assume responsibility for the organization of thousands of other "listening groups." For these the school should make available its housing facilities, its reception equipment, and equally important, the stimulation of its leadership. The modern school cannot well justify closed and darkened buildings or idle equipment in the face of community needs. From a purely selfish point of view such service to the community may well develop a greater community consciousness of the needs of the school.

3. What Are the Functions of the Radio and Television in School and Classroom?

Enriching the program of the school

Every school can through the radio and television greatly enrich the existing school program. Although it may not be feasible for schools, other than a few near Washington, to have their pupils visit sessions of the Congress, attend a presidential inaugural, or be present at other important occasions at the nation's capitol, it is possible to bring such events to thousands of American school youth through the use of radio and television during school hours. In recent months frequent broadcasts of prominent foreign leaders, particularly through activities at the United Nations meetings in New York, have given the schools an opportunity to stimulate the interest of pupils in international affairs. Almost every event of major importance, regional or national, is now put on the air. Important addresses and descriptions of events which are broadcast after school hours are frequently available through transcriptions at hours convenient for the school. The use of transcriptions is still new and its value in education is not fully appreciated. Alert teachers and school administrators can utilize these broadcasts to make the school a center of a wide range of experiences.

Providing supplemental materials and experiences

In addition to the enrichment of the whole school program the radio provides a wealth of materials to supplement existing resources of course offerings, and frequently to provide the equivalent of a course for which materials and facilities are not at the moment available. Many teachers who have not possessed the physical facilities for music production have utilized broadcasts to teach music appreciation. Teachers have used vocal and instrumental broadcasts to teach glee clubs, orchestras, and bands certain technical aspects of production which could not easily be taught by verbal explanation.

The science courses in the Chicago schools have been aided by the use of broadcasts during regular school hours. For the elementary grades, *Science Storyteller* and for the upper grades,

Science Reporter, are two series of broadcasts set up to supplement the regular class work in science. The titles of other programs, such as *Our World Today, America at Work, Wellsprings of
Music, This Living World,* suggest the use Chicago makes of radio
in the classroom.

Typical of the programs made available to schools by outside
sources are a few samples taken from the schedule of the Minnesota School of the Air, First Semester 1951–52, given over station
KOUM, of the University of Minnesota. The following programs
scheduled at certain hours and days each week were available to
the schools: *Old Tales and New, Let Science Tell Us, Books Bring
Adventure, Adventures in Music, Your Health and You, Penny and
Paul and the World of Ideas, Journeys in Art, Let's Sing, Current
Events, Following Conservation Trails.* A list of the sub-topics of
each program with the date each was to be broadcast was provided. In addition to these radio programs the University of Minnesota, during the summer of 1951, provided twelve television programs on *Family Life.*

Furnishing up-to-date material. At the present time, before a
geography text can be made available to the classroom it is likely
to be incorrect with respect to many boundary lines. The social
studies teacher now finds it exceedingly difficult to keep fully cognizant of all the social changes taking place, particularly those of historic interest. Invention and scientific discovery move so rapidly
that our science textbooks at many points soon become inaccurate.
Even in the matter of health knowledge many teachers are not up
to the minute in their knowledge. Many of our broadcasts attempt
to supplement or correct our textbook information with the most
recent developments in various areas of human knowledge and
activities. Presented by specialists in the areas reported and presented in non-technical language, these broadcasts make pupil and
teacher aware of the changes taking place and of the significance of
the changes.

Bringing the pupil into vital contact with his world

The school has tended to be isolated from the realities of the
world around it. The nature of education as conceived in the past
placed the emphasis upon the tested facts of history. Further, the
theory of "mental discipline," so prevalent up until the past two
decades, deprecated the value of contemporary developments.

Today the educational emphasis is laid upon the vital contact of the pupil with the realities of his environment. The task of the school is to push out beyond the cloistered four walls of the class-room and to help the pupil understand the world in which he finds himself; to help him acquire effective ways of adjusting to this world; and to help him develop some satisfying and wholesome attitudes with respect to his relationship to it. The radio is one of the effective ways of making youth conscious of the world outside the school and of vitally linking the school with this outside world. The pupil is introduced indirectly to important personalities whom he recognizes as the present makers of history, the leaders of politics, business, science. He has a chance to hear their voices, to realize they are real men and women who are determining the kind of world he must live in. He becomes acquainted with contemporary problems as these leaders discuss them, and he becomes highly conscious that there are many problems still unsolved.

Developing good listeners

The emphasis upon reading has led, quite unintentionally for the most part, to a lack of attention to listening. Good listening is an art. Few people realize how important is the ability to listen carefully and accurately. Few can do it. Since the radio has become such an important agency of dissemination of fact and near-fact the school can no longer neglect the social and educational function of listening. There is as much of technique involved in good listening as in good reading. When careful researches have been developed it is altogether possible that we shall recognize the techniques of good listening to be much greater than those of reading. Studies tend to show that the average person spends more time listening to the radio than he does in reading. When the other common instances of listening are also considered, it is obvious that the total time a person devotes to listening is considerable.

The primary requirement for the listener, assuming that his hearing is normal, is the ability to keep sustained concentration upon the words of the speaker. This concentration may be difficult for many reasons. The voice of the radio speaker is separated from the other physical aspects of his personality. There is no opportunity to check back on a previous statement if continuity is lost. Voice inflection and emphasis must be understood. The technique of proper note-taking in oral situations has been largely neglected, although much attention has been given in recent years to note-taking in library work.[8]

Developing critical thinking and discrimination

The development of critical thinking and discrimination is closely associated with the factor of good listening. One may listen in the sense that he can remember everything he hears but be unintelligent as to the meaning of what he hears. On the other hand, no one can be critical in his thinking if his thinking is not preceded or accompanied by careful listening.

Since the advent of the radio the American people have been subjected to a larger amount of dribble, propaganda, and false advertising than ever before. In recent political campaigns the nation was subjected to a terrific barrage of campaign oratory. The radio along with television gives every indication of becoming, if it has not already become, one of our major instruments of shaping public opinion. The school must undertake seriously the development of listeners who can listen critically and with discrimination to radio programs.[9]

Developing leisure time interests and appreciations

There is every indication that leisure time is on the increase. As working hours decrease and productive employment is further restricted for youth and old age, education for intelligent use of leisure becomes a major task of the school. Radio and television appear to be very important media for leisure time activities. It is necessary then for the school to help youth learn how the radio and television may be utilized to greatest advantage during this leisure time. Too, the school must help youth to acquire standards by which to distinguish the worth-while from the trivial. Present studies of the programs reported as most popular by youth and adult do not always indicate the exercise of discriminating tastes.

Developing standards of correct speech

Many sentimental admirers of our sectional speech peculiarities have lamented the possible threat of the radio to the continuance of these speech characteristics. They do not wish to lose the collo-

[8] See Chapter 7 on "How Can Good Study Methods Be Taught?" for a discussion of note-taking.
[9] See Chapter 7.

quialisms and peculiar pronunciations of the New Englander, the Southerner of the "deep South," or the Texas cowboy. Whether or not this point of view deserves a sympathetic hearing, certainly the radio will tend to bring uniformity into language expression and to give America a common language pronunciation. In addition the studied care with which correct speech is used in radio programs will influence the quality of language used by the listener. The school can utilize as models in the classroom the radio speech usage of respected and well-known personalities.

4. What Are the Techniques of Radio and Television Instruction?

Classroom procedure

Educational authorities in general are agreed that the three major phases of classroom procedure in the use of the radio and television are preparation, reception, and follow-up. The relative importance of each phase will depend largely upon the nature of the broadcast and upon its significance for the particular class which uses it. The value of the radio and television as of any educational medium of instruction depends upon the way they are used.

1. *Preparation.* In the initial use of radio many teachers unfortunately did not understand that the pedagogical principles which apply to instruction generally are applicable also to radio instruction. Careful preparation, which has been a *sine qua non* of classroom instruction, is of even greater importance when radio is used.

The instrument should be in perfect running order. It should be located so that all can hear and see without strain. The pupils should be prepared as thoroughly for a broadcast as for any class activity. They should understand the significance of the broadcast and should realize that a radio or television program is used because it makes some unique contribution to the work of the class not possible or readily feasible by other means. The class should anticipate the general nature of this contribution.

The preparation will, of course, be governed by the nature of the subject matter and by the particular broadcast or series of broadcasts. If contemporary history is the subject of the broadcast, the background data should be studied for a better comprehension of the issues to be presented. If a play is to be dramatized or a current best seller is to be reviewed, or a type of literature is to be described and critically evaluated, the student should know something about the play, the author of the book, the book, or the type of literature. The extent of the preparation will vary with the nature and purpose of the classroom use of the broadcast. Again, a broadcast may be scheduled in which the teacher anticipates the use of new or unfamiliar words or terms. Their meanings must be made clear. Readings and reports covering the use of terms and concepts likely to appear in the broadcast should be part of the preparation of the class. If geography is to be involved, as in current events or travelogue programs, some map study should normally precede the broadcast.

Occasionally the teacher must guess at the content of an advertised program. Preparation must be made less specifically therefore than when the general nature of the content of the broadcast is known in advance. There is a growing practice among educational broadcasters to make available to schools outlines or synopses of the program topics if content is not of a current nature. Typical of this kind of service now available to schools is the Teachers' Manual and Classroom Guide of the Texas School of the Air and the Teachers' Handbook of the University of Minnesota School of the Air. In these manuals weekly broadcasts for both elementary and secondary schools are listed for the school year. Hour, date, and title of the weekly topic of each program series are given. For each major program a brief description of the program with suggestions and references introduces the sub-topics. Each sub-topic is followed by a list of sources or materials used and by guide questions or teaching suggestions.

Radio education programs of this kind enable the teacher to plan the work of a course far in advance. He may check the radio programs within the reception area of the school which may contribute to some phase of his work, and plan the course to fit into the broadcast schedule. The teacher also has the opportunity to have such materials available as may be needed to make the broadcast most effective. In the sample programs cited above, the teacher would have for use in the classroom or for reference in the library the books listed.

2. *Reception.* The teacher, having prepared for a broadcast by assembling the materials needed, must now consider the second major phase of classroom procedure, reception. At the secondary level the reception phase will be essentially a listening activity.

The teacher must insure an environment conducive to listening activity. Provision must be made against interruption from without, or distractions from within, such as incorrect lighting, poor ventilation, an overheated room, or uncomfortable seating facilities. These difficulties are not so likely to arise if the class meets in its own room. The volume of the radio should be adequate so that all may hear. The seating of pupils in half circles about the radio or television set gives an air of informality and expectancy. When pupils are properly motivated from the preparation period, inattention and disturbance in the reception phase will be reduced to a minimum. The alert teacher will have an alert, enthusiastic group of pupils eagerly anticipating the broadcast.

The technique of "listening" discussed in an earlier part of this chapter is the major concern of the teacher and the pupil. Should the pupil take notes to supplement his memory and to insure continuity of idea? There is evidence that note-taking during radio programs tends to distract attention from the thought of the speaker. Most authorities approve of a few notes to fix main points or to suggest important data. A broadcast provides an opportunity for the teacher to teach pupils proper note-taking techniques under the most motivating conditions.

When travel or current events involving geography are topics of discussion, some authorities urge the use of large wall maps, with someone responsible for pointing out to the class the places of interest. In a large class this procedure may be impractical since pupils at the back of the room may experience difficulty in following the map and in listening at the same time. Unless an activity is recognized as definitely contributing to the better understanding of the pupils in a given situation, the teacher may better focus the entire attention of the class upon what is being said. During a television program obviously all attention should be focused on the screen.

3. *Follow-up.* Few broadcasts should be ignored after the class has heard or seen them. They were featured in the course because they were thought to have definite educative value. The program amplified, supplemented, or provided stimulation for the work of the class. The follow-up or third phase of classroom procedure is an important consideration for the teacher.

The nature of the contribution made by a broadcast determines, as a rule, the extent of follow-up attention which the broadcast receives. If the broadcast serves chiefly as a springboard for the study of a unit and is intended primarily as a means of motivating the introduction of the study, it may achieve its purpose with only incidental further reference. On the other hand, the broadcast may set the stage and raise the issues which become the heart of the new unit. Under these circumstances the class should give considerable attention to the issues raised and to the possible implications of the discussion towards their solution. A critical consideration of the way a problem is presented, the weight to be given to the evidence or arguments advanced, the impersonal or biased way a speaker approaches the subject, the lines of attack which remain to be made before the class feels a proper answer may be given to the issues involved — such considerations may well become the aftermath of a radio broadcast. If the broadcast adds valuable supplemental material for a course the pupil should understand in what way this material is significant.

The teacher should make every effort to derive maximum educational values from every broadcast used. Each pupil should have an opportunity to react to what he has heard.

Some general considerations

In addition to the major phases of classroom procedure in the use of the radio or television discussed above, there are some other items of importance in the instructional use of broadcasts.

1. *Danger of overvaluing radio and television.* Like all newly found instructional aids the radio and television are in danger of being overvalued by many teachers. They are not panaceas for all educational ills. Like the film and other visual-auditory aids which have their particular place in the broad program of instruction, the radio and television can be valuable supplemental aids. They cannot, however, replace the teacher. In emergency situations such as were created once by an earthquake in Long Beach and an epidemic in Chicago, when the schools are closed, the radio and television may keep some aspects of the educational program functioning to a limited extent. These instances have revealed both the values and the limitations of radios as an agency of instruction.

2. *Supplementing radio and television with other aids.* It is well to remember that radio is only an auditory aid to instruction, and television adds only a limited visual aid. Radio has the principal weaknesses characteristic of verbal instruction. In many situations

radio and television should be supplemented with visual aids such as maps, graphs, objects, slides, and the motion picture.

3. *Use of regular classroom where possible.* It is axiomatic in good instructional procedure that listening is facilitated under conditions which reduce distraction to a minimum. If the radio or television program can be received in the regular classroom under normal conditions of quiet, a maximum of concentration upon the program is possible. The room and surroundings are familiar. When it is necessary to move the class to some common center or auditorium where a radio or television is available for the use of the whole school, the unfamiliar room is a stimulus to distraction and the normal situation for the intimate rapport of teacher and pupil characteristic of the regular classroom is greatly weakened if not destroyed.

4. *Value of out-of-school listening.* The teacher should not be indifferent to the use of educational radio-television programs which are broadcast at other than school hours. Valuable programs that will contribute to many phases of courses taught are available to pupils at home. The alert teacher will encourage pupil use of such broadcasts and give recognition for contributions originating from out-of-school listening; such encouragement and recognition are important ways to teach discrimination and appreciation for leisure time use of the radio and television. The teacher may well utilize the leisure time radio and television listening of pupils to entertainment programs as a classroom activity. Discussion of these programs will help pupils to improve their standards of evaluating this form of entertainment.

5. *Use of radio-television equipment.* The larger question of broadcasting and reception equipment is not one of major concern to the teacher. He should realize that a modern radio or television receiving set is all that is necessary. If a large receiving set is not available a good medium-sized one will do especially where the class is small. Many schools have a central address system with a receiving outlet in each room. The same is being developed for television reception. Thus programs can be channeled to classrooms as may be desired. The writer was in a small school recently where such a system made possible the channeling of three radio programs to different rooms at the same time. Additional facilities of such systems provide for recordings as well. Some schools have a number of radio receiving sets on casters which are made avail-

14 *Using Radio and Television*

able to classrooms as teachers need them. It is more satisfactory
of course, to have a receiving unit as a regular item of schoolroom
equipment. In small schools one or two combination receiver and
recorder sets will prove satisfactory as general purpose radio units.

5. How Set Up Standards for Selecting Programs?

The good teacher will consider certain standards to guide him
in the selection of radio and television programs. These standards
will, of course, vary in certain particulars depending upon the
nature of the course taught or upon the specific purpose for which
the broadcest is desired. With some adaptation, however, the following standards may be applied to almost all educational programs.

Availability

A program is available if it is scheduled at a convenient time and
if reception is good. The hour of a broadcast may not coincide
with a particular class period and it may not be possible or convenient to have a class meet at the time scheduled for the broadcast. A program may appear to be most desirable for the purpose
of the course or occasion but it may be broadcast over a distant
station or network for which reception is known to be poor. Teachers should consider carefully the factors which affect the availability of radio programs.

Length of program

The time factor is important in the selection of programs both
with reference to the needs of the teaching situation and to the
proper planning of the instructional program. If no time is available for follow-up activities or if the values to be received do not
warrant the time required for the broadcast, the teacher must
decide on the advisability of including it in the teaching program.
Most programs do not exceed one-half hour in length although
some are longer. If the teacher plans follow-up activities after a
broadcast adequate time must be available to capitalize upon the
immediate stimulus of the program.

Applicability of broadcast

Radio or television programs are selected with reference to their assumed contributions to the activities of the classroom. A program may have valuable educational qualities but still be unsuited to the particular situation for which it is being considered. The teacher should determine what specific contribution each broadcast will make to the class. Will it add significant facts or create new attitudes? Will it clarify or help answer problems the teacher knows will arise in the development of the course? Will it cause the pupils to see implications which lead naturally into the next unit of work? In short, will the broadcast meet a need not readily met by other means? These are considerations which the teacher must weigh when selecting a radio program.

Stimulation of interest. The devices used in broadcasting are calculated to arouse and hold the interest of the listener. Speeches by outstanding personages of the day, "vignettes of history" and other dramatized sketches, broadcasts from museums such as the Smithsonian Institute or by distinguished scientists, televised events such as major UN activities, Congressional hearings, a variety of public happenings of general interest, and similar programs in other areas of school study stimulate interest and challenge thinking.

Effectiveness of presentation

Those who are responsible for radio or television programs of an educational character exercise great care in securing talent possessing superior radio personality, that is, persons with good voices, clear enunciation, a quality of magnetism, and a flare for the dramatic. However, many important personages in the educational or political world lack these important qualities. It is often difficult for an eminent specialist to present his material in non-technical language suited to the level of understanding of pupils. The teacher will do well to check the effectiveness of presentation which can be expected from the speakers on a program before deciding to use it. As one writer has commented: "No matter how worthy the content and objectives, a radio program is ineffective if poorly presented." [10]

Accuracy and authenticity of broadcast

The accuracy and authenticity of the facts and generalizations

[10] *How to Use Radio in the Classroom,* p. 7. Washington, D.C.: Association of Broadcasters, 1939.

presented in a program should be of major concern to the teacher. A radio or television program should meet the most rigorous test of accuracy that would be applied to any other material used in the classroom. To prejudge the projected program the teacher should check the source of the broadcast. If the sponsors are an educational group, the competence of those responsible for its production should be determined. If the sponsors are a commercial agency the teacher should determine why a particular program is being sponsored and to what extent the sponsors and producers have a reputation for fidelity to truth. The program may be worthwhile or it may be a propaganda broadcast of questionable accuracy. Students should be taught to question the accuracy of broadcasts and to apply the other standards of selection as a means of developing an ability to discriminate among the many programs available.

QUESTIONS AND PROBLEMS

1. Write a two-thousand-word paper showing the various types of educational radio programs now available for school use. Indicate briefly how each may contribute to the educational purposes of the school. Do the same for television programs.
2. What educational significance should be attached to the rapid development of "listening groups"?
3. What were some of the early educational uses of radio?
4. Account for the extensive development of educational programs via radio and television not originating through the agency of the public school.
5. What are some of the major national organizations concerned with educational broadcasts or the use of the radio or television for educational purposes? What distinct services may each render to the school or classroom teacher?
6. Do you think that sometime in the future, as many teachers have feared, there is a likelihood the radio and television may supplant the teacher? What reasons can you adduce to support your answer?
7. What are the psychological and pedagogical bases for the use of radio and television in education?
8. Can you enumerate a number of educational uses which might be made of the radio or television which are not now utilized?
9. What are some of the limitations in the use of radio or television to be recognized by the teacher?
10. a. What reasons may be advanced for the school's responsibility to utilize the radio and television for adult education?

b. Suggest legitimate ways of utilizing the radio and television for adult education through the school.

11. What are some of the problems of education accentuated through modern commercial practices in radio and television broadcasting?

12. In what ways will television contribute to the present educational values of radio?

13. Set up a list of criteria by which the teacher may evaluate the results of classroom use of radio or television.

14. What are some of the new technical advances in radio broadcasting and reception which promise much for educational radio use? Explain how these new developments may affect educational use of radio.

15. Explain some of the significant recent experiments which have been made in radio education.

16. What are some of the major problems confronting the school in developing maximal use of the radio?

17. There are many who believe that television will never be as useful as the radio in education. What basis have they for their opinion?

18. What are some of the distinct educational advantages which television has over radio?

19. How can television be used as complementary to the radio as an educational media?

SELECTED BIBLIOGRAPHY

Archer, G. L. *The History of Radio to 1926.* New York: The American Historical Company, 1938.

———— *Big Business and Radio.* New York: The American Historical Company, 1940.

Berry, Lola. *Radio Development in a Small City School System.* Boston: Meador Publishing Company, 1944.

Beville, Hugh M., Jr. "The Challenge of the New Media: Television, FM and Facsimile," *Journalism Quarterly,* vol. 25: 3–11 (1948).

Callahan, Jennie W. *Radio Workshop for Children.* New York: McGraw-Hill Book Company, Inc., 1948.

Cuthbert, Margaret. (Editor) *Adventure in Radio.* New York: Howell, Soskin, Inc., 1945.

Day, D. D. *Summary of Radio Research Studies.* Yonkers, N. Y.: The World Book Company, 1942.

Douglass, Harl R. and Mills, Hubert H. *Teaching in High School,* chapter XVII. New York: The Ronald Press Company, 1948.

Eddy, William C. *Television — The Eyes of Tomorrow.* New York: Prentice-Hall, Inc., 1945.

Education on the Air. Columbus, Ohio: Ohio State University, 1930–1944.

Education on the Air. Twentieth Yearbook, Institute for Education by Radio. Columbus, Ohio: Ohio State University, 1950.

Educational Radio Script Exchange Catalogue. Fourth Edition. Washington, D.C.: Federal Radio Education Committee, 1943.

Harrison, Margaret. *Radio in the Classroom.* New York: Prentice-Hall, Inc., 1939.

Herzberg, Max J. et al. *Radio and English Teaching.* New York: Appleton-Century-Crofts, Inc., 1941.

Hill, Frank E. and Williams, W. E. *Radio's Listening Groups.* New York: Columbia University Press, 1941.

Irwin, L. B. "Television as an Educational Medium." *Social Studies,* 39: 365–366 (December, 1948).

Kinder, James S. *Audio-Visual Materials and Techniques,* chapters XVI–XVIII. New York: American Book Company, 1950.

Kozlenko, William. *One Hundred Non-Royalty Radio Plays.* New York: Greenberg, Publisher, Inc., 1941.

Krulevitch, W. and Krulevitch, R. C. *Radio Drama Production.* New York: Rinehart and Company, Inc., 1946.

Lazarsfeld, Paul F. and Field, Harry. *The People Look at Radio.* Chapel Hill: The University of North Carolina Press, 1946.

Lazarsfeld, Paul F. and Kendall, Patricia L. *Radio Listening in America.* New York: Prentice-Hall, Inc., 1948.

Levenson, William B. *Teaching Through Radio.* New York: Farrar and Rinehart, Inc., 1945.

Lewis, Philip. "Television Goes to School." *Educational Screen,* 27: 439–441 (November, 1948).

———— "The Future of Television in Education." *Phi Delta Kappan,* 30: 157–160 (December, 1948).

Lohr, L. R. *Television Broadcasting.* New York: McGraw-Hill Book Company, Inc., 1940.

Palmer, Richard. *School Broadcasting in Britain.* London: British Broadcasting Corporation, 1947.

Radio in the Classroom. Madison: University of Wisconsin Press, 1942.

Reck, Franklin M. *Radio From Start to Finish.* New York: Thomas Y. Crowell Company, 1942.

Risk, Thomas M. *Principles and Practices of Teaching in Secondary Schools,* Second Edition, chapter XXVI. New York: American Book Company, 1947.

Rowland, Howard I. et al. *Criteria For Children's Radio Programs.* Washington, D.C.: Federal Education Committee, 1942.

Siepmann, Charles A. *Radio Television and Society.* New York: Oxford University Press, 1950.

Tyler, I. K. and Lowdermilk, R. R. *Radio As An Aid in Teaching.* Columbus, Ohio: Bureau of Educational Research, Ohio State University, 1937.

Umstattd, J. G. *Secondary School Teaching,* Second Edition, chapter XIII. Boston: Ginn and Company, 1942.

Willey, Roy D. and Young, Helen A. *Radio in Elementary Education.* Boston: D. C. Heath and Company, 1948.

Woefel, Norman and Tyler, I. Keith. *Radio and the School.* Yonkers, N. Y.: World Book Company, 1945.

Part
V

MANAGEMENT TECHNIQUES

IN TEACHING

17

How Can the Learning Environment
Be Improved?

---

1. What Are Some General Considerations?

Importance of good schoolroom conditions

Six or seven hours in schoolrooms under unhygienic conditions are likely to affect seriously the health of students. Certain unsatisfactory conditions may prove detrimental to the health of the teacher as well. The crowding of adolescents into congested schoolrooms, where they must live in close contact with youth from different types of home hygienic environments, requires the greatest care to safeguard the welfare of all. The rapid growth of body and bodily organs at the adolescent period — with uneven growth between some parts of the body such as heart and arteries — makes this age subject to ready overstrain of body and growth malformation. These facts necessitate the greatest care that the most healthful schoolroom conditions possible prevail.

Learning, too, is recognized as much more responsive to favorable physical classroom conditions than formerly thought. The much-worked psychological principle that pleasurable reactions facilitate learning is basically true. Modern education, on sound psychological and pedagogical grounds, is committed to the policy of creating the most favorable conditions possible for learning activity. Many innovations in the school, both in facilities and method, are the direct result of this policy.

It goes without saying that the teacher is favorably affected by good environmental conditions. When students approach their work with pleasure, if not eagerness, the teacher cannot but feel a buoyancy of spirit and satisfaction in his work not otherwise possible. In lesser degree, possibly, but none the less positively, unhygienic conditions in the classroom make serious inroads upon the health of the teacher. A teacher devitalized through illness or subjected to a constant feeling of exhaustion and depressed spirits, cannot be one hundred per cent efficient in the classroom. Enthusiasm, alertness, and a radiant spirit, so necessary to the success of the teacher, are the concomitants of good health and pleasant working conditions.

Teacher control of physical environment

Some factors that affect the classroom conditions are outside the province of the teacher and will not be dwelt upon here, except as they contribute to the teacher's understanding of the total problem. Discussion of these belongs to texts in school administration. If, for example, the construction of the building has been so ill adapted to the purposes for which it was built that no satisfactory scheme of ventilation is possible, and the provision for lighting, both artificial and natural, is inadequate at best, then the teacher is powerless to make the physical environment ideal.

On the other hand, there is much the teacher can do to make poor physical conditions better. Very often poor physical conditions exist because of negligence and indifference on the part of the teacher. The writer seldom approaches a class discussion of the items considered in this chapter without a feeling of semi-apology for not assuming that teachers in training, many of whom have had teaching experience, should be capable of proper supervision of classroom conditions without further instruction. So many of these considerations seem so obvious. However, each year of supervisory activity with teachers in training and the visiting of experienced teachers lead more surely to the conviction that few aspects of the teacher's work are more generally neglected.

2. What Are Proper Lighting Facilities?

Eye strain

Myopia, or shortsightedness, is probably the most prevalent form of defective vision found among those of school age. By the time the high school has been reached the use of eye glasses has become common among those of more studious inclination, at least. Some studies have shown all the way from 11 to 70 per cent defective vision among school pupils. Interestingly enough, the increase in defective vision has been found in some instances to follow a direct and accelerated ratio of advance in school from grade to grade.

The eye is the most sensitive of the bodily organs, and is most readily affected by conditions incident to the schoolroom. The nature of reading, which requires close application to small figures that make up the letters of words, tends to require a focusing of the eye not normal under non-reading conditions. Continued focusing of the eye in this manner leads to the adjustment of muscles of the eye so that permanent focalization on the basis of this reading results. Improper lighting, where additional strain is necessary to distinguish words, aggravates an already bad condition. Often incorrect position of the book while reading adds to the abnormal strain upon the eye. If the rays of light come directly from the front, or if bright sunlight shines directly upon the reading page, the eye strain is intensified.[1]

Proper lighting standards

Many of the things discussed here the teacher can do nothing about. If the teacher understands what constitutes good lighting, he will realize when it does not exist and do what he can to alleviate the evil. It is very difficult to judge the adequacy of light if one trusts one's senses alone. Many teachers have pulled down blinds because they thought a mellow light was desirable, when a casual glance at the deficient light area of the room, plus the dull atmospheric conditions outside, told the observer the standards were far more trustworthy than the teacher's judgment.

For many years it had been generally accepted in school building standards that at least one-fifth glass area to floor area was necessary, under normal conditions. Within recent years there has appeared a definite trend toward the recommendation of greater room illumination than the above standards make possible. In some sections of the country, where inclement weather is charac-

[1] For a most helpful discussion of the relations of proper lighting to the health and efficiency of pupils, in non-technical language, see *American School Buildings*, chapter XIII, "Light and Color," Twenty-Seventh Yearbook, American Association of School Administrators. Washington, D.C.: National Education Association, 1949.

teristic of the nine months of the season when schools are in session, one-fourth glass area to floor area is not considered enough.

For the teacher who does not wish to take time to determine by exact measurement the natural light available, it is only necessary to remember a few facts that will provide an approximate estimate. A room with a ceiling eleven and one-half to twelve feet high should have windows extending to within not less than four or five feet of each end of the room. They should begin about three feet from the floor and extend to the ceiling, with not more than five or six inches of space from glass to ceiling. The wall space between windows should not exceed one foot. These rough figures will give approximately one-fifth glass area to floor area when the room is not more than twenty-two feet wide and in normal rectangular form.

The past few years have witnessed much discussion of our school lighting standards. In the early thirties light with an intensity of five foot-candles at each desk was regarded as highly satisfactory if not ideal. Today there is a general tendency to think of several times that illumination as a minimum standard for our schools, with many responsible groups insisting upon twenty to thirty and even fifty foot-candles of artificial lighting as more nearly adequate.[2]

Below is given the proposed lighting standards set up by several groups concerned with proper school lighting. These lighting standards are typical of the recommendations now being made for schools. If anything, the tendency would be toward raising the standards for such activities as sewing and drafting.

Within the past few years there has been a change of emphasis with respect to school lighting. Basically attention is still given to the sufficiency of the light available, as Table 4 indicates; much concern, however, is now shown for a proper diffusion of light to avoid shadows, the avoidance of too sharp contrasts in amount of light surrounding the field of vision, and the elimination of glares. As one authority has stated: [3]

> For satisfactory visual environment the brightness of school room surfaces should not exceed 500 foot-lamberts and the glare factor should not exceed 15.

[2] "Recommended Illumination Levels for Classrooms and Other School Areas," *IES Lighting Handbook,* pp. 10–76. New York: Illuminating Engineering Society, 1947.

[3] Hamon, Ray L. *Lightning Schoolrooms,* Pamphlet No. 104, p. 4. Washington, D.C.: U.S. Office of Education, 1948.

TABLE 4. *Proposed Lighting Standards for School Buildings*

Types of Rooms	Minimum Operating Foot-Candles Recommended		
	*Illuminating Engineering Society — 1947	†National Education Association — 1946	**U. S. Office of Education — 1948
Class and Study Rooms	30	30	30
Corridors	5	5	
Drafting Rooms	50	50	40
Gymnasiums	20	20	
Laboratories	30	30–50	40
Lecture Rooms	30	20–50	
Lunch Rooms	10	10	
Sewing Rooms	50	100	40
Stairways	10	5	
Shops	30	30–100	30
Sight Saving Rooms	50	50	40
Store Rooms	5		
Wash Rooms	10	10	

* From *IES Lighting Handbook*. New York: Illuminating Engineering Society, 1947.
† From *Teaching About Light and Sight*, p. 45. Washington, D.C.: Research Division, N.E.A. 1946.
** From Hamon, Ray L. *Lighting Schoolrooms*, Pamphlet No. 104. Washington, D.C.: U.S. Office of Education, 1948.

Clear visibility requires a distinct brightness difference within the visual task or central field, but brightness differences outside of the immediate visual task should be held within limits which are conducive to eye ease and efficiency.

To achieve this, the writer goes on to say that:

Brightness balance will not be accomplished until color is considered an equal partner with light. The seeing conditions in many schoolrooms can be improved as much by painting as by adding wattage. High-reflection-factor surfaces in a room contribute to better lighting by the reducing brightness differences and by actually increasing the availability of light. If the room and furniture surfaces reflect a high percentage of light, the light is diffused and shadows are reduced.

He further suggests that *ceilings* should be so finished as to have a reflection factor of 85 per cent, *walls* down to the wainscoting should have a reflection factor of not less than 60 per cent, and from the wainscoting to the base board the reflection factor should not be less than 40 per cent, *trim* should have approximately the reflective factor of the surrounding walls, the *floors* should maintain a reflection factor of 30 to 40 per cent, and equipment, such as desks, tables, chairs, should maintain a reflection factor of 30 to 40 per cent.

The following table may help the alert teacher to judge the reflection value of the room color scheme. With a knowledge of what are desirable lighting standards and some idea of the reflection value of colors there is much that the teacher can do to provide the maximum light for the pupils which the physical conditions permit. Shades can be manipulated to advantage, light of greater wattage can be used, and if seats are not bolted down pupils can move about the room in search of the best lighting conditions available.

TABLE 5. *Average Reflection Factor of Certain Colors*

Color	Average Reflection Value	Color	Average Reflection Value
White	.88	Dark — Blue	.08
Light — Blue-Green	.72	— Yellow	.50
— Buff	.70	— Brown	.10
— Cream	.79	— Grey	.25
— Grey	.73	— Green	.07
— Blue	.55	— Black	.03
Medium — Blue-Green	.54	Wood finishes	
— Yellow	.65	Maple	.42
— Buff	.63	Walnut	.16
— Grey	.61	Mahogany	.12

Adapted from *Electrical World*, p. 107, October 25, 1947.

Suggestions for regulation of lighting

The suggestions offered here apply particularly to older traditional classrooms. Where teachers are fortunate enough to teach in school buildings constructed to facilitate a modern educational program, rooms are larger, lighting is plentiful and properly blended, and the freedom of the workshop atmosphere of the rooms makes it easy for teacher and pupils to adjust their activities in such ways as to take advantage of all lighting possibilities.

A universal *first rule* stipulates that light should come over the left shoulder of the student. This rule needs intelligent interpretation, as does almost every generalized suggestion. The rule assumes, first, that seating arrangements are more or less fixed; and the rule, therefore, must take into account this total situation. Writing, reading, drawing, etc., are presumably done under fixed seating conditions. The basis for the rule is to avoid shadows when writing, drawing, or otherwise so engaged with seat work as to produce them, should light come over the right shoulder. It matters not at all over which shoulder the light comes if the student is reading, or engaged in classroom discussion where writing is not required. The second assumption lying still further back of the rule is that students are right-handed. The rule violates its purpose if thoughtlessly applied by the teacher to left-handed as well as right-handed students. In these days when flexible seating arrangements are the vogue, this rule needs intelligent application. Where overhead lighting is ideal, and wall light reflection blends the light to avoid shadows, the rule does not apply.

The *second rule* is that glares should be eliminated, as far as possible. The source of light-glare may arise from improperly shaded or unshaded windows. Windows in front or on two sides of the room will produce glares and cross shadows. It is disconcerting to an observer to see a student twisting about most uncomfortably in an effort to avoid direct rays of the sun upon book or writing while the teacher looks on quite unconscious of any difficulty. Shiny surfaces, particularly shiny blackboards, are most annoying. The glare makes reading of blackboard work exceedingly difficult. Improper artificial lighting, as well as direct lights near the front of the room, is another source of harsh glare. Hard, brilliant colors in wall and ceiling decoration as well as dark floors, desks, and other equipment, add to the causes of room-glare. The teacher may have little voice in the remedy of incorrect building construction, but he can have much to do with the use of shades, and sometimes through education may induce a change from direct to indirect lights with adequate candle power, or proper choice of colors when the time comes for periodic room redecoration. It is safe to say that most teachers, either because of carelessness or ignorance of principles of correct usage, do not use the window shades available with even a 50 per cent efficiency. In this connection a good but simple rule for teachers to keep in mind is that for visual comfort and efficiency within the visual field no area or source of light "be brighter than the task, nor less than one-third as bright as the task, while the general level of illumination is high." [4]

The *third rule* is that on dull, cloudy days all shades should be up on windows on one side of the room, and artificial lights used

[4] Paraphrased and quoted from *American School Buildings*, Twenty-Seventh Yearbook, American Association of School Administrators, p. 222. Washington: National Education Association, 1949.

particularly along the side of the room opposite the windows. Because a room "seems" to the teacher to be sufficiently lighted does not make it so. Objective standards are safer guides for the teacher to follow.

A *fourth rule,* frequently violated, is that teachers should stand, when class attention is desired, at a position in the room considerably distant from the windows. Many teachers have a habit of standing before a window during recitation, or other form of class activity where students must give frequent attention to the teacher. The undesirability of this position should be obvious. The more teachers adopt modern classroom methods the less these cautions will be needed.

A *fifth rule* is that when fixed seating exists in traditionally lighted rooms the teacher should see that left-handed students are located near a window, so that the evil of light shadows upon their work may be reduced to a minimum. The alert teacher can do this tactfully, without the student's becoming sensitive to his abnormality and the special consideration given him.

3. What Constitutes Good Heating and Ventilating?

Recent research and standards

Few phases of classroom conditions have been subject to more intense study, within the past twenty years, than the heathful aspects of room temperatures and ventilation. Many conclusions tend to require a change of the standards previously set. For example, almost all text references to date have set a minimum of thirty cubic feet of fresh air per minute for classrooms, or a complete change of air every eight minutes. Recent studies tend to show that one-half that volume of air change does not endanger health, and in many respects is more desirable. Indeed, some recent studies have indicated more healthful conditions at the lower volume of air change.[5]

---

[5] For a thorough and authoritative study of this entire problem see *Heating and Ventilating Recommendations for New York State Schools,* New York State Education Department, Division of School Buildings and Grounds. Albany, New York: University of the State of New York Press, 1946. See also *American School Buildings,* Twenty-Seventh Yearbook, American Association of School Administrators, pp. 146–156. Washington, D.C.: National Education Association, 1949.

Schoolroom temperatures

A temperature of 68° has been considered the most satisfactory for efficient study and health. The New York Commission on Ventilation found that variations of 2° to 3° above or below 70° "do not exert a measurable influence upon respiratory-disease-incident." The Commission did find, though, that respiratory-illness-inattendance was definitely higher with temperatures above 73° and below 67°. The Commission further found that overheating does have a very important effect upon the amount of physical work done. It was found that 15 per cent less work was performed at 75° than at 68° with 50 per cent relative humidity and no air movement, while at 86° with 80 per cent relative humidity, work was reduced 28 per cent. The humidity may vary from 25 to 50 per cent without appreciable effect upon the health or comfort of the students. Slightly below 50 is best. The recommendations made in 1949 by the New York Board of Education are in general agreement. It suggests lower temperatures where physical activity is involved.

The teacher can do much to control healthful and efficient working temperature conditions in the schoolroom. Perhaps when the difficulty is in underheating, the teacher can do little but notify the office, in schools controlled by central heating plants. Overheat can be regulated to a large extent by turning off radiators and through a proper use of open windows.

Schoolroom ventilation

For years it was assumed that poor ventilation involved toxic poison through the presence of an oversupply of carbon dioxide in the air. The more recently accepted view, and the one maintained by the New York Commission on Ventilation, is that the discomfort experienced in poorly ventilated rooms is due "not to any chemical poisons, known or unknown, but to interference with heat loss from the body surfaces resulting from high temperature, excessive humidity, and lack of air movement. . . . The conclusion of all competent experts today is that the essential problem of ventilation — except where poisons or dusts due to imperfect combustion or industrial processes are concerned — is physical and not chemical, cutaneous and not respiratory."[6]

[6] "Final Contributions of the New York Commission on Ventilation"; in *School Ventilation Principles and Practices,* p. 3. Bureau of Publications, Teach-

If excessive heat, humidity, and still air are the causes of discomfort associated with poor ventilation, then the main objective of ventilation obviously is to rectify these conditions where they exist. The Commission contends that the removal of bodily heat is the major concern of ventilation, and that it can be achieved by lowered humidity, lowered temperature, and by air circulation. They suggest, further, that bodily exhalations in ill-ventilated rooms produce odors esthetically unpleasant, but that, other than the possible effect on health through lessened appetite that has been shown to result, no ill effects will be felt.

The teacher need not be concerned over the controversy that has waged over adequate ventilation systems. He can teach without anxiety if the air is not changed once every eight minutes. If temperature and humidity are controlled and some air movement assured, no danger to health need be feared. Experiments have shown that elaborate mechanical devices to purify air and circulate it at the rate of 30 cubic feet per minute per student are no better than simpler window-gravity types under normal conditions. In fact students and teachers complain of odors and uncomfortable drafts where air circulates so rapidly. When the teacher must aid ventilation, open windows, with sash boards that protect the student against draft, are considered satisfactory. The main things the teacher needs to watch are air movement without drafts upon students, heating, and excessive humidity.

4. What Are the Problems of Seating?

Hygiene of school seating

The hygiene of school seating has received careful study in recent years. Bennett, in his painstaking study,[7] cites data to show the bad effect improper school seating has upon correct physiological development and health. In one instance of 400 cases treated at the Boston Hospital for the Crippled and Ruptured, over 71 per cent of the cases were considered to have their origin in school. Girls are the greater sufferers from bad school posture.

ers College, Columbia University, New York, 1931. These conclusions are concurred in by the New York State Educational Department, and American Association of School Administrators in the sources referred to earlier in this chapter.

[7] Bennett, H. E. *School Posture and Seating,* chapters IV–V. Boston: Ginn and Company, 1928.

Seats are provided the teacher, but most schools are equipped with seats or desks of different sizes. The teacher may well see to it that the best possible seating adjustments are made, within the limits the schoolroom gradation in seat-size permits. The teacher should consult a scientific study of seating with its practical suggestions.

Light and seating

Under the consideration of light some aspects of good seating were incidentally discussed. On the assumption the teacher had the traditional seating and lighting conditions to contend with, it was suggested that the students be seated, except in special cases, in such a manner that light might come over the left shoulder. This is difficult to do because the students seated near the front of the room will be ideally located, while those midway back near the window may find light from the front, side, and rear. The student in the last row near the window will probably face the light. Where the teacher has moveable seats or tables and chairs adjustments should be made to overcome these difficulties.

The angle at which the book is placed before the student is important for ease of reading vision. The page should be on a direct vertical line with the eye if distortions are to be avoided. Often unconsciously the student will squirm into grotesque positions in an effort to approximate a vertical relation between eye and page. Desks with slanting tops are most desirable. Where these are not provided the alert teacher will suggest some way in which the student may improvise such a slanting effect for his book. Students are observed frequently with a couple of books under the upper portion of the one read, so as to form an angle that permits an approximation of a vertical line between page and eyes.

Defective hearing and seating

In most classes the teacher will have one or two students with defective hearing. In rare cases the defect will be so noticeable that the teacher can pick out the sufferer quickly. Generally the deafness is only partial; and, if it is of long standing, the student will have acquired a means of compensation so that the handicap is not noticeable to the casual observer. The author had a University student totally deaf in one ear and defective in the other. Four years of intermittent association with that student, however, did not suggest her difficulty until, one day while she was in the office, she casually remarked that an illness had left her hearing semi-defective. She resorted to lip reading to supplement auditory stimulus.

Most students are sensitive about any physical defect of this nature. The teacher should acquaint himself with the physical record of every student in his classes, and as unobtrusively as possible seat these students near the front and at an angle from the teacher's accustomed position before the class so that the disadvantage of left- or right-side deafness can be minimized.

Seating in relation to learning

The traditional classroom seating arrangement is based upon the equally traditional educational theory that learning is a "pouring in" process. The students are assumed to be empty vessels into which a golden stream of wisdom flows from the lips of the teacher into the eager ears of the learner. The teacher is the center of the educational situation; therefore the seating is so organized that attention is focused upon the teacher. It is what is known as the teacher-centered theory of education. Naturally the lecture method has been the dominant mode of teaching in this theory of education. In Europe, whence we appropriated much of our earlier theory and method, the lecture was the almost exclusive *modus operandi* of the secondary classroom. In America the classroom method gradually shifted from the lecture to the recitation, or "lesson hearing," as the latter has been called. The teacher still remained central, though the "pouring in" came via the textbook. The seating arrangement remained as satisfactory for the recitation as it had been for the lecture. To insure quiet and ease of administration the seats were fastened to the floor, in rows of military precision.

Today all is changed — in theory. Seating practice remains largely as in the past. Adjustment of our practice has not kept pace with theory. The lecture is considered incidental, and the traditional recitation is in ill repute. Other methods have to a large degree supplemented them in accepted educational theory, based upon a "child centered" concept of education. Activity rather than passivity is thought to be the key to learning. The seating organization in a large majority of our high schools, however, would fit admirably into the philosophy and practice of education of two centuries past. Gradually, loose-arm chairs and tables are supplant-

ing the rigid immovable desks. In these places the observer will
see students grouped about in circles with the teacher seated in
the circle, or clustered in small groups in various parts of the room,
or possibly silently at work at a table or chair with the teacher in
the background as educational guide and counselor. To fit the
newer theory of education seating must be flexible, so that, when
lecture or testing is in order, seats may be arranged to face one
way; when discussion or study is in order, the seats may be placed
singly, in a circle, or in small groups, to meet the needs of the
situation.

The teacher who accepts the newer theory of education may
find it difficult to fit into his own needs a seating plan adjusted to
a contrary theory. Adaptations are all that the teacher can make.
Salesmanship, after considerable orientation into the life of the
school, may bring about changes — movable desks at least — but
these must, if at all, come slowly. Patience here becomes a virtue.
The important thing is for the teacher to recognize what philosophy
of education and method lies back of traditional forms of classroom
organization so that every advantage may be utilized through intelligent adaptation and adjustment where these are possible.

5. What Is Good Classroom Equipment?

Need of classroom equipment

In Chapter 15 the problem of equipment was discussed in considerable detail and from the standpoint of visual aids. Only brief
mention will be made of equipment problems here. A recent
writer has said, "A good teacher might teach a lesson in appreciation without a picture before the class, but most teachers would be
doomed to failure without one." It is like the old Hebrews' complaint while in Egyptian bondage that they were compelled to
make bricks without straw. Teaching is more fortunate than many
other professions: one can teach with little equipment. The degree
of efficiency that might have been rendered with adequate equipment, however, is another story. The writer met a young graduate
of the law school a short time ago and, after congratulating him on
the degree and successful passing of the State Bar examination,
asked him where he had set up his practice. He replied he was
not practicing law because he had not been able to associate himself with any law firms; his home town did not have a court library

and, of course, he did not have money to procure the necessary equipment. No teacher is so dependent upon equipment, though the untrained public has not realized the absolute necessity for equipment if the best teaching is to be done. The fact that the teacher and the school can apparently "get by" without it should not lead the teacher to underestimate the value of equipment. A good professional library for himself is an essential for the teacher.

Equipment needed

Most smaller communities are woefully deficient in ordinary school indispensables. Office files, mimeographs or duplicator machines, maps — even decent blackboards, erasers, and chalk — are not always available, or, if they are, they are in bad condition and inadequate in quantity. Most of our larger schools are more fortunate. Many desirable things may be lacking, but necessities they usually possess, and these of good quality and quantity.

Blackboards have been considered indispensable to the school, and so they are. The extensive space devoted to blackboards is less needed than formerly. Some of this space could more profitably be used for display boards.

An extensive library is more and more becoming a *sine qua non* of a good school. The shift in educational point of view and method necessitates a working library of standard reference works of recent copyright and supplementary materials in each major and related field. A small high school library should have upwards of five thousand volumes, of comparatively recent issue. Ordinary books of fifteen to twenty-five years' vintage are of little value. Books of ten-year purchase, except in standard fields such as classics in literature, are likely to be obsolescent. In many sciences they become positively obsolete. In a recent state adoption of textbooks in which texts for twenty-seven subjects were considered, only six titles of the adoption six years previous were resubmitted by textbook publishers. Some of these the publishers must have known were obsolescent and superseded by more excellent texts then on the market. It is difficult for the very small rural high schools to secure sufficient money for books to enable efficient work to be done. Fortunately, many state libraries, even county libraries, are developing an extension service in which books in quantities of fifty or more are loaned for a given period to the school, subject to exchange for another quota of books. Valuable as this service is, librarians and school officials recognize it as a makeshift only, in lieu of a school-owned library of adequate proportions. Many educators rightly consider a large working library as the very heart of the modern school's equipment.

The attitude toward science equipment has been undergoing considerable change in recent years. Expensive, ingenious equipment is not looked upon as a necessity. A definite reduction in expensive laboratory equipment of the kind that used to clutter the shelves of school science rooms seems in order except for technical schools. These words will not have much application, however, to the very small high school. It has seldom provided enough equipment for good lecture-demonstration procedure, let alone the needs for good laboratory work. Many consider the use of inexpensive materials more advisable for physics or general science courses — materials with which the student is familiar — rather than expensive, highly complicated devices that attract attention more to their novelty than to the mechanical principles they are supposed to exemplify. Many mechanical contrivances about the home, particularly in rural communities, provide the basis for the elucidation of principles the students have repeatedly questioned as they observed the operation of these implements and devices. Radio sets, mechanical egg beaters, cream separators, and even old discarded automobile engines will serve the purpose of demonstration. The writer recently visited a rural high school where an old Ford Model T engine had been brought to the school by a member of the science class to study phases of combustion, electrical current, gear ratios, etc. Almost every phase of an elementary course in physics can be illustrated by equipment familiar to the student and in the natural environment of his interests, as well as his everyday usage.

Physical education, among the special subjects, has likewise undergone a revision of emphasis upon equipment. Elaborate equipment is not looked upon as necessary. Some apparatus especially designed for corrective work should be supplied. Calisthenics has given place in progressive practice to free sports and games intramural in nature. The day of excessive interschool athletics happily seems definitely in disfavor. Many schools have had the courage to abandon these competitive sports altogether in favor of a more wholesome balanced intramural form of sports. For such a program only a modest amount of equipment is necessary. The ingenious teacher will find it possible to get students to furnish much equipment of a personal nature, and various devices to raise money may be resorted to when the school budget does not care for all absolute necessities.

6. How Develop Room Atmosphere?

The nature of atmosphere

A nationally known educator likes to tell of an experience he had with a supervisor and principal in a class on "School Problems." They had been discussing "atmosphere" as an important factor in a good school situation. All agreed that it was very important to the morale of the classroom and the school. When they attempted an analysis of what constituted "atmosphere," there was considerable disagreement. One principal in particular insisted that "atmosphere" was intangible, largely associated with a vague something about the teacher's personality. She insisted that she could always tell when a good or bad "atmosphere" was present, but it was impossible to define it objectively or analyze it into constituent elements. She had had trouble with teachers who had bad "atmosphere" in the classroom, and had dismissed some from her building. After the beginning of school, the next autumn, this principal came to the educator in question and said: "I have an apology to offer. Never again will I say 'atmosphere' is an intangible quality that cannot be analyzed." Then this principal told of a certain room in her building that had been the source of trouble for several years. Teachers had been moved because they were judged unsatisfactory. The "atmosphere" was noticeably bad. The present teacher had not done well the year before, but this year something had happened. The class was different. She sensed a different attitude on the part of students and teacher — a changed "atmosphere." She tried to find a reason for the change. It suddenly dawned upon her that there were some very definite reasons for the transformation. She remembered this room for several years had been dingy with blackened coal-smoked walls, dark-stained woodwork, old rickety desks, shiny worn-out blackboards, dark, dirty oiled floors, etc. During the summer the room had been renovated. Now the floors had been finished like new, walls retinted mellow shades of cream and white, the woodwork restained in lighter color, and new desks, blackboards, and light-colored window shades installed. A few pictures had been placed upon the wall. "Now," said she, "I know some of the things that make up 'atmosphere.' Never again will I be guilty of blaming a teacher when part of the difficulty is in the condition of the room itself."

Sometime ago the writer was visiting a beautiful new school building, occupied but two or three years. Quite in contrast to many buildings, no writing on the walls, or carving or scratching on the desks was visible. The writer commented on this fact to the principal. With a note of pride the principal replied: "No, you will find no marks on building or desks. Our students take a pride in the building. They even move through the corridors with a decorum it was impossible to secure in the old building. There they did everything students usually do to walls and desks. Discipline has been much easier since we moved into this new building."

Teacher control of class atmosphere

Two major factors enter into the thing we call "classroom atmosphere" — room conditions, and the personality of the teacher. Over both of these the teacher has a large measure of control. Only infrequently can he secure the complete reconditioning of the classroom when floors, walls, woodwork, and desks are dull or in a dilapidated condition. Things are seldom so bad, however, that they might not be much worse. Teachers have been observed to work wonders with rooms of rather formidable appearance. Even good rooms may be made to have a bad appearance through careless disorder of room equipment, paper allowed to collect on the floor, some shades permitted to remain at half mast, others at rakish slants, while the teacher's desk and supply shelves are cluttered and disheveled. Neatness and orderliness are the first prerequisites of desirable class atmosphere. The teacher who senses the value of classroom atmosphere, as the stimulus to good work and good discipline, will see to it that students develop a pride in good classroom conditions. When efforts to secure administrative help to recondition the classroom are of no avail, the alert teacher will enlist the cooperation of the students to contribute pictures and a few house plants from their homes. The teacher can well afford, in the last extremity, to spend a few dollars in wall decorations. Student cooperation in minor money-raising schemes may be possible, in small schools, to buy curtains and pictures. Most P.T.A. organizations are more than willing to help the aggressive teacher.

The factors of personality, enthusiasm, tact, pleasantness, vitality, cheerfulness, etc., are all subject to the control and development of the teacher. These have a large place in the development of favorable "classroom atmosphere." The teacher should give as detailed and careful study to the development of desirable personality traits as he does to the physical conditions of the classroom. Indeed, it would seem that personality should receive much more attention, since personality is the much more enduring and pervasive factor of classroom atmosphere.

QUESTIONS AND PROBLEMS

1. Why is it especially important to overcome adverse schoolroom conditions in teaching adolescents?
2. What relation have satisfactory physical conditions in the classroom to the teacher's personal welfare?
3. If you were placed in a poorly ventilated schoolroom, what chief measures would you attempt to take in order to assure proper ventilation?
4. List the requisites for an ideally lighted classroom.
5. What is the reason for the rule that light should come over the left shoulder? How should the teacher adapt this rule?
6. Explain the importance of a teacher's position in relation to the source of light.
7. What are the standards of temperature regulation?
8. Why is the hygiene of seating such an important question?
9. What type of seating fits the newer ideas of education?
10. List and evaluate the most desirable forms of classroom equipment that should (a) be common to all classrooms; (b) be available to the classroom in your teaching major and minor subjects.
11. Discuss the value of an adequate school-owned library.
12. What is the modern attitude toward science equipment?
13. How can the expense of elaborate laboratory equipment be minimized?
14. What is a desirable minimum of equipment for the physical education work?
15. What are the most important factors of classroom "atmosphere"?
16. How do personality traits of the teacher play a part in classroom atmosphere?

SELECTED BIBLIOGRAPHY

Adams, B. "Reflectance Factor in School Lighting," *School Executive.* 70: 50 (April, 1951).
American School Buildings, chapters IX, XIII, XIV. Twenty-seventh

Yearbook, American Association of School Administrators. Washington, D.C.: American Association of School Administrators. N.E.A., 1949.

American Standard Practice for School Lighting. Illuminating Engineering Society in American Institute of Architects. New York: American Standards Association, 1948.

"Controlled Daylight in Classrooms." *Catholic School Journal.* 51: 30a (May, 1951).

Darley, William G. "Current Trends in School Lighting." *The Nation's Schools,* 41: 37–39 (April, 1948).

Hamon, Ray L. *Lighting Schoolrooms.* Pamphlet No. 104. Washington, D.C.: U.S. Office of Education, 1948.

Harmon, Darell B. *The Coordinated Classroom.* Grand Rapids, Michigan: American Seating Company, 1949.

Hathaway, Winifred. *Daylight in the Schoolroom.* New York: National Society for the Prevention of Blindness, 1946.

Heating and Ventilating Recommendations for New York State Schools. New York State Department of Education, Division of School Buildings and Grounds. New York: University of the State of New York Press, 1948.

Heating, Ventilating, Air Conditioning Guide. New York: American Society of Heating and Ventilating Engineers, 1948.

I.E.S. Lighting Handbook. New York: Illuminating Engineering Society, 1947.

Lewis, E. E. "Equipping the Classroom as a Learning and Teaching Laboratory." *American School Board Journal,* 101: 29–30 (December, 1940).

Lighting for Shops and Special Classrooms. Washington, D.C.: Research Division, National Education Association, 1947.

Nelson, H. W. "School Heating and Ventilating During the Past Fifty Years." *American School Board Journal,* 100: 37–38 (March, 1940).

"Schools." *Aspiration, An Air Conditioning Quarterly,* vol. 7, no. 2 (1951).

Seagers, Paul W. "A Different Approach to Ventilation." *The Nation's Schools,* 42: 60, 62, 64 (October, 1948).

Seagers, Paul W. "Visual Environment for Schoolrooms." *Indiana University School of Education Bulletin,* 26: 5–21 (May, 1950).

Specifications for Chair Desk Studies, Series VII. School Plant Research, No. 2. Washington, D.C.: American Council on Education, 1942.

Visual Comfort and Efficiency in School Buildings. New York State Department of Education, Division of School Buildings and Grounds. New York: University of the State of New York Press, 1948.

18

How Can Group Procedures Be Organized?

1. What Are Some Immediate Considerations?

Time to cover course

Unless the details of classroom procedure are most carefully worked out, the teacher is likely to discover that the hour has been frittered away, with little accomplished. Entire class periods have been wasted by the lack of organization which led to confusion, the attempt to retrace steps, the consequent interjection of problems foreign to the work of the hour, and a series of subsequent events that left both teacher and pupil bewildered to find the hour over and no progress made. Even where less serious losses of time occur, it is easy to waste ten minutes here, and another five minutes there because work has not been properly organized. Most teachers find it difficult to complete the work of the course in the usual time allotted This would not be of great concern, in and of itself. Modern education is concerned primarily with the development of desirable behavior patterns. It is important, however, that the work be so well organized that the pupils have as much significant experiencing as is possible.

Maintain student interest. Even more serious than failure to develop a consistent program of work is the devastating effect of lost motion on student interest. The student may not be able to analyze the situation and discover the reason for his lack of interest, but he is uninterested none the less. To maintain student

442

interest the class must reflect a definite healthy tempo. The teacher must guard against a too automatic sequence of movement from one phase of work to another, however, lest a sense of monotony develop. Spontaneity and freedom for the unexpected must always be present to challenge alertness on the part of the student.

Avoid waste of student learning opportunities

In a very real sense the teacher is the custodian of the learning opportunities of the student. Modern education is concerned with providing every student with the facilities that encourage and open the way for learning. The school is looked upon as the chief agency of society, outside the home, to provide these opportunities. Anything the teacher may do that inhibits these opportunities is a violation of his trust. While thoughtful people must reject the fatalism implied in the old adage, "Opportunity knocks but once," it is well to remember there is a very grave sense in which those words are true. If 10 to 25 per cent of the time the student spends in school has for any reason been wasted, he has lost opportunities that can never return. Furthermore, the teacher should think of his responsibility to the class not in terms, let us say, of five minutes lost in needless time-consuming methods of roll call for one individual, but rather in the larger perspective of thirty times five, or two hours and thirty minutes of precious time for members of the class, should there be thirty in the class. To visualize time wastage for students in these terms makes the picture an appalling one. No business concern of importance would tolerate such lack of economical procedure. Because the teacher is concerned with the learning potentialities of youth, it is infinitely more important that time for learning opportunity be conserved to the last degree.

Develop an appreciation of time

"Time and tide wait for no man." Even though we wish it might be otherwise, we are bound by the minute hand of time. The world is geared to an increasingly accelerated pace. There is a sense of urgency about modern life that has made itself felt in the schools. H. G. Wells gave expression to that sense when he said: "The future of civilization rests upon the results of a race between education and catastrophe." There is a widespread feeling of world crisis. Men in high places point the finger of responsibility for the future at the school. The school is faced with these problems. The world has become so complex and its problems have become so extensive and involved that opportunities to expose the student to experiences that promote understanding and provide competencies with which to grapple with them at best are limited. Besides, there are almost unlimited behavioral competencies the modern student must have, if he is to cope successfully with the more immediate problems of life, and, withal, a shortage of time in which to acquire the basic elements of this preparation exists. It has become necessary to determine the most desirable attitudes the student should have, and the extent to which techniques and skill in the solution of problems can be mastered while the student is in school.

The school can transmit no more important heritage to the student than a wholesome appreciation of the value of time. His future success depends in no small measure on his ability to sense time-values and to adjust his life to the tempo this age requires. The most effective way for the student to acquire such adjustment is by "precept and example" that require a similar adjustment within the school to that demanded outside. The teacher who organizes the detail of school life to maximum effectiveness, and requires the same efficiency in the learning activity of the students, has discharged well that part of his stewardship.

2. What Are Some Educational Problems in Classroom Organization?

Theory of management

Within recent years two sharply differentiated schools of thought have appeared — one demanding almost complete freedom for the child without let or hindrance; the other maintaining the older disciplinary organization akin to that of our military schools. The advocates of extreme freedom have given expression to their ideas in the "activity school." The other type might well be characterized by the examples Burton gives [1] of the pupils on the playground when the principal, who is always present with bell in hand, may decide to speak to some of the pupils:

The bell is tapped, and the children, some three or four hundred of them, stand stock still. The boys engaged in football or baseball

[1] Burton, W. H. *Supervision and the Improvement of Teaching*, p. 31. New York: D. Appleton and Company, 1922.

stop in their tracks, or if it be marble season, the lads remain on one knee until permission to arise comes from the upper regions.

Both theories claim to strive for the same goal: the "socially efficient individual," but they do not always agree as to what constitutes such an individual.

Apart from these two extremes, many who align themselves with neither school are in agreement that society does require conformity to its *mores* and conventions in limited degree, while at the same time society needs creative leadership and individual initiative if it is to advance. It is the position of this text throughout that neither socialization nor individualization can be sacrificed. It is a grave error to assume the student can be made a responsible citizen by unrestrained irresponsible individualism while in school, or that rigid training in lockstep conformity will develop initiative and creative genius. It is true that the student must come to assume a social point of view and adjust his behavior patterns in conformity therewith to an extent undreamed by his parents, if our present and anticipated future complex social organism is to function intelligently. The school must be figuratively the cradle in which the education for this new social order is vouchsafed to the student.

The dangers of mechanization

One apparent danger of a too thorough mechanization of classroom procedure is that a spirit of spontaneity may be destroyed. A situation that has been routinized to the nth degree leaves very little place for the unusual or unplanned to take place. Students like the zest of uncertainty and adventure. Creativeness cannot thrive under too rigid a classroom routine. Nonconformity is of the very genius of creative endeavor. Where all must work alike, the spirit of creative genius is likely to be crushed or effectively discouraged. Individual differences are ignored.

Then, too, mechanization tends to the blind acceptance of procedures without bother of question. An attitude is soon likely to prevail best expressed in the words of that famous poem, "Theirs not to reason why, Theirs but to do and die." Unfortunate the school where students accept this routine without question, or where teachers assume it is not the province of the student to inquire the reason for the rule. All of us, no doubt, have observed the deadening effect of such training. Intelligent social education is not won by this method. Students should understand and accept, as part of their social government, whatever routine is required. What is more, modern education for democratic living requires that the pupil have a real part in setting up the "rules of the road" he is expected to observe in school. It is a fundamental part of his educational experience.

A third danger is the tendency for the mechanization of classroom procedure to pervade the mental life of the students. Learning then becomes a matter of unquestioned acceptance of what the teacher presents, and is stereotyped in form. It is then that we see the student frequently as the smaller edition of his teacher as far as his mental reactions are concerned. It is this type of mind the demagogue can influence most easily. A critical attitude has not been developed. It is the kind of mind the totalitarian state idealizes in its citizens. It is the very antithesis of the kind of mind essential to the success of our American democracy.

Still a fourth danger lies in the tendency of the teacher to forget the democratic nature of his office. The older teacher is often regarded as dogmatic and arbitrary. Much of this notion was back of the protests of the opposition to the persistence of former President Woodrow Wilson when they said, "Never again will we have a schoolmarm as president." Whatever the actual justification for these strictures on former President Wilson, it is true that his immovableness in the face of what he regarded as moral principles led the old-guard opportunistic politicians to see in his actions the arbitrariness of the stereotype autocratic school teacher. The older ideas of education and classroom practice developed a spirit of autocracy on the part of such teachers that gave rise to these caricatures.

Advantages of mechanization

In addition to the more immediate advantages suggested at the beginning of this chapter, there is that of the training the student gets in socialization. Increasingly our complex social organism must limit the freedom of the individual in behalf of the welfare of the group. None can read the "signs of the times" without being impressed with the extent to which America is retreating from the old philosophy of "rugged individualism" in the direction of social cooperation. Business and industry have been experimenting rather radically with various schemes of co-operative endeavor. Social legislation designed to protect the interests of the larger group, it is safe to say, will increase rather than diminish. The school itself steadily becomes larger and more complex in organization as larger units supplant the historic one-room school. Complexity necessitates more mechanics of procedure to insure an efficient school society. Natural, not artificial, are the reasons that argue in favor of routinization of much of classroom procedure as a part of the larger social education needed outside the school.

A more direct advantage lies in the wider freedom mechanized routine gives the student. Paradoxical as it may seem, the student can readily see how conformity to routine procedure frees the school for greater achievement. Let a half dozen students try to talk at once in the classroom and observe the result. No one is able to get his ideas across to others. A stalemate is shortly reached, and corrected only when a mechanical rule is applied to govern the manner of address to the teacher, and recognition of the student by the teacher before the student tries to give expression to his ideas. The student can learn in the routinization of classroom procedures the valuable social principle of "liberty through law."

A third advantage involves the conservation of energy for the larger and more important issues that confront both teacher and student. The eminent psychologist, William James,[2] long ago expressed this idea thus:

> The great thing, then, in all education, is to make our nervous system our ally instead of our enemy. It is to fund and capitalize our acquisitions, and live at ease upon the interest of the fun. For this we must make automatic and habitual, as early as possible, as many useful actions as we can, and guard against the growing into ways that are likely to be disadvantageous to us, as we should guard against the plague. The more of the details of our daily life we can hand over to the effortless custody of automatism, the more our higher powers of mind will be set free for their own proper work.

Extent to which mechanization should take place

This problem is not a simple one to meet. In the abstract a ready solution may be given. But when specific applications are at-

[2] James, William. *The Principles of Psychology*, vol. 1, p. 122. New York: Henry Holt and Company, 1890. See the extended discussion of this point in a previous chapter (p. 352) where the above quotation was used.

tempted disagreement is likely to arise. Two closely related aspects of this issue immediately require the teacher's careful study.

First, to what extent may we reconcile uniformity with the recognition of creativeness and individual differences in education? At first there seems to be no basis of reconciliation — the one is the antithesis of the other. If we take two or three examples, however, it may be evident that adjustments are possible. Roll call, for example, need not interfere with individual differences of educational significance if made mechanical and routine. Neither should the form of recognition required of student by teacher for the privilege of expressing one's opinions. To require all to study the same materials or write exactly the same type of theme within the same time limits would sooner or later be destructive of individual needs and cramp creativeness at its best. To require a certain standard of work for all as a minimum, with variation to care for varied interests, to require that the work be completed on the same uniform paper, with a standard pattern of arrangement and a maximum of time in which to complete the work, would involve both conformity in broad categories and freedom for individualization of work within reasonably extended limits.

The *second* phase of the problem concerns the relation of classroom regimentation and creative individualism to the needs of society and the school. It has been pointed out before that society needs an oncoming citizenship trained in the social point of view and schooled in the practice of socialized activity and living. To accomplish such socialization rigorous education is needed in the discovery of those principles of harmonious group thought and expression necessary to the orderly well-being of society. Furthermore, many of these forms of thought and action must have been made habitual in individual behavior. Society cannot escape stagnation with conformity alone. It must have the creative individualist who refuses to be chained to the thought-grooves of the accepted majority. In some measure nonconformity in behavior is necessary as well, though far less so than is needful in thought. Again, experience has shown all too clearly the improbability that creative genius will suddenly assert itself in adulthood, if it is never exercised in youth. The school, therefore, has the dual responsibility of the preparation of the individual for the larger demands of his contemporary society, as well as that of adulthood, both in these elements of conformity for society's well-being and in the ability to contribute creatively toward the progress of society through individual thought and expression.

3. What Activities Should Be Mechanized?

Seating

If the class is small, with not over eight or ten students, designated seats are ordinarily not necessary. The class can be conducted informally and efficiently. Problems incident to the large class are not likely to arise, and individuals will feel more a sense of personal responsibility to the class. The members of larger classes may be assigned definite seats for the term if the traditional fixed type of seating in set rows is the vogue. Confusion can be avoided, special consideration given once and for all to those with physical defects or needs that warrant special attention, and the teacher will be able the better to visualize the class and its members as the daily preparation is made. Most seating is done alphabetically. Occasionally the alphabetical arrangement should be reversed to give equal opportunity for those to be seated near the front whose names place them far down the alphabetical list and thus toward the rear of the class. This caution is more necessary with junior high school than with senior high school classes. Immaturity requires more elaborate routine controls. The classes furthermore are usually larger in the lower grades of the high school. Modern education tends to frown on fixed seating, and as newer ideas in school buildings provide good lighting and table and chair equipment, less formalized seating should prevail.

Class roll

Class rolls should be carefully kept under all conditions. A definite mode of checking should be adopted and followed. The teacher should try to discover a way to do this, economical both of time and class distraction. Some otherwise very good teachers waste as much as five minutes with roll check. Very early establish a policy of checking either absence or attendance. Absences are fewer and more quickly checked. A roll book and a cardboard diagram of the seating arrangement in squares with names for each square enables the teacher to dispense with the roll quickly. Some teachers handle the roll check by the use of responsible monitors who check the roll and post the attendance slip at the door, when such a detail is required. The teacher then is free to begin class work the moment the bell rings, without the distraction usually attendant upon the check of the class roll. Further, the teacher should make it a routine detail to check the roll at the beginning of the hour. Many times teachers have been observed in confusion and the class distracted from the work in hand by the appearance of the office monitor to collect the attendance slip. The teacher should be aware that such irregularity does not make the best impression on the class when the teacher in turn properly demands care of detail.

Light, ventilation, heat

Few phases of classroom procedure are more important, and yet more frequently neglected, than lighting, ventilation, and heating. If there is to be careful attention to these important details the writer can suggest but one sure way to safeguard a fair room condition. At the beginning of every class hour the teacher should make automatic the practice of checking temperature, ventilation, and adequate light. If this is done at the beginning of the hour the chance of poor light, bad air, or over-heated rooms will be reduced to a minimum. Occasionally a very responsible student with good judgment may be assigned this duty as a monitor. The writer has always questioned this policy because of the inevitable distraction this responsibility imposes upon the conscientious monitor. Unlike roll check, these features need some attention throughout the period.

Use of materials and equipment

It is disconcerting to turn to the blackboard to write or draw a diagram illustrative of some item in the lesson, only to discover that no chalk is available. The writer has seen this recur repeatedly. The teacher should make it an inflexible rule, practiced until automatic, that before every class period a quick check is made to see that equipment needed for that hour is there and in usable condition. One of the most brilliant student-teachers the writer has worked with made a dismal failure of her training period by chronic negligence in the preparation of materials so that they would be in usable form for expeditious handling when needed. In spite of reprimand and pleading, Mary seemed constitutionally unable to reduce to mechanized routine a plan to handle materials for her class. She taught English literature, and the circumstances were such that she had to employ three sets of books of different publishers to supply her class needs during the class period. Five minutes elapsed between classes, but Mary never could utilize that time to collect the books into three stacks on her desk or on the book shelves of the room, decide how these books should be distributed when needed, or collected when the class was through with them. She was an honor scholarship college senior, yet her apparent inability to regularize simple routine for the expeditious care of classroom materials produced a very unwholesome classroom condition and stamped her a near failure as a teacher.

If certain materials are used frequently, such as books of the kind suggested above, and if papers for themes, examinations, etc., are to be distributed or collected, the class should become accustomed to uniform routine for the handling of these materials. If certain students are regular monitors, and certain mechanical schemes of distribution and collection have been taught the class, the teacher can save time and energy for more important things while the class avoids confusion, since it knows what is expected of it and in turn what to expect of the teacher and monitors. It should be a routine reduced to a rite that all laboratory equipment to be used in the class period be carefully checked in advance and conveniently arranged, so that class procedure may go forward with a minimum of confusion, loss of time, and misdirected energy. Much time is wasted and interest lost, also, by interminable dictation and the copying of materials that should be taken care of through the mimeograph or other means of duplication. "Just ten minutes to dictate this," some teacher will say, but when those ten minutes are multiplied by the class enrollment the result is startling. The teacher may well develop the habit of first asking, "How much time could be saved by mimeographing or duplicating this material?" and, "Is the permanent value of this material such as to make such duplication desirable?" If the teacher forced himself into the routine‑habit of first considering these questions, much time would be saved and classroom interest preserved.

Classroom courtesies

The writer had an unusual opportunity recently to observe the effect on the morale of a class of failure to establish definite mechanics to govern classroom discussion. As he conversed in the corridor with a supervisor, conversation was interrupted by the sound of voices raised in argument in a nearby room under the direction of a student teacher. It was obvious that several persons were trying to talk at once and that no one could be distinctly heard. As the voices became higher pitched and the tones evidenced growing excitement, the writer stepped into the room for the rest of the hour. The class was considering some very controversial theories of economics. The student teacher, a competent major in economics, was endeavoring to secure a judicious evaluation of various theories without in any way betraying his personal predilections for any one theory. His teaching pedagogy was excellent as he appealed for an unprejudiced weighing of the arguments for and against each theory. The class was electric with tense interest. All desired, and tried, to express their points of view simultaneously. The class hour closed with the class approximately where it was when the writer entered the room, except that prejudices had no doubt been more firmly established in the minds of many students through the emotional stimulus attendant upon an effort to express themselves. All this might have been avoided, without sacrifice of the keen interest displayed, had the teacher formulated a few clearly reasonable routine mechanics for class participation at the beginning of the course and rigidly adhered to them until the students conformed automatically. It was suggested to the student teacher that he immediately work out some definite mechanics governing participation in class discussion, take part of the class period the next day to inaugurate them, and lead the class to see how their operation would have permitted each student to express himself fully and thoughtfully the previous day without the excitement and rude discourtesy displayed toward other members of the class. The teacher had a supreme opportunity to show how blind prejudice, mob hysteria, and often mob violence in society results from just such failure to observe routine courtesies.

There should be definite rules adopted, with full cooperation and understanding on the part of the class, governing the relation of student to teacher and student to student in class discussion and other forms of class participation. These rules should be rigidly obeyed until response to them becomes automatic. The student should come genuinely to appreciate the fact that the etiquette of classroom courtesy does not cramp but actually releases the student to larger freedom. It is partly because this fact is not thoroughly understood that response to rules of courtesy does not sooner become automatic. A further difficulty is that genuine courtesy requires constant thought beyond a few obvious rules of conduct. In the high school, where much free movement within the classroom is more and more the practice, the establishment of definite mechanics of courtesy is essential.

Blackboard usage

Mass use of the blackboard by the class is disappearing under the impact of modern classroom methods. Where class use of the blackboard is still practiced, some routinization of procedures is necessary. It may be assumed in the upper grades of the high school when classes are of medium size that the maturity of the students will assure an automatic response to proper behavior-patterns without too much elaboration of class rules. In the junior high school or in large classes some routine must be established for the use of the blackboard, where the class is expected to make much use of it. Since there is seldom blackboard space sufficient for all members of the class, mechanics must be set up to avoid confusion and loss of time. A teacher in mathematics was observed to request the class to go to the board. A casual glance at the blackboard should have made the teacher aware that only about one-half of the thirty-eight students could conveniently work there. After considerable confusion and delay she recalled half the class to their seats, with some irritation evident among the students. In the board work that followed the students at their seats were forgotten for fully fifteen minutes, and then remembered only after idle hands and minds had contrived some mischief. Another teacher announced that problems would be worked on the board. For the first part of the period, rows 1, 3, and the first four pupils in row 5 would go to the board. Those at their seats should get out pencil and paper and work the problems too. The businesslike routine organization of procedure enabled the class to carry on its work smoothly and in an atmosphere of purposefulness.

Response to bells

Most high schools still use some signal system to begin and close class periods uniformly throughout the school. It is here that much time is lost and needless confusion produced because a definite routine has not been established. Teachers have been observed who frittered away the first five or ten minutes and allowed a situation to develop in consequence that noticeably affected the tone of class work the remainder of the hour. When the bell rings, it should be the established rule that all are quietly in their seats and automatically begin whatever may be the work for the hour. The teacher should be ready to begin his peculiar function for that class hour the moment the bell rings and without any hesitation. This should become an invariable habit. It means that everything must be well planned and in readiness. Probably no one thing contributes more to the tempo and atmosphere of businesslike seriousness in the classroom than this simple practice of beginning promptly with the bell. The students should be trained to respond to the closing bell with quiet poise. While passing to and from classrooms should be informal, as befits the maturity and social responsibility of high school students, yet successful informality can be achieved only by insisting upon the observance of certain mechanics that become part of the routine of the school.

4. How Secure Mechanization of Routine and Habit?

As has been frequently implied in the preceding discussion, the successful mechanization and routinization of classroom procedure require the formation of habits of response. Habit is simply the building up of patterns of response by repetition until response becomes automatic under appropriate stimulus. It is, therefore, exceedingly important for teacher and student to determine what activities should be routinized, then to adopt and practice acceptable forms of behavior until they are carried on regularly without recourse to serious thought. William James, the psychologist, emphasized the necessity of certain steps in habit formation that apply with force to this situation:

1. determine as early as possible what should be relegated to the category of habit or routine;
2. begin the practice of those activities which are to become habits with as much momentum as possible;
3. never permit an exception until the habit is firmly established.

It is not easy to mechanize classroom procedure and build up habits of routine ways of doing things. The teacher must establish firmly his own habits of routine, then with each new class get these accepted and *habitized*.

The teacher will find the task much easier if students are brought to see and understand the values of such mechanized routine, and the necessity for no exceptions to the rule. Students normally respond to rational situations when the situations have been made rational to their own minds. Furthermore, if the students are to get the educational benefit of the larger social implication of this routine they must understand fully the significance of every phase of classroom mechanization. The danger of blind routine will be overcome if the teacher always makes it a point to present the reasonableness of every phase of routine he wishes to establish.

5. How Is Mechanization of Routine and Discipline Related?

Every phase of school management is intimately related to school discipline, as commonly conceived. Few teachers fully realize the importance for school discipline of a well-organized, mechanized classroom procedure. A well-ordered classroom is likely to be free from disciplinary problems. The writer is convinced from his own observation that over 50 per cent of the teacher's disciplinary difficulties grow out of poor techniques in classroom procedures or failure of the pupils to understand and accept the procedures proposed. When the teacher organizes everything carefully, students know what to expect, and each phase of the work is handled with ease and dispatch. Seldom has the writer observed a case of poor room-discipline where the details of classroom procedure were carefully organized and routinized in cooperation with the pupils.

Most of the matters discussed in this chapter and in the preceding one should be so self-evident to the intelligent teacher as to make the discussion superfluous. To the contrary, however, experience has revealed the woeful lack of ability of many teachers properly to organize classroom procedure, and almost as fatal to their teaching has been their inability to connect cause with effect when bad classroom conditions resulted from improper routinization of classroom procedures.

QUESTIONS AND PROBLEMS

1. What are the main reasons that may be offered for the importance of economy of time in the classroom?
2. List the principal factors of time-saving in a classroom situation.

3. What is the relation between routine and discipline?
4. Why is loss of student interest a serious failure in classroom economy?
5. Give arguments for the two schools of thought in relation to classroom management.
6. What is the author's viewpoint in respect to these two theories? To what extent do you agree with it?
7. What is meant by the "democratic nature" of the teacher's office?
8. List the advantages of mechanization.
9. Under what circumstances may mechanization of classroom procedure become dangerous?
10. How is the teacher's success in the classroom linked with his ability to control routine?
11. Why should the teacher present the reasonableness of every phase of routine?
12. How do the steps in habit formation, suggested by the psychologist, William James, apply to the mechanization routine?
13. Why has the author given a chapter to these matters, most of which have little direct bearing on the subject-teaching method?
14. What principles should be observed in seating? What are the advantages of assigning seats to individuals? Why are modern methods getting away from fixed seating?
15. What is the importance of teacher-pupil cooperation in setting up class routine procedures?

SELECTED BIBLIOGRAPHY

Baxter, Bernice. *Teacher-Pupil Relationships.* New York: The Macmillan Company, 1941.

Burton, William H. *The Guidance of Learning Activities,* chapter XXII. New York: Appleton-Century-Crofts, Inc., 1944.

Dalton, W. T. "Classroom Atmosphere Reflects Quality of Learning." *Educational Leadership,* 8: 429–433 (April, 1951).

Gaffney, M. P. "Wholesome Classroom Environment." *National Association of Secondary School Principals Bulletin,* 34: 125–128 (December, 1950).

Goetting, M. L. *Teaching in the Secondary School,* chapter III. New York: Prentice-Hall, Inc., 1942.

Moody, G. F. *Teacher Manages the Class,* Second Edition. Minneapolis: Burgess Publishing Company, 1947.

Reinoehl, C. M. and Ayer, F. C. *Classroom Administration and Pupil Adjustment,* chapters IX–XIII. New York: Appleton-Century-Crofts, Inc., 1940.

Risk, Thomas M. *Principles and Practices of Teaching in Secondary Schools,* Second Edition, chapter XXIX. New York: American Book Company, 1947.

Rivlin, Harry N. *Teaching Adolescents in Secondary Schools,* chapter XI. New York: Appleton-Century-Crofts, Inc., 1948.

Schorling, Raleigh. *Student Teaching,* Second Edition, chapter V. Mc-Graw-Hill Book Company, Inc., 1949.

Seyfert, W. C. "Wholesome Classroom Environment." *National Association of Secondary School Principals Bulletin,* 34: 128–133 (December, 1950).

Williams, L. A. *Secondary Schools For American Youth,* chapter XIII. New York: American Book Company, 1944.

19

What Are Some Problems of the First Day?

This chapter will not have equal significance for all teachers. The teacher who has already had a year of classroom experience will find that much of the discussion does not apply to him. And this is true also for the teacher who is beginning work in a large school system in a metropolitan center. However, contemporary educational thinking stresses the importance of the teacher having as complete a picture of the background of every pupil when school begins as is humanly possible. This involves an understanding of the pupil's educational background, his emotional peculiarities, his social and home background.

The dominant high school in the United States is a relatively small school in a medium-sized community where the conditions presupposed as a basis for the considerations of this chapter prevail. Since teachers in these communities, furthermore, represent to a large degree those of short tenure and consequent inexperience, it is for them that the conditions assumed exist in fullest measure.

1. What Are the Critical Aspects of the First Day?

First impression

All authorities agree on the importance of the students' first impression of their teacher. Psychology has long emphasized the significance of "primacy" in memory, and its persistence even when

458

later impressions have shown the error of the first. There is something inherently stubborn in primacy of impressions. When one person meets another, each is likely to make a mental estimate of the other which often colors all subsequent relations between the two. It is safe to say that a very large percentage of the rank and file of the public places much store by these first impressions. Many individuals refuse to be influenced by evidence which contradicts a first impression until that evidence becomes cumulative beyond ordinary reasonableness. Some extremists, to be found in nearly every communuity, refuse ever to reverse their primary judgments.

The student is but a reflection of his elders. The same psychological elements which influence adults affect also the preliminary judgments of the student. As compared to the adult, however, he suffers one serious limitation: he does not have the maturity gained by experience to temper the absolutism of his first impressions. The teacher, therefore, faces a crucial test of his teaching experience when he confronts this group of young people for the first time. Those for whom school days have not receded too far into dim memory will have no difficulty in recalling experience after experience of the first meeting with the new teacher, the very definite mental set established toward him, and the effect of that impression upon conduct immediately thereafter, and until the teacher had confirmed or dispelled that impression. It might not be so serious if each student confined his impressions to himself, but he does not; he wants confirmation of his impressions and eagerly seeks to learn those of his classmates. The writer not only can recall from memory impressions of this character as a student, and the subsequent effect upon conduct, but also he is privileged every year to observe its consequences upon the success of the young teacher in training.

Community reaction

Students are quick to share their estimates of the new teacher with members of their family. It is the natural result of the exuberance of youth and its tendency to speak as it thinks. Often these judgments are not restricted to the immediate family. So much depends upon the attitude of the community toward the teacher that such gossip, if it be unfavorable, is likely to prove a serious handicap to his school success and opportunity for community leadership.

Natural confusion incident to first day

The very nature of newness and uncertainty in the situation makes some confusion inevitable on the first day. Students are entering new courses frequently under new instructors. Changes in classrooms add to the confusion. For good and sufficient reasons, "English IV" has been changed to a different room or teacher from that of last year. Textbook changes prove awkward to many students, and even to teachers. New students are present who were not enrolled the previous year; some of these are new to the community as well as to the school. The school, therefore, has had no advance information about them; and the teacher is unexpectedly faced with unforeseen problems of classification and adjustment within the course. These are but typical of the conditions that will exist at the opening of school, no matter how carefully administrative officers and teachers have tried to anticipate every eventuality.

Administrative recognition of importance of first day

So thoroughly have educational leaders come to recognize the value of making a good beginning that increasingly our better school administrators are insisting that teachers report for duty from two days to a week before school formally opens. Many schools now include in the teacher's contract a provision that requires teachers to be present a certain length of time before a school formally opens. This time is devoted to planning, coordinating, and getting every phase of the school program ready for the opening day, so that the machinery will function smoothly as the staff inducts the students into the new work of the year. Where the administrative office or Board of Education does not require it, the wise teacher will of his own accord arrive in the community several days in advance. He will occupy himself in preparation for his work, as will be indicated in the further development of this chapter.

Opportunity to set tempo of year's work

There is no better time than the opening day to "begin." By this is meant starting out at the sound of the gong with the businesslike precision you expect to characterize class work the succeeding days of the year. Again, you utilize the psychological principle of "primacy" as it bears on first impressions to give a "mind-set" toward the work. One writer aptly remarks that if we loiter along the first day with the expectancy that we will get under way the next day, the chances are that the week will pass before any serious beginning is made. Students will tend to react negatively, when, if ever, the pace is set which should have been established immediately. It will probably remain an extremely difficult thing to keep students working at the tempo desired. On the other hand, if the class begins without waste of time and continues with a dispatch that challenges the best effort of the students, they will tend to assume in a natural way that this is the pace expected in the course. They will not tend to question class requirements, but will put forth every effort to keep abreast of them.

There is no intention to imply the old military martinet type of beginning. It is possible for the teacher to start with a disarming sense of ease and apparent lack of haste, exploring with the class their interests, educational purposes, and how they think the school can help them realize their aspirations. From this the teacher can move easily but with assurance step by step toward the goals set for himself. It is the technique of group leadership dynamics that enlists the cooperation of the pupils; yet the teacher definitely leads and creates for the class a sense of confidence and a natural businesslike tempo.

The first day and school discipline

After all, school discipline is inextricably interrelated with every phase of school management. For the present, "discipline" is thought of as related to the accepted standards of wholesome class conduct. Every aspect of the critical nature of the first day thus far discussed has had back of it the tacit assumption that ultimately it would affect, for good or ill, the behavior of the student in the class and in the school. Weakness in one part of the school, like measles, is likely to be contagious. As suggested in the previous chapter, fully 50 per cent of our school problems are directly the outgrowth of improper school management. Many of them could easily be corrected by proper management techniques. One of the most important of these is to begin school in the right way. That means that if we are careful of the first day we assure ourselves a position of tactical advantage. Overt behavior is not so likely if the impressions of the first day have given students the idea that the teacher is in earnest, knows what to do and when to do it, and expects the class to do a full quota of work of such a nature as to demand the very best efforts of each student. The remainder of this chapter will be devoted to a consideration of those factors that contribute to a successful first day.

2. How Shall the Teacher Become Familiar with the Community?

Community attitude toward school

The teacher who has arrived in the community ahead of the regular opening of school should address himself to a thorough appraisal of the position the school occupies in the mind of the community. The teacher will do well to find out as much about the community as possible before his arrival. A few years ago, two enterprising young school men called at the writer's office to find out what he, along with other educationalists responsible for teacher training, thought was the feasibility of an informational bureau that would collect data on communities such as: size of community, location and availability by transportation routes, educational activities other than schools, social and religious interests, type of teacher-accommodations usually available, school enrollment, physical plant and equipment, etc. For this service they planned to charge one dollar to the teacher who sought information about a given community. The bureau never materialized, but the need for such information was none the less apparent.

In many places the teacher is placed upon a pedestal in community regard; the school is looked upon as its proud and most cherished possession. In others the teacher holds a position of low estate in the social scale, sometimes akin to a social parasite; education, too, is regarded as a questionable burden forced upon the community by the external authority of the state. Where the former of these attitudes prevails, the teacher will find his task much easier. The community will be ready to give moral support to all school problems and to aid in their solution. The teacher will be respected, and his personal relations in the community can begin in an atmosphere of pleasantness and potential leadership. Where the community does not appreciate the school, the teacher should early adjust himself to the prospect of limited equipment with which to work, little or no moral support from the community in the realization of the purpose of the school, and a situation in which he is looked upon with critical eye and held aloof from the life of the community. The teacher of vision and determination will accept the situation as it is, and begin marking out a quiet campaign of education that will create interest in the school and a sense of its community values. Incidentally, through his school leadership and personal bearing, he will undertake to produce a wholesome respect for the work and personality of the teacher.

Educational background of the community

Some time ago the writer was invited, through the superintendent of a certain small city school, to speak before its Chamber of Commerce at its weekly luncheon. As the meal progressed, the superintendent called attention to the personnel of that civic organization. Here was a man from Yale, another from Harvard, still others from Princeton, Michigan, Chicago, Stanford, etc. When he had completed the roll of university men from all parts of the United States present in that room, it was evident that this community was extraordinary for the number of men with excellent educational background who made up its business and professional life. The small city, possibly better deserving because of its size to be called a town, reflected the educational background of its responsible citizens. The schools were central in its thought; not merely adjuncts to the community life. The cultural life of the community gave prestige and leadership to everything connected with education, as the superintendent's position as chairman of the program committee of the Chamber of Commerce indicated. The school in a community of this kind has opportunities the teacher should be quick to see.

Social attitudes of community

The attitudes of the community on matters social, economic, political, and religious are of the gravest importance to the new teacher. Many communities are very liberal in their social views. The teacher might in all propriety accept, during the first week, invitations to social dances or card parties within such a community. In many other communities the attitude of the dominant group is very conservative. To accept such invitations in these places would be to jeopardize the teacher's standing in the community beyond redemption. A teacher in a community of over 2500 population reported that she fortunately discovered, when she first arrived in the town, that teachers could not attend the local motion-picture theater without serious loss of prestige. Such a condition is extreme, but communities are extreme — far more often than the unwary teacher realizes. A very good rule for the beginning teacher is to plead the pressure of school work as an excuse to refuse all such doubtful social participation until certain what the community sentiment may be. A little sacrifice of social levity during the opening days of school may later be more than repaid.

Teachers, too, find that economic-political views are not looked upon with the same degree of equanimity by all communities. It is wise to remain non-committal, or deftly to generalize any comments of a political, social, or economic nature until one has become well established. If the teacher is to be a leader in social, political, and economic affairs, later readiness to express convictions is another matter. It is the first reaction of the community toward the teacher that concerns us here. The advice of an older experienced clergyman to a group of younger men just entering the ministry is equally appropriate for the new teacher. Said he, "First get the people to love you, then you can say those things frankly you have it in your heart to say." Excellent advice!

Community factions — influential people

One of the most difficult situations for the new teacher in a small community is to avoid partisanship, or apparent favoritism with factional groups. When these exist in any intensity, the teacher is approached early and, unless unusually wise, is likely to say or do something, insignificant in itself, even possibly the only reasonable thing to do or say under normal circumstances, but highly prejudicial to the good will of one faction. If possible these conditions need to be learned long before arrival in the community. Selection of a place to room and board must be governed by many considerations such as these. Where factions exist it is fatal to a good beginning to take residence in a place which suggests alliance with one faction rather than another. A young woman, who gave good service in the high school and community, failed to be re-elected, insiders felt, because she was friendly to a very fine family, whom she had known for years — all because some members of the board bore personal animosities to the family. The new teacher should assume, by every device possible, a neutral attitude toward factions of whatever sort — at least at first. Individual situations must govern later decisions in these matters. In general, neutrality throughout is the part of wisdom.

The teacher should early discover who the influential people in the community are, and what their attitudes may be toward the school, and their outlook on life generally. The more the teacher knows about the parents and community leaders, the better he can prepare to meet the individualities in the classroom representative of these homes. Knowledge of this sort may also be of the utmost value if serious disciplinary problems arise in the school. If the teacher knows that the community or parent will support what he does, provided extreme measures become necessary, or vice versa, his action can be governed by this knowledge. There are certain communities where one or two people are the acknowledged leaders. When this is the case, it may not be out of place to make their acquaintance informally and learn, at first hand, their general attitudes toward education, the school, and school management. Fortified with this knowledge, the teacher can approach the first day with confidence and with intelligent plans.

3. How Shall the Teacher Become Familiar with Students?

Probable class enrollments

As a basis for any intelligent preparation the teacher should know the approximate enrollment of each of his classes. Supplies can then be calculated; and, if board work is planned, the routine for the use of the board can be determined. Seating, too, where such seems wise, can tentatively be arranged in advance. As indicated before, complete knowledge of enrollment is seldom possible unless in a very small community where migratory habits are poorly developed. Most forward-looking schools now carry on spring preregistration, so that approximations are normally possible in these schools. Even then, summer changes of family residence are likely to bring new students into the school and remove others.

School attitudes of students

Fortified with some knowledge of the community and of the individual parents, the teacher can quickly relate that knowledge with what he has learned about the attitudes and conduct of individual students. If the community or parents disparage education, the school, and the teacher, that attitude will probably be reflected in the attitude of the student. If the community or the parent places high value on the school and respects the position of the teacher, that, too, will be mirrored in the classroom reactions of the students. If the teacher knows that his mettle is likely to be tried on the first day, his reactions to comparatively innocent behavior problems will be governed accordingly.

The writer recalls a school situation where weak discipline led to the teacher's dismissal shortly after the holiday vacation. A new teacher, a young man, was employed. All went well until noon. The ringleaders, flushed with past triumphs, were not to submit without a test of the teacher's mettle. The instructor had carried forward the day's work as though he had been there all year. In an afternoon class a mild challenge of disobedience was offered. Before the students realized what had happened, the challenge had been met and the offending student, a ringleader, put in his place in such a manner as to serve notice upon all that no trifling would be permitted. No further challenges were offered the rest of the year, and the teacher became a favorite of the same students who were set to give him trouble at the beginning. Some students are followers and need not be watched or planned for as carefully as others. All students have their points of approach, if these can be reached. To challenge a student's interests or sense of responsibility may completely reverse his attitudes. Occasionally such a challenge can be given the first day.

Know student leaders

Every school has its student leaders. The teacher should make a thorough study of all who may be student leaders in his own class. If the school boasts a high school annual or something that substitutes for it, he can discover, to a large degree, the extra-curricular interests of the students. The leaders are easily picked out or verified if the teacher has previously been informed who they are. Very significant insights are furnished frequently by the comments made about them in school publications, as well as by the activities they have engaged in. To fit these leaders into the first day's program in such a way as to challenge interest and cooperation is no mean achievement. Even to lay well the basis for such cooperation could be regarded as a first-day triumph. Monitor service or some responsibility generally appeals to students. Trouble makers are often won over to the teacher if they can subtly be placed under obligation to the teacher.

The following story, not without point here, was related to the writer by a young woman who went out to teach a rural school. A large boy of fourteen years of age was in the eighth grade. Put out of a neighboring school because he was a "bully" and general classroom trouble maker, he was, she learned, to be in her school. She lay awake much of the night before the first day of school trying to figure out the best way to handle him. School opened, and Frank, an overgrown boy larger than the young teacher, appeared. The teacher asked him to clean some erasers. She noticed that he did this with alacrity and pride. Finally, she talked to him and commented on the fact that he was much larger and older than the others: she needed help about the school during the day, and someone at night to watch the children who walked home along the road to his house, so that they might be kept from fighting. She wondered if she could ask him to help her. Proud to be considered a responsible person, he met the challenge, proved to be a model student, a constant help about the school, and actually mothered the young brood of children home each night, whereas his previous reputation was one of "big bully" among those smaller than he. The potential liability became the teacher's asset and directly contributed to the teacher's success in the community.

To know the leaders, especially by their first names, on the opening day of school has a most salutary effect upon them. The teacher is recognized as alert, and is given credit for knowing much more about them than he probably does. In communities where enrollments are not in excess of one hundred students, the teacher should know something about every student likely to be in his classes and should be able to identify them on at least two important counts when face and name are associated.

4. How Should the Teacher Become Familiar With School Organization?

Administrative responsibilities

The teacher should have a very clear understanding of the administrative relationships in the school. If there is a department head, principal, and superintendent, the lines of authority exercised by each should be definitely understood. Textbooks on school administration clearly delimit each. In practical situations the ideal often is far from actuality. At times, even school-board chairmen have been known to run the school, with the principal in reality a glorified clerk and teacher. The teacher should know what the correct relationships ought to be, and then be governed by what they actually are. This knowledge may be very vital in the school where supplies, etc., are needed for the first day or week, and effectiveness in the classroom depends upon their availability when school opens. In the smaller schools, arbitrary division of authority is often agreed upon between principal and superintendent. The new teacher should know their respective fields of authority. If a head teacher is the immediate superior, the extent of that authority should be learned, and from the principal rather than from the head teacher himself. Some school officials grant considerable latitude for personal decision in classroom policies; others insist upon responsibility for even minor decisions. Regardless of the wisdom of the administrative responsibilities assumed or delegated, the teacher's success depends upon an awareness of what these are, and conformity to them on the first day and ever after.

General routine of the school

What are the usual plans for the organization of the first day? Is it the policy of the school to meet for organization and assignments only? Do the classes meet, organize, and begin regular work on the schedule to be followed thereafter? Does the school give placement tests for classification and gradation the first day? These are a few of the important questions on school organization that affect teacher preparation for the first day. It is desirable that the first day be taught much as the teacher expects to teach succeeding days. If the plan for the first day calls only for class organization, roll check, and assignment, then the teacher should learn what the usual form of approved organization is and plan each phase so that it is carried out with precision and little confusion. The students should not be permitted to loiter in the room when the work of the day is done. If classroom work is contemplated, then every detail should be planned with extraordinary care.

General attitudes of the administration

The new teacher must be prepared for any untoward eventualities, but it is not enough to know what he considers the wise step to take in a given situation. It is equally important to know what the principal, and ultimately the superintendent, may think of the teacher's methods. If it is necessary to discipline a student, and if the offense seems to require aid from the office, can the teacher depend upon full cooperation of the principal? If certain procedures to meet specific types of behavior are not thought wise by the principal, what is left for the teacher? To send a student to the office when the teacher feels the classroom situation demands it, only to find the student sent back, is a serious *faux pas* at any time, but particularly on the first day. The teacher should get the principal's point of view on a number of these items, and should find out just what kind of cooperation can be expected. What does the principal expect the teacher to do in the case of tardiness? Is it to be overlooked the first day? What is to be done later if tardiness is not checked upon the first day? These and numerous other questions should be answered satisfactorily before school begins. The teacher can no more afford to make an unfavorable impression on the administration than on students and parents.

5. How Should the Teacher Become Familiar With Equipment Facilities?

Equipment available for courses

The teacher of history may discover only a few reference books of the many desired. Maps are meager and, for certain sections of the course, of no value. At once the office should be approached and the teacher should learn just what additional supplies can be ordered. In the sciences, the equipment should be checked with utmost care, and the office consulted about the possibilities for additional supplies. Each teacher should know, before school begins, just what there will be to work with. If necessary supplies cannot be purchased, the teacher should find out what the attitude of the principal would be toward extra-legal plans to raise money by entertainments, etc., before plans for such are considered or student cooperation enlisted to secure from the community pieces of equipment or books that parents and friends may be willing to donate or loan.

Materials for the first day

Of the equipment available, the teacher should select that needed for the first day. This should be done with future needs and supply considered. Every piece of equipment should be gone over carefully to see that it is in working order, where mechanical elements are involved. This equipment should be properly arranged, so that it will be ready at hand when needed. Theme paper, pencils, chalk, and erasers should be ordered for the room, sufficient to meet any emergency. So important do some authorities consider the matter of supplies for the classroom that many recommend that the teacher appear at the school at least a half hour before classes begin, the morning of the first day, to see that the janitor has the room in order, blackboard clean, and chalk, erasers, and all other supplies requisitioned on the teacher's desk or supply table ready for use.

6. How Detailed Should the Planned Routine of Daily Program Be?

Organization of classes

The first task of the new teacher will be the tentative or permanent organization of the class. For this the teacher should bring to bear everything learned about the personnel of the class. As far as possible, physical needs should be met in the initial organization. If sight, hearing, or other defects require special seating adjustments, these should be cared for as tactfully as possible. Gratitude will be the teacher's reward from the sensitive ones thus helped. The evidence of detailed knowledge of each student by the teacher will not be lost on the keenly observant members of the class, who know all too well the physical limitations of their comrades. Problem cases can be deftly handled by the separation of those known to be leaders and mischief makers. When monitors are to be used, these can be selected in advance among the key students and seated to facilitate their service most effectively. If the seating is tentative, a minimum of readjustment later is likely to result from this careful organization. If books are to be used that day, these should be ready for distribution when supplied by the school on a free textbook basis. Otherwise, purchase should be arranged for. If the school organization does not permit the teacher to distribute books, and send in charge lists to the office or cooperating private book stores, this fact should be known and proper titles for purchase provided the student.

Acquaintance of students with routine procedures

When the class is organized, the forms of routine suggested in the previous chapter should be carefully explained. It is more in keeping with modern educational thinking to get the class to co-operate in the formulation of the "rule of the road" than that they should be routinized. The time will be well spent and pay large dividends in pupil understanding, good will and cooperation. Forms of recognition and response within the class, freedom of move-ment within the room, use of reference works, etc., need to be understood at once. The teacher ordinarily should not take up all the hour with organization and routine matters, if it is possible to do some regular class work. When details of organization have been properly planned in advance the teacher will be surprised to see how small a part of the class hour is actually needed for this purpose. There are some routine procedures that can await expla-nation another day. Only those incident to the needs of the day need be given special attention.

Where a mimeograph is available some list of suggested routine procedures should be handed the student in permanent form to file in notebooks for study and reference. Such foresight will pre-vent later arguments or excuses that certain routine suggestions were not agreed upon or not understood. Every effort should be made to get students to recognize the obvious worth and impor-tance of every routine procedure adopted. Indeed, the pedagogi-cally wise teacher will utilize the democratic way by enlisting the cooperation of the class in the formulation of a list of routine pro-cedures or rules of the road for the government of its members. Students will be brought to see quickly that every procedure thus outlined for the expeditious conduct of the group is planned to add to the freedom of the class and to enable every student to do his best work. The teacher cannot afford to let the student get the impression that he is unreasonably exacting; that the rules will cramp and stifle class spirit. The student must be brought to see at once that every procedure outlined for the expeditious conduct of the class has been planned to add to the freedom of the class, promote good understanding, and enable every student to do his best work. If this can be accomplished on the opening day of school, the teacher will have won his case with the students and a wholesome *esprit de corps* will result. If circumstances permit only of assignments and brief lecture, the routine factors may appro-priately be delayed until the second day.

Assignment and class activity

Class activity should be given a sense of precision and movement that keeps every student alert and in a state of expectancy. The lesson should move from one phase to another with smoothness and dispatch. Every effort should be put forth to make the class hour interesting. In the nature of the situation, the teacher must bear the brunt of the period. To avoid the danger that too much of the picture will be occupied by the teacher, and to give him a better idea of the mental reactions of students as well as of their preparation for the course, it is a good plan to have ten to fifteen minutes at least devoted to written work on significant phases of the course, calculated to indicate the adequacy of the students' previous preparation or advance knowledge of the work to be covered.

The assignment, without fail, should be carefully planned in detail. The teacher may not be able to approximate again during the course such minutiae of lesson planning, but it should be given every consideration the first day. Every possibility should be anticipated. Especial care should be given to reference works probably new to the students, the purpose of the course and the lesson. Everything possible should be done to get the students launched upon the work of the course with zest and enthusiasm. An assignment that leaves the students lethargic will be a serious handicap to the teacher's prestige with the class.

QUESTIONS AND PROBLEMS

1. Recall and analyze concise examples from your own experience of the important rôle of the psychological principle of primacy in regard to a new teacher. Consider its effect upon yourself as a child, and in turn, upon your family and community.
2. What are the reasons for the fact that the first day of school is likely to be a time of comparatively great natural confusion?
3. Why is it so important from the standpoint of interest and discipline to set the pace for the work of the course upon the first day?
4. From your own experience, give definite examples of adjustment problems of teachers to the various community attitudes regarding the school, the teacher, social and religious observances, etc.
5. What special seating adjustments may be made by the new teacher in order to assure the best arrangement of individual students for the good of the class as a whole?

6. What are the probable advantages to be gained by the teacher's having complete knowledge of the student leaders who are to be in her classes?
7. In what way might you as a teacher make a short period of written work of value on the first day?
8. Defend the requirements by some school administrators that teachers report for duty three to four days in advance of the opening day of school.
9. What specific things should the teacher know about his new work before the opening day of school?
10. How could you plan a "first day" in which you with the class cooperatively explored and agreed upon the general rules to govern class activities?

SELECTED BIBLIOGRAPHY

Burton, William H. *The Guidance of Learning Activities,* pp. 557–561. New York: Appleton-Century-Crofts, Inc., 1944.

Douglass, Harl R. and Mills, Hubert H. *Teaching in High School,* pp. 507–512. New York: The Ronald Press Company, 1948.

Green, I. "Starting off on the Right Foot," *Instructor,* 58: 22 (September, 1949).

Reinoehl, C. M. and Ayer, F. C. *Classroom Administration and Pupil Adjustment,* chapters II, III. New York: Appleton-Century-Crofts, Inc., 1940.

Rivlin, Harry N. *Teaching Adolescents in Secondary Schools,* chapter XV. New York: Appleton-Century-Crofts, Inc., 1948.

Simon, H. W. *Preface to Teaching,* chapter VII. New York: Oxford University Press, 1938.

20

How Can Discipline
Be Achieved?

1. How Are Conceptions of School Discipline Changing?

Discipline an evolutionary concept

No phase of education has shown a more radical evolution in theory and practice than that of school control — usually considered under the term "discipline." The picture of the ancient Roman schoolroom, in which the youth were undergoing a rigorous flogging at the hands of the schoolmaster is symbolic of the school of that day, but it would not find its counterpart in any picture that symbolized the modern school. It is not very long since a picture of the boy with the "dunce cap" might have been assumed as typical of disciplinary attitudes within the American school. That day, too, has passed, except in isolated places where primitive notions of education still prevail.

Some years ago the writer, visiting a fairly large and supposedly progressive junior high school, was interested in a little alcove in the rear of the auditorium, with the front closed with iron bars so that the one inside would be visible to all who chanced to pass. The room, which was approximately six feet wide, six feet long, and seven feet high, was of unfinished brick and contained a single chair as its sole article of furniture. This was spoken of as the "meditation room." Without, for the moment, passing on the value of "meditation" as an agency of correction, we may say that it is very doubtful that in any secondary or even elementary school built within the past dozen or fifteen years there would have been constructed or even set apart a room for such a purpose. To give a vivid picture of the evolution in disciplinary ideas, a writer in the late twenties [1] has set forth the change in theory and practice with special reference to American education.

Evolution parallels closely changing theological and ethical ideas. Every student of educational history is aware that the school through the centuries has been intimately associated with the institutions of religion of the Western World. Indeed, into the woof and warp of the whole fabric of the social and political thought of the Western World, religion has exercised a potent influence. The control of education in the United States was completely under the domination of the church in its early history. Harris, in reference to the New York school laws of 1840, quotes [2] with approval the words of Cubberley that, "The school remained religious in purpose, even though its control was beginning to pass from the church to the state." Secondary education felt the strong influence of the church through the Academy until the turn of the present century.

It is but natural, therefore, to expect that whatever the presuppositions of religion and theology may have been through the centuries, as they affect human behavior, there should be some influences traceable in the disciplinary ideas and practice found prevalent in the school.[3]

A careful study of the church and the school shows such an intimate relationship to have existed. No clear-cut lines of demarcation, however, can be found to separate the transition from the dominance of one point of view to another. Social evolution has seldom shown sharp mass transitions from one stage of thought to

[1] Harris, P. E. *Changing Conceptions of School Discipline.* New York: The Macmillan Company, 1928.

[2] *Ibid.*, p. 30.

[3] It is not necessary to enter into a consideration here of the opposing contentions as to whether enlightened social thought has modified theology or changing theology has modified social theory and practice. It seems more rational to conclude that experience has profoundly influenced our philosophy and, vice versa, our philosophy has shaped in large measure social theory and practice. It is important for the purpose of our consideration here only to recognize the parallelism between religious presuppositions and disciplinary theory and practice.

another. New ideas and consequent change in social practice, on the contrary, have shown a slow emergence, with periods of conflict as the struggles to gain recognition have gone forward. Even when new ideas and practices have gained general acceptance, significant sections of the general public may still cling to the old. Teachers should never forget that general acceptance of a theory by acknowledged leaders does not mean wholehearted recognition by the rank and file of folk or by local leaders. Even more serious, the general public may give lip service to a theory without a clear understanding of the direct implication which that new theory has for practice. Therein lies the frequent disparity between theory and practice. Such a disparity, between theory and practice, is particularly true in the evolution of religious thought and its consequent bearing upon social practice. It appears particularly in the practice of school discipline.

Evolution of theories of discipline

At least five theories of discipline can be traced in the evolution of human thought. These theories have found definite expression in the religion of the western world and in the social practice of the western peoples. Four have had their counterpart in schoolroom practice. Because different advocates of all five theories may be found in many communities, and because four of them applied to the school, it is well for the teacher to understand and appreciate the genesis and implications of each.

1. *The vindictive theory.* Strictly speaking, no disciplinary values of the social nature obtain in this most ancient conception of behavior treatment. To impute social significance to it is not exactly correct, as it grows out of an extreme individualism in thought. The theory was in harmony with the theology of primitive peoples. Deity was thought of as a capricious despot. A violation of his personal will was considered an affront to his dignity, honor, authority. He could wreak vengeance upon the culprit in personal satisfaction at will. He was not thought responsible to any code of rational behavior. Somewhat of the idea, crystallized into a phrase of a later age, "The king can do no wrong," dominated ancient theology. "'Vengeance is mine; I will repay,' saith the Lord" is typical of the viewpoint. This theory has no significance for the school except that too many teachers have permitted school problems to be considered personal, and in the emotional disturb-

ance that has resulted have themselves acted vindictively. They have been aided and abetted by the persistence of the vindictive attitude of social thought.

2. *The retributive theory.* The theory of retribution was a step beyond that of vindictiveness. No longer could irresponsibility in the infliction of punishment be condoned. A higher ethical plane was recognized or required of Deity. Even Deity had become amenable to a new sense of social justice inadequate though the primitive notions were. The Hammurabi and Mosaic Codes, both of religious origin and essentially retributive in ethical concept, have had tremendous influence on the social theories of discipline among western peoples. "An eye for an eye and a tooth for a tooth," or "He will visit the sins of the fathers upon the children unto the third and fourth generations," are typical maxims of a theology of retribution cast into a social mold. Even in the older theology the inadequacy of this theory was apparent to careful observers; as, witness the reaction against the theory in the books of Ecclesiastes and Job of the Old Testament literature. The influence of the Mosaic Code upon legal jurisprudence has long been recognized. A careful study of any modern legal code will reveal how intrenched is this ancient theory in our legal system, with its hair-splitting attempts to fit to the deed the correct proportionate measure of punishment.

While the retributive theory no longer has pedagogical acceptance as a dominant mode of school discipline, it has some values that cannot be entirely ignored. A cursory study of the inexorableness and retributory nature of some of Nature's laws are very uncomfortable to contemplate for those who seek through Nature's laws a less rigorous example of disciplinary practice. One does not violate the laws of health, for example, with impunity. Sometimes the penalties for infraction of her laws are exceedingly stern, or irreparable, and affect others besides the transgressor. Whether we will or no, as society is constituted, it seems as though the cessation of the operation of retribution in practice might be far remote. The school, while seeking a higher concept of disciplinary procedures, may well teach the student the sterner aspect of those retributive laws that operate throughout much of his relation to his environment.

A legalistic theory mechanically applied, however, may easily lead to transfer of attention from the main purposes of discipline

to the minutiae of its mechanics. The report of Henry Barnard of
the old German Schoolmaster is probably extreme, but typical of
the absurdities to which a legalistic approach may carry one. In the
diary of fifty-one years in the schoolroom had been recorded, with
the meticulousness of German thoroughness, the penalties applied,
with some suggestion of classification. The most common are
recorded, as follows:

Blows with a cane	911,527
Blows with a ruler	20,989
Blows with the hand	136,715
Slapped over the mouth	10,205
Boxed on the ears	7,905
Snaps on the head	1,115,800

In addition a vocabulary of over 3000 words was employed, one
third of which represented his own creation.

3. *The deterrent theory.* As history goes, this is a relatively
recent development in disciplinary theory. It is not necessarily
antagonistic to the doctrine of retribution. It may but use the
essence of retribution for an additional or primary purpose. The
deterrent theory is the first to begin to take on social significance.
True, retribution, while primarily individual in concept, had social
values as a deterrent of the individual. With the emergence of the
deterrent ideal, punishments in any form must look to one of two
results: the prevention of the individual from a repetition of the
social offense through fear of the pain, the consequent penalties
inflicted, or the example it brought to members of society to remind
them of the dire consequences of such behavior. The religious
doctrine of "hell and damnation" and the consequences of "falling
into the hands of an angry God," so characteristic of religious
teaching of an earlier period, breathes this atmosphere of deter-
rentism through and through. The earlier attitude toward human
nature that "man was conceived in sin and born in iniquity" led
naturally to a conception of the individual as of evil propensities.
The remedy for this condition was suppression, through the proper
establishment of inhibitions through external force. Not all religious teaching was so hard and stern, as was not all social theory;
but this emphasis was by all odds predominant.

In the social institution of penology the deterrent theory found
expression in the public whipping post, the stocks on the public

square, the public execution. It was an age that made possible the scene in Hawthorne's *The Scarlet Letter,* where the doctrine of retribution is coupled with the deterrent idea in the dramatic appearance on the scaffold of the man and the woman, violators of the social ethics of the day. England had its public hangings in hangman's square, where, we are told, women of culture and supposed refinement gathered to observe these hideous spectacles as a special form of entertainment, just as the women of France brought their needlework to watch and comment on the public executions at the guillotines.

In the schools the theory resulted in the "dunce cap," in making a pupil stand in a corner at the front of the room, and in other forms of punishment inflicted before the rest of the school. By precept and example the consequences of unsocial behavior, even though it might consist in a disregard of some arbitrary rules for which the student did not see the social significance, were brought to the attention of the student as forcibly as possible. The theory had as its basis the element of fear as a control of behavior.

One is inevitably led, at this point, to a consideration of the place of fear in education. There are some who insist that fear should be withdrawn entirely from modern pedagogy. Others cogently insist that fear cannot be eliminated from our relationship to natural environment, physical or social, and therefore should not be ignored in the school. A wholesome respect, if not downright fear, for the consequences of violating a physical law that jeopardizes health and physical well-being may well be considered almost inevitable and necessary to the safety of the individual. In that case it becomes a pertinent question whether the school can afford to ignore the place of intelligent fear in the formation of wholesome attitudes and conduct, even though at times the attitudes and conduct are controlled by negative considerations.

4. *The remedial theory.* Simultaneously with the deterrent theory of discipline has often been found a conception of discipline that has put more emphasis on a constructive reaction to individual and group behavior patterns. Society has not been satisfied with a more or less negative attitude in its penal institutions. Fear has its limitations as a disciplinary agent. The would-be law violator is deterred only so long as he is afraid of consequences. When fear is removed or when there seems to be some way to avoid consequences, no restraint is left for the still potent impulses. During

and following World War I society became rudely awakened to the thin veneer we had been pleased to call civilization. When the customary restraints of fear were removed, many persons found no adequate standards by which to govern conduct. To overcome this weakness there had been a growing conviction that something must be done to change the impulse itself. The individual should be brought to look upon conduct and the *mores* of society constructively. He should develop the desire and will to overcome unsocial attitudes and behavior, so that the impulse to observe the established *mores* of society will replace the old impulses to violate them.

Developing religious emphases fitted into this view admirably. The germs of the idea went back centuries, but slowly unfolded in its social implications. The idea that "man was conceived in sin and born in iniquity" led religious thinkers, who accepted the theology implied, to preach a transformation of the individual by the removal of evil propensities through divine grace and the substitution for them of a desire to be and do good. This good was identified with the advanced social *mores* of the times. It was but a step from the more religious personal transformation to a socially conceived transformation.

In keeping with the changing emphasis was ushered in the era of penal institutions built or managed, not as punishment centers, but as reform agencies. The prison farm, prison industries, prison libraries, educational classes for prisoners, recreational activities, wholesome living conditions, and "trusties" are all the outgrowth of this project of human reclamation. The changes led to the violent opposition of the non-progressive elements, and were capitalized by the political mountebank as "coddling criminals." A wave of reform-school building for youth swept the country. It is related of Horace Greeley that in a dedicatory address, given upon the establishment of a new reform school, he pleaded the value of reform schools and in a burst of eloquence asserted that, "If this institution reforms one individual assigned to it, it will have been worth all its cost." Afterwards a friend twitted him about his extravagant language. Said he: "You really didn't mean that. Just imagine the amount of money spent just to reform one boy or girl." To which Greeley promptly replied: "It wouldn't cost too much if it were my boy."

Pedagogy began to think of discipline as a means of changing the attitudes and conduct of students, so that they would desire and will to do the things laid down by the school to govern behavior within it. The problem became one of leading the student to see the seriousness for social, as well as personal welfare, of a continuance or a repetition of unsocial conduct. Every effort was now put forth to make the student see the reasonableness and advantages of acceptable behavior. Punishments, in consequences, have been reduced to a minimum in school guided by this theory of discipline, and in some schools the extreme position is taken that punishment should not be inflicted at all. It is the position of the advocates of this extreme point of view that reason and understanding guidance will correct all disciplinary difficulties that arise. When unpleasant disciplinary measures are regarded as necessary, it is thought that these should serve as the basis for reasoned reformation.

5. *The prophylaxis theory.* This theory takes one step beyond the remedial, and is now coming into general acceptance among thoughtful educators. It has found prophetic voices among sociological leaders. They insist that reform is proper and necessary in its place, but that it is like trying to cure a city of typhus disease without being forehanded enough to correct the evil at the source of infection. Society is spending more than fifteen billion dollars a year in America to take care of the costs incident to crime. Our crime bill is astounding. The advocates of prophylaxis reason that, if more money were spent to overcome conditions that lead to maladjustments, there would be less anti-social behavior and consequently less need for money to correct the bad situation which had been allowed to develop. In consequence, civic playgrounds, amusement centers, golf links, etc., are sponsored for the public good.

Vast areas of religious thought today see no reason for the old idea that man by nature is sinful and is conditioned to do wrong — to be anti-social. They maintain that man by nature would ultimately seek the highest. Unsocial attitudes and behavior are the result of misguided moral judgments or perverted ideals. They hold that the individual child is by nature non-moral, rather than immoral as the older theology maintained. For those who maintain this point of view, religion and morality are matters of education. Religious education, therefore, has had extensive development within the last decade and a half.

Fortunately, psychology has come to the aid of the newer point of view by discrediting the older ideas of human nature and the doctrine of instinct. Social psychologists, almost without exception in the past decade, have rejected the old rigid theories of instinct. They have placed great stress upon the education of emotions, and on patterns of thought and behavior. For them, training is the major determiner of personal attitudes and conduct.

Modern education, therefore, thinks of discipline as primarily that of attacking the causes of maladjustments in the school and environment so that the right patterns of thought and the right habits of conduct may be firmly established. According to this theory, an ideal situation would never necessitate the recourse to adjudication of an overt act; unsocial behavior would not occur. Of course, an ideal situation seldom exists. Adolescence is not maturity. The expediencies of present educational facilities and home situations require working conditions less than ideal. A recent book shows definitely the newer emphasis upon the discovery and removal of causes of maladjustment so as to correct behavior, as opposed to the assumption of individual perversity and of the need for reformation based upon that assumption.[4] Miss Smithies' *Case Studies of Normal Adolescent Girls* and Thom's *Normal Youth and Its Everyday Problems* are two admirable examples of the effort to apply this newer theory to a study of actual case-problems that arise in the school. The evaluation, then, of this theory, along with the others, must reckon with a practical situation. A close study of present trends in educational curricula and methodology will reveal how extensively the concept of prevention positively and constructively conceived has influenced modern education.

2. What Is Present Conception of Discipline?
Period of public confusion

The general public but dimly perceives the reasons that inspire the changes that take place within its midst. Oftentimes it is not fully aware of transformations until they are virtually accomplished facts. As suggested earlier in this chapter, progress is not made evenly through the social milieu. Some sections of the public mind are far advanced, while others remain sluggishly content with conditions as they have been. Even within a given community are to be found those keenly alive to newer ideas and developments in

[4] Tuttle, Harold S. *Dynamic Psychology and Conduct.* New York: Harper and Brothers, 1949.

practice, while others are insensitive to changes that take place about them. If mankind moved as a unit from one position to another in the evolution of human thought, little confusion would result, but it does not. Radicalism and conservatism strain at the leash. The progressive elements surge forward and are impatient of restraint, while conservative groups hold back and resent the efforts of others to disturb their complaisance.

This general social condition is mirrored in public comments upon the disciplinary practices of the school. The older theories of discipline are not without champions in the more popular literature. A cursory examination of articles that appear in popular magazines will reveal the critical veins in which the modern ideas of discipline are discussed. Most of these show a singular lack of understanding of the fundamental educational ideas involved. Some are definite flarebacks to ideas long outmoded in advanced social and educational thought. It is interesting to note the recurrence of theological ideas of human nature, and "spare the rod and spoil the child" conceptions of social controls, in these popular discussions. Even among people otherwise alive to social change, the conceptions of school discipline are close to the soil of their own childhood home and school training.

Divergence of emphasis in communities, and among schoolmen

The training school, with claims to modern theory and practice, finds difficulty at times in reconciling the training given its embryonic teachers with the demands of many communities and some local schoolmen. The teacher frequently learns that what he has been taught to consider good discipline is frowned upon by the community, sometimes by the administrative leaders of the school. Not long since a young woman, who had been considered one of the outstanding members of her class as a student teacher, went into a community of fair size to teach. She was soon called into the office and reproved for the methods she used and the discipline of her classes. Her principal judged her a disciplinary failure, yet she had been thought particularly strong in that respect while a student teacher in the training school. Other teachers in that system, known to have maintained excellent discipline in the training school, were found to be uniformily rated unsatisfactory in discipline. The principal was an advocate of the old military conception of rigid posture, and "pin-fall-quiet silence" in the schoolroom.

Discipline defined

Discipline has been defined functionally as "preparing boys and girls for life in a democratic society." This view envisages the whole of education and might be regarded as a very general definition of education. The broad implications would suggest the development of those attitudes and self-controls so necessary in an ideal democracy, where government depends upon individual recognition of responsibility for and participation in group life and social controls. One writer has suggested that discipline is always related to goal seeking, and thus "discipline may be thought of as organization of one's impulses for the attainment of a goal." [5] This concept of discipline is in entire agreement with the prophylaxis theory of discipline, positively interpreted. It is not out of harmony with the "remedial theory" when such remedial training is necessary.

In keeping with this larger view, but more specific in the visualization of the processes to operate within the school, Pringle [6] offers the following suggestion:

> What, then, is the modern conception of high school discipline? Stated negatively, it is not outward conformity, not coercion, not merely submission to authority and obedience to rules. . . . It is primarily concerned with a state of mind, not automatic execution of orders. It recognizes in the pupil the stages of continuous and concomitant development. It is the gradual transition from control by rule to control by reason. It implies a guarded shifting of responsibility for conduct to the pupils themselves, in the process of which the degree and kind of responsibility are always determined by the social maturity of the pupils.

Any conception of high school discipline, to be adequate, must recognize the classroom situation as an integral part of the larger discipline of the student outside the school. The life of the student, while at best somewhat artificial in a school situation where mass education obtains, must not be thought of as something apart from life outside the school. *It is life.* We can prepare the individual "for participation in a democratic society" only by recognizing his life in school as part of that democracy that embraces the

[5] Sheviakov, George V. and Redl, Fritz, *Discipline for Today's Children and Youth,* p. 4. Washington, D.C.: Department of Supervision and Curriculum, N.E.A., 1944.

[6] Pringle, R. W. *The Psychology of High School Discipline,* p. 6. Boston: D. C. Heath and Company, 1931.

totality of his existence. He must come to look upon the school as but one aspect of the total, and school discipline must reflect the larger implications of all life for the student. He must conceive of discipline as constructive and as concerned with the development of those attitudes and habits of conduct that contribute to the social well-being of the student and the effective achievement of the objectives of the school. As a basis for the proper development of controls, a school environment must be so set as to make life within it as normal and challenging as possible. Society must recognize that unsocial behavior is the result of maladjustments, either within the life of the student or of the school. The correct techniques of management and method, moreover, must be regarded as the principal agency of good discipline within the school.

Some implications of modern disciplinary theory

Baldwin, in an article on discipline, asks this pertinent question: "Is military discipline 'real discipline'?" He reports the statement of a student at Annapolis to the effect that discipline is a very prominent feature of the school life there, until after the diplomas are granted. Then may follow an "orgy of pranks resulting in the destruction of beds, chairs, and other furnishings." He goes on to say: [7] "It is a well known fact that such military discipline results in one kind of behavior when soldiers and sailors are on duty under surveillance, and quite another kind of behavior during shore leave." The discipline implied here is largely "deterrent"; when fear is removed, restraint is gone. The discipline implied in the above paragraphs requires intelligent ready response to positive standards of behavior, accepted by the student because he recognizes the social values inherent in the standards. Under such a conception discipline and character education become practically synonymous.

Another implication of this conception of discipline is that the attention of the teacher will be directed to the development of constructive attitudes and habits of conduct, rather than to regulations of control negative in nature. Tuttle has well stated the significance of this idea in these words: [8] "A large part of education for democratic living consists in the substitution of harmless forms

---

[7] Baldwin, W. A. "Discipline in Progressive Schools" in *Journal of Education*, vol. 115, p. 133 (February 8, 1932).

[8] From Tuttle, Harold S. *Dynamic Psychology and Conduct*, p. 174. New York: Harper and Brothers, 1949.

of satisfactions for those that injure and impoverish others. This is the constructive aspect of discipline." Aggressive leadership toward a positive desired goal is the emphasis demanded under the ideas of discipline. Instead of "keeping school" and priding himself upon no overt acts committed against the rules of the class, the teacher will searchingly seek to discover what advance the members of the class have made toward mastery of knowledge, attitudes, and understanding of the way to self-mastery and desirable social participation.

"He who governs least governs best," is a valid implication of the idea of modern school discipline. To the extent that the school is effective in the discharge of its training will it be unnecessary for the school to govern by authoritative means. The effort to effect a transition from "control by authority to a control by reason" is the essence of the goal of good discipline and education. Such a situation means freedom within the school to permit the exercise of self- and group-control. Adolescence is immature, and efforts to harness adolescent exuberance and to direct its energies constructively will require patience and tact on the part of the teacher. Nor should an "old head on young shoulders" be expected. Classroom order and quiet should not be expected of the old pin-drop-quiet variety, nor is it desirable for growing youth to maintain a military posture. It is at this point that criticism most frequently is directed against the newer expression of modern school discipline. We are accordingly led here to a brief consideration of what is good and bad discipline.

Good and bad discipline

In order to contrast the new and the old ideas of discipline, two examples are cited:

Some years ago the author found it necessary to assign a student teacher to an acting supervisor, considered a good teacher and a strong disciplinarian. The supervisor became very critical of the teaching of the student, and particularly of her discipline. She spoke of it as atrocious. Several visits to the classroom failed to reveal anything far amiss. The teaching technique lacked the touch of experience but was good, and the criticized discipline seemed not at fault. True, the youngsters in the junior high school age were wiggly, a trifle restless after forty-five minutes in one general position; but they were alert, eager, and readily responsive to the teacher. Sometime later it was necessary to tarry over a period in order to counsel with the supervisor. Her class was visited to obtain from her teaching method some clue to her idea of good technique. Almost the moment the bell rang her sharp staccato words brought the class to attention with a figurative bang. The sting in her voice and words caused the students to assume a rigid immovable posture for the hour — not a whisper nor a stray glance. The attitude was one of "answer when necessary, but speak only when spoken to." There was a strained tenseness about the class that did not suggest ease of mind or affection for the teacher. No smile emanated from the teacher to relieve the tenseness of the situation or the severity of her expression. The class was grave, almost solemn. When the period was over, the now-familiar criticisms were offered of the student teacher. The supervisor at heart desired to help the student teacher, and felt dismayed that the student was becoming nervously distracted by the critical attitude which the supervisor displayed. In the course of the conversation that followed the supervisor commented on a situation that greatly confused her. "I don't know why it is," she said, "but those students will work their fingernails off for that cadet teacher, and won't for me." The truth of her words was obvious. She condemned herself and did not know it.

Which was good discipline and which was not? Judged by the older conception of discipline, the older teacher deserved the reputation she bore as a good teacher and disciplinarian. By the same token the young teacher was quite poor. However, if the new conception of discipline be the standard by which these teachers were gauged, the judgments of the two would be reversed. The author carried away from that experience a settled conviction that he would elect without hesitancy, for a position on his staff, the student rather than the older teacher. Her kindly sympathetic attitude won for her the complete cooperation of the class. She was not disturbed by a little squirming on the part of adolescents with growing muscles, aching from forty-five minutes in approximately one position. She correctly estimated the worth of the eagerness displayed by the students, eagerness that produced noise unheard in the classes of her supervisor.

Whenever conditions in the classroom reveal an earnest, eager group of students working with enthusiasm and apparently without conscious restraint from the teacher, intent upon the accomplishment of the immediate task, the discipline of the class is almost certain to be good. The final test must be a wholesome class attitude, and a quiet enough room to permit effective work on the part of each pupil. When unnatural conditions that produce physical discomfort and strain, with unfavorable attitudes toward work and the teacher, are maintained in the classroom, an extremely poor disciplinary condition obtains, no matter how quiet and outwardly well-mannered the class may be.

3. Why Problems of Disciplinary Control?

Causes of disciplinary problems

The principal causes of disciplinary problems may be summarized under a fourfold classification, with a few suggestive examples of the problems that arise from each general source. The teacher who expects to gain a reasonably complete picture of the problems that may arise in this connection should consult a more complete treatment of the subject of discipline in sources given in the bibliography for this chapter.

1. *Physiological factors.* Two principal factors give rise to problems from this general source. Increasingly, educational leaders are recognizing the importance of health to school discipline. Many who heard Willis A. Sutton, formerly president of the National Educational Association, and for a long time superintendent of schools of Atlanta, Georgia, speak on health problems and discipline have gone away from that discussion with a conviction that, could the teeth of school children be properly cared for, most disciplinary problems would be at an end, so convincingly does he marshal the evidence from experience to show the effect of health upon school behavior. Bad health conditions often lead to irritability, restlessness, and sullen dispositions, with the myriad of bad behavior reactions that may flow from them. Some of these prove very serious indeed. Defective eyes, malnutrition, etc., may lead to apparent stubbornness and sullenness which are really an attempt to cover embarrassment or a baffled mental state that has resulted from a feeling of defeat, without fully understanding the reason for defeat. Abnormal glandular action may develop a sluggish, phlegmatic, indifferent student; it may also lead to a highly excitable individual — nervous, irritable, and difficult to get along with. A study of five hundred high school problem-cases traced disciplinary diffi-

culties to the malfunctioning of endocrine glands in over 10 per cent of the cases.

Closely akin to health factors are those physiological elements that determine adolescent characteristics. The rapid bodily growth, with the concomitant organic developments, makes high school youth restless, awkward, self-conscious, and bubbling over with energy and enthusiasm, and produces general emotional instability. These growth factors lead to natural restlessness in the classroom, giggling, self-assertiveness at times, and general mischievousness for idle hands and minds. They also make the student unusually sensitive to teacher influence. Nervousness and excitability in the teacher are likely to produce a corresponding condition in the members of the class. The writer has seen a class under the direction of a highly nervous teacher grow in excitability toward the end of the hour, with accelerated momentum until class control was gone. Neither teacher nor students understood why. Those same students the next period, under the soothing influence of a calm, poised teacher, became models of quiet behavior.

2. *Personal factors.* These factors classify themselves under a number of headings, as follows:

(*a*) *Egotism,* which is likely to find expression in a cocksureness of attitude, often challenging the teacher, and in definite disrespect for authority.

(*b*) *Immaturity of judgment.* From this factor flow all types of behavior problems — some of minor nature, others often vicious — but all the result of inability to see the consequences of the act. A group of high school boys with exuberant natures, and good general intentions but mischievous, decided to flicker the lights to torment a class play rehearsal. Incidentally, other groups were affected by their pranks, whom the boys did not realize would be affected, and through lack of knowledge of the switch one of the boys suffered a severe shock that might have proved very serious. When called to account, the boys readily admitted their pranks, and profusely and genuinely apologized for the unintentional inconvenience caused to others besides the play cast.

(*c*) *Low mentality.* During immaturity the individual of low mentality may not learn quickly by experience; in some situations he is unable to appreciate the implications of his behavior. The mentally dull student faces a further handicap in that he is unable to learn much through the observation of the conduct of others, or through a study of abstract principles of behavior. The lower the I.Q., the greater the inability of the student to profit by direct experience, and particularly by vicarious forms of learning.

(*d*) *Lack of social training.* This lack ranges from inadequate tutoring in the common standards of social courtesy to lack of ethical and moral perception. The overt acts that result from this factor may vary from simple discourtesies in speech and a lack of deference to others to stealing, lying, vandalism, and immoral conduct. Recently a junior high school boy, who was found guilty of a series of acts of immorality, was sent to the reform school. He readily admitted his guilt, but insisted he could see nothing serious about his offense. His mother, a divorcee, had not discussed sex problems with him, so that his sex information carried none of the inhibitions of the moral code of society.

(*e*) *Self-consciousness.* Unwillingness to do things before others, sometimes erroneously attributed to a stubborn disposition; inability to participate when called upon by the teacher, and attributed to gross negligence in preparation; giggling, etc., are forms of expression that result from self-consciousness.

3. *Social factors.* Social factors also are subdividable into a number of classifications, the more important of which are:

(*a*) *Desire for sensationalism.* The social emphasis of modern society puts a premium on the extraordinary, the spectacular. A military figure or a Lindbergh receives the attention of the multitudes. The newspapers give prominence to the sensational, often without regard to social consequences. As a result, gangsters assume the rôle of glorified heroes through the publicity gained for their anti-social behavior, as many have testified. The school, too, is permeated by desire for sensation. The youth, to gain recognition, often indulges in sensational behavior not because of pleasure in the act itself, but to gain the attention a developing inferiority complex demands. The teacher who is a social psychologist will recognize these symptoms of "showing off," vanities of one kind or another. To this group of factors belong many pranks that bring attention to the individual as a hero among his fellows, such as strewing match heads on the floor, placing Limburger cheese in places difficult to detect, and other pranks all too familiar to high school youth and experienced teachers.

(*b*) *Desire to be identified with the crowd.* In direct antithesis to the above, many students dislike nothing so greatly as to be considered different. They want to be like the majority, and avoid the feeling of being odd or different. If a majority are thought to act in a given way these individuals are likely to do likewise, though the action violates their better knowledge. The conformist often will do what the gang dictates, though the acts lead to very serious offense and personal inconvenience. A fashion prevails in the school and cannot easily be changed, because most students will imitate their heroes and what they think the crowd will do as led by these leaders. To get unwholesome fashions started is serious, because otherwise well-mannered young people of high ideals have not the strength of moral purpose to stand out against the crowd. These imitative fashions may extend from mere gum-chewing to gross lawlessness. Certain schools become noted for good discipline because it has been made the fashion; others become very disorderly because the school leaders have popularized a lawless attitude. Much has been borrowed from the elders, and ideas of uniformity have been instilled into youth in their homes and out-of-school environment. In such cases lawlessness should be recognized not as a peculiarity of high school, but as an echo of adult social life. As such it must be dealt with. Nor should group fashions be looked upon as undesirable. If intelligent, a fashion of behavior is a most wholesome instrument for desirable behavior control.

(c) *Resentment at control.* The old adage, "You can lead a horse to water but you can't make him drink," suggests the so-called perversity of temperaments. Adults stubbornly resist any limitations upon their "personal liberty," even though modern conditions make "personal liberty to do as you please" an anachronism in our complex social organism. The idea of personal independence has permeated popular social thought to the extent that it is difficult to get people to do even desirable things when to do them savors of acting under compulsion. Youth, with a natural impulsiveness, chafes at the restraints incident to the artificial social structure we call society-civilization. Modern youth has but intensified the prevalent somewhat natural opposition to control from above. A study, made on the basis of the seven causes of disciplinary problems given by Moorehouse, revealed that approximately 22 per cent of high school disciplinary problems might be classified as antagonism to imposed controls. Truancy, open disobedience, or disrespect to the teacher are characteristic of problems associated with student resentment. Unfortunately the curriculum and general attitude of the traditional high school tends to foster this student reaction through the subjects of questionable value required and the formal, deadening teaching methods so often employed.

4. *Schoolroom factors.* In the last sentence, allusion was made to some of the factors that give rise to discipline problems. These factors should not be overlooked, even though some cannot be corrected by the individual teacher. For the teacher to recognize them, though, is to be stimulated to make all adjustments possible to nullify their cramping influence. Where they exist the teacher can in some measure overcome the following conditions:

(*a*) *Unattractive room.* Students cannot develop a natural respect for an unattractive room or building. Beauty draws an involuntary respect and instills a spirit of awe. The incongruity of rowdyism in a beautiful environment seems a natural reaction of adolescents. Where beauty exists, it is easy to avoid defacements and rough handling of furniture. Without attractiveness rooms are subject to pencil or chalk marks and desks to clever engravings. A cheerful atmosphere acts as a buoyant force to arouse students' spirits and stimulate in them a desire to achieve.

(*b*) *Unhygienic room conditions.* Students in poorly lighted, overheated, poorly ventilated rooms are likely to become restless, irritable, or depressed. When symptoms of these conditions exist the source of the difficulty probably is near at hand.

(*c*) *Classroom method.* Method is directly related to poor disciplinary situations. Few teachers with otherwise normal conditions and good classroom methods have many disciplinary problems. The lecture or recitation method, conducted in an uninspiring manner with poorly organized materials, will almost inevitably end in expressions of indifference, boredom, note-writing, whispering, and pranks.

(*d*) *Indifferent organization of classroom routine.* Students appreciate definiteness and orderly procedures in their work. They like to get a more or less mechanical form for doing certain things that frequently recur. They show their disgust at once for constant change in matters that might be made routine. Facial expressions first register dissatisfaction; then more serious complaints and disorderliness may follow, culminating in any of the acts common to a disorderly school.

Direct and indirect means of control

In general theory, two principal methods of handling school discipline are recognized. By direct control is meant those steps that must be taken to correct an overt act once it has been committed. The main purpose of direct control is to restore the class or student to normal schoolroom activity. The indirect means of control contemplates primarily the prophylaxis ideal. Under this plan the work of the school is so organized, and possible difficulties so anticipated, that an overt act does not occur except as ideal conditions cannot be provided. The ideal of the high school especially is to achieve such working conditions that direct control will be reduced to a minimum and made entirely an incidental phase of school control.

4. How Secure Direct Means of Control?

The overt act

A writer [9] on discipline asserts that "there is something fundamentally wrong when a high school teacher finds it necessary frequently to resort to any means of direct control." Yet experience shows frequent situations where attention to direct means of control is necessary. It may be the fault of the classroom situation itself; it may be a carry-over from undesirable conditions in other classrooms; the general school organization may be at fault; or the difficulty may even originate in conditions beyond the school. Something may have to be done immediately to preserve class morale, before the teacher is free to seek out the causes and set processes to work to remove them.

There is no place in sound disciplinary theory for "soft pedagogy." The physical, social environment of the student is rigorous, often inexorable. For the school to prove wishy-washy or indulge in maudlin sentimentality would be a disservice to the student. The school should be a pattern of the total social environment, albeit a place shaded to relieve the student of some of the rigors so likely to attend error in judgment and conduct in his out-of-school relationships. He should be made fully conscious of the degree of favorable protection the school offers him during this period of intensive learning. In other respects he must meet the demands of citizenship, industry, and responsibility demanded in the workaday world.

Dangers in overfocalized attention on direct control

Two dangers are inherent in too close attention to the problems

[9] Pringle, R. W., *op. cit.*, p. 187.

of direct control. First, it is easy to over-emphasize the place of direct control in education. The teacher who does so will create problems instead of eliminating them. The old saying, "Look for trouble and you will be sure to find it," has its carry-over here. The teacher constantly on the lookout and in a state of expectancy will not long be unrewarded. Innocent behavior will be wrongly interpreted. Students will sense the lack of confidence, and consciously or unconsciously will be influenced to accommodate the teacher. The teacher unknowingly will be planting the suggestion for undesirable behavior that will produce its harvest.

Moreover, the teacher will tend to take the path of least resistance and form a habit of undue attention to undesirable overt behavior. We are all creatures of habit. Moreover, it requires more effort and alertness to seek out causes that may lead to undesirable behavior, and correct them before they lead to overt acts, than to wait until they occur and then use devices to provide a temporary correction. The teacher who emphasizes the direct modes of control is seriously in danger of losing sight of the importance of method and management, and of slipping back into traditional practices that tend to produce the very things the teacher wishes to avoid.

Principles governing the handling of overt acts

Whatever our emphasis upon modes of control, there are times in the experience of every teacher when direct control is necessary. Experience and a knowledge of the psychology of human reactions have led to some very generally accepted principles that should govern the use of measures to correct undesirable overt behavior. These principles look beyond the immediate to the educational values of permanent significance when direct control becomes imperative. Any intelligent application of these principles will recognize exceptions to every rule. The teacher should be fully persuaded of the justification of the exception, however, before it is made.

1. *The teacher should be responsible for his own discipline.* It is a recognition of weakness to be forced to refer discipline problems to the principal's office. The teacher should impress the class with his unquestioned ability to deal with every situation that arises. The students know the teacher and quickly estimate the degree of firmness the teacher will exhibit. There is less chance for trifling when the student deals directly with the teacher. A trip to

the office is accepted by most students as evidence of the inability of the teacher to handle the student. Moreover, the chance of escaping punishment when sent to the principal is accepted and utilized to the utmost. There is an opportunity for representing the case in such a way as to reflect on the merits of the charge, or to escape through the natural inclination of the principal in most schools to deal gently with the offender. In addition, to be sent to the principal gives the student prestige in the eyes of his fellow students, since his case is such that the teachers cannot handle it alone. There are times, however, when conditions make coopera- tion of the principal's office necessary. The teacher has the right under such circumstances to expect the fullest cooperation on the part of the administration.

2. *A class should not be punished for the individual.* Resentment at the injustice of being punished for another's crime will be the certain reaction of the class. If a large section of the class has been guilty of inexcusable confusion or participation in some major prank, it may be desirable to hold the entire class responsible un- less the individuals can be singled out. Such a course can be justi- fied on the social theory that to shield the criminal makes the inno- cent an actual participant in the crime, as fully recognized in legal jurisprudence. The class should be led to see the serious conse- quences for any democratically controlled society of an attitude that justifies the protection of the guilty in any manner. The teacher should be very careful in the exceptions to the rule, and should endeavor first to locate the guilty students. To bring the class into the picture, unless definitely aware that most of the class possess knowledge of individual guilt, is to court a resentment very diffi- cult to overcome. The writer will never forget the resentment of a class where reference books were used in a study of a number of topics for class reports. Some ten or twelve students chose a topic which involved the use of a certain book. The book disappeared. The teacher in anger posted on the board the names of all ap- pointed to that topic, and threatened to withhold grades for them until the book was returned. There was no way of determining who possessed the book, and little chance that those not guilty could possibly know who had taken the book. The resentment of the class became very pronounced. In spite of the years that have elapsed, the writer, though not one of the users of the book, feels a tinge of resentment at the memory of the palpable injustice.

3. *Discipline of the individual should not interfere with other*

educational opportunities. Whatever the nature of the overt act, the correction should not involve interference with other classes which the student should attend; or, if he is engaged in private lessons after school, these should not be interrupted through penalties imposed. Other teachers have their class plans, and it seriously jeopardizes whole class programs at times to have students absent through necessary detention at the office, or otherwise. A student teacher found a class very unruly; because they would not be quiet the class was held five minutes after the dismissal bell. Immediately complaints were forthcoming. It was a relief to the general supervisor to learn that the penalty had been exacted in the last class-period before the noon hour. To have used this form of correction at any time between classes would have disorganized the school.

4. *Correction should be impersonal.* "This hurts me as much as it does you, but the situation demands that it be done" is the attitude that should characterize all correction. The teacher should genuinely feel that way about it. The teacher who accepts the newer philosophy of discipline recognizes overt acts usually as serious reflections upon the technique of the classroom and the teacher, or as rising from remote causes that reflect serious deficiencies in student training. Correction of any sort, therefore, represents an unfortunate situation. The teacher and student should alike feel this, yet at the same time they should recognize certain penalties for breach of established order. If the teacher will think of misconduct as a reaction against societal standards, rather than against him personally, except as he represents these standards, an impersonal attitude will be more easily maintained. Under no circumstances should correction take place under the stress of emotion. The student will identify the correction with personal vindictiveness on the part of the teacher, creating personal resentment and withdrawing attention from the educational values intended in the correction. Further, emotion inhibits clarity of thought and the judicious application of corrective measures.

5. *Correction should be understood by the pupil.* Any attempt to correct overt behavior results in more harm than good, unless the reasons therefor and the justice of those reasons are made apparent to the offender. The remedial theory of discipline does not countenance any punishment of simple vindictive or retributive nature. There must be a definite expectation that the individual

corrected will have learned from the experience the value of approved behavior, not alone to avoid unpleasant consequences but also because the larger interests, personal and societal, are achieved by the adjustment of conduct to the approved social modes of the school. This is the principle that separates the remedial and the prophylaxis theories from the older ideas of discipline. It is desirable to talk over with the student all phases of the transgression so that the seriousness of the offense may be perfectly understood. If possible, the student should be brought to admit the need of the correction and cheerfully acept the penalty as a necessary sequence of the act.

6. *Correction should be private.* Exposure of the student to correction was the accepted method of the deterrent theory. There is a sense in which this is still a desirable part of correction technique. The class should be made to feel a sense of the inexorableness of school discipline as it obtains outside the school. This result cannot be accomplished by complete privacy, though what actually takes place in the privacy of the office of the teacher should not be revealed to others in the class unless the one most concerned cares to make the revelation. An exception might well be taken, however, when it is found that the class labors under the delusion that nothing serious ever happens. Then there are some acts which need prompt and effective handling while the class work proceeds. As little attention as possible should be called to the individual when classroom correction is necessary. In most situations it is possible to have private conferences with the student over matters that need correction. It is well to remember always that individual reformation is the primary goal of discipline whenever overt acts are concerned.

7. *Correction should be certain.* One of the reasons among many given for the extent of lawlessness in America is that punishment is not certain. In the case of only a small fraction of crimes committed is the criminal ever apprehended, and in a significantly smaller percentage of cases is there any definite meting out of punishment. The ability to "get by" is a most dangerous omen for the welfare of society, both for its failure to exercise a deterrent influence and for the education of those who "get by," and who tend to believe that some forms of anti-social conduct are personally most profitable. The student should be made to feel that the school does not with impunity permit breaches of its laws. If the

school can instill correct attitudes through experience, it will have contributed materially toward a wholesome civic atmosphere in the school and in the community. It is the gambling chance that too many are willing to take when it seems possible to escape punishment.

8. *Correction should be swift.* The most effective impressions are made when correction follows close on the heels of the act that merits it. There is a common tendency to disregard consequences in proportion as they are remote from the causes that produce them. If the student thinks the consequences are to be reckoned with shortly after the overt act, he is likely to be deterred far more than if he knew that the reckoning was in the distant future. The virtue of swiftness lies in its deterrent values and in certain identification in memory of cause with effect.

9. *Correction should be painful.* It is a maxim of discipline that when correction is necessary the offender should suffer severely as a result of the offense. There are two types of pain that may be inflicted — physical and mental. In the high school it is assumed that physical pain will not be inflicted except under most extraordinary circumstances. It is the least effective as a corrective. Yet there are some communities in which floggings are common and, indeed, necessary. Many small isolated communities are still primitive, and the fashion of the community requires rigorous controls. The teacher must take these into account.

The most common means of inflicting pain is mental. It is likewise much more effective. It may be devastating in its effect. The teacher should use this means with care lest psychological consequences for the personality of the student invalidate all the corrective values hoped to be obtained by its use. There are both very "tough-minded" and very "tender-minded" folk, as distinguished by Professor James, the psychologist. The tough-minded are not easily jarred by what is said to them. On the other hand, a very sensitive individual might suffer irreparable harm from a few words of disparagement from the teacher. The teacher needs to exercise extraordinary wisdom in the application of mental suffering appropriate to the nature of the individual and the desired corrective results to be obtained.

10. *Correction should be adjusted to the offense.* There is a measure in which a reversion to the old retributive theory of "an eye for an eye" is necessary and desirable. It is necessary if the

pupil is to gain some idea of the relative value society places upon various aspects of behavior, and the teacher should not for a moment forget that the school should be a microcosm of the democratic society the youth must be helped to understand and adjust himself to successfully. Some behavior is harmful but not serious; other forms carry very serious implications for the well-being of society. It is wholly incompatible with the offense of note-writing, let us say, to suspend the student from school. Vicious conduct, on the other hand, might make suspension or expulsion necessary to safeguard the rest of the student body. There was a justifiable basis for some differentiation in the importance of the deed as the old Mosaic Code attempted to recognize it, or as is implicit in the legal codes of today. The student needs to gain some perspective of the relative seriousness of offenses within the school. To show some discrimination in the teacher-evaluation of conduct will impress the student, both with the judiciousness of the teacher and with the impersonal nature of the correction.

11. *Correction should be adjusted to the offender.* Two general factors should be considered in this connection.

First, what form of correction will prove most effective with the individual concerned? Corporal punishment is the only effective means of control which some students recognize. These students, we have said, represent one extreme. They are found in backward, primitive communities where less rough and ready appeals have not become fashionable in the community; or they are pupils of low mentality, which renders them unable to see the more subtle values that reside in conduct relations. At the other extreme are to be found those who readily cooperate and whose violation of school *mores* may be charged to ignorance.

The second factor that needs always to receive consideration is the intent of the offender. This is very important if the fullest educational values are to be secured, yet it is one of the most difficult factors to determine because it is so subjective in nature. The guilty and the innocent alike will usually declare their good intentions. Mistakes do happen with the best of intentions. Where the teacher has reason, through the general tenor of previous behavior, to believe that the student's declaration of good intent is valid, he should take the good intention into account, but it is seldom wise to excuse entirely any failure to act in complete harmony with approved school *mores.*

12. *Teacher should be certain of guilt.* The problem here is closely akin to the problem of group punishment. Any unmerited correction will produce a rankling in the breast of the student, likely to embitter him toward the school as well as toward the teacher. An injury may easily be done that will alienate student respect and cooperation. If the student is aggressive, future trouble probably will result from the incident. The utmost care should be exercised, for, in addition to innocence falsely punished, the guilty person may "get by." To permit the latter situation is pernicious for the individual, who thus learns that he can violate law with impunity or with a good chance of avoiding detection.

Effective means of handling overt acts

There are no commonly accepted penalties which the teacher can accept with full confidence that they have met the test of practical experience. No scientific studies are available that have determined beyond doubt the values of various forms of corrective devices. It is doubtful if such values could be given. The best the teacher can do is to glean the devices recommended on the basis of experience. In the final analysis it must become clear to the teacher that every situation is unique and demands its own solution. The best the experiences of others can offer is a broad category of devices that may be effective if used with discretion. Possibly as suggestive a list of corrective devices as may be given, with some data on their effectiveness, is that of Belting, offered several years ago. A number of teachers contributed 755 cases of serious discipline problems as a basis for the study. These disciplinary cases were classified according to causes, and then the success or failure of nineteen forms of disciplinary devices as given, together with the percentage of success which the teachers agreed they had had with the application of each disciplinary device. The list of devices employed is given below, ranked in descending order of effectiveness, with the percentage of success entered at the right of the item.

Some cautions need to be offered in an appraisal of these items and their rankings. First of all the teacher should remember that these cases represent very serious cases. The usual type of disciplinary problem is not considered here. That fact will account for the high ranking of some correctional devices that modern disciplinary theory would justify as a last resort only, namely: No. 6,

TABLE 6. *Penalties Applied in Disciplinary Control and the Per Cent of Success in Case of Each* [10]

Penalties Applied	No. of Cases	Percentage Successful
1. Kindness and sympathy	18	94
2. Loss of privilege	48	77
3. Same treatment as the offense to offender	26	69
4. Placed on honor or probation	21	61
5. Parents' assistance	21	57
6. Handled by board	7	57
7. Extra work	59	52
8. Lecture	24	45
9. Ridicule	9	44
10. Expulsion	84	43
11. Reprimand	35	42
12. Failure in work	23	39
13. Ignoring	33	$33\frac{1}{3}$
14. Teacher's resignation	6	$33\frac{1}{3}$
15. Corporal punishment	56	30
16. Apology	40	30
17. Suspension	88	27
18. Sarcasm	8	25
19. Nothing	149	.6

Handled by board; No. 10, Expulsion; No. 17, Suspension; and No. 14, Teacher's resignation. Again, the disparity between case-frequencies for the several penalties applied should be considered in relation to the percentage of successes recorded for the use of a given penalty. Even then the high percentage sustained by the highest five in rank is noticeable.

A number of the items listed above, with a discussion of other disciplinary devices generally employed, may well be given individual consideration.

1. *Kindness and sympathy.* Modern educational theory maintains that normal adolescent youth at heart wishes to do right, but that lack of knowledge, immaturity of judgment, and emotional instability often lead him in moments of stress to do things he would not do were he informed or fully poised. Most of the disciplinary problems the teacher confronts are not serious, at least in the beginning. The student, therefore, is very amenable to a kindly, sympathetic approach when misconduct takes place. The teacher who reveals a genuine faith in the good intentions of the student will find that confidence honored. Even though the student were

[10] Data adapted from Belting, P. E. *The Community and Its High School,* pp. 234–237. Boston: D. C. Heath and Company, 1923.

not deserving of the assumption in most cases, he would endeavor to rise to the estimate of his teacher. In either case the student is challenged to his best. A quiet, serious conference with the student, in which the wise teacher asks well-directed questions that lead the student to discover for himself the seriousness of his behavior, is the most effective way of correcting a fault constructively. A study of the literature shows unanimity on the value of kindness and sympathy in the correction of overt behavior. This kind of treatment is psychologically sound. Even when reproof is necessary in the classroom, if it is given briefly, quietly, and kindly, with a note of challenge to the better self, it will be highly effective.

2. *Loss of privilege.* The two types of privileges that the student has: (1) those common to all, and (2) those he has earned as special honors, are dear to the average student, especially the latter. Experience seems quite generally to warrant confidence in the effectiveness of removal of privilege, particularly of special privilege, for failure on the part of a student to fulfill his obligations. Such deprivation should be employed only when failure in attitude or conduct has been somewhat pronounced. The teacher will need the cooperation and judgment of the principal to enjoin the student's special privileges. It is necessary to strike where the blow will be most seriously felt when grave overt behavior has taken place. To be denied participation on an athletic team, student-body office, etc., brings the individual face to face with the public opinion of his peers. A sense of disgrace as well as the sacrifice of cherished opportunity results. Loss of common privileges should not affect seriously his educational opportunities within the class.

3. *Same treatment as the offense to the offender.* This method carries the teacher back to the ancient principle of *lex talionis.* Its application is not retribution, but a convenient form of remedial device that insures a correction which will appear justifiable and merited in the light of the offense committed. For adolescence it seems to be a safe device that is recognized as fair. It should be used sparingly, however, for in many situations the principle leads to some absurdities and may involve others. Again if the teacher is the one involved, there is danger that the student will associate the punishment with personal pique or revenge.

4. *Placed on honor or probation.* This device usually has proved very effective. The failure to make good usually results in the curtailment of privileges. If the offense has been somewhat serious,

but the student insists he will make good if given a chance, it places him on his mettle. The teacher should so stage the setting that he appears to be in the position of placing confidence in the student, while at the same time giving him the assurance that a watchful eye will none the less be upon him during the probationary period.

5. *Parental assistance.* There are many values in parental co-operation, but the teacher must jealously guard against the appeal to outside authority for help. Today education stresses the cooperative nature of the education task between home and school. Where a spirit of cooperation has existed that has involved the total educational situation and not just overt behavior of children, then the home should be a source of great assistance. Unfortunately, in all too many communities the principal appeal to the home by the school has been when serious behavior problems arose. In the latter situation the teacher should try to avoid such an appeal. If such contacts can be made casually, or if the nature of the difficulty is such as to go beyond the confines of the school, then parental cooperation may be invoked.

6. *Corporal punishment.* Corporal punishment has been discussed at some length in relation to the use of painful correctives. As a disciplinary device in high school, authorities generally agree it cannot be used. Its use is justifiable, if ever, only in a backward community where rough-and-ready tactics are the fashion of the community. As quickly as possible a tranistion should be made to other more pedagogically sound procedures.

7. *Apology.* Because it is so frequently used, it seems well to give some attention to this device. An apology carries with it an assumption of inward recognition of wrong done and an unmixed desire to atone in the best way possible for the injury done another. Most apologies are to some members of the school staff. Generally they are forced. Compulsory expression of regret violates the spirit of disciplinary procedure. Most teachers recall lip-service apologies made because the part of valor dictated — not a transformed spirit. Pringle says,[11] in this connection:

> It is difficult to understand why anyone should think that the mere assertion of authority strengthens authority. If an offense is of such a character that an apology is the natural form of atonement and the apology is not forthcoming, then surely it is someone's duty to bring the offending pupil into an apologizing frame of mind, so that he will

[11] Pringle, R. W., *op. cit.*, p. 307.

seek an opportunity to apologize. If this cannot be done, then the trouble must be settled in some other way. To force an apology is to misuse authority.

5. How Secure Indirect Means of Control?

The ideal school would find discipline confined to indirect methods of control. Since the ideal is seldom found, much attention has been given to the practical exigencies of ordinary classroom situations. *Inasmuch as the thesis of this book envisages all that modern discipline embraces, only incidental attention will be given in the chapter to indirect modes of control. Curriculum classroom management, teaching techniques, and methods are the keys to this form of control.* The teacher should think of them as essentially a part of the problem of this chapter, and as partial answers to the question of how good discipline can be achieved. These "keys" have been adequately discussed in other sections of this book.

The teacher factor

The teacher becomes pivotal in any consideration of school discipline. A good teacher with dynamic personality and winning appeal can have a nearly ideal classroom situation, regardless of other factors that might prove valuable supplementary aids. A teacher lacking forcefulness — irritable and negative in manner — will probably have an unwholesome classroom condition, regardless of the physical environment, the perfection of routine organization, or the use of correct teaching techniques and method. Those traits of the good teacher that should be emulated were considered in some detail in Chapter 2. The teacher is but given emphasis here as the possible key to indirect disciplinary control.

Management factors

This chapter is but a segment of the larger treatment of class management to which Part V is devoted. As often pointed out in this section, every phase of management bears directly on the problem of discipline by indirect control. The teacher will learn very early the value of a smooth-running machine to obviate overt behavior. With a well-organized, smoothly operating school routine, and physical conditions made most agreeable, all geared in with a modern functional curriculum, the way has been paved for the removal of those elements most likely to give rise to classroom friction and undesirable conduct.

Teaching technique factors

The problems of motivation and natural procedures that facilitate learning are part and parcel of teaching techniques and methods. It has been long recognized that human beings do eagerly and with complete concentration those things that interest them most. Youth, to a greater degree than adult, will do with utter abandon that which challenges their interest. It is the province of teaching techniques and methods to arouse those vital interests and utilize the natural modes of learning, to the end that students will work happily and contentedly within the school at appropriate educational tasks. When this has been achieved in fullest measure, the ideal of modern discipline will be well on the way toward accomplishment. For this purpose, special attention should be given Parts II and III.

It is well for the teacher to remember that none of the three factors of indirect control thus far discussed stand alone. They are closely interrelated. The fullest realization of ideal discipline can be attained only when the three are operative at their best.

Extra-curricular activities

"All work and no play makes Jack a dull boy." It also makes Jack susceptible to irritation, quarrelsomeness, and restless dissatisfaction. Even with the most satisfactory schoolroom conditions, students need a more direct outlet for their social tendencies. Extracurricular activities, erroneously so-called, have found a definite place in modern secondary education to meet the needs of social outlets for students. Students wish forms of activity that provide more freedom for individual and group expression than normal classroom procedures provide. The original purpose and educational significance of extra-curricular activities has been well given in the words of one writer, "Social pleasure was their aim, and social training was the result." This statement also explains why educational leaders were so slow to recognize the values of extra-curricular activities. Today, progressive educators consider them an integral part of any adequate program to realize the objectives of modern education. Recreation and social expression are as much a part of education as any of the older traditional content subjects of the curriculum. Indeed, many of these activities have more fundamental worth for education than some of the time-honored subjects hoary with age. They provide for a classroom situation the needed supplement that gives a sense of completeness and normality to the school environment, closely akin to the normal life situation outside the school. Properly guided, the disciplinary values of extra-curricular activities are at once apparent.

The teacher should become fully informed of the philosophy and psychology of modern extra-curricular activities. The forms of organization, and the types of activities through which wholesome social expression may take place, are fully treated in the recent literature on the subject. Probably no phase of education has received more attention by educational writers in the past half dozen years. A glance at the bookshelf before the writer, as these lines are written, reveals a personal collection of over thirty titles on extra-curricular activities, and the collection makes no pretense at completeness.

Student participation in school government

No innovation of educational theory has suffered a more troubled history than that of "student self-government." Based upon the idea that the school should represent a pattern of adult democratic society, it has had for its objective the training of youth in responsible self-government along the lines of contemporary adult society. It found its apparent validation in the modern conception of education, and in the definition of discipline given earlier in this chapter as "the preparation of boys and girls for life in a democratic society." Further, the psychological principle that we "learn by doing," and the equally sound psychological fact that habits of correct social reaction are the basis for desirable traits of adult citizenship have led educational thinkers to hail the idea of student self-government as educationally sound. Experience, too, has not given confidence in the adequacy of older educational procedures to meet the needs of society in governmental relations.

Many experimenters have tried complete student self-government. It has not proved universally successful. Indeed, its patent failure in such a large proportion of the schools where it has been tried has produced open skepticism in many quarters concerning the practicality of the idea. The danger is that the fundamental soundness of the educational theory of *student participation* in government may be lost in the natural reaction to the failure of student government in practical tests. As in the case of all innovations, enthusiasts rush in to experiment without mature consideration of all the implications the new theory involves.

It is not the province of this discussion to consider extensively the reason for any failures of student self-government. It is sufficient only to call attention to the obvious failure of the old educational methodology to secure intelligent functional adult citizenship, and to the educationally sound basis for *student participation* in school government. The difficulty with student self-government, so it appears, has been the failure to recognize the limitations of adolescent immaturity in self-government, and to make the idea of self-government the "fashion" of popular opinion in the school. The fact that popular adult public opinion, in its superficiality, has frowned upon those aspects of self-government that are most essential to success, has effectively prejudiced the student against any attempt at a proper exercise of civic functions. This obstacle must be removed before *student participation* in school government can, in any measurable degree, hope to succeed. It is questionable whether full self-government is possible even under ideal conditions. However, the teacher who can get a large measure of responsibility for social control freely accepted and executed by the students will fulfill the larger objectives of discipline and education. As Pringle [12] and many educational writers maintain, *pupil participation in school government*, rather than the older idea of student self-government, is the practical method through which indirect control is to be fostered and disciplinary purposes achieved.

6. What Limitations Are Placed upon Disciplinary Procedures?

Legal limitations — states

An editorial from a daily paper is of interest at this point:

A Minnesota jury the other day imposed a fine of $750 on a school superintendent for spanking a boy who had put a tack in the seat of

[12] For excellent discussion of the place of student participation in school government in educational theory and practice, with practical suggestions for the establishment of cooperative school government between pupils and faculty, see Pringle, R. W., *The Psychology of High School Discipline*, chapter on "Pupil Participation." Boston: D. C. Heath and Company, 1931.

the little girl in front of him; and whether the ordinary citizen agrees
that the fine was deserved or not, he will at least read of the incident
with a good deal of interest. For it indicates that if one old American
custom is slipping, another one, equally venerable, is still thriving.

In the old days no jury would have dreamed of fining a school
master for flogging a juvenile culprit. In that respect American
schools have changed tremendously.

As the editorial suggests, a distinct change has come over the
social thought of the American public. It reflects a definite reaction against the cruelty and severity of older disciplinary practice.
As in the case of Minnesota, many states have laws that prohibit
absolutely, or under strict limitations, forms of corporal punishment; others have restricted the use of physical correctives, particularly the severity of the punishment. In some states, for example,
physical punishment may be legally used so long as an abrasure of
the skin does not result. Some states permit corporal punishment
with the one condition that the teacher or school official who inflicts
it have the written consent of the parent or guardian; otherwise the
parent may prosecute the teacher or school official who acted without his consent.

Administrative limitations

These limitations emanate from two sources; those that arise from
the policies of boards of education, and those that reflect the attitudes of the school administration itself, either the judgment of the
superintendent or of the principal.

Some boards of education deny the school staff the right of
corporal punishment of any kind. Others permit physical correction for certain causes, and under definite restrictions. A frequent
limitation imposed, where physical punishments are permitted, is
that at least one witness be present. This is a sensible safeguard to
the one administering the punishment, whether required by law,
school-board rule, or not. Boards of Education, too, normally frown
upon such drastic action as suspension or expulsion.

On these same questions of disciplinary procedures school administrators generally have very definite convictions. While the
legal limitations of states and the semi-legal restrictions of boards
of education usually concern only the more drastic of disciplinary
devices, the school administration may have policies that affect
every phase of the problem. It is well for the teacher to learn just

what the principal or superintendent favors in disciplinary procedures, before occasion arises to use them.

Community-parental limitations

Teachers will find their correctional practices often effectively circumscribed by community and parental sentiment. Teachers have felt virtually forced to use physical force at times, simply because the community attitude demanded it. Fortunately, it is more often true that enlightened community or parental sentiment forbids physical pain as a weapon of discipline.

It is disconcerting at times for the teacher to learn that the community may have some very definite notion of what constitutes good discipline. There are plenty of communities where rigid silence in the classroom is regarded as the symbol of the ideal school, and the measure of the teacher is taken by the degree of approximation to this ideal he is able to attain. Worse still, methods that do not produce this effect are sharply criticized. Newer methods are usually open to suspicion. When these produce a classroom situation other than the one which the community concedes to be ideal, the teacher need not be surprised to find his methods targets for attack. Teachers have sometimes found that the methods which they employed as indirect agencies of discipline are inadvisable because, as with a "socialized recitation," for example, they produce too much noise and unpardonable "arguing" in class. Or a teacher utilizing the supervised-study method has met with the criticism in a backward community that the "teacher just walks around the room or sits at his desk most of the time, and lets the students work rather than finding out what they know. And besides, the students walk around the room to get books as they please because that teacher is too lazy to have them hold up their hands and then to take the books they need to their desks."

The wise teacher will acquaint himself with all the limitations that restrict free exercise of his ideas of good disciplinary procedure, direct and indirect. It is a fatal mistake, at times, to act without full knowledge of the true limitations under which the teacher works.

7. What Is the Importance of Discipline?

The discussion thus far leaves but a word to be offered at this point. The importance of discipline is implicit in the definition accepted at the opening of this chapter and the discussion of discipline that follows. The practical identification of the purpose of education and of discipline as the same — the one approached through the other — raises discipline to a plane of importance not contemplated in the older narrower conception. This broader concept is made necessary with the acceptance of the prophylaxis theory of discipline. It is legitimate to say that without good discipline educational ideals cannot be achieved, and *vice versa*. When good discipline obtains, the realization of the best in educational purpose is in process of achievement.

QUESTIONS AND PROBLEMS

1. In what ways have religious presuppositions and disciplinary theory and practice in schools been related?
2. What is an adequate concept of high school discipline that fits the needs of a democratic society?
3. What evidence do we have for believing that most disciplinary problems are a result of maladjustments of the student rather than of the deliberate intent of the student to be mean or vicious?
4. What things in a classroom would you look for in order to determine the teacher's disciplinary ability?
5. What can a teacher do to maintain a discipline that will keep the students orderly and happy?
6. What is the prophylaxis theory of discipline and what are its social implications?
7. What are the causes of confusion that exists in the public mind about school discipline?
8. Given a schoolroom situation, how would you judge the discipline observed?
9. In what ways are disciplinary problems classified and what conception of discipline is involved in each classification?
10. Have a panel consider this statement of an eminent writer: "The school, then, is not a place either for the regimentation of pupils or for the indulgence or coddling of their whims or fancies."
11. What are the dangers of too much control in the classroom?
12. What are some physiological factors that affect the disciplinary problems of the classroom?
13. Evaluate the statement: "Serious overt behavior in the classroom is to be accepted in general as a reflection on the quality of teaching to which the students are subjected."

14. Outline the principles governing the handling of overt acts in the light of modern disciplinary theory.

15. What are some of the most effective corrective methods used in disciplinary cases?

16. What teacher qualifications insure the best indirect control of discipline?

17. What administrative limitations are imposed on direct discipline in many States?

18. How does the parental-community attitude determine disciplinary procedures?

19. What theoretical relation does discipline have to education?

20. Suppose you, as a case worker, had authority to deal with a problem child, who habitually played truant and learned very slowly; what measures would you take? Justify your procedures from the standpoint of the newer ideas on discipline. Smithies — *Case Studies of Normal Adolescent Girls,* or Thom — *Normal Youth and Its Everyday Problems.*

21. The new principal of a high school, in order to assure good discipline of the student body that had the reputation of being disorderly, told them in assembly that he would whip any boy who dared misbehave. The school became very disorderly. How do you explain the student reaction? What methods should the principal and teachers have used to establish and maintain an orderly school?

22. What are the chief contributing causes of the failure of student self-government in high schools?

23. What particular items of knowledge should one have concerning the pupil before one attempts to correct him for the overt act of throwing chalk at another? Substantiate your answer.

SELECTED BIBLIOGRAPHY

Baxter, Bernice. *Teacher-Pupil Relationships,* chapter IV. New York: The Macmillan Company, 1941.

Benjamin, H. R. W. "We Develop Discipline for Freedom," *Childhood Education,* 27: 199 (January, 1951).

Borgese, G. E. "Freedom and Discipline in a Vital Democracy," *Journal of Adult Education,* 12: 249–254 (June, 1942).

Butler, Frank A. *The Improvement of Teaching in Secondary Schools,* Second Edition, chapter XV. Chicago: University of Chicago Press, 1946.

Cutts, N. E. and Moseley, N. *Practical School Discipline and Mental Hygiene.* Boston: Houghton Mifflin Company, 1941.

Douglass, Harl R. *Organization and Administration of Secondary Schools,* chapters XI, XII. Boston: Ginn and Company, 1945.

Douglass, Harl R. and Mills, Hubert H. *Teaching in High School,* chapter VI. New York: The Ronald Press Company, 1948.

Edmonson, J. B., Roemer, J., and Bacon, F. L. *The Administration of the Modern Secondary School,* chapters X–XVI. New York: The Macmillan Company, 1948.

Goetting, M. L. *Teaching in the Secondary School,* pp. 58–68. New York: Prentice-Hall, Inc., 1942.

Hardin, A. A. "How Should the Council be Concerned with Discipline?" *School Activities,* 22: 89–90 (November, 1950).

Jenkins, R. L. "The Constructive Use of Punishment," *Mental Hygiene,* XXIX: 561–574 (October, 1945).

Mann, C. R. "Democratic Discipline," *Educational Record,* 22: 5–14 (January, 1941).

Maul, R. and Brodhead, A. "Self Discipline in a Modern School," *Understanding the Child,* 20: 56 (April, 1951).

Pringle, R. W. *The Psychology of High School Discipline.* Boston: D. C. Heath and Company, 1931.

Reinoehl, C. M. and Ayer, F. C. *Classroom Administration and Pupil Adjustment,* chapters XVIII–XIX. New York: Appleton-Century-Crofts, Inc., 1940.

Risk, Thomas M. *Principles and Practices of Teaching in Secondary Schools,* Second Edition, chapter XXIX. New York: American Book Company, 1947.

Rivlin, Harry N. *Teaching Adolescents in Secondary Schools,* chapter XII. New York: Appleton-Century-Crofts, Inc., 1948.

Scheideman, Rose. *Democratic Education in Practice,* chapter XVI. New York: Harper and Brothers, 1945.

Schorling, Raleigh. *Student Teaching,* Second Edition, chapter IV. New York: McGraw-Hill Book Company, Inc., 1949.

Shannon, J. R. "School Activities and School Control," *School Activities,* 22: 115–117 (December, 1950).

Smithies, Elsie M. *Case Studies of Normal Adolescent Girls.* New York: Appleton-Century-Crofts, Inc., 1933.

Spears, Harold. *Principles of Teaching,* chapter VI. New York: Prentice-Hall, Inc., 1951.

Stiles, L. J. and Dorsey, M. F. *Democratic Teaching in Secondary Schools,* pp. 237–255. Chicago: J. B. Lippincott Company, 1950.

Thom, D. A. *Normal Youth and Its Everyday Problems.* New York: Appleton-Century-Crofts, Inc., 1932.

Thut, I. N. and Gerberich, J. R. *Foundations of Method for Secondary Schools,* chapter XVIII. New York: McGraw-Hill Book Company, Inc., 1949.

Tuttle, Harold S. *Dynamic Psychology and Conduct.* New York: Harper and Brothers, 1949.

Part

VI

THE TEACHER IN EDUCATION

21

What Is the Teacher's Function in Modern Education?

1. How Important Is the Teacher?

Essential nature of the teaching service

Shortly after the turn of the century, one of the leaders[1] in education wrote as follows:

> The teacher is, by all odds, the most influential factor in high school education. Curriculum, organization, equipment, important as they are, count for little or nothing except as they are vitalized by the living personality of the teacher.

Of a more challenging nature is the statement of Dr. C. H. Judd, which appeared in a recent issue of the *Phi Delta Kappan*:

> The teaching staff of any educational institution is its most essential item of equipment. Providing suitable teachers for American high schools is a task so colossal that our civilization is staggered in its effort to meet the demand. . . . Our ability or inability to provide competent teachers will determine the success or failure of the American experiment of universal secondary education.

Less startling perhaps but of equal significance is the studied statement of another writer:[2]

[1] Brown, J. F. *The American High School*, p. 193. New York: The Macmillan Company, 1909.
[2] Brubacker, A. R. "Plain Talks to Teachers," in Holmes, H. W., and Fowler, B. P., *The Path of Learning*, p. 451. Boston: Little, Brown and Company, 1926.

515

The forward movements in human welfare become possible only from correct teaching. Civilization advances in accordance with the quality of teaching service. The influence of the great teacher extends through many generations, doing high service beyond the limits of his natural life. It transcends geographical and national boundaries. Witness Socrates and Jesus.

Reading such encomiums as these to the teacher brings to mind the familiar sentiment that a liberal education could be had with Mark Hopkins seated on one end of a log and the student seated on the other. The centrality of the teacher in any scheme of education seems indisputable. The galaxy of great teachers from every age whose influence upon succeeding generations continues to the present is clearly recognized, both in and out of educational circles. If supporting evidence were necessary, it would be simple for any student reading these lines to marshal before him the names of great teachers of history whose teachings have influenced the course of human development in economic, social, political, and religious life and thought.

As yet no substitute has been found for the impact of mind upon mind, personality upon personality. Even in advanced educational pursuits the graduate student recognizes that two of the chief contributions that can come to him arise from the shared point of view, acquaintance with the habit of thought of his professors, and, if he is very fortunate, the coveted intimate associations with these great scholars. Unfortunately, the mass formations in educational procedures in recent years have made this closer contact with the instructor a privilege of the graduate student, but rarely the opportunity of the undergraduate whose immaturity makes such contacts the more needful. The high school has suffered as well through the attempt to educate *en masse* at minimum cost. Education through mere acquisition of facts and development of the power to reason can never adequately replace the more intimate association between student and teacher that smaller classes and less excessive teaching loads make possible.

The secondary student is at the formative period in his development. Modern pedagogy recognizes more clearly than ever that in the learning situation the personal influence of the teacher is much more significant than subject matter achievement alone. Attitudes toward school work are more important than actual achievement. The personal reaction of the student toward the teacher will have very much to do with the conditioning of these attitudes. Most of us can, figuratively speaking, place our fingers upon the particular teachers whose influence conditioned our present likes and dislikes for certain school subjects. Furthermore most of us can point out the particular teacher who influenced us most in certain modes of thought. Generally we discover upon analysis, that the influence of such a teacher extended far beyond the subject matter studied under him.

As these lines are written, the author is quite conscious of the very definite influence upon his subsequent life of a teacher in the beginning of the junior high school period. In a real sense, without the stimulus of her influence this book might never have been attempted by the writer. It is to her influence, back in a little rural school, that the author owes his intellectual awakening and concomitant scholastic ambitions. To be sure, these did not find full flower at once. Their evolution, however, is clearly traceable in segmental stages over the intervening years. Persons, mostly teachers rather than facts learned, have added touches here and there. Many of these are clearly recognizable to the author. The witness of hosts of others to similar experiences makes imperative the recognition of the strategic place of the teacher in education.

2. What Should Be the Teacher's Personal Equipment?

Teachers' philosophy

The trend of teacher training for the past two decades has given thoughtful students of education cause for concern. Swept into the maelstrom of a materialistic emphasis upon education, we have had a tendency to measure educational values by such standards as could be applied by the yardstick of statistical formulation and immediate objective results. Whither we were ultimately bound and why, we were too impatient to inquire. Philosophy, or an attempt at the discovery of ultimate values or goals of a societal or cosmic nature, was regarded as fit for an age of luxurious contemplation but out of place in a world of rigorous action. As one educational leader remarked to a graduate student, just after World War I: "I am vitally concerned that your training in technique should function one hundred per cent." He was remonstrating against this student's giving too much time to the sociological-philosophical aspects of education and life. The result has been a generation of teachers and, unhappily, school administrators too, who know much about technique, buildings, and budgets, but little or nothing of the ultimate purpose of that knowledge. Like the dog at the railroad station who had eaten his tag, we have been on our way, but whither we were bound, or why, no one knew.

Almost four decades ago a warning voice was raised against the form of specious thinking and practice of educational leaders, and those responsible for teacher training, that emphasized mechanics and depreciated the careful inquiry into the fundamental reasons for these mechanics.

Professor Moore, then of Harvard, declared: [3]

Whether one's philosophy is home made or academically constructed, we must agree with Mr. Chesterton that the view of the universe which he keeps is the most practical and important thing about him. "We think that for a landlady considering a lodger it is important to know his income, but still more important to know his philosophy. We think that for a general about to fight an enemy, it is important to know the enemy's numbers, but still more important to know the enemy's philosophy. We think the question is not whether the theory of the cosmos affects matter, but whether in the long run anything else affects them." And to us it seems that by far the most important thing about a teacher is the kind of philosophy of education which he carries about with him. How one couples up his notions of education with the scheme of things seems to us to be the most illuminating item that can be known about him. Indeed, so thoroughly do basic conceptions determine conduct that if he will tell us definitely and clearly what he thinks education is, we, on our part, will undertake to tell what methods he uses and what success attends his work.

Strong words these! They fit poorly into the mood of expression teachers and schoolmen of this generation have listened to from outside the school, and often within the school as well. These years, however, have not been without "voices crying in the wilderness." Of similar import as those of Professor Moore's are the words of Rusk: [4]

There is probably no worker whose practice is more affected by his philosophy than the teacher's; it consequently behooves him, as he

[3] Moore, E. C. *What is Education?* pp. 13–14. Boston: Ginn and Company, 1915.

[4] Rusk, R. R. *The Philosophical Basis of Education*, pp. 22, 23. Boston: Houghton Mifflin Company, 1929.

cannot avoid it, to secure as adequate a philosophy as he can command. . . . From every angle of the educational problem comes thus the demand for a philosophical basis of the subject. There is no escape from a philosophy of life and education. Those who pride themselves on their neglect of philosophy, have their own philosophy — usually quite an inadequate one.

Today we face a new era in educational thinking. The last few years have brought much disillusionment. When at the close of the inflated period between World War I and 1929 the figurative "joy ride" ended, people realized with something of a jolt that they had enjoyed the ride but had thoughtlessly neglected to consider where they were going, or to set the relative value of what they were doing over against values that might be more enduring and, in the long run, more satisfying. All this has been further intensified by World War II. Education, too, has been brought up sharply and has been forced to take greater cognizance of the true values education should seek to achieve. While our most thoughtful educators have been giving serious consideration to these problems, the rank and file have not. Teacher-training institutions very generally, during this period, eliminated courses in philosophy of education and history of education. Even the courses in curriculum construction tended to deal with the more immediate and superficial, though necessary, problems of the curriculum.

There is a very definite feeling today that education must play a large part in the readjustment society must undergo, not only in the perfecting of the techniques by which this readjustment is to be accomplished, but also in formulating its goal. The demand is for teachers with a broad, deep understanding of life. Those who teach history or mathematics must see beyond historical dates and algebraic formulas to the goals of life and society, and be able to link their teaching with these ultimate values. Since life consists of more than raiment, so education must aid adolescents to sense values, both immediate and remote, societal and cosmic, in nature. The teacher who has not thought through these problems himself and accepted a fairly consistent philosophy that envisages the whole of life will be an inadequate guide and counselor of youth. He cannot be a wholly efficient teacher, no matter how thoroughly he knows his subject matter or how completely he is master of mere technique, important as both are.

Teacher personality

As evidence presented from careful research to show personality is important for the teacher it may be pointed out that in study made of the relation between teaching ability and personality factors by use of the Wilke Personality Rating Scale, Shuey found a correlation of .78.[5] One of the prerequisites all teacher-training institutions consider as the basis of a promising teacher is personality. Most educational writers and public school officials insist personality is one of the most important factors in the successful teacher's equipment. Says Burnham: [6]

> Psychology, education, history, culture, mental hygiene and religion — all put emphasis upon human personality. . . . In all countries during all periods, personality has been, usually perhaps unconsciously, the potent characteristic of leaders.

The late President Eliot of Harvard once said, "The supreme value of a teacher lies not in the regular performance of routine duties, but in his power to lead and inspire his students through the influence of his own mental and moral personality and example." The prospective teacher should take for granted the importance of personality, and consider it seriously as he evaluates his personal fitness and probable success in teaching.

Immediately two questions arise — "What is this thing called personality?" and, "Can teacher personality be developed?" To the first it must be answered that few terms are more widely used in discussions of the individual and his problems, or more generally disagreed upon as to meaning.[7] Many writers prefer rather to discuss the characteristics they believe make up personality than to attempt a complete definition. A common definition assumes "personality to be the sum total of an individual's reaction-tendencies." Burnham quotes,[8] with seeming approval as emphasizing an important phase of personality, the definition of Bekhterev: "The personality, objectively considered, is a freely active individual with mental uniqueness and an individual relation toward the external

[5] Shuey, Audrey M. "The Reliability of the Wilke Personality Rating Scale," *Journal of Educational Psychology*, 34: 273–277 (September, 1943).

[6] Burnham, W. H. *The Wholesome Personality*, p. 123. New York: D. Appleton and Company, 1932.

[7] Thorpe, L. P. *Psychological Foundations of Personality*, pp. 1–36. New York: McGraw-Hill Book Company, 1938.

[8] Burnham, W. H., *op. cit.*, p. 121.

world." He contents himself, however, with a list of fourteen factors that make up human personality. These are: (1) one's attention; (2) one's emotional tendencies and reactions; (3) one's psycho-physical energy or what is perhaps commonly called one's will; (4) one's moral character including one's obedience to organized or traditional authority; (5) one's conscience; (6) one's ideals and beliefs; (7) one's knowledge; (8) the mental attitudes; (9) the religious attitudes of dependence, reverence, and the like; (10) one's intelligence; (11) one's imagination and memory, especially habits of noting and recall; (12) one's sense of humor; (13) wisdom, including common sense and judgment; (14) the ego.

It may be well to postpone the answer to the second question, "Can teacher personality be developed?" until we attempt to discover what factors of personality are important for teachers. It is obvious that some factors given above are primarily the result of inheritance; others the product of environment. It is altogether probable that some personality factors especially essential for teachers are not important in other situations.

Qualities of a good teacher

For the past several years there has been increasing interest in the personal qualities that make for teaching success. It is clearly recognized that the problem of wise selection of teachers for training or employment depends upon the ability to determine what qualities make for teaching success. If misfits could be anticipated in the teacher-training institutions, much bitter disappointment, humiliation, and misdirected energy might be saved. The public school, too, could select with greater assurance those most likely to succeed.

A few significant examples of efforts at analysis of these qualities, and the general conclusions that may be warranted from the studies, will be given. These are selected to represent slightly different approaches to the solution of the problem. The first, no doubt, represents the most elaborate attempt at trait analysis of teachers. Twenty-five traits are "judged by competent critics of teachers to be most important," and again ranked for relative importance by twenty-five equally competent educational leaders. Table 7 is adapted from Charters and Waples.[9]

[9] Charters, W. W. and Waples, Douglas. *The Commonwealth Teacher-Training Study*, p. 18. Chicago: University of Chicago Press, 1929.

For convenience, the additional column at the right of the table is added to facilitate comparison with the findings of the second study given as an example.

The findings of the Barr-Emans study are not exactly comparable with the adapted table from Charters and Waples since the Barr-Emans data embrace all grades from the kindergarten through the senior high school, while it seemed desirable to give the Commonwealth Teacher-Training Study data for the secondary school only. The study made by Barr-Emans [10] attempted to find, from an analysis of the rating devices "collected from cities of more than 25,000 inhabitants, state departments of public instruction, and departments of education in universities," those traits considered important for successful teachers. Such rating devices, it was assumed, should reflect the items judged by responsible educators as important in teacher success. The results were compared with the Charters-Waples Rank List of Teachers' Traits.

Considerable dissimilarity is evidenced in the two rankings, though at some points the studies show close agreement. This dissimilarity may be due to the dissimilarities in the range of school grades covered, yet the ranking for all grades on the Charters-Waples study shows a much closer agreement with the rankings of the junior-senior high school sections of the study than the total rank averages do with the comparable total rank averages for the Barr-Emans study. The important consideration, for our purpose, is that the same traits appeared in both studies with some indication of broad agreement.

The Commission [11] on Teacher Education of the American Council of Education in an extensive study of the qualities of the good teacher listed the following: (1) respect for personality; (2) community-mindedness; (3) rational behavior; emotional surefootedness; (4) creative power; (5) skill in cooperation; (6) increasing knowledge, breadth and integration of scholarship; (7) skill in mediating knowledge; (8) friendliness with children; (9) social understanding and behavior; (10) effective citizenship in the school; (11) skill in evaluation; (12) faith in the worth of teaching.

[10] Barr, A. S. and Emans, L. M. "What Qualities are Prerequisite to Success in Teaching?" in *The Nation's Schools*, vol. 6, No. 3, p. 62 (September, 1930).

[11] Adapted from list presented in *The Improvement of Teacher Education*, Final Report, Commission on Teacher Education, p. 37. Washington, D.C.: American Council on Education, 1946.

TABLE 7. *Comparison of the Rank List of Teachers' Traits in the Commonwealth Teacher-Training Study with the Barr-Emans Study*

TRAITS	Grades X–XII Senior H. S.	Grades VII–IX Junior H. S.	Total Rank Jr.–Sr. H. S.	Barr-Emans List Ranked for Grades Kdg.–XII
1. Adaptability	8	10	8	13
2. Attractiveness, personal appearance	17	14	16	3
3. Breadth of interest (interest in community, profession, pupils)	1	10	4	4
4. Carefulness (accuracy, definiteness, thoroughness)	11	13	13	18
5. Considerateness(appreciativeness, courtesy, tact, sympathy, kindness)	17	3	10	5
6. Co-operation (helpfulness, loyalty)	11	9	10	1
7. Dependability (consistency)	14	19	18	19
8. Enthusiasm (alertness, animation, inspiration)	9	4	6	12
9. Fluency	23	24	24	9
10. Forcefulness (courage, decisiveness, firmness, purposefulness)	5	4	3	23
11. Good judgment (discretion, foresight, insight, intelligence)	2	1	1	20
12. Health	16	16	17	8
13. Honesty	7	12	9	22.5
14. Industry (patience, perseverance)	19	8	14	17
15. Leadership (initiative, self-confidence)	4	7	4	6
16. Magnetism (approachability, cheerfulness, optimism, sense of humor, sociability, pleasing voice)	11	4	7	2
17. Neatness (cleanliness)	20	16	21	21
18. Openmindedness	9	20	15	24.5
19. Originality (imaginative, resourcefulness)	22	22	22	14
20. Progressiveness (ambition)	23	23	23	22.5
21. Promptness (dispatch, punctuality)	21	14	20	7
22. Refinement (conventionality, good taste, modesty, morality, simplicity)	14	20	19	15
23. Scholarship (intellectual curiosity)	5	16	12	10
24. Self control (calmness, dignity, poise, reserve)	2	2	2	11
25. Thrift	25	25	25	24.5

Pupil rating of teachers

Another study attempted to find out what high school students regarded as the good qualities of teachers. Twenty-eight teachers in the Barberton High School, Barberton, Ohio, were ranked by their students, and the qualities they considered good and bad in teachers were listed. Thirty-five items were mentioned twenty times or more. These are listed [12] below in descending order of mention:

(1) Good disposition, kindness, patience; (2) impartiality; (3) ability to explain clearly; (4) discipline; (5) knowledge of subject;

[12] Light, U. L. "High School Pupils Rate Teachers" in *School Review*, vol. 38, pp. 28–32 (January, 1930).

(6) fairness in marking; (7) sense of humor; (8) helps pupils out of class; (9) understands high school students; (10) knows how to interest pupils; (11) honest, keeps his word; (12) good judgment; (13) good personality; (14) school spirit; (15) clear and definite in assignments; (16) distinguishes important and unimportant; (17) will-power; (18) leadership; (19) never laughs at pupil's mistakes; (20) makes no use of detention rooms; (21) general knowledge as well as of her subject; (22) does not get off subject; (23) good voice; (24) knows ability of class; (25) able to give good advice; (26) appreciates whatever weaknesses pupils may possess; (27) uses good English; (28) supervises study, allows study periods; (29) understands home conditions; (30) gives frequent tests; (31) practices Golden Rule; (32) ventilates room; (33) dresses conservatively; (34) cooperates; (35) good sport.

Another study of interest in this connection is that which was made in 1947 by Witty.[13] From nearly 12,000 letters written by children on "The Teacher Who Has Helped Me Most," the following traits are listed in descending order of mention: (1) Cooperative democratic attitude; (2) kindliness and patience; (3) wide variety of interests; (4) good appearance and pleasing manner; (5) fairness and impartiality; (6) sense of humor; (7) good disposition; (8) interest in pupil's problems; (9) flexibility; (10) use of recognition and praise; (11) superior teaching efficiency.

Possibly the most significant data concerning pupil judgments of what qualities are important in the good teacher are to be found in Hart's study of the opinions of ten thousand high school seniors. In this study students were asked to recall the best liked teacher they had ever had. This teacher was to be designated as "Teacher A." The students were requested to give the reasons why they liked this teacher best. Then the students were asked to designate as "Teacher Z" the teacher "you have liked least of all," and to give the reasons why this teacher was not liked. Finally, the students were asked to designate the teacher whom they regarded as the *best* teacher they had ever had. If such teacher was neither teacher "A" nor "Z" then such teacher was to be called "Teacher H," and the students were to indicate in what ways "Teacher H" was different from "Teacher A."

An adaptation of the tables given by Hart showing the different

---

[13] Adapted from Witty, Paul A. "Teacher Who Has Helped Me Most," *Elementary English*, 24: 345–354 (October, 1947).

qualities of these three types of teachers is given below. It is of great significance for the aspiring good teacher that the data reveals that "Teacher A" in four cases out of five enjoys the double distinction of being both the "best liked" and the "best teacher." [14]

The author, in collaboration with a graduate student, has carried on an extended research to discover, if possible, significant traits of good secondary teachers. This study was made by comparing the judgments of school superintendents and principals as to those qualities they deemed important for teachers to possess as they analyzed their own teachers. These judgments were then checked against data from the Appointment Bureau and the University Registrar's office records to discover other factors of value, particularly of a predictive nature. The study, which involved data covering several years, yielded the following teacher traits or qualities that appear significant.[15]

1. scholarship	10. cooperation	16. attention to individual needs
2. discipline	11. optimism	
3. teaching skill	12. school management	17. skill in motivating work
4. industry	13. promptness and regularity	18. health
5. care of routine		19. resourcefulness
6. use of English	14. self-control	20. voice
7. tact	15. initiative and self-reliance	21. enthusiasm
8. adaptability		
9 sense of justice		

There is a remarkable similarity in the findings of all these studies as to the composite traits or qualities that make up the picture of the successful teacher. The last named list, or the trait list of Charters and Waples, may be accepted as indicative of the qualities a teacher should possess.

Important teacher qualities affecting personality

If a careful analysis is made of the Charters-Waples Rank List of Teachers' Traits, in comparison with Burnham's fourteen factors

[14] Hart, Frank W. *Teachers and Teaching*, p. 279. New York: The Macmillan Company, 1934.

[15] Unpublished Master's thesis, University of Oregon, 1932. Godard, S. L., *Reliability of Superintendents' and Principals' Estimate of Success of Their Teachers and the Relationship of this Teaching Success with the Teachers' College Record.*

TABLE 8. *High School Seniors' Judgments of Teachers "A," "Z,"*
and "H" Ranked in Descending Order of Frequency of
Mention *

Reasons for Liking Teacher "A" Best	Rank	Reasons for Liking Teacher "Z" Least	Rank	Teacher "H" Differed from Teacher "A" as Follows:	Rank
Is helpful with school work, explains lessons and assignments clearly and thoroughly, and uses examples in teaching	1	Too cross, crabby, grouchy, never smiles, nagging, sarcastic, loses temper, "flies off the handle"	1	More exacting in standards of work, stricter in marking, "we learned more"	1
Cheerful, happy, good-natured, jolly, has a sense of humor, and can take a joke	2	Not helpful with school work, does not explain lessons and assignments, not clear, work not planned	2	Better at explaining lessons and assignments, work is better planned	2
Human, friendly, companionable, "one of us"	3	Partial, has "pets" or favored students, and "picks on certain pupils"	3	Knows the subject better and "can put it over" better	3
Interested in and understands pupils	4	Superior, aloof, haughty, "snooty," overbearing, does not know you out of class	4	Stricter, more rigid discipline	4
Makes work interesting, creates a desire to work, makes class work a pleasure	5	Mean, unreasonable, "hard-boiled", intolerant, ill-mannered, too strict, makes life miserable	5	Makes the work more interesting	5
Strict, has control of the class, commands respect	6	Unfair in marking and grading, unfair in tests and examinations	6	Is less friendly	6
Impartial, shows no favoritism, has no "pets"	7	Inconsiderate of pupils' feelings, bawls out pupils in the presence of classmates, pupils are afraid and ill at ease and dread class	7	More serious, more businesslike, keeps closer to the subject, more conscientious	7
Not cross, crabby, grouchy, nagging, or sarcastic	8	Not interested in pupils and does not understand them	8	Less understanding of pupils, less interested in pupils	8
"We learned the subject"	9	Unreasonable assignments and home work	9	More sarcastic	9
A pleasing personality	10	Too loose in discipline, no control of class, does not command respect	10	Less attractive	10
Patient, kindly, sympathetic	11	Does not stick to the subject, brings in too many irrelevant personal matters, talks too much	11	More cross and crabby	11
Fair in marking and grading, fair in giving examinations and tests	12	"We did not learn what we were supposed to"	12	More aloof	12
Fair and square in dealing with pupils, has good discipline	13	Dull, stupid, and uninteresting	13		
Requires that work be done properly and promptly, makes you work	14	Too old-fashioned, too old to be teaching	14		
Considerate of pupils' feelings in the presence of the class, courteous, makes you feel at ease	15	Not "fair and square" in dealing with pupils	15		
Knows the subject and knows how to put it over	16	Knows the subject but "can't put it over"	16		
Respects pupils' opinions, invites discussion in class	17				
Not superior, aloof, "high hat," does not pretend to know everything	18				
Assignments reasonable	19				
Is reasonable, not too strict or "hard-boiled"	20.5				
Helpful with students' personal problems, including matters outside of classwork	20.5				

TABLE 8 (*continued*)

Reasons for Liking Teacher "A" Best	Rank	Reasons for Liking Teacher "Z" Least	Rank	Teacher "H" Differed from Teacher "A" as Follows:	Rank
Dresses attractively, appropriately, neatly, and in good taste..............	22	Does not hold to standards, is careless and slipshod in her work......	17		
Young..............	23	Too exacting, too hard, gives no chance to make up work.............	18		
Work well planned, knows what class is to do.............	24	Does not know the subject..........	19		
Enthusiastically interested in teaching	25	Does not respect pupils' judgments or opinions........	20		
Gives students a fair chance to make up work..............	26	Too changeable, inconsistent, unreliable............	21		
Home-work assignments reasonable..	27	Lazy, not interested in teaching.......	22		
Recognizes individual differences in ability	28	Not friendly, not companionable ...	23		
Frank, "straight from the shoulder," a straight shooter ...	29.5	Shows boy or girl favoritism..........	24		
Personally attractive, good-looking......	29.5	Dresses unattractively or in bad taste............	25		
		Weak personality....	26		
		Insincere..........	27		
		Personally unattractive............	28		
		Does not recognize individual differences in pupils....	29		
		Voice not pleasant ..	30		

* This table is an adaptation of tables found on pages 131–132, 250–251, 278–279, in Hart, Frank W., *Teachers and Teaching.* New York: The Macmillan Company, 1934.

that make up personality, it becomes apparent that the lists are very similar, particularly if Chapters II–III of Burnham are studied in this connection. Almost every factor of personality is included in Charters-Waples trait list, although some are ranked very low. The failure to include in the Charters-Waples trait list reference to "religious attitudes" or "one's ideals and beliefs," emphasized in the Burnham list, represents the principal variation in the two classifications. This omission of reference to religious attitudes, ideals, and beliefs is but natural, since the education of those whose judgments are used as the criteria by which to establish such traits has led these men to depreciate the significance of philosophy in teacher training, or, in the case of the younger educational leaders, their professional training has ignored philosophy and related subjects as a legitimate part of an educator's professional equipment. While the absence of a philosophy of life and education may not affect the more superficial estimate of the teacher's success, such a lack must in a real sense seriously limit the largest usefulness of the teacher. It is safe to conclude that the emphasis upon personality in the past has not been misplaced. Indeed, the evidence from careful research gives it a central position in teaching success.

Educability of successful teacher qualities

A letter received by a colleague from a principal of a leading high school contained this interesting observation, "Every year that I spend in high school work I am more convinced that teachers are born, not made." This statement is closely related to the previous question, "Can teacher personality be developed?" The answer is, with qualifications, "Yes."

The degree to which intelligence is the result of inheritance rather than environment will limit the educability of that trait. Originality, adaptability, foresight, imagination, insight, appearance, voice, health, and scholarship are qualities that are interrelated, and in part assumed to belong to natural endowment; all of these, however, are capable of development to a greater or lesser degree. A careful study of the Charter-Waples trait list suggests a basis of natural endowment necessary for teaching success. Careful researches are steadily revealing the degree to which these inherited capacities may be developed through training. Many of the traits listed are obviously susceptible to extensive education. Many are matters of simple habit-training, such as neatness, honesty, self-control, promptness, carefulness, dependability, kindness, etc. Very often the failures of teachers are due more to these incorrect habit-traits than to qualities incapable of or subject to limited development. In the study carried on under the author's direction, scholarship was found to be the most significant index of teaching success. This trait is related to general intelligence. Within considerable limits it is the result of individual effort, and therefore improvable to a marked degree.

Health of teachers

"I Am Stober" is the attention-arresting title to a very significant article on the teacher's health.[16] Though written many years ago it is as timely today as when written. Stober was an ambitious student whose brilliant record made him leader of his classes both in

[16] Brooks, J. D. "I Am Stober" in *Journal of Education*, vol. 110, pp. 351–352 (October, 1929).

the Normal College and the University. He was the college grind. He prided himself that he made his body the ready servant of his will. By dint of hard work and personal sacrifice he achieved the degree of Doctor of Philosophy and an appointment to a professorship in a small college. Later a long-coveted offer of a professorship in a large State University came but he was unable to accept it, for the toll laid upon his body during the years as student and teacher forced him to the hospital with a severe attack of rheumatism. Ten years later a classmate visited him in his college town to find him a misshapen physical wreck, suffering from "Arthritis Deformans" and unable to feed himself. His parting words to his friend were these, "You are a teacher of teachers. This life of torment of mine will not be quite in vain if it can teach others one lesson through you. The Greeks were right," he said thoughtfully, "as fundamentally right when they emphasized the development and perfection of their bodies and made physical training an essential part of the education of their youth as they were right in every other field they entered." Stober's failure to keep a true perspective in regard to health is typical of the attitude of many teachers.

This factor of teacher health deserves special consideration. So many other traits are influenced by the state of the teacher's health that special attention should be given to it. Further, teachers are notorious for their negligence of elemental laws of health, so much so, indeed, that cartoonists long have pictured the pedagogue as an emaciated, highly surcharged neurotic.

If the factor of economic loss alone were considered, teacher health would loom large. One city with a population of 50,000 spent over $6,000 in one year for substitutes to replace sick teachers. Another city of 900,000 population spent $25,000 for substitutes because of teacher illness. The cost, of course, is not reckoned alone in monetary loss. The inefficiency of ill teachers who struggle to remain at their tasks, and the recognized fact that most substitute teachers do little more than hold the class organization together while the regular teacher is off for a couple of days of illness, mean serious loss of educational opportunity for the students.

Insurance companies consider teachers preferred risks because their mortality rate is not high. On the other hand, teachers suffer from certain types of diseases or disorders that could be greatly reduced with proper attention to hygienic rules. Studies seem to show that nervous disorders occur frequently among teachers. Colds, tonsillitis, and sinus troubles, stomach and other forms of disturbance in digestion are among the prevalent types of teacher illnesses. Some of the illness resulting in indigestion is directly traceable to the nervous difficulties that afflict teachers.

Many causes are assigned to explain teacher illness. Disregard for proper exercise contributes not a little. A recent study of teacher illness revealed that 63 per cent of those affected took no daily exercise. Improper diet and irregular and hurried eating affect proper digestion. Another serious drain on the teacher's health is the exposure to which he is submitted in the classroom. Close association for several hours each day with students in crowded classrooms makes the teacher liable to all forms of bacterial infection carried by them. Underheated, overheated, poorly ventilated, and poorly lighted classrooms, soiled books, and excessive night work under poor room conditions continually tax the health safeguards of the most careful teacher. A high school principal in a little community, as he worked each week with the school library books, found himself subject to a particularly obnoxious skin disease — impetigo. A serious complaint of teachers in smaller communities is their inability to find suitable lodging accommodations that provide proper privacy and light and heat conditions necessary for cheerful and comfortable work. To overcome such difficulty, many smaller rural communities are providing teacherages to accommodate the teachers and enable them to live near the school.

Many of the health liabilities of teachers can be overcome or greatly reduced. Adequate attention to proper personal health habits is largely within the province of the teacher. Anyone visiting classrooms will wonder at times how teachers can be so negligent of their own health as well as that of students. Superheated, and poorly ventilated and poorly lighted, classrooms are often the fault of the teacher. Health examinations ought to be required of students, and are in most progressive schools. The teacher, however, should check his own health through periodic medical examination. "An ounce of prevention is worth a pound of cure." Plenty of exercise, fresh air, wholesome food, sufficient sleep, the cultivated habit of refusal to worry, and occasional week ends away from the community, all of these will contribute to the teacher's health.

No teacher can attain his maximum effectiveness when harboring poor health. A sound rugged physical organism is basic to a dynamic wholesome personality. Vigor and vitality bring optimism, enthusiasm, poise, alertness, and that contagion of spirit so essential to good teaching.

Academic preparation

A broad general education is basic for the teacher in the secondary school. At this point, when the youth is climbing, more than anywhere along the educational ladder he should be stimulated by association with men and women of broad outlook and acquaintance with many fields of human knowledge. The culture of the ages should find interpretation and appeal through the teacher. If an eagerness to know how other people lived, thought, and wrought is to be the future possession of the adult, it must find its genesis in these formative years of the student. The teacher who has drunk deeply and appreciatively of the thought life of the past, and has tied these experiences to the present, consciously and unconsciously will open wide vistas that beckon the student to explore beyond his little world.

It is of even greater importance that the teacher be fully alive to the present. As pointed out in the earlier chapters, we live in a unique epoch of history. Change in every aspect of life about us is so rapid that much of the past has little significance for us today, and less for tomorrow. The teacher has a primary responsibility to have an awareness of contemporary change and to understand the significance of this change, at least, in its major outlines. This is a large order for the teacher, but without it the teacher will be an ineffectual guide of youth. This broad general training should emphasize the complexity and oneness of life, and the part that various fields of knowledge must play in the realization of the fullness of that life. Economics does not exist for itself; literature is incomplete taken alone; history or science cannot alone give an adequate picture of normal existence. All must contribute their part to the understanding of life and its complete realization. A background in history, political science, sociology, literature, economics, the natural sciences and the fine arts is highly desirable.

In addition to a broad training, the teacher must be especially a master of one or two fields of learning. These should be in the broad areas common to the high school curriculum. It is somewhat unfortunate that the segmentation of human knowledge has been permitted to develop as it has in the secondary school. What should be a period of widely generalized training has been made, in practice, one of undue specialization. The narrowing process has been aided and abetted by our institutions of higher learning with their emphasis upon specialization, and their demand that some of that specialized training be pushed down into the high school. A correction of this practice of segmentation of knowledge at the high school level is slowly taking place, but special preparation in certain broad fields will no doubt continue for some time to be a prerequisite of the high school teacher.

Preparation for extra-curricular activities

Increasingly, schools are insisting upon teachers who can do more than teach in the traditional subject fields. They want student leadership in other forms of educational activity, miscalled extra-curricular. The ability to direct recreational activities, coach dramatics and class plays, conduct glee clubs and orchestras, lead boys' and girls' scouting, Nature Study clubs, hiking clubs, camera clubs, book lovers' clubs, science clubs, etc., has become a very important requirement and often is the determining factor in teacher employment. Slowly these activities are being coordinated with the regular school curriculum. Activity periods are part of the regular daily schedules of many schools. An extensive library on extra-curricular activities is rapidly developing. The prospective teacher will do well, therefore, to prepare for this form of school activity as well as for the more formal subject matter fields.

Professional preparation

Most states require a specified number of hours in professional courses in Education before a teacher will be given a certificate to teach in the secondary school. Courses in Educational Psychology, based upon a course in General Psychology, Principles of Secondary Education, Methods of Teaching, and Supervised Teaching are among those usually specified in the fifteen to twenty semester hours required. The teacher who looks upon teaching as a profession rather than a stopgap to something else will do well to consider a more thorough preparation than the minimum courses provide. Man's mental and emotional adjustment to the cosmic aspects of his existence are even more fundamental than his immediate practical adjustments to his economic-social environment. Adolescence is vitally concerned, and, where it is not, should be led to be concerned with these larger problems that provide the true satisfactions and poise in life. Closely related to philosophy should be a good course in the history of education. Our educational practice is the result of many forces that the teacher should understand if he would deal intelligently with the present.

Earlier in the chapter attention was called to the lack of philosophical perspective with which the ordinary teacher approaches his task. Here may be re-emphasized the need for a good course in the Philosophy of Education, built upon a course or two in general philosophy from the philosophy department. It cannot be too strongly urged that the function of secondary education demands the type of educational direction which only that teacher can give who is prepared to speak intelligently on the deeper meaning of life and the purpose of education in relation to those values men hold to have abiding worth.

Many training schools provide courses in Genetic and Adolescent Psychology in their professional curriculums. To these might well be added a course in Social Psychology. A course in Educational Tests and Measurements is almost a necessity for the efficient teacher. Inasmuch as the teacher is now expected to make many public appearances, a special course in Public Speaking, designed to insure clear and forceful address, with some knowledge of the principles of speechmaking, would be of material assistance in public relations.

No doubt the reader of these pages will protest that much more is required than is possible of fulfillment. This preparation cannot be secured in four years of attendance at college or university. A definite trend toward a minimum of five years beyond high school is now in evidence. Some states, such as California and Washington, have moved to that standard. The time must come when preparation comparable to that for the professions of law, medicine, and the ministry are accepted for education. Wide reading and varied experience through rich experiential living must supplement the formal classroom work if the best possible preparation is to be made.

3. How Develop School Relationships?

Student-school relationships

Precept and example are two words the teacher should constantly bear in mind. Example is often much more potent than any item of equipment the teacher possesses — certainly more important than anything he may say. In the mind of the student the teacher is the embodiment of the ideas and ideals expressed. Dignity, poise, and self-assurance without a suggestion of egotism are important personality traits, both in and out of the classroom. Dignity and poise, without frigidness and an air of undue personal importance, are achievements not easily attained. There is but a narrow margin between dignity and coldness, yet many teachers carry, with apparent ease, an atmosphere of easy approachableness and at the same time just as definitely a "thus far and no farther" manner. A teacher who refuses to get excited, acts calmly and judiciously in trying situations, dresses neatly and appropriately, plays no favorites, and is clean in personal habits will tend to establish these modes of reaction on the part of the students, and at the same time keep their respect for himself and for his position.

The attitude of the teacher should always be that of friendly cooperation and sympathetic understanding. A readiness to go out of one's way to help a student is seldom abused as a student privilege. The teacher whose genuine interest in the student has been demonstrated will find that interest repaid in student loyalty and esteem. When such confidence has been reposed in the teacher, a chance for real help to the student is afforded. Adolescence gives all or nothing. Its loyalties are not likely to be halfhearted. The teacher whose interest is genuine can do much to mold the patterns of student thought both in the classroom and out. Confidences are readily given to those whose genuineness is accepted. Those who enjoy this coveted relationship know what influence is theirs; so do most observant parents. Teachers should learn to respect as inviolate confidences so given.

Many teachers have found the way to student confidence most quickly reached through wholehearted interest and assistance in extra-curricular activities. Every teacher should consider this one of the major responsibilities and opportunites he must assume in the school. Shortsighted, unprofessionally minded teachers often take the attitude that they are hired to teach. Only recently a superintendent was recounting to the author the reasons for the failure of a brilliant young man as teacher in his school. An example of a remark to students, which revealed an unfortunate attitude, was recalled. A student in the presence of others asked the teacher about certain events not immediately connected with his work but which an alert teacher would have known about. The reply, indifferently given, was: "I don't know. I am only hired to teach here." Superintendents frequently complain that some teachers seem to feel their obligations completed when the formal classroom work is complete for the day. Successful teachers know their school obligations are not so easily discharged. It is becoming increasingly difficult to decide just where school work ends. The extra-curricular activities, the newer ideas of student counseling, etc., extend the work of the school far beyond the classroom.

Staff relationships

The test of a teacher often comes in his relationship to the rest of the staff, rather than in the classroom. Teaching is a cooperative enterprise. It requires the cooperative effort of every teacher with every other teacher and with the administrative leadership of the school if the school is to succeed. The work of the school is closely interrelated. The curriculum should represent the careful coordination of every part. The teachers must necessarily work together if this unity is to be assured. Some teachers tend to regard their own area as the most important and become jealous of any encroachment on their field or time. Some are extreme individualists, and find it difficult to work with other members of their own departments or on committees with other teachers. The same spirit of ready cooperation and helpfulness shown toward the students should prevail among teachers.

The principal and the superintendent should be looked upon as friends. They have slightly different functions to perform, but all are working toward the same purpose. The attitude of the teacher should be complete loyalty to the leader of the school and school policies, once these are adopted. The fact that we do not all see alike should not prevent every teacher from giving wholehearted cooperation in the furtherance of any program designed to better the school. More and more teachers are having a substantial voice in the formulation of policies that directly affect them. More and more the concept of democracy in school administration is reducing the sharp cleavage that traditionally has separated administrator and teacher. They work together to determine large areas of school policy. As the cooperative nature of the school task becomes more fully accepted, more democracy in the school will be in evidence, and more cooperation actually necessitated.

While elaborate treatises are available on professional ethics for teachers, with which every teacher should become familiar, a few items deserve special mention. Some of these appear so self-evident that their mention would seem unnecessary if their violation were not so frequent.

First, the teacher should give full loyalty to the administration and to fellow teachers, and wherever it is possible for him to give assistance he should do so freely, when to do so does not require an unjustifiable sacrifice of his first responsibility. Such an attitude is of the essence of cooperation.

Second, the policies of the school should be defended when necessary, or the teacher should at least tactfully refrain from comment if those policies cannot be fully endorsed. It is well to remember that ultimately the administration is responsible to the school board, and behind them to the community for school policies. Presumably the school board is cognizant of these policies and has approved them. If they are unwise, be content that the fact will come to light quickly enough.

Third, the teacher should expect sympathetic, constructive supervision from his superiors; and the superior should consider it an obligation of his office to assist the teacher in every possible way to become a better teacher.

Fourth, teachers should not gossip about fellow teachers or criticize them unfairly to other teachers, to students, or to outsiders. Particularly is it a breach of fair play to criticize one's predecessor. The writer remembers an incident where a highly respected teacher was criticized by a successor. The criticism almost cost the critic her position. Her efficiency was greatly impaired.

Fifth, teachers should sedulously refrain from talking disparagingly about one student to another. Whatever the faults of the student, the chances are that he is sensitive to the teacher's good opinion. Furthermore, if the student to whom the teacher gossips possesses a keen sense of justice, he will lose his respect for the teacher.

4. How Meet the Social Problems of the Teacher?

Social conduct

No phase of the teacher's professional life is likely to prove more important to his success than that of social conduct. It is difficult for students who have spent four or more years in a college or university to adjust quickly to the different social customs of another community. Four years at the seat of teacher training often gives students an exaggerated notion of personal freedom in the ordinary modes of social convention. Those four years at best have been in a semi-artificial, unnatural environment. As likely as not the student is suddenly transplanted to a small, rather isolated community, where possibly the dominant group in the community is ultra-conservative in social thought and practice. In this type of community everybody's business is nobody's business, and the teacher's conduct is subjected to the most rigid scrutiny. Youth, impatient of what it regards as unreasonable backwardness and intolerance, may disregard community *mores* and soon is in serious trouble. Such difficulty is likely to arise out of a failure to sense the situation and the mistaken assumption that the same freedom enjoyed at the training school obtains in the new community. It is a wise teacher, indeed, who finds out what responsible elements in the community think about such relatively innocent pleasures as dancing and card playing before indulging in them.

Often the teacher finds himself in a very hard situation in an isolated community where the chief forms of amusement are forbidden fruit to teachers. People, too, are often most inconsistent. After a lecture at a teachers' institute some years ago, where some of these problems had been discussed, a young woman came to the platform and submitted to the writer this situation with the query: "What would you do?" The circumstances in which the young woman found herself were these. She was teaching in a little rural school some miles from a small town of less than 100 inhabitants. The chief social event for the countryside was the Saturday evening dance at the little town. Regularly, she said, the man and wife with whom she lived went to this dance Saturday evenings and left her alone at home. She said, "I know they would think it terrible if I so much as suggested that I would like to go along. The inconsistency and injustice of it outrages me." One must sympathize with a teacher in these circumstances. What should one say to her? Similar situations constantly arise. The community expects the teacher to observe a standard of conduct it refuses itself to observe. Many a school patron saturated with the unmistakable odor of tobacco becomes vociferous when he discovers that the teacher uses it even discreetly.

There can be no question but that the teacher is quite universally required to observe a high standard of personal conduct. If he can forget his irritation at the double standard set for teacher and school patron and ask the reason for this state of affairs, he may discover a very soothing answer. Is it not true that people demand exceptional standards of those they regard highly, and are quite indifferent to the actions of those they hold of no importance? The minister has always been held to a rigid standard of conduct by the community, because for the community he symbolizes their high regard for religion and for the sanctity of his office. By most parents the teacher is looked upon as the symbol of the ideals they wish their children to embody. Next to the clergy, and, for many, on a par with them, the teacher stands as the symbol of the ideals that the parents desire their children to embrace. The parent, therefore, insists that while he may not measure up to the standards he desires for his children, the teacher must. Most parents are wise enough to know the influence the teacher will wield over their children.

Social pitfalls

In almost twenty years of intimate contact as director of college and university placement bureaus, it is no exaggeration to say that over 50 per cent of teacher failures find their direct cause in social maladjustment in the community. A few, too many in any case, of these social difficulties involve serious moral delinquencies, but by far the major portion arise from differences in social conventions subscribed to by the teacher and by the community. An especial difficulty with young women is their failure to choose wisely the friendship of young men in the community where they teach. Time and time again the writer has been confronted with a positive demand that assurances be given that a young woman under consideration as a teacher "is the kind that will not keep company with high school boys, or go out with young men of doubtful community standing." A tendency to forget the dignity of the position and descend to the level of the students in an effort to win them, to become a party to a clique, to develop a "crush" on a high school student of the same sex or to permit a student to form such an attachment — a particular fault with women teachers in their relations with high school girls — these are the most common social pitfalls for the high school teacher.

While the seriousness of the problem must be recognized, sympathy rather than censure belongs to most of those caught in the meshes of social difficulties. Young people, single women mostly, are sent out into isolated communities with little opportunity for the social contacts enjoyed at college, with limited means of travel, and bound by social conventions not applied to men teachers that isolate her still more. Is it surprising that some cautions are disregarded in an effort to escape the crushing effects of sheer loneliness? Just recently two young women of unusually fine character, ability, and personal charm confided to the author that the social life in their school community was intolerable. The only eligible young man the community afforded was one whom, the teachers remarked, they would not have looked at in the University. The community and the profession cannot for always refuse to face this problem. In the meantime the price of teaching success places inexorable demands upon the aspiring teacher. To be forewarned is to be forearmed. When the young teacher is in doubt about community attitudes, it is a safe policy for him to consult level-headed members of the school board or responsible members of the community whose judgment he has discovered is respected by all.

Community residence

In these days of greater facility for travel, with good roads, automobiles, and bus service in addition to railroads, it is possible for teachers to live in larger social centers and travel to and from school each day or spend the week end outside the community. For most schools such practice presents a problem. Many communities desire to have the teacher participate in the social life. There are communities where the teaching staff constitutes no small part of the social life of the community during the nine or ten months of the year that the schools are in session. To have ten or a dozen college and university trained young people in a small community adds in no small measure to the tone of the social life.

Further, many of the social or extra-curricular activities of the school take place in the evening. It is highly desirable that the community have the benefit of trained leadership for its young people. Some schools have gone so far as to frame contracts that carry clauses stipulating residence in the community as a basis of employment. Moreover, one cannot entirely forget the pressure of certain materially minded members to insure the expenditure of salaries, as far as possible, within the community.

On the other hand, many districts do not provide adequate housing accommodations for teachers. Such a community this year is employing teachers with the definite arrangement that they live in the near-by city and travel back and forth by automobile, since there is no satisfactory rooming or housing accommodation available in this small place. There is much to be said for the efficiency of the teacher who is able to secure pleasant and convenient lodgings in the near-by city, and enjoy wholesome social life and the intellectual stimulation that larger places afford through lectures, music, libraries, etc. The school and the teacher both have their rights, and where these seem to conflict they should be satisfactorily adjusted at the time of contract.

5. What Are the Teacher's Civic Responsibilities?

Leadership within the community

The eternal problem of the teacher is to determine to what extent he is obligated by his position to give unstinted leadership to the community itself. Here again the teacher must have recourse to his philosophy of education and his concept of the function of the secondary school within the social milieu. If education involves preparation in part for a society that ought to be, as well as for a society that is, the psychology of learning would suggest that our educational endeavor will be seriously handicapped if the environment in which the youth must live eighteen hours of the day differs radically from the societal level maintained by the school. Many teachers are fully aware of the difficulty of teaching one thing in the school and discovering the community practice to be quite the contrary. The reconstruction function is just as important as the adaptive function in education. The province of education is rapidly being accepted as embracing the totality of the individual's present life. If the social environment is not conducive to the fruition of those ideals, attitudes, and behavior-patterns the school is endeavoring to develop, then the obligation of the school transcends the limits of its four walls. It must concern itself with the community.

The teacher should keep this broad picture of the function of the school clearly in mind as he approaches the problem of immediate community responsibility as teacher and citizen. The lodge, the grange, the service clubs, and the churches are the chief agencies that look to the teacher for participation and leadership. They have a right to the teacher's help, and the teacher owes such leadership as he can give. First responsibility, of course, belongs to the school. The question the teacher must ask is: "Where am I best fitted to serve, and what leadership will be most productive of results?" A graduate student, while principal in a certain community, had become Master of the Grange there. This agricultural community felt the force of his personality and leadership through this active service as in no other community effort he could have given. Some doubt the wisdom of too close identification with church activities because of sectarian rivalries, and because the teacher should have Sunday, at least, free from teaching activities similar to those of the schoolroom. Many factors must be considered before an answer can be given.

The teacher may well survey the influential agencies in the community early in his period of residence, and select the ones in which he feels sympathetic interest, and can render most effective service. It is better to do a few things well than to attempt many and neglect both the activities and the school.

It is well to remember, also, that while the teacher is thus an influence on the life of the community, there are reciprocal benefits. Such contacts enrich the life of the teacher and lessen the tendency to narrowness in outlook, or to the development of unsocial traits — a serious danger in teaching. Further, these contacts with the environment of the student will enable the teacher to understand many school problems otherwise baffling. Contact with parents leads to a wholesome appreciation of individual students, their modes of thought, possibilities, and reasons for behavior-patterns observed. Teachers should not forget the opportunities for parental cooperation in the school which these associations provide as incidental values.

Political activities

In the July, 1933, National Education Association convention held in Chicago, President Walter Dill Scott of Northwestern University challenged the teaching profession to drop its former attitude of aloofness from the political-economic affairs of the country, up to the present dominated by bankers and politicians, and assume leadership in these fields. He was ably seconded by other speakers at the convention.

If the point of view of this book is accepted as fundamentally sound, no other alternative remains. Possibly at no time in recent history has this country been more in the mood to accept leadership from the educational profession than now. The high esteem in which the industrial and banking interests of the country have been held for years has been irretrievably lost in the aftermath of the great disillusionment suffered with the recent financial reverses in this country, and the subsequent exposure of questionable practices in high places. As oracles of economic-social wisdom the bankers and great princes of industry have been found very commonplace. The politicians have succeeded in plunging the world into further chaos, so that their leadership is far below par in public esteem. The recent tendency of governmental agencies to seek the advice of trained educational leaders in economics, political science, and other social sciences suggests a readiness to consult trained minds rather than resort to political expediency, as has been too often done in the past.

Just recently a state university abrogated a rule of many years' standing that denied its professors the right of active participation in political affairs. Many notable leaders in civic affairs have been identified with educational institutions. . The record of intelligent, clean, civic leadership which these educators have given bodes well for further assumption of leadership in this direction.

A word of caution needs to be given the young teacher full of enthusiasm to reform the world. The first thing the teacher needs to consider well is that the world does not want to be reformed. It will accept reform only under protest. Participation then in political activities may not win the undivided approval of the community. Such participation means definite aggressive opposition to significant groups within the community. Until the community has been educated to teacher activity in civic-political affairs, care must be exercised, or the reaction may be detrimental to the school itself.

Political-economic-social theory in the classroom

With the new day in education must come a more intimate connection between the discussion of political-economic-social theories in the classroom and their practice outside. Instead of the purging of all textbooks of references to politico-socio-economic theories not in harmony with the views of certain portions of the community, as is now frequently tried by pseudo-patriotic groups, the students must face the worth of these theories. If municipal ownership or state ownership of utilities cannot be considered on its merits by the class with all the facts before it, the school becomes restricted to banal generalities, and its value to society as a training agency for intelligent citizenship is questionable. On the other hand, the school cannot permit itself to become indiscriminately propagandist. Its function should be to present all the facts and to permit impartial evaluation. When but one conclusion is possible, it should be possible to state that conclusion. Where room for differences of opinion is present, these should be recognized; and the teacher should sedulously refrain from influencing student judgment. The right of the teacher, as a citizen and leader, to advocate ideas of civic import must be stoutly defended. As a teacher in the schoolroom he is an impersonal leader of the students in the fearless search for truth; a propagandist for a controversial theory he may not be.

QUESTIONS AND PROBLEMS

1. In what way does a teacher's philosophy of life play an important part in his success as a molder of character?
2. Is the mastery of subject matter sufficient to assure good teaching? Substantiate your answer.
3. What are the individual factors that make up human personality?
4. Is there a high degree of relationship between the teacher traits considered desirable by high school students and those listed by educators? What relationship is there between scholarship and later teaching success?
5. To what extent can a good teacher personality be developed? What are the natural limitations?
6. What successful teacher traits as given by students and educators would one expect to find (1) invariably (2) not so frequently (3) and not necessarily at all in a good scholar? Give reasons for your answers.
7. What precautions should a prospective teacher take in preparing for the profession?
8. What place do appearance, voice, health, and general learning have upon teaching success?
9. What qualifications should a teacher have to meet the general demands of the average community?
10. What are the major items in a code of ethics that a successful teacher should observe?

544   *The Teacher's Function in Modern Education*

11. What social relations must a teacher maintain and avoid in the average small community? Assume that you are elected to a five-teacher high school in a small community. List the items of social relations you would need to consider positively and negatively at least until you were well acquainted with the social conventions and *mores* of the community.
12. What reasons may be advanced for and against the demand that a teacher live in the community in which he teaches?
13. How far should a teacher's civic responsibilities extend for his own and the community's good?
14. What should the teacher's position in the schoolroom on political and community questions be?
15. According to your experience as a student or a teacher in the average small community, what specific inhibitions in the life of the teacher markedly restrict her development? What specific measures might be used to overcome these difficulties?

SELECTED BIBLIOGRAPHY

Anderson, Vernon, Grim, Paul R., and Gruhn, William T. *Principles and Practices in Secondary Schools,* chapters XVIII–XX. New York: The Ronald Press Company, 1951.

Baxter, Bernice. *Teacher-Pupil Relationships.* New York: The Macmillan Company, 1941.

Beecher, D. E. and Bump, J. W. *The Evaluation of Teaching in New York State,* New York State Education Department. Albany: The University of the State of New York, 1950.

Bigelow, K. W. *Teachers for Our Times.* Washington, D.C.: American Council on Education, 1944.

Bossing, Nelson L. "The Measurement of Teaching Efficiency," chapter VII in Umstattd, J. G., et al., *Institutional Teacher Placement.* Detroit: College of Education, Wayne University, 1937.

Burton, William H. *The Guidance of Learning Activities,* chapter VI. New York: Appleton-Century-Crofts, Inc., 1944.

Butler, Frank A. *The Improvement of Teaching in Secondary Schools,* Second Edition, chapter VIII. Chicago: University of Chicago Press, 1946.

Douglass, Harl R. and Grieder, Calvin. *American Public Education,* chapter XIV. New York: The Ronald Press Company, 1948.

Douglass, Harl R. and Mills, Hubert H. *Teaching in High School,* chapter XXVII. New York: The Ronald Press Company, 1948.

Elsbree, W. S. *The American Teacher.* New York: American Book Company, 1939.

Faunce, Ronald C. and Bossing, Nelson L. *Developing the Core Curriculum,* chapter IX. New York: Prentice-Hall, Inc., 1951.

Fordyce, W. G. "The American Federation of Teachers: Its History and Organization," *American School Board Journal,* CXII: 23–26 (June, 1946).

Gruhn, W. T. and Douglass, H. R. *The Modern Junior High School,* chapters XI, XII. New York: The Ronald Press Company, 1947.

Hunt, E. C. *Education of Teachers.* Columbia, S.C.: University of South Carolina Press, 1944.

Kent, Rudyard K. and Kronenberg, Henry H. *Principles of Secondary Education,* chapter XVII. New York: McGraw-Hill Book Company, Inc., 1941.

Martin, T. D. "Code of Ethics for Teachers," *Encyclopedia of Education,* pp. 200–203. New York: The Macmillan Company, 1941.

Rasey, Marie I. *This is Teaching.* New York: Harper and Brothers, 1950.

Reavis, W. C. and Cooper, D. H. *Evaluation of Teacher Merit in City School Systems.* Chicago: University of Chicago Press, 1945.

Reavis, W. C. and Judd, C. H. *The Teacher and Educational Administration.* Boston: Houghton Mifflin Company, 1942.

Reinoehl, C. M. and Ayer, F. C. *Classroom Administration and Pupil Adjustment,* chapter XXIII. New York: Appleton-Century-Crofts, Inc., 1940.

Risk, Thomas M. *Principles and Practices of Teaching in Secondary Schools,* Second Edition, chapter I. New York: American Book Company, 1947.

Rivlin, Harry N. *Teaching Adolescents in Secondary Schools,* chapter XVI. New York: Appleton-Century-Crofts, Inc., 1948.

Schorling, Raleigh. *Student Teaching,* Second Edition, chapter III. New York: McGraw-Hill Book Company, Inc., 1949.

Sheviakov, George V. and Redl, Fritz. *Discipline for Today's Children and Youth.* Washington, D.C.: Department of Supervision and Curriculum Development, 1944.

Stiles, L. J. and Dorsey, M. F. *Democratic Teaching in Secondary Schools,* chapter II. Chicago: J. B. Lippincott Company, 1950.

The Legal Status of the Public School Teacher, Research Bulletin No. 2. Washington, D.C.: National Education Association, 1947.

The Improvement of Teacher Education. Washington, D.C.: American Council of Education, 1946.

Thut, I. N. and Gerberich, J. R. *Foundations of Method for Secondary Schools,* Part III. New York: McGraw-Hill Book Company, Inc., 1949.

Umstattd, J. G. *Secondary School Teaching,* Second Edition, chapter XVII. Boston: Ginn and Company, 1944.

Wahlquist, John T. *An Introduction to American Education,* chapters 2, 6, 7. New York: The Ronald Press Company, 1947.

INDEX

INDEX

Ability, special, as category of educational aims, 49; relation of successful study to, 177; measurement of, 243, 244

Academy, development and decline of, 4–6

Achievement, measurement of, 244; testing by use of questions, 328, 329

Activities, development of course around, 67; discipline and extra-curricular, 505, 506; preparation of teacher for extra-curricular, 532

Activity movement, limitations of, 67

Adams, John, *The Evolution of Educational Theory*, 236 n.

Adaptation, function of school in teaching of, 12–14

Administration, division of responsibilities in, 467, 468; general attitudes of, 468, 469; restrictions on discipline, 508, 509

Adolescence, characteristics of, 20–22; variation in, 23 n.

Adult education, through radio, 403–405

Affective life, function of school in training of, 14–16

Aims, educational, 47–50; examples of, 48, 49. *See also* Curriculum

Alberty, Harold, *Reorganizing the High School Curriculum*, 61 n.

Alexander, W. M., and Saylor, J. G., *Secondary Education*, 25 n.

American Association of School Administrators, "Light and Color," 425 n.; *American School Buildings*, 429 n., 430 n.

American Council on Education, *The Story of Our Calendar*, 364 n.; *The Story of Writing*, 366 n.; *The Improvement of Teacher Education*, 522 n.; on qualities of good teacher, 522

Anderson, John E., on adolescence, 21; *The Psychology of Development and Personal Adjustment*, 21 n.

Anderson, V. E., Grim, P. R., and Gruhn, W. T., *Principles and Practices of Secondary Education*, 243 n.

Answer. *See* Response

Apology, as penalty, 503, 504

Application, in Herbartian steps, 117, 118

Appreciation, teaching of, 204–238; nature of, 213–221; and values, 213–215; relation of emotion to, 215, 216; relation to mores, 216; types of, 216, 217; importance of education for, 219; technique for teaching of, 219–221; question used for development of, 331

Appreciation, aesthetic, 217, 218; development of, 229–238; definition of, 229; differing standards for, 230, 231; technique of teaching, 231–238

Appreciation, ethical-social, 218, 219; development of, 221–229; elements involved in, 221; technique of developing, 221–229; importance of teacher's personality in development of, 222, 223; precepts in teaching of, 223, 224; direct and indirect instruction for, 224–227; pressure in teaching of, 226; provision for expression of, 227–229; literature in teaching of, 228, 229; use of ritual in teaching, 229

Art, differing standards of, 230, 231. *See also* Appreciation, aesthetic

Arthur, T. S., influence of *Ten Nights in a Barroom*, 226

Assignment, nature of, 296–298; definition, 296; importance of, 296–298; properties of effective, 298–315; clearness and definiteness in, 300–302; conciseness combined with adequate detail, 302; anticipation of advance work, 303; relating new to past experiences, 303, 304; making clear importance of, 304, 305; arousing interest by, 305–308; provision for individual differences by, 308–310; suggested motivation by, 310; stimulation of thought by, 311; provision of directions for study, 311, 312; adjustment to time and opportunity, 312; variety and adaptability of materials, 312, 313; evaluation of, 313–315; technique of, 315–321; time of making, 315, 316; time devoted to, 316; difficulties in making, 317, 318; suggested procedure, 319, 320; types of, 320, 321; on first day, 472

Assimilation, in Morrisonian cycle plan, 119

Association of Broadcasters, *How to Use Radio in the Classroom*, 415 n.

Atmosphere, of classroom, 438–440; teacher control of, 439, 440

Atomistic theory, description of learning by, 61

549

Shaw, George Bernard, on thinking, 362

Sheviakov, George V., and Redl, Fritz, *Discipline For Today's Children and Youth*, 484 n.

Shuey, Audrey M., "The Reliability of the Wilke Personality Rating Scale," 520 n.

Siepmann, Charles A., *Radio Television and Society*, 401 n.

Situation, graph of practice related to, 354

Slides, use of, 386, 387

Slogans, teaching ethical-social appreciation by use of, 223, 224

Smith, B. O., Stanley, W. O., and Shores, J. H., *Fundamentals of Curriculum Development*, 63 n.

Smith, E. R., and Tyler, R. W., *Appraising and Recording Student Progress*, 265 n.

Socialization, democratic procedure of teaching by, 149–171; traditional recitation compared to, 156, 157

Socialized class procedures, techniques of, 158–171; important principles of, 165–169; conduct of informal, 169–171

Source materials, in the modern curriculum, 55

Spaulding, F. T., *High School and Life*, 403 n.

Staff, relationships of teacher with, 535, 536

Standardized tests. *See* Evaluation

State, contribution to curriculum, 57

Stevens, Romiett, *The Question as a Measure of Efficiency in Instruction*, 328 n.; on questions, 335

Stimulus-response theory, curriculum objectives related to, 47; related to practice, 353

Stowe, Harriet Beecher, influence of *Uncle Tom's Cabin*, 226

Strang, Ruth, *et al.*, *Problems in the Improvement of Reading in High School and College*, 181 n.

Stratemeyer, Florence, *et al.*, *Developing a Curriculum for Modern Living*, 44 n., 55 n.

Strebel, R. F., and Morehart, G. C., *The Nature and Meaning of Teaching*, 307 n.

Student, teacher's preliminary knowledge of, 465–467

Student government, relation of discipline to, 506, 507

Study methods, teaching of, 174–202; essentials of effective, 176–181; importance of reading in, 181–183; general techniques of, 184–199; importance of note taking, 189–191; note taking technique, 191–194; use of time, 197–199; special techniques, 199–202; types of learning, 199, 200; testing for effectiveness of, 247, 248

Subject matter, traditional organization of, 32–34; modifications of, 37; failure in logical organization of, 51

Sumner, W. G., on mores, 206, 207; *Folkways*, 206 n.; on habit, 211

Symbolism, effective use of word, 369–375

Sympathy, use in discipline, 501, 502

Symposium, nature of, 162, 163

Teacher, characteristics for good lecture, 144–147; importance in development of appreciation, 222; prerequisites for successful questioning, 326–328; techniques of questioning, 333–338; reaction to student questions, 338–340; reaction to student response, 340, 341; control of physical environment, 424; control of class atmosphere, 439, 440; responsibilities for own discipline, 494, 495; and effective discipline, 504; importance of, 515–517; personal equipment of, 517–533; philosophy of, 517–520; personality of, 520, 521; qualities of good, 521–523; table showing traits, 523; pupil rating of, 523–525; table showing pupil rating of, 526; educability of successful qualities of, 528; health of, 528–531; academic preparation of, 531, 532; preparation for extra-curricular activities, 532; professional preparation of, 532, 533; school relationships of, 533–536; relationships with students, 533–535; staff relationships of, 535; professional ethics, 535, 536; social problems of, 536–540; residence of, 539, 540; civic responsibility of, 540–543; community leadership by, 540, 541; political activities of, 541, 542; classroom presentation of political-economic-social theory, 542, 543

Teaching, diagnosis of effectiveness of, 246, 247; relation of discipline and techniques of, 505

Teaching unit, compared with resource unit, 92

Technique, relation of discipline to teaching, 505